The Cassiopaea Experiment Transcripts 1996

The Cassiopaea Experiment is unique in the history of channeling, mediumship, and parapsychology. For years prior to the first Cassiopaean transmission, Laura Knight-Jadczyk went to great lengths to study the channeling phenomenon, including its history, its inherent strengths, weaknesses, dangers, and the various theories and methods developed in the past. After having exhausted the standard literature in search of answers to the fundamental problems of humanity, Laura and her colleagues (including her husband, mathematical physicist Arkadiusz Jadczyk) have held regular sittings for more than twenty years.

With the goal of applying true scientific standards and critical thinking, Laura began her experimentation with the spirit board, chosen for the optimum conditions of conscious feedback it offers. As Laura writes, "We take the approach of a sort of scientific mysticism where mystical claims are submitted to rational analysis and testing, and the required scientific proofs are modified to allow for the nature of evidence from theorized realms outside of our own where ordinary scientific proofs might not apply."

The dynamics and content of channeling are in general tightly entangled with current global events and the lives of the participants and their interpersonal relationships. For this reason, clarifying context has been added, and questions and answers have been annotated extensively, giving unprecedented insight into the background of the Cassiopaea Experiment.

In this year, the dialogue with the Cassiopaeans revolved around the further exploration of various theories that were promulgated at that time in books and the internet, the solar companion hypothesis, the theorized states of being above our own, hypnosis, mind programming, false prophecies, the rediscovery of a possible ancient technology utilized in the pre-history of mankind, quantum principles and possibilities for their macroscopic application, as well as the process of gaining more protection by assimilating and applying knowledge and networking with like-minded people.

For the first time in print, this volume includes complete transcripts of 44 experimental sessions conducted in 1996.

The Cassiopaea Experiment Transcripts 1996

Laura Knight-Jadczyk

Red Pill Press
2016

Copyright © 2016 Laura Knight-Jadczyk and Arkadiusz Jadczyk
First Edition, first printing
ISBN 978-0692725733
Red Pill Press (redpillpress.com)

No part of this publication may be reproduced, stored in a retrieval system, or transmitted in any form or by any means, electronic, mechanical, or otherwise, other than for "fair use", without the written consent of the author.

Contents

Editor's Note	i
January 7, 1996	1
January 9, 1996	13
January 13, 1996	19
January 20, 1996	23
January 27, 1996	33
February 3, 1996	43
February 8, 1996	51
February 17, 1996	55
February 21, 1996	61
February 24, 1996	65
March 10, 1996	73
March 13, 1996	83
March 23, 1996	89
March 29, 1996	103
April 24, 1996	121
April 27/28, 1996	129

May 4, 1996	137
May 25, 1996	149
May 27, 1996	155
June 1, 1996	161
June 9, 1996	167
June 15, 1996	179
June 22, 1996	185
June 29, 1996	193
July 14, 1996	201
July 21, 1996	215
July 27, 1996	219
August 3, 1996	223
August 11, 1996	235
August 17, 1996	245
August 24, 1996	253
August 31, 1996	257
September 14, 1996	267
September 21, 1996	281
September 27 1996	297
October 1, 1996	305

October 5, 1996	319
October 12, 1996	339
November 23, 1996	343
November 30, 1996	353
December 8, 1996	357
December 14, 1996	367
December 21, 1996	377
December 28, 1996	395
Chapters of "The Wave"	411
Recommended Reading	415
Index	443

Editor's Note

In the last 20 years, session transcripts of the Cassiopaea Experiment were available only in an electronic format – first shared as text files in a private email group and later, in 2010, republished one by one in the public Cassiopaea Forum[1] for discussion.

Readers have been strongly discouraged from reading the Cassiopaean transcripts on their own, outside of the context provided by Laura's work, since it had been noted that readers often would understand them too literally, misinterpret them and would tend to project their own ideas, beliefs, and biases onto them. Therefore, readers were advised to read them *in context*, that is, by reading about the background of the Cassiopaea Experiment and the unfolding events 'behind the scenes'. For this reason, excerpts of the transcripts have been included, discussed and researched in Laura Knight-Jadczyk's books *Amazing Grace, The Wave* series Vols. 1–8, *The Secret History of the World* Vol. 1 and *High Strangeness*. In these and other books (see "Recommended Reading" section), Laura matches a small percentage of 'inspiration' from the Cs with a lot of 'perspiration', i.e. hard work in researching the issues and conveying them to the readers.

This third volume, published two years after the first volume, continues with 44 experimental sessions of the year 1996, for the first time published in paper and electronic books. The advice about getting the necessary context to better understand the material still cannot be emphasized enough. For this reason, the editors have included footnotes pointing to the location where certain excerpts are discussed in detail in the above-mentioned books. The footnotes hopefully will encourage the reader to look up and study additional context. A referencing footnote marks the first occurring line of a session excerpt contained in the mentioned books. The footnotes give the book title and the chapter number where the excerpts can be found (e.g. *The Wave* 46). The section "Rec-

---

[1] http://cassiopaea.org/forum

ommended Reading" and the table "Chapters of 'The Wave'" at the end of this volume give additional details about the inserted references.

The dynamics and content of channeling are in general tightly entangled with current global events and the lives of the participants and their interpersonal relationships. For this reason, Laura has added clarifying context, and annotated questions and answers extensively, giving unprecedented insight into the background of the Cassiopaea Experiment.

In this year, the dialogue with the Cassiopaeans revolved around the further exploration of various theories that were promulgated at that time in books and the internet, the solar companion hypothesis, the theorized states of being above our own, hypnosis, mind programming, false prophecies, the rediscovery of a possible ancient technology utilized in the pre-history of mankind, quantum principles and possibilities for their macroscopic application, as well as the process of gaining more protection by assimilating and applying knowledge and networking with like-minded people.

Question and response lines have been numbered in the margins for easier referencing and quoting of the material. An exhaustive index at the end of this volume will hopefully enable the reader to quickly find topics of interest, even though the entire transcripts can and should be read as an amazing, unfolding story, containing numerous gems of wisdom, advice, and information.

The spirit board with a few custom modifications.

January 7, 1996

Toward the end of the 1995 sessions volume, in the 16 December 1995 session, I mentioned that I had recently run into Pat Z. In the footnote to that remark, I wrote that this was the "woman who came for hypnosis session on the night that giant black boomerang-type UFOs were seen in several places in our area, including over my house. The episode is related in detail in *The Wave*, chapter 44." The story is so interesting, the reader is encouraged to consult that volume of *The Wave*; the high strangeness going on in our lives at that time was just crazy. And the so-called "alien weirdness" all started, more or less, with the hypnosis session I conducted with this woman, Pat Z.[1] Even though you can read a fuller account in *The Wave*, I'd like to briefly recap a few points about my "running into" Pat as I wrote it there so as to give the reader some background on the questions in this first session of 1996.

> One of the main reasons we wanted to go to the Gulf Breeze conference was because of the magazine. It was hoped that it would be an organ for the Cassiopaean material since I could really think of no other affordable way to make the material available. We planned to print a thousand copies and take them to the conference with us and give them away with a subscription form attached inside.
> As you might expect, the events surrounding the work on the magazine, *The Aurora Journal*, took on a *Twilight Zone*–like quality. The Matrix again went into overdrive to prevent the plan from being brought to fruition.
> One of the first things I wanted to do was to find a printer who would do a nice job for me at a reasonable cost since I was paying for it out of my own pocket. There was a print shop near the chiropractor I was still seeing three times a week for therapy, and I decided to stop in and find out what my options were and how

---

[1] This story also appears in the Tom French article in the *St. Petersburg Times* that was published in 2001 and is still available online.
See: www.sptimes.com/News/webspecials/exorcist

much I could do myself to keep the costs low. At the same time, I had printed up a large volume of the Cassiopaean material and thought that it might be cheaper to have it copied, so I hauled it in with me.

The young lady at the counter quoted me a very reasonable price for the copying but said that she couldn't tell me anything about doing a magazine layout because she was just there in a clerical capacity and I would have to come back. I left my material with an order for three copies, bound in a plastic spine.

Several days later I went back to pick up my copies. As the girl was getting them from the back, a woman emerged from the shop area, grinning widely, and said, "I thought that was you I heard out here!" I looked at her blankly because, frankly, I had no idea who she was! She realized that I didn't recognize her and she said, "Pat! You remember! I came to you for hypnosis!"

And then I realized who she was! She was the woman I had hypnotized back in 1993 the night the flying black boomerangs were sighted over the three-county area. She had been so upset by the idea of an alien abduction lurking in her subconscious that she never came back for any further sessions. I had always wondered what had happened to her since, and it was very curious to find her in this print shop since she had told me back then that she was in real estate. It was even stranger when you consider that I had selected this print shop over any other simply because it was en route between my house and the chiropractor I was seeing every other day as a result of an accident that I was certain was a deliberate attempt on my life by hyperdimensional forces. Not only that, I was in the print shop for the very purpose of having copies made of material that related to the events in which Pat had been involved at the very beginning. Further, that I was planning on inquiring about the printing of a magazine that was an offshoot of those same events.

I was shocked. She looked like she had aged about 20 years in the almost three years since I had seen her! As it turned out, Pat had recently bought the print shop as a business venture for her kids. She invited me into the back of the shop for coffee and we brought each other up to date on what had been happening in our lives since the incident of the UFOs. That event had upset her so badly that she completely retreated into denial and the "normal life" routine. I told her how that event had done just the opposite for me – I had been catapulted into a series of learning experiences that had completely shattered my previous world, and made it seem like I was on a continual roller coaster ride. I told her, "Honey! If you had any idea of the stuff that has happened to me since you were at my house and opened the door to those damned aliens, you would not believe it!" And we both laughed.

So, we spent an hour or so catching up. Pat was fascinated by the story of how the contact with the Cassiopaeans had developed the year following her hypnosis session and wanted not only to read the material, but to attend a session. It turned out that she was very interested in mysteries, or so she claimed. It never occurred to me to wonder why she wasn't interested in her own mystery!

I was, of course, thinking to myself how serendipitous this was for Pat to own this print shop since it just might mean that I could get my magazine printed at a really reasonable price.

As we talked, Pat began to reveal things about her past that were beyond strange. When she had come to me for hypnosis, she was working in real estate and caring for her retired and dying husband, who had been a former government employee. That was basically all she had said at the time. I had never asked her if her husband worked for the post office or any other specific agency, not realizing that it might be important.

Now she was telling me that he was a physicist who had worked at various government labs, including JPL on the Mars Observer, and had spent most of his time working in an underground laboratory somewhere in Maryland or thereabouts. She was telling me so many things that I found it difficult to assimilate all of it. It was as though, in the years since the door to the idea of aliens had been opened in her mind, all sorts of associations had come together. It never occurred to me that this might be bait to attract my interest.

On top of her husband's work, Pat, herself, had a high security clearance and had spent years working (or so she said) in certain office positions that gave her access to highly sensitive information. Finally I thought I understood why Pat may have been abducted. If her husband was a scientist and she had a security clearance, that might explain it. I shared with her that I had learned that families of government employees generally seem to be abducted more than the average person. She thought this was interesting, but still didn't think that it applied to her specifically.

I was pretty excited by all of this. A real, potential witness to weirdness! What a find!

We discussed the magazine, finally, and she agreed that if I would come into the shop and physically help assemble it, in addition to having camera-ready copy, she would be able to give me a considerable discount. So, I left feeling like the fates were in my corner and all was going to be right. I also thought that this was a big opportunity – perhaps the one the Cassiopaeans had mentioned when they had said back in October of the previous year:

> **Q**: *(L)* We need to create a forum.
>
> **A**: Yes. A direction will open if you persevere.
>
> **Q**: *(L)* So things will be brought to us and happen for us if we just persevere?
>
> **A**: Soon expect big opportunity.
>
> **Q**: *(L)* I assume that we are not to ask what it is, we are to have faith, is that correct?
>
> **A**: Yes. Danger you may misinterpret opportunity.
>
> **Q**: *(L)* Should we all be able to realize in congruence whether the opportunity is good?
>
> **A**: Varying degrees.
>
> **Q**: *(L)* If there is a danger we may misinterpret the opportunity, could you give us a couple of clues so that when it occurs we won't miss it?
>
> **A**: At least one of you will have instant recognition but others may not. Wait and see.

My first interpretation of this opportunity was the fact that RC wanted to dump her magazine. She did claim to "recognize" me as a connection from her past life, though I can't say that I had similar recognition. A magazine was a "forum."

The next interpretation I put on it was that Pat had "instantly" recognized me, but I hadn't recognized her. And having an inside line to printing, especially since we were planning a journal, was definitely a "big opportunity" in terms of "creating a forum," one would think.

Earlier, I had joined Mike Lindemann's ISCNI forum on AOL and had been invited to chat live, online, with his group in a sort of question and answer session. I felt sure that this, also, was part of the "forum" and might be the "big opportunity."

But, the fact that, in none of these instances had there been "instant recognition" by any of the group, with the others "doubting," still bugged me. What other big opportunity could there be?

So, it's funny how we anticipate things in ways that never quite fit, and yet how desperate we are to make them true.

And this is where we find me in the early months of 1996 ... moving slowly and inexorably to the threshold of the unknown; my conscious mind fighting tooth and nail against the forces of my own higher self, ignorant of the Predator's mind, ignorant of the Matrix, learning by experience and direct, painful interaction. There was the world of practical events in which this drama manifested; there was the underlying psychological drama, and there was, apparently, another reality – the theological reality – from which the energies emanated.

And learning to see this other reality and to be able to respond to it with no apparent proof seemed to be the big test.

Now you have been introduced to the guest at the next session, let us proceed!

Participants: 'Frank', Laura, Pat Z

Q: *(L)* Hello

A: Oops!

Q: *(L)* And who do we have this evening?

A: Turrin.

Q: *(L)* And where are you communicating from?

A: Cassiopaea.

Q: *(L)* We have Pat with us tonight...[2]

A: Hello Pat.

Q: *(L)* Now, with all of us here, we would like to ask why the black, flying boomerangs showed up on the night Pat first came for hypnosis?

A: Examine issue carefully.[3]

Q: *(L)* The first thing we thought about it was that this was a, if not necessarily rare, at least rarely observed type of craft, and the event itself was rare... Is this correct?

A: It is rare.

Q: *(L)* If it is rare for it to occur in response to a hypnosis session, which person were the UFOs particularly interested in?[4]

A: It was not a person, but information that is hidden in the subconscious memory of Patricia.

Q: *(L)* Were they wanting to get this information?

A: No. To monitor what would be revealed.

Q: *(L)* Does this mean that Pat has in-

---
[2] *High Strangeness* 8; *The Wave* 21
[3] *The Wave* 64
[4] *High Strangeness* "Appendix"

formation programmed into her before birth that she needs to access?

A: No. Abductions.

Q: *(L)* They wanted to see if anything would be revealed about their abductions of her?

A: Yes.

Q: *(L)* Okay, since she is here, can we ask who abducted her?

A: Grays.

Q: *(L)* How many times has she been abducted?

A: 4. Snow scene was only 3rd density.

Q: *(P)* Does that mean that the snow scene was only in this realm?

A: No. Abduction which occurred there was strictly physical.

Q: *(L)* Okay, the abduction that occurred in the snow was a physical abduction. Perhaps the others were not. Were they physical also?

A: The others were 4th density. 3rd density abduction only occurs rarely, and is of great import.

Q: *(L)* What is of great import that is connected to this abduction?

A: Review.

Q: *(P)* Was my son abducted?[5]

A: Frozen.

Q: *(L)* Why did they want Pat so bad that they would take her physically?

A: Do you have any ideas?

Q: *(L)* Yes, I have ideas. Maybe Pat has ideas and knowledge that she could access to work against these beings?

A: But real reason is more fundamental.

Q: *(L)* Were they abducting Pat to harvest eggs?

A: No.

Q: *(L)* To harvest energy?

A: Would you like to learn or play "20 questions?"

Q: *(L)* I would like to learn and get to the bottom of this.

A: You answered your own enquiry earlier.

Q: *(L)* Because she had information they wanted to get from her?

A: No, no, no.

Q: *(L)* What did I say?

A: Exposure.

Q: *(L)* Oh, they fear that she will act in some way to expose them...[6]

A: Government proximities!

Q: *(L)* Oh! When I was talking earlier about people who have someone working for the government, such people tend to be abducted more. And just because Pat was married to a scientist who worked at JPL doesn't mean she knew anything. Does she know something?

A: Not what she knew.

Q: *(L)* Was it because of where she lived?

---

[5] *The Wave* 64
[6] *The Wave* 64
[7] Pat is referring to the underground base where her husband worked on secret research.

52 **A**: Because of proximity to Consortium activity.

53 **Q**: *(P)* Was that activity in the tunnel?[7]

54 **A**: Implanted for possible future activation.

55 **Q**: *(L)* So, because of your proximity to the people you were living around and interacting with, you had an implant designed to control you if need be. *(P)* Was this related to what was going on under the mountain? *(L)* What mountain? What's under the mountain? *(P)* Just ask.

56 **A**: Not locator, personnel are factored.[8]

57 **Q**: *(L)* Okay, it is not where you were so much as who you were in contact with.

58 **A**: Yes.

59 **Q**: *(L)* Was it her husband?

60 **A**: Perhaps.

61 **Q**: *(L)* Maybe that is why there is a higher rate of abduction among family members of government employees, so that they can be activated or controlled? *(P)* But my husband wasn't really working on anything secret.[9]

62 **A**: He had access to sensitive facilities.

63 **Q**: *(L)* Did he have a security clearance or was he friends with others who did? *(P)* I had a security clearance. *(L)* So, Pat had an implant put in. An actual, physical implant. Where is it?

64 **A**: Behind sinus cavity.

65 **Q**: *(L)* What is this implant designed to do?

66 **A**: Activate behavioral control reflex and thought pattern generation and alteration.

67 **Q**: *(P)* Is that why I can't remember anything?

68 **A**: Some.

69 **Q**: *(L)* Did you ever have headaches or nose or ear problems? *(P)* No, but I do have this memory problem in a big way. *(L)* What is the main part of the memory problem Pat has? Can you give us any more on that?

70 **A**: No.

71 **Q**: *(L)* So, can I say that this UFO appeared over my house on the night Pat was under hypnosis, to reinforce the implant so that she would not be able...

72 **A**: To monitor.

73 **Q**: *(L)* If Pat had revealed the details of her abduction, would there have been any repercussions?

74 **A**: Not in this case.[10]

75 **Q**: *(L)* Are there cases when persons reveal details of their abductions, that there are repercussions?

76 **A**: Varied.

77 **Q**: *(L)* So, if Pat had gone to anyone, these craft would have appeared?

78 **A**: Yes.

79 **Q**: *(L)* You have already told us that this is extremely rare. Did Pat have an abduction experience of unusual significance?

80 **A**: 3rd density.

81 **Q**: *(L)* Okay, what else was unusual?

82 **A**: Discover.

83 **Q**: *(P)* Does this have anything to do with Camp David?

---

[8] *High Strangeness* "Appendix"; *The Wave* 21
[9] *High Strangeness* 8
[10] *The Wave* 10, 34, 39

84 **A**: Not the issue, its personnel![11]

85 **Q**: *(L)* Did you know somebody? Was it that she knew someone or interacted with someone in particular?

86 **A**: Many others!

87 **Q**: *(P)* If I started naming people, could we get to it?

88 **A**: Not necessary.[12]

89 **Q**: *(L)* Well, there is an issue here that we need to get to. *(P)* Do the planes have anything to do with it?

90 **A**: It is up to Pat, the extent she wishes to retrieve and divulge, the many unusual experiences that were met, by Pat, with unusual indifference.

91 **Q**: *(P)* The first thing unusual was the geographic location of our house. Directly west of us was the mountain that housed all the communications to be used in the event of nuclear war. We were 13 miles north of Camp David. And, while we lived there, many, many things took place at Camp David that were of global significance. And, we built a barn in 1982 and had bought the house in 1976, and never, in all the years that I lived there, did I ever notice these planes until we built the barn. If I had a stick in my hand, I could have touched them, that's how low they flew. Right over my barn. The same day every week. And there was always two of them, and they never had a single marking on them. And, they were propeller planes. And I wondered: what in the hell is this country doing flying planes, unmarked, propeller driven, and so low, over this area? This continued until we moved from that house. So, these planes came twice a week from 1982 until 1989. *(L)* What were these planes?

92 **A**: Search to learn.

93 **Q**: *(L)* Well, obviously we need to discuss this to develop our synapses. *(P)* Well, after the first couple of times, I sort of just said, "Well, there are the planes." So, what else is new?

94 **A**: Indifference.[13]

95 **Q**: *(P)* I thought the planes had something to do with the mountain. Did they?

96 **A**: Maybe.

97 **Q**: *(P)* We knew they were flying under radar. Now that I am thinking about this, nobody else ever talked about these planes. It was like we were the only people that ever saw them, or people who were at our house saw them too. My best friend who lived right up the road never saw them. I asked her, "Did you see the planes?" and she said, "What planes?" I mean, she was seven acres away and nothing in between!

98 **A**: Unusual experiences mount!

99 **Q**: *(P)* Vic also noticed these things and he would always say – he was less indifferent than I was – he would say, "What in the hell are those planes and what are they doing?" *(L)* Why was Pat so indifferent? *(P)* Well, it didn't affect *my* life, except that I was damn mad that it upset my horses. But then, the horses got used to them too, and they became indifferent! [Laughter] Well, they came so often, twice a week – "It's Wednesday, the planes will be here!"

100 **A**: More... continue probing...

---

[11] *High Strangeness* "Appendix"
[12] *The Wave* 24
[13] *High Strangeness* "Appendix"; *The Wave* 64

101 **Q**: *(P)* The planes came from east to west, and in the west was the mountain...

102 **A**: Catoctin.

103 **Q**: *(P)* That is the name of the mountain. *(L)* What is it? *(P)* The tunnel where all these facilities were... under Catoctin Mountain. Camp David is near, too.

104 **A**: And MUCH ELSE! Mount Weather, Virginia. And why did you live in area... helicopters?

---

[14]Wikipedia, "Fort Detrick": Fort Detrick is a United States Army Medical Command installation located in Frederick, Maryland. Historically, Fort Detrick was the center of the US biological weapons program from 1943 to 1969. Since the discontinuation of that program, it has hosted most elements of the United States biological defense program.

As of the early 2010s, Fort Detrick's 1,200-acre (490 ha) campus supports a multi-governmental community that conducts biomedical research and development, medical materiel management, global medical communications and the study of foreign plant pathogens. ...

During World War II, Camp Detrick and the USBWL became the site of intensive biological warfare *(BW)* research using various pathogens. This research was originally overseen by pharmaceuticals executive George W. Merck and for many years was conducted by Ira L. Baldwin, professor of bacteriology at the University of Wisconsin. Baldwin became the first scientific director of the labs. He chose Detrick Field for the site of this exhaustive research effort because of its balance between remoteness of location and proximity to Washington, DC – as well as to Edgewood Arsenal, the focal point of U.S. chemical warfare research. ...

From 1945 to 1955 under Project Paperclip and its successors, the U.S. government recruited over 1,600 German and Austrian scientists and engineers in a variety of fields such as aircraft design, missile technology and biological warfare. Among the specialists in the latter field who ended up working in the U.S. were Walter Schreiber, Erich Traub and Kurt Blome, who had been involved with medical experiments on concentration camp inmates to test biological warfare agents. Since Britain, France and the Soviet Union were also engaged in recruiting these scientists, the Joint Intelligence Objectives Agency *(JIOA)* wished to deny their services to other powers, and therefore altered or concealed the records of their Nazi past and involvement in war crimes.

The U.S. General Accounting Office issued a report on September 28, 1994, which stated that between 1940 and 1974, DOD and other national security agencies studied hundreds of thousands of human subjects in tests and experiments involving hazardous substances.

Jeffrey Alan Lockwood wrote in 2009, that the biological warfare program at Ft. Detrick began to research the use of insects as disease vectors going back to World War II and also employed German and Japanese scientists after the war who had experimented on human subjects among POWs and concentration camp inmates. Scientists used or attempted to use a wide variety of insects in their biowar plans, including fleas, ticks, ants, lice and mosquitoes – especially mosquitoes that carried the yellow fever virus. They also tested these in the United States. Lockwood thinks

105 **Q:** *(P)* Is it because of Fort Detrick?[14]

106 **A:** What brought you to Maryland?

107 **Q:** *(P)* Fort Detrick. *(L)* What does Mount Weather mean? *(P)* The underground tunnel – everybody in town called it "The Tunnel" – but there was nothing around there to ever give anybody the slightest clue as to what it was. In fact, I lived there for quite a long time before I knew it existed. And, on top of the mountain there was a weather station... *(L)* But, what about Fort Detrick? *(P)* Vic was doing electron microscopy – cancer research.

108 **A:** REALLY?

109 **Q:** *(P)* It was a photographic lab. *(L)* Do the instruments on top of the mountain have anything to do with these planes?

110 **A:** So what?

111 **Q:** *(L)* Does it have anything to do with those antennae that are reported as being connected to that project, that alter space-time?

112 **A:** Helicopters, Pat? We are asking you!

113 **Q:** *(P)* Well, the helicopters in Frederick went over our house every time the president was at Camp David. But, that was our house in Walkersville, not in Emmetsburg, when we first moved to Maryland. Sometimes the helicopters were unmarked...

114 **A:** You see, Pat is resistant due to experiences, things don't "phase" her easily, programming, etc.

115 **Q:** *(L)* So, all of these things happening around her, the planes, the mountain, the helicopters... *(P)* But the helicopters, I knew it was the president either going to or coming from Camp David.[15]

116 **A:** Resistant, not resisting.

117 **Q:** *(L)* Is the term "resistant" a clue?

118 **A:** All is a clue here!

119 **Q:** *(L)* Since Pat has only been abducted 4 times, can this mean that she is resistant to that?

120 **A:** No.

121 **Q:** *(P)* Isn't that just my personality, that if it doesn't affect me I don't bother with it?

122 **A:** Yes.

123 **Q:** *(P)* I don't get bothered about things that...

124 **A:** Shoot somebody in front of Pat, and she says: "Oh well, that's life" so, to discover spectacular things, one must be patient and probe carefully, no hasty assumptions, please!! There is much to be retrieved, revealed, studied.

125 **Q:** *(P)* Well, the helicopters went back and forth to Camp David. The president was supposed to be in them. And his entourage. There was only 3 helicopters. *(L)* Are these the helicopters referred to?

---

that it is very likely that the U.S. did use insects dropped from aircraft during the Korean War to spread diseases, and that the Chinese and North Koreans were not simply engaged in a propaganda campaign when they made these allegations, since the Joint Chiefs of Staff and Secretary of Defense had approved their use in the fall of 1950 at the "earliest practicable time". At that time, it had five biowarfare agents ready for use, three of which were spread by insect vectors.

[15] *The Wave* 21, 64

126 **A**: No. Let Pat digest it, and report back later.

127 **Q**: *(L)* At the time we had all those sightings around here on the night we did that session with Pat, why did so many other people see them?

128 **A**: Window was "blast."

129 **Q**: *(L)* Are there any craft over us at this time?

130 **A**: ?

131 **Q**: *(L)* Okay, we have the magazine ready to go out and the articles are somewhat controversial. Can we have an indication as to whether there will be a positive response to this issue or not?

132 **A**: Wait and see.

133 **Q**: *(L)* Will it be possible to 'channel' online as Mike Lindemann has suggested?

134 **A**: Sure!

135 **Q**: *(L)* Pat is having some serious problems at the present time. Can you help her with these?

136 **A**: Networking works!!![16]

137 **Q**: *(P)* Is there a light at the end of the tunnel?

138 **A**: Networking works!!!!!

139 **Q**: *(L)* So, if she becomes involved in a network of some sort, things will sort out for her?

140 **A**: What do you think networking is, Laura?

141 **Q**: *(L)* Well, just what we have been doing... *(P)* How can you network a federal contract?

142 **A**: Share ideas, ask others for their experiences and opinions.

[16] *The Wave* 64

143 **Q**: *(L)* Pat says her shop cannot support the salaries for three people. And her federal transcription business has gone kaput since the budget ran out and Congress has not passed a new one.

144 **A**: What harm is there in aggressively pursuing government contracts, what have you to lose? Even if it fails dramatically, what, then, have you lost? If someone has the capacity to do so in business, the ultimate advice is to diversify, not eliminate, in other words, "leave no stone unturned!!" Suggest chase state and local government work as a buffer. Networking works Pat, you have always solved dilemmas, you go into "automatic pilot" during crises, so why do you ask?

145 **Q**: *(L)* Can you give us a clue about when the budget battle is going to end?

146 **A**: It is in the process of ending. Monday will start to refire the machine, though it will be awhile before it runs at full steam again. Backlogs create opportunity.

147 **Q**: *(P)* But, the backlogs can't begin until the budget is passed and signed.

148 **A**: Will happen in quick succession. You need to concentrate on straightening your personal situation.

149 **Q**: *(P)* What does that mean? *(L)* It means that until you can do something else, concentrate on that.

150 **A**: Mercury retrograde favors continuances, not beginnings.

151 **Q**: *(P)* I would like to know about the apparitions of the Virgin Mary at Conyers, GA, as well as this book *Mary's Message to the World* and all the other

messages about the End Times that are coming out all over?[17]

A: The forces at work here are far too clever to be accurately anticipated so easily. You never know what twists and turns will follow, and they are aware of prophetic and philosophical patternings and usually shift course to fool and discourage those who believe in fixed futures.[18]

Q: *(L)* Anything further for tonight?

A: Goodbye.

End of session

---

[17] *High Strangeness* "Appendix"; *The Wave* 64
[18] *The Wave* 21

January 9, 1996

As I've written, the channeling experiment began in 1992 after I met Frank and we discovered a mutual interest in the topic. Looking back, a number of very strange steps led to the Cs and a whole lot of other things. I don't want to recap all of that here since it is covered pretty thoroughly in *The Wave* series and *Amazing Grace*. In the latter text, I describe a murder case in which I was peripherally involved and which led to the conditions under which I was induced, somewhat unwillingly, to consider the topics that led to the Cs experiment. Now, after the recent meeting with Pat Z, who had shown up to play a significant part in the drama, I began to think back over all of the connections and wonder just how oddly this world was made!

What was exercising my mind at the time of this session was the fact that it was looking into the murder case that led to the almost enforced opening of the door to the consideration of UFOs in the realm of paranormal phenomena. I began to wonder if there was some sort of connection between UFOs and murder, UFOs and serial killers, etc. I had read in one of the UFO books in the big grocery sack (see *Amazing Grace* for details) that there had been UFO sightings in the Pacific Northwest around the time of the first activities of serial killer Ted Bundy. And Ted Bundy had certainly taken up a lot of mental space for people living in Florida because of the murders he committed there, and because he was captured, tried and executed there. In fact, on the day he was executed, I had tuned in to the radio to follow the progress of the event. I was still struggling to understand how evil could exist in a world that was supposed to be perfect and good under the guidance of a benevolent deity or something similar: benevolence in general. Thus, the following session, which offered some gems of insight despite the fact that the Cs would not satisfy my curiosity and put me in possible danger thereby.

Participants: 'Frank', Laura

Q: *(L)* Hello.

A: Hello.

Q: *(L)* Who do we have with us tonight?

A: Xiooira.

Q: *(L)* Is that anything like exhilaration?

A: Close.

Q: *(L)* Well, if it is like exhilaration, I am all for it. And where are you from?

A: Cassiopaea.

Q: *(L)* Tonight I have a question for a friend. V___ was over today and wanted me to ask if her son is involved in some cult-type activities?

A: More like "kiddie gang."

Q: *(L)* She said she has noticed things missing. Are they using any of her personal items to try and put a 'hex' on her, if even in a kiddie way?[1]

A: No.

Q: *(L)* Is the action she is taking, which is to try to get him into a hospital drug treatment facility... Can you make any comments on this?

A: Futile.

Q: *(L)* Is there anything that she could do that would be helpful at this point?

A: Son follows in "shoes" of parents.

Q: *(L)* So, she needs to look at her past to know what would alter his behavior. Whatever would have worked with her will work for him, is that it?

A: And David.

Q: *(L)* Any other advice for her at this time?

A: Best to let kid salt his oats and take his lumps.

Q: *(L)* Okay, Pat Z will be here on Saturday, so we will leave a lot of my questions for then. I don't quite know how to ask this. It has become increasingly obvious to me that there is some sort of connection where JO[2] was concerned, some synchronous connections between that murder and my so-called 'awakening', if you want to call it that. And I also noticed a connection between the life pattern, or change in life pattern, of Ted Bundy and certain UFO sightings, and cattle mutilations that were in his area of the country. Now, we have another girl who has come up missing at the same time Pat and I were discussing the JO case, and this new case has a lot of things that seem to be common to that case. I see that there is an issue here that I would like to get to the bottom of. Can you help?

A: Vague.

Q: *(L)* I know that is vague. Did my involvement with the JO case[3] have anything to do with opening the door of my mind to other phenomena, particularly UFOs and aliens?

A: Possible.

Q: *(L)* You can't give me a clear answer on that?

---

[1] V___ had a pretty vivid imagination about that sort of thing on top of being something of a drama queen.
[2] An unsolved murder of a local 13-year-old girl; absolutely *no* clue.
[3] I was asked by law enforcement official to try to come up with some clues or hints through astrology and psychic impressions.

26 **A**: Learn!

27 **Q**: *(L)* Okay. I had dreams about it. The work that I did on the case astrologically, the dreams I had about it, as well as certain impressions I received, convinced me that a particular individual was the killer. Was that an opening of my instinctual awareness in some way?

28 **A**: Maybe.

29 **Q**: *(L)* Was there some soul connection between myself and JO?

30 **A**: No.

31 **Q**: *(L)* Was there some connection between JO's murder and 'alien' activity?

32 **A**: There is always this connection in one way or another, at one plane convergence or another.

33 **Q**: *(L)* Was the murder of JO a 'mini-plane convergence'?

34 **A**: What did we just say?

35 **Q**: *(L)* It seemed to me that was what you said, and I was trying to clarify it. Is that, in fact, a plane convergence, where one person's plane of reality converges with another person's plane of reality, and one or the other gets annihilated?

36 **A**: 4th, 5th and 3rd density is involved.

37 **Q**: *(L)* Is this true with all murders?

38 **A**: Discover and yes.

39 **Q**: *(L)* Was my interaction into that reality a sort of entering into a point of plane convergence?

40 **A**: Flirting with the edges.

41 **Q**: *(L)* So, when a person is working on a murder investigation, or thinking about it, or applying thoughts, talents, instincts or whatever to the solving of this kind of puzzle, they are interacting with a plane convergence?

42 **A**: This represents one manifestation of the always present desire to return "home" to 5th density.

43 **Q**: *(L)* Okay. Well. Now, I want to get to the 64,000-dollar question. In the JO case, was my conclusion correct?

44 **A**: "Correctness" takes many forms and provides a window to many conventions.

45 **Q**: *(F)* What does that mean? *(L)* I don't know. My evaluation was that [name redacted] was also the killer. Is that correct?

46 **A**: Learn.

47 **Q**: *(L)* Was the man who killed JO known to her?

48 **A**: We recall advising a cautious approach, in order to insure that your lessons are learned not only accurately, but painlessly as well.

49 **Q**: *(L)* Could you suggest, just to get me on track here, a form of question that would be a 'cautious' question? Then I can frame subsequent questions on that model.

50 **A**: The issue here is not how to "frame" a question in such a way as to lure us into answering in the way you desire, but for you to learn most effectively. Do not have prejudice that there is only one thing to be learned from each response. "You never know what there is to be learned when you inquire with innocence and freedom from supposition."

[Break to listen to response.]

51 **Q**: *(L)* I just played the tape back and it is all muddy. Could you tell us why we are having this problem with the tape?

52 **A**: Telekinetic wave transfer.

53 **Q:** *(L)* What is this telekinetic wave transferring?

54 **A:** Evolving energy.

55 **Q:** *(L)* Given off by us?

56 **A:** Both to and from.

57 **Q:** *(L)* From us to you?

58 **A:** You and others, not us.

59 **Q:** *(L)* Who are these others?

60 **A:** 4th density eavesdroppers, Pat's involvement should "heat things up."

61 **Q:** *(L)* Is Pat's involvement going to be beneficial to this work?

62 **A:** Yes, but also expect anomalies.

63 **Q:** *(L)* That is interesting. Are you going to tell me who killed JO? I am willing to give up my conclusion if necessary.

64 **A:** Learn. Review our previous response.

65 **Q:** *(L)* I would love to, but much of the answer was lost in the static.

66 **A:** It can be deciphered.

67 **Q:** *(L)* Okay. Learn. Was there something about Ted Bundy and the fact that his life seemed to disintegrate at the same time a lot of UFOs were sighted?

68 **A:** Yes.

69 **Q:** *(L)* Was Ted Bundy abducted?[4]

70 **A:** Yes.

71 **Q:** *(L)* Was Ted Bundy programmed to do what he did?

72 **A:** Yes.

73 **Q:** *(L)* What was the purpose behind that programming?

74 **A:** We must withhold answer for the present.

75 **Q:** *(L)* Okay. Bundy described his murdering urges as a 'pressure building inside' him that he couldn't overcome, and it seemed to cause him to stop being 'human', as we think of it. That seems to me to be an example of an implant being able to overcome a person's social behavior, or controls over antisocial tendencies. Is this also what happened to the person who killed JO?

76 **A:** Maybe.

77 **Q:** *(L)* Is there a connection between the newly missing girl, CB, and JO?

78 **A:** You are doing well in your probing of the knowledge within on this issue, we suggest continuance, after all, learning is fun!

79 **Q:** *(L)* So, it seems to me that there was a connection between the appearance of CB and JO. Could it be that the individual who killed one or both of them was programmed to respond to this particular type facial characteristic? Could that be part of the programming?

80 **A:** End subject.

81 **Q:** *(L)* What do you mean?

82 **A:** We have helped you all that is necessary for now on this matter. It is beneficial for you to continue on your own for growth.

83 **Q:** *(L)* Can I ask just one or two more little questions in a different direction? I mean, this is like walking away and leaving me in the dark!

84 **A:** No it is not!

85 **Q:** *(L)* I would like to be able to solve this because the families are in pain and have asked for help.

---

[4] *The Wave* 21

86 **A:** Why don't you trust your incredible abilities? If we answer for you now, you will be helpless when it becomes necessary for you to perform this function on a regular basis, as it will be!!!!

87 **Q:** *(L)* Well, frankly, I don't want to be involved in any more murder investigations. It is too upsetting. Am I supposed to do this sort of thing regularly?!

88 **A:** Not same arena.

89 **Q:** *(L)* Well, then how do you mean "perform this function"?

90 **A:** No, seeing the unseen.[5]

91 **Q:** *(L)* Okay, shift gears. I received a rather nasty letter from Jason D____. He said he was getting tired of listening to the Cs trash his favorite channel o'choice. After all, he *is* the one who *asked* me!

92 **A:** He will come around if he follows his instincts. J___ M___.[6]

93 **Q:** *(L)* Yes! That reminds me that I wanted to ask you about him. He wanted me to ask you if I should pull him out of school.

94 **A:** What do you think?

95 **Q:** *(L)* I think he is miserable, but he does not want to 'give up' or be viewed as a 'quitter', or a baby. He is torn between his misery and disgust with the system, and his desire for peace. I would like to know why that kid attacked him the other day?

96 **A:** Attack.

97 **Q:** *(L)* You mean stimulated through 4th density?

98 **A:** Yes.

99 **Q:** *(L)* Is there anything I can do to help protect him?

100 **A:** What do you think?

101 **Q:** *(L)* Well. I don't know what to think.

102 **A:** Don't avoid the issue, it is of paramount importance!

103 **Q:** *(L)* Yes, I think I ought to take [my son] out of school. There is just too much attack going on from all directions, and that is *one* that I can close off.

104 **A:** Instincts preserve 3rd density experience.

---

[5] It has only been after years that I have actually begun to understand the depth of meaning in this response: "Why don't you trust your incredible abilities? If we answer for you now, you will be helpless when it becomes necessary for you to perform this function on a regular basis, as it will be!!!! ... seeing the unseen." Only after our research into psychopathology began as a consequence of later events did it begin to make sense. I began to understand why so many individuals who set off on a path to becoming more awake and aware, to know and develop their inner core self, get side-tracked; it really is like the Fable of the Magician told by Gurdjieff as recounted in Ouspensky's book *In Search of the Miraculous*. "Seeing the unseen" is not seeing rainbows and unicorns and auras; it is quite simply being able to read the symbols of our reality, including human behavior. It is a survival skill that most people have lost entirely and therefore are continually at the mercy of negative forces.

[6] My son. It was arresting that the Cs so definitely reminded me of the fact that I wanted to ask questions about my son's experiences in middle school. There were gangs that had targeted him for bullying and the situation was extremely worrying.

Q: *(L)* What does that mean? You say that the issue is of paramount importance. Why?

A: Instincts preserve 3rd density existence.

Q: *(L)* There is some threat to his existence in 3rd density if I *don't* do something right away?

A: Yes.

Q: *(L)* Is this threat from outside sources?

A: Yes.

Q: *(L)* So I need to pull him out of school *now*.

A: Follow instincts.

Q: *(L)* That's clear enough for me. I have the feeling [my son] is here for a purpose and that is why he has so much difficulty interacting with persons who are not as concerned about things as he is. Is this correct?

A: Yes.

Q: *(L)* Now, I want to ask my Sheldon Nidle channeling question.

A: Suggest you not waste energy on this.

Q: *(L)* There are a lot of people who are convinced by Sheldon Nidle that there is going to be a photon belt and a mass landing of UFOs in the fall of this year. Is this, in fact, going to occur?

A: People are very convinced by Bo and Peep.[7]

Q: *(L)* Okay, I won't put any more energy in that. Thanks for the assist tonight. Goodnight.

A: Goodnight.

End of Session

---

[7] Reference to the Heaven's Gate cult? We hadn't even heard of them at this point in time. "Heaven's Gate was an American UFO religious Millenarian group based in San Diego, California, founded in the early 1970s and led by Marshall Applewhite (1931–1997) and Bonnie Nettles (1927–1985). On March 26, 1997, police discovered the bodies of 39 members of the group who had committed mass suicide in order to reach what they believed was an extraterrestrial spacecraft following Comet Hale-Bopp. Applewhite and Nettles used a variety of aliases over the years, notably 'Bo and Peep' and 'Do and Ti' (pronounced doe and tea)." (Wikipedia, "Heaven's Gate (religious group)")

January 13, 1996

This is one of several sessions that were made almost unintelligible due to static noise. This had never occurred with the particular tape recorder used in over two years, and only occurred in seeming relationship to the interaction of Pat Z. In fact, during *this* session, two recorders were used, and *both* tapes were nearly ruined. One is immediately reminded of the exchange from the previous session:

Q: *(L)* I just played the tape back and it is all muddy. Could you tell us why we are having this problem with the tape?

A: Telekinetic wave transfer.

Q: *(L)* What is this telekinetic wave transferring?

A: Evolving energy.

Q: *(L)* Given off by us?

A: Both to and from.

Q: *(L)* From us to you?

A: You and others, not us.

Q: *(L)* Who are these others?

A: 4th density eavesdroppers, Pat's involvement should "heat things up."

Q: *(L)* Is Pat's involvement going to be beneficial to this work?

A: Yes, but also expect anomalies.

Obviously, things were getting very strange. Despite the transmission anomalies, there are a couple of items in this session that are just fascinating, particularly the bit about communicating with the dead and the monitoring process described in respect of Pat.

Finally, we meet here PatrickZ, the son of PatZ who is going to have a significant role in the soap-opera that our lives became as a consequence of the connection with this extremely strange family. Patrick was with his mother in the car on the night of her alleged abduction that is described in *The Wave* and the *St. Petersburg Times* article referenced in the previous session. I don't know if all families with close secret government connections are as dysfunctional as this one was/is, but there was a similar dynamic in the family of Sue V.

Participants: 'Frank', Laura, Pat Z, Patrick Z (Pk)

Q: *(L)* Hello.

A: Hello.

Q: *(L)* What name do we use this evening?

A: Yommor.

Q: *(L)* And where do you transmit from?

A: Cassiopaea.

Q: *(L)* Okay, we have Pat and Patrick here with us this evening. I would like to ask, as the first question, about the invitation to do online chats and channeling through Mike Lindemann's IS-CNI. Is this an acceptable mode of communication for this source? Because, if so, we think we can figure out a way to do it.

A: Okay.

Q: *(L)* Is this a desirable forum?

A: Yes.

Q: *(L)* I have worked on preparing a little biographical sketch about the Cs, and would like to know if it is acceptable as is?

A: This is up to you!

Q: *(L)* What is going on with Val Valerian? He was calling every week, and I have not heard from him in almost a week.[1]

A: He lost track of time.

Q: *(L)* Why did he lose track of time?

A: Busy with many projects. You must contact him because we see his desk topped with mounds of "stuff." He is interested, but just not for some period. [Short pause] Isis has uterine or cervical abrasion from birth process.[2]

Q: *(L)* What can I do to help her?

A: Vitamins A, D, E and a solution of Goldenseal root to be placed in food.[3]

Q: *(L)* Next question: I guess I ought to let Pat ask about it. *(P)* A man came to our shop last Monday and ordered a phenomenal amount of work and promised more work in the future if he is satisfied.

A: Good intentions. Is like a "self-styled" wheeler dealer.

Q: *(P)* Does he have the money to back up his good intentions?

A: Strings projects along ... Kiting, as in checks. Repeat: good intentions.

Q: *(S)* There are people who know they will have their pay on Friday, and they write checks on Thursday. *(P)* Yes, but it really is against the law. If it is not in the bank when you write the check, you are breaking the law.

A: Beware of errors in timing ... suggest that you be conservative in the processing of especially big orders. Take the checks to bank of writer to cash, when possible, and beware of out of area checks ... Steady in decisions regarding monumental tasks, do not attempt to

---

[1] *The Wave* 64

[2] Isis was my dog, who had given birth to five puppies, two of which died a short time after birth because Isis was unable to care for them. It had been several days, and Isis had been moved into the kitchen for warmth, but had been 'down' for several days. This comment was volunteered with no question asked.

[3] These instructions were carried out and Isis recovered completely within 10 days, with definite improvement noted after two days.

tackle large projects unless you are certain of the efficacy of fund transfers offered.

Q: *(P)* Next question: How does one determine if they are channeling a 3rd density dead dude, or a higher-density being?

A: Corrections and clarifications needed: "Dead Dudes" are 5th density beings. Either they are stuck in 3rd density, or they are communicating from 5th density, not 3rd density!! They are not 3rd density! 1st density includes all physical matter below the level of consciousness. 6th density is uniform in the level pattern of lightness, as there is complete balance on this density level, and the lightness is represented as knowledge. 7th density is union with the one ... it is timeless in every sense of the word, as its "essence" radiates through all that exists in all possible awareness realms. The light one sees at the termination of each conscious physical manifestation is the union, itself. Remember, 4th density is the first that includes variable physicality!! Ponder this carefully!!! And, remember, there is only one "God," and that the creator includes all that is created and vice versa![4]

Q: [Three names were given of scientists who worked for the U.S. government, asking if they were part of the reason Pat had been abducted and implanted, as was described in a previous session attended by Pat. All three names were lost in static bursts, but the response to all three names was "yes." The last name was recorded in the notes and was Bob Nathan at JPL. Then, the following remark was made.]

A: Big involvement there! Microwave technology has many applications. Laser, ELF, electromagnetic.[5]

Q: *(P)* Was Vic's last assignment ...[6]

A: Was used, but not consistently.

Q: *(P)* Was what Vic was told about the job he was doing a complete lie, or was it the truth?

A: Close, but a few details off.

Q: *(P)* Was it because he was too strong

---

[4] The topic of 'going into the light' as a trap has recently come up in our forum discussions. It seems that there are a number of sources that promulgate this idea, which goes against everything the Cs have said (particularly in this statement) as well as my years of experience doing spirit release therapy. I made a series of videos explaining the process of SRT and the interested reader should refer to them for very detailed information. Part One begins here: https://www.youtube.com/playlist?list=PL6A5636AF74D4C560. As to why anyone would wish to propagate the idea that going toward the light after death is a trap, I can only suggest that it might be part of the plot of the Lords of Serpent Power; re-read the session from 11 November 1995. As I note in my SRT videos, over the years, I became painfully aware how much suffering has been brought on humanity by wrong beliefs and expectations about death and the afterlife.

[5] *The Wave* 64. Also, check out the interview with John Lear here: http://www.bibliotecapleyades.net/sociopolitica/sociopol_lear03d.htm. There's quite a bit about Bob Nathan there.

[6] Remainder of question lost in static noise. Vic was Pat's husband, who had worked on secret government research at an underground facility and was now dying.

willed to be controlled by an implant, that he was retired?

A: He was trained in applications, not reversal of command instructions.

Q: *(P)* Does that mean that he wouldn't have sold out to the ones who put in the implant, that he was loyal to his employer?

A: Not quite correct concept, it means that he could not be relied upon to reverse "course" upon activation of subliminal instructions.

Q: *(P)* How could I be used to monitor personnel when I never noticed anything as being unusual?

A: Very complex, in fact, parallel subject. Pat is "locator probe" for the purpose of monitoring those in her midst. Telling is not important, reading is. Besides, most of the work performed did not involve conscious awareness.

Q: *(L)* Is this still going on?[7]

A: Partly, but also, Pat could be used as a probe to monitor all events taking place at JPL and other laboratories by examining aural imprints of her husband and others with whom she was acquainted. All events leave permanent imprints upon aural energy fields. This explains, for example, some sightings and apparitions. "Ghosts" are sometimes merely spontaneous activations of the aural records of the natural surroundings.[8]

Q: *(P)* [Question lost in static burst, but it was something about seeing a blue light ahead on the side of the road the night she and Patrick experienced 'missing time' on their journey home.]

A: No, Pat, the "blue thing" you saw was not an aural imprint reading, it was a 4th density craft partially transferred into 3rd density. Your deep subconscious memory remembers much, much more.

Q: *(L)* Patrick wants to know about the sound he hears in his head that he was describing earlier.

A: It is Patrick.

Q: *(L)* You mean his own internal sound?

A: Close.

Q: *(Pk)* What does it mean?

A: Discover.

Q: *(P)* Does the knife incident have anything to do with it? The memory of Patrick cutting his thumb with a knife, immediately after the blue light?[9]

A: Yes.

Q: *(P)* What did the knife have to do with it?

A: Screen memory. Goodnight.[10]

End of Session

---

[7] *High Strangeness* 8; *The Wave* 21

[8] What strikes me as intensely interesting about this remark is "All events leave permanent imprints upon aural energy fields." Does everything in existence have an "aural energy field"? Does the Earth itself have one? The entire cosmos?

[9] See *The Wave*, chapter 44, for details of the abduction experience.

[10] I really should have taken note of this abrupt ending and the fact that all sessions where Pat was present were anomalous.

January 20, 1996

In this session we meet MM. As the reader already knows, this was during the time I was putting the first issue of our new magazine together. To quickly recap for those who may not have read the previous volume of sessions: The owner of the New Age bookstore in Tampa mentioned in previous sessions, Marti, referred MM to me. I've written about this in *The Wave* beginning at Chapter 18. MM wanted to talk to me about placing an ad in the magazine.

MM claimed to be a somewhat well-known New Age teacher of many subjects including Reiki, meditation, aura-reading, create your own reality, and a slew of other interesting things. She was quite attractive, very blonde and Nordic looking, and a real 'ball of fire' at getting things organized for her many classes and seminars. She claimed that her lectures drew big crowds, that she received great reviews for her work, and was generally quite popular in the New Age communities around the country. (I recently looked her up on Facebook and found that she got 'saved' and is now a Fundie.)

MM traveled to many New Age or UFO seminars, expositions and conferences, making new contacts and connections, spreading the word (whatever it was she was spreading) and taking aura photos. She also said that she was occasionally invited to appear on television and radio as a paranormal expert, and at one point I heard that she was claiming she had gotten a Ph.D. in metaphysics by mail and published a book, though I have never been able to find it at any bookstore or on the Internet.

Anyway, MM called me about placing an ad in our magazine. She wanted a quarter page, which we were selling for $350.00. However, she didn't have the money to pay for it, so she asked me if I would be willing to do an exchange. I asked her what she had in mind, and she said that she would come to one of our sessions with her Polaroid aura camera and take photos of all the participants as well as the process itself. That sounded completely cool, so I agreed. It also happened to be the same session that Pat Z was going to attend. Well, the more the merrier!

Early on the evening of the session, MM arrived before anyone else to haul in and set up her equipment. I examined it all as she did so and realized that it was a pretty simple concept. It was pretty much just an ordinary Polaroid camera mounted on a tripod. The so-called aura photos are the result of photomontage technique where an illusion of an aura is created. There is a light source inside the camera that illuminates the film directly based on the measured electrical skin resistance that the camera gets when you hold some metal rods or put your hands on metal plates; this creates the alleged 'aura'. At the same time, the camera is photographing you in an ordinary way. That is why I was so amazed at the 'aura photographs' of myself and the board, which pretty much went against the rules of how this setup should work, as you will see below.

Sue arrived late and came in while we were in the middle of all this photography. She was very quiet and soon complained of a headache and declined to participate in the aura photography.

After we were done with all the pictures, MM announced that, except for my photo and the photo of the board, she expected to be paid for her 'services'! She quoted exorbitant prices that she claimed she received for this work, as well as a special 'fee' for having brought the equipment to us!

I was, needless to say, a bit surprised with this 'bait and switch' routine, but not wanting to engage in a dispute over it, I decided that I would just pay for all the participants since I was the one who had told them that MM was bringing the camera as an exchange, and they had all participated believing that there was no additional charge. However, the group, seeing the situation for what it really was, came to my rescue and paid for their photos. In the end, my aura photo and the aura photo of the board were quite expensive: about $175 apiece! That's a pretty pricey Polaroid considering that the camera used ordinary Polaroid film that sold for about $12 a pack of ten photos! Only one pack was used in this case.

After what seemed to be a fleecing of my guests, MM declined to stay for the rest of the session. This puzzled me, because I thought she had said she wanted to ask specific questions. She packed up her equipment and left.

After MM was gone, we resumed our session.

Participants: 'Frank', Laura, Pat Z, Patrick Z (Pk), SZ (daughter of PZ), Sue V, MM (local 'aura photographer'), Wilma (friend of MM)

1 **Q**: *(L)* Hello. We have a lot of guests tonight!

2 **A**: Hello. No need to direct traffic.

3 **Q**: *(L)* What name shall we use tonight?

4 **A**: Yodnor.

5 **Q**: *(L)* And where do you transmit from?

6 **A**: Cassiopaea.

7 **Q**: *(L)* MM is here tonight with her aura camera. Is it possible to take a picture of us while channeling, and will anything show up?

8 **A**: Try it and see.

9 **Q**: *(L)* We certainly will, but we want to ask a question before we get started on that. There are rumors out that Betelgeuse has gone supernova and it can be seen with a telescope, but not yet with the naked eye. When did this occur?[1]

10 **A**: You better check the data.

11 **Q**: *(L)* Okay. Is this going to have any effect on us?

12 **A**: No.

13 **Q**: *(L)* Is it going to have any effect on us in an ethereal sense?

14 **A**: No.

15 **Q**: *(L)* Is it just something that has happened that is going to be interesting to look at?

16 **A**: Open.[2]

17 **Q**: *(L)* We are going to take a little break and let MM set up the camera. [Camera is set up, metal plates are arranged so that L puts right hand on one and F puts left hand on one, and their other hands are kept on the planchette.] *(L)* Hi, guys! What do you think of all this equipment?

18 **A**: Yes, neat!

19 **Q**: [Preparations being made for aura photos. L and F draped in black cloth.] *(S)* Laura, you have something stuck in your hair! *(F)* It's a pen. *(S)* She's always got things stuck in her hair. No telling what else is in there! *(P)* Yeah. It's pretty wild tonight. You look like a witch! *(L)* Well, you people are so nice tonight!

20 **A**: Which?

21 **Q**: [Laughter] *(L)* Okay, everybody... settle down! We had some plans for questions tonight.

22 **A**: Okay.

23 **Q**: *(L)* Yes, does anybody remember the questions? Where is the list? Wilma, ask a question because I just went blank! [Laughter]

24 **A**: Ask Wilma. [Laughter]

25 **Q**: *(L)* We were curious as to what was photographed by MM and SV when

---

[1] This rumor was conveyed by MM who, apparently, had been told it by Wilma.

[2] I would suggest that the Cs' brief responses to this topic indicated that it simply was not true, but they were not inclined to state that clearly, since MM and Wilma were so invested in believing it.

they were in Central America? There was some fuzzy image on the photo. Chichen Itza, I believe.

26 **A**: Aural imprints.

27 **Q**: *(L)* Of what? [Aura photo taken of Frank]

28 **A**: Representations in zero space/time of members of "Quan" sect of supreme spiritualists who vacated the body simultaneously.

29 **Q**: *(W)* Well, I am just coming in in the middle and I don't know what has been asked before. Who is the most likely candidate to be elected president this year?

30 **A**: Well, this is not of great importance, as the president does not make the decisions, but it is likely to be Dole, as the points are aligning now. But, there is a lot to be seen between now and then. Future is open.[3]

31 **Q**: *(MM)* Let me move the camera around, I want to get one of Laura now. *(S)* Look at Frank's photo. It looks like there is a hand around his arm! *(F)* It doesn't look like anything to me. *(MM)* I am going to try to get one of the middle of the board where their hands are. *(L)* Guys! Are you here and ready for a mug shot?

32 **A**: Yes.

33 **Q**: *(MM)* Take a deep breath and hold ... [Aura photo of Laura is taken.]

(L) [After a few minutes, looking at aura photo of self.] This is very strange, guys. How come I am not in this picture and Frank shows up in his? Why have I physically disappeared?

34 **A**: Learning builds spiritual growth, and awareness "solidifies" knowledge.[4]

35 **Q**: *(L)* Okay, guys, smile for the camera! [Aura photo of board is taken with Laura's and Frank's fingers on planchette.] *(L)* Okay, but that does not explain why I disappeared.

36 **A**: Because the energy field enclosure was unifying you with the conduit, as is usual during channeling sessions between 3rd and 6th density level communications.

37 **Q**: [Photo of board develops, and geometric figure appears to sounds of amazement from group.] *(L)* What is this geometric figure?

38 **A**: Was a visual representation of the conduit, indeed!!! The reason for such clear luminescence is that thought centers were clear and open in you at the moment of the photograph. In other words, there was an imbalance of energy coming from 6th density transmission point. So, what you are viewing is 100 per cent pure light energy of uncorrupted knowledge transmitted through you. This has never been seen in 3rd density ever before. You do not completely realize the ramifications of this

---

[3]Obviously, the Cs were wrong about the presidential election. Turnout was registered at 49.0%, the lowest for a presidential election since 1924. President Clinton's chances of winning were initially considered slim in the middle of his term as his party had lost both the House and the Senate in 1994 for the first time in decades; he had reneged on promises to cut taxes in order to reduce the deficit, enacted a Federal assault weapons ban, and had a failed healthcare reform initiative. After the election, there was a scandal about campaign finance. (See Wikipedia, "United States campaign finance controversy".)

[4]*Secret History* 12; *The Wave* 3, 20, 46

yet, but you will. We have made history here tonight folks!!!!!⁵

[Break while more individual aura photos are taken. When finished, MM and Wilma pack equipment and depart. Discussion of grammar.]

39 **Q**: *(L)* I would like you to comment on our discussion on grammar. Does acquiring knowledge in a spiritual sense assist in the development of knowledge in other areas, such as communication?

40 **A**: Correctness in all areas, as agreed upon by convention, can only serve to help or improve or strengthen all processes.

41 **Q**: *(P)* I would like to know what I can do to improve my memory?⁶

42 **A**: You have sleep disorders that are short circuiting what would ordinarily be utterly spectacular psychic and mental abilities. When you were very young, your senses were 10 times sharper. But then, the "interferences began."

43 **Q**: *(P)* That is absolutely true. I have had a sleep problem for years. *(L)* Is there anything Pat can do to overcome this? Physically or otherwise?

44 **A**: Cleansing of a very intensive nature; hypnotic regression; spirit release and dietary adjustments. Also, stress-inducing life circumstances of a very "ordinary" nature must all be deviated! Ordinary, in this instance, means not of an ethereal nature directly.

45 **Q**: *(P)* Well, I have taken several steps in that direction.

46 **A**: Some, but it is like putting a "bandaid" on a gunshot wound.

47 **Q**: *(P)* What is the implant I have made of?

48 **A**: Silicon based micron definitive construct.

49 **Q**: *(P)* Is this why I have this scar?

50 **A**: Scar is manifestation of scar in being.

51 **Q**: *(S)* I have been having some serious problems with joint pain in my fingers and I would like to know what to do to make this better, because I think that taking pain pills is something that hides the symptoms and does nothing for the cause.

52 **A**: Not true, S__, sometimes pain killers cure cause as well as symptom. This is simply reversal of therapy. The symptom dies, thus cutting off the energy flow of the causative problem. Then the root cause dies if its "fuel supply" is interrupted for an adequate duration.⁷

53 **Q**: *(L)* Will this work on me?

54 **A**: You need to utilize herbal therapies and nerve or neural blocking techniques, such as self-hypnosis and Reiki and acupuncture.

55 **Q**: *(L)* Well, I have been having a horrible pain in my leg that makes me un-

---

⁵See images at the end of this session. Even today I have no explanation for the extraordinary photograph even if the processes of 'aura cameras' have been more or less debunked. A Polaroid instant camera has a pretty well understood process and what happened here defied that process completely.

⁶*The Wave* 64

⁷I've always found this to be a fascinating perspective on pain as a feedback system that can be broken from either direction.

able to walk without a cane. What is causing this pain?

56 **A:** Tissue nodular grains passing through vascular region affected by mild thrombosis. Try nutragina and roots of water based plants such as spirulina, for starters.

57 **Q:** *(L)* Isn't neutrogina a soap?[8]

58 **A:** Base is edible and topical.

59 **Q:** *(L)* Anything else on that?

60 **A:** Chlorella.

61 **Q:** *(L)* Where do I get that?

62 **A:** Leafy green vegetables.

63 **Q:** *(L)* Pat has been having almost an identical pain in her leg. Is it a similar condition?

64 **A:** Psychological pressures register in the physical. When acute psychological pressures are evident.

65 **Q:** *(P)* When is this acute pressure going to end?

66 **A:** Open. We recommend ginseng and guarana also for herbal remedies for displaced fatigue.

67 **Q:** *(L)* I am getting tired.

68 **A:** Goodnight.

End of Session

---

[8]I was assuming that "neutrogina" was what the Cs meant, but they spelled out "nutragina" which may be something else entirely.

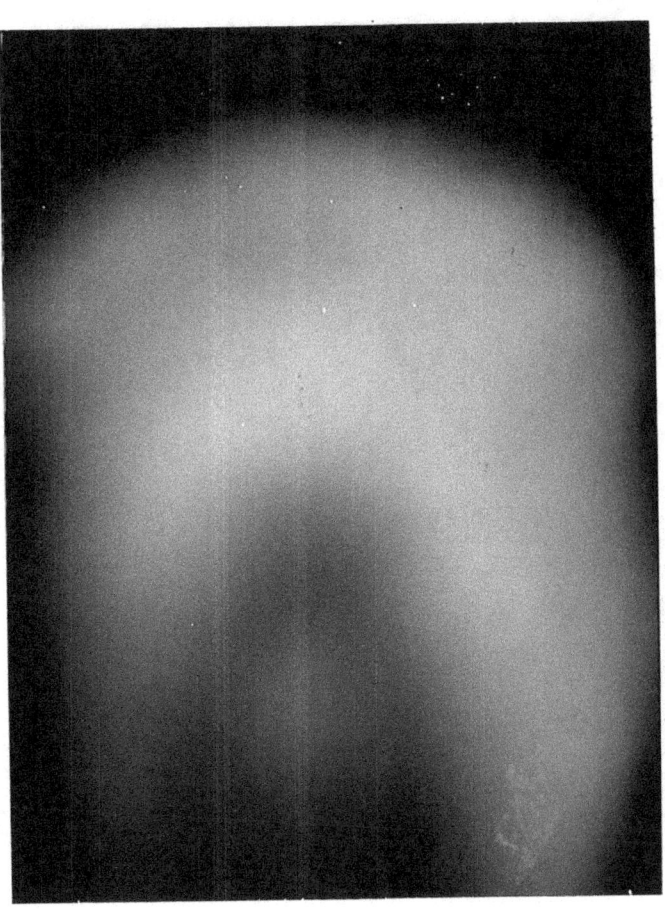

Image 1: Image taken of Laura (Scan of Polaroid instant film).

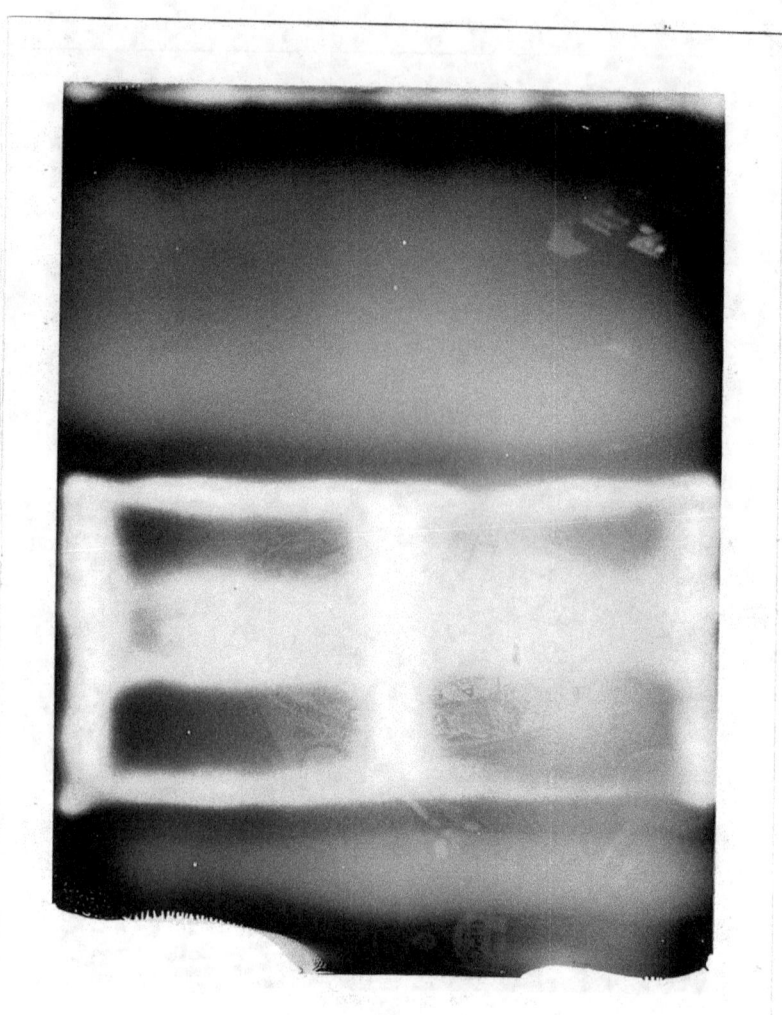

Image 2: Image taken of Laura and Franks hands on the spirit board (Scan of Polaroid instant film).

Image 3: Scan of Polaroid instant film in which Image 2 was exposed and developed. The bright, rectangular outlines in Image 2 even appear on the chemical reagent layer. Without knowing the exact mechanism of the used "Aura camera", it is impossible to explain why this particular rectangular shape was burnt even into the reagent layer. What is notable is the fact that the central image of the rectangular form was a pair of hands, Frank on the left, Laura on the right. They seem to be the main features of the image. The emulsion of the film pack was sucked away from the non-image areas to more or less force the brilliance of the light structure.

January 27, 1996

Now things really begin to get strange. As the reader knows, Sue and I had become quite close as friends and she was also my physical therapist (one of them), helping me to recover from the accident injuries from the December 1994 auto accident. We had also set up her mother and my mother in a house together so that they could live comfortably, though that situation was *not* turning out very well. The Cs kept giving hints and clues about this, but it seems that I was pretty dense and naive. There were some really strange things going on in the background here regarding Sue V that I want to go over briefly, using mostly my text from *The Wave* where I described the whole situation.

First of all, you may have noticed all the encouragement the Cs were giving me to "network via computer". I was doing my best, exploring the possibilities, though I was really a tech dummy. I was, however, able to manage email and navigate around AOL a bit. One of my net correspondents sent me the famous/infamous 'Greenbaum Speech' and something entitled 'Elaine and the Sisters of Light', which was drawn from a book entitled *They Came to Set the Captives Free* by a 'Dr. Rebecca Brown'.

The Greenbaum material offered a partial explanation for many strange things via exposure of a secret government mind-programming project. A quick and basic description is kind of like what was presented in the movie *The Manchurian Candidate*. What I began to wonder was: what if the descriptions of alleged satanic ritual abuse that emerged in the memories of various psychiatric patients was really an implanted memory engineered by the Greenbaum method for the purposes of hiding the real source and purpose of the Greenbaum programming?

Another question was: what if alleged alien abductions were also engineered memories just like the 'Elaine' and other ritual abuse material? Engineered, that is, via the Greenbaum program; again, to conceal the Greenbaum program?

Then, there was another way of thinking about it: what if the Greenbaum program and the Elaine program were both 'screen memories' of alien abductions?

In any event, I thought that the Greenbaum text deserved wider distribution and I planned to publish it in the first issue of the *Aurora Journal* along with a commentary giving my ideas as above. And, of course, it is just at the point that I am getting this magazine done that MM enters the scene.

Keep the previous session in mind. The next day, after that session, MM called and hemmed and hawed a bit before saying, "I have a question that I just have to ask you. Where did you meet Sue? How well do you know her?"

I was a little taken aback by this question, and, of course, I was still a bit put out by her behavior the night before, but told her that I knew Sue from a Reiki group and that, due to the accident, she had been one of my therapists for almost a year now.

"Are you guys connected with that coven up there in Hernando County?" MM next asked.

"What?!" I was flabbergasted. "What coven? Do you mean Wicca or something like that? Absolutely not! I don't mess with that mumbo jumbo stuff! What in the world made you think that?"

MM explained that she recognized Sue and she knew that she was involved in some sort of group that was deeply into ritual magick.

I was absolutely stunned. I was also a little angry because, after experiencing MM's double face the previous night, I was sure that there was some serious misunderstanding.

But, I wanted to understand why this woman would just call me on the phone and tell me that a member of our little close-knit group was a member of some cultic coven-type thing.

MM launched into a history of having been in a healing class of some kind with Sue back whenever. After the class graduated, they all went on a trip to the Yucatan to visit the Mayan ruins. I vaguely remembered Sue being absent from the Reiki group at one point and that when she reappeared, she talked about her trip to the Yucatan. So, I knew that MM must know something since that was a fact.

She went on. Apparently, she had been the one who shared the cruise ship cabin with Sue and had also been assigned to her on their 'buddy system' while they were sightseeing. She explained how Sue had tried to convert some of the members of this class to some of the ideas of this cult/coven saying that they were able to "really get results" with their rituals and so forth. She had approached MM with an invitation, but MM had declined, sensing that there was something unsavory about it.

She went on with some more details, many of which coincided with things I did know to be true and as she talked I became sicker and sicker. I realized now that there was an explanation for a lot of strange 'absences' and funny behaviors of Sue's that I had just shoved under the rug. It also explained her quietness the previous evening when MM was there – and maybe even why she didn't want her aura photo taken.

I was completely devastated. I just didn't see how Sue could have a whole secret life like that! Yet MM cited details about her that I knew were true! And at the same time, some of the missing pieces of Sue's own puzzle were falling into place.

My mind was racing for an answer. I knew that a well-to-do older couple – pillars of the community – had adopted Sue in the same area of the country that was the setting for the Elaine story; but that was just too crazy! And of course, my own mother was living with that woman!

I also knew that Sue had spent many of her early years as a Motorcycle Mama with the Outlaws motorcycle gang. Frank and I had discussed what a great epiphany Sue must have had to leave that life to go into massage therapy and metaphysical studies. We knew, from things that she had said, that there were some very dark things in her past. Frank had questioned her closely on one occasion and she had admitted to having been involved in covering up a murder, though she made it explicit that she had not participated in the actual murder.

But she was so soft-hearted toward animals, and refused to even kill roaches, that I was convinced that her attitudes were certainly from the heart, and whatever reason had driven her out of her home to live with known criminals, she must have been horribly abused! I had nothing but sympathy for her. Plus, since we had made the living arrangements for the mothers, I had a lot invested in defending Sue.

So, I explained to MM that, even if that was the case a few years ago, Sue was definitely a reformed person now! There was just no way she could participate in something like that on one night of the week and then sit in on our sessions on another. She had been so devoted to me in helping me to recover from my accident that I simply could not believe that she was still connected to any of those people who, as I have described in *The Wave*, worked hard to do me bodily harm.

I then told MM about the metaphysical church folks and all that had transpired there, that Sue knew all about it and was definitely not involved with those people anymore.

MM was reassured and asked if she might now attend a session in the future. She had some very definite issues she wanted to deal with involving the many strange things that had been happening to her.

She claimed she was in an abusive marriage, her son had been hospitalized for a minor illness but was nearly killed by the anesthesiologist, and she had recently met a man who demonstrated signs that he might be her 'soul mate' and she was desperate to know what to do. All kinds of 'synchronous events' were happening between her and this man, she said, and I had just been through that scenario with another abductee, so I tried to warn her that it can be as much a warning as an indicator that one is going in the right direction.

I was wary of MM because she had already demonstrated that what she said at one time could not be relied upon in a consistent way. Nevertheless, against my better judgment, I agreed reluctantly. She then asked if she might bring her friend, Wilma, too.

However, before MM attended another session, we had one that was a bit more private. At this point, I'm aware of Sue's alleged hanging out with the Magick gang and had discussed it with Frank. However, Pat Z knew nothing about it. I should also note that I had come down with some kind of bug that almost wiped me out. I was dreadfully sick and it showed no signs of clearing up anytime soon. Also, right after the phone call from MM, Sue V had called me to tell me about a very strange dream she had that is discussed in this session. It was as though she knew that MM had 'given the game away'.

Participants: 'Frank', Laura, Pat Z, Patrick Z (Pk), Sue V

1 **Q**: *(L)* Hello.

2 **A**: Hello.

3 **Q**: *(L)* Who do we have with us?

4 **A**: Sorria.

5 **Q**: *(L)* And where do you transmit from?

6 **A**: Cassiopaea.

7 **Q**: *(L)* If you will bear with us tonight,

---
[1] *The Wave* 64

we would like to ask a couple of health related questions.[1]

A: Yes.

Q: *(L)* First, is this sickness that I am experiencing part of an 'attack'?

A: As always.

Q: *(L)* Is there anything I can do to terminate this kind of attack?

A: No. Prevent? Yes!

Q: *(L)* What can one do to prevent these kinds of attack?

A: Always watch all portals! Those around you are all portals always!

Q: *(L)* So, we are all portals. If everybody is a portal, it seems that you could spend all your time watching all of them and never get anything else done!

A: Incorrect, when portals are activated, you will know if you are watching!!! Your problem has been "falling down on the job," especially not being aware of the danger presented by those closest to you. You tend to expect attack to always come from more or less disassociated parties, and you frequently confuse issues: mode and source![2]

Q: *(L)* Well, is this especially true as we are on the verge of getting the magazine out and getting some things out on the internet?

A: Of course, that should be obvious.

Q: *(L)* Does that also include Pat's aches and pains every time we try to get the work done?

A: Yes, and expect more.

Q: *(L)* Well, I am so sick that I am ready to throw in the towel.

A: Throw in the towel?!? It's too late!! And besides, your life will dramatically improve if you persevere, as we have told you.[3]

Q: *(L)* Susan has had several dreams about a storm coming and having to batten down the hatches and relocating ...

A: Susan must inquire.

Q: *(S)* In my dream, it was either a physical move, or a moving on to something. Am I moving out of town in a physical way, is it a spiritual moving on, or am I moving in a different direction in terms of my path?[4]

A: That is four questions at once.

Q: *(S)* Am I going to be leaving the area?

A: Do you desire to?

Q: *(S)* No, I don't.

A: Then why would you expect that you would?

Q: *(S)* Well, that's what the dream was, but I know it's symbolic. Do you think maybe I could be moving on, hopefully spiritually? What does it mean, my moving on or relocating?

A: Vague.

Q: *(S)* Well, I just wonder in what way ... *(L)* Susan has said that she

---

[2] I would say that this was almost a direct warning about Sue because she was not only close to me friend-wise, but was also one of my physical therapists and that meant she worked directly on my physical body.

[3] Yet another of the hints that something big was around the corner.

[4] It seems obvious in retrospect that Sue knew exactly what she was talking about but was dissimulating.

thinks this dream means she is going to die ...[5]

A: Susan, ask your questions directly, please! If you "beat around the bush," we will also!

Q: *(S)* Will I be moving into 5th density soon?

A: What is "soon?"

Q: *(S)* Will it be sometime this year?

A: Only if you do something that might best be described as "ill advised."

Q: *(S)* Because of all these dreams about me moving on, could it have something to do with, like, in an earlier session you said that I was a, um, I was held over in 5th density as a learning channel. Now, I must have been learning [something] important to be held over as many times as I was. Will whatever I was learning in 5th density come in handy in this lifetime, maybe?

A: What do you think you have been doing for the past year, as you measure "time?" And, what is "moving on?"

Q: *(S)* Progressing?

A: Yes!!

Q: *(S)* You mean that what I am learning here, the knowledge I am getting here?

A: That is beside the point, somewhat.

Q: *(S)* The only other thing is therapy ... Is it the channeling?

A: Both, and more to come.

Q: *(S)* Well, I feel like I am just wasting my time in doing the therapy ...

A: Let it flow, Susan, don't worry about what all the twists and turns along the way mean ... It is the destination that matters, and that is not for you to know yet.

Q: *(S)* In all these dreams, I am repeatedly packing up to move. *(L)* Why are you worried about it? Let it flow. *(S)* Because I have never had dreams that repeated over and over. This is a first for me ...

A: Have you ever had other "firsts?"

Q: *(S)* Yes.

A: Did you panic over those?

Q: *(S)* Sometimes.

A: And what happened?[6]

Q: *(S)* I survived.

A: So...?

Q: *(S)* I just learn from them and grow from them ... *(L)* And don't we just answer our own questions? *(P)* I have a question. The lady who took the aura pictures the other night told me that I can astrally project. Is this true?

A: Everyone can.

Q: *(Pk)* Am I special?

A: Vague.

Q: *(Pk)* America has a flag, does Cassiopaea have a symbol? I want a symbol for my magazine ... I mean your magazine.

A: We have given two.

Q: *(L)* The wheel with seven spokes and the triple pyramid with the circle. *(P)* Together?

---

[5] This was the high drama that Sue had presented to me when she told me about the dream. Obviously, in retrospect, it was designed to elicit my sympathy and put me off any suspicions.

[6] *The Wave* 5

64 **A**: No. Ask more, Patrick, as two very recent events have served to blast open your learning channel.

65 **Q**: *(Pk)* Then they must know exactly what I am going to ask. I want to know if they can put something in my subconscious for the cover design. I need proof.

66 **A**: Proof, what is that?

67 **Q**: *(Pk)* What is proof? Never mind. I'm afraid to ask.

68 **A**: Ask, what do you think we will do? Disintegrate you where you sit?

69 **Q**: *(Pk)* The rumbling ... Does everybody have this? The rumbling sound in my head?

70 **A**: Vague, but we will answer if "everyone" were to choose to have it, then everyone would have it.

71 **Q**: *(L)* What is it that Patrick perceives as a rumbling in his head? Apparently, when he turns it on, it has a pronounced effect on his aura.

72 **A**: Turn on a radio between channels, and what do you hear?

73 **Q**: *(L)* Static. *(Pk)* Buzzing. More than one channel? *(L)* What are the channels?

74 **A**: That is not the issue. Turn on a radio that has its tuner between channels, and what do you hear???

75 **Q**: *(L)* You hear static. And this would imply that the radio could be tuned.

76 **A**: Yes.

77 **Q**: *(Pk)* And that is what I need to work on?

78 **A**: If you wish.

79 **Q**: *(L)* I don't know too many people who can turn this on and off ...

80 **A**: But you know people who have it "on" all the time, and always tuned.

81 **Q**: *(L)* I guess. *(Pk)* Does it have anything to do with why the aliens did not abduct me back in 1987 on the road trip through Pennsylvania?

82 **A**: That is not important.

83 **Q**: *(L)* Yes. They wanted his mom, not him! *(Pk)* Do I have an implant?

84 **A**: No.

85 **Q**: *(Pk)* Will I have an implant?

86 **A**: ?

87 **Q**: *(L)* Sheldon Nidle has written a book called *Becoming a Galactic Human*. He has said that the Earth is going to go into a photon belt sometime this summer, that there is going to be three days of darkness, and the poo is going to hit the fan, so to speak, the aliens are going to land in the late summer or the fall, and they are all coming here to help us. Could you comment on these predictions?

88 **A**: No.

89 **Q**: *(L)* Is a fleet of aliens going to land on Earth and be announced by the media in 1996?

90 **A**: No.

91 **Q**: *(P)* In 1997?

92 **A**: No.

93 **Q**: *(L)* Could you comment on the source of this book: *Three Days of Darkness*, by Divine Mercy?[7]

---

[7]Both of these books were very popular at the time, and the book by 'Divine Mercy' was shown to me by Pat Z who was very taken by it. She was a great believer in apparitions of the Virgin Mary.

94 **A**: Source?!?

95 **Q**: *(L)* Well, is there going to be three days of darkness in 1998 like it says?

96 **A**: Why does this continue to be such a popular notion? And, why is everyone so obsessed with, are you ready for this, trivia...? Does it matter if there is three days of darkness?!? Do you think that is the "be all and end all?" What about the reasons for such a thing? ... at all levels, the ramifications? It's like describing an atomic war in prophecy by saying: "Oh my, oh my, there is going to be three hours of a lot of big bangs, oh my!!"

97 **Q**: *(L)* Well, you didn't say it wasn't going to happen in the fall of 1998. Is it?

98 **A**: First of all, as we have warned you repeatedly, it is literally impossible to attach artificially conceived calendar dates to any sort of prophecy or prediction for the many reasons that we have detailed for you numerous times. And we have not said that this was going to happen.

99 **Q**: *(L)* I know that you are saying that this three days of darkness is trivial considering the stupendous things that are involved in realm crossings. But, a lot of these people are interpreting this as just three days of darkness ... then wake up in paradise. I would like to have some sort of response to this question.

100 **A**: Trust us to lead you when and how it is appropriate. You should already know that to attempt apply 3rd density study and interpretations to 4th density events and realities is useless in the extreme ... This is why UFO researchers keep getting 3 new questions for every 1 answer they seek with their "research." If you will trust us, we will always give you not only the most correct answers to each and every inquiry, but also the most profound answers. If the individual does not understand, then that means they are either prejudiced, or not properly tuned in.

101 **Q**: *(L)* Previously you told us about the Southwest region of the United States becoming 4th density. Will the people who live there become 4th density beings? Or will they be 3rd density beings in 3rd density?

102 **A**: Some of both bleed-in and bleed-out.

103 **Q**: *(L)* Recently Frank had an experience where he heard me calling him as he was going in his door. Then, he heard [my son] talking to him here in my kitchen when [my son] was up in bed. He was worried that it meant something had happened, but it was apparently nothing of the sort. So, what was it?

104 **A**: Increased awareness of ethereal imprints.

105 **Q**: *(L)* When I was standing at the washer the other night, I heard someone clap their hands very loudly right behind me. Nobody was there.

106 **A**: Same.

107 **Q**: *(L)* You said earlier that if I just persevere that my life will improve dramatically and immediately. So, when you say this, do you mean really sudden and in a big way?

108 **A**: Open.

109 **Q**: *(L)* Are you going to give me any clues on this?

110 **A**: No.

111 **Q**: *(Pk)* Do you ever laugh?

112 **A**: Yes.

113 **Q:** *(Pk)* Do you miss being in 3rd density?

114 **A:** Do you miss being in 2nd? Or first?

115 **Q:** *(Pk)* Are you laughing at us?

116 **A:** Yes. And no, Patrick, we were 3rd density beings in fact we are you in the "future!" We were you, and we are you, and we were 3rd density. Do you understand the significance of the last statement, or would you rather just brush it off? We are you and we were you and we were 3rd density but we are not now 3rd density and you are not yet 6th density.

117 **Q:** *(L)* How do you spend your 'time'?

118 **A:** Teaching, sharing, assisting.

119 **Q:** *(L)* What do you do for fun?

120 **A:** That is fun!

121 **Q:** *(PZ)* With each other?

122 **A:** No.

123 **Q:** *(PZ)* With who?

124 **A:** Densities 1, 2, 3, 4, 5.

125 **Q:** *(PZ)* Do we all have a guardian angel? Each and every one of us? One to a person?

126 **A:** Not correct concept.

127 **Q:** *(L)* What is the correct concept?

128 **A:** Not possible for you to comprehend.

129 **Q:** *(L)* How do we get assistance from higher realms?

130 **A:** By asking and ...

131 **Q:** *(L)* What is the limit to the kind of assistance we can receive?

132 **A:** Limit?!? We live within a realm that includes no such thing!!!

133 **Q:** *(L)* Well, the 'angel thing' is pretty big nowadays. There are an awful lot of angels running around. My first thought was, 'What better way for the bad guys to deceive than to appear as angels?'

134 **A:** Not true!!! STS *can* appear as entities incorrectly perceived as "angels," but if it is really a sixth density being, incorrect perception is not possible.

135 **Q:** *(L)* I don't understand. There are a *lot* of beings who deceive people. They produce phenomena, they do any number of things including making people 'feel good,' have dreams, and all that. What do you mean that incorrect perception is not possible? It happens all the time!

136 **A:** No.

137 **Q:** *(L)* Well, what is the story here?

138 **A:** Your perception abilities are short-circuiting due to vibrational interaction.[8]

139 **Q:** *(L)* If you there is anywhere in you a question about what you are perceiving, then that question is an indication that all the rest of what you are perceiving could be false?

140 **A:** Part of the equation.

141 **Q:** *(L)* So, if it is really a 6th density being, it will blow you away to such an extent that there is *no* question?

142 **A:** Yes.

143 **Q:** *(L)* Now, what is the other part of the equation?

---

[8] I think the Cs were giving me a little hint here that the current company was, perhaps, not the most beneficial. Notice how the session ends abruptly. The Cs really weren't terribly fond of Pat Z and her kids and I think Sue was on the list too.

144 **A:** Well, why do you question us? First of all, you question us because the communication is limited at this point ... you are not yet prepared for stronger envelopment.

145 **Q:** *(PZ)* So, I should continue to pray?

146 **A:** All goes to 6th density.

147 **Q:** *(PZ)* Okay, let's say that I have a little child who is dying of leukemia, and I am praying with everything in me, and the child dies anyway. I don't get it. What's the deal here?

148 **A:** Wrong. If child dies, that is your lesson profile.

149 **Q:** *(PZ)* Well, why isn't my lesson profile with this particular situation that is going on in my life right now, why isn't it continuing? I thought that maybe I need to ...

150 **A:** Is it over yet, Pat?

151 **Q:** *(PZ)* No, it isn't over yet, but ...

152 **A:** So, what is your question, if it is not yet concluded?

153 **Q:** *(PZ)* Can you feel what I am thinking?

154 **A:** Yes.

155 **Q:** *(PZ)* So, why do I need to ask?

156 **A:** Because we never interfere with free will.

157 **Q:** *(PZ)* If I continue to pray, things will continue to get better?

158 **A:** Things will stay on their intended course.

159 **Q:** *(PZ)* Are you telling me that my life has been predestined?

160 **A:** No. If you continue to pray, there is no chance of your lessons being interrupted or deferred. Clarify.

161 **Q:** *(PZ)* Well, that sounds like it is going to continue, it is not going to stop.

162 **A:** No, clarify means to solidify your understanding of the answer.

163 **Q:** *(PZ)* Well, I don't understand. *(L)* I think it is pretty clear that the things you are experiencing are part of the lessons.

164 **A:** Whatever that is ... i.e.: que sera sera.

165 **Q:** *(PZ)* But then, we are back to predestiny?

166 **A:** No, lessons.

167 **Q:** *(PZ)* Well, how many damn lessons do you have to get?

168 **A:** As many "damn" lessons as you need!

169 **Q:** *(S)* What about the prayers that are directed to Jesus?

170 **A:** Jesus is one of us in "special service" sector.

171 **Q:** *(L)* Like a 'green beret'?

172 **A:** No, more like a "beige beret."

173 **Q:** *(L)* What is a "beige beret"?

174 **A:** Just our term.

175 **Q:** *(PZ)* Well, I have just always wondered if this praying business is a bunch of malarkey. *(L)* Oh, no. *(PZ)* If I pray a rosary, I am praying to the Virgin Mary. Who is she? Where is she?

176 **A:** "She" is here too.

177 **Q:** *(PZ)* Does that prayer go directly to her and does she then send you out to do whatever?

178 **A:** She is not really a she. And when you write to "Ann Landers," does she really see it? And goodnight.

End of Session

February 3, 1996

There are a number of things about this session that ought to be said. First of all, as usual, when Tom French of the *St. Petersburg Times*, and photographer Cherie Diez, were present, the energy was off in some way. It was, I think, a reflection of Frank's anger that he was not the subject in which they were particularly interested. That doesn't mean that answers are incorrect, because Frank was quite interested in 'showing off'.

The second thing is that, again, Pat Z and her kids were present and that also contributed to static because of their strong Catholic beliefs. MM, the 'aura photographer' discussed previously, was also present.

Finally, my dear friend, Sandra DeP was present. Though we did not know it, she would be dead in about two months, so it is curious that she was asking about death issues. I don't recall what Sue V was talking about as the session began that prompted the opening remark; however, it rather indicates that someone – me or Frank, or both of us – was not very happy with her. Though it started slowly, this turned out to be one of the strangest exchanges with the Cs we ever had. (I have no idea why I describe any of them as being 'the strangest'! The whole thing is bizarre as all get-out!)

Participants: 'Frank', Laura, Sue V, Pat Z, SZ, MM, Wilma, Sandra, Tom French, Cherie Diez, Patrick Z (Pk)

1 **Q**: *(L)* Hello.

2 **A**: Words mean little.

3 **Q**: *(L)* What does that mean?

4 **A**: Your commentary.

5 **Q**: *(L)* My commentary?

6 **A**: Sue V___'s.

7 **Q**: *(L)* Okay, who do we have with us this evening?

8 **A**: Vostokokki.

9 **Q**: *(L)* Where are you transmitting from?

10 **A**: Cass.

11 **Q**: *(L)* Why are you not spelling Cassiopaea as is usual?

---

[1] Right away I was suspicious because of this curt response about the curious abbreviating of "Cassiopaea." In retrospect, I think that it indicated quite clearly that the

A: We have addressed this in prior sessions. Please review.[1]

Q: *(L)* We have several questions tonight. Do you have any particular messages for anyone here first?[2]

A: The need to deliver messages flows naturally, there is no way to "choreograph" it by requesting a specific "time" for this procedure. And, please tell SV to relay specifically when we place words in quotes!!!!! It is annoying to not get messages properly transmitted when it is important for each entity receiving to absorb every detail of the given messages as it is intended. We have up until now not said anything about this, in the hopes that she would learn this by herself, but alas, she has not. Therefore, we regret the necessary reprimand. Sorry SV, but now please be aware that you have been told, and do not make this error ever again![3]

Q: *(L)* Goodness! All I did was ask if there was a message for anyone!

A: But it is important for you to continue at the same steady pace.

Q: *(L)* Can I continue with the questions now?

A: Obviously, it is always possible to do all that you desire to attempt.

Q: *(L)* First question: there were rumors on the internet that a respected scientist described a 'ship' in orbit around the planet Saturn, which was said to be as large as the planet Earth. And, supposedly, he said that the photographs from the space probe that sent back the pictures of Saturn's rings showed this ship clearly with portholes in it. Is this thing seen in orbit around Saturn, described by this NASA scientist on television, which I cannot confirm because I did not see it; is it, in fact, an artificially constructed craft of some sort?

A: No.

Q: *(L)* What was being seen?

A: It was an artificially constructed tale.

Q: *(L)* Okay, there is a fellow, TF, who has been hanging around PZ's print shop, who has a very strange story about his past and present. The funny thing is, all the odd things about his story that we were discussing recently, he explained point by point the following day as though he had been listening to our conversation and knew of our doubts and suspicions. Who is this guy and what are his objectives where PZ is concerned?[4]

A: Best not to discuss issues which threaten to interfere with free will directive. Suggest you stay "on your toes" with this one!

Q: *(L)* Is there anything about this that

---

[1] Cs' input to this session was 'abbreviated' somewhat.
[2] *The Wave* 45, 64
[3] This kind of reprimand was completely unlike the Cs and reflected more Frank's anger and resentment.
[4] This phenomenon is actually something we have become more familiar with over the years; we refer to it as the activation of a 'cryptogeographic being'. That is, there is some kind of connection between individuals who are activated as agents in the lives of people and some sort of transmission of information between them. It may appear to be 'synchronicity', but it isn't.

you can tell us that does not interfere with free will?

26 **A:** Have you not thought to gently inquire of the individual in question? And if not, why not? Generally, those involved in a ruse, be it simple or complex, are uncomfortable with graduated incremental disclosure!

27 **Q:** *(L)* Is one of the reasons you cannot discuss this more freely because we have such a large group this evening?

28 **A:** Who says we are not discussing it freely? Subtle answers that require effort to dissect, promote intensified learning.

29 **Q:** *(L)* Okay. I made the observation that if the fellow was a government spy, he would certainly have had a better cover story that the one presented. Am I on the right track?

30 **A:** Maybe.

31 **Q:** *(L)* And, sometimes it seems that alien-programmed or -controlled individuals do not have stories that make sense, or are consistent, because maybe there is some lack in their understanding of human culture. Am I on the right track here?

32 **A:** Sometimes is not all times.

33 **Q:** *(L)* Well, the guy is really huge and has size 17 feet ... he looks like a Nephilim to me! Am I on the right track?

34 **A:** It would be more fun if he had size "35" feet![5]

35 **Q:** *(L)* Who has size 35 feet?

36 **A:** If you meet them, "give us a call!"

37 **Q:** *(L)* Are you joking with me? All kidding aside ...

38 **A:** You need to be aware of all "guys."

39 **Q:** *(L)* Does PZ have anything to be afraid of?

40 **A:** What have we told you about knowledge as opposed to ignorance?!?

41 **Q:** *(L)* PZ wants to know what his intentions are.

42 **A:** Review answer two.

43 **Q:** *(PZ)* Was he paranoid about the questions we were asking a week prior to tonight?

44 **A:** What happens to those who become uncomfortable?

45 **Q:** *(L)* Well, they get out of the situation. So, start grilling him ...

46 **A:** Not "grill." We suggest subtle approach, or grill him "rotisserie" style.

47 **Q:** *(L)* Tonight, it seems that everyone wants to know who or what is this El Chupacabras?

48 **A:** We were not finished with the other subject. That is weighing heavily on some minds present here. Ask, that is how one learns!!

49 **Q:** *(PZ)* Do I have any reason to be concerned about my actions regarding him, that I called to check on him with the police and reported him to the State Attorney's office?

50 **A:** Possibly.

51 **Q:** *(PZ)* Is it possible that there are 'moles' in the tiny little police department here?

52 **A:** Open.

53 **Q:** *(PZ)* Do I need to get a bodyguard?

54 **A:** You are straying, please review.

---

[5]Probably a reference to the '3-5 code' discussed in the 11/11/95 session.

Q: *(L)* Was it a clue that if she stays "on her toes" he won't step on her with his size 17 feet?

A: No.

Q: *(PZ)* Patrick seems to believe everything he says.

A: Ask Patrick.

Q: *(L)* What do you think, Patrick? *(Pk)* I think he does a little bit of double-talk, but not as much as everybody thinks.

A: That is not the issue.

Q: *(L)* Is the specific issue whether this guy has any alien connections ...

A: No, that is not it.

Q: *(PZ)* Is he monitoring us?

A: Review answer two.

Q: *(L)* It must be the one about inquiring in subtle ways.

A: Now, ask yourself Pat: How likely is it that anyone with a tremendous ability to supposedly create such massive amounts of income, would just "walk in the door" and offer you a partnership in an endeavor that is going to produce such riches, as the person in question has described to you? If this individual has such tremendous acumen, why would he want to share the "bounty?" Remember the old saying: if something sounds too good to be true ...

Q: *(L)* Okay, can we ask now about El Chupacabras?

A: It is what it is.[6]

Q: *(L)* It is a 'goatsucker.' Where does it come from?

A: Review transcripts re: "window fallers."[7]

Q: *(L)* If it is a window faller, does it come from another density, or a lateral dimension?

A: Closer to the latter.[8]

Q: *(L)* Okay, so it is like a horizontal dimension. What allowed it to enter our realm?

A: This is complex, but best described as "EM wave bursts along frequency border variation."

Q: *(L)* Is there some way to capture or stop this creature?

A: You do not yet completely understand all the "mechanics" of the window faller phenomenon. The physicality is entirely transitory and partially dependent upon consciousness variabilities, as well as expectations of witnesses.

Q: *(L)* Does the energy of the fear of the witness enable the creature to continue its existence? Does it feed on the excitement and fear, and is that what makes it manifest?

A: Close, but off a little. It is the other way around, and retro-factored by one half.

Q: *(L)* What do you mean by that?

A: It is mutual, rather than unilateral. Also, remember that a window falling represents a cross-energizing of realities, equally represented from each "dimension" in question. In other words, because the dimensional curtain has been "torn," half of one and half of the other contributes to the whole reality.

---

[6] *High Strangeness* 7; *The Wave* 9
[7] 9 June 1995.
[8] *The Wave* 3, 68

81 Q: *(L)* Does this mean that something from our reality is also scaring something in that other reality?

82 A: No, it does not "work" that way at all.

83 Q: *(L)* Is there any possibility that this mutual creature is going to turn its attention from animals to humans?

84 A: Ditto last answer. And review response prior to that!

85 Q: *(L)* Okay, now, there are a lot of current teachings that say that the 'dregs' of other planets are being sent to Earth to 'refine' them, so to speak, and that this is why the human race is so divided and antagonistic ... that the interactions are supposed to result in annihilation of the weak and survival of the strong in both physical and spiritual terms.

86 A: First of all, confusion abounds here due to incorrect interpretations of the last subject discussed. Dimensions are not densities!!!! Dimensions are strictly the result of the universal consciousness as manifested in the imagination sector of thought. Density means level of development as measured in terms of closeness to union with the One ... Cycle. So, obviously, the "chupacabras" is a manifestation of human consciousness, and, human beings are a manifestation of the Chupacabras consciousness. Get it? Now, a shocker for you: You would not exist if someone didn't "dream you up."

87 Q: *(L)* Who dreamed me up?[9]

88 A: Not important just yet. You literally are the "figments" of someone's imagination, and nothing more!!!

89 Q: *(L)* You mean God dreams and brings us into existence?

90 A: Remember, "God" is really all existence in creation, in other words, all consciousness. This is because all existence in creation is consciousness, and vice versa.

91 Q: *(L)* So, the issues of racial superiority that are brought up in the Urantia book can be answered by 'anything is possible'?

92 A: Close, but remember, all there is is lessons!

93 Q: *(L)* Is it true that the 'dregs' of other planets are being sent to Earth?

94 A: That would be subjective.

95 Q: *(MM)* I would like to know if the Cassiopaeans are familiar with the entity that was on the three-dimensional level known as Paramahansa Yogananda?

96 A: Third density, not three dimensional. And yes, but this entity had many aliases: Thorn, Christian, Mobson Singh, etc.[10]

97 Q: *(MM)* Where is Paramahansa now?

98 A: Fifth density.

99 Q: *(MM)* Is he the Avatar?[11]

100 A: That is a subjective, artificial concept of the self-styled variety.

101 Q: *(MM)* Who came up with the concept? *(W)* I don't know. I read it in a book somewhere. *(L)* So, someone said he is now an avatar?

102 A: Is Debbie a "shaman," is Billy a "hero," is Oscar a "blade runner?"

---

[9] *The Wave* 25
[10] *The Wave* 64
[11] An 'avatar' is claimed to be a manifestation of a deity in bodily form on Earth.

103 **Q**: *(L)* I read Yogananda's book and it seemed that he might be a very holy person. He seemed to have very loving concepts and practices in his life. *(MM)* I just wanted to know where he is now. *(L)* 5th density, they said. *(MM)* Does 5th density have anything to do with Venus?

104 **A**: That is not a proper conceptualization.

105 **Q**: *(L)* Well, 5th density is the contemplation and recycling 'zone'. *(MM)* Well, at the centers, the ashrams and shrines, people swear that he appears to them. I was curious also about the entity in my home.

106 **A**: This is a hanger-on from visit with Wilma at her domain. It is an E. energy seeking renewal.

107 **Q**: *(L)* Is MM's critter an STS or STO entity?

108 **A**: Open.

109 **Q**: *(L)* How does it make you feel? *(MM)* I am tired all the time. *(L)* How can she get rid of it?

110 **A**: Spirit release.

111 **Q**: *(MM)* Was it attached to Wilma first?

112 **A**: Yes.

113 **Q**: *(MM)* Is this what set off my fire alarm?

114 **A**: Energy therefrom.

[Break]

115 **Q**: *(L)* Sandra wants to know about her uncle who just died in January. *(S)* Where is he?[12]

116 **A**: He is at 5th density.

117 **Q**: *(S)* Is he having a hard time adjusting?

118 **A**: No, but remember, there is no "time" there.

119 **Q**: *(S)* Many members of the family have reported having visions and dreams of him. What are these caused by?

120 **A**: Various processes.

121 **Q**: *(L)* I guess you have to ask about specific ones. Are any of these caused by Uncle Andrew himself visiting?

122 **A**: That is too simplified.

123 **Q**: *(L)* I guess you have to specify ...

124 **A**: No, you don't understand. We meant that your comment was too simplified. The question is: are any of these manifestations Uncle Andrew?

125 **Q**: *(S)* He appeared to his oldest daughter ...

126 **A**: The concept is faulty.

127 **Q**: *(L)* The idea of any of them being Andrew, I guess. *(S)* So, the appearances are all their own expectations?

128 **A**: No, not always, but we are trying to teach.

129 **Q**: *(S)* Is he at peace?

130 **A**: Yes. Do you want to learn, or would you prefer to assume?

131 **Q**: *(L)* What are these manifestations?

132 **A**: They are 5th density thought projection energy waves.

133 **Q**: *(L)* So, his family are picking up these 5th density thought energy waves.

134 **A**: You are not following well.

135 **Q**: *(S)* So, when the family members are seeing negative things, it is just their own guilt?

---

[12]Sandra, herself, died a couple months after this session.

136 **A:** There is no time on 5th density. All event sequences happen eternally and for an instant only at once.

137 **Q:** *(L)* How does that relate to the question?

138 **A:** Because you asked if he was at peace, and if he was "adjusting." Do you not see that by the "time" you realize someone is "dead," they have already, in essence, experienced their entire 5th density incarnation recycling, learning and contemplative experience in "zero time?!"

139 **Q:** *(L)* Sandra wants to know how many times she has been 'recycled' as a human being?

140 **A:** 84.

141 **Q:** *(S)* I knew it! That's why this body is breaking down in pieces![13] *(PZ)* What about me?

142 **A:** 73.

143 **Q:** *(L)* S___ Z___?

144 **A:** 73.

145 **Q:** *(L)* Pat?

146 **A:** 65.

147 **Q:** *(PZ)* Have Shayna[14] and I known each other in another life?

148 **A:** Yes, all have and do. Number of incarnations does not predetermine schedule for graduation. And you, my dear, are too fatigued, so goodnight.

End of Session

---

[13] As noted, Sandra died not long after this session.
[14] Her daughter.

February 8, 1996

In this session, which was just me and Frank, and Sue to take notes, I addressed the issues of the previous session. Again, the Cs are trying to warn Sue and probably me, too, but we are rather oblivious.

Participants: 'Frank', Laura, Sue V

1. **Q**: *(L)* Who do we have with us tonight?
2. **A**: Wikijia.
3. **Q**: *(L)* And where are you from?
4. **A**: Cassiopaea.
5. **Q**: *(L)* Last Saturday night we had a very large group of people here and I experienced very unpleasant sensations. I would like to know the source of these.
6. **A**: The question is vague.
7. **Q**: *(L)* Was the channel corrupted?
8. **A**: Not corrupted, diluted. Static EM discharge from two entity sectors.[1]
9. **Q**: *(L)* What is the source of these entity sectors?
10. **A**: We have explained in detail these structures of this in prior sessions.
11. **Q**: *(L)* Was this due to the presence of any one or more persons in the room?
12. **A**: One but two.
13. **Q**: *(L)* One person but two entities?
14. **A**: Yes.
15. **Q**: *(L)* Who was the one person?
16. **A**: Open.
17. **Q**: *(L)* Well you said, at the time, that MM had an attachment and needed spirit release. Is this the same person?
18. **A**: You learn by answering, using your own learnings, not from ceaseless confirmations by us.
19. **Q**: *(L)* Well, I am obviously not learning too well, because I was dead wrong on the missing girl, and you were telling me about my 'amazing abilities', which were not so amazing in that case![2]
20. **A**: All who have amazing abilities must too guard against corruptive forces from within and without having to do with prejudice, assumption, and the anticipatory desires involving patterning presumption. i.e. keep an open mind, always!!!

---

[1] *The Wave* 45, 64
[2] A missing girl case similar to the missing girl a few years earlier who was found murdered. There were similarities between that previous case and this most recent one, but this one turned out to be a runaway. See 9 January 1995 session for details.
[3] My mother and SV's mother had moved into a house together and it was not working out, to put it mildly. Her mother required way more care than had been stated

21 **Q**: *(L)* Well, this leads me to the situation with the mothers: can you give us any immediate advice on this? A clue as to how to settle this situation.[3]

22 **A**: Advice was given; not followed!

23 **Q**: *(L)* What advice was given that was not followed? *(SV)* Only about the living will for my mom.

24 **A**: Did we identify source of the advice?

25 **Q**: *(L)* What is the source of the advice?

26 **A**: Transposed by Susan!!!

27 **Q**: *(L)* Do you mean the advice Frank gave Susan?

28 **A**: First things first! Please, Susan, try to be accurate!

29 **Q**: *(L)* Well, the situation is gummy right now ...

30 **A**: You were warned, Susan! Please, please, please, please, when you call or cry out for help and or guidance, know that we will always, always, always answer. It is up to you to be aware and then trust and follow. If your deep-seated stubbornness prevents this, it will result in nothing short of your total undoing! This is because we never give such warnings, except when vitally necessary! This applies to all others present equally as well!![4]

31 **Q**: *(L to SV)* Well, remember that you don't want to work your way into your own undoing, I guess, so you ought to begin to overcome your stubbornness about not facing things that need to be dealt with, and doing it. And, from what they are saying, you will get all the support you will need from us and them if you just ask. *(SV)* Lesson learned, I hope. *(L)* This is a tough subject. Any more on it?

A: Up to you.

33 **Q**: *(L)* Is there anything further you can add?

34 **A**: The situation will resolve naturally as all situations do ...

35 **Q**: *(L)* Is there any advice you can give for mom so that she is better able to cope with the situation?

36 **A**: Reading will help relieve her stress. She can get the correct materials herself.

37 **Q**: *(L to SV)* So, I guess it is up to you to see that she gets time to relax and read. Okay, next issue: the computer problem. Is it an attack to prevent the magazine?

38 **A**: Could be viewed as such.

39 **Q**: *(L)* Is it going to be resolved quickly?

40 **A**: Yes.

41 **Q**: *(L)* Is our involvement with PZ fortuitous or potentially disastrous?

42 **A**: Either.

43 **Q**: *(L)* You said before that when we got things going that everything would improve suddenly and dramatically, and immediately. We understood that to mean getting online dialogues

---

at the beginning and was very temperamental and demanding. My mother was exhausted and her health was breaking down as a consequence.

[4]Notice that the Cs added in a consequential way that this warning about "total undoing" applied to others present as well. This warning is interesting particularly since the Cs used the word "vitally", which was a variation of Sue's surname. It will come up again in a future session where the topic of discussion is Sue again, though I wasn't yet putting the puzzle pieces together.

going and also getting the magazine out. Are we going to be able to do this soon?⁵

A: As soon as needed.

Q: *(L)* Thank you. Goodnight.

A: Goodnight.

End of Session

---

⁵I didn't know that I was only five months away from meeting Ark and that the magazine name – *Aurora Journal* – was more symbolic than anything else. Also, "online dialogues" was how I met Ark.

February 17, 1996

Sue was still attending sessions because I was still trying to figure out what the heck was going on. There were the claims made by MM, hints from the Cs, and my own inclination to 'make nice' and just try to get along. Sue had indicated she wanted to ask financial questions. This led to a very interesting series of exchanges about the economy that have since proven to be very insightful and useful. At the same time, in respect of my own activities, it seems that Frank's perspective was dominating here and you can probably pick up my hurt and frustration at being accused of things that were not true. Sometimes I even think that these episodes occurred to try to get me to pay attention to exactly such dynamics.

Participants: 'Frank', Laura, Sue V

1. **Q:** *(L)* Hello.
2. **A:** Hello.
3. **Q:** *(L)* We have several questions on the list I would like to get to before anyone else gets here. Actually, SV has some questions about her investing strategy.
4. **A:** Who are we?
5. **Q:** *(L)* I'm sorry. Who do we have with us tonight?
6. **A:** Piliannah.
7. **Q:** *(L)* And where do you transmit from?
8. **A:** Cassiopaea.
9. **Q:** *(L)* Okay, now that we are connected ...
10. **A:** Ask specific questions.

[1] See session 25 November 1995.

11. **Q:** *(L)* In rereading the session on the economy and investing and so forth, I was wondering if we are, at least, on schedule or the right track?[1]
12. **A:** Yes.
13. **Q:** *(L)* One thing noted was, "if you play by the rules, you cannot survive, if you don't play by the rules, you will do quite well, indeed." What specific rules do you mean?
14. **A:** Vague. Review the text.
15. **Q:** *(L)* Well, one of the rules was 'working very hard and earning your bread by the sweat of your brow'. You said that was trap number one ...
16. **A:** No, working for someone else; not how "hard" one does it.
17. **Q:** *(L)* The other thing was about investing. You said that storing it in

banks was useless, and you suggested to invest ...

A: These were suggestions, not limitations.

Q: *(L)* You also suggested publishing ...

A: We suggested you ask directly to be published.

Q: *(L)* I talked to Val, and he has apparently become enamored of Drunvalo Melchizidek, and Frank De Marco bounced back the material.

A: That is two only, and of neither did you ask directly and with humility. Remember, sophistication and the upkeep of an appearance of "stature or professionalism" are to be avoided here! Forget "images," and concentrate on intent with sincerity. You are very skilled at "getting your point across," if you are sufficiently motivated to do so. Do not let self-importance interfere!

Q: *(L)* What are you talking about!?! Do you have any idea how much work I have done? How much I have sent out? The numbers of people?!

A: Just ask: Please publish this work.

Q: *(L)* I do not think you are grasping the situation here! There are two choices: a publishing house that pays *you* or a publishing house *you* pay!

A: You have not contacted all sources.

Q: *(L)* Of course I haven't contacted all!!! Do you have any idea how much money it costs to mail out that manuscript? There is no way I could possibly send it out to them all! You are being completely unrealistic for 3rd density here!

A: Then, network.

Q: *(L)* This is ridiculous! You don't know what you are talking about. You are in 6th density, this is 3rd density. *(S)* No, look at that computer. There are a lot of people who know other people. Surely somebody knows somebody who works for a publisher? *(L)* Sue, you aren't getting it ... I have a file of rejection letters. Do you want to see them?

A: What text did you send?

Q: *(L) The Noah Syndrome.* It is the only thing that is in readable form.

A: Who says?

Q: *(L)* Well, for goodness sake, you ought to know that the transcripts are not suitable to send out to anyone in the chopped up and scattered shape they are in!

A: Avoid prejudice!

Q: *(L)* So, what you are talking about is sending out the transcripts of the sessions. Is that it?

A: Yes.

Q: *(L)* Well, that's not what I was talking about! If you guys know so much, how come you didn't know that?

A: We did.

Q: *(L)* Well, "Tales are easy to sew, when the past is yours only to know!"

A: Good one!

Q: *(L)* Yeah, I got it from you!

A: If you ask to be published, you will be published! Also, we suggest it not be piecemeal, but all inclusive! And use your networking skills.

Q: *(S)* Look at how many people write to you asking questions ...

A: It need not be further "organized." We have done that for you. Just have faith!!!! We have told you, we do not give false advice.

Q: *(L)* I am confused here.

46 **A**: Then inquire.

47 **Q**: *(L)* We were thinking that putting out the magazine with Pat Z was the way to go. And, all the other things that could go in there ... Is that a vain assumption?

48 **A**: Things, maybe, but not a book. Magazine is "cool," but not the book. Publish the book elsewhere!

49 **Q**: *(L)* Well, since you could give me the name of a chiropractor, why can't you give me the name of a publisher?

50 **A**: Because it violates learning directive. But note: it is close at "hand."

51 **Q**: *(L)* I don't get it.

52 **A**: What do you spend so much "time" doing with your hands?

53 **Q**: *(L)* I type ... letters to people on the Net ...

54 **A**: Light bulb?

55 **Q**: *(S)* Bright idea! *(L)* No, it has to be more complicated than that.

56 **A**: Look for a directory of publishers, and their mail addresses, for example.

57 **Q**: *(L)* Well, I have had enough on that subject. That's enough.

58 **A**: No, it is not!!!

59 **Q**: *(L)* Okay. I look for a directory of publishers ... then what?

60 **A**: What do you think?

61 **Q**: *(L)* Anything else?

62 **A**: Ask.

63 **Q**: *(L)* Well, how will I know the right one when I find them? I can't just send it out all over the place!

64 **A**: No.

65 **Q**: *(L)* What else is there?

66 **A**: Much else ... You know how you like treasure hunts, Laura?!? Then learn to like this one.

67 **Q**: *(L)* Okay, what is the next clue in this treasure hunt?

68 **A**: Network!!! Do you yet understand what we mean when we say that? Yet?

69 **Q**: *(L)* I guess that means that you share information on the Net?

70 **A**: Yes. And... Read John Naisbitt. We have direct communications with him, too!

71 **Q**: *(L)* Who is he?

72 **A**: "Megatrends."

73 **Q**: *(L)* Oh, I have the book. Are you telling me that you communicate with him?

74 **A**: Yes. Now, read chapter headings!!!

75 **Q**: *(L)* Okay: 'Industrial Society to an Information Society', 'Force Technology, to High Tech', 'National Economy to World Economy', 'Short Term to Long Term', 'Centralization to Decentralization', 'Institutional Help to Self Help', 'Hierarchies to Networking', etc. Page 211, interesting numbers. Okay, anything else you want to add?

76 **A**: In your "spare time," read and absorb, and look for the clues there. This will allow you to use your resources more efficiently, thus quickly achieving goals.

77 **Q**: *(L)* Okay. *(F)* With an open mind. No prejudice!

---

[2]Interestingly, it was because I sent the transcripts out in more or less raw form that they attracted the attention of certain people and eventually ended up in Ark's email. So, the Cs weren't wrong in this discussion, they were simply trying to get me to open my mind to various ways of 'publishing'.

78 **A**: Yup.[2]

79 **Q**: *(L)* Can I ask my other questions? Some people on the Net want me to ask about this HAARP thing ... seems to be some sort of antennae thing ...

80 **A**: Disguise for something else.[3]

81 **Q**: *(L)* What is that something else?

82 **A**: Project to apply EM wave theories to the transference of perimeters.

83 **Q**: *(L)* What does that mean?

84 **A**: If utilised as designed, will allow for controlled invisibility and easy movement between density levels on surface of planet as well as subterranially.

85 **Q**: *(L)* Who is in charge of building this thing?

86 **A**: More than one entity.

87 **Q**: *(L)* What groups?

88 **A**: INVELCO is one guise as well as UNICON and banking interest.

89 **Q**: *(L)* Who is in disguise as INVELCO and UNICON? Are they just dummy companies for cover?

90 **A**: Close.

91 **Q**: *(L)* Can you tell us if this is a human organization or aliens, or a combination?

92 **A**: Human at surface level.

93 **Q**: *(L)* Whose idea was this project?

94 **A**: Not applicable.

95 **Q**: *(L)* Is there more you can tell us about this?

96 **A**: It has nothing to do with weather or climate. These things are emanating from 4th density, as we have told you before.[4]

97 **Q**: *(L)* Is this something like a transdimensional atomic remolecularizer?

98 **A**: No.

99 **Q**: *(L)* Is it something like what you said about the whole Southwest going into 4th density?

100 **A**: No.

101 **Q**: *(L)* So, HAARP has nothing to do with the weather?

102 **A**: And also EM associated with same as reported.

103 **Q**: *(L)* So, when is this HAARP thing scheduled to go into operation?

104 **A**: Open.

105 **Q**: *(L)* Is it currently in operation?

106 **A**: Experimental.

107 **Q**: *(L)* How long have they been working on this thing?

108 **A**: Since the 1920s.

109 **Q**: *(L)* What?! The 1920s?

110 **A**: Yes.

---

[3] *The Wave* 22, 57

[4] In addition to the statement in the 30 July 1994 session, that the cosmic war was being fought at other dimensions and densities and appeared to us here on Earth as weather, this is another clear declaration that climate change and erratic weather emanates from 4th density and are *not* a consequence of 'weather wars' being waged by the secret government against people. There will be further comments on this as we proceed, so stay alert to this!

[5] I think that what I was reading was about Uri Geller. See Wikipedia for a list of books by and about Uri.

111 **Q:** *(L)* Well, that certainly is strange. Change gears. I read the other day about an association between UFOs and breaking things. Is there?[5]

112 **A:** Some, yes.

113 **Q:** *(L)* In the experiences that I had myself, where a lot of things either broke in some strange relation to me, or disappeared, and specifically the incident when Chloe G and I were coming back from North Carolina and the window in the car exploded, were any of these events related to UFO activity?

114 **A:** Maybe.

115 **Q:** *(L)* Well, Chloe wanted me to ask about the trip. Could you comment on that?

116 **A:** Maybe you should continue to probe Chloe to see what other experiences she has had, and why? There is much hidden there.

117 **Q:** *(L)* Well, I recounted to her the flash of memory I had of the incident that happened back in 1987 when I woke up and the house was surrounded by a super bright light. My first thought was that there was a whole bunch of trucks and cars surrounding the house with their lights shining on it, that it was people my husband knew, therefore he should handle it. I thought it was a joke and decided that I didn't need to worry about it. Later I woke up, reversed in the bed, the bottom half of my gown was wet, and instead of going nuts about this, I crawled out of the bed, which was against a wall, and turned around and crawled back in and went to sleep. I told this to Chloe, and pointed out to her how exceedingly crazy a thing it was. To know that there was all this light shining on your house, and to just go back to sleep, and then to wake up in such an odd condition, and think nothing of it ... just sweep it under the rug. This happened around the same time the things were breaking. What happened?

118 **A:** What do you think?

119 **Q:** *(L)* Well, it could have been a dream. It could just be a very lucid dream.

120 **A:** Seems dreams do tend to reverse one's position on the bed, as a general rule, don't they?

121 **Q:** *(L)* Well, no need to be funny. The fact that my physical body was reversed and I was wet would indicate an actual physical abduction, I guess.

122 **A:** Yup.

123 **Q:** *(L)* Well, haven't you said that actual physical abductions are somewhat rare?

124 **A:** Yes.

125 **Q:** *(L)* That was when my hands started going numb, the horrible headaches began ...

126 **A:** Probe Chloe, to see what things she is repressing.

127 **Q:** *(L)* She did tell me that she was beginning to see some things ... We will leave that. On the news the other night, there was a new type of AIDS reported. Where did it come from?

128 **A:** Mutation of virus.

129 **Q:** *(L)* The story is that it came from Thailand. Is this true?

130 **A:** Maybe.

131 **Q:** *(L)* Is it already in the U.S.?

132 **A:** No.

133 **Q:** *(L)* Well, it is supposed to be eight times more contagious ...

134 **A:** But still transmitted in the same mode.

Q: *(L)* Is AIDS transmissible by, for example, insects?

A: No.

Q: *(L)* By any means other than what is taught?

A: No.

Q: *(L)* How many people have died of true AIDS in the U.S.?

A: 189,000.

Q: *(L)* How many people have it at present?

A: Approx 1 million are HIV positive. Only 39 per cent will ever develop AIDS.

Q: *(L)* Anything that I ought to have asked that I did not? Can you tell me anything that will help?

A: Proceed with caution, as publishing soon to "explode."

Q: *(L)* We do have this online 'chat' with Mike Lindemann on ISCNI tomorrow night. Any advice?

A: Keep to the point, use simple English, avoid excessive verbiage, or concepts not universally understood, unless accompanied by an adequate explanation.

Q: *(L)* Okay, I guess we just press on with the networking and the magazine for now ... hope it creates some cash flow because all that paper and printing is costing me an arm and a leg!

A: Soon to be solved!!

Q: *(L)* Well, I need to know if I am pouring money into a useless project here!

A: No you don't! Discovery is fun!

Q: *(L)* Is anything unusual going to happen at the conference next month?

A: Wait and see!

Q: *(L)* Thank you and goodnight.

A: Goodnight.

End of Session

February 21, 1996

We were still discussing attending the Gulf Breeze UFO conference. Sue's finances were also on her mind as well as the issues surrounding her mother who was now sharing a house with my mother and things were not going well. Sue's mother was nasty-tempered and demanding and my mother had about had enough. I told Sue that she needed to tell her mother that if she didn't make an effort, she would go back to the nursing home which she hated. It seems that Sue was completely unable to make this clear statement to her mother. It was totally astonishing to see how she turned into practically a groveling servant in the presence of this mother (by adoption) who was certainly unable to harm her in any way. Whatever had been done to Sue as she was growing up to create this control over her must have been horrifying. I told Sue she shouldn't be spending anymore of her capital because I was pretty sure she was going to have to put her mother back in the home. Again, I would suggest that the Cs' "financial advice" came from Frank who was sure that he was an investing superstar.

Additionally, in this session, I pointed out that I was following the Cs' instructions from previous sessions to just send out raw transcripts.

Participants: 'Frank', Laura, Sue V

Q: *(L)* Hello.

A: Hello.

Q: *(L)* Who do we have with us?

A: Yona.

Q: *(L)* Where are you transmitting from?

A: Cassiopaea.

Q: *(L)* Sue has some issues tonight, and I guess that the first one is that she is concerned about flying to Gulf Breeze. She wants to know: Is the plane we are taking safe?[1]

A: Why would you expect otherwise?

Q: *(S)* Well, the Lizzies could come

---

[1] What is so darned strange about this session is that the first issue was Sue's concern about flying on our trip to the UFO conference in Pensacola/Gulf Breeze. When you read the session that discusses what happened on our flight home, you'll see that there is definitely something odd going on here, though what it is, exactly, I can't say.

along and blow the plane out of the air!

A: "Lizzies" could come along and blow up your cars.

Q: *(L)* Do we have any protection from them?

A: Knowledge/awareness acts as a shield, as we have told you.

Q: *(L)* Well, speaking of that, Sue had questions about investment back in December and you described a strategy ...

A: One possible course of action, but not exclusive in nature.

Q: *(L)* A couple of weeks ago you said "advice was given" that Sue didn't follow. You then said that when she calls on you for advice, that it was up to her as to whether she chose to trust and follow the advice. Then you said that if her "deep-seated stubbornness" prevented this, it would result in her "total undoing". She wants to know what advice you gave that she did not follow?

A: All.

Q: *(L)* She thought she was handling it.

A: You left portals "unwatched."

Q: *(S)* What portals were these?

A: Emotions in motion.

Q: *(S)* Relating to what?

A: Ask yourself.

Q: *(L)* Well, my thought is that it has to do with her mother.

A: What specifically?

Q: *(L)* Well, her mother and her emotions relating to her mother?

A: Interconnected.

Q: *(S)* I have been concerned.

A: What about potential for discourse?

Q: *(S)* What do you mean, discourse? *(L)* Discourse or discord?

A: Either/or.

Q: *(L)* We knew there was potential for discord. *(S)* Yes, we talked about it.

A: And what did you, Susan, do to prevent discord? Does talking about it amongst yourselves solve it?

Q: *(L)* What did Susan not do?

A: Ask Susan!!

Q: *(S)* I talked with them ...

A: Talking about weeds does not solve a bug problem, does it?!

Q: *(L)* What do you mean?

A: Think! Avoidance does not solve!

Q: *(L)* Did you ever say to them that you would put them back in the home if they did not cooperate? *(S)* No, I never said that. *(L)* So, you just talked about the weeds, and did not address the bugs. And, your mom and Dick are so devious and manipulative that you really have to tell them in a firm way about the consequences of their behavior and what you *will* do if it continues. And, you have to make it stick. You are just simply avoiding the whole issue. *(S)* Well, I am going to take them to my house on Saturday and ask them how they feel ... *(F)* That's not going to solve the problem. Of course they are going to lie to you about everything and continue exactly as they are doing. *(L)* Sue, that is not dealing with *your* issues with your mother. Her control over you. You need to break that!

A: Yes.

Q: *(L)* Is that what Sue has not done?

A: Partly.

Q: What else?

44 **A:** Discuss for learning purposes!

45 **Q:** *(L)* I have been getting the strong feeling that Sue should not be taking any more risks with her finances. Sue paid off all her debts with her capital instead of investing it to make more money. Was that a good idea?

46 **A:** What is a "good idea?"

47 **Q:** *(L)* Well, she no longer has any investment capital, and if anything happens to her mother ... *(S)* I only have about 8K left, but I believe that I should just do the best with what I have ... maybe I won't have tons of money coming in, but a little here and a little there ...

48 **A:** Okay, here comes one last financial suggestion: take one half of your remaining capital and buy gold.

49 **Q:** *(S)* Gold or gold options?

50 **A:** Up to you.

51 **Q:** *(L)* So, you are saying that now the whole deal has changed?

52 **A:** Well of course, the situation has changed due to change in circumstances brought about by Sue's choices.

53 **Q:** *(L)* Would it be advisable for her to get the cash out of her credit line for investment?

54 **A:** We advised on this. It is up to her.

55 **Q:** *(L)* And, there is another thing: she is always stressed because of the place she works. *(S)* Well, I can't take the time to go to every single chiropractor for stuff like that ...

56 **A:** Take time and go to one single computer terminal! And you can't presume "stuff like that!"

57 **Q:** *(S)* I want to know what you mean about "deep-seated stubbornness"?

58 **A:** We mean what we said, self-explanatory.

59 **Q:** *(S)* I think everybody is stubborn in one way or another. *(L)* Let's change the subject. I have been getting a lot of mail on the internet from the portions of transcript that I have posted.

60 **A:** Tip of the ice-berg.

61 **Q:** *(L)* Well, if it keeps up, I will need a secretary because it seems that all I do is write answers to questions or send copies of answers to questions to people asking the same questions ...

62 **A:** What fun!

63 **Q:** *(L)* I am trying to keep up will all of it and I am being worn out. I am working 18 hours a day ... I am trying to keep up with all the stuff that is coming in ...

64 **A:** And those of wisdom, know to follow paths most easily grooved.

65 **Q:** *(L)* I have written to a *lot* of people about the publishing ... When am I going to find what I am looking for? I am amazed at how many people want to read the material after I have sent out these excerpts.

66 **A:** Then you should know our response.

67 **Q:** *(L)* Wait and see?

68 **A:** Bingo!! Did we not tell you, did we not advise you about the network??!??

69 **Q:** *(L)* Of course ...

70 **A:** And what did you do?

71 **Q:** *(L)* Well, I did it as soon as I could ...

72 **A:** And what happened?

---

[2]I was referring to the fact that the very day after I had first signed up for an internet account and obtained the software and installed it, I was in the auto-accident that nearly did me in completely and the effects of which I was still suffering.

73 **Q:** *(L)* The Lizzies tried to kill me! [Laughter]²

74 **A:** The Lizard Force, i.e. STS, has been attacking you since day one. We have been advising you only for 1.5 years, as you measure it.

75 **Q:** *(L)* The situation is such that I am running out of force from working against this constant oppression and opposition. Can you tell me if I will ever have some peace of mind so that I can continue to function?

76 **A:** Have we?

77 **Q:** *(L)* I guess. Okay, there is some valley in Canada³ that is supposed to be very mysterious and it seems that no one will go to the area anymore because they all end up dead with their heads cut off. Who is doing this? Is there some Indians or cave people or what?

78 **A:** STS beings, density 4.

79 **Q:** *(L)* Oh, goodness! Well, I think that I ought to ask something else because I have this feeling that there is something right around the corner, or something just out of my line of sight that I do not see. I guess I am asking for unknown knowledge.

80 **A:** Knowledge of an unknown nature is not knowledge.

81 **Q:** *(L)* Okay. Anything else from anybody? Sue, I guess you know what you are supposed to do now ... you screwed up big time ... *(S)* Well, I was always taught that ...

82 **A:** Rules.⁴ Goodnight.

End of Session

---

³"Headless Valley is a specific region (Lat: 61.25 Long: -124.5) of the South Nahanni River valley (Canada) said to encompass a lost world complete with tropical forests, murderously savage natives, and a myriad of mysterious creatures ranging from 'Bear Dogs' to Sasquatch. The legend of Headless Valley is unusual in that it is fairly modern, having originated in 1908, following the discovery of two decapitated miners in the region of the South Nahanni River. Since that time, several other disappearances and murders have been documented in the region." (http://arcana.wikidot.com/headless-valley)
   See also:
http://raven-talesoftheweird.blogspot.com/2011/02/valley-of-headless-men.html

⁴Referring to the previous financial discussion where the Cs had described the "rules" of financial success.

February 24, 1996

Notice that Pat Z and her daughter are present here, but not her son. Patrick had asked my eldest daughter out. This relationship will play an interesting background role through the rest of this year, so stay tuned.

Participants: 'Frank', Laura, Sue V, Pat Z, Shayna Z, MM, Wilma

1 **Q**: *(L)* Hello.

2 **A**: Hello.

3 **Q**: *(L)* Who do we have with us this evening?

4 **A**: Vorta.

5 **Q**: *(L)* And where do you transmit from?

6 **A**: Cassiopaea.

7 **Q**: *(L)* First item: it seems that everyone in this room has been experiencing some sort of major, cumulative problems, all on the same day. Would you comment on this, please?

8 **A**: Exception.

9 **Q**: *(L)* What exception?

10 **A**: Frank. Move board over to left. Your left. [Adjustment made.] More. [Further adjustment.] OK. Better centered.

11 **Q**: Can you comment on Sue's situation since she is the most upset?

12 **A**: Not unless you ask specifics.

13 **Q**: *(S)* I know I am under attack and I am going to deal with it the best way I can. It's hard, but there is nothing else I can do. I knew I was coming under attack because the clock that does not work was humming again and that is always a sure sign.

---

[1] To be 'bereaved' means to be deprived of a close relation usually through death. I still don't quite understand what the Cs meant here. The situation with the mothers had hit a sort of crisis and I had decided that I would move my mother out of the house she was sharing with Sue's mom and her mom's boyfriend. The two of them were so manipulative and childishly demanding, my mother simply couldn't cope with it. So, Sue was faced with having to sort out the situation since neither of them was capable of taking care of themselves much less each other. So, the only bereavement that was in the offing was that it was putting a severe strain on the relationship between me and Sue. Putting that together with other things the Cs had said to Sue, plus the situation that MM had revealed previously, I guess that's what they meant: death of a friendship. In retrospect, it seems obvious that Sue was concealing things from us, too; her mother was so deceitful and manipulative it would not have been surprising if Sue had acquired such habits herself,

A: Concealment causes bereavement.[1]

Q: *(L)* Who is bereaved?

A: Who is concealing?

Q: *(L)* Are you trying to hide your emotional state? *(S)* Of course. It's my problem. *(L)* Well, remember what they told me: when I hurt, everyone else suffers. *(S)* But, if I don't tell anyone else, then no one else has to suffer.

A: Networking provides solutions, and not just on the computer!!!

Q: *(S)* Well, I am upset with everything about my mother. I know it is my own fault ... If I had left them at the home, everything would have been fine.

A: No.

Q: *(S)* Well, it's not fine now. Everybody is upset. Everybody is miserable. *(F)* It is certainly not a good situation. *(S)* I want to know about this clock. Is it really a warning signal as I think it is?

A: What do you think? Remember, you learn on an exponential curve, once you have become "tuned in." This means that you become increasingly able to access the universal consciousness. Please learn to trust your increasing awareness. All who are present here are at one point or another on that cycle, or one point or another on that cycle of progression, some further along than others. If you properly network without prejudice, you may all wind up at the same point on this cycle. We also mean that you can access the universal consciousness to find the answers to otherwise unseen truths, such as the clock vibrating as a sign of increased 4th density STS presence, for but one example.[2]

Q: *(L)* Well, along this line, MM has a very strange object appearing in 'aura photographs' in her house and more or less with her. It appears to be a column of light, or a luminescent tube of some sort. What is it?

A: Represents conduit created by presence at locator which is in direct communication with higher density levels. And, in fact, there is some degree of convergence between same.

Q: *(L)* What presence are we talking about?

A: Many and varied.

Q: *(L)* And this is also a convergence point of densities?

A: Not exactly; convergence is taking place to some degree.

Q: *(L)* Are these presences STS or STO?

A: Both.

Q: *(L)* It is like a portal?

A: Not a portal, it is a conduit. A portal is an opening allowing influences to manifest from higher density levels and downward. A conduit is a "two way street."[3]

Q: *(W)* What do they want MM to do?

---

[1] though at the time, I couldn't perceive it and was always trying to put a positive spin on things. I suspect she was still hanging out with the Magick gang and they were giving her advice contrary to what the Cs would suggest and she wasn't being forthcoming about it.

[2] The Cs were clearly trying to encourage Sue to come clean, but she didn't; I guess it was the stubbornness the Cs had pointed out in an earlier session.

[3] This is an interesting distinction and ought to be kept in mind.

34 **A**: That is not the correct concept. Correction: A conduit develops both because of locator and ... the entities present. It is not locator fixed.

35 **Q**: *(L)* What should MM do in regard to this opening and these presences?

36 **A**: Nothing in particular ... But it is up to MM to decide how to handle the situation.

37 **Q**: *(L)* Are any of these presences connected to the statue?

38 **A**: Yes.

39 **Q**: *(L)* What kind of entity is connected with the statue?

40 **A**: Fifth density holdover.

41 **Q**: *(L)* Why is this being there?

42 **A**: Chooses to be. And no, Laura, it is not a Lizard!!!

43 **Q**: *(L)* Well, then what is it?

44 **A**: Didn't we just tell you?

45 **Q**: *(L)* Yes. We were talking about that earlier. How dead dudes can attach to things or people or houses or whatever. How are we going to solve this?

46 **A**: What needs to be solved?

47 **Q**: *(L)* Can she use this conduit?

48 **A**: Of course. And has already!!! If she had not, the conduit would not exist!

49 **Q**: *(MM)* How can I use it more effectively?

50 **A**: This would violate learning directive.

51 **Q**: *(MM)* What is the connection between the statue and myself?

52 **A**: All is interconnected. Please refer to our first few responses of this session!

53 **Q**: *(L)* She can use it to access universal consciousness?

54 **A**: Yes.

55 **Q**: *(L)* Well, what can she do to maximize the STO presence and minimize the STS use of the conduit?

56 **A**: Oh Laura, my dear, seems you need a refresher course in the transcripts. Maybe suggest you read them and relax and privately listen to the ones you have not as of yet transcribed a little more. This would be extremely helpful in your many and increasing communications via the "net" as well. Remember, we help you to unlock answers that have been placed in your superconsciousness files from before the "time" of the birth of your physical body. Also, false information is worse than no information at all.[4] Now, for Pat: Please denote quote marks in your reading back of the answers, in order to preserve the greatest possible meaning! Thank you!

57 **Q**: *(MM)* What is happening to me when I feel I am being touched in a sleep or semi-sleep state?

58 **A**: Various entities.

---

[4]This was a particularly interesting remark. It was true that I was getting way behind in transcribing the sessions. In earlier days, I would transcribe right away so we could re-use the tapes (wish we hadn't!), but now, I was just letting them pile up because I was so busy with the magazine and trying to follow leads on the internet to see if anything would develop. But *most* interesting is the remark about answers that are "placed in your superconsciousness files from before the 'time' of the birth of your physical body". It was almost a direct statement that I had been compelled to begin the whole experiment for that very purpose.

59 **Q:** *(MM)* What is their purpose for doing this?

60 **A:** Too vague to explain and this is learning material. Consult karmic references.

61 **Q:** *(MM)* I would like to ask about my karma with Wilma?

62 **A:** Remember two things: Number one, there are better ways to access this information than to expect us to lead you by the hand, this is not learning. Number two, too many personal questions begin to restrict the channel!

63 **Q:** *(L)* Mike Lindemann asked us if we would be interested in utilizing ISCNI as a forum for the material. Is this an acceptable forum?

64 **A:** Okay.

65 **Q:** *(L)* You also said that publishing would 'explode'. Can you give us any more on that?

66 **A:** Is this "personal data night?"

67 **Q:** *(L)* Well, I didn't think it was personal data.[5] I have a number of questions from people all over the world that I need to get answered, and it seems that people are interested, and I would like to get the material out there.

68 **A:** We have advised on this subject already, and patience is a virtue which builds strength!

69 **Q:** *(L)* Mike Lindeman has proposed that we submit the channeling to 'rigorous testing'.[6]

70 **A:** Mike Lindemann does not channel, now does he? What sort of rigorous testing does he propose?[7]

71 **Q:** *(L)* He didn't say. I guess they want short-term predictions and all sorts of little tests ...

72 **A:** Precisely, now what does this tell you?

73 **Q:** *(L)* It tells us that he wants proof.

74 **A:** Third density "proof" does not apply, as we have explained again and again. Now, listen very carefully: if proof of that type were possible, what do you suppose would happen to free will, and thusly to learning, Karmic Directive Level One?

75 **Q:** *(L)* Well, I guess that if there is proof, you are believing in the proof and not the spirit of the thing. You are placing your reliance upon a material thing. You have lost your free will. Someone has violated your free will by the act of *proving* something to you.

76 **A:** If anyone CHOOSES to believe, that is their prerogative!

77 **Q:** *(PZ)* [Unintelligible but sarcastic sounding remark.]

78 **A:** You did not completely understand the previous response, Pat. And what would constitute proof?

79 **Q:** *(L)* Predictions that came true, answers that were verifiable about a number of things.

80 **A:** Those would still be dismissed by a great many as mere coincidences. We

---

[5] And no, it wasn't a personal question so the Cs' response was interesting and possibly a clue, since the publishing 'explosion' actually turned out to be my meeting Ark, which was, indeed, personal.
[6] *The Wave* 20
[7] *The Wave* 11

have already given predictions, will continue to do so, but, remember, "time" does not exist. This is a 3rd density illusion. We do not play in that sandbox and cannot and never will. The primary reason for our communication is to help you to learn by teaching yourselves to learn, thereby strengthening your soul energy, and assisting your advancement.

81 **Q**: *(L)* Are you saying that your primary reason is just to teach us? This small group?

82 **A**: Because you asked for help.

83 **Q**: *(L)* So, you came through because we asked. Is this material being given to others, or is it designed to or intended to be shared with others?

84 **A**: If they ask in the necessary way. Otherwise, the sharing of the messages we give to you will teach millions of others.

85 **Q**: *(L)* What is the "necessary way"?

86 **A**: How "long did it take you?"

87 **Q**: *(L)* Well, it took all our lives and a *lot* of hard work.

88 **A**: Okay, now what did we mean when we referred to "millions of others?"

89 **Q**: *(L)* Are you saying that this information will be transmitted in some way to millions of others?

90 **A**: In what way?

91 **Q**: *(L)* Well, the only thing I can think of is through books.

92 **A**: Bingo!!

93 **Q**: *(W)* That's a lot of work.

94 **A**: The work has been ongoing, Wilma!

95 **Q**: *(W)* Well, it all has to be typed, and edited, and correlated and put in a cohesive form, and it will be a couple of years ...

96 **A**: All will be taken care of, and no, Wilma!

97 **Q**: *(L)* Well, that's a clue! A concession! *(W)* Well, I was thinking of the time frame and so many things are getting ready to happen any time now. It seems like the information needs to get out there soon or it will be obsolete.

98 **A**: Prejudice serves no purpose! Also, who says that the information is going to be obsolete?

99 **Q**: *(PZ)* What is the matter with just making photocopies and binding it?

100 **A**: Wait and see. And don't be surprised if events supercede such options.

101 **Q**: *(L)* Well, that's a clue! I wonder what they mean?

102 **A**: Wait and see.

103 **Q**: *(W)* I would like to know about this comet that is being talked about on the internet that people say is going to crash into the Earth on April 7th ...

104 **A**: Nonsense!!!

105 **Q**: *(L)* Well, I am curious about Pat's and MM and Wilma's mysterious phone calls, and the strange guy who has been stalking Pat being seen peering in the window at Frank's job. Are all of these things interconnected?[8]

106 **A**: No comment. All of these things can be discovered by utilising the methods we have taught you and the talents you possess and have learned elsewhere.[9]

---

[8]See Chapter 45 of *The Wave*

[9]Well, the Cs were definitely declaring that they were not particularly inclined to answer certain questions with the present company.

107 **Q:** *(L)* Well, group, have we answered all these questions yet?

108 **A:** Facetiousness is humorous, so long as all present understand intent!

109 **Q:** *(L)* Recently I heard a clapping sound behind my back, and I spun around and there was no one there. Gene B mentioned hearing the 'clapping' sounds behind him when he was meditating once. I understand that this is like breaking the sound barrier when something comes through from another density ...

110 **A:** Not "sound" barrier, just "barrier" will do!

111 **Q:** *(L)* Well, in regard to Pat's situation ...

112 **A:** Pat has had "situations" going on for some time, as you measure it.

113 **Q:** *(L)* Well, considering her husband's work, her own work, her security clearances ... and that it is very common to get the funny phone calls, and now Wilma has also had these phone calls ...

114 **A:** Greys.

115 **Q:** *(L)* Well, there was a woman on television who had claimed that she was being abducted. She left a voice-activated tape recorder on her night table, and during the night a strange, metallic-sounding voice was recorded which said, "Don't wake up," and it was the strangest thing you ever heard. And, Karla Turner had the same sort of thing going on with her. *(MM to W)* Should we tell them who this was that was calling? *(L)* Who, God? *(MM)* No. Go ahead. *(W)* I can only tell you who he claimed to be. He died in 1952. It was Paramahansa. *(MM)* Yes. I went out and found a tape of Yogananda, and it was *his* voice! And then the tape fried my karaoke machine. *(L)* Well, it either was, or it wasn't. Was the voice that of Yogananda? Can we ask?

116 **A:** You can ask.

117 **Q:** *(L)* Well, was it?

118 **A:** Was it?

119 **Q:** *(L)* Well, where is Yogananda now?

120 **A:** Fifth density.

121 **Q:** *(L)* So, Yogananda is in 5th density. Cayce once said that he would return in 1998 as a 'liberator'. Did he mean that he would be born in 1998, or 'activate' in 1998?[10]

122 **A:** That is not important.

123 **Q:** *(L)* Now, my memory for dates and times has always been, at best, a little vague. But, lately, it has been really bad. What is the cause of this loss of ability to keep a sequential record of what one does, who one sees, etc.? It is really strange.

124 **A:** It is not strange. As one "ages" the illusion of time passage begins to deteriorate because your "higher mind" begins to understand the illusion.

125 **Q:** *(L)* I was reading some of the transcripts earlier today. One of the things I read was about the Nephilim and their interactions with human beings and about other planets and molecularization, etc. Then, I was reading about the planet Kantek. Are there any human beings, on Earth, at the present time, who carry in them the Nephilim genes?

126 **A:** Yes.

---

[10] I could see that the Cs were not going to give an answer to the Yogananda question that would satisfy MM and Wilma, so I thought I would just change the subject.

127 **Q:** *(L)* MM has a six-foot-tall daughter. I have a kid who is pretty tall. Could this be a manifestation of Nephilim genes?

128 **A:** Maybe, maybe not.

129 **Q:** *(L)* Is there any way one can tell?

130 **A:** Would you want to?

131 **Q:** *(L)* Yes.

132 **A:** No you wouldn't!

133 **Q:** *(L)* Would these Nephilim genetics be passed down in the natural way, or would they be the result of genetic manipulation by genetically altering a fetus and then putting it back?

134 **A:** No to latter. One clue: double Y chromosomes.

135 **Q:** *(W)* That's male ...

136 **A:** Nephalim were.

137 **Q:** *(L)* They, were male. Women are a double X, men are XY.

138 **A:** Prisons are filled with double Y's with monstrous personality disorders, almost always Caucasian and oversized. Also, "bikers" often carry the gene. We suggest you not share this in a general way on the Net!!!

139 **Q:** *(L)* On TV they interviewed a serial killer. He was *huge*! He described killing. The shrink who was analyzing said he did it because he wanted to get caught. I did *not* get that feeling. I think he did it just because it was what he did. Bikers often carry the gene ... and this is why they form 'gangs'. Nephalim. Bikers. Big. Caucasian. My, my, my. Is there any other clue you can give?

140 **A:** Nephalim are not currently on your world, just trace residuals.[11]

141 **Q:** *(L)* Trace residuals in people. And there are supposed to be 36 million of them coming ...

142 **A:** With the Wave.

143 **Q:** *(L)* That reminds me: is it possible that this comet cluster you have talked about exists in 4th density?

144 **A:** No.

145 **Q:** *(L)* The comet cluster is in 3rd density?

146 **A:** Transcends 3rd and 4th.

147 **Q:** *(L)* Okay, so it is both in 3rd and 4th ...

148 **A:** It will be visible to you.

149 **Q:** *(L)* Well, everyone is having fits over Hale Bopp. Is it related?

150 **A:** ? Many space objects currently or recently visible are mysterious.

151 **Q:** *(F)* Well, on the news last night they reported that something had been sighted in 1991 and 1992 that had not reappeared ... they thought it was a comet, then they said it wasn't that, and they also said it appeared to be pulsating. Even the astronomers were at a loss about this thing that has disappeared.[12] *(PZ)* Is this thing that was seen in 1991 and 1992 going to be part of this Wave?

152 **A:** No.

---

[11] I just recently read a fascinating book on the topic of giants with a lot of documentation included: *"Giants on Record: America's Hidden History, Secrets in the Mounds and the Smithsonian Files"* by Jim Vieira and Hugh Newman (2015). It sure gives a lot of food for thought.

[12] See Wikipedia, "Lost comet", for a discussion of lost space objects.

Q: *(PZ)* I understand that they are building the largest telescope ever on top of a mountain in Peru. Is this telescope going to have the ability to forewarn about the Wave?

A: There is the ability to forewarn of the comet cluster, but not the Wave as it is not visible. Question is whether or not warnings will be given due to clandestine and political factors.

Q: *(W)* Well, they already have the technology and are searching the skies with the SETI telescope in Puerto Rico.

A: SETI Schmetti, Wilma! SETI stands for "search for extra terrestrial intelligence," now why don't you all start a search for a method to invent indoor plumbing?

Q: *(W)* Well, you know, Carl Sagan ... *(L)* Oh, I know. And they are always asking for money. Every time I get their mail-outs I write across the top: "They are already here! When will you guys wake up?!" And I send it back. Does Carl Sagan know that we have already been 'invaded'?

A: Close.

Q: *(L)* So, he is just lying?

A: Open.

Q: *(L)* Is there anything we ought to cover that we haven't asked at this point? *(MM)* Yes. Was it Yogananda?

A: Learning is fun. Otherwise, you would still be riding your bicycles, complete with training wheels, and on that note, goodnight.[13]

Q: Goodnight. Thank You.

End of Session

---

[13] And that was about all the Cs were willing to say about Yogananda.

March 10, 1996

At this point, things began to get really weird. Recall a few sessions back when I brought up the Greenbaum speech and the 'Elaine and the Sisters of Light' material, which, in conjunction with what MM had revealed about Sue V, got me to wondering about what was really going on in Sue's life? Well, it wasn't just Sue's life that was some kind of metaphor for me (not to forget Pat Z and her husband working on secret government research!), but now, MM came onstage with a really scary drama that is the subject of this next, very short session. Again, I'll draw from *The Wave* for some of the details.[1]

She called early one morning shortly after that last session. She was in a panic and quite obviously on the verge of collapse. Apparently she had suffered a terrible nightmare in which a Lizard-type being raped her. That was bad enough, but what really sent her plunging over the edge was when she woke up, she was covered with welts and a rash exactly as if she had been exposed to something violently allergenic.

In the dream, she said, the Reptoid had nipped her on the solar plexus, telling her that it was a 'love bite' so she would remember him. When she looked at the area after awakening, there were scratches that corresponded exactly to the teeth she remembered in the dream.

She also had another puncture on her leg added to a long series of them that had appeared at various points in her life, and assorted other marks and scratches all over her body.

I was pretty skeptical. It was my thought that the woman had just gone hysterical and maybe had done something to herself for attention. After all, from her own description, she was in a horrible marriage, may have been sexually abused as a child, and had a whole host of issues just waiting to erupt in her life. Her public persona was one thing; her private life was a disaster waiting to happen!

It would not have been at all unusual for a woman in her situation to

---

[1] *The Wave*, chapters 18 and 19.

deliberately manufacture such an event to get attention, create drama and excitement, or to use it as a platform from which to launch other difficulties for those around her. I thought it was a cry for help.

I figured that if she was making it up or over-dramatizing it, I would be able to catch it eventually, and gradually she would be able to look at her life in more realistic terms. It was a bit inconvenient to deal with her at that moment, but she was so desperate and insisted over and over again that she needed help now. She didn't have the money to pay for the hypnosis, but I have never let that be a factor in whom I accepted to work with, so even though I was very pressed for time, I decided to rearrange my schedule to accommodate this sudden eruption of something into her life.

She seemed genuinely at a loss to explain what had happened to her, and I was at a loss to explain it either. I had never heard of a Reptilian being raping anyone. In fact, I knew little about so-called Reptilian aliens at all other than what the Cassiopaeans had said, and that didn't tend to make me think that they went around raping women. How does a hyperdimensional being, who is somewhat ephemeral by definition, have the physical solidity necessary to perform rape?

But, MM was hyperventilating, having palpitations that terrified her, and every time she tried to talk about the event she would start shaking uncontrollably to the point that her teeth chattered loudly. Serious post-traumatic stress indications, for sure.

It took a little while to get her terror under control, to get her to relax, and finally, to get her under hypnosis. As it turned out, she was an excellent subject. When she did go, she went deep. After setting up a safe environment in which to view the event, I asked MM to describe what had happened that night.

Apparently, she had had an argument with her husband and MM decided to sleep in the living room on the sofa. She went immediately to sleep as though she were drugged. The next thing she was aware of was some sort of disturbance, like a noise or a sudden bump. She was awake, but paralyzed. She could see a glow in the corner of the room she was facing, and saw a shimmering 'opening' in the ceiling. This opening of shimmering light began to expand in a columnar way so that it became like a shaft of light coming through the ceiling to the floor. As she watched, she struggled unsuccessfully against the paralysis and her heart started pounding so hard she thought the blood would burst out of her ears.

The light began to have 'sparkles' in it – like swirling dust motes in a sunbeam – and these sparkles began to coalesce into a figure. And it was a figure out of a nightmare, for sure! A huge, muscular Lizard man who was soon joined by two others. She was too distressed when trying to describe them accurately, but she did manage to say that they had scales, claws, and lips that were vaguely fish-like.

The beings didn't talk to her, but simply came over; one took hold of her arms and the other took hold of her legs so as to position her for the third that immediately leaned over her and began to copulate.[2]

Well, after working through the rape during the hypnosis session, we went through some processing of the emotions. As I was doing this, I had the idea that I should test my hypothesis about the Greenbaum material[3] by asking some of the Greenbaum questions. It was really just an idea and I certainly did not expect to get a positive response from my subject!

Following the Greenbaum program, I set up the ideomotor finger-signals and suggested:

> I want the central inner core of you to take control of the finger-signals. And I want that central inner core of you to take control of this hand of these finger-signals and what it has for the yes-finger to float up. I want to ask the inner core of you, is there any part of you, any part of MM, who knows anything about Alpha, Beta, Delta, or Theta?

I nearly dropped my teeth when I got a 'yes' response.

Okay, that was the 'red flag'. I was sailing in unfamiliar waters here and really wished I hadn't started down this path without more training. But, it was like surgery: the patient was open, so I needed to see what I could find, do no damage, and hopefully, fix something before I closed her back up.

---

[2] There are photos of the wounds on MM's body and extracts from the hypnosis session in *The Wave*.

[3] My idea was that alleged alien abductions could be implanted memories designed to cover up Greenbaum programming.

After receiving the 'yes' answer I said, "I want a part inside who knows something about Alpha, Beta, Delta, and Theta to come up to a level where you can speak to me, and when you're here say, 'I'm here'."

A voice that was quite different from MM's voice said, "I'm here." I asked for the name and the response was "Gatekeeper".

Well, the only thing to do was to press on and identify as much as I could in the time I could do it. I definitely identified seven different programs and one of them was "Delta". Now, remember what Dr. Hammond said about Delta? "Deltas are killers trained in how to kill in ceremonies."

I went through the programs asking for the 'erasure codes', and was given some of them. On some others, the very mechanical response "Access denied!" came back.

The freaky thing was, I was getting an almost textbook series of responses from this woman that exactly matched the information in the Greenbaum speech! I was utterly dumbfounded. I mean, what are the odds that a very short time after I became aware of this sort of thing a person would just sort of 'enter' my life who had this very situation active in her life? It just boggled the mind.

I went on with my probing, and it was in this process that the most stunning information that I have ever confronted in this work came out.

One of the programs identified itself as "Master Programmer". I began to inquire what type of program this was.

Master Programmer was designed to turn MM into a dynamic New Age/metaphysical teacher whose job was to travel the country, giving classes and seminars in many and various subjects, in order to turn on the already installed programs of other Greenbaum-type victims.

I asked how this could be done. The answer was simple: not only her words, but guided meditations, mantras, tones and symbols incorporated in some of the 'metaphysical jewelry' she carried to sell at her various lectures were used as program triggers. She was also using inaudible frequencies emitted by various gadgets she used in her 'healing classes'.

Further, the teachings, even though they were ostensibly of 'love and light', were designed to use certain word sequences that were standard program triggers. Not only that, but some programs were set up in such a way that even if a person were confronted with the logical inconsistency of their belief system, they would be unable to break through the 'coded thought loop implant' to understand their own faulty logic! In other words, when a person was confronted with truth or obvious factual information, the program would 'turn on' and deny them the ability to think anything other than the 'pre-coded' thoughts that would go around and around in their head like a 'message from God' or their 'guides' or whomever.

I asked what would happen if MM stopped doing this. The answer was, "Compliance is necessary to the mission; not performing the task is noncompliance."

I asked what would be the result of noncompliance. The answer was, "Termination of subject by activation of self-destruct program."

Well, that was pleasant! Definitely not what one would think of as a 'loving guide', 'angel', or 'higher self!'

I asked some questions about where, when and how the programming might have been installed. I wanted to see if she had the same information about 'Dr. Greenbaum'. It was during this portion of the session that the information was revealed that the real reason MM knew Sue was because they had been in the same 'programming set' as children! They had then been brought together in the healing class in Tampa because the teacher of that modality was another such as MM: a Master Programmer.

I was probing to get the code to deactivate some of the programs and suddenly MM began to moan and cry, "It hurts! It hurts!" and her hands went to her ears and she was trying to block out a sound that was obviously quite painful. She was twisting and turning in pain.

I kept speaking to her, attempting to get one of the programs or the 'core' to come forward when the most horrible voice came out of her repeating over and over, "Access denied! Access denied!"

I was finally able to get the Gatekeeper to come back and he stiffly informed me that any further attempts to probe or deactivate would result in immediate destruction of the subject.

Hoo, boy! That was heavy! We were playing with some nasty bullies here!

At this point, MM had been under hypnosis for a lot longer than usual for most subjects, so I released the Gatekeeper with assurances that no harm would come to MM from me, gave her some 'feel good' suggestions, and ended the session. There just didn't seem to be any other option.

After the session, I didn't know what to tell MM. She obviously didn't remember anything about the latter part of her session, but she felt a lot better and her rash was definitely calmed down by at least half, so I ventured to broach the subject of her program. I wanted to know what, exactly, was she doing in her classes? What kinds of things were being used to 'turn on' other people's programs? I had the idea that if it was brought to her conscious attention that she could begin to learn about it and to further evaluate exactly what she was doing. I even had hopes that she would be able to combat the influence and recover from her programming.

The only things I can tell you are that as soon as I began to talk to her about it, there was a definite shift in her personality and a fanatical look began to glow in her eyes.

She began to recite all the standard 'love and light' philosophy and how she was a 'lightworker' and it went on for a few minutes with my growing awareness that I was actually listening to a program!

It was eerie beyond imagining hearing this 'tape' running. Yes, she was saying all the 'right things' to inspire confidence and warm and fuzzy feelings! Yes, she was espousing a philosophy that is more or less standard in the 'New Age' theatre. But now, I was hearing it in a different way. It was no longer just the content of the words that was significant – it was something between and behind them – something sinister and lurking in wait to jump out at any moment.

I was fully aware that there were other programs in MM that could, at a moment's notice, be turned on and that one of these was a killer. There was nothing to do but agree with her that she was doing a 'great work for mankind' and send her home. I remembered what Dr. Hammond said about such individuals being programmed to kill their therapists. I hoped I hadn't been classified as such and marked for death. Seeing the fanatical fire in her eyes, there was no doubt in my mind that she could kill just as she was programmed to do.

The very next day, MM called me and began to chat in a normal way. I asked her how she was feeling, and she said fine! She was bright and sunny in her words and manner. I was listening carefully to her to determine if I was hearing the 'real MM'. Everything seemed to be okay, and she didn't sound like she was going to come over and kill me – at least not at that moment – so I relaxed and chatted casually along, staying alert for any signs of a switch to an alternate personality. Nothing was out of line.

I began to think that maybe we had just encountered a particularly crafty entity attached to MM who had used all this Greenbaum idea to avoid being sent into the light. Heck, maybe I was imagining things altogether! How could I possibly think that there was anything sinister or bizarre about MM?! What a great gal! So bright and easy to talk to. So engaging and funny and charming. Sheesh! This UFO business was really getting to me! I was getting paranoid! I was going off the deep end! That's it! It was me who needed a therapist!

But then, just as she was getting ready to hang up, she remarked, "We need to get together soon! There are a lot of things I want to talk about since I saw you last on Saturday night." That was the night of the session with the Cassiopaeans, not MM's hypnosis the very night before.

I said, "You mean something has happened since last night?"

MM said, "Last night? What do you mean?"

I reminded her of the previous night's hypnosis.

MM laughed and told me I must be dreaming because she had gone to bed early the previous night – she had been exhausted from her classes that day! She certainly had not been with me doing a hypnosis session!

One of us was missing some time here or one of us was going off the deep end and I was pretty sure it wasn't me. Not positive, just pretty sure!

I assured her that we had, indeed, done a hypnosis session. I reminded her that she had called me about her dream of the Reptoid rape and that she had come to my house covered with a rash and scratches. I told her to look at her abdomen to see the scratches.

At that point, MM became quite angry and screamed that I was crazy and slammed the phone down. A sort of 'cloud of unreality' descended over me and I really wondered for a moment if I was losing my mind.

I called Frank and he assured me that I had, indeed, done the hypnosis session, that he had been there manning the recorder, and we had the tape and the notes and the photographs.

Even though I was seeing glimpses of this bizarre reality beneath the surface, my mind really did not want to accept it. Of all the many synchronistic events that had been falling fast and furious upon me, this business of receiving the Greenbaum material and then just sort of having a real subject of it more or less drop into my life was pushing the limits of credulity. Just what in the heck was going on? So, naturally, we brought the subject up at the next session.

Participants: 'Frank', Laura

Q: *(L)* I have a number of questions that I want to get into tonight. Frank and I have been discussing the nature of attack. The first thing I would like to ask is: I did a hypnosis session with MM and utilized some of the Greenbaum techniques. She responded in the affirmative. I was told that she had several alter personalities: "Master Programmer, Gatekeeper, Alpha, Beta, Theta and Delta, Aero," and that there were over 3,000 installed programs. Were these responses valid?

A: Validity is subjective.

Q: *(L)* Does MM have over 3,000 of these 'programs'?

A: Be careful of data which originates from sources which mislead.

Q: *(L)* Which is the misleading source?

A: May mislead.

Q: *(L)* Which is misleading: MM or the Greenbaum text?

A: No it's the center of origin.

Q: *(L)* That which I perceive as a negative attachment?

A: This "subject" appears to be fragmented.

Q: *(L)* So, MM is suffering from MPD?

A: Not that simple.

Q: *(L)* Are her fragments caused by abductions?

A: She has had abductions and the like, but not the issue here. She is "searching," and when one is searching ...[4]

The session was interrupted at this point by a long-distance phone call and was never resumed.

Obviously, that was a timely interruption.

I can't swear that MM did not know anything about the Greenbaum speech and its description of mind-programming experiments. She may have known that material and may have been confabulating the whole situation for drama. The Cs were not terribly impressed by it. They did, at other points, confirm the existence of Greenbaum programming (or something similar), but it is almost as though the Cs were saying that the misleading source was MM herself, or some part of her. But then, isn't that the essence of such mind programming: fragmented

---
[4] *The Wave* 19

personalities? Perhaps what the Cs were going to say at the end was that when a person is searching, they sometimes open the wrong doors and let in things that should not be admitted and this was the source of the misleading information? Was I being misled to think that MM was mind programmed by some secret government project, when in fact, she was being abducted by hyperdimensional beings? Or vice versa? Read *The Wave* chapters indicated for more discussion of this topic.

I was still somewhat concerned about MM's revelations about Sue and the remark under hypnosis that she and Sue had been part of the same 'programming set', which I took to be a group. Not only that, but there was the receipt of the 'Elaine and the Sisters of Light' material at precisely the time that MM made her revelations to me about Sue.

Was I looking at another aspect of the 'hidden control mechanism'? The whole thing was so unlikely and so crazy that I was really stretching my credulity to even deal with it on a rational basis. But heck! When you talk to '6th density light beings' via a board on Saturday nights, how unlikely and weird can anything be?

March 13, 1996

The trip to the UFO conference in Gulf Breeze was all Frank could talk about. I had the idea that we would drive up in my van, split the expenses three ways, and we could park on one of the great beaches up there and camp out with sleeping bags. Frank would have none of that. He would have a hotel room or nothing.

Okay. Well, I couldn't afford a hotel room. But Frank pointed out that Sue could. Frank decided that she ought to fund this trip. As he pointed out, Sue had certainly been providing printing supplies, paper, ink, and tapes to me for the sessions and printing excerpts and copies of sessions. Why shouldn't she pay for a trip to Gulf Breeze?

I didn't like it, but Frank said, "If we don't go in style, I ain't goin'!" And I most definitely wanted Frank to go. "Just let me handle Sue," he assured me.

I didn't want Sue to have to discuss this with Frank alone, since I was already certain that she couldn't see through his little manipulations that I generally swept under the rug when he tried them on me and made every effort to protect other people from them. (Again, I was waiting for Frank to come into his own, and I tolerated his flaws until he did, which I was sure he would eventually.)

After Frank had made his proposal to her in a more or less direct way, which could not have been faulted, I mentioned the fact that my idea had been to drive up and camp out to save money. Sue thought my idea was more fun, but Frank again interjected that he wasn't going to go if he couldn't stay in a hotel.

So, Sue said, "Sure! That would be fun! We can just all share a double room!"

"Nope!" Frank declared. He would not go if he couldn't have his own room. I could see the chances of going to the conference and distributing the magazine dwindling. But Sue agreed. Sure, she'd pay for two rooms if that would make Frank happy.

However, that wasn't all that Frank wanted. Now he announced that it would undoubtedly be cheaper all the way around if we were to fly up instead of drive. I could see the chances of going to the conference and distributing the magazine dwindling again. But Sue agreed. Sure, she'd pay for round-trip tickets for the three of us.

And Frank just beamed with delight.

But the problems with getting things ready for this conference began to multiply like mushrooms after a rain.

Participants: 'Frank', Laura

Q: *(L)* Hello.

A: Hello.

Q: *(L)* Who do we have with us tonight?

A: Vinxyoh.

Q: *(L)* And where are you from?

A: Cassiopaea.

Q: *(L)* You once said that you are always with us. If so, then you must have heard the earlier discussion to the effect that, since we have been doing this project, the magazine and all that, it seems to bring on the most awful attacks from every imaginable corner. I am really tired. I get it from the people out there, and I get it here at home. I'm tired of the dramas. I am tired of the complaints and aggravation. I am tired of doing all the work, and everybody else just coming up with more problems for me to solve. I am tired of being sick. I am tired of pain. I am tired of not knowing the answers. I am just tired. I am ready to stop. To quit. To just sit in my room and vegetate. Any comment?

A: What do you want to know?

Q: *(L)* I want to know if all of this activation of Murphy's law is going to stop.

A: This is not the problem.

Q: *(L)* Well, for beings who are supposed to be able to read minds, you aren't helping much! Why don't you just read my mind and tell me what I need to know?

A: You need to read your own mind!

Q: *(L)* Considering the state of mind I am in right now, that almost sounds like a facetious answer!

A: No.

Q: *(L)* What is in my mind?

A: Ask yourself. Discover.

Q: *(L)* Well, the closest I can come is to say that I am suffering from the most serious loss of faith I can ever remember experiencing. Sue and her mother. Pat and the games with getting the magazine printed. The school board. The lunatics at ISCNI. Mike Lindemann ...

A: We warned you that there would be attack.

Q: *(L)* I am at the point that I don't want any more attack. We can stop the channeling, the writing, the internet ... everything. I just want to quit.

A: And what do you think that would do for you?

Q: *(L)* Well, maybe some of the attack would stop.

A: And maybe not!!

23 **Q:** *(L)* Then I need you to tell me what I can do. I am drowning here! I need to know how to shield myself.

24 **A:** Re-aim direction somewhat.

25 **Q:** *(L)* Toward what?

26 **A:** Ask yourself.

27 **Q:** *(L)* Obviously, since the magazine has been so incredibly stressful, doing everything with no help, I guess I will have to give it up.

28 **A:** If you wish, or perhaps change format?

29 **Q:** *(L)* Change the format to what?

30 **A:** Anything that brings less stress.

31 **Q:** *(L)* Well, the whole point of doing it was to create a vehicle for the transcripts. And that seems to be what is causing the stress, because people just don't want to hear it!

32 **A:** That is not true, it is how it is presented!!

33 **Q:** *(L)* We sent it out to hundreds of addresses. I have a mailing list. It cost a fortune for the bulk mail permit and the postage, not to mention the printing. I sent one to D___ and Val and tons of other people. D___ told me the other night that Val called him and said that he just didn't want anything to do with the material because it was so choppy and disorganized. It was a mess.

34 **A:** If the magazine is just our messages, would not this be less stressful?

35 **Q:** *(L)* Well, there won't be another issue if it is going to be this stressful. My point was to get enough in there so that a broad range of people would be interested and subscribe.

36 **A:** Is your "point" the only one?

37 **Q:** *(L)* Of course not! But I'm the one who has fallen heir to this and I am just doing the best I can without a whole hell of a lot of help!

38 **A:** Because you wish to direct without guidance.

39 **Q:** *(L)* Now wait a minute! That is *not* fair. I have asked for guidance and was told to figure it out myself. This is what I did according to what I thought was the best way to do it!

40 **A:** We are trying to help you, not hinder, but you must be willing to understand what is being said. And this requires willingness to have faith and really be guided. Not good to "get lost," as can happen when other problems intercede, such as prejudice and the lack of conduit mindset, i.e. obsession.

41 **Q:** *(L)* This is precisely what I am getting at here. How does one maintain a conduit mindset, or lack of obsession, or any of these other things? Those are not the problems, those are only the results of the problems. The problems are the attack, such as the situation with my mother, Sue and all of her problems, the kids, the husband, the magazine, Pat and Patrick ...

42 **A:** Try to avoid encumbrances, when at all possible. Also, suggest that you try to stop trying to solve problems for others, especially when your instincts tell you this! Remember, all are on a different learning "schedule," or path.

43 **Q:** *(L)* Well, that is all fine and good, but when other people's problems interfere with getting the work done, the magazine out, and having peace of mind so that I can focus, it is hard for me to not try and help and solve these problems!

44 **A**: Now, give an example of how one's problems interfere with getting the magazine published, please.

45 **Q**: *(L)* Well, Pat's kid in the print shop, being unable to keep any part of the process straight, much less keep his head on straight, caused me to have to go down there repeatedly and work like a lunatic physically assembling copy just so it would be done in time. And this was *after* spending 18 hours a day typing or formatting! I can assure you that, had I not done so, there would be no magazine. Meanwhile Sue is acting like a jerk because her mother is acting like a jerk ... Come on! You guys can see this stuff!

46 **A**: We can also "see" what you cannot!

47 **Q**: *(L)* Which is why I am sitting here asking. And why I asked you before ... and all you gave me was 'open,' and 'up to you' and 'wait and see'. And now, I am physically exhausted, worn out, I have been constantly sick for months ... You could have just told us! Sue could have left her mother in the nursing home! I just want to crawl into a hole and *quit*!

48 **A**: If we had told you that, you would not have learned!!!

49 **Q**: *(L)* You could have just told me that Sue was a flake to begin with, and that she would cause me all this grief!

50 **A**: Subjective.

51 **Q**: *(L)* I know it is subjective and I don't really mean it that way, but if Sue had been doing what was her own responsibility and not continuously crying to me on the phone, or coming over here and putting guilt trips on me, then I could have handled what I needed to ... and she hasn't done a damn thing she didn't want to do, and I am the one that's paying for it!

52 **A**: If you had done nothing, the situation would have solved itself.

53 **Q**: *(L)* I hate to tell you this, but not helping people when they call and ask for help sounds like a pretty STS position.

54 **A**: No.

55 **Q**: *(L)* I'm sorry, but that is what it sounds like. To say to somebody, 'That's your problem, sayonara!' doesn't sound very helpful to me!

56 **A**: That is not what needs to be said.

57 **Q**: *(L)* I am very offended by a lot of things that have happened. I am very offended by the fact that when I asked Sue to do one tiny little thing for me, which was to go to the store after I had been up for over 24 hours doing lay-out, and get me a ream of paper, she couldn't do it because she had a stiff neck. And, she said this to me! Me, with pus running out of my eyes. And I am offended by Pat and her hours and hours of complaining, and any single thing that she could do herself to straighten her own affairs, she completely ignores it, or does the opposite. And Sue did not handle her mother with the result that my mother was calling me on the phone and essentially saying, "You got me into this, it is terrible, and what are you gonna do?" And, in a sense, she was right. I felt responsible. I believed Sue, Sue lied to me, and everything got completely screwed up.

58 **A**: If your focus had been on the project only, none of these problems would have resulted. And, furthermore, this is not an STS stance. Nothing of the sort!!! If you listen to your inner

"voice," it is easy to differentiate between an actual request for helpful assistance, and just another trap, otherwise known as a portal of attack.

59 **Q**: *(L)* Well, do you understand the rock-and-the-hard-place concept? I was not in a position to help my mother, and I am still human. And, I didn't like seeing Sue's mother suffer and do without, either. It seemed like such an ideal solution.

60 **A**: Interesting alternative: what if you had suggested to Sue that her mother move in with her?

61 **Q**: *(L)* I did suggest that.

62 **A**: And ...

63 **Q**: *(L)* Well, we said that she would have to give up her job and her life to take care of her mother and she couldn't do it.

64 **A**: And this is the crux: if that were true, Sue then would have had to have found an alternative which was always open to her. Also, your mother had other alternatives open to her, but chose to "sit back" and let you handle it, as you have always done. This is a karmic circle, which, though difficult, accelerates the learning process, thus soul progress and karmic advancement.

65 **Q**: *(L)* Well, I felt some sense of obligation to help Sue because she was always buying me and the kids things and bringing them over and insisting that I keep them. What were her motives?

66 **A**: "Buying your friendship." Still continues ...

67 **Q**: *(L)* Well, there are other things here that are related to this issue here. I was not able to buy some of those things, and she knew it. I was sinking a *lot* of money in the magazine, and that leads to another problem. Finances. And this seems to be an ongoing portal of attack here. A whole lot of problems would be solved if I did not have to worry about survival!

68 **A**: We have told you we would help with the finances, and have, and will continue to do so.

69 **Q**: *(L)* Okay, is the magazine, as it is done, going to work out and carry itself forward?

70 **A**: We suggest being open to alterations.

71 **Q**: *(L)* It can be altered next time ... but not now, it is printed.

72 **A**: Okay. How a book can be created ... just concentrate on editing our messages, and nothing else, with each issue, unless camera ready "canned" copy, and at the end, just consolidate for publisher!!

73 **Q**: *(L)* Okay. I already thought of that. Okay. Before we stop for the night, I want to ask one question that is unrelated to all we have been discussing. I asked once before about Nephilim genes, and you said, "You don't want to know." So, let me make a statement. We already know that people get used for 'lunch' or experiments, to be tossed into the blender, milked for emotional energy, made to suffer in infinite ways for infinite reasons. And, we are not talking about something to which I am very much attached, in terms of these missing babies of mine, because it was a long time ago. But, what I would like to know is, what is it about these Nephilim children when I asked if I had children with Nephilim genes that made you respond that way...?

74 **A**: What specifically?

Q: *(L)* I don't know. So, we will shelve it. I am exhausted. Goodnight.

A: Goodbye.

End of Session

March 23, 1996

The very beginning of the second side of the tape has a noise anomaly as follows: it starts out sounding like the taped voices are soft, far away and coming from the bottom of a well. This clears up; the voices are clearer and nearer. Then, they sound far away and faint again. This continues; on the tape recorder's speakers you can actually 'hear' the rotation from one speaker to the other. It almost sounds like either the microphone or the people speaking are actually 'spinning' around each other. It was checked out on another tape recorder, one with only one speaker, and it is not on the other side of the tape, so it is not a physical aberration of the tape itself, or my tape recorder. —Transcriber, Jan R.

At some point during the magazine preparation period, Sue made an offhand remark about her relations with several people that I knew to be deeply involved with ritual magic and other unsavory activities. I was surprised. After all we had learned so far, didn't she think it was a bit dangerous to be hanging out with those people? Sue explained that she really wasn't hanging out with them, she was being paid to do therapy with them. It was purely and simply a business relationship.

But she knew that this was the same group of people who had previously tried to harm me, and I felt a tremendous sense of betrayal. I knew I couldn't ask her to give up a massage client in solidarity with me, but I certainly hoped she would.

Having this sudden revelation just before our trip did not make the prospects all that pleasant for me. But, I was committed to getting the magazine out, and that was that.[1]

Now, the reader has to understand the problem here. Sure, the Cs were telling us all kinds of things about agents and theological struggles between forces and that those forces act through human beings, and that

---

[1] See also *The Wave*, chapter 45, for additional details of the chaos that reigned at that time.

people can be activated as agents and that everybody was controlled to one extent or another by a vast, bizarre system that was basically run by a sort of Evil-Magician complex; but having them tell us this, *applying it in our lives so that we made life decisions based on it was another thing altogether.*

However, the situation was becoming unbearable at the time we made the trip to Gulf Breeze. I decided to closely observe Sue during this time we were going to be together day and night and see if I could discover what, exactly, the problem was. I certainly did not want to jump to conclusions and exclude her if it was just a matter of personality. I have always believed that people can get along if they have some things in common, or at least a common goal, even if they have very different personalities. The question was: what was Sue's goal? What were her intentions? Why did she so eagerly seek to join our group? It had been gratifying, of course, to think that she was so excited over the material, as she claimed to be; that she was truly being helped by participation; and that she was the most faithful attendee! But, was there a motive behind this that was not so benevolent?

Just prior to this trip, Frank asked me one day, didn't I think it was strange that Sue had been involved with the Outlaws motorcycle gang, and Pat's agent had also been involved with the Outlaws?

I had never given the matter much thought. Sue was adopted and really knew nothing about her biological family, but that was not the issue. At a young age, she had rebelled, as is generally considered normal, but her mode of rebellion was a little extreme: she became involved with a member of a notorious motorcycle gang!

Of course, by the time we knew her, all that was in the past. She had long been disassociated from them, had gone to school to become a massage therapist and had become actively involved in the local metaphysical community. She had experienced an 'awakening' and 'conversion', and her declared form of service was to be a part of our group.

But still, as Frank pointed out, she could talk about mayhem and even murder in the most disconnected way imaginable. It was as though she had no emotion about it at all. This was very disturbing. Frank pointed out how on the several occasions when he had asked her questions about her experiences, rather than seeing them as dreadful, she talked and laughed about some of them, and she never seemed reluctant to talk about it at all. Frank drove home the point that this simply did not mesh with her reformed persona. How could someone decry the extermination of roaches, and pass off the murder of human beings as though it were nothing?

I had no answer, but Frank did. He was convinced that this was the root of any problems with the group. It was Sue who was to blame for attitudes, atmosphere, strange connections that are too numerous to describe. But, most of all, it was now clear that this was the reason the Cassiopaeans would not be as forthcoming in her presence as they had formerly been. It also explained the reason they had changed the subject when I was talking about the Coral Castle and, instead, brought up the fact that Sue's background was unusual ... all were clues for me to pick up on, designed to not violate my free will.

No sooner had we discussed it, than something manifested to explain it or counteract what we were thinking and talking about. During the trip up to Gulf Breeze, all of a sudden, Sue was a literal bundle of emotions. She more than made up for all the emotions she had never displayed before, all in a three-day period. It was as though she had been able to hear our thoughts and was now counteracting them.

Tom French and Cherie Diez met us in Gulf Breeze for the conference. When we arrived after a trip that was probably more exhausting than driving up in the van would have been, we settled in our rooms and went looking for Tom and Cherie. There was a bulletin board in the hotel lobby where Tom had left a message for a rendezvous, and we made our way to the vendors to unload a stack of magazines to our friend who promised to distribute them.

Having done that, we attended a few lectures, met Tom and Cherie for lunch, attended a couple more lectures with Tom and Cherie, and at the end of the day, everyone went out on the beach for a UFO watch.

I have read that people who have visited all the most famous beaches in the world say that the beaches along the Florida panhandle are the finest in the world. I have to agree. They are absolutely gorgeous.

But, no UFOs showed up, and we finally retired for the evening, Frank to his private room, and Sue and myself to our shared double room. I was soon asleep. And then, the dream.

I dreamed that there was someone far away, in a room full of people who were planning to do something to harm him, only he didn't know it. I tried to get his attention and signaled that he should meet me in the next room. He followed me in there and I told him that I was afraid for his safety. He told me not to worry, that he would be all right, and that I should go back home and wait for him because as soon as he could make the arrangements and extricate himself from this danger, he would come to me. And then he kissed me. I couldn't see his face clearly, but I most definitely felt that kiss.

The only thing I can say about it is that it was like being Sleeping Beauty and being kissed by the Prince, because *I woke up*. Not just figuratively, but literally, too. I woke up and sat bolt upright in bed with the sensation of having been kissed still on my lips. I stared around the unfamiliar hotel room in bewilderment and heard Sue snoring lightly. I reached up to touch my lips with my fingers as if by doing so I could detect some trace of who had kissed me. But there was nothing, no clue. Just an incredible feeling that something amazing had just happened. I laid back down and went back to sleep. I dreamed again. This time, I was with the man who had kissed me, though again, I couldn't see his face. In the dream, my then husband came to me to ask me to come back to him, and this other man put his arms around me protectively and said, "She belongs to me. She always belonged to me. You were supposed to protect her until I came, and all you did was hurt her. Now go!"

At breakfast I shared the dream with Sue and Frank, and later told it to Tom and Cherie. I still had the sensation on my lips of having been kissed. Now, as so many years have passed and I understand more – even understanding what "We are You in the Future" really means – I realize that this dream, this kiss, was the 'appearance of the Cs' at the UFO conference.

The flight back was a real doozie. We went through a major thunderstorm that there was no way to fly under, over or around. We just had to brace ourselves and the plane bucked like a bronco. I had to laugh because this was only the third time I had ever been on a plane in my life, and Frank had spent hours before the trip recounting all his memorable flights and how much he loved to fly. And now, he was popping motion sickness pills, looking as green as a tree frog, and I was having the time of my life.

Curiously, Sue, who had been so terrified of getting on a plane on the trip up to Gulf Breeze, just *slept through the whole thing*. And lest you think I am exaggerating, at the end of the flight, even the captain was green as he stood there shaking everybody's hand on their way out. They were all thanking him for still being alive!

Participants: 'Frank', Laura, V

1 **Q**: *(L)* Hello. Is anybody there?

2 **A**: Fopilion from Cassiopaea.

3 **Q**: *(L)* Good evening to you, we are glad you came to join us. We have some situations we want to look at, and then we want to ask some questions of a more universal nature. Is that all right for the evening?

4 **A**: Maybe.

5 **Q**: *(L)* What's the maybe refer to?

6 **A**: Your inquiry.

7 **Q**: *(L)* The first inquiry I have is our situation relating to Sue, and the different clues that we have received, and the different observations that I have made myself, and the discussions or the networking interactions that we have had on the subject. Can you tell us anything in a general way, or do we really have to ask specific questions about the subject?[2]

8 **A**: Sue is storehouse of vital information, clue for you was in name, but you failed to notice![3]

9 **Q**: *(L)* Okay, but Sue ...

10 **A**: This is why the frustration is for you; nothing of value comes without a price!!

11 **Q**: *(L)* Number one, Sue has lied to us.[4] Number two, it seems that she began to demonstrate emotional affect only after we had discussed the fact that there was a serious lack of emotional affect, after you had told us that these robot people

---

[2] *The Wave* 45

[3] Recall the previous use of the word "vital" in respect of Sue from the 8 February session: "You were warned, Susan! Please, please, please, please, when you call or cry out for help and or guidance, know that we will always, always, always answer. It is up to you to be aware and then trust and follow. If your deep-seated stubbornness prevents this, it will result in nothing short of your total undoing! This is because we never give such warnings, except when **vitally** necessary! This applies to all others present equally as well!!" I was beginning to feel that I had some deep-seated stubbornness about something and that it was leading to my destruction! And of course, in retrospect, I did, indeed. I was stubbornly choosing to think and believe the best of everything and everybody and to take them at face value, and to look for excuses to explain any kind of clues that there was a deeper, unseen reality. And of course, this reminds one of the session when we talked about Ted Bundy and the necessity to learn to 'see the unseen', session 9 January 1996.

[4] I was referring here to the information given to me by MM regarding Sue's continued involvement with the Magick gang that had tried to harm me.

[5] See the 21 October 1995 session for the first discussion of robot types. That was interesting because Sue was present and we were discussing another individual named Susan S. The Cs said, at that time, that they named only one such individual but

are people who spend a lot of time alone and have ...[5]

A: The price, my dear, continues ... [Referring to previous answer: "nothing of value comes without a price!!"]

Q: *(V)* By continuing the relationship?[6]

A: The Nordic Covenant was a duality.[7]

Q: *(L)* Sue comes from that area where that Nordic Covenant ... what is it, Minnesota, she's from Minnesota? Oh, I never made that connection! Holy Frijoles! "Nordic Covenant was a duality" ... so, when you made mention of the Nordic Covenant, and the banking scandal, was that a double-layered statement to us?

A: Maybe, but you are missing the point! All persons of Nordic heritage hold secret power centers, can be of darkness, or of light ... Sue is of Teutonic bloodline leading directly to such super power source such as Thule Society and others, and she is aware of her powers and mission. It is of positive orientation. However, you are being tested by 4th through 6th density forces to determine if you have the strength and wisdom for continuance!

Q: *(L)* The whole thing just doesn't make sense ... I mean, with that nasty red aura she has ...

A: Red aura needs much further study on your part. Your sources for such information could be deceiving you.

Q: *(L)* Well then ...

A: And we are the Cassiopaeans, but it is of your will to live as you desire.

Q: *(L)* Well ... Then why was she told by you guys that if she didn't do certain things that it would lead to her total undoing?

A: Go back and study that message again, with assistance of tape, and with mind open to all angles. Check intent, however, malice is in absence. Notice the difference. The duality of covenant!!!

Q: *(L)* Well, Frank is of Nordic extraction. Is he a member of this covenant, also?

A: Maybe.

Q: *(F)* If so, it's news to me. (Laughs) *(L)* Do you say she is aware of her mission?

A: Some are.

Q: *(L)* Is her mother something in the way to block her from performing her mission?

A: Mother is inconsequential.

Q: *(V)* Her mother, her adopted mother ... inconsequential. Okay, so does ...

A: Curious how background is murky, yes!

"cannot give you others at this juncture". We discussed later the fact that Sue did not seem to display emotional affect. She could talk about the most awful things as though she were giving a recipe. Not very long after Frank and I had this discussion privately, Sue all of a sudden started acting all emotional and crying about stuff and making dramas, especially in respect of the mother situation.

[6] *The Wave* 62

[7] See the 3 December 1994 session for the first mention of the Nordic Covenant. Then also see 24 September 1995 for further discussion of Nordic types in humans and 4 March 1995.

31 **Q:** *(L)* Yes, that is curious. *(V)* Something tells me that this can go further ... *(L)* Well, yes, but they were also talking about her birth, and her adoption, and all that kind of thing in another session. Stuff that's so unclear, she doesn't know anything about it, and claims she doesn't. So strange ... Is Sue a 'walk-in'?

32 **A:** Not correct terminology.

33 **Q:** *(L)* Well, then what is the correct terminology? What is Sue?

34 **A:** Birthright.

35 **Q:** *(L)* Now, what does that mean?

36 **A:** Discover.

37 **Q:** *(L)* Are you saying that when we make mention of the Nordic Covenant and the Thule Society, that there's some possibility that Sue has been programmed, or has layers of programs, and that some part of her program knows what she's doing, and maybe other parts don't?

38 **A:** Yes, but this is not a negative thing.

39 **Q:** *(L)* Okay, now let me go a little bit deeper. Could Sue be what you described as a robot person, but programmed for a positive purpose?

40 **A:** No, robot "people" do not have bloodlines.

41 **Q:** *(L)* So, this is something that's programmed genetically in a bloodline?

42 **A:** Not exactly, those that have the bloodline have the corresponding soul alignment.

43 **Q:** *(L)* We are talking about a genetic bloodline that activates certain abilities and genes that interface with the corresponding soul that has prepared for this manifestation of the bloodline?

44 **A:** Yes.

45 **Q:** *(L)* Is there any significance to the fact that Sue spent all of those years living with the Outlaws motorcycle gang and this covenant?[8]

46 **A:** Yes, and that is what has led and is leading to the destruction of the "Outlaws," a group associated directly with 4th density STS.

47 **Q:** *(V)* Her presence there caused them to break up? This was a good thing. Is this what is meant here? That her presence was uplifting to them? *(L)* Well, it's not uplifting them, it's breaking them; they are all going to jail!

48 **A:** Yes and because of circumstances planted by "Agent Sue." This is why the perceived lack of emotion connected with that whole situation. Sue is the bravest human you have ever known! All evidence to the contrary is veil; part of the testing process.[9]

49 **Q:** *(L)* If we're being tested, why are you telling us? *(V)* So that you do not fail?

50 **A:** Yes.

---

[8] *The Wave* 62

[9] And notice that just above, it was me that was being 'tested'. Here, they mention a 'veil' that is part of the testing process. So, which way to see this?

[10] Again they use that word which takes us back to: "If your deep-seated stubbornness prevents this, it will result in nothing short of your total undoing! This is because we never give such warnings, except when **vitally** necessary! This applies to all others present equally as well!!"

51 **Q:** *(L)* Is Sue aware that this is going on?

52 **A:** Vital that you do not fail.[10]

53 **Q:** *(V)* Is Sue aware that ...

54 **A:** Yes.

55 **Q:** *(V)* Is there a pivotal word that might break this open to a clearer understanding?

56 **A:** Discover.

57 **Q:** *(L)* Now, when we were flying back home [from UFO conference in Gulf Breeze] and we were flying through that storm, was that storm, which began before we left, and we flew through it on the way back, was that a byproduct or bleedthrough of a battle between the forces?

58 **A:** Yes.

59 **Q:** *(L)* Was it trying to harm us in any way, because we had to fly through it, and couldn't fly over it? I mean, even the pilot was worried, and he had been flying for years!

60 **A:** Yes.

61 **Q:** *(L)* What brought it to an end?

62 **A:** Sue. Notice how "unaffected" she was?!?

63 **Q:** *(L)* I told you that the whole thing about being scared was a fake! *(F)* Yes, she was scared on the way up, when there was nothing to be scared of, and on the way back, when we were bouncing around like a pinball in a pinball machine, she's sleeping, I'm getting sick, and Laura's going, "Ride em, cowboy!!" [All laughed] *(L)* Okay, so how are we supposed to react to this situation?

64 **A:** Up to you.

65 **Q:** *(L)* Okay, we knew that was coming. It wouldn't have been a good night without it! *(V)* Some things never change, huh? *(L)* Well Frank seems to think there's a whole lot more there in terms of background than she was letting on. Is that correct?

66 **A:** Maybe.

67 **Q:** *(L)* Well, okay, I'm going to trust you guys, and I'm going to go with the flow, and I'm going to assume that you are right, and I'm going to assume that this is for the best and for the good, and I'm going to stop my knee-jerk reactions, and stop worrying about such things.[11]

68 **A:** Suggest you look before you leap. All can be wrong in their quick judgments, whether the result be acceptance or rejection. All is not as it seems ... Remember, those that come into your group, or your circle of influence can be different than you think.[12]

69 **Q:** *(L)* You said we were being tested. Tested for what?

70 **A:** Continuance.

71 **Q:** *(L)* Continuance of what?

72 **A:** All.

73 **Q:** *(L)* Continuance of all. Okay, and we are being tested through Sue?

74 **A:** Currently.

75 **Q:** *(L)* Are you saying that what we have been considering attacks were just tests?

76 **A:** The ones associated with Sue. And no, all with that name are not of this

---

[11] *The Wave* 62

[12] That this response came right after I announced I was going to accept that Sue was one of the 'good guys' really shook me up!

orientation, but this clue was installed for you.

77 Q: *(L)* Are you saying that Sue is our 4th density Nordic?

78 A: ?

79 Q: *(V)* Maybe just by the purpose of her being, she's vital for you! *(L)* Okay, Whitley Strieber wrote back and told me that he was familiar with this school that I experienced in the dream and I think I asked you guys about this once, and you said I needed to discover some more about it. He says that he is familiar with all of it ...

80 A: All is not as delivered.

81 Q: *(L)* He says that he is one of the patriarchal dudes who was teaching ...

82 A: Ditto.

83 Q: *(L)* Well, my feeling is that this was a school on an astral level, it was a school of a higher density, that it was not ever a physical, 3rd density school. That was my impression of it, and that I was being sent forth from another density, to experience, after being instructed by this group of patriarchal-type beings. [They were actually seen as more like how one would imagine Greek philosophers.] Is that correct?

84 A: Yes.

85 Q: *(L)* So, the school that Whitley describes, and him thinking that he is one of the higher-density beings, he's misinterpreting this as a physical school. Is that correct?

86 A: Maybe.

87 Q: *(L)* Is he, is he, well ... They're not going to answer that one, are they? Why do I even bother thinking that I'm going to slide that one by ...

88 A: Now, for the remainder of this session, we wish to address the so-called Earth changes for your benefit, as you are stuck here. Those present need to be equi... [sound anomaly on tape begins here, on second side] ...pped to stop buying into popular deceptions once and for all! Reread Bramley.

89 Q: *(L)* Funny, I took him off the shelf today ... *(V)* What's Bramley about? *(L)* Well, hold on. Do you want me to read it right now?

90 A: No.

91 Q: *(L)* Okay, address the subject.

92 A: All such changes are caused by three things and three things only! 1) Human endeavors. 2) Cosmic objects falling upon or too near earth. 3) Planetary orbital aberrations.

93 Q: *(L)* All right, carry on.

94 A: Don't believe any of the nonsense you hear from other sources. It is designed to facilitate mass programming and deception.

95 Q: *(L)* Okay, okay.

96 A: Just as your Bible says; "You will know not the day, nor the hour." This means there is no warning. None. No clue. No prophecy. And these events ... [anomaly starts again here, briefly] are of the "past" as well [and ends here].

97 Q: *(V)* What events of the past, as well?

98 A: Cosmic and "man made" cataclysms.

99 Q: *(L)* Well, since you put 'man-made' at the top of the list, am I to infer that perhaps some of the activities of the Consortium, the secret government, are going to precipitate some of these events?

100 A: No.

101 **Q**: *(L)* Yes. Okay, is there any more that you want to say on this? Go ahead, you have the floor. Please.

102 **A**: Ask away.

103 **Q**: *(L)* Well, you've said that there's a comet cluster that's coming this way. Is that still correct?

104 **A**: Yes.

105 **Q**: *(L)* Is this body that has been called Hale-Bopp, is this that comet cluster?

106 **A**: No.

107 **Q**: *(L)* Is this comet cluster that's coming, and you've indicated that it could arrive anywhere between 18 years, something like that, is that correct?

108 **A**: Maybe.

109 **Q**: *(L)* Now, is this something that can be seen from a great way off?

110 **A**: No.

111 **Q**: *(L)* Is this something that's going to impact our particular immediate location, and appear suddenly, as this comet that has flown overhead just did? Nobody saw it until a very short time ago, and all of a sudden everybody sees it?

112 **A**: The cluster is a symptom, not the focus.

113 **Q**: *(V)* What is the focus?

114 **A**: Wave, remember, is "realm border" crossing ... What does this imply? Consult your knowledge base for Latin roots and proceed.

115 **Q**: *(L)* So, the Latin root of realm is *regimen*, which means a domain or rulership or a system for the improvement of health. Does this mean that, and as I assume, we are now moving into the STO realm, now, out of the STS realm?

116 **A**: Partly.

117 **Q**: *(L)* And also, can I infer from this, that the comet cluster exists in the other realm?

118 **A**: Partly.

119 **Q**: *(L)* Well, previously, you had said that the comet cluster would come before the realm border. Which indicated that the comet ...

120 **A**: Yes.

121 **Q**: *(L)* Well, how can something so ... you said it appears to be one single large body, and that our government knows that it's on its way, and that apparently somebody has spotted it. Which direction is it coming from?

122 **A**: Direction?

123 **Q**: *(L)* Well, the comet cluster. That comet cluster, is, I am assuming, a real body, in 3rd density experience, right? A part of a real cluster of bodies in 3rd density experience. Is that correct?

124 **A**: Cluster can approach from all directions.

125 **Q**: *(L)* So, can I infer from what has been said, that we are going to move into this comet cluster, as into a realm?

126 **A**: Border changes rules.

127 **Q**: *(L)* But if we run into the comet cluster before we cross the border, then, I mean, I would understand if we were going into the realm border first ...

128 **A**: Part in part out.

129 **Q**: *(L)* Okay, is this so-called HAARP project instrumental in any of these realm border changes, these realm changes?

130 **A**: All is interconnected, as usual.

131 **Q:** *(L)* Anybody got any questions on this? What is the thing that is going on nowadays ... let me ask about this. Roxanne sent me some information about the Do-ma, or space goddesses who rule the Grays, supposedly. Apparently there is a whole group of people, including government officials, involved in this Do-ma cult.

132 **A:** Yeah, right!

133 **Q:** *(L)* Well, that was my feeling. I sent ...

134 **A:** Deception is everywhere! Scrambled brains, anyone?

135 **Q:** *(L)* Gotcha. I sent several chunks of the Cassiopaean transcripts off to [Hampton Roads publishers]. As I was requested to ...

136 **A:** Wait and see.

137 **Q:** *(L)* In a nutshell, could you tell us what the re-emerging goddess images represent, nowadays? *(V)* Programming?

138 **A:** Close.

139 **Q:** *(L)* Frank, is there anything you need to know? *(V)* I just want to know if they have anything they want to share with me, that's all. They know what all my questions are.

140 **A:** Open to all possibilities. Rigidity does not pay!

141 **Q:** *(V)* What are they talking about? *(L)* I guess that last comment was for everybody. Be open to all possibilities. Okay, well, we'll stop for the night. Goodnight.

142 **A:** Goodbye.

End of Session

After the end of the session, I read over the notes quickly, and noted that, in response to my acquiescence to the idea that Sue was a positive being exactly as the Cs were saying, the Cs had said: "Suggest you look before you leap. All can be wrong in their quick judgments, whether the result be acceptance or rejection. All is not as it seems ... Remember, those that come into your group, or your circle of influence can be different than you think."

I realized suddenly that their high praise of Sue had been so exaggerated that I was supposed to catch the fact that the truth was the exact opposite of what the Cs were saying. I knew that I was so uncomfortable with the situation that I simply wanted to find a way to bring our association to an end amicably and without any ugly confrontations. With those thoughts firmly in mind, I asked for the Cs to come back and comment.

143 **Q:** *(L)* Hello. Are you there? I am not comfortable with this information about Sue. It seems to be contradictory to everything

I can observe and feel.[13]

A: Hiklu Cassiopaea. Worry not further! Discomfort is not necessarily danger, and is indicative of growth and learning. So, proceed and celebrate!![14]

End of Session

Apparently, I had passed the test. But there were so many more yet to come!

I was beginning to get the idea that there was a lot being said to me that required study and contemplation. Obviously, getting the truth through the Matrix was not so easy. I was beginning to feel like a spy in enemy territory needing to decode messages that were double and triply encoded.

And it was *Vital* to succeed.

At this point, I am going to begin including some extracts from Ark's journals of 1996 insofar as they may relate to the hints and material the Cs were delivering. Ark generally gives titles to his journals because they are not just personal ruminations, but also research records of what he is working on at any given time. The journal that he began for 1996 was entitled: 'Master Gravitation'. That is, he was giving himself a task to master this topic beginning in the year 1996. The reader may wish to refer to the first session when gravity was discussed with physicist Ruggero Santilli, 27 May 1995, close to 10 months prior to this present session. The next discussion of the topic was on 31 May 1995 followed by 17 June 1995. Then, there is the now famous (in my mind, at least!)

---

[13] *The Wave* 45, 62

[14] This was a most interesting result. Because, even thought the Cs had more or less praised Sue to the skies – though using some strange language in the process – I just decided that I couldn't accept what they were saying, that I *had* to go with my instincts at this point and conclude that, if Sue was connected to some Nordic Covenant or the Thule Society or whatever, it was *not* a positive thing. This is what I meant by "everything I can observe and feel". Their response that my discomfort in making this choice did not indicate danger is actually quite interesting, because I had spent my life avoiding having to deal with such unpleasant decisions and usually ended up in the soup as a consequence. Here, I was making a decision that was difficult and unpleasant, even including rejecting what the Cs were saying, and their response to that was, "Discomfort is not necessarily danger, and is indicative of growth and learning. So, proceed and celebrate!!" So, perhaps that means I passed the test of trusting my instincts and was learning to 'see the unseen'?

session of 22 June 1996 when the Cs suggested that I should "learn, read, research all you can about unstable gravity waves."

> Notes from correspondence with Jim, March 23, 1996:
>
> ...
>
> Gravitational drive reverses the gravitational wave. Not negative gravity or antigravity.
>
> This reverses gravitational wave.
>
> Gravity has some attributes that we do not fully understand. It is this lack of understanding that we will be studying.

Jim was a funny New Age–type guy who had contacted Ark via email and presented himself as very knowledgeable in esoterica. Ark was intensely interested in such subjects mainly because he had the idea that no area of potential knowledge should be excluded in the search for the answers to the truths of our reality. Jim was a member of Col. Steve Wilson's 'Skywatch' email discussion list. Wilson was retired after forty years in the Air Force and claimed that he was head of Project Pounce for MAJI (MJ-12) that conducted alien disc crash-retrieval operations and had seen subterranean bases in operation. He was also dying of cancer, which was his ostensible reason for attempting to publicize the real nature of the alien infestation of Earth. He apparently died in the latter half of 1997. The organization was taken over by Bill Hamilton of AstroScience Research (astrosciences.info).

Anyway, returning to Jim, it seems he contacted Ark via his web contact form on his website sometime in January of 1996. This means that he became aware of Ark's work via his writings there. Jim's internet handle was "SecElijah". He will be mentioned again a few times in future sessions.

March 29, 1996

Background: I had just asked my husband for a separation.

The important thing for the reader to remember as they go through this recapitulation of events, relations, and my thoughts regarding same, is that there was no Cassiopaea website for me to read, there was no Wave Series for me to read, and there was no real concept of the Matrix, as such, available to me by which I could evaluate my experiences. I was in uncharted territory, slashing through the jungle, and hardly able to fully grasp the nature of the beast, much less articulate it.

If we keep in mind the programs of family, religion, and society, which are more or less the same for everyone with only slight variations, we realize that it is not so easy to go against the programs of 'give the benefit of the doubt', 'turn the other cheek', 'forgive and forget', 'kiss and make-up', 'make it nice', 'if you can't say something nice, don't say anything at all', and so forth. We are taught by our culture, via various psychological theories, to 'compromise and work it out', or to deal with our own issues so that what other people do won't have any power over us. We are taught to heal our wounded inner child, or blame everything on our parents. We can learn to reframe our experiences and achieve rapport with anyone in three days of neuro-linguistic programming, or, as a last resort, we can solve the problem with a little Prozac or something similar.

The fact is that, even though the Cs were telling me about these theological dynamics, that didn't necessarily mean that I was buying it. Just because the Cs said it, didn't mean I believed it. And that still applies. Sure, there are many things the Cs have said that we have experimented with – 'try before you buy' – and have observed results that indicate that they are presenting a view of our reality that is objectively testable. There are many other things that we have researched based on the clues the Cs have given us and have discovered again and again, "Damned if they aren't right!" And very often, these have been things about which we were most skeptical.

Even though I was being given a higher-density view of human relations and dynamics as the medium through which higher-density forces engage and do battle – the Matrix Control System – I was still in it, and still controlled by it to a great extent. In this sense, the Cs were very wise in not telling me anything directly as to what I ought or ought not to do in terms of my choices and actions. They were, indeed, giving me a new perspective about higher-density affairs, giving clues about our own level of reality so that I could research these matters and determine the interaction between the two, but if they had just told me the answers or told me what to do, they would have violated my 'free will learning directive'. That is to say, it seems that all of existence is for the purpose of gaining knowledge.

The point is that if we are here in this reality to learn, it doesn't do us any good for somebody else to do our homework for us. We can't learn to ride a bicycle by watching somebody else do it, or by reading a book about it. Indeed, we will have clues, and some idea of what we ought to do, but we cannot master it unless we get up and try it. And very often, we may think it looks easier than it is, and we discover on our first try that falling down and scraping our knees is what teaches us how not to fall down.

So it was that, in the places where discussions of the matters of the theological reality were taking place as recorded in the transcripts, that didn't mean that I was ready to get on the bicycle just yet. Even if Sue or Pat or any other given person was identified as being an agent or in a close relation with purported STS forces, didn't mean I was going to jump up in their faces and shout, "Lizzie lover!" or "Gray hugger!" and ditch them as a friend or associate.

However, after the "kiss", I woke up.

My perceptions had certainly changed, but I was not really able to say how or why. All kinds of thoughts and realizations about reality were shaping themselves in my mind, but as usual, I was keeping it to myself to observe and ponder it before I attempted to explain it to anyone. The first concrete manifestation of this awakening was right after we returned from the conference and I drove to the high school to pick up my daughter as I did every day. I was sitting there in the parking lot watching all the kids pouring out of the different doors of the building onto the school yard. There were kids who were racing to their cars or to their buses, and there were many others who were milling about, congregating in their little groups and cliques. I couldn't hear anything anyone was saying since I was observing from a distance, but I could most definitely see certain dynamics – something like a pecking order – playing out before my eyes.

Each group consisted of about seven or eight people – maybe as many as ten. In each group there was a dominant person who was the focal point of the gathering. Watching the eye contact, the touching, and the fawning behavior of the 'low man' in the group was a fascinating study. And as I watched, I noticed something else: the dominant person actually seemed to swell and grow, while the submissive persons gathered around him literally seemed to shrink. Of course, this was a trick of posture and the way they were all holding their bodies, but it was definitely clear that there was a form of feeding taking place. And when the submissive persons ran out of 'juice', they were dismissed to the outer fringes of the circle and a new submissive moved in to take their place. The eye contact and touching went through the same series of gestures, and the dominant person stood taller and taller, and his or her eyes opened wider and glowed brighter, while the submissives were diminished one by one, shoulders slumped, and they often crept away.

I found myself actually holding my breath as I watched this amazing display. Of course I thought of Jane Goodall and her years of observation of chimpanzees, and I knew I wasn't thinking anything terribly original here. The big difference was that I was seeing it not just in terms of psychological dynamics, but an actual energy transfer – the theological reality. It was this theological reality that had suddenly been opened to my perception as though I had withdrawn into space and was viewing it from a distance.

All around us in the natural world there are wonders and horrors. On almost every corner of the planet, from the highest mountains to the lowest valleys, from the hottest to the coldest climates, above the oceans and within them, there are populations of interdependent plants and animals. Most of the time this term interdependence really means that they 'eat' one another.

I thought about the garden behind my house. There are birds and lizards, insects and plants of all sorts. The lizards eat many insects and they are, in turn, eaten by the birds or the cat, who also eats the birds if she gets a chance. There are roses – beautiful but deadly – which grow in soil composed partly of plant detritus – dead plant matter – converted by earthworms into usable nutrients. There are also grubs and mole crickets that seem to do nothing but destroy what I work so hard to produce and maintain. In the evenings, the bats and mosquitoes both come out in force, the former preying on the latter (thankfully), and the night blooming jasmine opens to feed a particular species of night moth that delights in its nectar.

There is spring, when I spend eight hours a day getting the garden in shape; there is summer, when I relax and watch my efforts grow and blossom; there is fall, when I pull up the dead annuals and prune the overgrowth; and there is winter, when everything rests and builds strength to burst forth the following spring, to initiate a new cycle; cycles within cycles; birth, growth, maturity, reproduction, decline and death; to everything there is a season.

Now, imagine that you are observing the Earth with a high-powered telescope from a point out in space. This telescope gives you detailed close-ups of any point on the planet, but you cannot hear anything. You can only see. Forget everything you think you know about the principles of biological life or psychology. Forget that you think you know anything about what living things are or how they are supposed to behave. Now, what do you see?

The first thing you notice is that the surface of the planet is teeming with activity. This includes areas under the soil and deep within the ocean. The activity on the surface of the planet consists of an immense number of different shapes and sizes of living things going about in circles *eating each other*.

Further, you notice that there is a whole class of these living things that are, essentially, immobile; incapable of escaping being eaten. In fact, they don't seem to object being eaten at all. Maybe if they could run away, they would, but they can't, so it may only seem that they don't object. But, the fact of the matter is that these immobile beings (call them plants) use this fact of being eaten to their advantage. By being eaten, they are often able to propagate themselves in far distant places that they would otherwise be unable to populate on their own.

However, all the other living things clearly resent being eaten. They very often make strenuous efforts to not be eaten.

I began to see a certain pattern emerging: the variations of biological systems have to do with whether or not, under specific and ever-changing conditions, one variety of creatures can survive the competition in the terrifying planetary game of life and death. It was clear that danger is omnipresent and only the most vigorous and adaptable survive.

I also saw that there was a sort of balance. Many of the creatures that are most often considered prey are equipped with elaborate sensing organs that help them to stay out of harm's way. Many of the creatures that are the predators have horrifyingly efficient organs of destruction such as teeth and claws. If predators became too numerous, they quickly devoured all but the cleverest of prey, and then turned on each other. In this way, both populations were culled. What I also was seeing was that populations that existed in herds, where there was sharing and protection of weaker members by stronger ones, had a far better chance of survival in the presence of voracious predation.

I realized with absolute horror that this was exactly the case with human beings, though it occurred at a different level: humans were an interface between the strictly material and ethereal realms, and it was through them that the energies of prey and predator manifested at the theological level. From the strictly human perspective, such a realization was monstrous. The psychological and spiritual environment in which we live is the infrastructure of the theological reality which is accurately represented in the wild world in which animals live out similar dramas. 'As above, so below', the ancient teachings have repeated for millennia, and I realized that this was part of what they intended to convey. When they tell us that the Great Secret can be learned from Nature, they weren't kidding!

On the one hand, I was seeing a terrible vista that shattered my illusions of 'God in his heaven, and all is right with the world'. On the other hand, I could see that it wasn't just mindless cruelty; that it was purposeful activity from another level of being.

As simple as this insight may seem to the reader, having access to all of the other information that has become available about these matters over the past few years, it was a stunning revelation to me.

I then began to think about Sue and the 'vital information' that could be conveyed to me. The first thing I realized was that human beings at a certain point in their development reach a crossroad where they can choose which dynamic they will develop in spiritual terms: predator or prey, and it had nothing to do with material considerations. In fact, I wasn't even sure if it was a choice and not just simply the inherent nature of an individual.

I could see that Sue was, indeed, as the Cs had described her: a simple, giving soul. But in her dynamic interaction with her mother she was literally acting out the role of prey to her mother's role of predator. As her mother grew older and less able to hunt on her own, she manipulated Sue to engage in interactions whereby she became a sort of lure to induce other prey into her mother's range of operation so that the feeding could continue. In a sense, it was very much like a weakened member of a herd that keeps wandering away into the realm of the predator, and when others would go after her to save her, they become prey as well; they leave the protection of the herd, or the network. In this sense, some individuals become a sort of predator by proxy – a lure to destruction, a decoy. On the other hand, I wasn't too sure if that was exactly accurate either. Perhaps there were predators who stalked their prey in long, slow, silent exercises in patience and concealment?

I could instantly see that nearly all of humanity was in a terrible predicament by being unaware of this infrastructure of theological prey and predation. In the animal kingdom, who was who and what was what in terms of predators and prey was pretty easy to see because they look different and their behaviors are out in plain view. But in the human dynamic, it is masked from us. And it seemed to be masked for a reason: the masking is utilized to separate the herd, to divide and conquer.

Of course, that such a condition could be possible seemed to have no explanation in positivist terms until I thought about the culling factor, and the idea that spiritual vigor might be the objective. Using the animal kingdom as a template, it seemed obvious that those creatures that most correctly assessed and responded to their environment had the best chance of survival and reproduction. Those members of herds that remained in the symbiotic networked environment had strength and safety and numbers on their side. Those that strayed from the herd, those that exposed themselves to danger, were eaten. It was that simple.

It was at this moment that I saw myself as a cog in a vast global mechanism – a feeding machine – and I was nothing more than food. It literally made me sick to see it. What was more, I needed to understand where all this energy was really going. Who was getting it? Who was at the top of the food chain?

A day or so later, my husband came in and initiated another of the endless series of diatribes he habitually generated, which always started with him picking at one of the children. I would defend the child, trying to reasonably explain to him that each of them was different, that they had a right to their own opinions, likes and dislikes, and that they were not little clones of him who existed just to reflect what he believed, or to do what he wanted. The other children would join in and try to support my reasonable remarks with examples of their own. They all loved their father and all of us knew that he had a 'problem' because of his religious fundamentalism. He was bigoted and judgmental, harsh and even cruel in his judgments, and if the children did not immediately agree with him, they became outcast also, damned and doomed to perdition unless they quickly changed their ways and views – to his ways and views, of course.

As usually happened, the discussion ended up with him becoming more and more antagonistic and harsh and saying many mean things to all of us, couched in Christian theology that was for our own good, of course. As the dynamic progressed, and I tried harder and harder to soothe and make nice, trying to mediate and sustain his parental authority, even though I knew he was completely wrong, and protect the children from this psychological destruction, I saw with horror that what was really happening was that he was feeding on all of us.

I instantly stopped trying to reason with him at all, told him that he was entitled to his beliefs, and I was entitled to mine, the children were entitled to theirs, and I wasn't going to discuss it at all with him anymore. He left in a huff with some parting shots directed at all of us that I can't even remember.

The children were upset, I was upset, and I sat there pondering what I had just seen. As I did, one of my daughters came in to hug me and tell me that she was sorry that I had to go through such things over and over again. Then she said something that nearly knocked me over: "I don't know how you have lived with it for so long; he's just not like us. He's like a cat in a house full of dogs."

Out of the mouths of babes.

Actually, he was like a cat in an aviary of birds, but she made her point. He wasn't 'like us'. At that moment, I realized that I had to do something. The Universe had been giving me clues for years, and I had been ignoring them, stubbornly clinging to my self-sacrificing, make-everything-nice, shove-it-under-the-rug, let's-work-it-out view of things. I had read all the pop-psychology books; I had tried all the guaranteed methods of self-help, taking the brunt of the burden of making things work on myself; I had expended untold amounts of energy in trying to compromise, to work it out, to support and sustain this man and to simultaneously protect the children and myself from his clear predation. I had done all of this for years in the firm belief that all could be made right, all could be healed, all could be worked out with sufficient devotion and giving.

But now, suddenly, I was seeing it all in a completely different way. He was a predator, and we were prey. We, the children and myself, were his sources of energy. Where his energy was being drained to, I didn't know, but I had a pretty good idea.

What is important for the reader to understand is that I didn't blame him for being 'bad' or for being 'wrong', or for anything at all like that. I simply realized that he was not like us in terms of the theological reality, and therefore, something had to be done. It was one thing for me to be aware and willing to sacrifice myself to this energy-feeding dynamic. It was something else altogether for me to pass it to my children by example and to oblige them to live in it. A mother's primary role is as advocate and protectress of her children. And in this case, I saw that the one my children needed to be protected from was their own father.

The toughest part is the fact that I also knew that I had to do something for my husband as well. Cats that feed on pigeons have as much right to be and exist as the pigeons do. They are not bad because they are cats and because they eat pigeons if given the chance. What was even more difficult was the knowledge that even if I explained to him what I was perceiving, he wouldn't get it; he wouldn't believe it; he wouldn't agree. He would insist to his dying day that his mode of being – his 'catness' – was right.

In the end, I knew that I had to bear the burden of doing what was right for him – strange as it may seem – because he was neither able nor willing to see it or understand it. I remember thinking that the only way I was going to be able to get through it was to take all the blame, to completely release him from any responsibility, because, on the many occasions I tried to get him to be responsible for anything he said or did that hurt me or the children, it was a dead end.

For example: if he was being a steamroller toward the children, I would spend hours explaining child psychology to him, and how damaging it was to a child to not be accepted and allowed to have their own likes and dislikes – that telling them things like "that's stupid" or "you'll go to hell for that" and so on was abuse. I tried to engage him in a cooperative work with raising the children. He would seem to listen and I would think I was getting somewhere, and then a glassy look would come into his eyes and he would say, "Well, if nothing I do is right, I'll just not do anything. You raise the kids and I'll stay out of it."

Then, I would try to explain the importance of both parents being involved and united for the sake of the children and the glassy look would come and he would twist that around and tell me that since he wasn't wanted, his way wasn't accepted, he wasn't respected ... well, to heck with all of us. And that was not what I was saying! I was saying that, as parents, we had to put many of our own things aside for the sake of the children.

He simply could not think beyond himself.

So, when the time came, and it came within a day or so, I knew this and I knew that no amount of explaining would be effective in any terms other than just repeating, "I made a mistake when I married you and now I am correcting it," and words to that effect. That put all the blame on me. My objective was not to put him down, to lay blame, to do anything but get myself and the children out of this situation.

And the war began in earnest. He was fighting to retain his position, to reclaim his feeding territory. And I was equally determined that he was not going to feed on any of us any longer.

When he said, "I knew you would do this. All women are alike. Blah blah," I just agreed, even though I knew that his view was completely twisted. It was not necessary for me to be "right" because I knew that when I was right, it didn't matter because he was going to see it the way he saw it anyway.

I just kept remembering a funny thing that I had read about how to get proper service from a store clerk who keeps trying to sell you something you don't want: just keep repeating what you do want, and when they say, "What about this over here?!" say, "No, I don't want that. I want this."

So, I knew what I wanted to accomplish, I knew I would be subjected to a 'sales talk' of some kind, and I knew that I had to keep repeating over and over again what I wanted and insist that the focus stay there. Whenever he tried to engage me in a discussion, I said, "That's fine. I know you see it that way, but I don't and this is what I want." Over and over.

When he started listing all the things that he had done, I just agreed that he had done them and that it was good that he did, but it didn't change the fact that I had made a mistake, and it needed to be corrected and I was going to do it.

Then came the name-calling and accusations ... and I agreed with everything. "Yes, you are right. I lied to you. I never loved you, blah blah." I just agreed that everything he said was right, but it didn't change the fact that I was going to do what I was going to do and that was that.

In his initial declaration of territorial rights, he made it clear that he wasn't giving an inch. If I didn't want to be around him, if I had decided that it was over, then I was the one who was going to have to leave. If I didn't want to sleep with him, I would have to sleep somewhere else because he wasn't giving up his right to sleep in the master bedroom.

I didn't argue with him. I moved into the baby's bedroom and slept with her. After a day or two of this, of sleeping somewhere other than on the special orthopedic mattress that had been bought after my accident, the children told their father that he was being very selfish to make Mom sleep on a bed that hurt her. Of course, he wanted to appear to be the injured party, so he immediately moved into the playroom and slept on the sofa in there, giving me the bedroom back.

After failing to change my mind with argument, insult and manipulations of the overt kind, he went into the pity-trip mode. He claimed that he had nowhere to go, that he would have to build a camper on his truck and live in the woods somewhere. He then asked for several days to make his preparations.

I just wanted him out of the house. I was hanging on to my resolve by a thread, and I knew I couldn't take much more of the pity-me trip, because that had always been my weak point. I knew that, for the sake of the children, I had to win this battle. I had already spent too many years teaching my children by example how to be prey and now I needed to teach them by example how not to be prey.

It was at this point that something completely bizarre happened. I went to the kitchen to get a drink of water in the middle of the night and had to pass by the door to the playroom. As I did, I heard him talking in there. I wondered who in the world was he was talking to. In the low, ambient light of the house, I could see that he was stretched out on the sofa, alone and apparently asleep. But he was talking. I stood there very quietly and listened. He seemed to be having a long conversation with someone in a dream and I could only hear his end of it. The thing that was so amazing was that in all the years of our marriage, he had never once talked in his sleep. Not once. And now he was saying things like, "Yes, I know I failed in the mission, but I won't fail again." "Please don't punish me! I won't fail again!" There was a long series of 'yes' responses as though he were receiving instructions, and the subservient nature of his end of the dialogue gave me the absolute willies. An air of evil emanated from the room and I understood that the subject of discussion was me. Somehow, he had been assigned to do something in regard to me, and the present situation was unacceptable to the overseer of this 'mission' he kept mentioning.

If my resolve had been growing weak, it was increased a hundredfold by this little encounter. I made up my mind that I had to get him out of the house. His physical proximity was dangerous. He was slowly but surely wearing me down, he was playing on the emotions of the children, and the situation had to end now.

I talked to my friend Sandra about it. She was a supervisor of the Child Support Enforcement Unit of the State Department of Health and Rehabilitative Services. She told me that I needed to apply for assistance and make it clear to him that he had to be out of the house or he would be subject to legal sanctions. I was already receiving a supplemental check from Social Security because I was unable to work due to my health problems, so this seemed the logical thing to do until the insurance case related to the accident was settled. I reasoned that, since our house was paid for, the children and I would be able to survive – though just barely – until he could get himself settled and the court could set a reasonable amount for him to pay as support for the children.

So, that's what I did. I made it a legal matter, and because Sandra was behind me and he knew that he couldn't play any games with the state legal system with Sandra watching, he packed up his things and moved back to his parents' house.

It was at this point that something akin to physical withdrawal began to manifest. Sandra explained to me that I had to keep repeating over and over in my mind why I was doing what I was doing. She told me to make a list of all the times when we had gone through the feeding episodes, and how when I had reached the end of my rope and declared that I couldn't take it anymore, we had gone through the same deal and all the promises that were made and not kept.

I realized that I had to just keep hitting myself over the head to stay awake.

Then there came the fear of not being loved, of being judged a 'bad girl' or a 'bad wife and mother'. This was the program that had kept me in the situation for so many years. It had been inculcated into me (and millions of other women) as a little girl. It is the chief program of women in general: to cover the bad things up, to shove them all under the rug, to make things nice – to be a 'good girl' by being a doormat.

I had to keep reminding myself that I was Bluebeard's wife. And Bluebeard had a secret room in the castle with the bodies of all his other wives – symbols of the fact that he was a predator, feeding on our energy because he had none of his own. And he had none of his own because he was inured in the Matrix, a source of energy in the food-chain pyramid of the theological reality of higher-level dark forces that feed on humanity. We can feel sorry for such people, as they may only become Bluebeard because of damage to them as infants or children. But they cannot be fixed, and their damage spreads like an infection to everyone with whom they are in contact.

What was ultimately important to me was the fact that I knew I had to become what I wanted for my daughters. Children do what they see, not what we tell them. And the greatest gift we can give anyone is to become what we would have others be: free.

March 29, 1996

Participants: 'Frank', Laura

1 **Q:** *(L)* Hello.

2 **A:** Hello.

3 **Q:** *(L)* Who do we have with us this evening?

4 **A:** Womol.

5 **Q:** *(L)* And where are you from?

6 **A:** Cassiopaea.

7 **Q:** *(L)* In the past week I have been going through some fairly severe trauma because of certain ideas and realizations I have been forced to face ...[1]

8 **A:** Stress, yes, trauma, no.

9 **Q:** *(L)* Well, it has felt traumatic to me. The first question I would like to ask is: in reading and analyzing the Bluebeard fairytale as a map of consciousness, am I correct in my understanding, that I am basically living the life of Bluebeard's wife?

10 **A:** Close enough for now.

11 **Q:** *(L)* My application of this map of consciousness, so to speak, is not only in the area of my marriage, but also a number of other interactions. Is this correct as I understand it?

12 **A:** Maybe.

13 **Q:** *(L)* What part is the maybe?

14 **A:** Learning is a complex process, answers follow study.

15 **Q:** *(L)* I studied the situation at length. One of the first things I determined was that my assessment on ...

16 **A:** Interference from blossomer nearby.

17 **Q:** *(L)* Do you mean right now?

18 **A:** Yes.

---
[1] *The Wave* 46
[2] *The Wave* 46

19 **Q:** *(L)* [Child was discovered nearby, sent to bed.] What kind of interference do you get from a 'blossomer', as you call them?

20 **A:** Soul discharges caused by efforts made by influences attracted by channel attempting to take over body of child in order to experience sensation of total euphoria!!

21 **Q:** *(L)* So, as a general rule, is this euphoria produced by watching television?

22 **A:** Can be enhanced. Warning!! Littlest one is most susceptible to total possession by extremely STS-oriented forces during sessions, and must be kept away at all costs!!!! There have been instances where perceived health disturbances by this one and others have been, in reality, up to 30 percent possession! Lungs are the "weak link," and it is your psychic abilities that have caused the troubles in the past.

23 **Q:** *(L)* You mean that what I am doing is causing problems for my children?

24 **A:** No.

25 **Q:** *(L)* Then why have my psychic abilities caused health troubles in the past?

26 **A:** Because you were less aware at that point, and your abilities went into a surge.

27 **Q:** *(L)* Well, it seems to me that I have a strong tendency to manifest my psychic and emotional state physically; not only in my own body, but also in manifestations and events around me.[2]

28 **A:** Yes.

29 **Q:** *(L)* Back when we first moved into this house, we had a burglar break in

during the night. I have always been troubled by the fact that a strange man broke into my house, the symbology of it. The other night, I was reading about dreams of people breaking into one's house being a warning that there is extreme danger from the deep subconscious. These dreams always have a strong physiological manifestation. Well, I had an 'intruder dream', and it *was* like this. But then, I thought about the actual intruder being a psychically manifested warning in the flesh.

A: Yes.

Q: *(L)* Was the fact that it could manifest in a physical way any kind of indication of the seriousness of the threat?

A: Yes.

Q: *(L)* Is there any particular thing that I ought or could do to further protect the children?

A: Open, but suggestion would be to organize more.

Q: *(L)* In what sense?

A: The children.

Q: *(L)* I don't understand. Do you mean being more strict in terms of regimen?

A: Close.

Q: *(L)* In the sense of bedtime rituals or something? Prayers?

A: Maybe, but also other.

Q: *(L)* Limiting watching television?

A: We have told you some things ...

Q: *(L)* Okay ...

A: Imagine an interruption that leads to problems.

Q: *(L)* Are you saying that 'idle hands are the Devil's tools'?

A: No, because free will is paramount.

Q: *(L)* Just give me more of a hint.

A: Organize.

Q: *(L)* Send them to bed before we channel?

A: Up to you.

Q: *(L)* Is A___ also susceptible?

A: Not blossoming.

Q: *(L)* Are they alright in their bedrooms?

A: Yes.

Q: *(L)* Does it have something to do with physical distance?

A: Awareness.

Q: *(L)* Are you saying that their awareness of what we are doing establishes the connection?

A: Close.

Q: *(L)* And I should organize them more. So, I should have them ready and in bed before we work.

A: Yes.

Q: *(L)* Back to my question: the intruder dream the other night was *very* disturbing. In the dream, I tried to wake my husband to tell him that someone or some thing was in our house. I discovered that he was paralyzed. He was like my friend Keith ... can you help me with this image?[3]

A: Learning is fun!

Q: *(L)* Well, it was not fun! My heart was about to pound out of my chest, and I ended up sitting in a chair half

---
[3] *The Wave* 46

the night. There was a realization that I have been being drained by a lot of people for a long time ...

64 **A**: Yours to look and discover. Not ours to help you "cheat!"

65 **Q**: *(L)* No cheating, huh. I can't look at the answers in the back of the book. Okay, let me ask you this: is there any significance to the fact that L___'s mother's maiden name was Rheindress?

66 **A**: Open.

67 **Q**: *(L)* Well, you are not helping! I have been seeing things so completely differently lately. I even see that you have given all sorts of clues about this that just went over my head ...

68 **A**: Laura, please learn just to trust your expanding insights. They will bring you to ever-increasing knowledge and ability. But, you want us to lead you by the hand. All this can do is ultimately lead this channel and conduit into an STS vehicle!

69 **Q**: *(L)* That is not what I am trying to do here! I am trying to expand on a learning experience to help other people.

70 **A**: You have the ability to do that all on your own!! Cannot you see this yet?[4]

71 **Q**: *(L)* I am still in the process of making major changes in my life based on such insights ...

72 **A**: And, how do you feel when you make a decision to make one of these changes?

73 **Q**: *(L)* It hurts to make some decisions, even if I feel that it is the right thing to do. It can be painful and scary.

74 **A**: Relief?

75 **Q**: *(L)* Definitely relief!

76 **A**: And ...

77 **Q**: *(L)* I have some little hope that maybe something else will happen to help with the work if I make sure that my own life is clean. I am cutting off my financial support, and that is frightening. But, right now, I had another thought ... I recently received some information about the Denver Airport. It seems that there is confirmation that this airport does have some connection to something very mysterious. And, you brought this up in the very first contact. Is there something more on this?

78 **A**: Wait and see.

79 **Q**: *(L)* I also learned that the sighting of flying boomerangs over in England, quite some years back, was also accompanied by messages that came through a board to some kids in a town some distance away, and that those messages were very similar to some of what we have received. In fact, the opening messages were warnings about alien bases! I am very curious about that. There were so many things about that particular case that are so similar in dynamics ... When something very negative happens in the Earth, does it necessarily make an opening for a balancing of positive energy?

---

[4]Here, again, the Cs are pointing me in the direction of realizing that the entire purpose of the communication was to prepare me for the task of utilizing what I was learning through this personal initiation process so that it would be of benefit to others. Of course, at this particular moment in time, I was not feeling terribly confident about anything. I was having trouble with my eyes – an inflammation had taken hold and I had to keep medication in them that made it difficult to see.

80 **A**: Maybe.

81 **Q**: *(L)* Can you tell me anything else about it? The Clapham Wood incident back in the 70s?

82 **A**: No.

83 **Q**: *(L)* Well, that is not helping me.

84 **A**: It is, but not as you think. Stonehenge power. Vortex. Magnetic principles understood by you when you occupied other bodies, ask Hilliard, ole boy.

85 **Q**: *(L)* There have been a number of hints that Hilliard has some knowledge that he may be withholding. Does he have knowledge that is important, and how can I persuade him to tell me?

86 **A**: Massive, and probe directly after promising absolute confidence ... and don't break it!!!

87 **Q**: *(L)* Okay, I will. Well, back to the situation. I am between a rock and a hard place.

88 **A**: Not really.

89 **Q**: *(L)* Easy for you to say.

90 **A**: Wait and see.

91 **Q**: *(L)* Well, rereading back over the transcripts, there seems to be some very interesting stuff about the Thule Society and some things about a Nordic Covenant, and this seems to be very mysterious and connected with activities going on in Antarctica. Well, I read the place where it was said that the Lizard beings were slaves and pets of the Orions. That seems to be extremely significant.

92 **A**: When you get money, pay someone to transcribe.

93 **Q**: *(L)* I will do it myself as quickly as possible ... Sue was supposed to help me with this, but obviously she is fading from the picture here ...

94 **A**: Maybe, maybe not, you are not completely in control of all possible factors.

95 **Q**: *(L)* Well, however things work, I don't really care right now. As soon as I can see again, I will get back to transcribing. I have sent some samples out to a couple of places. I have had some *very* positive responses ...

96 **A**: Have fun!

97 **Q**: *(L)* What is that supposed to mean? I don't like the sound of that! The other day when you said 'celebrate!' all I did was suffer!

98 **A**: Stop suffering!

99 **Q**: *(L)* I can't help it! I feel so sorry for L___! He is a master at being a victim! It tears me apart! Back to my questions. Is the Nordic Covenant what has charge of this genetic project to prepare a 'breeding ground' for the Nephilim?

100 **A**: No.

101 **Q**: *(L)* What does the Nordic Covenant do?

102 **A**: Discover.

103 **Q**: *(L)* How am I supposed to do that? I can see myself going up to somebody: "Hi! Are you a member of the Nordic Covenant? I'd like to know what is going on in your head?! What do you think about?" Right! Well, I am tired. Anything else for the protection of the children?

104 **A**: We have told you.

105 **Q**: *(L)* Anything I need to know about my situation? I feel pretty desperate.

106 **A**: Has it been "desperate" before?

107 **Q**: *(L)* Yes.

108 **A**: Did you turn into dust?

109 **Q**: *(L)* No, but I thought I would!

110 **A**: What about your settlement?

111 **Q**: *(L)* God knows when that will happen! You won't tell me!

112 **A**: If we did, you'd become a "softie."

113 **Q**: *(L)* It seems that over the course of time, you have turned us more and more in the direction of learning on our own. Does this mean that it is winding down to come to a halt?

114 **A**: No.

115 **Q**: *(L)* Can you tell me what this means?

116 **A**: You needed more assistance earlier.

117 **Q**: *(L)* Well, am I correct in the MPD idea regarding Sue?

118 **A**: Pursue with an open mind and cross check all analyses.

119 **Q**: *(L)* Okay. I am concerned about the baby. Should I do a spirit release for her?

120 **A**: Why?

121 **Q**: *(L)* Well, her lungs seem to be pretty reactive right now. She is having a rough time right now.

122 **A**: Regulate diet, it is abysmal!!

123 **Q**: *(L)* What about her diet?

124 **A**: Sugar, out!!! Fats reduced, leafy vegetables increased, sleep coordinated.[5]

125 **Q**: *(L)* Okay, speaking of diet ... the Atkins diet seems to be logical ... but it increases fats and proteins.

126 **A**: Waistline okay, heart smart?! Naah![6]

127 **Q**: *(L)* You talked once about passing a test, that I was being tested in some way ... that this had something to do with Sue ... I would like to know if this was the test?

128 **A**: Open.

129 **Q**: *(L)* Well, I have to get up early, and my mind is drifting, so I will say goodnight.

130 **A**: Goodnight.

End of Session

---

[5]Except for the sugar part, this was not very good advice.
[6]Again, not very good diet advice, in my opinion.

April 24, 1996

The reader will notice that it is almost an entire month between this session and the previous one. As I wrote in the comments to that previous session, what I was going through was a kind of 'withdrawal'. And it definitely manifested with as much discomfort as the worst drug withdrawal I have ever read about. In addition to the psychological and emotional pain, I was having trouble with my eyes – an inflammation had taken hold and I had to keep medication in them that made it difficult to see. The infections became so severe that I was bedridden for almost a month. My ears, eyes, and lungs were infected and I had been ordered by the doctor to not read or look at a computer screen for a month. I had to spend several periods a day with hot compresses on my eyes. In a funny sort of way it represented my human reaction to what I was literally seeing, hearing, and experiencing. I was also depressed almost beyond endurance. During that period from the dream of the Kiss in March, to the moment when I realized that everything I had ever believed in was a lie, and I was being asked by the universe if I was willing to pay everything. And pay I did; in advance. During the period following my separation, as my energy was no longer being drained daily, the manifestation in the body was the evidence of the price I was paying. Everything in my physical system cried out against this view of the world of human affairs, the view of predators and prey, and I wept tears of blood and pus from my eyes to the point that I nearly lost my sight altogether.

During the same period, one of my elder daughters was also so depressed that she could barely get out of the bed. Even though I was struggling with my own health issues, I was more concerned about her than anything and I took her to the doctor several times to have her checked for any kind of physical illness. Our family doctor had been part of our lives for about seven years at this point, and he was intimately familiar with all of the ups and downs of our situation, and he was concerned as well. He ran every test known to medical science and finally just said that if I was patient and supportive with this most sensitive of children, that she would pull through it. Being of the 'old school', he didn't think that medication was the right option. He knew my daughter too well.

The next disaster was that my next-to-youngest daughter broke her ankle on the trampoline in the back yard. I had been gone from the house only long enough to pick up the eldest from school, and when we returned, there was another crisis to deal with.

I was on the phone with my friend Sandra almost every day and she kept me going through this terrible time. In view of my closeness to Sandra, take notice the comment added to this session regarding 'thrombosis'. That will become very important.

Participants: 'Frank', Laura

1 **Q**: *(L)* Hello. Is it okay to work in this room since [my daughter] has taken our work room tonight?

2 **A**: Necessities produce changes.

3 **Q**: *(L)* And who do we have with us tonight?

4 **A**: Siril.

5 **Q**: *(L)* And where are you transmitting from?

6 **A**: Cassiopaea.

7 **Q**: *(L)* I would like to deal with certain issues relating to the progress of this 'mission' or 'project' as you have described it. As you know, we have experienced serious disruptions and 'attack' in recent months. I came to a conclusion that my husband is a robot person. But, I am not going to ask you to confirm or deny that. I came to that idea through information in the transcripts. What I do want to know is: is it likely now that much of the attack will cease since that energy has been removed from my environment?[1]

8 **A**: Maybe, but not necessarily in the ways you think![2]

9 **Q**: *(L)* Well, since I have been through such a terrible ordeal in the past year, what is there to encourage me?

10 **A**: Vague.

11 **Q**: *(L)* Okay, is my husband a robot person?

12 **A**: Listen. Open.

13 **Q**: *(L)* What do I need to listen to?

14 **A**: See.

15 **Q**: *(L)* Am I going to see something?

16 **A**: Robot or not, all are programmed.

17 **Q**: *(L)* All are programmed including myself and Frank?

18 **A**: Yes.

19 **Q**: *(L)* Well, considering a lot of my internal experiences, I had already come

---

[1] *The Wave* 46

[2] That was certainly to prove to be true! The Universe is about balance and there will be ups and downs no matter what you do. Gurdjieff suggests that you can choose your suffering, and this proved to be true.

to this conclusion. What is the objective of this programming?

A: It is too complex to explain yet.

Q: *(L)* What was the source or cause of the complete loss of my voice for several weeks?[3]

A: Q plasma bacterial infection. Ask Wu.

Q: *(L)* You mean Dr. Vu?

A: Yes. Pronounced Wu in southern oriental inflective tone.[4]

Q: *(L)* I was analyzing some of the material regarding the recent episode with Sue and her mother. To this point, she still has done none of the things that you advised her to do in response to her requests for advice. I told her that I was very angry that she took so much of my time and energy and still did none of the things advised, resulting in *everyone* being upset. Now, I had someone call me and tell me that Sue was involved in some sort of coven or very dark organization. I just have a very difficult time believing this. How can she speak so disparagingly of such things and then be a part of such? Yet, the source of the information knew things that 'clicked' and could not possibly have been said unless this was true. Is it possible that Sue could have multiple personalities and one of her other 'selves' is doing this? As in Greenbaum?[5]

A: Sure!

Q: *(L)* Is it possible for either Frank or I to be involved in such and not be aware of it?

A: Yes, but it is not that.

Q: *(L)* Does that mean that there *is* some other thing that we are involved in, in some other aspects of our selves, that we are not aware of?

A: Close.

Q: *(L)* Is this something that happens in altered states or in sleep states?

A: Not happens, happened.

Q: *(L)* Something that happened in the past?

A: Laura, you need to consult a powerful, practiced, effective hypnotherapist to unlock these questions for you.

Q: *(L)* Is this something I could do for Frank in the meantime? Obviously Frank could have a big piece of the puzzle locked up in there ...

A: Both of you and others. The locks have been installed in such a way that it is literally impossible for you to unlock them, as they were installed with full knowledge of present circumstances.

Q: *(L)* Who installed these locks?

A: Supremely powerful STS consortium!!

---

[3] *The Wave* "Appendix C"

[4] Yes, it *is* Wu, and I *did* ask. This is a definition of an 'unknown' or 'unidentifiable' bacteria which the medical profession labels 'quelle' to indicate its unknown origin.

[5] This concerns my growing awareness of the Matrix that conceals the theological reality and how difficult it is to break free of the illusion that our reality is as it presents itself to be. Though I didn't realize it as I went through it, all of the events of this period were simply the results of forces that activate to terrify the awakening individual, to convince them to go back to sleep, or if that is not possible, to wear them out, destroy their health, or otherwise make it impossible to awaken.

39 **Q:** *(L)* And what circumstances were they aware of, as you have mentioned, when they installed these locks?

40 **A:** All.

41 **Q:** *(L)* You are the Cassiopaeans, correct?

42 **A:** Yes.

43 **Q:** *(L)* And you are STO?

44 **A:** Yes.

45 **Q:** *(L)* And you are telling us that we have locks on knowledge installed in us, installed by supremely powerful STS consortium. Can we not, in our conscious state, reject this programming, and ask you to inform us of this information?

46 **A:** Not possible!

47 **Q:** *(L)* What is not possible?

48 **A:** What you just asked.

49 **Q:** *(L)* You mean we can't change our minds, or you can't inform us?

50 **A:** Incorrect analysis.

51 **Q:** *(L)* Give me the correct analysis.

52 **A:** You cannot unlock, and we cannot tell you details of what, or why.

53 **Q:** *(L)* Why can you not tell us?

54 **A:** Free will violation, and endangerment of you if done thusly.[6]

55 **Q:** *(L)* Is there some way to do it that does not endanger us?

56 **A:** We have told you.

57 **Q:** *(L)* Is it a danger to us to *not* unlock these things?

58 **A:** In a sense.

59 **Q:** *(L)* When I was kidnapped at the age of three or four in Jacksonville, how many days was I missing? My mother simply has a blank about it, which amazes her.

60 **A:** 12 days.

61 **Q:** *(L)* Who was it that kidnapped me?

62 **A:** Jan.

63 **Q:** *(L)* Who was Jan?

64 **A:** Corps member.

---

[6] Even though I was being given a higher-density view of human relations and dynamics as the medium through which higher-density forces engage and do battle – the Matrix Control System – I was still in it, and still controlled by it to a great extent. In this sense, the Cs were very wise in not telling me anything directly as to what I ought or ought not to do in terms of my choices and actions. They were, indeed, giving me a new perspective about higher-density affairs, giving clues about our own level of reality so that I could research these matters and determine the interaction between the two, but if they had just told me the answers or told me what to do, they would have violated my 'free will learning directive'. That is to say, it seems that all of existence is for the purpose of gaining knowledge. Hopefully, the reader has read P. D. Ouspensky's *Tertium Organum*, and is familiar with his writings on this subject. The point is that if we are here in this reality to learn, it doesn't do us any good for somebody else to do our homework for us. We can't learn to ride a bicycle by watching somebody else do it, or by reading a book about it. Indeed, we will have clues, and some idea of what we ought to do, but we cannot master it unless we get up and try it. And very often, we may think it looks easier than it is, and we discover on our first try that falling down and scraping our knees is what teaches us how not to fall down.

65 **Q:** *(L)* What corps is this?

66 **A:** Select division of economic legion under control of G5.

67 **Q:** *(L)* Economic legion? What is G5?

68 **A:** Intel.

69 **Q:** *(L)* What was the purpose of this kidnapping?

70 **A:** To install self-destruct programming.[7]

71 **Q:** *(L)* So, this Jan was known to us as 'Cecil Brien'.

72 **A:** Yes.

73 **Q:** *(L)* And he more or less overwhelmed my mother and persuaded her to marry him just to get at me? I find this to be incredible!

74 **A:** It was easy at the time. She was vulnerable.[8]

75 **Q:** *(L)* So, I have a 'self-destruct' program. And Frank has one also?

76 **A:** Similar, but not an exact copy so as to mask.

77 **Q:** *(L)* Was Frank abducted in a similar fashion?

78 **A:** Close, but not exactly.

79 **Q:** *(L)* Was Frank's pneumonia when he was a child, that nearly killed him, part of this self-destruct program?

80 **A:** Yes.

81 **Q:** *(L)* Was Frank's father also programmed?

82 **A:** Semi.

83 **Q:** *(L)* Well. I think we can safely assume that every member of our families has had some sort of program installed, if only to facilitate our programming. This whole situation is beginning to sound inexpressibly grim.

84 **A:** Grim?!? You have lived decades after these episodes! How many brethren? Multiples of millions!

85 **Q:** *(L)* That is why I am saying it is pretty damn grim ...

86 **A:** And it is part of a natural process, do not forget.[9]

87 **Q:** *(L)* Well, we need some help from the good guys. Or, is it that unless we can figure it out we are stuck?

88 **A:** No.

89 **Q:** *(L)* It sounds so dreadful. We need some help here. I am becoming *very* tired.

---

[7] *The Wave* 19

[8] This event is described in detail in *Amazing Grace*, Chapter 1.

[9] If we keep in mind the programs of family, religion, and society, which are more or less the same for everyone with only slight variations, we realize that it is not so easy to go against the programs of 'give the benefit of the doubt', 'turn the other cheek', 'forgive and forget', 'kiss and make-up', 'make it nice', 'if you can't say something nice, don't say anything at all', and so forth. We are taught by our culture, via various psychological theories, to 'compromise and work it out', or to deal with our own issues so that what other people do won't have any power over us. We are taught to heal our wounded inner child, or blame everything on our parents. We can learn to reframe our experiences and achieve rapport with anyone in three days of neuro-linguistic programming, or, as a last resort, we can solve the problem with a little Prozac or something similar.

90 **A:** You only need knowledge.

91 **Q:** *(L)* Have any of my children been programmed?

92 **A:** Open.

93 **Q:** *(L)* My daughter A___ has been going through a terrible time. I have taken her to the doctors several times. Can you tell me what is wrong with her?

94 **A:** Desire for acceptance.

95 **Q:** *(L)* What will help?

96 **A:** Patience. She is headstrong.

97 **Q:** *(L)* You can say *that* again! Recently I talked to a fellow who was telling me about discovering the trainload of Nazi treasures in a cave in the Harz Mountains. He was asking for investors. If I were to get my [insurance] settlement in time, ought I to invest in this?

98 **A:** Does herpetologist study his/her subject by travelling naked into a snake pit?

99 **Q:** *(L)* Okay, that settles that. What about the settlement?

100 **A:** Your settlement is being delayed by those purporting to be on your side.

101 **Q:** *(L)* Is [my ex] going to give me any further problem?

102 **A:** Not if you "cut him loose" completely.

103 **Q:** *(L)* What does that mean?

104 **A:** Give him ultimate freedom.

105 **Q:** *(L)* Well, I want to have a little direction here.[10]

106 **A:** Concentrate on settlement. This can be a problem solver if handled wisely, a curse if not so! Use some of the funds to locate a "super-hypnotherapist."

107 **Q:** *(L)* Who might this person be? A clue?

108 **A:** No.[11]

109 **Q:** *(L)* Is there some progress that we can make on our own?

110 **A:** Yes.

111 **Q:** *(L)* Give me a clue ... I want something that will blow me off my chair and enrich my life which is so grim ... produce knowledge that will protect me ...

112 **A:** Won't succeed until locks are blown off in proper way.[12]

113 **Q:** *(L)* Well, I hope I survive until then.

114 **A:** Refer to previous answer.

115 **Q:** *(L)* If you guys were here, I'd throw something at you!

116 **A:** We'd dodge!

117 **Q:** *(L)* Well, you see my problem here ... I guess I just want to know that there is someone out there who cares ...

118 **A:** You should by now.

119 **Q:** *(L)* Then you guys ought to get behind my lawyer and jack him up ...

120 **A:** We do, through you.

121 **Q:** *(L)* Tell me about D___ F___, who is supposed to be part of the intel network.

122 **A:** Not so.

123 **Q:** *(L)* What is not so?

---

[10] *The Wave* 19, 46

[11] Notice that this is the second time they have mentioned this in this session. One has to wonder what a 'super-hypnotherapist' would be. I *did* find out further down the road, but it would be over a year before the meaning of this became clear.

[12] Which refers again to the 'super-hypnotherapist'!

124 **A:** Intel.

125 **Q:** *(L)* You mean, the claimed intelligence connection?

126 **A:** "Remember the Brockinton!"

127 **Q:** *(L)* Well, D___ F___ does not go around exactly claiming he is connected like Andrew B___ does ...

128 **A:** Intel does not spew on the internet.[13]

129 **Q:** *(L)* So, we have a *lot* of stuff locked up inside and all we have to do is find the key ...[14]

130 **A:** Yes, exactly.

131 **Q:** *(L)* Anything else ...

132 **A:** Beware of cardiac concerns. Not what is, what may be. Possible thrombosis in future.

133 **Q:** *(L)* What can I do to avoid such?

134 **A:** Many things, but most important is your attitude. You must decrease your anger.

135 **Q:** *(L)* Well, I thought I had basically done with that when I asked [my ex] for divorce. What am I angry about?

136 **A:** Much, but especially dark past occurrences, some locked, some not.

137 **Q:** *(L)* What past occurrences?

138 **A:** What was done to you.

139 **Q:** *(L)* You mean the kidnapping and possible alien interference?

140 **A:** And other.

141 **Q:** *(L)* Do you mean [my ex]?

142 **A:** Not mainly.[15]

143 **Q:** *(L)* Well, can I ask this: did [my ex] ever, at any point in our marriage, care for me at all?

144 **A:** The way he does.

145 **Q:** *(L)* That says it all. But, what are they talking about? What was done to me?

146 **A:** Violations.

147 **Q:** *(L)* In the process of programming me to destroy myself, was I physically and sexually violated? I have absolutely *no* memory of *any* of that. Are you talking about when I was a child?

148 **A:** Yes. And other.

149 **Q:** *(L)* Can you tell me what ages?

150 **A:** 2, 4, 7, 10, 17, 22, 44.

151 **Q:** *(L)* When I was two, I was abducted?

152 **A:** Yes.

153 **Q:** *(L)* And when I was four? I was kidnapped and programmed?

154 **A:** Yes.

155 **Q:** *(L)* And when I was seven, I was abducted?

156 **A:** Yes, and ...

157 **Q:** *(L)* I was programmed then, too?

158 **A:** Yes.

---

[13] This was a short exchange about a local MUFON character who was exciting some discussion among people in the New-Age/metaphysical/UFO-abductee community.

[14] Here I dropped the "DF" discussion and returned to the burning issue.

[15] I was, in fact, very angry at my ex. However, it is interesting that this issue of heart concerns/thrombosis was brought up at this moment because *within just a few days of this session,* my close friend, Sandra, suffered a thrombosis that caused cardiac arrest and her death. This suggests that some information that gets 'picked out' can relate to someone close rather than to the individual specified. It also highlights the peculiar 'impressionistic' nature of psychic transmissions.

159 **Q:** *(L)* When I was ten ... abducted?

160 **A:** Yes ...

161 **Q:** *(L)* Well, I am just going to have to think about all this ... Looks like a good lotto number![16]

162 **A:** Open.

163 **Q:** *(L)* [That was a joke.] Don't you guys believe in *fun*?[17]

164 **A:** Yes. Goodnight.

End of Session

---

[16] Considering the fact that the remark about thrombosis actually ended up applying to Sandra, I can't help but wonder if the items related to it also applied to her, at least in part.

[17] Fairly typical reaction from me at the time: when really upset, make light of it!

April 27/28, 1996

This was an interesting session night. If you refer back to the immediately previous session of 24 April, you'll note the reference to cardiac concerns. On the 25th of April, my close friend Sandra, my main support throughout the terrible ordeal I was going through, suffered cardiac arrest, probably due to thrombosis. She was found by a janitor cleaning the offices where she was working late. She was supposed to stop by my house that evening on her way home from work, but never showed up. I figured something came up and she would call me. When another day went by and I had not heard from her, I called to find out what was going on and learned about her collapse, that she was in the hospital, but that she had been found too late; she was on total life support only until all of the family could assemble.

With the permission of the family, I was allowed in to see her. I spent some time talking to her and found it hard to believe that she was gone, because her eyelids would flicker and her fingers would move when I talked to her. Anyway, I was very distressed, and that night, after the visit, I determined to either try to communicate with her or ask the Cs about her. So, the first part of this session was dedicated to that. Unfortunately, the tape for this part of the session was damaged and I had to reconstruct parts of it from the handwritten notes. It was around 11:30 p.m. to midnight when we began, which is why there are two dates.

Participants: 'Frank', Pat Z, Laura

1 **Q**: *(L)* Hello.

2 **A**: Hello. You wanted to contact Sandra?

3 **Q**: *(L)* Who do we have with us tonight?

4 **A**: Yturso.

5 **Q**: *(L)* And where are you communicating from?

6 **A**: Cassiopaea.

7 **Q**: *(L)* I would like to know if it is possible to communicate with Sandra?

8 **A**: Maybe. If you wish to speak with her, we must "step out of the way".

9 **Q**: [Question lost]

A: With, not "to."

Q: *(L)* Is there any chance that she will recover?

A: No.

Q: [Question lost]

A: In order for you to contact her in any way, we must leave!! Temporarily, of course!

Q: *(L)* Is it safe for you to give up the channel?

A: Yes.

Q: *(L)* Well, I'm a little skeptical.

A: Try it.

Q: *(L)* How will I know it's really Sandra?

A: Discover.

Q: *(L)* Okay, let's try it.

A: Done!

Q: *(L)* Sandra, are you there?

A: Yes.

Q: *(L)* When I was talking to you at the hospital, were you trying to respond to me?

A: No.

Q: [Here, there followed a series of 'no' responses that indicated that Sandra was not coming back to her body. I asked her how she felt.]

A: Good. I'm just getting started!

Q: [Then, more or less out of the blue the following came:]

A: Don't shoot! Let the young girl go!

Q: *(L)* What do you mean?

A: You'll see. Station. Radio.

Q: [That was rather puzzling and since it didn't seem to be anything but static, we didn't pursue it.]¹

Q: *(L)* Are you having problems communicating?

---

¹It was only on the following day that we learned that the Port Arthur, Tasmania, massacre was taking place at exactly that time. The Port Arthur massacre of 28–29 April 1996 was a killing spree in which 35 people were killed and 23 wounded. It occurred mainly at the historic Port Arthur former prison colony, a popular tourist site in southeastern Tasmania, Australia. The Port Arthur massacre remains one of the deadliest shootings worldwide committed by a single person. The entry on Wikipedia is sufficient to realize that Sandra – or whatever was going on in this session – was most probably influenced by these events on the other side of the planet. "Ahead of him were Nanette Mikac and her children, Madeline, 3, and Alannah, 6. Nanette was carrying Madeline, and Alannah was running slightly ahead. By this point, they had run approximately 600 metres (660 yd) from the car park. Bryant opened his door and slowed down. Mikac moved towards the car, apparently thinking he was offering them help in escaping. Several more people witnessed this from further down the road. Someone recognised him as the gunman and yelled out "It's him!" Bryant stepped out of the car, put his hand on Nanette Mikac's shoulder and told her to get on her knees. She did so, saying, "Please don't hurt my babies". Bryant shot her in the temple, killing her. Next, he fired a shot at Madeline, which hit her in the shoulder, then shot her fatally through the chest. Bryant shot twice at Alannah, as she ran behind a tree, missing. He then walked up, pressed the barrel of the gun into her neck and fired, killing her instantly." (Wikipedia, "Port Arthur massacre (Australia)")

35 **A**: My first time. I'm better on the other side of the board. [Sandra had sat with us to communicate with Cs on a number of occasions.]

36 **Q**: [I asked something about whether she was in and out of her body.]

37 **A**: Yesterday was last time. I just came in for a little while.

38 **Q**: [Several 'no' answers which I think were about whether she suffered any pain. Then I asked her what was she thinking about when she suffered the 'event'.]

39 **A**: Dinner.

40 **Q**: (L) What did it feel like?

41 **A**: Felt like fainting. I had a funny feeling in my stomach. Weak in the arms, then a tingling in my fingers. Then lights flickered then flash then a popping in my head then a dream. Then I saw myself on the floor. I felt good.

42 **Q**: (L) Were you afraid?

43 **A**: No. I thought, well of course I'm dead, who wouldn't be after all that?

44 **Q**: [Then I asked her something about whether she was stuck or could she go into the light.]

45 **A**: No, Laura. You really don't know about this. I am in the light.

46 **Q**: (L) I just don't want you to get stuck anywhere.

47 **A**: When have I ever been stuck? This is fun! There is no right or wrong here either. This is like a school. This is fun! Do you know when I last had fun?

48 **Q**: [I said something about how much I would miss her.]

49 **A**: Laura, don't be a spoilsport!

50 **Q**: [Here I asked how could I be sure that I was talking to Sandra.]

51 **A**: Figures in file cabinet. Think. Tom was mad.[2]

52 **Q**: [I said something like I couldn't be sure ...]

53 **A**: Oh, Laura, I'm doing my best! Do you want my fingerprints?

54 **Q**: [At this point, I said my farewells with great sadness and we let Sandra go and then asked for the Cs to return.]

55 **Q**: (L) Hello.

56 **A**: Hello.

57 **Q**: (L) And who do we have with us this evening?

58 **A**: Vordkon.

59 **Q**: (L) And where do you transmit through?

60 **A**: Cassiopaea.

61 **Q**: (L) As you know, we just had a little chat with Sandra and we thank you for that. Now, we have been discussing a lot of different things here, and the main thing that I have been focusing

---

[2] This referred to a practical joke she and I pulled when we worked together at the state welfare office, HRS. We had put little dressmaking mink heads and tails in a file folder, sticking out like the whole critter was in there, and then sent the secretary to get a file that would be found in that drawer. When she opened it, she threw a whole stack of files she was carrying into the air and ran screaming from the room. And yes, the lead worker, Tom, was really upset with us. No one else in the room while I was communicating with Sandra (Frank and Pat) knew about this.

on is the trap of emotions. I would like to know if this trap is foisted upon us from external sources?

62 **A:** The formula is "foisted."[3]

63 **Q:** *(L)* What is the formula?

64 **A:** Set pattern, like a maze.[4]

65 **Q:** *(L)* Okay. And what is the most effective way to get out of this maze of emotional control?

66 **A:** Calculate.[5]

67 **Q:** *(L)* Is there anything that can be done when one is in process of extricating oneself from an emotional trap to cut off or ease the pain of it? It quite literally hurts.

68 **A:** No need to ease.

69 **Q:** *(L)* Well, once you have done it and gone through it, or, more particularly, once you see that it is a trap, it doesn't hurt anymore – or lessens. Another thing is that we all have been affected by being sucked into emotional traps, seemingly since birth. Is this common for all people?

70 **A:** All? No, most, yes.

71 **Q:** *(L)* Would it be a fair statement to say that people who have potential to do very positive things in terms of clearing away and understanding the reality in which we exist, might be primary targets for this emotional turmoil?

72 **A:** Yes.

73 **Q:** *(L)* Can you tell us what might be the characteristics of a person who is not caught in the emotional trap?

74 **A:** Embracing? No. Uniting? Yes.[6]

75 **Q:** *(L)* Ah! So, you are saying that peo-

---

[3] *The Wave* 46

[4] This is actually an interesting remark considering the work of social psychologists. "In psychology, social psychology is the scientific study of how people's thoughts, feelings, and behaviors are influenced by the actual, imagined, or implied presence of others. In this definition, scientific refers to the empirical method of investigation. The terms thoughts, feelings, and behaviors include all psychological variables that are measurable in a human being. The statement that others' presence may be imagined or implied suggests that we are prone to social influence even when no other people are present, such as when watching television, or following internalized cultural norms. Social psychologists typically explain human behavior as a result of the interaction of mental states and immediate social situations. Social psychologists therefore deal with the factors that lead us to behave in a given way in the presence of others, and look at the conditions under which certain behavior/actions and feelings occur. Social psychology is concerned with the way these feelings, thoughts, beliefs, intentions and goals are constructed and how such psychological factors, in turn, influence our interactions with others." (Wikipedia, "Social psychology")

[5] I still have no idea what the Cs meant by "calculate" in respect of getting out of mazes of emotional control unless they meant "to determine by reasoning, common sense, or practical experience; estimate; evaluate; gauge."

[6] I guess the difference is that when you 'embrace' you may take hold of someone who is not necessarily colinear; when you 'unite' you are connecting to someone who is colinear.

ple who can clear the emotional traps can unite in a higher emotional sense?

76 **A**: Emotions are chemicals only.

77 **Q**: *(L)* So, if emotions are chemical only, is it true that when one is in physical proximity to certain people, that perhaps their frequency vibrations cause these chemicals to be stimulated or generated within us?

78 **A**: Okay.

79 **Q**: *(L)* And, that it takes great force of will and mental power to counteract this physical action?

80 **A**: No, just practice.[7]

81 **Q**: *(L)* Okay, once you have done it a few times in small ways, you can build up to big ones?

82 **A**: Not quite correct concept.

83 **Q**: *(L)* I was reading this piece sent to us on the internet where this Cosmic Awareness source talks about people who deliberately have [incarnated] because, since the good guys really can't interfere from the outside, because it would violate free will, that many of them incarnate and thereby partake of the physical experience, and then wake up and are able to do the things that are needed on the planet. The object being to try to make sure that they will awaken to their purpose, and that emotions and emotional traps are used repeatedly and continuously to try to prevent them from awakening. What I am getting at is: what are the things that we can do to awaken? You have told us many times that we need to awaken. Obviously we are not fully awakened. We are aware of that. Is there some other thing we can do?

84 **A**: Let it happen naturally. If you are on a path, do you seek to jump up into the air and fly to the end of the path? If you did, you would regret missing the "rest of the path."

85 **Q**: *(L)* A lot of very strange things have been happening ... Sandra and her heart attack, [my daughter] and her [broken] ankle, the terrible sicknesses I have had in the past months, [my other daughter] talking about the things that have happened in her experiences ... it seems like, to me, that the situation in terms of attack is really heating up. Can you comment on this?

86 **A**: No.

87 **Q**: *(L)* Well, thanks a lot! Can we ask questions about it?

88 **A**: Yes.

89 **Q**: *(L)* Well, my eye infections, the ear problems, the loss of my voice for so long ... were these part of the attack process?[8]

90 **A**: Yes.

91 **Q**: *(L)* My mother also fell down and has a black eye. I am trying to find the portal. What is the portal through which all this attack is coming?

92 **A**: Discover.

---

[7]This actually proved to be correct. Of course, the first few times you act against your emotions and for reason, common sense and experience, it is very scary and painful. After a while, you find out it is not as scary and painful as you imagine it to be.

[8]See comments to previous session for description of this ordeal that was still ongoing at the time of this session though there was improvement.

93 **Q:** *(L)* Did we already discover it in part, i.e. Sue and her mother and that situation?

94 **A:** No.

95 **Q:** *(L)* Are you saying that Sue is not a portal?

96 **A:** People are not portals!!! They are only victims of the things that come through the portals. Otherwise, many could describe you as a "portal."

97 **Q:** *(L)* Well, I never said that I wasn't. Speaking of that ...

98 **A:** When you concentrate on the people as portals, you falsely direct negative energy upon the soul units themselves. Rather like treating acne with the therapy to be found in a shotgun!

99 **Q:** *(L)* What is the appropriate response when you are in a situation and you know that the person is being victimized, yes, by the forces coming through the portal, but their victimization is causing you a great deal of problems? What is the appropriate response here?

100 **A:** How do you view those afflicted with disease? Do you throw rocks at them?!?

101 **Q:** *(L)* Well, no, you don't throw rocks at them ...

102 **A:** What do you do, then?

103 **Q:** *(L)* Well, a person with a disease: you send or take them to a doctor or suggest that they go to a doctor.

104 **A:** For what purpose?

105 **Q:** *(L)* To discover the diagnosis of the disease, to obtain medicine, to either relieve the symptoms or cure the disease.

106 **A:** Bingo!

107 **Q:** *(L)* We are talking about people who won't even admit they have a disease! How do you tell someone to go to a doctor when they don't think they are sick? Most people do *not* believe that they are subject to control or manipulation from other densities! You have told a number of people that they were going to be subjected to attack and manipulation and they have blithely said, "Oh, there is nothing in our lives that would permit that."

108 **A:** Denial is not incurable until you give up. Patience combined with kind invitations to participate in the learning process eventually allows the victim to awaken, thus to be open to cure. This helps you to build the "army" you seek.[9] Isolation cures nothing. Thereby stifling progress, as any and all will ultimately be seen as "portals." Rather like "spinning one's wheels," yes??

109 **Q:** *(L)* So, in other words, you are saying I should remain married to my husband, I should have Sue and other disruptive and destructive people over here constantly to 'participate' in the learning process?

110 **A:** The point is not to rigidly adhere to specific lifestyles, nor maintain exact patterning of behavior, merely to not close doors completely and permanently.[10]

---

[9]The remark about building an army was puzzling at the time, but considering the way world affairs have gone in the years since that time, it makes much better sense.

[10]This was good advice then and since! It is all too easy to learn a little bit about attack and portals and hyperdimensional realities and then just start having knee-jerk reactions against things. Of course, I was suffering a lot at the time of this

111 **Q:** *(L)* Okay, if a person were, say, a robot person, when a person becomes a robot person, what happens to the soul of the robot person?[11]

112 **A:** Same process.

113 **Q:** *(L)* As what?

114 **A:** Death.

115 **Q:** *(L)* So, a person can die and leave their body, their body can be taken over and reanimated and controlled to function and do a lot of things for a long time. Meanwhile, the original soul has completely departed to 5th density, ready to recycle?

116 **A:** Yes, but body is replaced, not reanimated.

117 **Q:** *(L)* Is this what happened to [my ex] when he had that surgery back in 1981?

118 **A:** We caution that, even though you have met 7 "robots," in your entire lifetime, not to "see" them under every bush or around every corner. You have met so many people in your life. We gave you one, and only one!![12]

119 **Q:** *(L)* What was the source of the dream where this was stated to me quite clearly?

120 **A:** Dreams are the best forum for disinformation that exists.

121 **Q:** *(L)* Okay. I can see that. But, at the same time they are also one of the best ways to get information from the subconscious and the higher conscious. Is this not true?

122 **A:** We have mentioned dualities a lot!!

123 **Q:** *(L)* Skipping the disinformation part, and just getting to the analysis part, the story of Bluebeard ... I am still of the opinion, robot person or not, I am doing the right thing. Is it possible that, even in this situation, that I am caught up in an emotional trap?

124 **A:** Sure. This learning thing is anything but easy!

125 **Q:** *(L)* Yes, that's all fine and dandy, but we are talking about breaking up my whole life here ...

126 **A:** Maybe, maybe not.

127 **Q:** *(L)* What good is channeling if it does not help you to make decisions once in a while? Once in a while, I say. Not all the time. Or to help clarify things! To put additional light on it instead of muddying the water!

128 **A:** We are not "muddying" the water," only you can do that!

129 **Q:** *(L)* Well, enough of that ...

130 **A:** No, not enough of that. And a much needed pointer for you: answers to questions of global or universal significance provide for a greater personal learning than direct personal inquiries. If you disagree, check transcripts and especially un-transcribed sessions for validation! You will see, my dear!![13]

---

session and I felt the Cs were being a little hard on me, but sometimes one needs a little kick in the backside to get one's attention!

[11] *The Wave* 21

[12] You can see here my own 'knee-jerk' reaction in assuming that my ex was a 'robot type'. I no longer think so, but perhaps, at the time, thinking that helped me to sustain my determination to end the relationship.

[13] Yes, I had been so depressed and sick that I had allowed the session transcribing to back up.

131 **Q:** *(L)* Well, that is why I said that was enough of that, because I don't want to talk about my personal stuff anymore. I did think that the thing about the robot people was pretty significant, but obviously it is not that significant or important. There's two million of them on the planet, and I have been told that I have encountered seven. I did think that this was a pretty high ratio of robot people for one person to encounter ...

132 **A:** Yes, but your life path has been unusual. And you have met 4588 people personally!

133 **Q:** *(L)* How many people has Frank met?

134 **A:** 2754.

135 **Q:** *(L)* How many were robots?

136 **A:** 3.

137 **Q:** *(L)* How many has Pat met?

138 **A:** 3856.

139 **Q:** *(L)* How many robots?

140 **A:** 1.

141 **Q:** *(L)* So, why seven for me? Yeah, we know the path is unusual ...

142 **A:** Yes.

143 **Q:** *(L)* Can you tell me in what sense it is unusual?

144 **A:** Can't you?

145 **Q:** *(L)* Well, I thought I would trick you into telling me ...

146 **A:** No tricks, we only treat.

147 **Q:** *(L)* Oh, okay ... *(P)* Will they tell us who are the robots we have met? *(L)* Probably not ...

148 **A:** Susan S___.

149 **Q:** *(L)* That was the one they named before ... no cigar.[14]

150 **A:** What better disguise? A nudist![15]

151 **Q:** *(L)* That was funny! I tell you, the emperor has no clothes! *(P)* Won't you tell me who it is that I have met?

152 **A:** Nope.

153 **Q:** *(L)* I am so tired now that I cannot formulate a legitimate, reasonable, intelligent or coherent question of global or universal significance; we will say goodnight.

154 **A:** Goodnight.

End of Session

---

[14]See session 21 October 1995: the 'nutritionist'.

[15]Here the Cs are exhibiting their sense of humor, only I wasn't feeling much like humor at the time.

May 4, 1996

This was a really interesting session because of the two guests. Tom H__-__ was an old friend of mine about whom I wrote in *Amazing Grace* in the chapter entitled 'Graveyards, Psychopaths, Psychics, and Meetings on the Bridge'. By this time in my life, Tom was an old friend and he would drive over from Brooksville once a year or so to pay a visit. He never announced his arrival in advance, he just showed up. So, this was the day he showed up. At the same time, my brother Tom K___-had come down for a weekend visit, which he did now and then on no definite schedule either. The last time he had attended a session (14 October 1995), there had been a very interesting discussion.

Looking back on the situation I was in, and my references to the Bluebeard story in Pinkola-Estes's book *Women Who Run With the Wolves* in previous sessions, it seems as though it was a manifestation of the archetype, with my 'brothers' showing up as they did for the heroine in the story. In any event, the energy the two of them lent to the session resulted in an extraordinary exchange. We decided to continue the line of questions that had been part of that previous session my brother attended. Obviously, what is discussed in this session, if true, is a frightening picture of how our reality/society can be manipulated. Considering global developments since the time of this session, one just has to go "hmmmm?!"

Participants: 'Frank', Tom H, Tom K, Laura

1 **Q:** *(L)* Hello.

2 **A:** Hello.

3 **Q:** *(L)* And who do we have with us this evening?

4 **A:** Lorra.

5 **Q:** *(L)* And where do you transmit from?

6 **A:** Cassiopaea.

7 **Q:** *(L)* One of the things we talked about the last time Tom was here[1] was about the underground bases and military interference in civilian affairs and civilian interface with military affairs.

---
[1] See session 14 October 1995.

What further can you tell us about this?

A: Ask specific questions, please.

Q: *(L)* One of the questions we were dealing with was the use of warfare to create situations in which bodies could be taken ...

A: Warfare has many "uses."

Q: *(L)* Could you list for us some of the most common uses of warfare?

A: Generation of environment to facilitate inconspicuous replacement of gene pool. Factors in paradigm shift through stimulation of conception activity, replacement of key personnel according to frequency vibration pre-readings ...[2]

Q: *(TH)* Who or what in the gene pool is being replaced? *(TK)* Whoever they want replaced. *(L)* Well, you know how it is in the movies ... everybody is indiscriminately making love before they go into battle ... *(F)* Yes ... they said "factors in paradigm shift through stimulation of conception activity". *(L)* "Replacement of key personnel according to frequency vibration pre-readings" ... Okay, do you mean to say that war ...

A: Creates "environment" for unnoticed genetic modifications because of greatly heightened exchange of both physical and ethereal factors.[3]

Q: *(L)* What do you mean by "replacement of key personnel"? Key personnel according to whose definition?

A: 4th density STS.

Q: *(L)* Are these key personnel human?

A: Yes.

Q: *(L)* When you say replacement, do you mean something as simple as someone dying, such as a head of state, and being replaced by another person who comes to power? That would be the simplest scenario that would fit this explanation.

A: Your scenario is not simple.

Q: *(L)* I mean simple in terms of the machinations ...

A: Both.

Q: *(L)* Would it also be that key personnel could also be replaced as in duplication?

A: Yes. And removing to secret activity realm. Enough wars have taken place to effectively create entire new "underground race" of humans, both from direct capture followed by "reeducation," and spawning activity using these persons and others.

Q: *(L)* What do you mean by spawning activity?

A: Those captured have reproduced offspring, these never having seen your world.

Q: *(L)* Are you saying ... *(TK)* They have given birth and these children have never seen our world ... *(L)* How can an entire race of people, or groups of people, live under the surface of this planet, without the whole six billion of the rest of us on top, or at least a large number, realizing that there is anything going on? This is so wild an idea ...

A: No. How much space exists underground, as opposed to that on the surface?

---

[2] All of this carries a lot heavier meaning in view of the rampant war-mongering since 9/11.
[3] *The Wave* 21

29 **Q:** *(L)* A lot, I suppose. You aren't saying that the Earth is hollow, are you?

30 **A:** No, not exactly.

31 **Q:** *(L)* Well, how deep is the deepest of these underground cities?

32 **A:** 3,108 miles.

33 **Q:** *(L)* That's pretty deep! But wouldn't it be too hot at that depth?

34 **A:** No. Temperature averages 68 degrees F.

35 **Q:** *(TK)* That's pretty comfortable! *(L)* How do they have light?

36 **A:** Magnetic resonance.

37 **Q:** *(L)* Well, aren't they subject to being crushed by earthquakes?

38 **A:** No, earthquakes are not felt deep underground!!

39 **Q:** *(L)* Does any of this underground civilization activity have any relation to this massive underground base the Russians are building?[4]

40 **A:** No.

---

[4] At the present time, considering the appearance of Putin on the global stage, it's interesting that I asked this question about Russia then. Anyway, Wikipedia tells us about this base:

> Mount Yamantau ... is in the Ural Mountains, Bashkortostan, Russia. The name means wicked mountain in the Bashkir language - Яман тау . It is also known as Mount Yamantaw. It stands at 1,640 metres (5,381 ft) and is the highest mountain in the southern Urals. Along with Kosvinsky Mountain (600 km to the north), it is suspected by the United States of being a large secret nuclear facility and/or bunker. The closed military town of Mezhgorye - Russian: Межгорье - is situated nearby. As late as 2003, Yamantaw was not yet fully operational.
>
> Large excavation projects have been observed by U.S. satellite imagery *as recently as the late 1990s*, during the time of Boris Yeltsin's government after the fall of the Soviet Union. Two garrisons, Beloretsk-15 and Beloretsk-16, were built on top of the facility, and possibly a third, Alkino-2, as well, and became the closed town of Mezhgorye in 1995. They are said to house 30,000 workers each. Repeated U.S. questions have yielded several different responses from the Russian government regarding Mount Yamantaw. They have said it is a mining site, a repository for Russian treasures, a food storage area, and a bunker for leaders in case of nuclear war. Responding to questions regarding Yamantaw in 1996, Russia's Defense Ministry stated: "The practice does not exist in the Defense Ministry of Russia of informing foreign mass media about facilities, whatever they are, that are under construction in the interests of strengthening the security of Russia." Large rail lines serve the facility.
>
> Mount Yamantaw is near one of Russia's last remaining nuclear labs, *Chelyabinsk-70*, raising speculation that it already houses nuclear weapons. Russian newspapers reported in 1996 that it is a part of the "Dead Hand" nuclear retaliatory command structure.
>
> In 1997, a United States Congressional finding, related to the country's National Defense Authorization Act for 1998, stated that the Russian Federation kept up a "deception and denial policy" about the mountain complex after U.S. officials had given Cheyenne Mountain Complex tours to Russian diplomats, which the finding stated "...does not appear to be consistent with the lowering of strategic threats, openness, and cooperation that is the basis of the post-Cold War strategic partnership between the United States and Russia." (Wikipedia, "Mount Yamantau")

41 **Q:** *(TK)* Is any of this under the ocean?
42 **A:** Yes.
43 **Q:** *(TK)* Well, we'll never explore all of what is under the ocean. *(L)* It just staggers the mind to think about it. What do they want these people for?
44 **A:** To replace you.
45 **Q:** *(TK)* And why? Because they can control them better, right?
46 **A:** Completely.
47 **Q:** *(L)* Do these people being bred and raised in these underground cities have souls?
48 **A:** Yes, most.
49 **Q:** *(TK)* Are they just like us only raised differently?
50 **A:** More complicated than that.
51 **Q:** *(L)* How long have they been doing this?
52 **A:** 14,000 years, approximately.[5]
53 **Q:** *(L)* If they have been doing it that long, obviously the ones they have taken at the beginning have croaked and are of no use to replace anybody on the Earth unless they have been replacing people from time to time for various reasons ...
54 **A:** No, their technology makes yours look like Neanderthal by comparison! Hibernation tubes ... One heartbeat per hour, for example.
55 **Q:** *(TH)* That means that for every year we live, they would live 4200 years ...

(L) Does any of this have anything to do with that crazy pit at Oak Island?
56 **A:** In an offhand way.
57 **Q:** *(L)* How do we fit into all of this? *(TK)* We don't!
58 **A:** You have been the "preparation committee."
59 **Q:** *(L)* What have we been doing? Is it part of the plan for us to destroy the planet, destroy the ozone layer, pollute the seas and so forth to make it more habitable for them?
60 **A:** Those things are inconsequential and easily repaired.
61 **Q:** *(TK)* With their technology, they can fix all of that. *(L)* This is really horrible, you know! To think of all this ... *(TK)* Apparently, from what I am understanding, they can't just come in and wipe us out and replace us, because the 'rules' won't allow it.
62 **A:** Yet the natural cycles within the framework of the natural order of things will allow all these things to fall into place.
63 **Q:** *(L)* Is there some law within the realm of these beings, sort of like the law of gravity, that prevents them from just coming in and taking over?
64 **A:** No.
65 **Q:** *(TK)* I don't think it is like the law of gravity ...

---

[5]The time designated for the beginning of this activity is interesting since it was right around the last glacial maximum, following which many changes began to occur on earth. Basically, that was the time of the beginning of the modern warm period, at which time, human populations, previously forced into refuge areas as a result of Ice Age climatic conditions, gradually begin to repopulate the Northern Hemisphere's Eurasian landmass. This was followed by a period of relatively brief cold oscillation, referred to as the Younger Dryas.

66 **A:** What "law" is there that inhibits you from manipulating 2nd density beings at will?!?

67 **Q:** *(L)* Well, I don't go out and deliberately hurt or manipulate anything or anybody. *(TK)* Of course, in our handling of these 'critters', we are conserving them in some ways so that we will have an ongoing food supply ... I think there are rules to the game. It's like a chess game. They can't just come in and change things, it has to progress in some way. But, there are loopholes and they can sneak in and manipulate and get away with some things ... *(TH)* Then, there aren't rules – there are just guidelines.

68 **A:** Two important points there: 1) When we said "you," we meant 3rd density collectively. 2) You missed our statement about the natural cycle and order of things almost completely. We suggest you reread and ponder ... Also, what if your race is manipulated to destroy yourselves, or, just hang around until the next natural cataclysm?[6]

69 **Q:** *(TK)* Well, it seems like there is another side that is trying to prevent them from gaining control.

(L) Well, from what I understand, the only thing the good guys are able to do is, because of free will, they have to wait to be asked for help, and the only they thing they can really do is give information.

(F) Well, this is valuable if used by the right people at the right time.

(TK) You have to come up with the right questions, too. You have to have enough information to be able to come up with the right questions. I am sure the information is there. You have one group with all these people underground and they want to take over the planet. This group likes being 4th density – they don't want to advance. They want to block advancement. Then, you have the group that want to advance, they want the natural order to proceed. This negative group wants to stay there and keep everyone they can there.

(L) And because they deplete themselves and diminish in numbers, they keep having to supply their needs and existence.

(TK) If, by some odd chance, the Earth is the only place where people come to advance, then sooner or later it is going to stop, if these other guys take over, then it will just stop ... implode.

(TH) I know! The Earth is a 4th density theme park!

(L) We already thought of that ... we all have an 'E' ticket ride!

(TK) Obviously we have the information, but we haven't really dug deep enough; we don't know the questions that we need to ask. Is this true?

70 **A:** No.

71 **Q:** *(TK)* Is what I was saying close to the truth?

72 **A:** Yes. Total truth is elusive.

73 **Q:** *(TK)* So, what I said was the gist of what is going on here. So, we have to figure out what we are supposed to do so that the Earth can be maintained ...

74 **A:** You will do what you will do.

75 **Q:** *(TK)* This is true.

76 **A:** Do you, in general, control 2nd density beings on earth?

---

[6]This discussion and its implications are a lot scarier now, in the years since 9/11.

77 **Q:** *(L)* Yes.

78 **A:** So, what is "fair" about that?

79 **Q:** *(L)* Nothing.

80 **A:** Okay, so what is the difference?!?!???

81 **Q:** *(TK)* So, basically, we control 2nd density, and 4th density controls us. There are the good guys and bad guys. *(L)* And we will do what we will do. Either we choose to align ourselves with the good guys, or with the bad guys.

82 **A:** It's up to you.[7]

83 **Q:** *(TK)* However, if too many people align themselves with the bad guys, then the balance tips in their favor, and there is no more advancement, so there has to be education so that people will know ...

84 **A:** Tom, you are close, but you are missing the point.

85 **Q:** *(L)* What is the point?

86 **A:** The point is, there "has to be" nothing. You will do what you will do. You choose. We have told you this repeatedly, but you still suffer from self-centered perspective.

87 **Q:** *(TK)* Everybody is worried about themselves. They all want to be saved and not worry about others.

88 **A:** More to the point, everybody in an STS realm views themselves as somehow "special, chosen, or protected." This is simply not so!!

89 **Q:** *(TK)* What is going to happen, is going to happen. The people ...

90 **A:** The body does not matter. It is the soul that either progresses or digresses, just ask Sandra!

91 **Q:** *(L)* Did Sandra progress or digress?

92 **A:** Open.

93 **Q:** *(L)* So, in other words, we could just sit around and live our lives and have a good time and not worry about a damn thing. Is that the point?

94 **A:** No.

95 **Q:** *(L)* It's our choices?

96 **A:** Yes.

97 **Q:** *(TK)* The point is it's going to happen ...

98 **A:** But, nobody is there to intervene on your behalf as many would like to believe.

99 **Q:** *(L)* So, we are here on this planet, and we will either make it or we won't, just like Dorothy and Toto in Oz, based on our own ability to figure it out, to overcome the odds, the witch, monkeys and soldiers ... *(TK)* Maybe what they are trying to do is give people the information, or make the information available so that people can make the choice, do they want to stay ...

100 **A:** We are not "trying" to do anything. We are here to answer questions if asked. We cannot interfere.

101 **Q:** *(TK)* Yes, the non-interference idea is pretty clear and understandable. So, they cannot interfere ...

102 **A:** And, even when we answer, you may not believe, it is up to you!

103 **Q:** *(L)* So, we are really on our own!

104 **A:** You always have been, and so have we, and all others, too!!

105 **Q:** *(TK)* I guess then, it is a matter of asking the right questions so that you will know what course of action to take.

---

[7]This appears to be acknowledgment that my statement was correct: "Either we choose to align ourselves with the good guys, or with the bad guys."

I mean, do you want to advance? Do you want to go to 4th density? Or do you want to go higher? Or do you want to stay here? How can you make an informed choice if you don't know the true conditions and what your options are?

(L) Is it that the religions that have been generated and foisted on the human race, have been designed to give people a feeling of complacency or faith in something outside themselves, and that this prevents them from seeking knowledge, opening their eyes, facing the facts of their existence, and therefore keeps them in bondage?

106 **A**: It's just obstacles, as always. You employ those too, for your 2nd density friends!![8]

107 **Q**: *(TK)* What state of mind do you have to have to want to advance?

(F) Well, you know you are on the path when you can see that the words don't match the facts of life. Think of all the people you have met with whom you may have had a philosophical conversation. How many will say, "Oh, all I need is the Bible. That's all I pay any attention to"?

(TK) I don't have many philosophical conversations with people, because I rarely agree with anything that is said.

(F) Well, you must have decided on this because you tried it and found it didn't work.

(TK) I have a real problem ... yes, the Bible has been around for a long time, and religion has been around for a long time ... but I have a real problem believing something that is so obviously produced by humans with agendas of their own!

(F) But most people that you tell that to will say, "Oh, no! People didn't write the Bible, God did!" Or, they could be a complete atheist and believe only in the religion of science.

(TK) I believe that a person is supposed to live by rules and treat people with respect and honor life ... and some of the ideas of religion are good, but they just go over the edge.

(F) That is how they suck people in. Mix lies with the truth.

(L) Yes, a lie sandwiched between two truths makes it easier to swallow.

(F) Yes, if it was *all* false, the vast majority of people would have figured it out immediately. Or, very quickly.

(TK) The vast majority don't care. They just want to be led like sheep. They don't want any responsibility.

(F) And what happens to the vast majority of cattle? They munch away in their pasture until time to get in the truck to go to the butcher.

(TK) Well, after all my years in the military, I have gotten to the point that I just don't trust anybody with authority.

(F) And, if you talk to the religious types, they will say, "Oh, I don't have any answers ... I just follow the Bible."

(L) Not only do they not have any answers, they don't have any questions, either. And, I think that is the clue: the people who are still asking questions after wading through all the religions and mystical mumbo-jumbo. The ones who

---

[8]Seems to be a confirmation of my remarks about mainstream religions, even referring to them as 'fences', more or less.

think they have found the ultimate answer are – well – lunch!

(TK) The whole purpose of life, it seems to me, is to obtain knowledge and advance. You are stuck on this level until you figure it out. But what are you supposed to figure out?

(L) I think that the knowing is the doing.

(TH) "Ye shall know the truth and the truth shall set you free." It's in the Bible!

(L) Is the knowing the key?

108 **A**: Yes.

109 **Q**: *(L)* I think that knowing changes your frequency. Is that true?

110 **A**: Yes.

111 **Q**: *(L)* The acknowledging and the seeing?

112 **A**: Yes.

113 **Q**: *(L)* What did they tell us once ... "it's not where you are, but who you are and what you see that counts." *(TK)* So, we aren't gonna change what happens. There is no way we can have any appreciable effect on the underground armies ... it is just a matter of changing ourselves and whomever else we can share with.

114 **A**: Correct, the cow has no effect on the health of the livestock industry ...

115 **Q**: *(TK)* The cow has no effect on the herd. One cow doesn't ... or even a lot of cows.

(F) But there might be one or two cows that follow one that breaks out of the herd.

(TK) Yes, you might be able to affect somebody else's life, but not the whole group. So, worrying about the underground stuff is immaterial.

(L) But, knowing about it is.

(TK) All those survivalists, the militias and so forth. It is a complete waste of time.

(F) It is good to know what is going on.

(TK) But, could you know if you had an implant? *(L)* Yes ... *(TK)* How, by asking?

(L) Well, that and examining your life and comparing with others. When you read the material, you find a lot of clues. It really opens your eyes.

(TK) Isn't the implant and the brainwashing a little bit past the interference that the 4th density STS should be allowed?

(L) We have learned that knowing you have an implant and what it can do, you then can cancel it out by choices. Those who believe that their implant is for their own good, are, of course, completely subject to them.

(TK) Have I ever been abducted?

A: Ask Tom about your kidnapping ... 116 Tom must learn.

117 **Q**: *(L)* What could be done ...

118 **A**: Why do you suppose Tom "chose" to enter the Navy?

119 **Q**: *(L)* Because he was manipulated to do so?

120 **A**: Was led.

121 **Q**: *(L)* What things happened in the Navy?

122 **A**: Ask Tom.

123 **Q**: *(L)* It seems that he has been living rather on the surface ... have you

just gone along from day to day without thinking too much about it? *(TK)* Mm-hmm.

124 **A**: No. That is what your "memory" tells you.

125 **Q**: *(TK)* I am getting a headache. *(L)* That's interesting. Why does he get the headaches?

126 **A**: Research the problem in order to learn. If we told you the answers to all these things, at this point, you would just shrug your shoulders and forget about it.

127 **Q**: *(L)* Is the shrugging of the shoulders a programmed response in him?

128 **A**: To an extent.

129 **Q**: *(L)* Okay, he mentioned the headaches beginning when he went on a particular camping trip. And, he is now trying to remember it, and it is causing him pain.

130 **A**: Hypnosis.

131 **Q**: *(TK)* The worst headache I ever had was when we were on our way to Japan and stopped in Hawaii. I went over to another ship to get some hydraulic fluid ... on the way back, as I was coming back on the ship, I had a headache that was so bad I couldn't even tolerate light or sound. *(L)* You mean the kind where it hurts even to breathe? *(TK)* Mm-hmm. *(L)* Well, I started having those after I woke up one night reversed in my bed with the bottom half of my nightgown wet. I know what they are like. Unbelievable pain.[9]

132 **A**: Yes.

133 **Q**: *(TK)* Yes, nothing helps. *(L)* Can you give Tom a little help here?

134 **A**: Sorry. Tom is at the point where it will not help him for us to "give him a little bit."

135 **Q**: *(F)* Well, they never gave us point blank answers either. *(L)* Well, of all the people who have come to the sessions, he is the first who has immediately understood what is going on and what it means. *(F)* Most everyone else thinks they already know the answers ... *(L)* Getting back to the underground bases, is the HAARP project connected to these underground bases?

136 **A**: Not directly.

137 **Q**: *(L)* You once said that HAARP was something that was to be used to 'transfer perimeters'. I am assuming that this means to manipulate space, time and density.[10]

138 **A**: Yes.

139 **Q**: *(L)* Is it possible that they are planning to use this to bring up the Atlantean crystals to utilize?[11]

140 **A**: Not so much to "bring up," as to utilize.

141 **Q**: *(L)* Is there anything to BRH's idea about the 'harmonics', that it must be ready to function on a certain day and time?

142 **A**: No.

143 **Q**: *(L)* In terms of what we understand – I know you aren't gonna answer it that way – if Tom tries to bring up the memories and understand, the headaches

---

[9] *Amazing Grace* gives details of these events.
[10] *The Wave* 62
[11] *The Wave* 22
[12] *The Wave* 46

ought to go away ... *(TK)* I haven't had any since I have been out of the Navy.[12]

144 **A:** O'Brien is "lyin'"[13]

145 **Q:** *(L)* What is it about O'Brien?

146 **A:** Discover. Why is Tom there, of all places?!?

147 **Q:** *(L)* Is there something in that area, some frequency from the Earth, some electromagnetics or something, that can tend to ...

148 **A:** Maybe, maybe, maybe, maybe ....

149 **Q:** *(L)* It keeps a person quiescent and in the dark?

150 **A:** Stalling frequency ... And by the way, can anyone come up with a purpose for the existence of Camp Blanding? Well?? ...

151 **Q:** *(TK)* Ask about Dave Wh___. He lives nearby ...

152 **A:** First, some blockbuster stuff for the Knighted ones ... Look upon a detailed map, and reflect, remember lonely journeys from long ago, and begin to unlock shattering mysteries which will lead to revelations opening the door to the greatest learning burst yet!![14]

153 **Q:** *(F)* Oh, my. A *lot* of questions ... *(L)* Was there more than one journey to Camp Blanding?

154 **A:** No.

155 **Q:** *(L)* Only one?

156 **A:** For you.

157 **Q:** *(L)* More than one for Tom?

158 **A:** ?

159 **Q:** *(L)* You said "knighted ones", as though there were some significance to the name ...

160 **A:** Discover ...

161 **Q:** *(L)* Is there some genetic engineering here?

162 **A:** No, not in the sense you are thinking. But, all are in some sense.

163 **Q:** *(L)* Why did my mother marry men who kept affecting our lives in such terrible ways?

164 **A:** Ask her.

165 **Q:** *(L)* She has no answer. She is baffled herself.

166 **A:** So, get her to discover. That is where the clues lie.

167 **Q:** *(L)* So, the clues lie with some of these people ... We remember the trip with one of them – to North Carolina – when we were taken to school ...

168 **A:** Why did he insist you go to boarding school? And why did your mother acquiesce?

169 **Q:** *(L)* All this comes back to the original question, why Tom is in O'Brien, near Camp Blanding ...

170 **A:** EM waves curdle the mind producing complacency in the face of contrived misery. Numbs the mind through isolationist influences. Why are you there, Tom? Who begged you to stay there? EM waves emanate from?? Suggest you, Laura, go to library and research Camp Blanding. You may find a "black hole," so to speak!![15]

---

[13] *The Wave* "Appendix C"

[14] *The Wave* 21, 28

[15] "Camp Blanding Joint Training Center is the primary military reservation and training base for the Florida National Guard, both the Florida Army National Guard and certain non-flying activities of the Florida Air National Guard. The installation

171 **Q:** *(L)* A black hole. Okay. Well, there is sure a lot of stuff that has gone on in our lives for which there is simply no rational explanation. *(TK)* They sure have been giving a lot of stuff tonight without a lot of questions ...

A: Visits through trees, forests, leading 172 to a perfectly square clearing ...

is located in Clay County, Florida, near the city of Starke. The site measures approximately 73,000 acres (300 km) and includes Kingsley Lake. It also hosts other Reserve, Army National Guard, Air National Guard, and some Active Component training for the U.S. Armed Forces.

"Additionally, Camp Blanding serves as a training center for many ROTC units, both Army and Naval. Jacksonville University and University of South Florida NROTC Battalions continue to conduct their week-long orientation at Camp Blanding each August before the college semester starts. Camp Blanding also hosts the Audie Murphy field training exercise where Army ROTC units from more than a dozen Florida, Georgia, and Puerto Rican universities gather to conduct a five-day field problem focusing on small-unit tactics, land navigation, and leadership development every April. ...

"Camp Blanding owes its location on the shore of Kingsley Lake to the United States Navy's desire to establish a Naval Air Station *(NAS)* on the banks of the St. Johns River, south of Jacksonville, in the late 1930s. The site that would eventually become Naval Air Station Jacksonville was already the location of the Florida National Guard's Camp Foster and negotiations were started for a land-swap. In mid-1939, the transaction was accomplished and the state armory board chose as compensation a tract of 30,000 acres (120 km) in Clay County as a National Guard camp and training site. The National Guard Officers Association of Florida recommended the new camp be named in honor of Lieutenant General Albert H. Blanding. The War Department agreed and Camp Blanding's history began. ...

"In 1940, Camp Blanding was leased to the United States Army as an active duty training center. The post was originally used by New England and Southern troops preparing for deployment overseas. However, during the course of the war, Camp Blanding served as an infantry replacement training center, an induction center, a German prisoner-of-war compound, and a holding center for 343 Japanese, German and Italian immigrant residents of the United States. ... At one point during the war, the camp contained the population of the fourth largest city in Florida. There were 10,000 buildings, 125 miles (201 km) of paved roads, the largest hospital in the state. It was one of the largest training bases in the country.

"After the war, the state's 30,000 acres (120 km) were returned to the armory board and by 1948, most of the buildings were sold or moved off post. In the early 1950s, the Federal Government deeded additional land to the State of Florida for use as a National Guard training facility, but until 1970, the post saw only limited use by the military. ... From 2001 until 2008, Camp Blanding was used by the Southeast Region of the Civil Air Patrol to host their South East Region Encampment for CAP Cadets. The Florida Wing of Civil Air Patrol continues to utilize Camp Blanding for their wing-level Summer Cadet Encampments." (Wikipedia, "Camp Blanding")

173 Q: *(L)* Hmmmm. Is Aunt H___ one of the generators of EM frequencies?

174 A: No, she is merely an unwitting agent.

175 Q: *(L)* Well, L___ is very isolationist in her tendencies. Is that a result of being in that area?

176 A: Same.

177 Q: *(L)* Well, what I *really* want to know is, *why* have we had all of these *crazy* things happen in our lives, and all of these people ranged all around us seemingly placed there, or manipulated deliberately to affect us negatively? I mean, am I wrong, or is this not a *very* unusual and crazy situation?[16]

178 A: Why do you think?

179 Q: *(L)* Well, I have no idea!

180 A: Because you are of the extremely rare and few who have the abilities to put the puzzle together.[17]

181 Q: *(L)* So, what are we supposed to do? *(TK)* Discover.

182 A: Yes. And, for tonight, goodnight.

End of Session

---

[16] *The Wave* 21, 28

[17] As my readers know, I generally don't trust any kind of channeled response that might be seen as 'ego-feeding'. I had the same reaction to this remark as usual: "Oh yeah?" However, let it be noted that I have spent years looking for someone else to be a 'teacher' and to put things together in a way that is not riddled with logical inconsistencies, mostly to no avail.

May 25, 1996

This is another very interesting session where an external event triggered a discussion that led to unusual ideas and recommendations.

Between the previous session on the 4th of May and this one, Ark wrote in his journal:

> Journal 12/5/1996
>
> Where am I going? It's year 1996. Four years till the end of the century. What has changed? I was asking the same question 30 years ago. Anything has changed? Nothing. Nothing? I was writing then: I see only one goal – Knowledge, cognizance. I was having then one goal: to master gravity. Quantum Future moved this goal into the background. Today I am again close to that goal. But what is my plan?
>
> [Skipped technical scientific research to-do list]
>
> What do I need to remember? That in everyday life I do not care about the results. I care about action, no matter what will be the results. But in science matters only results count, not intentions and not action.
>
> Public life -> Action no matter what results
> Scientific life -> Results no matter what actions
>
> In public life: current without resistance.

Then, a day later he wrote:

> 13/5/1996
>
> [Skipped to-do list, preparing for power games in the Institute.]
>
> It will be a game. I need to remember that results are not important. What is important is to be awake, to be aware, to see what is dark. Jim is telling me that dragons need to be rebuked. Which means I need to be awake. Not to be daydreaming. I need to be superconducting. Therefore I am not conspiring, I am nice to people, yet I am telling them the truth. It all comes from the

observation that fighting the evil takes from me the energy. The energy that I need for other things.

I need to remember what is the most important. And the most important is my work. Work on what? That's the question.

[Skipped to-do lists, progress reports, description of power fights in the Institute over several days.]

Participants: 'Frank', Laura, Sue V

1 **Q**: *(L)* Hello.[1]

2 **Q**: *(L)* Hello.

3 **A**: Hello and hello.

4 **Q**: *(L)* Who do we have with us this evening?

5 **A**: Yxorra.

6 **Q**: *(L)* And where do you transmit from?

7 **A**: Cassiopaea.

8 **Q**: *(L)* That was strange. Can you tell me what was the meaning of the bursting of the pool hose as we began a few minutes ago?

9 **A**: Weakened plastic fibers.

10 **Q**: *(L)* I expect so. But it was so synchronous that it happened at that precise instant!

11 **A**: Coincidence.

12 **Q**: *(L)* Well, I don't think there are coincidences. Who are you kidding?

13 **A**: We are not kidding.

14 **Q**: *(L)* Well, okay. We have several issues just now ...

15 **A**: Flute.

16 **Q**: *(L)* What does that mean?

17 **A**: You have one.

18 **Q**: *(L)* I don't have a flute. Tell me about the flute.

19 **A**: Ponder.

20 **Q**: *(L)* Flute as in playing a tune? Another clue?

21 **A**: No.

22 **Q**: *(L)* And you want me to stop and ponder this right now? Well, you play music on a flute. Usually you play happy music on a flute.

23 **A**: Not point. On or not.

24 **Q**: *(L)* You guys are being really obscure tonight. Is flute significant in some way?

25 **A**: Maybe.

26 **Q**: *(L)* Is there another word or two you can give me for a clue?

27 **A**: D.

28 **Q**: *(L)* Fluted?

29 **A**: Yes.

30 **Q**: *(L)* Does 'fluted' have anything to do with 'grooving'?

31 **A**: Columns.

32 **Q**: *(L)* What columns are we talking about?

33 **A**: Ionic.

---

[1]At the exact instant the planchette began to move, the outflow hose from the pool pump burst and began to shoot water straight into the air, making the sound of a downpour on the roof of the house. We all rushed out to see, a temporary repair was made, and we came back in and settled to begin again.

34 **Q:** *(L)* Why are we talking about Ionic fluted columns?

35 **A:** Because they are a link to previous direct contact between humans and density 4 STO!

36 **Q:** *(L)* Okay, Ionic columns fluted and grooved ...

37 **A:** Plastic hoses, fluted and grooved.

38 **Q:** *(L)* Well, you are getting more and more obscure. How do we establish this direct link between us and 4th density STO through the concept of fluting, and grooving, and columns?

39 **A:** Magnetic telemetry profile.[2]

40 **Q:** *(L)* Are you suggesting that the hose with the water rushing through it can transmit something from 4th density STO to us?

41 **A:** Transceive.[3]

42 **Q:** *(L)* The original Ionic column structure was a hollow tube?

43 **A:** Not the point.

44 **Q:** *(L)* It is the fluting, grooving and spiralling that are important?

45 **A:** Yes.

46 **Q:** *(L)* Okay, once you mentioned that I ought to move the pool and install a maze, or spiral. Well, I am hoping to get some money from the insurance company soon, and I was thinking about putting in an in-ground pool as part of my improvements. Couldn't I have the spiral inlaid in the bottom of the pool in tile?

47 **A:** Good. Suggest that you install a triple Ionic column with top beam and base, as the Romans and Greeks did,[4] near the deep end. Two-sided triangle when seen from above, flat top of beam, no gables. 1.3 meters between bases of the three columns. Columns 1.6 meters tall. Base set at 30 degree angle. Center column placed to the east of the pool. Use pure spiral, counterclockwise, corresponding to northern hemisphere of the planet.

48 **Q:** *(L)* Okay, once we have set this up, what is it going to do for us?

49 **A:** Empower 4th through 6th density STO channel transceiver.

50 **Q:** *(L)* Well, I guess I need to make some really big bucks to do this!

51 **A:** Yes.

52 **Q:** *(L)* Well, will I be able to do this soon?

53 **A:** That is up to you. If you follow guidance, yes.

---

[2] "Telemetry is the automated communications process by which measurements are made and other data collected at remote or inaccessible points and transmitted to receiving equipment for monitoring and analysis. The word is derived from Greek roots: *tele* = remote, and *metron* = measure." (Wikipedia, "Telemetry")

[3] Transmit and receive.

[4] Are the Cs suggesting that it was the ancient Romans and Greeks who had direct contact with 4D STO?

[5] The story of D4, as we called him, aka 'Blue Resonant Human' or BRH, aka Brother Blue,, unfolded as unmitigated tragedy. He was a major figure in online ufological circles at that time. His handle was sort of a humorous dig at those who followed the Mayan calendar. Blue, as I began to call him, and I hit it off immediately, and I have entire disks full of email discussions we carried on through the years 1996

54 **Q**: *(L)* Okay, Blue Resonant Human, aka D4,[5] wanted me to ask a question for him. He has recently been in touch with a guy who claims to be a magician after the ilk of Aleister Crowley ...

55 **A**: D4 has not followed our guidance. If D4 seeks answers, it is not wise for him to ignore "leads," and seek inappropriate pathways instead!

56 **Q**: *(L)* Well ... there is nothing I can do. He keeps sending me stuff from Cosmic Awareness and says, "Gee, I wish the Cs could churn out stuff like this ..." And yet, this Cosmic Awareness talked a lot about 1996 being the year when there was going to be a mass landing and a bunch of other stuff that obviously did *not* happen ... so, what do you want here? Verbose and fancy, or clues that must be worked out? It is incredibly frustrating! Why would we want to churn out crap like that?

57 **A**: Push the man's buttons.

58 **Q**: *(L)* Well, what do you mean?

59 **A**: Mount Palomar.[6]

60 **Q**: *(L)* Oh, you really want him to go out to Mount Palomar?

61 **A**: And no, his contact is not a magician ... Lay off the mind-altering substances, D4, or else you will lose it!!!

62 **Q**: *(L)* But, D4 says that he no longer uses drugs, so what do you mean?

63 **A**: Ask D4. When you say "drugs are bad," do you expect those who want you to like them to admit to partaking?

64 **Q**: *(L)* Of course not. I guess I am too hard on that subject. Now, as you know, [my ex] was here earlier and we had a discussion. I would like to know if there is any chance that he will be able to open his mind and get help.

65 **A**: Open.

66 **Q**: *(L)* He really needs help. Is there anything that you can tell me that will ease my mind?

67 **A**: Worry not.

68 **Q**: *(L)* I know you say that, but sometimes it is really *hard*! Okay, once we build our little columns and pool and other toys, what then ought we to do once we are in this pool?

69 **A**: Up to you.

70 **Q**: *(L)* Any particular exercises?

---

until he disappeared; my last email from him was on 20 July 2009. Basically, it seems that he lost his mind. The last few emails were utterly tragic.

In the very early days, when I was attacked by the crowd on Mike Lindemann's ISCNI discussion board for daring to suggest that aliens might not have our best interests at heart, Blue jumped to my defense, and I witnessed words being used in a way I had never thought possible – literally like swords. The Lindemann harpies fled in terror, and I decided that participating in their discussions was a waste of time and energy. But Blue and I chatted on, and I have him to thank for many, many enlightening posts. I was naive in the extreme, and he undertook to protect me and educate me in matters that were crucial to my survival. We had a number of long phone conversations, and Blue attended a few sessions with Cs via telephone. He will come up again, so I'll leave it at this for the moment.

[6] A few people have made much of this 'Mount Paolomar' clue but I think it was specific for BRH and related to some of his doings, meetings with strange and dangerous characters and so forth.

71 **A:** No.

72 **Q:** *(L)* Just *be* in the pool?

73 **A:** Yes.

74 **Q:** *(L)* And then what?

75 **A:** Wait and see!

76 **Q:** *(L)* You are just making my night! *(S)* I don't want to sound paranoid, but all the reports about mind programming ... is it as widespread as we have been lead to believe? That it could be the guy next door, and a certain color, or word or sound could set them off?

77 **A:** Vague.

78 **Q:** *(L)* That's not exactly vague. What is the percentage of programmed people?[7]

79 **A:** 2 out of every 100.

80 **Q:** *(L)* How many are programmed by human means?

81 **A:** 12 per cent of the .02 per cent.

82 **Q:** *(L)* So, out of every 1,000 people, there are 20 that are programmed, and 18 of these are programmed by aliens, as in 4th density STS?

83 **A:** Understand that 4th density is physical, indeed. You are drifting further and further toward an ethereal only perception/theoretical position.

84 **Q:** *(L)* You are saying that the humans working on these kinds of things ... and ...

85 **A:** No, Laura, we are saying that there is really a very strong "nuts and bolts" reality to this phenomenon, and don't ignore it![8]

86 **Q:** *(L)* Gotcha! We were watching television, and they showed a video of a man and his daughter who videotaped a very large object in the sky, and it was there for a long time, and I also understand that someone else taped it from another location. It was a long, white, tubular object. It was estimated to be about a mile long, because they figured this out by the perspectives from the two tapes, sort of by parallax, and it had moving lights on it, and it just hovered, or sat there for a very long time. What in the world was this thing?

87 **A:** A "mother" ship of Orion STS scanning vectors of the reality continuum fabric.

88 **Q:** *(L)* Well, they talked about a report of a similar happening at this very same spot, only it was 78 years previous to this. Was there a connection?

89 **A:** Yes. Space/time coordinates linkage.

90 **Q:** *(L)* Was this ship doing anything other than what you have said?

91 **A:** No.

92 **Q:** *(L)* Does a mother ship carry a lot of small ships?

93 **A:** Yes.

94 **Q:** *(L)* How many can be carried in one mother ship?

---

[7] *The Wave* 18

[8] What was missing from our understanding was the broad, overall, influence of society and culture as programming agents. Such systems can be created and maintained by a small elite, operate totally naturally within the world system, and only limited, direct hyperdimensional influence is even required. But still, having said that, the Cs were pretty emphatic that we should not ignore that there *is* a 'nuts and bolts' reality to 4D STS.

95 **A:** 150,000.

96 **Q:** *(L)* Holy Shi'ite Moslems! What size are they? And, we have to remember that these ships are bigger inside, as a rule, because of some sort of strange principal at that level.

97 **A:** Exactly, remember, there is variability of physicality on 4th density, but not lack of physicality.

98 **Q:** *(L)* There was apparently a sighting in Gulf Breeze either last night or the night before. The triangular ships with the orange lights. Were they human or alien?

99 **A:** Alien.

100 **Q:** *(L)* Who did they belong to?

101 **A:** Same.

102 **Q:** *(L)* Why are there so many kinds of alien ships?

103 **A:** See previous statements. VOP.

104 **Q:** *(L)* Variability of physicality. Okay, I have also been reading about cattle mutilations, that specific parts of the body are taken ...

105 **A:** Rumen.

106 **Q:** *(L)* What is that?

107 **A:** Cattle part.[9]

108 **Q:** *(L)* Why do they take an eyeball? What do they want wth only one eyeball?

109 **A:** Study soul pattern.

110 **Q:** *(L)* Can you study a soul pattern through an eyeball?

111 **A:** Like a tape recorder.

112 **Q:** *(L)* Why do they take part of a lip?

113 **A:** DNA library.

114 **Q:** *(L)* Well, how many eyes and DNA libraries do they need? This is happening a lot.

115 **A:** Some is copycat by "secret government."

116 **Q:** *(L)* I have heard a recent rumor that the Chupacabras makes three puncture marks, and that one of them extends all the way up into the brain. Is this true?

117 **A:** No.

118 **Q:** *(L)* Are the stories being heard from the Southwest and Mexico, and even from South Florida, are they all the Chupacabras?

119 **A:** Some.

120 **Q:** *(L)* How many people in the United States have implants?

121 **A:** 2 per cent.

122 **Q:** *(L)* Why did I lose my voice recently?

123 **A:** Inflamed vocal cords. Suggest you go buy, then read, Oeschler book for enhanced learning. Okay for now, Goodnight.

End of Session

---

[9] The rumen, also known as a paunch, forms the larger part of the reticulorumen, which is the first chamber in the alimentary canal of ruminant animals.

May 27, 1996

I was slowly, but surely, pulling out of my depression and illness following my separation and then Sandra's death. After the Cs had lectured me about 'portals' and my knee-jerk reactions, that I should not 'close doors' on people, Sue attended another session despite the fact that things were a bit tense where she was concerned. Terry and Jan had pretty much stopped attending sessions because of her presence. She had called and talked about the forthcoming visit of her sister and I was pretty astonished at how afraid she seemed to be of this woman. In any event, I decided to just ask about things that were not too sensitive.

Frank, of course, was happy as a clam that I was getting a divorce. He now had the run of the house, and I was so wounded that it wouldn't have taken much to push me over the edge. Frank's plans are quite evident in the following session, and they included getting his hands on Sue's inheritance, and getting Tom French out of the picture. Nevertheless, in spite of the powerful emotional skewing that Frank was producing, the Cs were still able to utilize his agenda to get a message through to me.

Participants: 'Frank', Laura, Sue V

1 **Q:** *(L)* Hello.

2 **A:** Hello.

3 **Q:** *(L)* Who do we have with us tonight?

4 **A:** Soroca.

5 **Q:** *(L)* And where are you from?

6 **A:** Cassiopaea.

7 **Q:** *(L)* We would like to ask some more questions about the architectural project mentioned the other night.[1] We were given the height and distance apart of the three-column structure. Would it be okay to build this on the perimeter of the existing pool?

8 **A:** No. You must wait until you have the financial resources to construct an inground pool. The spiral must be below ground level by at least 1 meter, must be constructed of blue, gold ceramic tile perfectly cut and even. Columns cannot be purchased as prefabricated. Must be constructed onsite. Cap should be 18 centimeters in height,

---
[1]Previous session, 25 May 1996.

2 meters in length, same dimensions for cap and base.

9 Q: *(L)* Can or should we do this with our own hands?

10 A: Hire a contractor ... you are not adequately skilled.

11 Q: *(L)* How many grooves in each column?

12 A: Diameter of columns should be 10 to 14 centimeters, width of fluting should be 2 centimeters. Use illustrations of authentic ionic columns as a guide.

13 Q: *(L)* The counterclockwise spiral of tile, how many turns?

14 A: Turns not important. Width should be 1.6 meters.

15 Q: *(L)* Blue tile with gold border?

16 A: Mixed blue and gold.

17 Q: *(L)* Blue with specks of gold?

18 A: Close. Translucent.

19 Q: *(L)* Is azure an appropriate blue?

20 A: Close.

21 Q: *(L)* Should anything be incorporated into the cement mix to pour the columns?

22 A: No.

23 Q: *(L)* Should the columns be hollow and used for flowing water?

24 A: No. Place fountain or hydrable pond in front of columns.

25 Q: *(L)* Pool shape: square on one end then rounded at one end. Rectangular with a curved end. [Planchette is drawing shape of pool.] (Curved end to follow guide of columns at end).

26 A: The fountain should be in between and the spiral in the middle of the pool.

27 Q: *(L)* Are you having fun designing a 3rd density pool?

28 A: 6th density is always "fun!"

29 Q: *(L)* What about the turns on the spirals at the top of the columns?

30 A: Up to you.

31 Q: *(L)* Is this pool meant to be built here, on this property?[2]

32 A: Up to you.

33 Q: *(L)* Well ... *(S)* Had you planned on moving? *(L)* Well, I hadn't planned on it, but that is a strange answer. I guess I will do whatever presents itself as the right thing to do. *(S)* Well, you have to get the money first ...

34 A: Sue, invest now![3]

35 Q: *(S)* What should I invest in?

36 A: Market.

37 Q: *(S)* Penny stocks? Should I sell my gold?

38 A: No.

39 Q: *(S)* I could get advances on my credit cards ... What kinds of stocks?

40 A: All the reference materials you need are at your disposal. Magazines, newsletters, "papers," etc.

---

[2] *The Wave* 47

[3] My feelings about the 'investment' advice that came from Cs now and again was that it was mostly Frank who was convinced that he was an investing genius of some sort. He spent a great deal of time reading about this topic and complaining that he had no money to invest, that if he did, he would be a millionaire. So, take all of this exchange with a grain or two of salt.

41 **Q:** *(S)* I am getting an investment magazine, but I haven't really been reading it because of everything else ...

42 **A:** Is "everything else" earning you money?

43 **Q:** *(L)* Okay guys, you gave advice before that Sue did not follow, can you be more specific now that her situation is changed?

44 **A:** If we did that, she would balk.

45 **Q:** *(S)* I would not balk!

46 **A:** Yes you would!

47 **Q:** *(S)* In order to go to Argus tomorrow ...

48 **A:** We did not say to go to Argus tomorrow. "Now" means without unreasonable delay. The reference materials as well as networking will provide you with all the answers you need. [This was delivered *very* fast and strong!] Use your mind to find low-priced stocks in the areas of conservation, environmental protection and medical, telecommunication and computer technology ... Also, information processing, such as software development, etc... Precious metals and related is a good area too.

49 **Q:** *(S)* Well, I was brought up to not borrow money and to keep all the bills paid first ... then if there is anything left over ...

50 **A:** Sue, for heaven's sake, why limit yourself? When you exercise your credit lines and use the capital borrowed, as long as you have a steady income, the worst that can happen is you store your money. The best that can happen is that you become wealthy ... So, why sell yourself short?!?

51 **Q:** *(L)* Are you saying that she should extend her credit, use the borrowed capital to invest, and that she will make money?

52 **A:** Yes. Now: All three of you are uniquely oriented toward generating unearned income at a meteoric level.

53 **Q:** *(L)* Is this something that requires an interaction between the three of us, or is it individual?

54 **A:** Are three gold bars worth more than one? Laura! Turn over stones, sell apples, do whatever you have to do to get your computer refitted to accommodate the internet, including the online market system, as soon as absolutely possible!!!!!!

55 **Q:** *(L)* Well, I am not really in a position to spend that money right now! And what do you mean to "turn over stones and sell apples"?

56 **A:** Figures of speech! Do what you have to do ... take care of the mechanics, my Dear, the rest will fall into place ...[4]

57 **Q:** *(L)* Well, I don't know how we got off onto this thing about making money ... what is all of this making of money supposed to do for us? *(S)* Build the pool ...

---

[4]This more or less spontaneous interjection about my online status was odd and only in retrospect does it become apparent that it was the Cs making sure that I made the connection with Ark, which was, at this point, just a bit over a month away. It's also interesting that the Cs mentioned stones and apples since, at present, we live adjacent to a huge apple orchard and have spent many hours removing river stones from our property. The apples are actually growing in what was once an ancient freshwater sea bed loaded with stones!

58 **A**: And other ...

59 **Q**: *(L)* Now, back to some of my other questions: I want to know why Frank used to pound the ground with a stick when he was a child, a habit that caused his parents to think he needed to see a psychiatrist ...[5]

60 **A**: Channel.

61 **Q**: *(L)* But it was such an odd way to go about it. What did this particular activity do to create or alter or modify a channel, or...? *(S)* Maybe he was 'grooving' himself?

62 **A**: All of the above ... Did you not study hypnotic states?

63 **Q**: *(L)* But he described it as such a random rhythm ... the changing ... the running about to pound the ground here and there ...

64 **A**: It was not random.

65 **Q**: *(L)* Was there something on another density that this activity represented?

66 **A**: No, it just opened the channel.

67 **Q**: *(L)* Okay. What is going on with Pat Z? I am just completely baffled by this behavior ...

68 **A**: She thinks you are "out to lunch."[6]

69 **Q**: *(L)* Well ... why?

70 **A**: Her conditioning.

71 **Q**: *(L)* Well, she seems to be going down the tubes fast ...

72 **A**: Yes.

73 **Q**: *(L)* And there is nothing I can do about it ... I feel sorry for her.

74 **A**: She hoped that you would be a money maker for her, and so, she put up with your "eccentricities...."

75 **Q**: *(L)* Well, I sort of figured that out finally.

76 **A**: Beware! Tom French has a similar thought pattern!

77 **Q**: *(L)* I have been thinking that I ought to write to Tom and ask him to just write me *out* of the whole project ...

78 **A**: Suggest you not waste "time" on your suggestion, and make certain it includes all others.

79 **Q**: *(L)* What suggestion? Suggest that I not waste time in contacting Tom?

80 **A**: Yes.

81 **Q**: *(L)* Then I will just e-mail him ...

82 **A**: And.

83 **Q**: *(L)* What do you mean by "include all others"?

84 **A**: Who else has Tom French met through you?[7]

85 **Q**: *(L)* Well ... okay. *(F)* Why were you thinking about that? *(L)* Well, I don't know ... I went to a psychiatrist recently for stress [following break-up of

---

[5] See *Amazing Grace* for a discussion of this activity.

[6] *The Wave* 47

[7] I would say that the attempt to derail Tom French was more of Frank's jealousy coming through. Notice that it comes after an exchange about his early childhood channeling experiences. This was an interesting session since the energies definitely alternated!

[8] I actually didn't go back to the psychologist (not psychiatrist) because I gave a lot of thought to what he had initially said to me: that there are just areas of the mind that one should cordon off and not go there. I didn't think that was very helpful.

marriage] ... and I am wondering if going again is going to help me deal with all the things going on right now ...

86 **A**: Yes ...[8]

87 **Q**: *(L)* Okay, Sue's sister and niece are coming, and I have the feeling that this is going to be a serious disruption?

88 **A**: Yes.

89 **Q**: *(S)* Is there anything I can do to minimize it?

90 **A**: Take control, after all, it is your house!

91 **Q**: *(S)* I know that ...

92 **A**: But you don't do it!!! Okay, folks, Goodnight!

End of Session

Obviously, the Universe had its own plans. We notice that the Cs sent an urgent message in the midst of Frank's favorite subject: stock market investing, which he firmly believed would make him rich if he could only get his hands on some money to invest with. The Cs said: "Laura! Turn over stones, sell apples, do whatever you have to do to get your computer refitted to accommodate the Internet, including the online market system, as soon as absolutely possible!!!!!! ... Do what you have to do ... take care of the mechanics, my Dear, the rest will fall into place ..."

Well, since Frank was so taken with the idea of the stock market and being in control of an investment portfolio in real time via the Internet, he persuaded Sue to pay for the computer upgrade that made it possible for me to do more than just run a mail program. So we see how the Cs utilized Frank's greed and semantic aphasia to get me online, which enabled Ark and me to connect exactly 40 days later.

June 1, 1996

This session followed a rather heated exchange between Frank and myself. He had started another of his 'pity me' rants and I had just told him in a joking way that if he started on that again I was going to throw something at him. He became all upset that I had used a word describing a physical act of violence. I pointed out that the violence was only words spoken in defending myself against his words which were, effectively, doing violence to me because they were draining my energy. What was more, it was merely a metaphor, and he knew I really wasn't going to throw anything at him. But he just wanted to argue, so I suggested that sometimes, one had to do or say something to make the point. What is interesting about this session is the fact that it generally contradicts the information given in the session about Frank's many rants as being his way of "fighting back".[1] Which, of course, raises the question of why it was okay for Frank to fight back with words, but it was not okay for me to do it! This session might relate back to the previous session where it was suggested that I ask Tom French to cancel his writing project about me and my work. It was becoming abundantly clear that Frank was extremely jealous of this and his jealousy came through not only in his verbal harassment of me, but also in this session. The fact that we were not giving him star billing over all the other participants as 'The Channel' seems to have begun to prey on Frank's mind at some point. All attempts to move the channeling to trance format with Frank channeling alone were rejected, though we most certainly gave it a spin a few times. Our vigilance to keep the material as uncorrupted as possible worked for the most part even when he was direct channeling. So, keep in mind, what went on here still brought forth some valuable information!

---

[1]See sessions 7 November 1994 and 2 January 1995.

Participants: 'Frank', Laura, Sue V

Q: *(L)* Hello.

A: Hello.

Q: *(L)* Who do we have with us this evening?

A: Viror.

Q: *(L)* And where do you transmit from?

A: Cassiopaea.

Q: *(L)* Frank and I would like to have a comment on our dispute.[2]

A: Ask.

Q: *(F)* I don't know what to ask. *(L)* Well, Frank says that violence is *never* an appropriate response to words no matter how hurtful the words may be.

A: Okay.

Q: *(L)* I say that under some circumstances, it may be the only response.

A: Why do you say that?

Q: *(L)* Because there do exist situations where words are used repeatedly to harm another. One example is the Nazi propaganda machine. If someone had shot Goebbels, it might have saved a lot of people from dying.

A: No.

Q: *(L)* Well, of course. There would have been someone else. Still, the point is, words can be used to destroy, and words of power can be used to kill. Sometimes words can be a lot more hurtful to the soul than physical acts.

A: Not directly.

Q: *(L)* Well, directly, or indirectly, it still amounts to the same thing.

A: No.

---
[2] *The Wave* 41

Q: *(L)* Well, I know you are not going to agree with me.

A: This is a subject that demands further exploration, in order to bring about a definitive answer.

Q: *(L)* Go ahead. Explain it to me.

A: Words only have power if the receiver believes they do.

Q: *(L)* But, in many cases, that belief exists.

A: The power to control belief lies exclusively within the receiver.

Q: *(L)* Let me put it this way: Frank often says things that are not precisely soothing to the soul, to say the least. Most often, I ignore them. But, sometimes I am not in an ignoring mood, and my response is no more violent toward him than his toward me. I merely speak metaphorically. When I do, I am only saying "Stop doing that!" in a figurative way. But, he finds this to be as irritating to him as what he says that irritates me ...

A: And ...

Q: *(L)* Well, that is about it. I have lately been verbally attacked by numerous individuals ... so I am not in a mood to tolerate much in this line from those around me.

A: And if this irritates you, it is because you allow it to.

Q: *(L)* Fine and dandy. And it is true, and I know it. Which is why I am beginning to think that I ought to simply do nothing, because my feelings are too sensitive.

A: And do you really believe that that is an unalterable condition?

June 1, 1996

31 **Q**: *(L)* Well, why should I be the one who is obliged to become less sensitive, and other people are not obliged to become more thoughtful about what they say?

32 **A**: You cannot control others.

33 **Q**: *(L)* I don't want to control anyone. I am just saying that the obvious thing is for me to simply withdraw into my own little world of reading and thinking and writing, and if nothing ever comes of any of it, it is utterly immaterial to me.

34 **A**: That is your choice, but not a wise one!!!

35 **Q**: *(L)* Well, you say that, but it is, as several people have pointed out to me, only since we have begun this channeling project that all these dreadful things have happened in my life. My life is a shambles!

36 **A**: "Dreadful is subjective."[3]

37 **Q**: *(L)* I would say that the physical things that have happened to me, the collapse of my marriage, the things that have happened to my children, are pretty damn dreadful, subjectively or otherwise!

38 **A**: Before these changes began to manifest, you were deeper into the "deadly illusion" than you are now. Emergence is, by its very nature, uncomfortable. But, it has and will, empower you, we promise!!!!!!!!

39 **Q**: *(L)* It is a very trying time now. I am having a difficult time just coping.

40 **A**: And there have been others, and will be others, but that does not mean that the rewards will be slight.

41 **Q**: *(L)* Well ...

42 **A**: You are on a path of destiny, and there is no turning back now.

43 **Q**: *(S)* What happened in specific? *(L)* Well, I was trying to explain some of the material to several people, and the end result was that they decided that I was possessed and that the C's were evil because they say that we have to figure things out ourselves in order to graduate to the next level. Including my husband. [In short, I experienced a whole lot of verbal abuse.]

44 **A**: Why does this bother you? It does not bother us. They can all decide that we are the "Queens of Satan," if they wish. It is free will.

45 **Q**: *(L)* I don't like the implied hardness ... I am not a hard person.

46 **A**: It is not hardness. The "feelings" you describe are related to ego, and by relation, pride, two things that were deliberately implanted into the 3rd density human psyche by the 4th density STS 309,000 years ago, as you measure time. Refer to the transcripts with regard to DNA alteration and the occipital ridge. Believe it or not, you, Laura, will be rid of these, eventually. It is not what some individuals respond to you that matters. It is sharing the information that counts. Also, remember, these persons do not perceive your feelings and sensitivities as keenly as you

---

[3] *The Wave* 5

[4] That was all fine and good, and I certainly couldn't argue with it in principle. However, I was having some difficulty understanding how feeling hurt after being attacked for sharing some of the Cs material was related to ego and pride. What is more, this didn't seem like the Cs I was used to. Indeed, there comes a time when

do, nor do you perceive theirs, likewise.⁴

Q: *(L)* There is someone who wants to ask some questions ...

A: We are not finished with this subject. Also, it is important to note that, in most cases in which you have suffered "attack" from those on the internet, you were not directly conveying the information we have given to you. You were presenting thoughts that you claimed as your own, or knowledge that you have gathered strictly through your own efforts, thus, it was responded to in kind. This you must expect if you are going to plant the bulk of the credit upon yourself, then you open up yourself to direct criticism. This is not wise if you are not prepared for negative reactions. Third density beings will always perceive knowledge that is being given to them before they are ready to receive it as "preaching," and they resent this because of the very same ego-related issues we discussed earlier. So, suggestion: better to frame knowledge transference with a preamble such as, "this is what was given to me, it is up to you to decide for yourself whether or not you are comfortable with accepting it, or not."

Q: *(L)* Well, that is *not* true, by *any* stretch of the imagination. I don't want to talk about it anymore with you. You are being completely wrong! Talk about

---

a person needs to toughen up, but considering the beating I had been taking for so long, these remarks were singularly cold. Yes, they offered the carrot that "you are on a path of destiny", and "rewards" that were not slight were indicated. But as a general rule, I am on guard against such lures, considering them to be ego hooks. I realize in retrospect that yes, it may be true that there is some destined activity, but the entire interaction with Frank was designed to divert that destiny to some other agenda, and to prevent the real destiny, if there is one, and whatever it may be.

⁵What was so shocking about the above remarks was that it was entirely and altogether untrue. In fact, it had always been as a direct result of presenting the raw material that I had suffered attack! I was most definitely directly conveying the information, and I was most definitely not presenting thoughts that I claimed as my own! And that's a cold hard fact because I still have the emails and message board discussions from that period. There is no doubt whatsoever that this was Frank using the board to express what he believed to be true. He felt that he was not being sufficiently revered as the channel, and this led him to create wild theories in his mind that everyone was conspiring against him to 'cut him out' of something, including credit for being the channel. What is more, for a very long time I presented all material as simply from the 'Group', with no names designated at all. I was so stunned by this attack from the Cs that I knew it was not them at all and I terminated the session.

But again, let me point out to the perspicacious reader that, even though there was skewing, again, there were remarks that were made that were right on the money, most especially those comments about DNA alteration and our need to hone our skills as warriors by divesting ourselves of self-importance in the sense of being subject to offense. Indeed, when I am offended, it is an effect of self-importance. But in the above case, I was most definitely not guilty of the offenses for

assumptions!⁵ End of Session

Interestingly, on the same day that this session took place, Ark wrote in his journal:

1/6/1996

Life is difficult. Around me is the politics. I am banging my head against a brick wall. One can hear the bangs. Nothing good comes from all all this rumbling. But it is necessary. It is a normal situation with those who fight in order to accomplish something. They are being discouraged by the environment. That I am making errors? So what? The point is to learn from these errors. The point is to remember:

"Never do as others do. Either do nothing, just go to school, or do something no one else does."

And this is my task. Therefore keep the direction and work full speed.

[Skipped to-do lists]

The following day Ark mentions that he was experimenting with "time traveling in the mind" via meditative reverie:

2/6/1996

Experimenting with time travel: visiting Max Planck in 1930 in Berlin. Drawing, writing. "There are other dimensions". Max Planck is too scared by meeting time traveller. Does not want to talk.

And then he was invited to Florence, which resulted in a brief note:

26/6/1996

What is happening? On Sunday I am going to Florence.

[Skipped to-do list]

---

which I was being blamed.

By now the reader may be getting the idea that sometimes the transmissions were like trying to watch television while someone runs the vacuum cleaner (no pun intended!). The degree of interference can vary by the position of the vacuum relative to the television, as well as other factors including the strength of the broadcast signal. So, even though the picture might get very snowy or distorted, the real picture can still be seen and interpreted.

June 9, 1996

As I mentioned in a previous session, I had gone to see a psychologist in an effort to come to terms with the terrible suffering I was going through as a consequence of my decision to end my marriage. Not receiving anything particularly helpful from that quarter, I turned to my library in search of answers. My eye fell on a book that had been on the shelf for a while but which I had never opened: William Chittick's *The Sufi Path of Knowledge*. I took it down and began to read it off and on. It didn't take long for me to realize that much of what the Sufis thought and taught – at least that which came from Ibn al-Arabi – was very, very similar to the cosmology and anthropology of the Cs. I talked to Frank about it to some extent, and he appeared interested that there was an ancient source that agreed with what we were receiving in this experiment. I asked about it in this session, but only after trying to deal with a list of questions that had been sent to me to ask the Cs as a result of my sharing transcripts on an online discussion.

The first part of this session was extremely unpleasant in feeling and tone. It could have been partially due to the nature of the questions sent in by others, but since the Cs were always talking about networking and interacting with people on the internet, and then went after me for 'self-importance', it seems odd that they would give such answers to persons writing in with questions. There was a certain feeling of impatience with ignorance that I felt was emanating from Frank, who appears to have dominated this session – probably because my own energy was rather low. Perhaps he exerted some control over the short answers – which were true enough as far as they went – as a way of covertly lobbying for his aim to act as trance channel.

The second part of this session was truly amazing. After I asked my Ibn al-Arabi question, the whole atmosphere changed. I felt that I gained energy as the session went on, which counterbalanced Frank's negativity.

Participants: 'Frank', Laura

Q: *(L)* Hello.

A: Hello.

Q: *(L)* Who do we have with us this evening?

A: Ehou.

Q: *(L)* And where are you transmitting from?

A: Cassiopaea.

Q: *(L)* I have several questions that have been submitted by other people ...

A: Ask.

Q: *(L)* The first one is from Phillip P., for whom we have asked a couple of questions in the past. He wrote and called to tell me that his sister had hand prints, bruises, and the description was very similar to the ones I saw on Scarlett H___'s legs.[1] Also, the sister had three little puncture marks in a triangular pattern on her ankle. He would like to know what happened to her.

A: What does Phillip think?

Q: *(L)* Well, he just wanted to have a brief run-down on this. He thinks she was abducted, and I tend to agree.

A: The point here is that learning involves reaching the stage where confirmation by a third party is no longer needed, once one has adequate knowledge.[2]

Q: *(L)* I know that. But, Phillip just wanted to know that he could ask a question and get an answer specifically for him. I guess he just wanted to think that somebody out there in the cosmos cares about Phillip P. and his sister.

---

[1] When I wrote about this in *The Wave*, Volume 2, Chapter 14, I mentioned that I was changing the individual's name to a pseudonym. I wrote:

> I decided to tell pretty much the whole story that was on my mind, changing only the names of those involved for protection of their privacy.
>
> One problem remained: three of the names of the people involved were part and parcel of the Symbol System under discussion. So much a part, in fact, that one of my children contracted an illness with the name of one of these people. I was thinking how I was going to convey this dynamic and still use a pseudonym for this person. I finally resolved it by finding another name that was both a disease and a woman's first name.
>
> As I was writing about the situation, I was asking myself some questions about this particular person's role (and we are going to call her Candida, or Candy for short) in the soon-to-be-revealed bizarre drama.

As you see above, her name was actually Scarlett, and the disease my daughter contracted was scarlet fever which was quite a bit more dramatic than candida.

See also *The Wave*, Chapter 19, for a discussion of the bruises on Scarlett's arms and legs. In that chapter, I also include a transcript of the hypnosis session following Scarlett's alleged abduction.

[2] Here I ask why the Cs would give such a response when they were otherwise so anxious for us to connect with people online?

[3] If the Cs were interested in winning friends and influencing people, this was certainly not the way to go about it! What is more, there are other places in the transcripts that contradict this statement.

A: Nobody does.³

Q: *(L)* Nobody cares about Phillip and his sister?

A: Nobody "cares" about individual units of the universal consciousness.

Q: *(L)* We realize that, but we, as units in bodies of flesh ...

A: One must get past the idea that there is some sort of "cheerleading squad" attached to individual consciousness units if one is to progress ... it just doesn't work that way!

Q: *(L)* Well, does this mean to just forget the rest of the questions?

A: No. All questions have great value if the answers are comprehended.

Q: *(L)* Is there anything you *can* tell Phillip for his sister? What are the three puncture marks on her ankle?

A: You know this.⁴

Q: *(L)* Was this a sampling device, or an implanting device, an energy drain, or a monitor?

A: Maybe.

Q: *(L)* Since this also happened with Scarlett – the four-fingered hand prints on the backs of the calves – what kind of beings leave these marks?

A: We are regressing.⁵

Q: *(L)* I just wanted to ask a question for the guy, get something, and go on to more interesting subjects, for God's sake! I don't think this is worth the amount of time and energy that it is taking. I don't even think it will be useful to the guy. I just want an answer for the guy!

A: And you have one!

Q: *(L)* Phillip has another question for this David, who would like to know what happened to them in January 1991, outside of Athens, Ohio; and who was 'Tim'? They saw a UFO speed past them and stop behind a hill and they have never seen Tim since.

A: Very vague and directionless as presented.

Q: *(L)* That is all I have on that, so let's move on. Who was Tim?

A: Pick up.

Q: *(L)* They saw a UFO speed down towards them and then stop behind a hill. What do you mean by "pick up"?

A: Someone who was.

Q: *(L)* Picked up as in picked up by the UFO?

A: No.

Q: *(L)* Picked up as in sexual or a hitchhiker?

A: The latter.

Q: *(L)* Did Tim have any connection to the UFO?

A: Yes and no.

Q: *(L)* What is the 'yes' part?

A: Everyone has some connection to UFOs.

Q: *(L)* What is the 'no', that he had no connection to this one in specific?

A: In the sense that your inquiry suggests.

Q: *(L)* Was there an abduction that took place when they saw this?

---

⁴Notice that in the previous session, I had been castigated for 'independence' and here I'm being castigated for not just answering the guy's question.

⁵The Cs were definitely *not* being nice here.

46 **A**: No.

47 **Q**: *(L)* Did any unusual event occur in connection to this UFO?

48 **A**: No.

49 **Q**: *(L)* Was what they saw a UFO?

50 **A**: No.[6]

51 **Q**: *(L)* Well, that settles that. Bob Tietz, publisher of Bill Baldwin's book, writes and asks: "What can the C's tell me about Dr. Mahlon Loomis? Have the C's been in contact with him?"

52 **A**: No.

53 **Q**: *(L)* Alright. If the Cs are not in contact, do you know who is?

54 **A**: These questions are difficult to deal with because the questioner is making assumptions.

55 **Q**: *(L)* Is the assumption that there is anything or anyone at higher levels in contact with this Dr. Mahlon Loomis?

56 **A**: Yes. And there are no such.

57 **Q**: *(L)* Is Dr. Loomis putting him on?

58 **A**: No, he is "out to lunch."[7]

59 **Q**: *(L)* Okay! Next question: "Do the C's know the whereabouts of one Jessica Goode?"[8]

60 **A**: Yes, deceased.

61 **Q**: *(L)* You just said that Dr. Loomis is out to lunch – can you explain the process whereby he is given data?

62 **A**: This happens to those who fall prey to lower-level contacts, believing them to be otherwise.[9]

63 **Q**: *(L)* Bob asks: "Do the C's know of an entity claiming to be a Sirian named Anitra?"

64 **A**: Yes.

65 **Q**: *(L)* "If so, what can they tell me about the information that Anitra, or any Sirian, is communicating?"

66 **A**: Hocus pocus.

67 **Q**: *(L)* Tell us about the Sirians?

68 **A**: There aren't any.

69 **Q**: *(L)* Why are all these people coming along and claiming to be Sirians?

70 **A**: Why are all these people coming along claiming to be Jesus?

---

[6]It seems to me that the entire exchange was a complete waste of time.

[7]At the time, I had no clue who Mahlon Loomis was. Here are a few assembled snips from his Wikipedia bio:

> Mahlon Loomis (21 July 1826 – 13 October 1886) was a dentist, the inventor of artificial teeth (patent #10,847 May 2, 1854), and the **earliest inventor of wireless communication** (patent #129,971 July 30, 1872). He claimed to have transmitted signals in October 1866 between two Blue Ridge Mountain-tops 14 miles apart in Virginia, using kites as antennas, but without having identified the names of independent witnesses. Loomis was actively promoting his idea of using atmospheric electricity for telegraph communication. Loomis noted that transmission was possible only when the kites were flown to the same altitude above ground, which seemed to confirm his hypothesis that he was completing a DC circuit through layers of the atmosphere that he hypothesized carried such currents.

[8]I have no clue who this Jessica Goode was/is.

[9]Obviously, the Cs were out to lunch on this one!

71 **Q:** *(L)* "Do you know an Andalusian named Lucatron?"

72 **A:** Yes.

73 **Q:** *(L)* "Who is this Andalusian, and what can you tell him about the information coming from this source?"

74 **A:** This "Andalusian" is delusional.[10]

75 **Q:** *(L)* "Can you express an opinion about Swedish genes, and any specific properties of these genes?"

76 **A:** Yes. They tend to produce blonds with the greatest of proficiency.[11]

77 **Q:** *(L)* "Are there any specific properties to those genes that are of specific interest to aliens or extraterrestrials?"

78 **A:** Only that which we have already told you, that this was the last "race" to be seeded on Earth in 3rd density.

79 **Q:** *(L)* Okay. D4 is apparently still mucking about in the mire a bit. His questions were: "1) I had a very serious chat with God, in which I asked the following questions. First, who is this Melchizedek fellow and why is Jesus said to be a priest after the order of Melchizedek? Who was this Melchizedek who was said to have received tithes from Abraham?"

80 **A:** False prophet.

81 **Q:** *(L)* "Why is Jesus described as being a priest after the order of Melchizedek?"

82 **A:** We told you that 70 percent of the Bible is false.

83 **Q:** *(L)* Well, 70 percent would equal an amount that could consist of the entire Old Testament.

84 **A:** Yes.

85 **Q:** *(L)* Did Abraham pay tithes to Melchizedek?

86 **A:** No.

87 **Q:** *(L)* Did a Melchizedek live at the time of the patriarch Abraham?

88 **A:** Yes.

89 **Q:** *(L)* It was said that he was the priest king of Salem, which became Jerusalem, and that he had neither father nor mother, and that he came into being by his own will. Are any of these parts of the story correct?

90 **A:** No.

91 **Q:** *(L)* D4's next question: "What did Paul see during his out-of-body experience, and why were these things not 'lawful for a man to speak'?"

92 **A:** Jesus said: "Give to Caesar that which is Caesar's."

93 **Q:** *(L)* How does that apply to this question?

94 **A:** Ponder for learning.[12]

95 **Q:** *(L)* D4 asks: "What did the seven peals of thunder say and why was John commanded to seal up the things which

---

[10] The Cs continue with giving an example of how *not* to win friends and influence people!

[11] This response was downright sarcastic and insulting. Yes, it may have been true – as many of the answers the Cs were giving in this session apparently were in some sense – but they were given in such a cold and abrupt way.

[12] This response, in view of my research into the Jesus question over the past ten years, is particularly interesting. As some of my readers know, I think there is good evidence that the mythical Jesus of Nazareth was a story based in large part on the life and death of Julius Caesar and that it was Paul who made that connection.

the seven peals of thunder have spoken?" Well, he would know a lot about these things if he would read *Noah*.

96 **A:** This is an exercise in futility!

97 **Q:** *(L)* What, asking these questions, or dealing with these people?

98 **A:** There is much hope for D4, but he must discover it for himself.[13]

99 **Q:** *(L)* Okay. Let's toss that. My question is: Is the information we are receiving similar to what al-Arabi calls an 'opening'?

100 **A:** Yes.

101 **Q:** *(L)* You say that you are unified thought forms in the realm of knowledge.[14]

102 **A:** Yes.

103 **Q:** *(L)* Al-Arabi describes unified thought forms as being the 'names of God'. His explication seems to be so identical to things you tell us that I wonder ...[15]

104 **A:** We are all the names of God. Remember, this is a conduit. This means that both termination/origination points are of equal value, importance.

105 **Q:** *(L)* So, it is a blending of the aspects of God?

106 **A:** No.

107 **Q:** *(L)* What do you mean? Does this mean that we are a part of this?

108 **A:** Yes.

109 **Q:** *(L)* So, it has to do with ...

110 **A:** Don't deify us. And, be sure all others with which you communicate understand this too!

111 **Q:** *(L)* What quality in us, what thing, enabled us to make contact? Because, obviously a lot of people try and get garbage.

112 **A:** You asked.

113 **Q:** *(L)* A lot of people ask![16]

114 **A:** No they don't, they command.

115 **Q:** *(L)* Well, a lot of people do ask or beg or plead, but they get all discombobulated with the answers.

116 **A:** No, they command. Think about it. You did not beg or plead ... that is commanding. After J___ W___ left, purification began.[17]

117 **Q:** *(L)* This recent 'awakening' or period of seeing things with such clarity, as they really were, and the whole picture of the interactions between people and how truly ugly it can be ... I plunged into a terrible depression. I needed to get my balance from seeing so much all at once. Can you explain to me what was going on?[18]

---

[13]See session 25 May 1996.

[14]*Secret History* 12; *The Wave* 17, 26, 46

[15]I had the feeling at this moment, when I asked the question about al-Arabi, that the energy of the session changed to a more positive line.

[16]*The Wave* 71

[17]A former participant who was very gung-ho on Zecharia Sitchin.

[18]What I wrote about this in *The Wave*, Volume 2, was the following:

> Taking my first breath in the new reality, I made a conscious choice to limit my participation in this deception foisted on mankind. I consciously decided that ... I was no longer going to lie to myself about reality at all.
> When I looked at a flower I was going to remember the decay and death in the

118 **A**: Growth.

119 **Q**: *(L)* I tried to share this perception with other people, and almost without exception, when I said to people that I was finally seeing things in their true state and it was *not* a pretty picture, they all said, "Well, you are obviously seeing this through the eyes of some major spirit possession!" Why would they say this?

120 **A**: First of all, it is not correct to perceive "everything in such darkness and gloom, etc." That is merely the result of a cocoon of falsehood being removed. Celebrate the balance. Don't mourn the death of an illusion of an imbalance.

121 **Q**: *(L)* Where do I go from here? Where do we all go?

122 **A**: Everywhere.

123 **Q**: *(L)* We were talking earlier about sleeping and dreaming. It seems to me that sleeping cannot be an evolutionary benefit, because sleeping would not evolve as something beneficial, because when you are asleep, you are completely vulnerable to any munching monster that passes by. Therefore, it is not conducive to evolution to sleep. And, I think there is some other reason for this thing we call sleeping. Obviously it is not to rest the brain, because the brain is as active asleep as when awake. And the bodily functions ...

124 **A**: Bodies may get munched; souls don't, however!

125 **Q**: *(L)* Okay, yes, but still it makes me think that there is something to this sleeping business that does not meet the eye in strictly physical terms. Nobody seems to know why we sleep. You made a remark once that dreams were a prime opportunity for the implanting of negative information and suggestions. This makes me think that we are even more vulnerable during sleep than previously thought. Are we induced to sleep genetically for the purpose of control by other density beings? Could you comment?

126 **A**: Ask specifics.

127 **Q**: *(L)* Is it essential, in an evolutionary sense, for the human body to sleep?

128 **A**: Yes.

129 **Q**: *(L)* Why is it that carnivores need more sleep than herbivores, and on down?

130 **A**: Physicality, my dear, physicality.

---

soil from which the flower drew its nourishment. When I looked at a cat or a dog, I was going to remember the fleas and parasites and killing and eating of other creatures that goes on all the time in the animal world. When I looked at a beautiful and peaceful lake, I was going to remember the loads of disease-causing organisms multiplying prolifically beneath the shining, mirrored surface.

Sounds pretty bizarre, yes? But it had a strange effect.

Because I was no longer lying to myself about anything that existed, least of all myself, my nature, my being, I was free to choose what to manifest in every instant. Knowing that all of these shadows existed within me, in my very DNA, my flesh, my evolved self; knowing that I had experienced many lifetimes dealing death and destruction on my own, or suffering the same at the hands of others, I was free to choose. And further, I knew that the choice was free! ... There was no longer any blame for anything. It was just what is. This is nature. This is God. And God has two faces: Good and Evil. We can love them both, but we can choose which face we manifest, while always loving unconditionally both faces.

131 Q: *(L)* What is it about physicality that necessitates sleep? What are we doing while we are sleeping?

132 A: Body recharge.

133 Q: *(L)* Where is the body being recharged from or what is it being recharged by?

134 A: Rest.

135 Q: *(L)* What is the soul doing while the body is sleeping?

136 A: Same, it taxes the soul greatly to be embodied.[19]

137 Q: *(L)* Is this why, when people suffer sleep deprivation, they go psychotic?

138 A: Yes.

139 Q: *(L)* Why are the results of sleep deprivation, psychosis, delirium tremens, and psychedelic drugs and some mystical states so similar in their expressions and manifestations? What is being seen?

140 A: Openings.

141 Q: *(L)* Well, if doing without sleep provides an opening, what is it an opening to?

142 A: Density levels 4 and up.

143 Q: *(L)* It would seem to me – well, why is this not good?

144 A: Who said it wasn't?

145 Q: *(L)* Well, apparently a lot of people who have psychotic episodes, literally go out of their minds. They can no longer function in this world. They *lock* them up!

146 A: Yes ...

147 Q: *(L)* Why does melatonin induce these openings?

148 A: Gentle hallucinogen.

149 Q: *(L)* Sue's mother took it and got all discombobulated with it!

150 A: Perception is key. If you really "dig" 3rd density, it makes you uncomfortable to see into the higher densities.[20]

151 Q: *(L)* Can one use something like this and grow accustomed to the higher densities?

152 A: Ask Timothy Leary.

153 Q: *(S)* It's too late now! He's in 5D! *(L)* Ask him for us.

154 A: We did, and he liked it a lot!

155 Q: *(L)* Did all of his use of hallucinogenics make it easier for him to transition?

156 A: Yes.

157 Q: *(L)* Where is he now?

158 A: 5th density.

159 Q: *(L)* Moving along ... recently I read *On the Trail of the Assassins* by Jim Garrison, the New Orleans attorney. This is the book about his investigation into the Kennedy assassination. I know that we asked one or two questions about this earlier, but I think that now, with expanded perspective, we could ask a few more. Was the purported Cuban agenda what was really behind the assassination of JFK?

160 A: Not in its entirety.

161 Q: *(L)* Was there, in fact, any connection between this murder and JFK planning to reveal the government's knowledge of alien interaction?

162 A: Maybe, or that was feared, based upon a sophisticated psychological profiling system.

---

[19] Looking back, this was one of the Cs' seriously profound short remarks.
[20] Another truly interesting remark with loads of implications!

163 **Q:** *(L)* One thing that we noticed was that Lee Oswald was 'sheep-dipped'[21] in many areas around the country, well before the election of Kennedy. Why would this be the case?

164 **A:** Consortium.

165 **Q:** *(L)* What was the intention in using Oswald in this way? Was it just to have a handy person around, or did they already know, in advance, that Kennedy would be elected and that they would assassinate him?

166 **A:** Time alteration.

167 **Q:** *(L)* Do you mean time alteration in the sense that these events did *not* actually occur at the noted times, or that they were able to go back in time and do this to put more confusion into the picture?

168 **A:** Latter, see Montauk.[22]

169 **Q:** *(L)* Obviously the consortium was operating through the FBI, the CIA, the Mafia, and God knows who else, but, can you tell us who fired the shot that caused JFK's death?

170 **A:** No, because it would put you in grave danger.

171 **Q:** *(L)* Speaking of Montauk, Roxanne quoted at length some information received from some Native American about Montauk being used to change the weather on the planet, and also sending out energy waves to generate anger and other negative emotions. Is this one of the uses for the HAARP assembly?

172 **A:** No.

173 **Q:** *(L)* Once before you said that the HAARP assembly was a continuation of the Montauk project, and was being used to 'transfer perimeters'. I guess

---

[21] "The phrase 'sheep dipped', is commonly used in intelligence circles. It's a way of saying someone has been given an alternate identity. The best known example being Air America, but also in many other covert ops applications. Not necessarily military. 'Those who were accepted got "sheep-dipped" and vanished.' Dipping a sheep gets rid of creepy crawlies. Dipping a person figuratively gets rid of details of his/her former life. SHEEP-DIPPED: Stripping a soldier of his military uniform and identification so he can pose as a civilian during a covert mission. Lee Harvey Oswald was 'sheep dipped' in order to carry on his involvement in the CIA's clandestine activities." (Urban Dictionary.com, "sheep dipped")

[22] *The Montauk Project: Experiments in Time* by Preston B. Nichols and Peter Moon is the first book in a series detailing supposed time-travel experiments at the Montauk Air Force Base at the eastern tip of Long Island as part of the Montauk Project.

The 1992 book and its follow up books are written in a first person style and are widely believed to be science fiction. The real photographs of the base and crude drawings of the project electronics in the book contributes to the authentic feel prompting the project to assume a cult status whereby websites declare it is true or false.

Using a time travel theme, the characters alter history with visits to Jesus Christ, altering the outcome of Civil War and World War II battles and often doing battle over the Scientology characters. (Wikipedia, "The Montauk Project: Experiments in Time")

[23] *The Wave* 62

this meant space-time travel, correct?[23]

A: Yes. And resurrect Atlantean crystal principle.

Q: *(L)* Do they plan to actually attempt to bring up the Atlantean crystals?

A: No.

Q: *(L)* Do they plan to use this for mind control?

A: And other uses.

Q: *(L)* Can you give us a few of these uses?

A: Technical.

Q: *(L)* Is the HAARP assembly in operation now?

A: No.

Q: *(L)* Is there an estimated date of its activation?

A: No.

Q: *(L)* Is there anything you can tell us about when and if it will go into operation?

A: No.

Q: *(L)* Is there anything further you can tell us about this HAARP project?

A: Time to read Bielek.[24]

Q: *(L)* But didn't you tell us that Bielek was a disinformation artist?

A: Yes, but can you weed?

---

[24]"The Philadelphia Experiment is an alleged military experiment that is said to have been carried out by the U.S. Navy at the Philadelphia Naval Shipyard in Philadelphia, Pennsylvania, some time around October 28, 1943. The U.S. Navy destroyer escort USS *Eldridge* (DE-173) was claimed to have been rendered invisible (or 'cloaked') to enemy devices. The story is widely understood to be a hoax. The U.S. Navy maintains that no such experiment was ever conducted, that the details of the story contradict well-established facts about the USS *Eldridge*, and that the alleged claims do not conform to known physical laws.

"The story was adapted into a time travel film called *The Philadelphia Experiment* (1984), directed by Stewart Raffill, which was re-made in 2012 as a straight-to-video film. Though only loosely based on the prior accounts of the 'Experiment', it served to dramatize the core elements of the original story. In 1990, Alfred Bielek, a self-proclaimed former crew-member of the USS *Eldridge* and an alleged participant in the 'Experiment', supported the version as it was portrayed in the film. He added details of his claims through the Internet, some of which were picked up by mainstream outlets." (Wikipedia, "Philadelphia Experiment")

[25]"Jeremy Michael Boorda (November 26, 1939 – May 16, 1996) was a United States Navy admiral who served as the 25th Chief of Naval Operations. Boorda is notable for being the first American sailor to have risen through the enlisted ranks to become the Chief of Naval Operations, the highest-ranking billet in the U.S. Navy.

"Boorda, a Vietnam War veteran, died in May 1996, at the age of 56, when he deliberately shot himself with a firearm. The reason for his suicide was reportedly given as his being distraught over a media investigation into the legitimacy of him having worn on his uniform two service ribbons with bronze 'V' (valor) devices which were generally perceived to indicate heroism in combat. The two medals represented by the ribbons were authorized, but the two ribbon devices (Navy combat distinguishing devices or Combat 'V's) he wore on his uniform for several years

191 **Q**: *(L)* Now, Admiral Boorda recently committed suicide ...[25]

192 **A**: Time to read Oeschler.[26]

193 **Q**: *(L)* Did Admiral Boorda really commit suicide?

194 **A**: Yes. Culmination, as is usually the case.

195 **Q**: *(L)* A culmination of other things?

196 **A**: Yes.

197 **Q**: *(L)* Did any of this have to do with human–alien interactions?

198 **A**: No. He was not aware of any of that.

199 **Q**: *(L)* What about Vince Foster?[27] Did he commit suicide?

200 **A**: Yes.

201 **Q**: *(L)* For the reasons proposed?

202 **A**: Partly.

203 **Q**: *(L)* What was the main reason?

204 **A**: Depression.

205 **Q**: *(L)* Back to Kennedy, people say that Marilyn Monroe committed suicide, some say she was murdered. Was she murdered?

206 **A**: Yes.

207 **Q**: *(L)* Was she murdered by the Kennedys or someone else?

208 **A**: Both.

209 **Q**: *(L)* Was it because she was going to reveal things?

210 **A**: Yes.

211 **Q**: *(L)* Can you tell us what?

---

were not authorized. Although Boorda participated in combat situations off the coast of Vietnam and had been given permission to wear the devices, it was determined before and after he died, that he did not meet the requirements to wear the devices. Boorda had removed the two ribbon devices and wore his uniform without the devices almost a year before he died." (Wikipedia, "Jeremy Michael Boorda")

[26]"In 1989, former NASA scientist Robert Oeschler claimed that he had been invited by top USAF officials to participate in an exercise to finally reveal the existence of extraterrestrials to the public. He was shown photographs, including one of a 'typical grey alien', and was taken to a 'top-secret tracking station' off the Florida Coast where he was allowed to see what was described as UFOs being monitored during their flights over US and surrounding airspace. Oeschler publicised this information, although the promised official revelations did not materialise." (http://www.thelivingmoon.com/41pegasus/12insiders/Bob_Oeschler.html)

[27]"Vincent Walker 'Vince' Foster, Jr. (January 15, 1945 – July 20, 1993) was a Deputy White House Counsel during the first few months of President Bill Clinton's administration. Before that he was a partner at Rose Law Firm in Little Rock, Arkansas, and a colleague and friend of Hillary Rodham Clinton. At the White House he was unhappy with work in politics and spiraled into depression. According to multiple official findings, he committed suicide. However, his suicide remains disputed by several conspiracy theories. ... What became interpreted as a suicide note of sorts, in actuality a draft resignation letter, was found torn into 27 pieces in his briefcase. The letter contained a list of complaints, specifically including, 'The title*(WSJ)* editors lie without consequence' and lamenting, 'I was not meant for the job or the spotlight of public life in Washington. Here ruining people is considered sport.'" (Wikipedia, "Vince Foster")

A: Any and all, but it does not matter, because the "bottom line" was that she knew too much.

Q: *(L)* Next, Aleister Crowley, who claimed to be the most evil man on the planet: was he capable of doing the things he claimed in his magical operations?

A: No.

Q: *(L)* Was he used by other people?

A: Yes, and for now, goodnight!

End of Session

June 15, 1996

There are a few oddities about this session that deserve comment. First of all, this was the topic that, 19 days later, after it was shared on the internet, would attract the attention of Ark Jadczyk. Secondly, notice the mention of my book *The Noah Syndrome*, which is, effectively, about my search for 'the Ark'. At this particular moment in time, as we were conducting this session, Ark was in Florence, Italy, sitting on a megalith, writing in his journal about 'gravity waves'.

I mentioned in the comments to the previous session my reading of the work of William Chittick, *The Sufi Path of Knowledge*.

Participants: 'Frank', Laura, Sue V

1 **Q:** *(L)* Hello.

2 **A:** Hello.

3 **Q:** *(L)* And who do we have this evening?

4 **A:** Uquoppe.

5 **Q:** *(L)* And where are you transmitting from?

6 **A:** Cassiopaea.

7 **Q:** *(L)* As you know, I have been studying the Sufi teachings, and I am discovering so many similarities in these Sufi 'unveilings' to what we have been receiving through this source, that I am really quite amazed, to say the least. So, my question is: could what we are doing here be considered an ongoing, incremental 'unveiling', as they call it?[1]

8 **A:** Yes.

9 **Q:** *(L)* Now, from what I am reading, in the process of unveiling, at certain points, when the knowledge base has been sufficiently expanded, inner unveilings then begin to occur. Is this part of the present process?

10 **A:** Maybe.

11 **Q:** *(L)* My experience has been, over the past couple of years, that whenever there is a significant increase in knowledge, that it is sort of cyclical – I go through a depression before I can assimilate – and it is like an inner transformation from one level to another. Is there something we can do, and if so, is it desirable, to increase or facilitate this process in some way?

12 **A:** It is a natural process, let it be.

13 **Q:** *(L)* One of the things that al-Arabi writes about is the ontological level of being: concentric circles, so to speak, of states of being. And, each state merely defines relationships. At each higher level you are closer to a direct relation-

---
[1] *Secret History* 12; *The Wave* 5, 25, 46

ship with the core of existence, and on the outer edges, you are in closer relationship with matter. This accurately explicates the seven densities you have described for us. He also talks about the 'outraying' and the 'inward moving' toward knowledge. My thought was that certain beings, such as 4th density STS, and other STS beings of 3rd density, who think that they are creating a situation where they will accrue power to themselves, may, in fact, be part of the 'outraying' or dispersion into matter. Is this a correct perception?

14 **A**: Close.

15 **Q**: *(L)* Al-Arabi says, and this echoes what you have said, that you can stay in the illusion where you are, you can move downward or upward. Is this, in part, whichever direction you choose, a function of your position on the cycle?

16 **A**: It is more complex than that.

17 **Q**: *(L)* Well, I am sure of that. Al-Arabi presents a very complex analysis and he probably didn't know it all either ... Nevertheless, it almost word-for-word reflects things that have been given directly to us through this communication.

18 **A**: Now, learn, read, research all you can about unstable gravity waves.[2]

19 **Q**: *(L)* Okay. Unstable gravity waves. I'll see what I can find. Is there something more about this?

20 **A**: Meditate too!

21 **Q**: *(L)* Yes. Well, they have been telling us to meditate. Have you been meditating, Frank? *(F)* Not lately.

22 **A**: We mean for you, Laura, to meditate about unstable gravity waves as part of research.

23 **Q**: *(L)* Okay. Would it be alright to ask a few more questions about the Sufis?

24 **A**: Not unless you wish to get off the track.

25 **Q**: *(L)* That would be off the track from the way we are moving at present?

26 **A**: Not until you have memorized Sufi teachings to the extent that you can cross reference with Bible and similar works.

27 **Q**: *(L)* Okay. So, we are on to something with the Sufi teachings. But, we don't need to get off the track. I guess that they did with the Koran what some other mystics have done with the Bible. It is clear that there is something under the surface of it, but it is corrupted and twisted. And, I was convinced by seeing this underlying pattern that it was possible to penetrate the veil, and that gave me the impetus to push for a breakthrough.

28 **A**: Unstable gravity waves unlock as yet unknown secrets of quantum physics to make the picture crystal clear.[3]

29 **Q**: *(L)* Can we free associate about these gravity waves since no bookstores are open at this hour? Gravity seems to be a property of matter. Is that correct?

30 **A**: And ....

31 **Q**: *(L)* And hmmmm ...

32 **A**: And antimatter![4]

33 **Q**: *(L)* Is the gravity that is a property of antimatter 'antigravity'? Or, is

---

[2] It is interesting to notice in retrospect the fascinating topics that were triggered by my questions about Ibn al-Arabi and the Sufis!
[3] *The Wave* 25
[4] *The Wave* 5, 7, 57

it just gravity on the other side, so to speak?

34 **A**: Binder.

35 **Q**: *(L)* Okay. Gravity is the binder. Is gravity the binder of matter?

36 **A**: And ...

37 **Q**: *(L)* Is gravity a property of light?

38 **A**: Not the issue.

39 **Q**: *(L)* What is the issue? Can you help me out here, Frank?

40 **A**: Gravity binds all that is physical with all that is ethereal through unstable gravity waves!!!

41 **Q**: *(L)* Is antimatter ethereal existence?[5]

42 **A**: Pathway to.

43 **Q**: *(L)* Okay.

44 **A**: Doorway to.

45 **Q**: *(L)* Are unstable gravity waves ... no, hold everything ... do unstable gravity waves emanate from 7th density?

46 **A**: Throughout.

47 **Q**: *(L)* Do they emanate from any particular density?

48 **A**: That is just the point, there is none.

49 **Q**: *(L)* There are no unstable gravity waves?

50 **A**: Wrong ...

51 **Q**: *(L)* There is no emanation point?

52 **A**: Yes.

53 **Q**: *(L)* So, they are a property or attribute of the existence of matter, and the binder of matter to ethereal ideation?[6]

54 **A**: Sort of, but they are a property of antimatter, too!

55 **Q**: *(L)* So, through unstable gravity waves, you can access other densities?[7]

56 **A**: Everything.

57 **Q**: *(L)* Can you generate them mechanically?

58 **A**: Generation is really collecting and dispersing.

59 **Q**: *(L)* Okay, what kind of a device would collect and disperse gravity waves? Is this what spirals do?

60 **A**: On the way to.

61 **Q**: *(L)* So, if were to focus on collecting unstable gravity waves ...

62 **A**: When you wrote "Noah" where did you place gravity?

63 **Q**: *(L)* I thought that gravity was an indicator of the consumption of electricity; that gravity was a byproduct of a continuous flow of electrical energy ...

64 **A**: Gravity is no byproduct! It is the central ingredient of all existence!

65 **Q**: *(L)* I was evaluating by electric flow and consumption ... and I was thinking that electricity was evidence of some sort of consciousness, and that gravity was evidence that a planet that had it, had life ...

66 **A**: We have told you before that planets and stars are windows. And where does it go?

67 **Q**: *(L)* The windows?

68 **A**: The gravity.

69 **Q**: *(L)* Oh. Gravity must go into the ethereal dimensions or densities. I mean, you have my head going in so

---

[5] *The Wave* 25
[6] *The Wave* 5
[7] *The Wave* 25

many different directions that I feel like I have popcorn in there.

70 **A:** Good!

71 **Q:** *(L)* Well, where does gravity go. The sun is a window. Even our planet must be a window!

72 **A:** You have it too!!

73 **Q:** *(L)* So, gravity is the unifying principle ... the thing that keeps things together, like the way all the fat pulls together in a bowl of soup.

74 **A:** Gravity is all there is.

75 **Q:** *(L)* Is light the emanation of gravity?[8]

76 **A:** No.

77 **Q:** *(L)* What is light?

78 **A:** Gravity.

79 **Q:** *(L)* Is gravity the same as the strong and weak nuclear forces?

80 **A:** Gravity is "God."

81 **Q:** *(L)* But, I thought God was light?

82 **A:** If gravity is everything, what isn't it? Light is energy expression generated by gravity.[9]

83 **Q:** *(L)* Is gravity the 'light that cannot be seen', as the Sufis call it: the Source?

84 **A:** Please name something that is not gravity.

85 **Q:** *(L)* Well, if gravity is everything, there is nothing that is not gravity. Fine. What is absolute nothingness?

86 **A:** A mere thought.

87 **Q:** *(L)* So, there is no such thing as non-existence?

88 **A:** Yes, there is.

89 **Q:** *(L)* Do thoughts produce gravity?

90 **A:** Yes.

91 **Q:** *(L)* Does sound produce gravity?

92 **A:** Yes.

93 **Q:** *(L)* Can sound manipulate gravity?

94 **A:** Yes.

95 **Q:** *(L)* Can it be done with the human voice?

96 **A:** Yes.

97 **Q:** *(L)* Can it be done tonally or by power through thought?

98 **A:** Both.

99 **Q:** *(L)* Then, is there also specific sound configurations involved?

100 **A:** Gravity is manipulated by sound when thought manipulated by gravity chooses to produce sound which manipulates gravity.

101 **Q:** *(L)* Now, did the fellow who built the Coral Castle spin in his airplane seat while thinking his manipulations into place?[10]

---

[8] *The Wave* 57
[9] *The Wave* 25
[10] See session 23 October 1994 and *The Wave*, Chapters 25 and 44.
[11] "Coral Castle was built in the early 20th century by an eccentric Latvian recluse named Edward Leedskalnin. Edward Leedskalnin was a 100 pound, 5 foot tall man – who wound up in Homestead, Florida – on a ten-acre tract of land just south of Miami, Florida. Somehow he managed to single-handedly lift and maneuver blocks of coral weighing up to 30 tons each and create not only a castle but other things. How Edward did his work has never been discovered, though he labored for 30 years.

102 **A:** No. He spun when gravity chose to manipulate him to spin in order to manipulate gravity.[11]

103 **Q:** *(L)* Does gravity have consciousness?

104 **A:** Yes.

105 **Q:** *(L)* Is it ever possible for the individual to do the choosing, or is it gravity that *is* him that chose?

106 **A:** The gravity that was inside him was all the gravity in existence.

107 **Q:** *(L)* Well, I thought the Sufis were tough! *(F)* Well, it's probably because of your studies that this door opened. *(L)* Good grief! What have I done? Alright. I am confused.

108 **A:** No you are not.

109 **Q:** *(L)* Then, just put it this way: I am befuddled and overloaded.

110 **A:** Befuddling is fun!

111 **Q:** *(L)* Well, I guess that if any of this is going to be of particular significance to us, then we will certainly find out the details as we go along.

112 **A:** How many times do we have to tell you?!?!

113 **Q:** *(L)* Learning is fun! Right!

114 **A:** The entire sum total of all existence exists within each of you, and vice versa.

115 **Q:** *(L)* Then what is the explanation for the 'manyness' that we perceive?

116 **A:** Perception of 3rd density.

117 **Q:** *(L)* So, the entire universe is inside me ... okay, that's ... I understand. Oddly enough, I do. The problem is accessing it, stripping away the veils.

118 **A:** That is the fun part.

119 **Q:** *(L)* So, the fellow who built the Coral Castle was able to access this. Consistently or only intermittently?

120 **A:** Partially.

121 **Q:** *(L)* According to what I understand, at the speed of light, there is no mass, no time, and no gravity. How can this be?[12]

122 **A:** No mass, no time, but yes, gravity.

123 **Q:** *(L)* A photon has gravity?

124 **A:** Gravity supersedes light speed.

125 **Q:** *(L)* Gravity waves are faster than light?

126 **A:** Yes.

He worked alone – at night – and seemed to know when he was being watched. On those occasions – he never lifted any of the stones. Many articles claim that he found the same secrets of levitation as those used by the supposed builders of the Pyramids of Egypt – among other megalithic sites around the world whose creation remain unexplained.

"Edward Leedskalnin was quoted as saying, "I have discovered the secrets of the pyramids, and have found out how the Egyptians and the ancient builders in Peru, Yucatan, and Asia, with only primitive tools, raised and set in place blocks of stone weighing many tons!"

"In total, Edward quarried over eleven hundred tons of coral rock for his castle, using tools fashioned from wrecking-yard junk, never revealing how he managed to raise, and position, the massive coral blocks that make up the compound." (http://www.crystalinks.com/coralcastle.html)

[12] *The Wave* 57

127 **Q**: *(L)* What would make a gravity wave unstable?

128 **A**: Utilization.

129 **Q**: *(L)* I feel like I am missing a really big point here ...[13]

130 **A**: You are, but you can only find it at your own pace.

131 **Q**: *(L)* Well, I think I need to do some reading and research so that I can come back to this.

132 **A**: And, on that note, goodnight.

End of Session

---

[13] *The Wave* 46

June 22, 1996

This is an excellent session with good material and which felt good. Notice that there are two other women present. When either of these ladies was there on her own, things could be problematical; but together, they sort of balanced each other and both of them contributed feminine energy to counterbalance Frank.

My ongoing reading of *The Sufi Path of Knowledge* was inspiring new directions for questions.

Participants: 'Frank', Laura, Sue V, VG

1 **Q**: *(L)* Hello.

2 **A**: Hello.

3 **Q**: *(L)* And who do we have with us this evening?

4 **A**: Firson.

5 **Q**: *(L)* And where are you transmitting from?

6 **A**: Cassiopaea.

7 **Q**: *(L)* Tonight, I would like to ask about 5th density. How does the 'dividing line' between the four physical densities and 5th function?

8 **A**: Recycling zone, one must have direct contact in perfect balance with those on 6th density in order to fulfill the need for contemplation/learning phase while in between incarnations of 1st through 4th densities.[1]

9 **Q**: *(L)* When a person finishes all their experiences on 1st through 4th density, do they then remain at 5th for a period before to moving to 6th?

10 **A**: Yes.

11 **Q**: *(L)* When you die in 3rd and go to 5th, do you pass through or see 4th?

12 **A**: No.

13 **Q**: *(L)* When you are in 5th density, is part of your service to be a guide? Are there two kinds of beings on 5th: those who are there for the recycling, and those whose level it simply *is*?

14 **A**: No. All are as one in timeless understanding of all there is.

15 **Q**: *(L)* If, at 5th density a person has timeless understanding, what is it about them that determines that they will 'recycle' as opposed to moving to 6th from 5th?

16 **A**: Contemplation reveals needed destiny.

17 **Q**: *(L)* So, being united with other beings on 5th, you come to some sort of understanding about your lessons ...

---

[1] *The Wave* 6

18 **A**: Balanced. And this, my dear, is another example of gravity as the binder of all creation ... "The Great Equalizer!"[2]

19 **Q**: *(L)* In this picture in my mind, the cycle moves out, in dispersion, begins to accrete and return to the source. Is this correct?

20 **A**: Close.

21 **Q**: *(L)* Is it, in fact, that exactly half of all that exists, is moving into imbalance, while the other half is moving into balance?

22 **A**: Close.

23 **Q**: *(L)* All the cosmos? All that exists?[3]

24 **A**: Yes.

25 **Q**: *(L)* Is it possible that one area of the cosmos has more of the balance-seeking energy while another has more of that which is seeking imbalance?

26 **A**: Oh yes!

27 **Q**: *(L)* Is the Earth one of those areas that is more imbalanced than balanced at the present time?

28 **A**: Yes, but rapidly moving back toward balance.

29 **Q**: *(L)* Is the realm border part of this balancing?

30 **A**: Yes.

31 **Q**: *(V)* A few weeks ago several of us began to suffer from internal heat, insomnia, and other things. What was this?[4]

32 **A**: Image. Deep conjunction of fibrous linkage in DNA structure.

33 **Q**: *(V)* Well, I want to know if it is in my mind that I get so hot, or does my body temperature actually elevate?

34 **A**: Only on 4th.

35 **Q**: *(V)* I don't understand.

36 **A**: Bleedthrough, get used to those!

37 **Q**: *(L)* Does this mean we are actually experiencing a bleedthrough of 4th density?

38 **A**: Image.

39 **Q**: *(V)* Are the little flashes of light I see also a manifestation of this?

40 **A**: Maybe so, but try to concentrate on the ethereal significance, rather than the physical.

41 **Q**: *(L)* When you say "deep conjunction of fibrous linkage", does this mean that we are conjoining with a linkage to a 4th density body that is growing, developing?

42 **A**: Slowly, but surely. Now, get ready for a message: We have told you before that the upcoming "changes" relate to the spiritual and awareness factors rather than the much publicized physical. Symbolism is always a necessary tool in teaching. But, the trick is to read the hidden lessons represented by

---

[2] The Cs were really pushing the gravity thing for some reason of which I was as yet unaware!

[3] *The Wave* 22

[4] This was an odd phenomenon. I would start feeling really hot on the afternoon before a session. I had mentioned it to VG and she, too, reported that after attending sessions she would suffer with the same thing. Neither of us was quite yet ready for menopause, so it was a puzzle.

the symbology, not to get hung up on the literal meanings of the symbols!⁵

43 **Q**: *(L)* You say that the symbology has to do with hidden meanings. The symbology that you used was "image" and "deep fibrous linkage" of DNA. Now, is that a physical, symbolic image?

44 **A**: Yes.

45 **Q**: *(L)* What is your definition of 'image'? We have many.

46 **A**: Learning is fun, Laura, as you have repeatedly found!

47 **Q**: *(L)* Well, I am so hot now that I really want to know! And, how come I am always the one who gets assigned the job of figuring everything out?

48 **A**: Because you have asked for the "power" to figure out the most important issues in all of reality. And, we have been assisting you in your empowerment.⁶

49 **Q**: *(L)* Image. DNA linkage. *(V)*

---

⁵This was a much needed reminder. The Cs had warned several times against taking esoteric/spiritual things too literally and misreading physical things and giving them esoteric significance when none is there. Recall session 26 November 1994, where they said:

> Now would be a good 'time' for you folks to begin to reexamine some of the extremely popular 'Earth Changes' prophecies. Why, you ask. Because, remember, you are third density beings, so real prophecies are being presented to you in terms you will understand, i.e. physical realm, i.e. Earth changes. This 'may' be symbolism. Would most students of the subject understand if prophecies were told directly in fourth density terms?

As we have learned in the twenty years since this session, a lot of what the Cs have said relates to spirit and awareness, particularly in terms of human consciousness on this planet. Some folks think that it is enough to 'spiritualize' or 'gain esoteric knowledge' by studying or speculating, but turn their nose up at the hard interpersonal work that is actually needed. They think that they can just go along and live their lives until 4D comes and then, if they have been pretty good, and we are all hooked up together, they'll be in 4D and everything will all be easier. I don't think it is gonna happen that way.

As the Cs pointed out, 4D is more or less *here* all the time – as are the other densities – so what is it that is preventing us being part of it right now? Also, as the Cs pointed out, 4D is as much state of awareness as it is change of state. Your state won't change until your awareness does, and your awareness won't change until you change your state. It is kind of a Catch 22. It is only with super-efforts, as Gurdjieff said, and with the help of a network, that you can bootstrap yourself out of the old state into a new one.

They gave lots of clues about this, like 'seeing the unseen', which I talked about in some detail in *The Wave*, but we have learned oh! so much more in the past 20 years of our ongoing hands-on experiment!

⁶And apparently, I asked for this "power" when I was at 5th density between incarnations! But it was nice that the Cs mentioned that they were helping me, which, of course, goes completely counter to some of the unpleasant things that came out in some sessions when Frank was dominating.

'Power' was in quotes.

50 **A**: Leave that alone for now, you will know soon enough.[7]

51 **Q**: *(V)* Is this 4th density body something that already exists so that we could communicate with it?

52 **A**: Habeas corpus?

53 **Q**: *(V)* Well, they just said ... *(L)* Well, what they must mean is that you *are* it – you are transforming little by little and all of the unpleasant little side-effects are just part of it.

54 **A**: Yes.

55 **Q**: *(V)* Righteous! *(L)* Terry showed me a couple of acupuncture points that seem to induce an altered state. Is this, as he says, a way to open the door to the subconscious?

A: Stimulates endorphins.

57 **Q**: *(L)* Is there any point on the body that *can* be used to assist in opening the gate to the subconscious?[8]

58 **A**: No such assistance is needed. First, we would like to suggest that you seek a "spin" doctor for your quest!!

59 **Q**: *(L)* Would a "spin" doctor be a Sufi master?

60 **A**: One example.[9]

61 **Q**: *(L)* Yes. We are supposed to do several things involved with spinning.

62 **A**: Hilliard. Leedskallen. Coral Castle.

---

[7] As I am reading over this right now, it occurs to me what the Cs meant by "image" and "deep fibrous linkage", especially combined with "you will know soon enough" and the frequent mentions of gravity: the Cs were indicating the almost imminent arrival of Ark on the scene! But the DNA thing is still curious to me: "deep fibrous linkage"? In the 19 November 1994 session, the Cs remarked that "Level 1 changes" cause pain and suffering and that such suffering is "closely followed by dramatic life changes". At a later point in time, which we will come to, the Cs remarked: "Suffering activates neurochemicals which turn on DNA receptors". I had certainly been going through the most intense and prolonged psychological and emotional suffering of my life.

Just over a year before, on 27 May 1995, we had the session with physicist Ruggero Santilli during which gravity was discussed. As it happened, on that very night something really strange happened. The guests had gone home and I was trying to settle myself down for sleep. I closed my eyes and began meditative breathing to try to relax, since I was rather hyped up. Suddenly, I saw a face before my eyes of a man with blond or white hair and very kind eyes looking right at me. The face was so real that I felt that I could reach out and touch it; it looked like living flesh and was totally three dimensional. I was so startled by what was obviously a serious hallucination that I opened my eyes to see if it would stay – it didn't. I closed my eyes and the vision was gone, but I was left with a very strange feeling. I didn't know at the time that I was seeking Ark's face, but I was soon to know! That is what I think the Cs meant when they said "image"; they were referring to this incident.

[8] *The Wave* 7

[9] The arrival of Ark on the scene was just days away – at the time of this session, only 12 days – and a quantum physicist is certainly a 'spin doctor'.

63 **Q:** *(L)* Well, they are really pushing on this gravity thing.¹⁰ Can I ask a question on another subject?

64 **A:** You can ask about the Easter Bunny, if you wish.

65 **Q:** *(L)* Is 3rd density awareness the only density with perception of time?

66 **A:** No.

67 **Q:** *(L)* Well, what others?

68 **A:** 4, 5, 6, 7.

69 **Q:** *(L)* But I thought that time perception was an illusion?

70 **A:** YOUR perception of it is an illusion. Remember the example of the dogs and cats riding in a car?

71 **Q:** *(L)* Yes. Ouspensky and the horse. So, time, as an essential thing, *does* exist?

72 **A:** But not as you know it. When we refer to "timelessness," we are speaking from the standpoint of your familiarity only.

73 **Q:** *(L)* Does time then exist, and does space have a limit?

74 **A:** You are getting confused because your inborn linear perception is clouding the image your efforts are trying to produce.

75 **Q:** *(L)* Okay, let's go back to the 'balancing' of Earth. How can this be done?

76 **A:** Vague question.

77 **Q:** *(L)* Let me try this: the 'buckets of love and light' group say that it is going to be balanced because everyone is going to think nice thoughts, and all of their buckets of love and light are going to eventually reach a critical mass and spill over onto all the rest of humanity and all of the bad guys are going to be transformed into good guys. This is the standard version. Is this what you mean?

78 **A:** No.

79 **Q:** *(L)* Is the energy that is being manifested in the positive, on and around the planet, is it going to reduce the level of negativity in the beings existing on the planet?

80 **A:** This is not the point. When "Earth" becomes a 4th density realm, all the forces, both STS and STO shall be in direct contact with one another ... It will be a "level playing field," thus, balanced.¹¹

81 **Q:** *(V)* I am wondering about the significance of the quoted words. Is it some kind of code?

82 **A:** Maybe you should go back to the beginning, and arrange all our quoted statements in sequential order?

83 **Q:** *(L)* Do you mean *all* the transcripts?

84 **A:** Yup!

85 **Q:** *(F)* Well, they mentioned twice to be careful about putting in the designated quotes. *(L)* One of the crop circles you interpreted¹² was an 'astronomical twin phenomenon'. What is an astronomical twin phenomenon?

86 **A:** Many perfectly synchronous meanings.

---

¹⁰I just didn't understand the gravity thing; I had no idea that my life was about to change suddenly and dramatically and that, because of the 'image' I had seen a year previously, that I would instantly recognize Ark.

¹¹*The Wave* 22

¹²Session 7 May 1995.

Q: *(L)* Synchronicity is involved. Does this have something to do with "image"?

A: Duplicity of, as in "Alice through the looking glass."

Q: *(L)* Double images. Does this relate to matter and antimatter?

A: Yes, and ...

Q: *(L)* Gravity and manifesting on one side and manifesting a mirror image on the other ...[13]

A: Yes, and ...

Q: *(L)* And images of 4th density bodies with tenuous fibers connecting to DNA as in manifesting imaginal bodies on 4th density?

A: Astronomical.

Q: *(L)* Okay, that relates to stars and planets ... astronomical in terms of another universe, an alternate universe composed of antimatter?

A: Yes, and ....

Q: *(L)* And is this alternate universe going to merge with our universe ...

A: No.

Q: *(L)* Is this alternate universe of antimatter the point from which phenomena occur or are manifested in our universe?

A: More like doorway or "conduit."

Q: *(L)* Is this alternate universe the means by which we must travel to 4th density? Is it like a veil, or an abyss of some sort?

A: Think of it as the highway.

Q: *(L)* So, we must travel through this universe of antimatter in order to reach 4th density?

---
[13] *The Wave* 6

A: No.

Q: *(L)* Is something going to happen in terms of interacting with this antimatter in order to bring about some sort of transition?

A: No. Realm border is traveling wave.

Q: *(L)* Okay, you say "traveling wave", and then you say that antimatter is the highway. Does this mean moving through antimatter or interacting in some way with antimatter via the impetus of the traveling wave, or realm border?

A: Bends space/time, this is where your unstable gravity waves can be utilized.

Q: *(L)* Utilizing antimatter by creating an EM field, which destabilizes the gravity wave, allows antimatter to unite with matter, creating a portal through which space-time can be bent, or traveled through via this 'bending'. In other words, producing an EM field, bringing in the antimatter, *is* the bending of space-time? Is that it?

A: Yes.

Q: *(V)* Is there a portal for each person, or one large portal?

A: No.

Q: *(V)* So we move through a portal in masses?

A: No.

Q: *(L)* Is this generating of EM fields to destabilize the gravity wave what the HAARP assembly is designed and built for?

A: No.

Q: *(V)* If there are not personal portals for one person, or portals for groups of people ...

118 **A:** Portal is where you desire it to be.

119 **Q:** *(V)* So it could just be a state of mind?

120 **A:** No. With proper technology you can create a portal where desired. There are unlimited options.

121 **Q:** *(L)* Proper technology. Unstable gravity waves. And once you told us to study Tesla coils ... antimatter ... destabilizing the gravity waves through EM generation allows the antimatter to interact with matter which then creates a portal ... Is it in the antimatter universe that all this traveling back and forth is done by aliens when they abduct people?

122 **A:** Close. They transport through it, but most abductions take place in either 3rd or 4th density.

123 **Q:** *(L)* Is this movement through the antimatter universe, is this what people perceive in their abductions as the 'wall of fire'? The coming apart? The demolecularizing?

124 **A:** No. That is transdimensional atomic remolecularization.

125 **Q:** *(L)* Okay, if a person were passing into the antimatter universe, how would they perceive it?

126 **A:** They wouldn't.

127 **Q:** *(L)* Why?

128 **A:** No space; no time.

129 **Q:** *(L)* Antimatter universe has no space and no time ... so, the antimatter universe is possibly where the poor guys of Flight 19 are?

130 **A:** Yes.

131 **Q:** *(L)* And you can get stuck in this place?

132 **A:** Yes. And if you are in a time warp cocoon, you are hyperconscious, i.e. you perceive "zero time" as if it were literally millions of years, that is if the cycle is connected or closed, as in "Philadelphia Experiment." And, on that note, goodnight.[14]

End of Session

---

[14] And I sure got in deep water this night!

June 29, 1996

I had been quite stirred up by the Cs' recent references to gravity waves and had been giving it a lot of thought. I wrote about this in *The Wave* as follows:

> After a couple of years of holding everything they [the Cs] said in deepest suspicion, looking for the flaws, being a super skeptic, I was now beginning to think that I had invented the wheel! After all, it seemed they could hold their own in a discussion with a 'real' scientist; they produced information that was initially thought to be incredible or nonsense, which then checked out in amazing ways; and most of all, they very carefully avoided any kind of interference in our personal lives in a direct way, while the information they were imparting to us, if considered and added to our criteria for evaluating our reality, seemed to help enormously in sorting through problems and understanding what was going on under the surface.
>
> They were, in effect, not giving us fish, but teaching us to fish.
>
> And, of course, with this growing confidence, I decided to run a tighter ship, so to speak. No more fun and games. Let's get right down to business here and solve this puzzle and go home!
>
> Since the Cassiopaeans had suggested that I do research on gravity waves, that is exactly what I decided to do. I went to the library and struck out. Nothing there. I did a rather primitive internet search (I wasn't very computer smart at the time) and found a couple of odd references that made no sense, and finally decided to do something rather more daring.
>
> I figured that Dr. Santilli must be the answer! If he had lost interest in the Cassiopaeans, maybe I could rekindle it. I put together the material from the Santilli session with the subsequent gravity wave material delivered over a year later, and typed it all up very nicely and faxed it to him along with a request that he have a look at what had come up since he had visited. I was sure he would be interested and things would just take off from there.
>
> Nope. Barely a flicker of a response.

Okay, Plan A flopped; Plan B: obtain permission from Dr. Santilli to use his name and then post the material on the internet in the hopes that someone would read it who knew something about gravity waves and would reciprocate with more information I could work with. Fortunately, he was gracious enough to consent, and I dutifully sent the whole sequence of remarks to Col. Steve Wilson for his opinion, and to ask if he would post it to his Skywatch mail group. Col. Wilson was very interested in the material, and the Cassiopaeans as well, since we had exchanged a number of previous e-mails on many subjects. It was his opinion that the Cassiopaeans were certainly revealing information that was accurate and that he could verify. But some of the information he could neither verify nor comment on.

Col. Wilson posted the Santilli session to the mail group on June 27, 1996, and I settled down to wait and see if anyone who could point me in the right direction for my research would read it. The subject field of the message read: 'Dr. Roger Santilli and the Cassiopaeans...' I thought it was catchy enough that people wouldn't just delete it out of hand.

I admit to having been more than a little paranoid about sending this material out this way. After all, I had already experienced some pretty vicious attacks from various sources that I will detail another time, and it was clear to me that there was possibly some danger to myself in making public the Cassiopaean information in some of the more 'sensitive' areas. But, I was desperate, and understood that being desperate called for desperate measures.

Nothing happened. Nobody commented on the post. Nothing was said by a single soul on that supposedly humongous mail group. I had played my cards and lost. There would be no more information about gravity waves.

So, I was on my own. I had some silly fantasy that I would solve the greatest mystery of science if I could just find the right specific questions to ask in order to extract the answer! I pretty quickly learned that I was way out of my depth. Also note that when dealing with such 'cold' subjects that carry no emotional load for any of the people present, things go generally rather smoothly.

Participants: 'Frank', Laura, Sue V

Q: *(L)* Hello.

A: Hello. We are the Cassiopaean transmitting 6th density beings of light, and for purposes of an identifier for your familiarity pattern, we will label this consciousness unit "Jarrah."

Q: *(L)* Well, that is an interesting opening. I guess you have been tuned in during the week and have been aware of the stuff going on in my head. I would like to get directly to my questions as they have developed during the past few days. The first thing is in regard to the Santilli session: is awareness equal to gravity?

A: It is a part therein.[1]

Q: *(L)* Does accumulation of knowledge and awareness correspond to an increase in gravity?

A: No.

Q: *(L)* You said that energy can change the value of the density. The value of the density, as I understand it, is either plus or minus. Does this mean that pumping energy into 3rd density from another realm of space-time can intensify the gravity to such a state that it changes its unit and becomes antimatter?

A: No.

Q: *(L)* You said that EM was the same as gravity. Does an increase in EM, the collection of EM or the production of an EM wave, does this increase gravity on those things or objects or persons subjected to it?

A: Gravity does not ever get increased or decreased, it is merely collected and dispersed.

---
[1] *The Wave 7*

Q: *(L)* If gravity is collected and dispersed, and planets and stars are windows, and you say that human beings 'have' gravity, does that mean that the human beings, or the life forms on a given planet or in a given solar system, are the collectors of this gravity?

A: No. Gravity is the collector of human beings and all else! Make "collector" singular.

Q: *(L)* Is STO the equivalent of dispersing gravity?

A: No, STO is a REFLECTION of the existence of gravity dispersal.

Q: *(L)* Is STS also dispersal of gravity?

A: No. Collection is reflected. STS is reflection or reflected by collection of gravity.

Q: *(L)* You said that changing the unit involves movement to another density. You also said that antimatter realm is the door to, or the pathway to, ethereal existence. Is 4th density, therefore, an antimatter universe?

A: No.

Q: *(L)* Do the beings in 4th density manifest in an antimatter state?

A: Both.

Q: *(L)* Is 4th density a density where both matter and antimatter are in balance?

A: Not in balance, in evidence.

Q: *(L)* So matter and antimatter are both available for utilization by individuals according to will and awareness?

A: Close. Antimatter and matter are balanced everywhere.

Q: *(L)* What effect does collection of gravity – you said gravity was collecting human beings – what effect ...

A: No, we did not say that. You don't learn when you "skip over" the material.

Q: *(L)* What did I skip over? You said that "gravity is the collector of human beings"?

A: Yes, but all else is the key. When one says that, there is no differentiation.

Q: *(L)* Yes, well I am asking these questions at *our* level here. What effects does gravity have on the body?

A: Too complicated. Try breaking your question down.

Q: *(L)* You say that increasing awareness was "a part therein" of gravity. So, if a person is increasing awareness, do they also increase in gravity?

A: No.

Q: *(L)* What is the relationship between the increasing awareness and gravity?

A: Nothing direct.

Q: *(L)* I am trying to find out what effect increasing awareness has on human beings in relation to this unstable gravity wave you have mentioned, as well as the oncoming 'Wave'.

A: You are trying to "marry" two parallels.

Q: *(L)* We have two parallels ... okay ... so if one is exponential increasing in awareness, the sign of the units of bodily energy does not change?

A: You are still attempting to generate.

Q: *(L)* Well, I am just trying to get a grip on some ideas here ...

A: Then change the thought pattern. Gravity is the "stuff" of all existence, therefore it has an unchanging property of quantity.

Q: *(L)* So, gravity is not being 'used', per se?

A: Close.

Q: *(L)* You said that light was an energy expression of gravity. Then you said ...

A: You can utilize gravity, but you cannot "use" it. You cannot increase or decrease that which is in perfectly balanced static state.

Q: *(L)* So, gravity is in a perfectly "static" state. Yet, it can be "utilized". Can you make clear for me the transition from the static state to instability. What occurs?

A: There is no transition, just application.

Q: *(L)* What occurs from the perfectly static state to the application mode? Is anybody following me?

A: No, including us!

Q: *(L)* Wonderful! What I am trying to get at is, 1) gravity exists in a static state; 2) light is an energy expression of gravity, therefore it is utilization? Correct?

A: No. Light is an expression of gravitational energy.

Q: *(L)* Well, when one has an expression, it expresses onto, into, or to something somewhere ...

A: It does?

Q: *(L)* Well ...

A: If a tree falls in the forest, and nothing is there to hear it, does it make a sound?

55 **Q:** *(L)* You are saying that gravity is everywhere in balance and static, and then you say that utilization causes unstable gravity waves. And then you say that gravity is God, and that God is all creation, and we are a part of all creation, and, therefore, we are of God, and gravity. So, what I am trying to get at here is, what is the thing, the event, the manifestation, the mode of utilization that takes gravity from a perfectly static state to an unstable state, if you are saying it is always perfectly balanced? That does not make sense to me.

56 **A:** Instability does not automatically mean non-static. Unstable waves can be static in their instability.

57 **Q:** *(L)* None of this makes a whole lot of sense. I thought I was beginning to understand it, and obviously I don't have a clue. Let's try a different direction. You said that the universe consists of equal amounts of matter and antimatter. Are the first three densities, densities of matter?

58 **A:** And antimatter.[2]

59 **Q:** *(L)* Are there equal amounts of matter and antimatter at all densities?

60 **A:** Yes. Remember, density refers to one's conscious awareness only. Once one is aware, all [many spirals of the planchette] conforms to that awareness.

61 **Q:** *(L)* What is it about the oncoming Wave that is going to make any given person aware?[3]

62 **A:** Not yet ... First: your prophets have always used 3rd density symbology to try to convey 4th density realities. You are attempting to gather 3rd density answers to explain 4th through 7th density principles. This is why you are getting frustrated, because it doesn't "mesh."[4]

63 **Q:** *(L)* Are manifestations in 3rd density loci of collection of gravity?

64 **A:** In part. But, so are manifestations on all densities.

65 **Q:** *(L)* Okay. So, if ...

66 **A:** What do you suppose the opposite of gravity is?

67 **Q:** *(L)* Antigravity?

68 **A:** Yes.

69 **Q:** *(L)* So, if all that exists were like a blown-up balloon, and the surface of the balloon represents the static state of gravity, 7th density maybe ... and it begins to bump out in different places ... and all these little bumps are loci of manifestation of various densities – and this is very simplified, I am just trying to get an image – is this getting, even very simplistically, an idea that I can work with?

70 **A:** As long as you have an "anti-balloon" too.

71 **Q:** *(L)* So, can we make the outer surface of the balloon a balloon, and the inner surface or the air the 'anti-balloon'?

72 **A:** No.

73 **Q:** *(L)* Two balloons next to one another?

74 **A:** No. A non-balloon.

---

[2] *The Wave* 5, 57
[3] *The Wave* 8
[4] Another warning that we may have no real way to understand higher realities from our state of being. It's interesting to think about this statement while reading something like 1 Enoch.

Q: *(L)* A non-balloon? You are making me *crazy*! You are saying that *nothing* exists! We are just not even *here*!

A: No.

Q: *(L)* Well, for God's *sake*! Help me out with a visual on this! Okay, a balloon in front of a mirror, the reflection of the balloon is the non-balloon.

A: No.

Q: *(L)* The non-balloon is when the balloon switches off – but it does it so fast you are not aware of it – like a pulsation...? I mean, I am desperate here!

A: You see, my dear, when you arrive at 4th density, then you will see.[5]

Q: *(L)* Well, how in the heck am I supposed to get there if I can't 'get it'?

A: Who says you have to "get it" before you get there?

Q: *(L)* Well, that leads back to: what is the Wave going to do to expand this awareness? Because, if the Wave is what 'gets you there', what makes this so?

A: No. It is like this: After you have completed all your lessons in "third grade," where do you go?

Q: *(L)* So, it is a question of ...

A: Answer, please.

Q: *(L)* You go to fourth grade.

A: Okay, now, do you have to already be in 4th grade in order to be allowed to go there? Answer.

Q: *(L)* No. But you have to know all the 3rd density things ...

A: Yes. More apropos: you have to have learned all of the lessons.

Q: *(L)* What kind of lessons are we talking about here?

---

[5] *The Wave* 24

[6] I would suggest that this may be one of the most important things the Cs ever conveyed: that we should concern ourselves with the lessons of this reality and learn them well and thoroughly, and people should stop trying to be avatars or adepts or whatever, thinking that they can just spiritualize themselves without having learned how to function in the present world effectively. Gurdjieff referred to it as being a 'good obyvatel', or basically, a 'good householder' who is successful in things of the world before thinking he can apply himself to things *out* of this world. Castaneda wrote about it also as what he called the 'three-phase progression'.

> "One of the greatest accomplishments of the seers of the Conquest was a construct he called the three-phase progression. By understanding the nature of man, they were able to reach the incontestable conclusion that if seers can hold their own in facing [human] petty tyrants, they can certainly face the unknown with impunity, and then they can even stand the presence of the unknowable.
>
> "The average man's reaction is to think that the order of that statement should be reversed," he went on. "A seer who can hold his own in the face of the unknown can certainly face petty tyrants. But that's not so. What destroyed the superb seers of ancient times was that assumption. We know better now. We know that nothing can temper the spirit of a warrior as much as the challenge of dealing with impossible people in positions of power. Only under those conditions can warriors acquire the sobriety and serenity to stand the pressure of the unknowable.
>
> "The seers of [the Conquest] couldn't have found a better ground. The Spaniards were the petty tyrants who tested the seers' skills to the limit; after dealing with

92 **A**: Karmic and simple understandings.⁶

93 **Q**: *(L)* What are the key elements of these understandings, and are they fairly universal?

94 **A**: They are universal.

95 **Q**: *(L)* What are they?

96 **A**: We cannot tell you that.

97 **Q**: *(L)* Do they have to do with discovering the *meanings* of the symbology of 3rd density existence, seeing behind the veil ... and reacting to things according to choice? Giving each thing or person or event its due?

98 **A**: Okay. But you cannot force the issue. When you have learned, you have learned!

99 **Q**: *(L)* I just want to make sure that I am doing the most I can do. I don't want to have to come back to 3rd density. If I can accelerate things a little ...

100 **A**: You cannot, so just enjoy the ride. Learning is fun!

101 **Q**: *(L)* Now, you told me to research and meditate upon unstable gravity waves. And, that once I understood this, quantum physics would be perfectly clear to me, and basically everything would be perfectly clear. Now, I have been struggling with this ...

102 **A**: That is just the point, Laura! When it is a struggle, you are not learning. So stop struggling and meditate. i.e. enjoy the ride.

103 **Q**: *(L)* So, you say that if I am struggling I am not doing it right. Well, I struggled with myself to get out of my marriage, and that was and still is a struggle. Was that an erroneous approach?

104 **A**: Yes, because all that happened would have happened anyway.

105 **Q**: *(L)* So, it was the wrong approach?

106 **A**: Yes.

107 **Q**: *(L)* What was the right approach? Wait for him to choose to leave?

108 **A**: ?

109 **Q**: *(L)* Well, at this point, I was brought to the point of death.

110 **A**: That is not the point, but yes, if you had not struggled to be something other than who you are while IN the relationship, and struggled to make the relationship work every time it came to a point of termination, it would have happened sooner.⁷

111 **Q**: *(L)* When we went through the transcript to get some of the quoted words, there was a sequence that came out: "Time caused alpha level suffering." Is there such a thing?

112 **A**: Maybe. Mix and match.

113 **Q**: *(L)* You mean in putting the words and phrases together?

114 **A**: Yes, but don't struggle with it! You try too hard when you feel upset with others, this is why see: ISCNI, LM, D4, and others ...

---

the conquerors, the seers were capable of facing anything. They were the lucky ones. At that time there were petty tyrants everywhere." (Castaneda: "The Fire From Within", (New York, Pocket Books, 1985), p. 19)

⁷So, so true! I was struggling the wrong way at the wrong times. An example of the "karmic and simple understandings" that human beings need to learn while they are in this reality.

115 **Q**: *(L)* So, you are saying that I should not do anything that makes something inside me feel compressed or denied ...

116 **A**: Do without expectations. When you conform or change your behavior in the expectation of creating a change in others, then you are expecting something. So, do it. See what happens. But be patient and see what happens! [8]

117 **Q**: *(L)* Okay, let me ask about a dream. My daughter and I both had dreams night before last. The nature of both dreams were very similar, although the participants were different. Was this some sort of prophetic energy?

118 **A**: Natural cycles caused psychic "link."

119 **Q**: *(L)* You mean as in hormonal cycles?

120 **A**: Yes. And goodnight. [9]

End of Session

---

[8] More excellent advice about "karmic and simple understandings". How many people actually think that when they are changing something essential about themselves in order to get along that it is actually a negative thing?

[9] The Cs left rather abruptly, so it was rather obvious that they were not going to go into that topic. But, considering the remarks made in the previous session about "deep fibrous linkage" and DNA and so forth, this response about "psychic link" was curious. In fact, the dreams my daughter and I had concerned me getting married to someone. In each of our dreams, the new husband was a real person of our acquaintance, though certainly not someone either of us would think of me marrying in real life. But still, the idea of starting a new relationship was the link between the two dreams, which were very vivid. I didn't know that a member of the email discussion group I had sent the Santilli session to had forwarded it to Ark.

July 14, 1996

The reader will notice that it had been two weeks since the previous session on June 29. I cover this period in *The Wave*:

> The Fourth of July was coming up and my aunt invited me to come to her house to celebrate since there were also a couple of family birthdays – one on the third and one on the fifth – so we were going to do the whole family celebration thing and go to a fireworks exhibition and barbeque. I was pretty depressed, but the kids wanted to go, and since I was finally recovering somewhat from my months of disability, I thought I would chance it and make the trip. Besides, my cousin is an aerospace engineer and I had decided that I would sort of 'come out of the closet' about my channeling activities and enlist his help in looking at the material and seeing if he could come up with any 'real' physics or math that would further the project. Heck, who knows? Maybe he would know something about gravity waves!
>
> So, we went. It's about 150 miles there and usually takes over three hours with the traffic, but it seemed like a lot less with the kids so excited and happy to be 'on the road'. We barreled along through the North Florida woods with the tape player blasting us with U2 and Pink Floyd all the way. I must have heard "Are we there yet?" at least a hundred times.
>
> The barbeque was nice and I won a fishing rod in a raffle for the local volunteer fire department. The kids had a great time with the cousins, but I was tiring rapidly and couldn't keep up with all the activity. My aerospace engineer cousin either knew nothing about gravity waves or thought it wasn't a suitable subject to discuss with a woman. His attitude seemed to be humorously condescending, so the conversation went nowhere. So there I was, wandering around in the heat, humidity, and bugs, wondering just what the heck was I going to do next. We stayed overnight and I had a strange experience there sleeping in a strange bed. I was feeling so completely alone – more than I ever had in my life – and I wanted so badly to solve these problems about our reality, our existence, our place in the universe, but I just couldn't seem

to connect with a single, solitary person who was as driven as I was to understand *why?* *How?* And all that. I actually began to cry from the frustration, and I was shouting the question at the universe in my mind. It seemed to echo and re-echo endlessly into the vastness of space, which frightened me, but then an odd sensation of comfort, of destiny, seemed to settle over me like a blanket. I just knew that an answer would come if I persisted.

The strangest feeling of disconnectedness from that environment of mindless celebration grew in me all through the next day, and I got more and more restless with each passing moment. I felt like I was going to jump out of my skin.

Meanwhile, Ark was writing in his journal in Florence:

4/7/1996

Since Sunday in Florence. Again in Florence. It was three years ago. I need a new vision. I need a new inspiration. How to get it? I came on Sunday driving Nexia (car brand). I was driving fast and not always safely. At the edge of safety. Yet I knew that nothing is going happen. So I am in Florence. I need a complete, absolute clarity of vision. I need a walk.

Now, return to my side of the account:

Finally, I could stand it no longer and I told the children that as soon as the fireworks were over we were going home. Thankfully, they were tired enough from all their activities that the thought of sleeping in their own beds made them agreeable. We made our apologies for not staying the full three days and headed out with the last 'rocket's red glare' showering down over the softball field in that little backwoods, North Florida town which boasted a single traffic light but one of the best fireworks shows I have ever seen!

On the road again. Night driving in the Florida backwoods – one of life's great pleasures. Minimal traffic, soft scented air blowing in the windows, smooth, two-lane blacktop between towering pine trees for miles and miles. The children were soon asleep and I drove straight home, arriving not long after midnight. I put everyone to bed and had a long, relaxing soak in the tub before putting myself to bed. But, just before turning in, I decided to check my e-mail to see if anybody had sent me anything at all.

"You have mail!" the computer informed me.
And I did.

Subject: Dr. Roger Santilli and the Cassiopaeans...
Send reply to: ajad@physik.uni-bielefeld.de
Date sent: Fri, 5 Jul 1996 19:07:43 +1
Hi, Which is the address (e-mail?) of Dr. Roger Santilli? I would like to take a look at his papers.

Thanks.

ark

What a funny name! And what a funny feeling it gave me. Subtle, indistinct, like a small draft of warm air across my cheek.

"Nothing," my conscious mind scolded! After all, this person with the funny name only wanted Santilli's e-mail, and had nothing at all to say about the Cassiopaeans. What a disappointment! But, it was the first 'nibble' in the eight days since I had sent out the material.

I swallowed my disappointment and decided to be as helpful as possible.

Meanwhile, a few days later Ark wrote in his journal:

13/7/1996

The most incredible thing that has happened is that now I know the person who talks to Cs. What then?

What next? What now?

I Ching, Hexagram 29, Water, changing line 1
Superior man constantly preserves his virtue
And practices the task of education. Avoid excessive drinking.

L. Knight Martin
New Port Richey
SE corner of Montana and Harrison streets

And so the end result was this: indeed, the Cassiopaeans were correct when they said that our little demo at the MUFON meeting was "predestined". Because it created a situation that caught the attention of Santilli, and because, a year later, I posted the Santilli session on a mail list on the internet, it was forwarded to a physicist who was interested in the Cassiopaean material. And not just any physicist – a physicist with a good reputation, a Humboldt Prize–winning physicist with a list of publications as long as my arm, and a specialist in the areas necessary to work on the very problems that had haunted my mind all my life.

Moreover, he was as driven to understand and solve them as I was. And, the curious fact is that he was actually writing about gravity waves in his research journal during the same time period that the Cassiopaeans were urging me to research them, as noted in my comments at the end of the 23 March 1996 session.

At the point in time when Ark found me as a result of the message posted to Steve Wilson's email discussion list, I was as close to dead mentally, psychologically, and even physically, as I had ever been. I had been stripped of everything I ever believed in, my life was basically at an end as far as I could see, and all I wanted was peace for whatever time I had left. There had been a partial revival of my interest in the world as a result of the Cs' hints about gravity waves, and I thought it would be a fairly simple matter of doing some little research, finding the clues, and voila! The Secrets of the Universe would be all laid out for mankind, and then I could die in peace and get some much needed rest.

Now we are at nine days after that first e-mail. However, I was keeping things low key and to myself, though I tried to see if I could indirectly get some guidance, as you will see below in my question about the book I read when I was 11 about the Polish Underground.

Notice also that VG and MM, the aura camera woman with the apparent 'Greenbaum programming', are present.

Participants: 'Frank', Laura, VG, MM

Q: [Last bit of discussion prior to session beginning, which related to the several mentions the Cs had made of the symbolic nature of prophecy, etc.] *(L)* I am just wondering if a lot of things are going to happen that may not be necessarily multi-density, or 'other density', in the strictest of terms, but may in fact be simply actions of 'human agents' of these beings on other densities. That it will not so much be a 'space invasion' as more like the Nazis under the control of 4th density STS? Hello.

A: Hello.

Q: *(L)* And who do we have with us this evening?

A: Derom.

Q: *(L)* And where do you transmit

from?

A: Cassiopaea.

Q: *(L)* Has there been some participation in the discussion we have been having?

A: Monitoring, not participation.

Q: *(L)* Would you care to comment, or shall we just ask our questions?

A: Ask specific questions, as always.

Q: *(L)* Then let's start with some basic things. First of all, I have had some contact with a physicist who is interested in the material. And, because of this, I was motivated to pick up a book I had read many years ago about the German occupation of Poland [*Story of a Secret State* by Jan Karski], and there were some very strange things said in this book, and some funny synchronous numbers ... It just seemed to be a prototype of the present reality in global terms. My question is: is there some synchronous implication between this contact, the reading of this book when I was 11 years old, and the material we have received through this source?

A: Open.

Q: *(L)* You have said that the Holocaust was basically a 'practice run' for the ultimate space invasion. Is this invasion supposed to take place as an actual 'aliens invading the planet' scenario, or ...[1]

A: Too many thought patterns at once. Step by step, please.

Q: *(L)* Let's boil it down. Was Hitler's agenda a practice run for a future scenario?

A: Close. Was a "testing" of the will.[2]

Q: *(L)* Whose will was being tested?

A: Yours.

Q: *(L)* Me specifically, or the planet?

A: Latter.

Q: *(L)* In terms of this scenario, is there some lesson that we can learn about what may or may not occur through this book I have mentioned?

A: Maybe, but suggest you learn to blend mosaic consciousness.

Q: *(L)* What is mosaic consciousness?

A: Thinking in internally spherical terms, rather than using linear "point blank" approach. The whole picture is seen by seeing the whole scene.[3]

---

[1] *The Wave* 8

[2] *The Wave* 7

[3] At the time, this seemed like an impossible suggestion, but over the years, I actually have come to think that way! There is a very clear distinction between service to self and service to others in terms of seeing. The former is subjective and sees only what it wants to see; the latter is objective and sees all. I have tried to convey to many people the amazing changes in my own life as a result of the change in my awareness – the burning away of what I had believed, or wanted to believe about our world for so many years.

What I have had difficulty describing is the completely new feeling that the universe has for me. It is truly like I went from a completely different universe to the one I presently occupy, and all the rules are different – commensurate with my awareness. As I gained more and more knowledge about the way things worked, I began to apply it to all that I experienced in my daily life. This brought about

25 **Q**: *(L)* Well, I guess that is why I get into so many thought patterns ...

26 **A**: Picture yourself as being at the center of a mosaic.

27 **Q**: *(L)* Okay, I know what you are saying, but I just don't think that there is any way I can *do* this!

28 **A**: Yes you can!

29 **Q**: *(L)* Okay. Okay. This whole situation, this Polish connection, this German connection, the American and alien things, the soldier/Nephilim thing, these are all manifestations of a realm border crossing, am I correct?[4]

30 **A**: Close.

31 **Q**: *(L)* And some of the manifestations of a realm border crossing are that some people graduate or transition to 4th density, that their awareness changes, everything changes, the playing field is leveled. So, what happened in Germany was a 'practice run', but what is going to happen is that the 'playing field' is going to be leveled, so it will not be exactly the same scenario. Is this a correct assessment?

32 **A**: Maybe. Alright, my dear, you want the facts, so we will give them to you, and hopefully you will comprehend. If not now, then when necessary maybe ... Fact number one: All there is is lessons. Fact two: this is one big school. Fact three: Timing as you perceive it, is never, NEVER definite. Fact four: What is to happen, as you state it, is a ways off, and will not occur until you have reached that point on the learning cycle, and you are not close yet. Now ponder before more facts are given!!

33 **Q**: *(L)* Okay, this being one infinite school, and we all seem to be wandering around in the darkness ...

34 **A**: Fact five: The learning cycle is vari-

---

many changes, because I made different choices about things than the choices I would have formerly made. Yes, many of these choices were based on things unseen, things that went against the standard, indoctrinated, cultural view of our world with which we are brainwashed by our society, and many of these choices were simply incomprehensible in ordinary terms. But, the fact is, I made them, acted on them, and the results were nothing short of amazing. I was learning to read the subtle clues about the world and the interactions of people that are veiled from us. And these clues were well beyond the usual psychic impressions of your standard 'psychic sensitive', I can assure you! Quite often, it required very hard work to 'see' beyond what I wished to see based on emotional inclinations, or what 'felt good'. Sometimes, seeing the truth feels very 'bad', but only because we are conditioned that way. See: *The Wave*, Chapter 8.

[4]The past-life situation described in *Amazing Grace* is what is referred to here. All my life I was haunted by dreams and images of a past life in Nazi Germany where I was married to a Jew who was arrested. Our four children were also taken away to camps. I committed suicide as a result of my grief for my family. I spent my whole life wondering where my husband of that time was. Upon meeting Ark, both of us experienced phenomena that suggested strongly that he was, indeed, that 'Lost Love' from another life, perhaps even many other lives. As the Cassiopaeans remarked at a later point, we were "complementary souls".

[5]Many people have written to ask me about 'wanting knowledge'. It seems to them

able, and progress along it is determined by events and circumstances as they unfold.⁵

35 **Q**: *(L)* So, the events and circumstances of our lives, individually and collectively, can indicate where we are on this learning cycle? And we are asking to have things told to us, or revealed to us about things which are, in themselves, the necessary lessons? And it would be virtually useless to be told about them since they must be experienced?

36 **A**: Partly correct. If you want hints, then hints shall we give. But, if you are looking for a "road map?," forgetitski!!

37 **Q**: *(L)* Okay, we want some hints. And Ark wants some hints, too! He wants to know if we can invent a tool that enhances free will?

38 **A**: No tool is needed because of facts 3, 4, and 5.

39 **Q**: *(L)* Ummm ... So, when a person is being hypnotized and controlled from outside – because that is the matter of concern we were discussing earlier – they are hypnotized and controlled until they learn to stop it?

40 **A**: Yes.

41 **Q**: *(L)* So, using the analogy of the pigsty, they just have to wallow in it and suffer until they have had enough?⁶

42 **A**: Using your analogy of the bicycle: Is there a tool which makes it unnecessary for the child to learn how to ride the bicycle in order to know how to ride it?!?

43 **Q**: *(MM)* Don't you get more free will by assimilating knowledge?

44 **A**: Yes!! Yes!!

45 **Q**: *(L)* So, in other words, knowledge and awareness makes you aware that you have free will, and also makes you aware of what actions actually *are* acts of free will, and therefore, when you know or suspect the difference between the lies and deception and truth, then you are in a position to be in control of your life?

46 **A**: Yes.

47 **Q**: *(L)* Ark also wants to ask ... well, his problem is faith, as he said it to me.

48 **A**: Faith comes also from knowledge, and as we have stated before ... False knowledge is worse than no knowledge at all!!!!!!

49 **Q**: *(L)* So, it is important to take each and every thing that is being learned or analyzed, and take it completely apart and dig in every direction around it, and

---

that the gaining and gathering of knowledge is an STS activity, but as the Cs say in the same session, "That is not passion; it is soul questing."

Then, of course, there is the question of making 'leaps' – wanting to skip over the 3rd density part and go right back to where all is wonderful and happy and peaceful. One has to realize that this sort of thinking is more deeply STS than it might at first appear because, in the end, what is wanted is to escape the hard work of learning the lessons of this density. What is wanted is ease and comfort and no work. Such individuals want to sit in circles, contemplate their navels and chant "Oooommmm", while bombarding the planet with their 'unconditional love and light' so that everybody else will get with their program, and we can all go home now! (Note that 'their program' contradicts the unconditional nature of the love and light they send!)

⁶*Secret History* 12; *The Wave* 27

even in related directions, to *fully* ascertain that it is true? As C.S. Lewis said, knowledge is like a rope ... as long as you are using it to tie up a box, it doesn't matter whether it is perfect or not, but if you have to use it to hang over a precipice, then it behooves you to make absolutely certain that it is strong enough to support your weight.

50 **A**: Yes.

51 **Q**: *(L)* Okay, Ark asks about this: "In 1979, Project Phoenix,[7] with the assistance of the Grays, was successful in producing a mind amplifier." Is this true?

52 **A**: Nope!

53 **Q**: *(L)* Okay! That was pretty precise! Next: "Is it possible that, under drug influence, psychics, or those with mental capabilities above the norm, can be hooked up to some type of machine and are enabled thereby to create some type of physical form?"

54 **A**: Possible.[8] Now review: The "Greys" are cyber-genetic probes of the "Lizard" beings, so just exactly who is doing the assisting? And who is behind the Lizard types?? Could it be your ancestors, perhaps!?!

55 **Q**: *(L)* It says here [reads text]: "The fire within man that is characterized as passion is the secret that can be utilized. The secret to all things is passion. With passion all things are possible. The amplification experiments of the Phoenix Project have been explained as having amplified brain waves. In fact, it amplified the passion of the subject. It was that 'inner will' of the subject that was amplified, that inner spirit within all of us is that driving force is manifested as electrical energy. Master that force and you cannot be controlled, the universe is yours. Master the inner spirit and you shall master the physical." Comments please.

56 **A**: First things first: Who is doing the assisting? And how is the assisting being done?!!!!!!???

57 **Q**: *(L)* Well, they say that the Grays are assisting the Consortium – this is the Hopi material ... Who is doing the assisting? Hmmmm ... give me a clue ... I think that the Nordic aliens are controlling the Lizards, who created the Grays, which are probes of the Lizards, and are purportedly assisting the Consortium ...

58 **A**: Assisting? Or maybe influencing?!? And if so, how so?!? And, is not this the whole point? Are you not ultimately influenced always?!? In EVERYTHING you do? We have stated thus numerous times ... So, please let us not get off the track, okay?

59 **Q**: *(L)* In other words, as long as we are in the pigsty, we are in the pigsty, and until we get *out* of it, we are *in* it?[9]

60 **A**: Until you reach that point on the learning cycle.

61 **Q**: *(MM)* What is this chemical they use with these psychics, per se? Is it the 'akashic chemical'?

62 **A**: That information you refer to is false in its entirety!

63 **Q**: *(L)* So, does that mean that the whole thing is false?

---

[7]Also known as the Montauk Project. See session 9 June 1996.
[8]It's actually kind of scary that the Cs say this is possible!
[9]*Secret History* "Afterword"

64 **A:** "Passion" does not set one "free," quite the opposite!¹⁰

65 **Q:** *(L)* But what if your passion is for knowledge?¹¹

66 **A:** That is not passion, it is soul questing.

67 **Q:** *(L)* What is it that gives some people this drive, this steamroller effect that they are determined to get to the absolute bottom of everything and strip away every lie until there is nothing left but the naked truth? What is the source of this desire?

68 **A:** Wrong concept. It is simply that one is at that point on the learning cycle. At that point, no drive is needed.¹²

69 **Q:** *(L)* So, you more or less are there because some critical mass has been reached that 'jumps' you to the point where seeking truth is simply who you are? It defines the parameters of your being.

(MM) Are these learning cycles similar to the layers ... all over the earth – remember the red dust all over the earth?¹³

70 **A:** No.

71 **Q:** *(L)* Is it more like a 360-degree circle, and each person is at a different point on the circle, and the whole thing cycles, and you never change relative to the people behind and in front of you, and the only real thing you can do to help anyone is to move the circle by moving yourself, thereby pushing the one ahead of you up, and pulling the one behind you into your previous place? And where you are on the cycle determines what you do?

72 **A:** It is a single cycle, yes. There is only one learning cycle, and where you are upon it, determines your EXPERIENCES, and vice versa.¹⁴

73 **Q:** *(L)* Is there ever any point where

---

¹⁰ *The Wave* 27
¹¹ *The Wave* 8
¹²The great Sufi shaykh Ibn al-Arabi wrote about these very things. William Chittick both translates and comments on the Sufi teachings in *The Sufi Path of Knowledge*. The following are extracts of both al-Arabi and Dr. Chittick's remarks:

> "Are they equal," asks the Koran, "those who know and those who know not?" (39:9) Knowledge is a divine attribute of all-encompassingness, so it is the most excellent bounty of God ... For man, the seeker of knowledge, the acquisition of knowledge is endless, since the objects of knowledge are endless. This is the secret of man's felicity. Knowledge, the greatest good, is also the greatest joy and the greatest pleasure. The never-ending trajectory of man's life in the next world has to be explained in terms of his constant growth in knowledge.
> For the felicitous, this knowledge is totally congruent and harmonious with their souls, which have been shaped in this world throughout faith and practice, and hence every increase in knowledge is an increase in felicity. For the wretched, knowledge of things as they actually are is a searing torture, since it contradicts their beliefs and practices in this world. Every new knowledge – every new self-disclosure, recognized now for what it is – is a new misery.

¹³I have absolutely *no* idea what MM was referring to here.
¹⁴Notice that they did not negate my concept above that the only way to move was to help the person ahead of you and behind you.

lines connect from one point on the cycle so that you can 'jump' from one point to another? Like a wormhole in space or something?

74 **A:** Refer to facts 1 and 2 and 3.

75 **Q:** *(L)* So, no short cuts?

76 **A:** Now, refer to 3, 4 and 5.

77 **Q:** *(L)* So, certain events and circumstances could help a person to make 'leaps'?

78 **A:** No "leap," acceleration.[15]

79 **Q:** *(L)* One thing, previously when we were talking about unstable gravity waves, and I asked what caused them to become unstable, you said "utilization", and that STO was dispersion, and STS was collection of gravity. I have made a few conjectures about this and would like to ask, does this mean that in giving to others, even if what you are giving is a withholding of assistance because you know that assistance would only prolong the lesson, is dispersing gravity, and exerting mental or other control over others, even if one is unaware that they are attaching energy drains to another, is collecting gravity?

80 **A:** Close.

81 **Q:** *(L)* So, when you collect gravity, you become like a black hole, you cave in on yourself?

82 **A:** Ultimately.

83 **Q:** *(L)* And it seems to me that one of the objects of what we are doing is releasing the gravity collected in ourselves?

84 **A:** If that is your choice, or if that is your path.

85 **Q:** *(L)* Is choice as intimately connected with the path as I am understanding it? Is it just simply part of how you are configured in your soul essence?

86 **A:** Close.

87 **Q:** *(L)* And there are people for whom STS is simply their choice. It is their path.

88 **A:** Close.

89 **Q:** *(L)* So, it is a judgment and a disservice to try to convert someone to your path, even if you perceive the end result of the path they are on, that it leads to dissolution? It is still their path?

90 **A:** Yes.

91 **Q:** *(L)* And, if you send 'buckets of love and light' to such a one, and that is their path, you are violating their free will?

---

[15]This reminds me of what the Cs said on 24 February 1996: "Remember, you learn on an exponential curve, once you have become 'tuned in.' This means that you become increasingly able to access the universal consciousness. Please learn to trust your increasing awareness. All who are present here are at one point or another on that cycle, or one point or another on that cycle of progression, some further along than others. If you properly network without prejudice, you may all wind up at the same point on this cycle. We also mean that you can access the universal consciousness to find the answers to otherwise unseen truths ..."

[16]"Justice is to put everything in its proper place, while wisdom is to act as is proper in every situation. Proper activity is impossible without discernment of the right relationships. The 'sage' or 'possessor of wisdom' is He who does what is proper for what is proper as is proper.

92 **A:** You might as well send "buckets" of vomit as that is how they will react.[16]

93 **Q:** *(MM)* Why send anything? Just be neutral?

94 **A:** Judgment is STS.

95 **Q:** *(L)* You told us before that stars and planets are portals, or openings into other densities. Is it possible that this oncoming Wave, this realm border crossing, will be accessed through these types of portals, that it is not something that is actually in our 'space', but that it would emanate through stars and planets? Am I onto something here?

96 **A:** You may be starting down a long path.

97 **Q:** *(L)* So, it is complex. When I was re-reading *Noah* ...

98 **A:** Just remember: All prophecies attached to calendar dates are useless unless you wish to be sucked up by the 4th density STS forces![17]

99 **Q:** *(L)* Speaking of being sucked up by 4th density STS forces, MM was told by her local Hindu gathering that she was vacuuming up their energies. What

---

"The Prophet said, 'Give to everyone who has a right his right.' Here the term may also be translated as 'rightful due'. The right of a person or a thing is that which he deserves on the basis of his nature and in keeping with the Law.

"The person who gives each thing its due is not only wise, but also courteous.

"The Divine root of courtesy is that God creates the world in order to manifest the properties of His names, and each name requires specific situations. Among these names are the 'secondary causes,' or the 'created things' of the Cosmos. God has established the secondary causes for a purpose, and the man of courtesy gives each its due. This means letting each reality play its proper function. The person who wishes to 'abolish' secondary causes shows discourtesy toward God.

"The divine man of courtesy is he who affirms what God has affirmed in the place where God has affirmed it and in the manner in which He has affirmed it.

"God did not establish the secondary causes aimlessly. He wanted us to stand up for them and rely upon them with a divine reliance. The Divine Wisdom makes this known ... So the divine and courteous sage is he who places the secondary causes where God has placed them. No one abolishes the secondary causes except him who is ignorant that God has put them there. No one affirms the secondary causes except a great learned master, a man of courtesy in knowledge of God.

"The sage among God's servants is he who puts each thing in its place and does not take it beyond its level. He gives to each that has its due, and does not judge anything according to his individual desire or his caprice. The sage considers the abode where God has settled him for a fixed term and he considers, without increase or decrease, the scope of the activity within this abode that God has laid down for him in the Law. Then he walks in the manner which has been explained to him and he never lets the Scale which has been set up for him in this abode drop from his hand." (Chittick, *The Sufi Path of Knowledge*)

[17] Yet again the Cs warn about trying to get, or take, prophecies literally!

[18] That is apparently what motivated her to contact me and ask to attend a session. If you recall, the last time she was present, she was certain that she and her friend Wilma were communicating with Parahmahansa Yogananda directly. She didn't

kind of an interaction was this? Why were they so uncomfortable?[18]

100 **A**: Because they wished to be worshipped.

101 **Q**: *(L)* They wished to suck her energy, because being worshipped is the equivalent of sucking energy?

102 **A**: Close.

103 **Q**: *(L)* Now, I am curious about the doggie image that was on the aura photo that MM took?[19]

104 **A**: In these times, 2nd density creatures will collect more and more attachments.

105 **Q**: *(L)* Are these attachments like other entities?

106 **A**: Yes, and others.

107 **Q**: *(L)* When they are collecting these attachments, are they collecting them from us, as in protecting?

108 **A**: No.

109 **Q**: *(L)* Are they being used to collect attachments to be detrimental to us?

110 **A**: Yes.

111 **Q**: *(L)* You mean we are gonna have to do depossessions on our dogs, too? *(V)* Holy Toledo!

112 **A**: That won't work.

113 **Q**: *(L)* Why are our animals picking up attachments?

114 **A**: Because of vibrational frequency intensifications.

115 **Q**: *(L)* Is there something we could do? I mean, are we supposed to get rid of pets?

116 **A**: We would never suggest something as harsh as this. However, beware: 3rd density STS orientation includes the thought of "dominion" over 2nd density, and this is merely a continuation of the energy buildups of the approach of the Wave ... Some of the lessons are interesting indeed. When you assume that capture and imprisonment of those of lesser capacity than you is for "the good," why should not you expect those of greater capacity than you to assume the same regarding you?!?[20]

117 **Q**: *(MM)* Well, I want to know what is the deal with this portal in my house?

118 **A**: Before we discuss that, we would like you to ponder further the previously given responses. We suspect there is much to be gained from insights lurking there. Now: Portals ... Ionic column ... hmmm ...

119 **Q**: *(V)* Are portals archetypal?

120 **A**: Are they? Hmmm ....

121 **Q**: *(MM)* So, my column is an Ionic column? *(L)* I don't think that is exactly what they mean. I think that they are saying that an Ionic column represents a portal into the next density. It is an archetype.

122 **A**: Third density facsimile.[21]

---

like that the Cs would not confirm this for her.

[19] MM took a photo with her aura camera (or so she told me), and in this aura photo there was an image of a dog in the aura area. Not really clear, more a suggestive image.

[20] Excellent point. The Cs are suggesting that, in some cases, higher-density beings look on us as pets; rather quelling to the ego!

[21] Recall the session of 25 May 1996 where the Cs discussed building a swimming pool as an inter-density transceiver.

123 **Q:** *(V)* So, this is how we choose to see it with our eyes? *(L)* I think they mean that it is a representation, that it follows in its form the 4th density form, only it is material here.

124 **A:** And 5th density, etc...

125 **Q:** *(L)* Okay, MM's portal – she has been experimenting with it, with this trans-density transceiver ...

126 **A:** No, she does not have a trans-density transceiver, she has a portal presence.

127 **Q:** *(L)* What is the function of a portal presence?

128 **A:** Function is not the correct concept.

129 **Q:** *(L)* What is it?

130 **A:** The presence of a portal.

131 **Q:** *(L)* Is this portal that is present related to any person in her house, or related to the area?

132 **A:** It is.

133 **Q:** *(L)* Which?

134 **A:** It just is.

135 **Q:** *(L)* Was it there before she moved there?

136 **A:** That is not important.

137 **Q:** *(L)* What is important?

138 **A:** Ask yourself that. Awareness.

139 **Q:** *(L)* On the one hand you could think it is a good thing and be wrong, and on the other hand you could think it is a bad thing and miss a good thing?

140 **A:** Learning is fun.

141 **Q:** *(MM)* I'm getting ready to work with it in meditation. But, I have been working with it and finding out more about it, and I was just wondering ...

142 **A:** Hey lady, don't you get it yet?[22]

143 **Q:** *(V)* Who is 'hey lady'? It must be me ...

144 **A:** No.

145 **Q:** *(V)* That is very odd. *(MM)* I was wondering if it goes to other densities?

146 **A:** Yes, but so what? This does too.

147 **Q:** *(L)* Why was this portal represented by a completely different figure?

148 **A:** None.

149 **Q:** *(L)* Is she supposed to channel through this portal?

150 **A:** The portal is not "importaltent!"

151 **Q:** *(L)* I guess that implies intent ... The portal is not important, what is important is what is going on inside you. And only you can know that.

152 **A:** On that note, goodnight.

End of Session

---

[22] The Cs did not seem very happy with MM and her 'portal'. They were mimicking the way she always started a sentence with "Hey..." Not surprising considering the revelations about MM as reported in previous sessions!

July 21, 1996

I had been keeping Terry and Jan informed about the sessions and other developments, and after Ark's arrival on the virtual scene, their interest was revived to a certain extent. (They had also indicated that their channeling experiment with Andrew B was going nowhere.) However, they (and Frank) spent something like 6 hours repeating to me that Ark must be an agent and I had to be very careful. I appreciated their concern and decided that maybe we ought to ask a few questions along that line. However, the Cs were having none of that. It was almost comical that I was trying to get a hint and they were determined to give nothing at all on this topic. As later events proved, it's obvious in retrospect why: some things are predestined events and must be entered into and managed entirely on one's own. Also, there was the fact that they had been giving me clues all along, but because I had been so depressed, I had not kept up with transcribing the sessions and could not review them so as to see those hints.

Participants: 'Frank', Laura, Terry, Jan

1 **Q:** *(L)* Hello.

2 **A:** Hello.

3 **Q:** *(L)* And who do we have with us tonight?

4 **A:** Vimon.

5 **Q:** *(L)* And where are you transmitting from?

6 **A:** Cassiopaea.

7 **Q:** *(L)* Is there any sinister intent toward me by Ark J? His thoughts toward me?

8 **A:** Too many, fragmented.

9 **Q:** *(L)* His thoughts?

10 **A:** No. Your questions.

11 **Q:** *(L)* Okay, more specific: I am having a dialogue with a man who contacted me via the internet.

12 **A:** Yes.

13 **Q:** *(L)* And it seems that there are a lot of synchronous events happening in conjunction with this.

14 **A:** Maybe.

15 **Q:** *(L)* Is it possible that some of these seemingly synchronous events are being created to deceive me?

16 **A:** Sure it is possible!

17 **Q:** *(L)* What does Ark J feel toward me.

18 **A:** "Feel" is not the point!

19 **Q**: *(L)* What is the point? What are his intentions?

20 **A**: Multiple.

21 **Q**: *(L)* Could you tell me at least two primary ones?

22 **A**: No we will not.[1]

23 **Q**: *(L)* Can you give me any of them?

24 **A**: How do you learn?

25 **Q**: *(L)* I know. But, I am also somewhat fragile and don't want to dive into the soup!

26 **A**: By using the powers existent within your mind, which are unlimited, as we have told you.

27 **Q**: *(L)* I know you are not going to give me a roadmap, but you can give me a hint! What are the extent of the hints you can give me about this?

28 **A**: One and only hint: always transcribe and review material from the sessions if you wish to learn properly, and avoid possibly fatal mistakes!!![2]

29 **Q**: *(L)* So, that is the one and only hint. I will start back on the transcribing.

30 **A**: Little by little makes a seemingly daunting task seem effortless. Learning is enhanced by timeless, enhanced pondering.

31 **Q**: *(L)* How do you enhance pondering?

32 **A**: With patience ... You see, Laura, it is better to be the tortoise than the hare!

33 **Q**: *(L)* Why did my air conditioner break down today when I was talking about the heat to Ark J?

34 **A**: Maybe it is time to enhance your pondering. Drastic measures are only necessary when one's stubbornness places one upon the precipice!

35 **Q**: *(L)* Well, if you guys did that, I hope you thought of the fact that there won't be any sessions until it gets fixed!

36 **A**: Do we need sessions?!?

37 **Q**: *(L)* No, you don't, but don't we?

38 **A**: What good are they when the messages are lost?

39 **Q**: *(J)* What is the significance of Terry's and my presence here tonight? Is it significant?

40 **A**: Yes! And road maps available at the Mobil station.

41 **Q**: *(L)* Well, we're glad to see you too!

42 **A**: Thank you! And likewise.

43 **Q**: *(J)* Well, how about a hint?

44 **A**: Answers are known. Doubt is sometimes relieved by pause.

45 **Q**: *(J)* Well, I think we ought to take a hiatus and get all the sessions transcribed.

46 **A**: Do it step by step. Do not attempt a marathon here. "Time" is not of the essence!

47 **Q**: *(L)* Well, then I will just do them as I go along – is that what you mean?

---

[1] The Cs were always pretty adamant about *not* interfering in any way with my choices, lessons, etc. And it's a good thing, too, I think!

[2] Obviously, the "fatal mistake" referenced would have been to listen to Terry, Jan, and Frank in respect of Ark. Over and over again they had hinted that he – and great changes – were just around the corner. When we connected, there was instant recognition. But Frank was convinced that Ark was an agent of some sort who was going to ruin everything. Well, in a sense, it did for Frank.

48 **A**: Partially. You need review, study, contemplation.

49 **Q**: *(L)* What I need is a vacation and less stress!

50 **A**: We would say that too! There are untold treasure troves locked up in those transcripts. You will be "blown away" by that which you have forgotten!!

51 **Q**: *(L)* Well, then we have a plan! Carry on!

52 **A**: Okay, folks, goodnight!

End of Session

July 27, 1996

The initial interaction with Ark was similar in some ways to the interaction with Frank's dad – it opened a huge door in my psyche, and again I began to remember. But it was quite different in flavor, texture, and context. All of the memories of lifetimes with Ark centered around the efforts of outside agents to separate us from each other, to make us suffer for our attempts to be together, and repeating scenarios of being horribly and brutally killed for seeking to work together for the betterment and freedom of others. Hopefully, such lessons will help us to avoid similar traps in this life, though it will become clear that the same types of forces have been activated against us.

There was a strange byproduct of this remembering and integration: I began to cry on that first day of the connection with Ark, and cried almost daily for the next year and a half. It was as though an ocean of grief was locked up inside and every single instance of suffering had to be re-experienced and fully mourned in order to integrate it. As a person who seldom cried, who had always had some measure of control over emotions, this inability to stop this flow of soul-deep grief was disconcerting to say the least. But there was another interesting side-effect of this releasing of the waters of life in such copious production of tears: my eyes began to heal.

It was now 22 days since Ark first wrote to me. I wish I could convey to the reader the overpowering sense of recognition that we both felt in reaction to the words and 'essence' of each other. The problem was that we had both been so burned by relationships that we were overly cautious. This was good in a way, however; we avoided making mistakes. But when the emotions are like horses that want to take the bit in their teeth, it was torture!

Having spent the previous three months in utter pain and misery, recognizing Ark as 'the one' I had given up on completely had a really strange effect. Well, it could also be the 'deep fibrous linkage in DNA' that the Cs mentioned a few sessions back. Whatever it was, I felt as though I was living between two completely different worlds simultaneously, and it was crazy-making! In retrospect, it was probably the effects of literally changing realities, changing timelines, but I couldn't know that then. I only know that the events of high strangeness in my life went off the scale. And this was true for Ark, too. Thus, this session where I was practically begging the Cs to tell me what the heck was going on.

But I wasn't the only one who was 'remembering'. This 'superhypnotherapist' action of the awakened superconsciousness had also apparently been activated for Ark as well.

Participants: 'Frank', Laura

Q: *(L)* Hello.

A: Hello.

Q: *(L)* And who do we have with us this evening?

A: Wonikha.

Q: *(L)* And where are you transmitting from?

A: Cassiopaea.

Q: *(L)* I am worried about my daughter. Is she alright? [She was out later than usual and hadn't called. I was a nervous wreck.][1]

A: Yes.

Q: *(L)* Will she be home soon?

A: Open.

Q: *(L)* Well, I worry about her lately.

A: She must experience that which she must experience.

Q: *(L)* That's true for everyone, even children.

A: Sort of.

Q: *(L)* I have been going crazy wondering about Ark J. Can I please ask some questions?

A: You may ask whatever you wish.

Q: *(L)* Well, one day it is one way, and I think I know what is happening, and the next day it is like something grips him and the whole mood changes. Can you tell me what is going on?

A: Why?

Q: *(L)* What is it that I said that caused him to be so cool to me?[2]

A: Are you learning?

Q: *(L)* Probably. I think I am. But what is in his mind? What have I said or done?

A: Not important.

---

[1] I already discussed the fact that my kids were having a very hard time with the separation and impending divorce. My second daughter was particularly affected, as I described previously.

[2] I really wasn't thinking about the fact that it was just as difficult for Ark, who was looking at what seemed to be the fact that he, too, had 'lost his mind' and was contemplating changing his whole life because of an online encounter! Every once in awhile he would try to be rational (as I did, too), but it was hopeless. Whatever force was drawing us together was impossible to resist.

23 **Q:** *(L)* What is important here? Is it important at all?

24 **A:** Wait and see.

25 **Q:** *(L)* Is there anything I can ask? What is going on with me? I am an emotional wreck ... Is the past life connection that I perceive part of this?[3]

26 **A:** Do you learn when we lead you by the hand? You have all the necessary tools to discover this.

27 **Q:** *(L)* Well, I thought *you* were one of those tools! That you are here to help us ...

28 **A:** But not by giving the answers to "Level One" questions.

29 **Q:** *(L)* Just one thing I would like to know is, what is the source of this emotional energy that is practically tearing me apart? Is it coming from outside or inside me?

30 **A:** The one thing we would like to know is: how much transcribing have you been doing?

31 **Q:** *(L)* I have been going through the notebooks and reading, I have been sorting things ... I am getting ready to start typing ...

32 **A:** The "answers" are there.[4]

33 **Q:** *(L)* Well, one thing I came across was a mention almost two years ago that something would happen, and one would have instant recognition, but the others may doubt. For me, it was instant recognition. But, recognition, by definition, is to know someone again. So, I think maybe that you were using the term recognition because you were talking about a person and not an event, necessarily.[5]

A: And learning helps you in immeasurable ways. 34

35 **Q:** *(L)* One last question, if there is a question that I could ask, to which I could receive a clue, consider it asked ... I am baffled!

A: Baffled yes, but buffeted, no. 36

37 **Q:** *(L)* So, I am not being buffeted by something outside, I am being baffled from inside.

A: Yes. 38

39 **Q:** *(L)* Is Ark J taking energy from me in some way? [This was what Frank had suggested.]

A: Open. 40

41 **Q:** *(L)* Is that all you can give me?

A: Maybe. 42

43 **Q:** *(L)* What are his thoughts and intentions toward me?

A: No. 44

---

[3] In *Amazing Grace* I wrote about the many dreams and psychic experiences I had about a past life in Nazi Germany where my husband was shot by the Nazis, our children taken to a concentration camp, and I committed suicide. That was one of the overlapping 'worlds' I was experiencing at this time, along with a number of other experiences of past lives, or so it seemed. I wouldn't just 'remember' things, I would actually find myself *in* those experiences – at least partly. I never lost my connection to this reality, but I could see things, hear conversations, experience emotions, all belonging to another person who was both me and not-me at the same time. It was crazy and I was sure I was losing my mind.

[4] Yes, the Cs were telling me all about the coming of Ark all along, but rather subtly!

[5] Session 28 October 1994.

45 **Q:** *(L)* Well, you have answered this kind of question before! You have told me about so many other people! How come you won't answer me about him?

46 **A:** It is not appropriate.

47 **Q:** *(L)* Why is it not appropriate? I am just trying to understand! I am in such a whirlwind inside ... pleeeeeease ...

48 **A:** Wait and see.

49 **Q:** *(L)* Does that mean good or bad?

50 **A:** It means what is Anna doing with those keys?[6]

51 **Q:** *(L)* What are you talking about? Anna doesn't have any keys!? I am exhausted, and you are being too obscure. Is there some clue as to how to conduct myself? Is he in any danger by talking about coming here?

52 **A:** No more than usual.

53 **Q:** *(L)* He believes that we can do things, that they can be done, that we can have a positive effect [for humanity].

54 **A:** Then focus on that!

55 **Q:** *(L)* Well, how did we get sidetracked on this other thing? Is that a form of attack?

56 **A:** Maybe.

57 **Q:** *(L)* Well, I don't want to put him in any danger.

58 **A:** There are ways.

59 **Q:** *(L)* Is there anything we can do with this gravity wave business? He is also very interested in this.

60 **A:** Then work on that with him!! Review the transcripts and that which has not yet transcribed.

61 **Q:** *(L)* Okay. I will start.

62 **A:** But slowly.

63 **Q:** *(L)* Okay, slowly but surely. And I am tired. So, goodnight and sorry this was such a short visit.

64 **A:** Short but sweet. Goodnight.

End of Session

---

[6]The odd question "what is Anna doing with those keys" made no sense to me at the time, but that was because I didn't know that Ark's soon-to-be-ex-wife was named Anna. I thought that the remark was about my daughter of the same name. However, it seems that Ark was the 'spin doctor', the 'super hypnotherapist' who had keys to unlock what was in my subconscious.

> 24 February 96:
> **A:** Oh Laura, my dear, seems you need a refresher course in the transcripts. Maybe suggest you read them and relax and privately listen to the ones you have not as of yet transcribed a little more. This would be extremely helpful in your many and increasing communications via the "net" as well. Remember, we help you to unlock answers that have been placed in your superconsciousness files from before the "time" of the birth of your physical body. Also, false information is worse than no information at all.

Note in the above the reference to communications via the net in relation to "unlocking"; I met Ark via my communications on the internet.

August 3, 1996

In the discussion period before this session, I let the group know that, at this point, plans were already being made for Ark to come to Florida so that we could meet. I felt that most of what passed between us was too personal to discuss with anyone else, so I was not giving much away, but at the same time, I was trying to figure out ways to ask the Cs innocuous questions that would get me answers without revealing too much.

I was going through some of the most bizarre experiences of my life in terms of states, visions, dreams, psychokinetic phenomena, physiological reactions, and so forth, but I didn't want to talk about that to anyone in any detail. I kept recalling what the Cs had said back on 28 October 1994:

Q: *(L)* Since the energy is high at this time, we would like to know if you have anything to give in the form of a teaching?

A: Not ready for that yet; establish clear channel and forum first; one step at a time.

Q: *(L)* What is the forum?

A: What do you think?

Q: *(L)* Do you mean that we need to bring more people into this work?

A: Close.

Q: *(L)* We need to create a forum.

A: Yes. A direction will open if you persevere.

Q: *(L)* So things will be brought to us and happen for us if we just persevere?

A: Soon expect big opportunity.

Q: *(L)* I assume that we are not to ask what it is, we are to have faith, is that correct?

A: Yes. Danger you may misinterpret opportunity.

Q: *(L)* Should we all three be able to realize in congruence whether the opportunity is good?

A: Varying degrees.

Q: *(L)* If there is a danger we may misinterpret the opportunity, could you give us a couple of clues so that when it occurs we won't miss it?

A: At least one of you will have instant recognition but others may not. Wait and see.

Q: *(L)* This misinterpretation, does this mean we can count on this misinterpretation?

A: Open.

It was certainly true that I had "instant recognition" of Ark and that the others in the group did not; in fact, they were not just doubtful, Frank was antagonistic. But, of course, that wasn't the only clue, just the one that guided my controlling of what information I revealed to the rest of the group; I didn't have the strength to fight them so I kept things to myself for the most part.

In any event, after the first few personal questions were out of the way, this session took a very, *very* interesting turn ... apocalyptic, even.

Participants: 'Frank', Laura, Terry, Jan

1 **Q:** *(T)* I think we ought to take a road trip. *(L)* Where to? *(T)* Down to Homestead, the Coral Castle. *(L)* Yes, I want to do that too. Okay, Hello!

2 **A:** Hello.

3 **Q:** What name will we use tonight?

4 **A:** Jopoye.

5 **Q:** *(L)* And where are you from?

6 **A:** Cassiopaea.

7 **Q:** *(L)* Before I give up the floor to everyone else, I would like to know if you have any comment about Ark? My experience here is so strange, and I don't want to be caught in a trap ...[1]

8 **A:** New.

9 **Q:** *(L)* New what? What does that mean?

10 **A:** What it is.

11 **Q:** *(T)* New as in 'renewed'?

12 **A:** Yes.

13 **Q:** *(L)* Beginning?

14 **A:** See how one simple word causes you to use your minds?

15 **Q:** *(T)* Yes.

16 **A:** And if we had given you a long and eloquent response, as you desired, you would not have!

17 **Q:** *(L)* Any more words on this subject?

18 **A:** No, thank you!

19 **Q:** *(L)* Let me just ask this *one little thing* ... I am trying so hard to restrain myself – like the tortoise – but sometimes I am overwhelmed. Can you advise me on my conduct? It is such a struggle ...

20 **A:** Discover.

21 **Q:** *(L)* Ark used some of the material in a lecture today, given in Germany.

---

[1] *The Wave* 39

[2] When Ark first wrote to me on July 5, he was in Florence. Since then, he had traveled to his home in Poland, and then had gone to Hamburg to attend a conference where he gave a talk (The Deutsches Elektronen-Synchrotron AKA DESY). I had a small photo of him that he had posted on his personal website, but he wanted one of me. This was in the early days of my computer education and I had to get help from a friend to scan a photo and instruct me how to send it. It took several tries for me to do the deed and the email with the photo arrived on Ark's first day at the conference. He loaded the photo and, apparently, went through the same thing I had gone through when I saw his photo and realized that it was the face of

Were you aware of this?²

22 **A**: Aware, yes.

23 **Q**: *(L)* I wonder if he is one of the less than 100 'aware ones' on the planet that you have told us about?

24 **A**: You have just said too much for us to answer.³

25 **Q**: *(L)* Because it would violate free will?

26 **A**: Or because it was "mishmash."

27 **Q**: *(L)* Okay. No more questions for me! They aren't going to tell me anything anyway! That is clear!

28 **A**: Oh yeah?

29 **Q**: *(L)* So, what are you going to tell me?

30 **A**: Discover!

31 **Q**: *(T)* Okay, word association. What words will get the answers we are looking for?

32 **A**: Sensible questions.

33 **Q**: *(L)* Well, you ask the questions, Terry. *(T)* I am often at a loss as to what to ask. I am never sure whether I am asking dumb questions or smart questions.

34 **A**: We will let you know.

35 **Q**: *(T)* I want to ask a personal question to start with. As you know, we have been proceeding in our campaign against the construction of a cellular tower across the street from us. We are feeling good about it. Shall we continue with what we are doing, in the way we are doing it? I don't know exactly how to ask this so you won't answer "discover, open, up to you, or whatever." *(L)* All of the above, Terry. You just answered your own question!

36 **A**: What you are doing is what you must do, or you would not be doing it!

37 **Q**: *(T)* Well, we are having fun, and it is helping our neighbors.

38 **A**: Instincts guide one to lessons.

39 **Q**: *(L)* This is kind of an off-the-wall question that just popped into my head. Did we ever ask anything about Hale-Bopp?

40 **A**: Yes.⁴

41 **Q**: *(L)* Is Hale-Bopp going to turn planet Earth into a super-conductor?

---

the man I had seen in my vision almost a year before. There is no way to describe the feeling of seeing someone and knowing for certain that you know that person at a soul level; you feel like you have been lifted out of your body and off the planet. (Now you know why I thought I was going crazy!) Anyway, he didn't want to sit and stare at the screen of his laptop so he thought he would print the photo and put it in his pocket so he could look at it privately. So, he did. No sooner than he had printed it than he sent me a quick email saying that he could not speak, he had to go out, and right at that moment, the power went out at the DESY conference and everything was down for hours, so I heard nothing further from him and nearly went nuts trying to figure out what was going on. Things were finally back to normal and he wrote about his lecture which utilized some of the ideas the Cs had referenced, and he ended with "Knowledge protects, ignorance is dangerous."

³This response is, in itself, a definite clue, even if the Cs were trying to put me off in the next response.

⁴See sessions 24 February 1996 and 23 March 1996 for brief mentions.

A: No.

Q: *(L)* Is Hale-Bopp the herald of the transition into 4th density?

A: No.

Q: *(L)* Is Hale-Bopp going to do anything other than pass by with a nice nighttime show?

A: No.

Q: *(T)* Is all the brouhaha over Hale-Bopp a smoke screen?

A: No.

Q: *(L)* Well, what is it then?

A: Hale-Bopp: Flopp!

Q: *(T)* Oh! The Kahoutek[5] of the nineties! *(J)* The cosmic OJ Simpson trial! Something to keep us busy ...

A: Since you have broached the subject: are you familiar with the "twin sun" theory?[6]

Q: *(L)* No. What is it? *(T)* Referring to our sun and the possibility of Jupiter being a sun in the making?

A: No.

Q: *(T)* Okay, what is the twin sun theory?

---

[5]"Comet Kohoutek, formally designated C/1973 E1, 1973 XII, and 1973f, was first sighted on 7 March 1973 by Czech astronomer Luboš Kohoutek. It attained perihelion on 28 December that same year.

"Comet Kohoutek is a long-period comet; its previous apparition was about 150,000 years ago, and its next apparition will be in about 75,000 years. At its apparition in 1973 it had a hyperbolic trajectory (e > 1) due to gravitational perturbations from giant planets. Due to its path, scientists theorized that Kohoutek was an Oort-cloud object. As such, it was believed that this was the comet's first visit to the inner Solar System, which would result in a spectacular display of outgassing. Infrared and visual telescopic study have led many scientists to conclude, in retrospect, that Kohoutek is actually a Kuiper-belt object, which would account for its apparent rocky makeup and lack of outgassing.

"Before its close approach, Kohoutek was hyped by the media as the 'comet of the century'. However, Kohoutek's display was considered a let-down, possibly due to partial disintegration when the comet closely approached the Sun prior to its Earth flyby. Since this was probably the comet's first visit to the inner Solar System, it would have still contained large amounts of frozen volatiles since its creation. Although it failed to brighten to levels expected, it was still a naked-eye object. Its greatest visual magnitude was −3, when it was at perihelion, 0.14 AU (21,000,000 km; 13,000,000 mi) from the Sun. Its orbital inclination is 14.3°. Its best viewing was in the night sky after perihelion, when it had dimmed to fourth magnitude. The comet also sported a tail up to 25° long, along with an anti-tail." (Wikipedia, "Comet Kohoutek")

[6]Notice that we hadn't said anything about a twin sun, but obviously, according to the Cs, there is a relationship between comets – the actual subject of discussion – and a companion star. It is really curious that the Cs communication began at the moment of the Shoemaker-Levy comet impacts on Jupiter, and they had told us about comet clusters in various prior sessions but had never mentioned this companion star business. Here, following the mention of the comet *du jour*, they brought up the twin sun or companion star topic. It's obvious from our responses that we didn't have a clue about it.

56 **A**: Theory that the sun is really a double star.

57 **Q**: *(L)* Well, if it is a double star, how come we don't see the other one? Where is the other one and why don't we see it? *(T)* I don't think I have ever heard of that, have you? *(F)* It seems vaguely familiar for some reason. *(L)* Is this factual, correct?

58 **A**: Wait a moment ...

59 **Q**: *(T)* They are bringing in their twin sun expert ... *(L)* No doubt! [Planchette spins numerous times.]

60 **A**: Now, where were we?

61 **Q**: *(L)* We were talking about the twin sun phenomenon ...

62 **A**: Theory.

63 **Q**: *(T)* Which is that Sol is one part of a twin system?

64 **A**: Yes.

65 **Q**: *(L)* Is this theory correct?

66 **A**: Not yet, you are "jumping the gun."

67 **Q**: *(T)* Okay. You brought this up. You indicated that, yes, our sun is one part of a dual system ...

68 **A**: Yes ...

69 **Q**: *(T)* ... and that there is another star, another sun here ...

70 **A**: Yes ...

71 **Q**: *(L)* Can we see it? *(T)* Can we see it at this point in time?

72 **A**: Can you?

73 **Q**: *(L)* No. Not that I am aware of. Is the reason we cannot see it because it is always on the other side of the sun from us? That it orbits in such a way that we can never see it?

74 **A**: Orbits, yes, assuming it is there, however, we did not confirm that, now did we?[7]

75 **Q**: *(L)* No, you didn't, but you *did* bring it up! *(T)* Let's go back to the beginning. Okay, you brought up the twin sun theory and then indicated that our sun is one of two suns in this solar system ...

76 **A**: Maybe.

77 **Q**: *(T)* The sun that we designate as Sol is one member ...

78 **A**: Maybe.

79 **Q**: *(T)* Is Sol two stars combined?

80 **A**: No. What is "dark" matter, and what are dark stars?

81 **Q**: *(L)* Are dark stars something like black holes?[8]

82 **A**: No.

83 **Q**: *(L)* Are they ... *(T)* I think it would be a star that has collapsed upon itself and the gravitational field of the star no longer allows light to escape.

84 **A**: No.

85 **Q**: *(T)* Okay, that is a black hole.

86 **A**: Yes.

87 **Q**: *(T)* Dark matter – that I have read about – is what the astronomical community calls all the loose stuff floating around out in the cosmos that must exist because of the equations, but they can't see it.

88 **A**: Yes.

89 **Q**: *(T)* Would dark stars be part of this?

90 **A**: Yes.

---

[7]This caginess was odd.
[8]Our ignorance of these things at the time is actually embarrassing now!

91 **Q:** *(T)* So there is dark matter and dark stars?

92 **A:** Yes.

93 **Q:** *(T)* The dark matter they cannot see because it is dark.

94 **A:** Yes. How about "brown stars?"

95 **Q:** *(T)* Okay, brown stars I have heard of. There is yellow, red, blue, green ... Okay, our star burns as a yellow star because of the matter it is composed of – hydrogen, etc.

96 **A:** Close.

97 **Q:** *(T)* Other stars burn different colors in the visible spectrum because of the make-up of the star ...

98 **A:** Yes, but not "brown" ones.

99 **Q:** *(T)* Brown ones are not brown because of the make-up ...

100 **A:** Okay, you have white, red, yellow, and blue ...

101 **Q:** *(L)* Do those colors represent temperature?

102 **A:** Partially, but that is not the point!

103 **Q:** *(L)* Is Hale-Bopp a brown star?

104 **A:** No.

105 **Q:** *(T)* No. Hale-Bopp has nothing to do with this discussion. Hale-Bopp is just another flop. Okay, brown stars. The colors we see are part temperature and part material ... *(L)* How about the spectral shift which determines direction?

106 **A:** Yes, but that is not the point!

107 **Q:** *(L)* What is the point of a brown star? Black body ...

108 **A:** No, silly! Try the most obviously apparent.

109 **Q:** *(L)* Well, is it one that just hasn't started cooking yet?

110 **A:** Opposite.

111 **Q:** *(L)* Okay, it has burned so long it is about to run out of gas?

112 **A:** Yes.

113 **Q:** *(T)* Is its running out of matter that gives it color?

114 **A:** Why did we put "brown" in quotes?

115 **Q:** *(L)* Because a brown star is assumed to be one that is burning out, but is the opposite?

116 **A:** No.

117 **Q:** *(L)* Because ... I don't know.

118 **A:** How easy is it to see brown against a black background?

119 **Q:** *(T)* Not easy at all! That is why they can't see the dark matter ...

120 **A:** That is why scientists dubbed it "brown."

121 **Q:** *(L)* How does brown star connect to twin sun theory?

122 **A:** Guess!

123 **Q:** *(T)* Okay. Let's talk about this. For some reason we have to work through this to maintain free will. *(L)* Is this star small enough that it is orbiting with the planets?

124 **A:** No, we are leading you to something, if you will be patient.

125 **Q:** *(L)* Okay, lead on ... we want to know about this. *(T)* They just asked if we understood what a brown star was.

126 **A:** Do you?

127 **Q:** *(L)* What is the significance of the brown star?

128 **A:** Dark star.

129 Q: *(L)* It is a dark star ... okay ...

130 A: If it is there.

131 Q: *(L)* Well, will you put me out of my misery and tell me? *(T)* Wait, a dark star is dark because it doesn't give off light. It is still a star, and acts like a star ...

132 A: Yes. And if it has an elliptical orbit ... would it, maybe, like, "come and go?"

133 Q: *(T)* What science – astronomy – has described as double stars, are two stars that are close together with some sort of interactive orbit. But that is not necessarily the only way two stars can exist.

134 A: Close. As you perceive from your vantage point. But how would you like to embark on a bicycle trip between them?

135 Q: *(L)* So the ones that we are aware of and see can be so far apart that there can be a lot between ... *(T)* So our astronomers have not recognized this possibility?

136 A: Yes they have.

137 Q: *(T)* They know, but don't talk about it. So, we may have, in this theory, a dark star orbiting ...

138 A: And what would happen if you did?

139 Q: *(L)* Well ...

140 A: And it, like, comes and goes?

141 Q: *(T)* Like every 3600 years?

142 A: Maybe.

143 Q: *(T)* And maybe this dark star also has some planets orbiting it?

144 A: OK, change of direction: Oort cloud and comet cluster and sun twin occasionally passing through the former like a bowling ball through pins.

145 Q: *(L)* How does the dark star passing through the Oort cloud relate to the comet cluster?

146 A: Cause and effect.

147 Q: *(L)* So, the comet cluster is caused by the dark star smashing through the Oort cloud? *(T)* Well, not necessarily smashing, but passing close enough for its gravity to change things ... *(L)* But they said "like a bowling ball through pins." *(T)* The gravity of that star would cause the comets to be flung in all directions. *(J)* Is the Earth like a pin? A bowling pin? *(L)* No, that's the Oort cloud.

148 A: Explain what the Oort cloud is, Laura.

149 Q: *(L)* Does everybody know what the Oort cloud is? *(J)* I don't. [Explana-

---

[9]"The Oort cloud, sometimes called the Öpik–Oort cloud, is a theoretical cloud of predominantly icy planetesimals believed to surround the Sun to as far as somewhere between 50,000 and 200,000 AU (0.8 and 3.2 ly). It is divided into two regions: a disc-shaped inner Oort cloud (or Hills cloud) and a spherical outer Oort cloud. Both regions lie beyond the heliosphere and in interstellar space. The Kuiper belt and the scattered disc, the other two reservoirs of trans-Neptunian objects, are less than one thousandth as far from the Sun as the Oort cloud.

"The outer limit of the Oort cloud defines the cosmographical boundary of the Solar System ... The outer Oort cloud is only loosely bound to the Solar System, and thus is easily affected by the gravitational pull both of passing stars and of the Milky Way itself. These forces occasionally dislodge comets from their orbits within the cloud and send them toward the inner Solar System. Based on their

tion of Oort cloud.]⁹ Okay, so we are looking at something ...

150 **A:** Now, think of how your Biblical prophecies speak of a very terrifying period, followed by an apparent renewal of normalcy, followed by the "End."

151 **Q:** *(T)* We learned about a 'comet cluster' very early on. Now you are going beyond that and giving us a reason as to why this comet cluster ...

152 **A:** Laura, please clarify exactly what the prophecies say.

153 **Q:** *(L)* Well, actually, *The Noah Syndrome* is primarily prophetic exegesis with a little science thrown in to help clarify why such occurrences must be along a 'natural' order. [Discussion of primary passages in *Noah*.] In the prophecies it is said: "If those days were not shortened, would no flesh be saved. But, for the elects' sake, will those days be shortened." Now, can you tell me what this means?

154 **A:** Not yet.

155 **Q:** *(T)* Where are we? We have a dark star flinging comets like bowling pins ...

156 **A:** Your Biblical prophecies speak of a period of terror and chaos followed by calm, and then, unexpectedly, amidst seeming overwhelming peace and renewal and prosperity, the end.

157 **Q:** *(L)* Okay, elucidate, please.

158 **A:** No, you elucidate, please!

159 **Q:** *(L)* Okay, I would say that this 'end' is the passing through the 'realm border', the 'Wave'.

160 **A:** Yes, but don't you know of the prophecies we are referencing?

161 **Q:** *(L)* Are you talking about the Epistle of Peter where it says the heavens will end with a thunderous crash and the Earth will burn up with fire?

162 **A:** No.

163 **Q:** *(L)* Thank God! Are you talking about the book of Daniel where a number is given regarding the time period between the one event and the other?

164 **A:** Close.

165 **Q:** *(L)* Okay. I know where to go to find it and study it. So, we are talking about the number 6.3, as in years?

166 **A:** Yes, but that is not correct.¹⁰

167 **Q:** *(T)* The number of years is not correct. *(L)* Okay, is it possible – since you

---

orbits, most of the short-period comets may come from the scattered disc, but some may still have originated from the Oort cloud.

"Astronomers conjecture that the matter composing the Oort cloud formed closer to the Sun and was scattered far into space by the gravitational effects of the giant planets early in the Solar System's evolution. Although no confirmed direct observations of the Oort cloud have been made, it may be the source of all long-period and Halley-type comets entering the inner Solar System, and many of the centaurs and Jupiter-family comets as well." (Wikipedia, "Oort cloud")

¹⁰I have no idea why I was being so dense at the time. The prophecy is from 1 Thessalonians 5:2-4, and goes: "For you are fully aware that the day of the Lord will come like a thief in the night. While people are saying, 'Peace and security,' destruction will come upon them suddenly, like labor pains on a pregnant woman, and they will not escape. But you, brothers, are not in the darkness so that this day should overtake you like a thief."

have brought this up on other occasions – through technology, to either skip this event by creating a means of travel to the next realm, or to create a parallel universe ...

168 **A**: No.

169 **Q**: *(L)* Well one thing we can establish ...

170 **A**: What would happen if the brown star that is the sun's twin were to get close enough to be illuminated by the sun?

171 **Q**: *(T)* Well, if it were close enough to be illuminated, the obvious result is that it would be *seen*. People would panic ...

172 **A**: Yes.

173 **Q**: *(T)* Governments would fall ...

174 **A**: And terror and chaos. And when it departs again?

175 **Q**: *(L)* Everything will seem to be fine! But, they won't realize that the Oort cloud has been hit! Oh, sugar!

176 **A**: And then what?

177 **Q**: *(L)* It is not the Oort cloud or the comets that is going to cause all this terror and carrying on; it is going to be the seeing of the illuminated brown star, which will go away, and then no one will see what is coming! And this *is* talked about in both the Bible and Nostradamus – but it was incomprehensible before! Okay, how long will it take the comets to get from the Oort cloud to here?

178 **A**: Let us just say that the cluster travels much faster than the usual cometary itinerary.

179 **Q**: *(T)* And this is because they are traveling in the wake of a large sun-sized gravity well ...

180 **A**: And we have spoken of the comet cluster before, and we have told you that this time, it rides the Wave.

181 **Q**: *(L)* Is the Wave the energy from this brown star?

182 **A**: No.

183 **Q**: *(L)* The Wave is the Wave. *(T)* So, the dark star is going to come through the Oort cloud, and it doesn't have to get too close. Any star that gets that close is *too* close. Its gravity will propel these comets in our direction. And, on top of that, they are being propelled by the Wave from behind, so they are being both pulled and pushed.

184 **A**: No.

185 **Q**: *(L)* Are they being 'kicked' and then they get on the Wave that is already on the move?

186 **A**: Yes. This time. You have had the comet cluster before in antiquity, but the Wave was last here aeons ago.

187 **Q**: *(L)* Is this Wave a gravity wave?

188 **A**: Interrelated.

189 **Q**: *(L)* Okay, now ... *(T)* Well, the Wave is a form of energy. *(L)* Yes, they once told us that it was 'hyperkinetic sensate'.

190 **A**: Realm border, this is your quantum factor, Laura, so plug it into "Noah" accordingly, and check out the results.

191 **Q**: *(L)* Does this brown or dark star have planetary bodies of its own, other than sharing planets with Sol?

192 **A**: No.

193 **Q**: *(T)* Okay. No correlation to Sitchin and his 'planet Nibiru'. *(L)* If the Wave is the quantum factor for the transition of the solar system, what is the factor for the transition of an atom?

194 **A**: Electrons emit what?

195 **Q:** *(L)* Photons ... *(T)* An electrical charge of some kind. *(L)* I thought that an electron didn't have any parts ... that it is an elementary particle ...

196 **A:** Right ...

197 **Q:** *(L)* What the heck does an electron emit? *(T)* An EM field?

198 **A:** What did we say about gravity? What did we say?!?

199 **Q:** *(T)* What was it? *(L)* That gravity collects ... *(T)* What you were reading earlier ...

200 **A:** Read it.

201 **Q:** [Reads segment from previous session about gravity.] *(L)* Is gravity emitted by an electron?

202 **A:** Yes.

203 **Q:** *(L)* What ...

204 **A:** Electromagnetically.

205 **Q:** *(L)* What is it that causes a quantum transition? A collecting and dispersing of gravity. What is it about an atom that causes it to collect or disperse?

206 **A:** How does the electron fit into the equation of the "atom?"

207 **Q:** *(L)* Well, it orbits the nucleus ... *(T)* Planets orbit the sun. *(L)* The energy that an electron collects, or any other part of an atom collects, that causes a quantum transition, comes to it from outside of it? A wave?

208 **A:** How many electrons orbit the nucleus?

209 **Q:** *(L)* It depends on the atom. The number of electrons determine what an atom is an atom of ... the number of particles it has orbiting ...

210 **A:** Yes.

211 **Q:** *(T)* And they orbit in specific shells ...

212 **A:** Yes ... And how does the sun relate to this macro-dynamically?

213 **Q:** *(L)* Okay, something from the nucleus of the atom acts upon the electrons to cause a transition?

214 **A:** How many electrons orbit the nucleus?

215 **Q:** *(L)* Of the sun? Are you asking how many electrons orbit the nucleus of the sun? Different atoms have different numbers ...

216 **A:** Of any atom?

217 **Q:** *(L)* Okay, it varies.

218 **A:** From what to what?

219 **Q:** *(L)* From one to somewhere in the nineties or hundreds ...

220 **A:** And what determines the number?

221 **Q:** *(L)* Well, that is a damn good question! *(T)* What makes one atom helium and one atom oxygen? How do they know how to become what they are?

222 **A:** No.

223 **Q:** *(T)* Well, what determines the number?

224 **A:** Is it the composition of the nucleus?

225 **Q:** *(L)* Yeah. That's right. We forgot. What causes or determines the number of protons or whatever in the nucleus?

226 **A:** What composition would cause the orbiting of one electron?

227 **Q:** *(L)* One proton?

228 **A:** Now, think macro-dynamically.

229 **Q:** *(L)* Well, you once said that the sun is a window, or transition point to another density. Are you saying that the nucleus of an atom is also a window?

230 **A**: What we are saying is the sun is a proton and its twin is an electron!

231 **Q**: *(L)* Well, I am still trying to get at ... the Wave causes transitions in the macro-cosmic atom, what causes the microcosmic atom ... what causes a quantum jump? What accumulates in an atom that causes it to transition? *(T)* Is it a case of accumulation, or something being given off?

232 **A**: Completion of Grand Cycle.

233 **Q**: *(J)* It just is. *(L)* No, no ...

234 **A**: And who says that the sun's twin appears every 3600 years?

235 **Q**: *(L)* Okay, we have the 3600-year comet-cluster cycle, the sun twin is another cycle altogether, and then we have the Wave, which is a Grand Cycle. So, we have three things causing a transition in nature?

236 **A**: Like "biorhythms."

237 **Q**: *(T)* And we have a triple bad day coming up! Or a good day, depending on which way you look at it.

238 **A**: Bad day if you are John D. Rockefeller, good day if you are Mahatma Gandhi.

239 **Q**: *(L)* So, does something like a three-cycle event also occur in subatomic transitions, like the biorhythm?

240 **A**: Yes.

241 **Q**: *(L)* So, there are three factors to be considered ... or more than three?

242 **A**: Either, or.

243 **Q**: *(L)* Can it be a random, arbitrary number of events?

244 **A**: If you wish.

245 **Q**: *(L)* Is it partly the observer that adds one of the factors? Consciousness?

246 **A**: Yes.

247 **Q**: *(T)* So, we see three separate cycles coming together here ...

248 **A**: Everything reflects macrodynamically and microdynamically. We suggest you absorb for now; and, fear not! For it is not imminent![11] Goodnight.

End of Session

---

[11] When they said "fear not! For it is not imminent!", remember, that was 20 years ago. One thing I wonder about when reading over this is if much of the theorized dark matter in the universe is actually concentrated in dark stars?

August 11, 1996

The discussion before this session was apparently all of us comparing notes about intentions and outcomes and whether or not intent had influence on outcomes as is normally theorized. This is the session where the Cs discuss the problem of anticipation. The energy was good and comfortable, as was most often the case when Terry and Jan were present.

Participants: 'Frank', Laura, Terry, Jan

1 **Q**: Hello.

2 **A**: Hoparb.

3 **Q**: And where are you transmitting from tonight?

4 **A**: Cassiopaea

5 **Q**: *(L)* I want to ask a real quick question first, and then just kind of leave everything else open for whatever else can happen. On several occasions with my conversations with Arkadiusz in Poland, and in Germany and in Florence, there have been some real serious computer problems. I would like to know if there is any connection between myself and these electronic failures?[1]

6 **A**: If we answer this, you will not limit it to one question.

7 **Q**: *(L)* Do I have to limit it to one question? *(J)* You said you would.

8 **A**: You placed that restriction upon yourself: It's not nice to fool mother nature, or the Cassiopaeans!!

9 **Q**: *(L)* All right, well let it go until it runs out. Is there some energy interaction that's causing these electronic failures? Is there an indication of some ...

10 **A**: Yes, and "it just ran out."

11 **Q**: *(L)* What just ran out? *(T)* The question string.

12 **A**: Yes.

13 **Q**: *(T)* You said you'd let it run out, and it just ran out! *(J)* They're playful tonight! *(L)* Oooh! So, yes, there's a connection, and that's all I get! *(J)* Hoisted upon your own petard, as they say! *(T)* Mirth! Mirth!

14 **A**: Bingo!

15 **Q**: *(L)* Stinkers, stinkers! Okay ... *(T)* Shall we run like we did last week, and just let them ...

16 **A**: You would have asked 29 questions about you and "Ark," and that is a "No-No."

17 **Q**: *(T)* Ah, but would she have asked the 64,000-dollar question in there somewhere?

---

[1] See previous session notes about the event at DESY.

18 **A**: Yes!

19 **Q**: *(J)* And what would the answer have been!?!? [Laughter]

20 **A**: Open.

21 **Q**: *(L)* Okay, we've been talking earlier this evening about intent, and of course, our own experiences with intent have really been pretty phenomenal. We've come to some kind of an idea that intent, when confirmed repeatedly, actually builds force. Is this a correct concept, and is there anything that you can add to it?

22 **A**: Only until anticipation muddies the picture ... tricky one, huh?[2]

23 **Q**: *(L)* Is anticipation the act of assuming you know how something is going to happen?

24 **A**: Follows realization, generally, and unfortunately for you, on 3rd density.

25 **Q**: *(L)* Is this a correct assessment of this process?

26 **A**: Both examples given are correct. You see, once anticipation enters the picture, the intent can no longer be STO.

27 **Q**: *(L)* Anticipation is desire for something for self. Is that it?

28 **A**: Yes.

29 **Q**: *(L)* Okay, so it's okay to intend something, or to think in an intentional way, or to hope in an intentional way, for something that is to serve another, but anticipation defines it as a more personal thing.

30 **A**: And that brings realization.

31 **Q**: *(L)* So, desire to serve others, and to do something because it will help others, brings realization ...

32 **A**: But, realization creates anticipation.

33 **Q**: *(L)* Well, how do we navigate this? I mean, this is like walking on a razor's edge. To control your mind to not anticipate, and yet, deal with realization, and yet, still maintain hope ... *(J)* They said it was tricky ... *(L)* This is, this is, um ...

34 **A**: Mental exercises of denial, balanced with pure faith of a non-prejudicial kind.[3]

35 **Q**: *(L)* Okay, so, in other words, to just accept what is at the moment, appreciate it as it is at the moment, and have faith that the universe and things will happen the way they are supposed to happen, without placing any expectation on how that will be?

36 **A**: Yes.

37 **Q**: *(L)* This is – and I'm not asking about Ark – this is something that he has talked about in terms of shaping the future. He talks about *shaping* the future as an intentional act of shaping something good, but without defining the moment of measurement. In other words, adding energy to it by intent, but not deciding where, when or how the moment of measurement occurs. When the quantum jump occurs, it occurs on its own, and in its own way. Is this the concept he's dealing with here?

38 **A**: Anticipation.

39 **Q**: *(L)* In other words, is what he's talking about anticipation?

---

[2] *The Wave* 23

[3] The only way I can describe such faith is that one just assumes that the Universe knows what it is doing and one learns to 'dance' with it.

40 **A**: No.

41 **Q**: *(L)* Well, what do you mean, anticipation in response to what I said?

42 **A**: That is the key to shaping the future ... Avoiding it.

43 **Q**: *(T)* Okay, because we're not anticipating in what we're doing ...

44 **A**: Yes.

45 **Q**: *(T)* What we're doing is not anticipatory, it's just happening. We were talking about it on the way up, that with interactions with others, we are facilitating, we are creating reality. This is what they all say about reality.

46 **A**: When it hits you, it stops.

47 **Q**: *(L)* When what hits you? *(J)* The realization. *(T)* The fact that it's happening.

48 **A**: Yes unless you cancel out all anticipation.[4]

49 **Q**: *(L)* Well, this is very tricky. *(J)* Well, hang on a second, I have a kind of a corollary question. The way I perceive what has happened with us in the campaign against the microwave towers – the article in the *Times*, and the editorial, and speaking to the people ... The way I view it is that when things like that happen, I look at them, and the synchronicities tell me that I am on the right path. Is that a true statement, that they are an indication that I'm going in the right direction?

50 **A**: Semi.

51 **Q**: *(T)* It's a road sign, an indicator. *(J)* Okay, thank you! That's good, it's an indicator. *(L)* Okay, shaping the future ... *(J)* In what way is it not? The answer was semi; part of it is true ...

52 **A**: We have told you.

53 **Q**: *(L)* Well then it seems to me – excuse me in this one – it seems to me that Ark may understand this one better than I do.

54 **A**: Yes.

55 **Q**: *(L)* That's all I wanted to know. *(J)* So, let him teach you! *(T)* He'll teach you what you need to learn from him, and you'll teach him what he needs to learn from you! And as a result, you'll both gain!

56 **A**: Imbalanced upon the former.

57 **Q**: *(L)* What was the former? *(T)* He can teach you more, maybe, than you can teach him? Because he's farther along? Is this correct?

58 **A**: Close.

59 **Q**: *(L)* This guy is, like, out there! *(T)* This is good! *(L)* Now, this is a funny little thing, I just want to bring this up. MM[5] called and told me that she had a vision that when Ark arrives, that the Cassiopaean transmissions will cease, that somehow he is some deep, dark, evil person who will cause everything to just fly apart ...

60 **A**: Baloney![6]

61 **Q**: *(L)* Thank you for that! That was so succinct! That's what I thought myself, but I just thought I'd throw it in there! *(J)* That's her anticipation! *(L)* Well, that's what she'd like! *(T)* Does MM's camera show real Kirlian fields and all that stuff? Is it actually showing the truth?

---

[4] *The Wave* 23
[5] Aura camera woman from previous sessions.
[6] Just goes to show that there's more than one way to get an answer from the Cs!

62 **A:** Discover.

63 **Q:** *(L)* Well, it showed a damn interesting thing when she took a picture of this board! *(T)* Ah, but is it the truth? *(L)* Well, they said it was! *(T)* They did? *(L)* They told us, "What you are seeing is the actual light picture of a conduit."

64 **A:** Do you think, Terry, that all things are either "black" or "white?"

65 **Q:** *(T)* Not in those photos! No, I'm only asking because I feel that the pictures are not only influenced by the subject in front of the camera, but also by the subject behind the camera. [Discussion ensued about workings of aura cameras] *(L)* Okay, is it true that if we were to bring an ordinary camera in here, that we would be able to get some interesting photos from our interaction? *(T)* I think that would be an 'open' or a 'maybe.'

66 **A:** No, it would be a "discover".

67 **Q:** *(L)* That was your third choice! *(T)* Thank you!

68 **A:** Too much bibble/babble.

69 **Q:** *(L)* Okay, then we'll stop bibble-babbling, then! [Planchette began a series of large spirals]

70 **A:** Crank away!

71 **Q:** *(T)* Okay, this is one I wanted to ask last week, and couldn't figure out how to phrase it. I'm not sure now, but I'll just plunge ahead. I got a copy of *Awakening to the Zero Point*, by Greg Baron, while we were in Atlanta, and I've read through it. He had a lot to say about the sacred geometries, and especially the circle, and the sphere. A while back we were talking with you about this,[7] and we got to a certain point, and got totally lost. We all kind of put it off to the side for the time being. Is what this fellow has to say in his book about the sacred geometries, and the sphere, is he on to what's going on here, is this what you were talking about?

72 **A:** Maybe.

73 **Q:** *(L)* Let me ask this. Is there any word that you can give us as a word association as to why my pool pump has decided to die, so that my pool is sitting there green, making me ill?

74 **A:** How about metal fatigue?

75 **Q:** *(L)* So, the pump is gone, it has nothing to do with any ... *(T)* You didn't do that one! *(L)* God, I hope not! *(T)* I was going to say a word ... how about chlorine? *(J)* Sometimes, what is, is ...

76 **A:** Sometimes circumstances are just ordinary, 3rd density boring, everyday "stuff."[8]

77 **Q:** *(L)* Well, I just wanted to make sure that it was not symbolic of [anything negative in the environment]! *(T)* Is there any direction you'd like to see us move in tonight?

78 **A:** How about the good old fashioned standby: UFOs and aliens? That is always a fun one!

79 **Q:** *(L)* Okay, I've got a question on that. Chloe called today, and in her conversation about the Ra material, she asked me: was I aware that in the Ra

---

[7] I don't recall, and can't find, any previous discussion about 'zero point energy', so I have no clue as to what Terry was talking about. Perhaps he had been talking to someone else about it?

[8] And this point should always be kept in mind!

material, they designated Cassiopeia as the residence of some real negative, icky, Orion-type STS aliens? Can you make a comment on these [aliens]?

A: ?

Q: *(L)* Also, the picture of the mantid-type beings in that document that I lent to Shawn has these beings designated as Cassiopeians. Who are these Cassiopeians? *(T)* Before they answer, can I make a comment here? There is no star called Cassiopeia on our star charts. *(L)* Oh, I know ... *(T)* It's a constellation. So for her to read this in the Ra material and go along with that there's a bunch of people called the Cassiopeians who are horrible people on a planet someplace called Cassiopeia, there is no place called that. So there can't actually be anyone called Cassiopeians because there is no Cassiopeia. *(L)* Okay, can we get commentary on this?

A: Sounds good to us!

Q: *(L)* Where do the mantid-type beings come from? The ones that we're aware of?

A: The ones you are speaking of come from active human imaginations!

Q: *(L)* Are there mantid-type aliens that we're not aware of?

A: Yes, there is damn near everything that you are not aware of!

Q: *(T)* As you said, there are mantids that we are unaware of, and they told us there's damn near everything we're unaware of! It's a big universe! *(L)* In other words, our awareness is ...

A: Yes.

Q: *(L)* ... extremely limited, from what I've been able to figure out. *(T)* They told us that in a couple of years – we have 2% now – it will grow to 30 to 40% of the knowledge of the smartest people on the planet, not the universe.

A: Yes.

Q: *(L)* So, in other words, what we can know in this level is just like dipping a needle in the ocean and the wetness of the needle is what we know compared to the ocean. *(T)* Big time! *(L)* Yes, this is not good! *(T)* We know one cigarette butt out of the whole tobacco crop!

A: That was a good one!

Q: *(T)* What did they say previously about the mantid beings? *(J)* "The ones you are speaking of come from active human imaginations."

A: Cassiopaean variety.

Q: *(L)* Oh, the Cassiopaean variety is the product of an overactive imagination. Okay, since the Ra material is considered to be a kind of primer to the Cassiopaean material, could you give us a percentage on the accuracy of this material?

A: 63.

Q: *(L)* 63%. Well, that's pretty good, considering ... *(J)* It's not bad ... *(T)* A lot of it's very good stuff ... *(L)* Can you talk to us a little bit about the concept of Wanderers? Is the Ra concept of Wanderers a valid ...

A: Yes.

Q: *(L)* Okay, is there anything about Wanderers that you can tell us, that would help us to identify them?

A: Specifics, please.

Q: *(L)* Okay, is it a correct point of reference that Wanderers are individuals who feel alienated in the world system?

102 **A:** Yes but they can partially adapt.[9]

103 **Q:** *(L)* Okay, do they also sometimes have physical ...

104 **A:** Revulsion to physicality.

105 **Q:** *(T)* Revulsion to physicality? They don't like physicality? But they're here! *(J)* Just because they're here, they don't have to like it! *(L)* Okay, is that always a clue?

106 **A:** Yes.

107 **Q:** *(L)* Anything else about them that ... *(J)* Wait, I have another question. Revulsion to physicality – does that refer to a dislike of the fact that in 3rd density is all physical, and it's fixed, as opposed to upper densities, where there's variability?

108 **A:** 3rd density is not "all" physical.

109 **Q:** *(L)* Well, there's spiritual ... *(J)* I understand that, but the physical body itself, is fixed. *(L)* Well, I don't think that's what they're getting at ... *(J)* That's what I'm asking. *(L)* I think that what they're getting at is like a fine division between somebody who focuses on physical sensation as opposed to spiritual or mental or emotional sensation as being the point of reference.

110 **A:** Yes.

111 **Q:** *(L)* And this is something that I was reading in this book the other day, that he talks about: the body is animal, and the soul is spirit. He says that animal people just seek animal experiences, and they glorify them, and they stimulate their physical emotions.

112 **A:** 3rd density natives tend to concentrate and, to an extent, revel, in the physical.

113 **Q:** *(T)* And boy, they're reveling right now! *(L)* Yes. *(T)* There's major reveling going on. And it's intensifying every day. *(J)* I think the point that I was trying to make was, having to stay in 3rd density, would they miss the variability of physicality? *(L)* Well, Wanderers, remember, are 6th density beings.

114 **A:** The lack.

115 **Q:** *(T)* The lack of physicality?

116 **A:** Yes. Is missed.

117 **Q:** *(L)* They miss the lack of physicality. *(J)* Right. Exactly. Okay, that was what I was getting at. I just didn't say it right.

118 **A:** Not so much "miss," as much as difficulty of adjustment.

119 **Q:** *(J)* Yes, like if you went blind, you'd miss being able to see, etc... *(T)* If you had the freedom of non-physicality, being limited, you'd miss the non-physical.

120 **Q:** *(L)* Okay, what's the scoop on this Mars rock? *(T)* That's kind of UFO-ish!

---

[9] *The Wave* 10

[10] On August 7, 1996, NASA made a press release:

Meteorite Yields Evidence of Primitive Life of Early Mars A NASA research team of scientists at the Johnson Space Center *(JSC)*, Houston, TX, and at Stanford University, Palo Alto, CA, has found evidence that strongly suggests primitive life may have existed on Mars more than 3.6 billion years ago.

The NASA-funded team found the first organic molecules thought to be of Martian origin; several mineral features characteristic of biological activity; and possible microscopic fossils of primitive, bacteria-like organisms inside of an ancient Martian

121 **A:** Vague as can be![10]

122 **Q:** *(L)* Is it the Mars rock that's vague as can be, or is it my question?

123 **A:** Latter.

124 **Q:** *(L)* Okay, latter, my question. Is this rock from Mars?

125 **A:** Yes.

126 **Q:** *(L)* How long have they known that rocks from Mars are on the planet?[11]

127 **A:** 12 years.

Q: *(T)* About the same length of time it took them to analyze the soil samples that they got from Mariner probes.

---

rock that fell to Earth as a meteorite. This array of indirect evidence of past life will be reported in the August 16 issue of the journal *Science*, presenting the investigation to the scientific community at large for further study. ...

The igneous rock in the 4.2-pound, potato-sized meteorite has been age-dated to about 4.5 billion years, the period when the planet Mars formed. The rock is believed to have originated underneath the Martian surface and to have been extensively fractured by impacts as meteorites bombarded the planets in the early inner solar system. Between 3.6 billion and 4 billion years ago, a time when it is generally thought that the planet was warmer and wetter, water is believed to have penetrated fractures in the subsurface rock, possibly forming an underground water system.

Since the water was saturated with carbon dioxide from the Martian atmosphere, carbonate minerals were deposited in the fractures. The team's findings indicate living organisms also may have assisted in the formation of the carbonate, and some remains of the microscopic organisms may have become fossilized, in a fashion similar to the formation of fossils in limestone on Earth. Then, 16 million years ago, a huge comet or asteroid struck Mars, ejecting a piece of the rock from its subsurface location with enough force to escape the planet. For millions of years, the chunk of rock floated through space. It encountered Earth's atmosphere 13,000 years ago and fell in Antarctica as a meteorite.

It is in the tiny globs of carbonate that the researchers found a number of features that can be interpreted as suggesting past life. Stanford researchers found easily detectable amounts of organic molecules called polycyclic aromatic hydrocarbons (PAHs) concentrated in the vicinity of the carbonate. Researchers at JSC found mineral compounds commonly associated with microscopic organisms and the possible microscopic fossil structures.

The largest of the possible fossils are less than 1/100 the diameter of a human hair, and most are about 1/1000 the diameter of a human hair – small enough that it would take about a thousand laid end-to-end to span the dot at the end of this sentence. Some are egg-shaped while others are tubular. In appearance and size, the structures are strikingly similar to microscopic fossils of the tiniest bacteria found on Earth.

The meteorite, called ALH84001, was found in 1984 in Allan Hills ice field, Antarctica, by an annual expedition of the National Science Foundation's Antarctic Meteorite Program. It was preserved for study in JSC's Meteorite Processing Laboratory and its possible Martian origin was not recognized until 1993. It is one of only 12 meteorites identified so far that match the unique Martian chemistry measured by the Viking spacecraft that landed on Mars in 1976. ALH84001 is by far the oldest of the 12 Martian meteorites, more than three times as old as any other. (http://www2.jpl.nasa.gov/snc/nasa1.html)

---

[11] *The Wave* 57

(L) Okay, Why all of a sudden are they revealing, or releasing this information about this Mars rock? In such a big and manipulative way? *(T)* You just said it!

A: You have already figured it out yourselves.

Q: *(L)* Well, Sheldon Nidle, the author of *Becoming a Galactic Human* ...

A: No.

Q: *(T)* Not Sheldon and the Galactic Humans! *(L)* Well, I know they said no, but Sheldon has made an announcement which was put out on the Net ...

A: No.

Q: *(L)* So, there's not going to be a massive UFO landing between August 29th and December 31st of this year? *(T)* Only if you go and see *Independence Day*!

A: No comment!

Q: *(L)* Well, I just ... *(T)* That's what the press secretary says for Clinton: "No comment!" "Can you describe this woman?" "No comment!" *(L)* Is that so pusillanimous as to not deserve a comment? Okay, well, so we won't have to worry about Sheldon Nidle's aliens coming and taking over ... *(T)* They can come and take Sheldon away! *(L)* Well, okay, but is this Mars rock, and is this opening of the doors concept, is this leading up to some definite, overt interaction with aliens? *(T)* They told us, we know it, yes!

A: Gradually.

Q: *(T)* That's what it's all about. They're opening it up, and they're going to take the money ... If they want to go to Mars to look for civilizations and stuff, which they're going to lead up to, and back to the moon here, and all this, and they're going to make Hoagland feel really good, because he's right! They've already done that!

A: Notice how you heard nothing about the Mars probes until the rock announcement?

Q: *(T)* This is the new stuff? *(L)* Is this right?

A: The excavation robot spacecraft. One probe is already on its way, another to follow. No further explanation about "loss" of Mars Explorer.[12]

Q: *(L)* What did happen to the Mars Explorer?

A: Blacked out. You see, "Too risky." And too much too soon, due to pressure from Hoagland and others.

Q: *(T)* My own opinion is that they've already been there, and they know what's there.

A: No. Microbes are easier to swallow than humans in togas![13]

Q: *(T)* Cleopatra and Antony are not going to go over real big this week! Especially with the Bible scholars. *(F)* And the scientists! *(L)* I want to throw in a quick one about this plane

---

[12] *The Wave* 57

[13] The reference to togas is curious since that was a particular Roman phenomenon. "The toga, a distinctive garment of Ancient Rome, was a cloth of perhaps 6 metres (20 feet) in length which was wrapped around the body and was generally worn over a tunic. The toga was made of wool, and the tunic under it often was made of linen. The toga was worn almost exclusively by Roman men, whereas women were expected to wear the stola." (Wikipedia, "Toga") One is also reminded of the Cs' odd response in relation to Paul in session 9 June 1996.

crash. Several people have written and asked me. We've discussed it ourselves. There's all of these plane crashes, with the possibility that we are actually in some state of conflict, and that we just don't know about it. It was suggested that they've been shot down by the Lizzies, or something along that line?

146 **A**: No.

147 **Q**: *(L)* Okay, well, then forget it. Okay ...[14] *(T)* Back to Mars. Okay? *(L)* Forward to Mars.

148 **A**: Yes.

149 **Q**: *(T)* Okay, you just mentioned that somebody from this planet already launched a Mars probe. A new Mars probe, that no one in public knows about. Because it's never been talked about. So, it's a secret probe. Who does it belong to?

150 **A**: Was secret US government.

151 **Q**: *(T)* Was it something that one of the Shuttle missions put out?

152 **A**: No.

153 **Q**: *(J)* When did it go up?

154 **A**: September of 1995.

155 **Q**: *(T)* Last September, a year ago. So, it's gone for a year. It takes it a year, two years to get there? Maybe not that long. So, it's over half-way there at this point.

156 **A**: Yes.

157 **Q**: *(T)* What's it going to do?

158 **A**: Next year.

159 **Q**: *(T)* Next year for the next probe?

160 **A**: Yes.

161 **Q**: *(T)* Is this going to be one of those public ones? A publicly announced one?

162 **A**: They both are.

163 **Q**: *(T)* What is the purpose of these probes?[15]

164 **A**: Excavation to display living organisms.

165 **Q**: *(T)* Display? *(L)* Yes, for public consumption. In other words, not only do we have a rock now, that shows evidence that there was ... *(T)* Oh, display, as when they find it and dig it up, they're going to show it on camera! *(L)* Yes! *(T)* Katie Couric will interview it! *(L)* Right! *(F)* First they said they found no evidence, then they said it was inconclusive ... Now, who the hell knows what they found! In revealing things, we'll start with fossilized life, and then move on ... *(L)* So, they're going to display the discovery of living organisms on Mars to take the next step to acclimate ...

166 **A**: Yes.

167 **Q**: *(L)* So, in other words, this process is going to be something of an on-going

---

[14] The topic will be brought up again in the future in a surprising way. At this point, all the Cs were saying was that it was not an alien/Lizzie action. See Wikipedia, "TWA Flight 800": "Trans World Airlines Flight 800 (TWA 800), was a Boeing 747-100 which exploded and crashed into the Atlantic Ocean near East Moriches, New York, on July 17, 1996, at about 8:31 p.m. EDT, 12 minutes after takeoff from John F. Kennedy International Airport on a scheduled international passenger flight to Rome, with a stopover in Paris. All 230 people on board were killed in the third-deadliest aviation accident in U.S. territory."

[15] *The Wave* 57

thing, and that all of these people who are cranking around about, you know, alien landings ...

A: No faces, though.

Q: *(L)* There's not going to be any 'Faces On Mars'? They are not going to show us ...

A: Won't be revealed, what do you think happened with Mars Explorer?

Q: *(L)* Well, what did happen with the Mars Explorer? *(T)* Now, now, now, let me ...

A: Hoagland forced their hand.

Q: *(T)* What do we think happened to the Mars Explorer? I think they switched channels. They just moved it from one communication post to another, and it's doing exactly what it's supposed to be doing. And they did it in such a way that the NASA people really didn't know what happened, so that when they were asked, they could say, "We don't know what happened to it!" Because they really don't know what happened! *(L)* When we're talking about attack, as we were before, as in plane crashes, the Olympics, all these different things – this dealing with these Mars Explorers – is all this stuff, or most of this stuff, coming from the 4th density manipulations of human minds, rather than ...

A: Yes.

Q: *(L)* ... rather than actual, physical entry and doing of deeds? Is that it?

A: Yes.

Q: *(L)* Okay, so what these people are doing with this Mars probe, with all of these things, they're being manipulated to do these things, and there's obviously an objective. What is the objective?

A: Too complex.

Q: *(L)* Too complex. So, it's not just control, there's control for a reason.

A: To explain to you.

Q: *(T)* Because there's 4th density, 5th density and 6th density reasons involved.

A: Just 4th.

Q: *(T)* I have a question. They're going to display live organisms, like, how did they put that? "Living organisms"? How big are these living organisms going to be? How advanced?[16]

A: Teeny-tiny.

Q: *(T)* So, we're still talking about microscopic organisms here?

A: Yes.

Q: *(J)* So, they won't wave at us!

A: But these will be alive. Can't you see the progression here? "Don't want to scare Grandma Sally Bible Thumper/Stockmarket Investor!"

Q: *(L)* Do you have any more for us tonight?

A: No. Goodbye.

End of Session

---

[16] *The Wave* 57

August 17, 1996

We started this session with a short exchange about the fact that I only had one blank tape left, so we needed to be careful not to run over time.

Participants: 'Frank', Laura, Terry, Jan

1 **Q:** *(T)* Good evening!

2 **A:** Hello.

3 **Q:** *(L)* And who do we have with us this evening?

4 **A:** Wokuhia.

5 **Q:** *(L)* And where are you from?

6 **A:** Cassiopaea.

7 **Q:** *(T)* Is Ark's computer going to continue to work okay?[1]

8 **A:** Attention: Please do not restrict session to limit of tape. Just be careful to write answers carefully. Tell Arkady to approach his career/move in more than one way: suggest he contact "Enterprise Florida," headquartered in Orlando, and propose that his potential hiring by any of four Florida universities would be a potential boon to State economic development efforts, due to his stature.[2]

9 **Q:** *(L)* Okay, any further on that? *(T)* They might even have a Web site! Check under Florida Chamber of Commerce. *(L)* All right, anything further on that?

10 **A:** Yes. What Terry just said is true. And one should know that while the University of Florida is somewhat "set in its ways," the same cannot be said for the University of Central Florida, which is in Orlando and has a massive, new, research park immediately to the east of its campus, where much research in advanced physics is slated to begin soon. You see, it is the "angle" or approach that one utilizes that determines the degree of success. Also, F.S.U. has re-

---

[1] Ark's computer kept going kaput and we were having trouble communicating. This was very upsetting on both sides!

[2] This was actually *not* the case, so I can only suppose that it was Frank in his role as 'expert financial advisor'.

[3] This must have been a bit of data that Frank picked up reading tech and/or investment journals. Indeed, there was a bit of activity at FSU to try to get a supercollider, but it didn't go through.

> While the thought of forging new paths in high-energy physics is pretty heady stuff, physicists remain plagued by an inability to communicate the importance of such basic research to the public. "We're not planning to produce new forms of electricity or solve the ozone-hole problem," says Hagopian [of FSU].
> But some physicists feel that not all of their colleagues are this candid, that

cently constructed a super collider. Yes, access in your libraries, if you do not believe ...[3] Remind Arkady that in the United States, it is the money that matters, unlike the Poland he grew up in, and the key is to "sell one's self," as if a commodity!![4]

Q: *(J)* I have a feeling they aren't going to let us ask any questions tonight. Ask them if they're going to let us even ask any questions tonight.

A: Yes, but wait a moment ... impress upon Arkady to discreetly sell himself as a valuable asset, if he wishes to have things move more quickly and smoothly. We suspect that "Gainesville," may have not appreciated what they are up against.

Q: *(T)* Elaborate "up against", please!

A: Means that they do not recognize the value ... He has been offered a position that is way below his station![5]

Q: *(L)* Okay, anything further that you would like to convey to him tonight?

A: Not at this "time."

Q: *(L)* All right, let's get on to our questions here. Let me ask a quick one about the tetrahedron. Terry, you ask it, because you know more about it. *(T)* The tetrahedron, triangle mathematics that Hoagland is working with in conjunction with the Mars/Cydonia region where he supposedly discovered this ...

A: Energy consolidator. EM wave capturer.

Q: *(T)* Okay, so it's an EM wave capturer. Does it also expel EM waves?

A: Close.

Q: *(T)* From the same points? The 19 points, whatever it is ...[6]

A: Channels and enhances, when used properly, and in pristine conditions.

Q: *(T)* Hoagland is not talking about ... whatever he's talking about, as far as the mathematics go, of the tetrahedral triangles within the sphere, which I'm assuming this planet is calling the sacred geometries, but are physics-type things of different densities, which may not actually be right. Okay, this doesn't apply just to Mars, this is, every sphere has these same properties...?

A: Yes.

Q: *(T)* ... a golfball, a baseball – I know they're not perfect spheres, they have dimples – all the way up to the sun, and so forth and so on, of any size, made out of any material, as long as it's a sphere, it will have the same properties.

A: No.

Q: *(T)* Okay, it has to have certain kinds of materials?

A: No, must be magnetized.

---

they tell the public what they think it wants to hear just to win funding for their research. In fact, some are convinced that it was exactly this sort of over-sell that was the downfall of the Superconducting Super Collider *(SSC)*. (http://www.rinr.fsu.edu/winter94/features/top.html)

[4]Again, that was not the case and things did not turn out that way. My guess was that Frank had been doing too much reading in his stock-market journals.

[5]This was certainly true.

[6]He obviously meant the points on the planet that Hoagland talks about that are located at about 19 degrees of latitude if you place a tetrahedron inside a sphere.

Q: *(T)* Okay, it's a magnetized sphere, something that has a magnetic field around it. *(L)* Is the tetrahedral configuration a property of the magnetism?

A: Yes. No.

Q: *(T)* Yes to my question, no to Laura's question?

A: Yes.

Q: *(T)* Okay, my question is, the sphere has to be able to generate a magnetic field, like the Earth has a magnetic field, like Mars generates a magnetic field ...

A: Or be magnetized by installation of internal magnetic generator.

Q: *(L)* Okay, what's the purpose of this? What's the purpose of these tetrahedrons? What are the ...

A: Purpose is not proper term.

Q: *(T)* That's right. It's not a purpose, it just exists this way. These spheres that are magnetic, or are able to be magnetized, this happens just because they are what they are, and this is how the physics works?

A: Reflection of universal balance.

Q: *(L)* Okay, they just simply ... and is it that something occurs at the points of these triangles that is noticeable? I mean, is it like a power point?

A: No.

Q: *(L)* Okay, well, this guy Jim [who is in communication with Ark] says that they are designated by different monuments on the planet's surface ...

A: Nonsense!!!

Q: *(T)* Thank you! *(L)* ... and that they are visual sighting ...

A: Artificial constructed tetrahedrons are placed on strategic locations on the planet's surface in order to utilize magnetic fields properly.

Q: *(L)* Who places these artificially constructed tetrahedrons at these points?

A: The artificial constructors.

Q: *(L)* And who are they?

A: Whomever they may be.

Q: *(T)* In other words, they can be anybody. They're artificial constructors, they could be anybody ... *(L)* If people know about them, they can do this ...

A: No, no, no. Nineteen degrees north and south.

Q: *(T)* Correct, those are the numbers that Hoagland came up with, with his stuff. On most of the planets, and our sun, we seem to have major events happening, or have happened ...

A: Hawaii.[7]

Q: *(T)* Yes, Hawaii, Puerto Rico ... let's see, 19 degrees north and south, Philippines, I think, is somewhere close, on the south side. Major volcanos ... *(F)* Philippines is on the north side, that's not in the Southern Hemisphere ... *(T)* I'd have to pull out a global map to see what the 19 degrees are. On Mars, Cydonia resides at approximately 19 degrees, the giant volcano, the dead volcano on Mars is approximately 19

---

[7]Yes, on his website, Hoagland mentions the Hawaiian Caldera, the Largest Shield Volcano on Earth, as being part of this configuration. My opinion in retrospect was that Frank was way too taken with Hoagland and emotionally attached to his ideas. Ark found Hoagland to be much less than he was promoted to be and wrote an article about his interactions with same: http://quantumfuture.net/quantum_future/bearden.htm

degrees, the stuff that they found on Venus, the major things, are at approximately 19 degrees. The sunspots are approximately 19 degrees, the red spot on Jupiter ... *(L)* Is there anything else we want to get on this tetrahedron? Is there anything else we could ask about this subject, that we haven't thought of ourselves ... *(T)* I'm sure there's a lot ... *(L)* Oh, I know ... that you could give us?

54 **A:** Unlimited.

55 **Q:** *(L)* Do the tetrahedrons spin within the sphere? Do these power points of the tetrahedron spin?

56 **A:** Energy fields flow in balance.

57 **Q:** *(T)* So they're spinning to keep balance?[8] *(J)* Like a gyro. *(T)* Is there ... now, am I correct in the fact that there's a direct relationship here to the real Hebrew Star of David, to these tetrahedrals?

58 **A:** Yes.

59 **Q:** *(T)* And that everything that has been done to it for the last 500 years or so has been done to screw things up?

60 **A:** Yes.

61 **Q:** *(T)* Yes. So that that symbol is not a religious symbol, as such, but a very important ... *(L)*... power symbol?

62 **A:** Yes.

63 **Q:** *(T)* It describes a physics that transcends the densities.

64 **A:** So is pentagon.

65 **Q:** *(T)* So is the Pentagon? *(J)* A pentagon. *(T)* The pentagon shape. These are part of what humans describe as the sacred geometries.

66 **A:** Yes.

67 **Q:** *(T)* So, in that 'Bear' book that I have ...

68 **A:** You as Atlanteans knew this, and lived by it in many ways. For example, the pyramid recharges by capturing exactly half the energy points, thus allowing a positive imbalance buildup to be captured, then expended.

69 **Q:** *(L)* Okay, are we finished, or ... okay, we know we are not finished, but we know we want to cover a couple of things ... is there something more about the tetrahedrons that is important for us to know now? *(T)* That we can pass on to Ark? *(L)* Yes, essential to know now? A real 'goodie'?

70 **A:** Open.

71 **Q:** *(T)* Send him what we've got now, and we can come up with some more questions ... *(L)* Yes. Until he's here, and can ask questions ... *(T)* Maybe it's something we can tap into ... *(L)* Okay, Jan has written down a question that I've been curious about myself lately, so I think we'll just kind of throw it in on the top ... that has to do with the unusually high historically recorded lightning strikes in this area. Does this have any correlation to psychic abilities?

72 **A:** Vaguely constructed inquiry.

73 **Q:** *(L)* Okay, is there any correlation between the extremely high lightning

---

[8]Notice that the Cs did *not* say that anything was spinning, only that energy was flowing.

[9]What I was trying to get at was: if you are born and raised in an area where there is a lot of lightning, as the Tampa Bay area, does it enhance psychic abilities, assuming one has them?

strikes in this area and our work? In this area?⁹

74 **A**: Maybe.

75 **Q**: *(T)* Is there a correlation to the lightning strikes in this area, in this immediate area – not right here, around this house, but in the Bay area – because it's so built up, because there's so much metal around?

76 **A**: Maybe.

77 **A**: *(L)* Is there any correlation between the lightning strikes and so forth that have been going on, seemingly coincidental moments in the communications I've been having with Ark?¹⁰

78 **A**: Lightning has been striking elsewhere a lot more too.

79 **Q**: *(L)* So, just in general. There's been more lightning strikes all over the place in general. *(T)* Okay, on the correlations things, to skip from lightning to another question I just thought of. Is there a correlation to the massive power blackouts on the West Coast that have been happening recently, to the government messing around with the HAARP Project, and other related weapons testing systems?

80 **A**: Not HAARP.

81 **Q**: *(T)* Okay, not HAARP. Something else that they're messing with? *(L)* Well, why don't we just ask, what's the cause of the blackouts? *(T)* Okay, what's the cause of the blackouts? Good question!

82 **A**: 4th density bleedthrough has many "fun" possibilities.

83 **Q**: *(L)* Oh, fun! *(T)* 4th density bleedthrough? This is part of the bleedthrough from the different bases on the West Coast?

84 **A**: More or less.¹¹

85 **Q**: *(T)* Are you aware of the Greenbaum effect? Dr. Greenbaum and his mind control experiments, that we've been looking at lately?¹²

86 **A**: Yes.

87 **Q**: *(T)* Is what's said there factual? I won't say true, but is it factual? Most of it?

88 **A**: Close.

89 **Q**: *(T)* Okay, the question is, is the fellow that just shot three professors in San Diego,¹³ I think it was, the university, before they read his thesis, because he was afraid they would throw his thesis away, and make it look bad, and

---

¹⁰Considering that we had been communicating over the summer, the rainy/storm season in Florida, having lighting strikes wasn't so unusual, but they did appear to me to be rather strange in the way that they picked exactly the worst times to happen!

¹¹There is absolutely no way to confirm or deny this exchange.

¹²*The Wave* 14

¹³"The 'San Diego State University shooting was a school shooting that occurred at the San Diego State University *(SDSU)* engineering building on August 15, 1996 in San Diego, California. Three professors were killed by master's degree student Frederick Martin Davidson. ... After the shooting, Davidson himself called 9-1-1. Police arrived to find Davidson in the third-floor hallway still holding the handgun. He was reportedly sobbing and begging for police to kill him. He soon surrendered to police without further incident." (Wikipedia, "San Diego State University shooting")

flunk him. Was he a Greenbaum subject?

90 **A**: Yes.

91 **Q**: *(T)* Why did they turn him 'on' at that point?[14]

92 **A**: Not correct concept. What if: those programmed in the so-called "Greenbaum" projects are preprogrammed to "go off" all at once, and some "malfunction," and go off early?[15]

93 **Q**: *(L)* Oh!!! Can you tell us at approximately what time they're programmed to go off? Because it is a program ...

94 **A**: Nope.

95 **Q**: *(T)* No, they can't. Free will! *(L)* Okay, can you tell us how many of them there are?

96 **A**: No.

97 **Q**: *(T)* Do you know how many there are?

98 **A**: Yes.

99 **Q**: *(T)* Are you 'tuned in' for ...

100 **A**: Tuned in!?!

101 **Q**: *(T)* Mirth! Mirth! *(L)* Okay, because we're going to run out of tape, let's get Jan's last question here. She wants to know if there's any significance to these three Scorpio/Aquarius couples in our circle? As in Terry and Jan, Laura and Arkadiusz, and Margaret and Michael? Well, Margaret and Michael are not really in the circle ... *(J)* Well, all three are known to me ... *(T)* She means finding that there's this Scorpio/Aquarius matchup.

102 **A**: No. Coincidences are the spice of life for those with higher knowledge.

103 **Q**: *(T)* Do you have a question? *(L)* Well, since things have progressed as far as they have, what do you think of Ark now? Is he the Orion?[16]

104 **A**: No commentski.

105 **Q**: *(L)* I guess you could read that in the way of a yes! *(T)* Well, we may not be able to read it in the way of a yes. Maybe he knows the Orion. He's bringing him with him.

106 **A**: Wait and see.

107 **Q**: *(L)* Okay ... *(T)* I'm excited about him coming now, too! I want him to get here, and talk to him in person. Yes! *(L)* Wait your turn!! *(T)* When you get back from your world tour! *(L)* Right, yeah!

108 **A**: You are all Orion manufacture.

109 **Q**: *(L)* Okay, that's cool! *(T)* I hope they build their cars better than Ford!

110 **A**: Still in testing phase.

111 **Q**: *(T)* Yeah, we're beta models! And somebody's reprogramming us, on top of it all! *(L)* Okay, let me say this. In reading through all these transcripts [that were being transcribed apace], you guys were right. My mind was blown. I was completely blown away at all the things that I missed ...

112 **A**: You ain't seen nothin yet!

113 **Q**: *(T)* "Dark star, see you in the morning ..." Still can't think of the name of that group! *(T)* Do you all have anything more to say this evening?

---

[14] *The Wave* 18

[15] This response has become far more interesting in the years since 9/11, and appears to have a certain amount of circumstantial evidence to support it. See: www.globalresearch.ca/mass-shootings-in-america-a-historical-review/5355 990

[16] See session 4 March 1995.

114 **A:** Do you have any more questions?

115 **Q:** *(L)* Well, we've got loads of questions, but we need to get ourselves formulated, we need to get tapes, we need to get organized, we need ...

A: Oh, by the way, Laura: You may 116 help Ark on the things we mentioned earlier, if he requests, what with your communication skills ... and on that note, goodbye.

End of Session

August 24, 1996

As I wrote in my introductory comments to session 27 July 1996, I began to remember what seemed to be past and parallel lives after my initial interactions with Ark, and began to cry almost daily from that first day of the connection with him. This 'superhypnotherapist' action of the awakened superconsciousness had also apparently been activated for Ark as well. I won't detail *all* the strange instances where this sort of thing manifested with each of us, simultaneously on opposite sides of the Atlantic, for the present. Suffice it to say that these incidents included visions, bilocation, synchronized dreams; effectively, so much strange activation of the inner psyche that Ark later said that if we hadn't lived through these utterly bizarre experiences, and someone else had recounted them to us, we wouldn't have believed it.

Background: As noted in comments to previous sessions, I had been in twice-weekly physical therapy for almost two years following the auto accident on Christmas Eve, 1994. I usually didn't mention it in the sessions, but at this particular point in time, probably due to the intensive body-work that was being done, I was truly in so much pain that I wondered how I could go on.

Participants: 'Frank', Laura, V

1 **Q:** *(L)* Hello.

2 **A:** Hello. Louritha of Cassiopaea and we welcome V___, it is good to have your presence!!

3 **Q:** *(L)* Why do I have this persistent, overwhelming pain in my shoulder? I am simply unable to do anything with this pain. If it were not so bad, I would not ask, but I am in such constant pain that it is difficult to even concentrate.

4 **A:** Soft calcium tissues.

5 **Q:** *(V)* How can she work that out?

6 **A:** Through re-energization of the body, combined with cleansing at the same time.

7 **Q:** *(L)* Are you talking about fasting?

8 **A:** A fast would not be good, except one day per each ten.

9 **Q:** *(L)* Okay, you say re-energization combined with cleansing. What is the proposed protocol to accomplish this?

10 **A:** You have been spending too much "time" being static.

11 **Q:** *(L)* You are saying that I need to get out and move around?

12 **A**: 1.5 hours per day. We recommend the first order of business is to clean the pool, then swim 100 circular "laps" each day. Swimming gets the entire body to move and purge, thus your cleansing.

13 **Q**: *(L)* Well, speaking of that. I cannot do that until I can afford to replace the pool pump. So, since you guys are so full of all this advice, maybe you will tell me how to do this? That is impossible right now.

14 **A**: Ask Ark.

15 **Q**: *(L)* I can't ask him!

16 **A**: Why do you think we sent him?

17 **Q**: *(L)* You are completely crazy. I couldn't do *that*!

18 **A**: Yes you could, and phrase it directly.

19 **Q**: *(L)* I can't do that! *(V)* Let me ask you, if Ark loves you, do you think he wants you to be in the situation you are in? If he loves you that much ...

20 **A**: In that sense, he is as you say, "loaded."

21 **Q**: *(L)* I can't *do* that! God! Guys, come on!

22 **A**: No, we are not at 7th density yet, but we appreciate the compliment!!

23 **Q**: *(L)* I can't do that! *(V)* Well, you can't as long as you keep telling yourself you can't! *(L)* Could you ask a man for money? *(V)* Yes. *(L)* You could? *(V)* If I was in a relationship where there was love, of course I could. And you can! *(L)* No, I can't. *(V)* What makes you think he wants you to suffer? If he knew how you are suffering, don't you think he would care? Am I right?

24 **A**: Yes.

25 **Q**: *(L)* Frank! You are pushing that! *(F)* I am not! *(L)* Well, I have a hard time asking anyone for anything. *(V)* Where does that come from? *(L)* I don't know. *(V)* How about pride and ego? A relationship is not about ego. A relationship is about soul connection and love.

26 **A**: Yes.

27 **Q**: *(V)* Thank you! See, I'm getting good! *(L)* Okay, let me ask why I have such an internal restriction [in respect of asking for help]?

28 **A**: You do not. You have always had high expectations relating to your own powers, when you let those go, good things happen.

29 **Q**: *(V)* Does this relate to the 'I must be perfect' syndrome? Or do you think that it diminishes your worth to need from someone else and to not be the one who is doing the giving? *(L)* I suppose that it makes me feel worthless to need.

30 **A**: What do you think he thinks you are?

31 **Q**: *(L)* I don't know. What does he think?

32 **A**: That is not what we asked you. Please answer us.

33 **Q**: *(V)* Well...? Think about it ... It is so intense, so fast ... *(L)* What does he think? I don't know. I only know what he says. But, what he says and what he really thinks may be two different things. He says that I am his other half, his completion. That's what he says. Who knows, he may be telling the truth.

34 **A**: So, where does ego enter into that?

35 **Q**: *(L)* I guess it shouldn't.

36 **A**: Do you think he will reject you if you are honest and open?

37 **Q**: *(L)* No.

38 **A:** Then we suggest you spell out to him your exact circumstances, and hide nothing!

39 **Q:** *(L)* You mean I have to tell him that my husband has left me with five children and no money and is playing games to force me to take him back or starve? That I have used all the money I had to live on and what [my ex] has given me isn't enough? That is completely humiliating! It makes me look stupid! What kind of a woman would put herself into this situation? Waiting for an insurance settlement which could take God-knows-how-long!

40 **A:** And how does one adult raise 5 kids these days? Do you not think the truth is better than fiction?

41 **Q:** *(V)* That's how you live your life! Based on truth. *(L)* But I never thought that it would include having to tell someone my personal problems, my financial difficulties! That is going a bit far with this! I expected the insurance money in July ... *(V)* You accept what the Cs say, correct? Then, you need to apply it in real life! *(L)* Guys! You are putting me in an impossible situation! I cannot do this!

42 **A:** Well, the internet expense angle is there too.

43 **Q:** *(L)* Yes. I will soon have to cancel my internet account and I will have to tell him that eventually.

44 **A:** Which has a funny ring of truth to it!

45 **Q:** *(L)* All things considered, how soon before I get the money from the lawsuit?

46 **A:** Up to you.

47 **Q:** *(L)* Now, you said that you 'sent' Ark. I want to know exactly what you meant by that. I don't like to be manipulated!

48 **A:** "Sent" may not be the exact term, more like nudged.

49 **Q:** *(L)* Well, you have certainly been nudging *me* in his direction! Are you sure I don't have an attachment in this arm? It is excruciating just now!

50 **A:** Yes. It is floating calcification.

51 **Q:** *(L)* Wonderful. Just what I always needed. More pain. Okay. I am in so much pain I will do just about anything to get out of it. Okay. I will tell him. But I want you to know that I do it under protest. And, if I never hear from him again, well ... it's better to know now. V___, ask your questions. *(V)* I have been helping a woman who has cancer.[1] I see her cancer as a sideline even though it is in the lymph system. Is this correct?

52 **A:** Cancer is always a "sideline."

53 **Q:** *(V)* When I was working with her, I felt a lot of energy flow coming up from her solar plexus. Was this the disease energy leaving?

54 **A:** Constriction easing. If she wants to remain on third density, she must change a 28-year-long outlook, and purge feelings, rather than collecting them as a "sponge." Also, dietary changes are needed. We suggest sauerkraut extract and fruit juices and broccoli. She needs colonic therapy, and if diagnosis is "terminal," why are poisonous treatments a consideration? We strongly recommend that you suggest a change in the 28-year-long outlook. She must purge and cleanse her

---

[1] Via Reiki.

mind, body, and soul, as with ALL cancer patients.²

Q: *(V)* I want to address another issue: that of charging for Reiki and other similar work. I mean, if this is a spiritual gift ...

A: Offer the opportunity to give donations in any amount or form as deemed appropriate by the receiver.

Q: *(L)* Okay, I have two quick questions. Last Sunday morning, after the session the previous night, I had a very strange experience similar to what al-Arabi describes as being in a 'state'. It was like being taken up into a condition of near madness, Ark was there [in a sort of vision], and then, when [the intense emotion of the visionary state] became unbearable, [I pulled myself back deliberately and fell into a state of] cold, shaking and rocking. I was shivering like I would never get warm and I could *feel* my soul rocking in my body [the same feeling that comes with an OBE]. I would like to know exactly what this was?

A: Balancing of half-self.³

Q: *(L)* What is a half-self?

A: Your starter version, relating to birth karmic imprint.

Q: *(L)* What in the world does *that* mean?

A: What you were assigned with at the onset of this incarnation.

Q: *(L)* Do you mean that this was 'starting' something? Like a starter in a car?

A: No, what you started with. This must be periodically re-balanced at apex of significant junctures.⁴

Q: *(L)* The next thing that happened was that a few days later, I went unconscious and Ark saw me come in the window [of his office in Wroclaw, Poland]. What happened?

A: Learning is fun!

Q: *(L)* Well, my night would not have been complete without that! *(V)* I am interested in more Reiki symbols. Yet, there is nowhere else to learn these things. Can you direct me?

A: Vague.

Q: *(L)* Is it possible at this point to learn more Reiki symbols?

A: We would be happy to give you one. [Draws symbol] This is called Ohnh tu shayti sunehn.

Q: *(L)* And what energy does this symbol produce or encourage?

A: Completes spiritual awakening. And goodnight.

End of Session

---

²This was excellent advice and I've recently read a few books by psychologists advocating the same approach, notably Gabor Mate's book *When the Body Says 'No'*.
³*The Wave* 3
⁴None of this made much sense at the time; it was only after reading Mouravieff's *Gnosis* trilogy and then re-reading Gurdjieff that more understanding came in terms of the lower centers and higher centers. I think the 'half-self' that the Cs referenced above was their way of describing the lower centers. Thus, this was probably an inflow of energy from the higher centers. Trust me, it was almost annihilating!

August 31, 1996

As I had been advised in the previous session, I gritted my teeth and wrote to Ark explaining my financial situation. Basically, I had only my disability income since my soon-to-be-ex was providing no support at all, and the lawyers working on my accident claim were dragging their feet. The kids and I could get by, but there were *no* extras such as a new pool pump, internet accout, or anything that came up needing repair. I was completely astonished when he wrote back and asked me to write up a budget of what I needed each month and also sent me an immediate bank transfer and credit card to cover the immediate problems plus replacing the pool pump. So, the pool was ready, as the reader will note from this session.

I was also concerned about my daughter who had been quite ill since the separation from my husband (see the notes for session 24 April 1996). Following the advice of our family doctor, she began to feel a bit better, and wanted to try to go back to school, though she had missed over a month. So this issue is also brought up.

Then, I thought I would bring up a topic of general interest regarding "underground bases" and that took a very interesting turn!

Participants: 'Frank', Laura, Terry, Jan, V

1 **Q:** *(L)* Hello.

2 **A:** Hello.

3 **Q:** *(L)* And who do we have with us this evening?

4 **A:** Kiork.

5 **Q:** *(L)* And where are you from?

6 **A:** Cassiopaea.

7 **Q:** *(L)* Does anybody have any questions this evening? *(V)* Yes, I do. What should I do for this rash? Could you please give me some insight? It feels like I have a chemical burn on my face, and my skin is itching.

8 **A:** So why is this?

9 **Q:** *(V)* I'm thinking it's because of hormones, the reaction to ...

10 **A:** No. No.

11 **Q:** *(V)* Why does it only happen to ...

12 **A:** Guess again, and remember, learning is necessary for growth.

13 **Q:** *(V)* Well, I notice it happening within the last few months right before

I cycle ... That's why I guessed that it's due to hormonal fluctuations.

A: And what are your usual practices around the cycling?

Q: *(L)* This is getting a little personal, V___! You shouldn't have asked this one! *(T)* It's something you're doing ... *(J)* Yes, what are you doing? That is what I was going to ask! *(V)* Well ...

A: OK Laura, hand on, thank you, now, rashes are usually an evidence of toxicity ...

Q: *(V)* From a food source?

A: We asked you.

Q: *(L)* So V___ has some toxicity in her system, and we're fairly certain it's not pot, because she's not smoking it anymore ... *(V)* And it's not alcohol, I'm not drinking. *(T)* Do you get any particular craving for any kind of food that you don't normally eat? *(V)* That's the thing! I eat chocolate all the time, I drink soda all the time ... *(T)* Is it a food type that's interacting?

A: But your "cycles" are not "all the time."

Q: *(L)* So, in other words, things that you eat at that time of the month will affect you negatively ... then you need to experiment with it. Is that the solution here, that there's something here that she's taking in that ordinarily doesn't bother her ...

A: Well, we alluded to "practices," did we not?

Q: *(L)* Is there anything that you do at that particular time of the month that you don't do ...

Q: *(V)* [Embarrassed] You guys! Well, I guess ... *(J)* You need to look at what you're doing at that time, and ... *(L)*

Just kind of eliminate some things, eat very simply and plainly, and be very careful with your system, physically, mentally, and emotionally and spiritually, at that time of the month. *(T)* You know, just change your whole lifestyle! [Laughter] *(L)* Okay, okay, have you heard enough yet, V___? *(T)* And stay out of San Francisco, too! *(L)* Let me ask real quick, on another health issue, last week you told me that I should swim circular laps. Is there some particular advantage to these circular laps, as opposed to back and forth across laps?

A: Yes.

Q: *(L)* Are you going to tell me what the advantage is?

A: Try it.

Q: *(L)* Well, I intend to. *(T)* Circles. It's spinning. It's the same idea. Thirty-three circles ... *(L)* They told me to do a 100 a day. *(V)* Not only that, it's a continuous motion. If you go from one end to the other, you have to stop ... *(J)* You're breaking ... exactly, that's true. *(T)* It's one continuous motion all the time. *(L)* Well I want to take the time to tell you guys that I really appreciate the tiny bit of advice you guys gave me last week; it certainly didn't turn out as I expected ...

A: Tiny?!?!?

Q: *(L)* Well it was really, really quite outstanding, and it had quite outstanding results. I'm impressed all to heck and back, so ... I don't know what to say ... *(T)* Genuflect! *(L)* Yes! Several times! So, anything further on that?

A: Any more questions of faith?

Q: *(L)* No, I don't think so! I think I'd be crazy if I had any! *(T)* I think you've gotten more than enough feedback on that. *(L)* Very quickly, let me ask for A___ [daughter]. We have been discussing whether she should, or should not, go to school. I support her either way. There are valid reasons for both. She asked me to ask you guys if you would give her a little guidance on the school issue, and she is open to anything that you may suggest.

33 **A**: Hmmm ... This one is difficult because there'll be regrets either way.

34 **Q**: *(L)* I know, and my thought is that she should go ahead and go, simply because of the fact that she is so moody a person, that it will make her, by her own willing herself to do it, to get out there and be active and interact with other people, and keep her out of the dumps. That's my feeling about it. She needs to get out of the dumps. *(T)* She needs to interact with people her own age. *(L)* Yes ...

35 **A**: Her "dumps" are not caused by that.

36 **Q**: *(L)* What are they caused by?

37 **A**: Her secrets.

38 **Q**: *(L)* And what are her secrets?

39 **A**: Open.

40 **Q**: *(T)* That you have to talk to her about. *(L)* Anybody got any clues? *(J)* How old is she? *(L)* Fifteen. *(J)* She's 15. It could be anything! *(T)* She's probably jealous of her sister. *(L, J, V)* No!

41 **A**: No.

42 **Q**: *(L)* Do these secrets have to do with physical things?

43 **A**: Vague.

44 **Q**: *(L)* Are they secrets about the way she thinks or feels?

45 **A**: Some.

46 **Q**: *(L)* Are they secrets about things she's done?

47 **A**: Not much.

48 **Q**: *(L)* Are they secrets from past lives?

49 **A**: Maybe.

50 **Q**: *(T)* She's very sensitive, as in psychic sensitive ... *(L)* Does she need spirit release? *(T)* Is the interaction with the other people, is she picking up on all their feelings and thoughts and ideas, and it's making her very, very uncomfortable?

51 **A**: Have you not travelled that path to your satisfaction yet?!?

52 **Q**: *(L)* Well, that was kind of obscure! *(V)* Didn't you have secrets when you were a teenager?

53 **A**: Spirit release.

54 **Q**: *(L)* She needs spirit release ... *(T)* No, they mean haven't you travelled that path already? You're not doing spirit release anymore, remember? She doesn't need that, no. *(L)* Yes, everybody's got to do their own ... *(T)* Is she reacting to the divorce? *(V)* That's what I was thinking. *(T)* That's got to be hard on her ... *(V)* Aren't secrets just a part of growing up? A natural part of growing up? *(J)* She's 15, remember.

55 **A**: No not for everyone. Secrets.

56 **Q**: *(J)* She's 15, and she's got secrets ...

57 **A**: No, no, no. Secrets are not for everyone to have and to keep.

58 **Q**: *(L)* Is this a seriously disturbing secret, or series of secrets, or ...

59 **A:** Ask A___ [daughter] how many secrets she keeps.[1]

60 **Q:** *(L)* Okay, let's drop it. What's next? *(T)* The last few where they've led off have led to some very interesting things. *(L)* Go ahead. *(T)* Would you all like to start the ball rolling here this evening and point us in a direction you'd like us to go?

61 **A:** No, you point.

62 **Q:** *(L)* Question, this may take us somewhere. I noticed when I was redoing these transcripts for Ark to read that when we were discussing the origin of the Celts, that the question was asked, by me, were they in any way superior to the indigenous people of this planet? And the remark was, that they were sturdier in some way. And then I commented that they didn't appear to be sturdier than, say, some of the big Black people, because Celts are very fair, and very thin-skinned looking, and very delicate. It just seemed to me to be kind of an odd remark to make. However, the response that I received, which I didn't pick up on at the time, which blew me out of the water, was that they were sturdier, but not necessarily *on the surface of the planet* ... *(J)* No, they didn't say on the surface of the planet. They just said, on the surface. *(L)* On the surface ... Uh-huh. So, does that surface mean surface of their appearance, or does that surface mean surface as in underground? That's my question.

63 **A:** Both.

64 **Q:** *(L)* Now, in talking about these large underground cities or enclaves that we've talked about on a couple of occasions, it has been said that these beings come and actually may take human babies. I mean, this is like fairy lore, legends, of different kinds of creatures that come and steal people's babies, and they go and live underground, and sometimes, one or another will escape. Is this what we're talking about here? These kinds of situations, these underground cities and caves and civilizations and so forth?

65 **A:** Vague.

66 **Q:** *(L)* Well, I know it's vague ... *(T)* Are the Celts part of these underground

---

[1] Just to avoid torturing the reader, I had a long talk with my daughter and it turned out that a big part of her depression was a complete loss of faith in the world. She described how her father had drilled into her head, when I was not around, that any little mistake she makes will send her straight to hell. And she was afraid constantly. Afraid if she was away from me and did the tiniest thing wrong that God would take me away, or if she did not do as her father asked, which often was detrimental to me, that God would take her father. And when my youngest daughter was born, she was so attached to her and then became afraid that God would take her ... and how she would get up at night and check doors and windows, and never felt safe. It was a beginning of her recovery. I told her that she did not have to worry about being perfect ... that I wasn't perfect and God was good to me, so there was an example. I also told her that it was my job to keep her from falling into the abyss and that we would have to have a secret word for her to use to tell me she was falling in again so that I could stop what I was doing and talk to her and pull her out again, as often as necessary, until she stops falling in and has her faith back.

civilizations?

67 **A**: Yes.

68 **Q**: *(T)* And they came to the surface some time ago ...

69 **A**: No.

70 **Q**: *(L)* No, they came here, and they were taken underground ...

71 **A**: No.

72 **Q**: *(L)* No, well, what's the story?

73 **A**: Went.

74 **Q**: *(L)* They went underground? Is that it? *(T)* When did they go underground?

75 **A**: Several occasions, the most recent being, on your calendar: 1941 through 1945.

76 **Q**: *(L)* That's when they went underground? 1941 through 1945?

77 **A**: Last episode of mass migration, mostly Deutschlanders.

78 **Q**: *(T)* Underground. We're talking underground, as in under the surface of the earth. Is this what we're talking about?

79 **A**: Antarctica. Under there.

80 **Q**: *(T)* Under Antarctica, under ... Oh, in one of the big... OOOhhh!

81 **A**: Entry port.

82 **Q**: *(T)* They went underground in Antarctica, they built a large underground base there. This is where the Germans, as in the Nazi Germans, claimed as Vineland, I think it is, where the older maps that show Antarctica, where the Germans, claimed as Vineland, I think it is, where the older maps that show Antarctica, where the German territory was claimed, it's in that section that's south of ...

83 **A**: Yes, but they entered through their constructed base, as instructed, then were assimilated.

84 **Q**: *(L)* They were assimilated into the population already existent? Underground cities, underground bases?

85 **A**: Yes.

86 **Q**: *(L)* So, they didn't build them, they entered into them as instructed, and were assimilated into the population?

87 **A**: They did build a base.

88 **Q**: *(T)* Well, they'd have to keep expanding! Now, you said instructed ... *(L)* Instructed by whom? *(T)* They were instructed to go there?

89 **A**: Those identifying themselves as "Antareans."

90 **Q**: *(L)* And who are the Antareans?

91 **A**: STS humanoid Orion linkage.

92 **Q**: *(L)* What is an STS Orion kinkage? *(T)* That's the ... *(L)* We have a new concept here. *(T)* They would be ... the ... the ... the ... *(V)* Mutant race! *(T)* Yes! Those that were part of the creation ...

93 **A**: No.

94 **Q**: *(L)* What is an STS humanoid Orion linkage?

[Part of tape seems to be missing here, questions in square brackets are reconstruction]

95 **A**: An STS race from Orion that is humanoid.

96 **Q**: [Something about who or how they got hooked up with the Nazis. Probably a question related to the group that 'handled' Hitler.]

97 **A**: The Thule Society originated contact.

98 **Q**: [Something about them "waiting to take over the world".]

99 **A**: Waiting?[2]

100 **Q**: [Terry's question about what Admiral Byrd may have seen over the South Pole.]

101 **A**: Yes, but he was led to believe he was chasing what amounted to merely an encampment of detached Nazis.

102 **Q**: [So Byrd must have *seen* something and was then led off the track ...]

103 **A**: Yes.

[Tape resumes here.]

104 **Q**: *(T)* ... the U.S. just assumed, and Churchill, between the two of them, was it Roosevelt and Churchill? They didn't even tell the Russians too much about what they were doing down there. They just assumed that this was a base, another one of their underground bases that was manned by the Nazis, but there wasn't anything that they could do, because they were too far away, and we were keeping them out of the war. So, there wasn't much that they could send back. So, they let them come in, and figured they were stranded. They've been coming back out ...

(V) Are they coming back out now in the shape of the White supremacists that are like popping up all over the place?

(T) They've been coming and going all along. Admiral Byrd was sent down there, supposedly to go to the South Pole, the first Admiral Byrd expedition to the South Pole; but he took a large military force with him. He was still a U.S. Admiral at the time. The large military force encountered resistance and got their asses whupped real good down there. But, they kept it real quiet, because nobody knew what was really going on down there. So, they just said, "Oh, it was a scientific expedition." It was really Captain Picard and the *Enterprise* going to find a new planet! And in reality, what they'd done was to go down there to root out this base out after the war, and they didn't do real well at all!

(J) Bit off more than they could chew.

(T) They lost a whole lot of people and a whole lot of ships, and a lot of equipment down there. That's why all these bases ring around the outside, all the scientific bases from different countries; Russia, the U.S., Great Britain, all these countries have these scientific bases all along the outer edge of the Antarctic. They're scientific, they use them for study, but they are there to monitor what's going on, that's why they don't go into the Antarctic [interior].

(V) You know, my father was a Seabee[3] down there.

(T) I'll bet he has some very interesting stories about it.

(V) That's why my father is an alco-

---

[2] This remarks was incomprehensible at the time, but after the events following 9/11 until the present day, it makes a lot more sense. So many things have been revealed, leaked, or exposed about the Secret Government since then that it is astonishing; and we were all so ignorant at the time!

[3] "A Seabee is a member of the United States Naval Construction Forces *(NCF)*. The word 'Seabee' comes from initials 'CB', which in turn comes from the term 'Construction Battalion'." (Wikipedia, "Seabee")

holic and can't see straight.

105 **A**: Yes.

106 **Q**: *(L)* What do these guys plan on doing?

107 **A**: This is where "The Master Race" is being developed.[4]

108 **Q**: *(L)* And what is the timeframe they have planned for this activity?

109 **A**: Never mind.

110 **Q**: *(L)* Is Ark going to be able to help us with technology, to help other people, or to protect ourselves in some way? In this really bizarre stuff going on here on our planet?

111 **A**: Too much, too soon, my dear. Curiosity killed the cat.[5]

112 **Q**: *(L)* Well, satisfaction brought him back!

113 **A**: Not in this case!!!

114 **Q**: *(T)* You've got to let this go along. It's picking up momentum every day, it seems. So, just let it roll along and let it see where it goes. *(L)* All right, let's ... *(T)* He's coming to protect you. That's what he said.

115 **A**: Maybe, but there is so, so, so much more in store than that!!!!!!

116 **Q**: *(L)* Stop...! Is that an ominous, "Maybe, but there's so, so, so much more in store"? Or is that a positive, "There is so, so, so much more in store"?

117 **A**: Why would you think it ominous?

118 **Q**: *(L)* Well I don't know ... because I'm scared of what I don't know! *(T)* Faith, we're back to faith again.

119 **A**: What have we helped you to discover so far? Would you rather discontinue this operation?

120 **Q**: *(L)* Oh, hell no! *(T)* After two years, you know she's always going to ask those kinds of questions!

121 **A**: Not two years, eternity.

122 **Q**: *(L)* Did I just get zinged? *(T)* No. No. Mirth! *(J)* Yes, we haven't had mirth in a while! *(T)* Just a little mirth there!

123 **A**: We have helped you build your staircase one step at a time. Because you asked for it. And you asked for it because it was your destiny. We have put you in contact with those of rare ability in order for you to be able to communicate with us. Again, because you desired it, in order to realize your path. By now, you should recognize the signs ... Those who display thinking patterns which in many ways deviate from that which is considered ordinary. The more unusual, the more telling. They have past lives on 3rd density Earth,

---

[4] *The Wave* 34
[5] *The Wave* 39
[6] This was an extremely enigmatic response and I still puzzle over its possible meanings. It seems to me that the first individual mentioned – "We have put you in contact with those of rare ability in order for you to be able to communicate with us" – described Frank. Then, the final description, since the exchange began about Ark, obviously was describing him: "Those who display thinking patterns which in many ways deviate from that which is considered ordinary. The more unusual, the more telling. They have past lives on 3rd density Earth, but not recently, but for this one. And they are not oriented to the Earth frequency vibrations." What it all ultimately means, I do not know since we haven't reached the end yet!

but not recently, but for this one. And they are not oriented to the Earth frequency vibrations.[6]

[Group discussion ensued on the last response.]

124 Q: *(T)* It is destiny for you to find out what your path was, you had to make this contact, because it was what you were supposed to do. *(L)* Are we not talking about Frank in terms of being put in contact with someone who enables me to communicate with you, so you can put me on my path, which is building the staircase, etc., etc.? Is that not what we've got going here?

125 A: He is one, but not the only one, just the one who awakened your sense of recognition.[7]

126 Q: *(L)* I know this is probably not the time to ask this question – this is the kind of discover, open, find out, open, that kind of thing – but it seems to me almost that you are leading up to say something, so maybe I can help you along by asking, what is this staircase, what is this destiny?

127 A: Discover.

128 Q: *(L)* I knew it was coming! *(T)* Why don't we ask who else is involved? *(L)* You ask, I'm trying to ... *(T)* Well, if Frank is one. Who else is involved?

129 A: We have given the signs, but they are not necessarily the same with each individual.

130 Q: *(L)* Well, I know it's kind of a bizarre idea, but ... *(T)* Let me ask this: all this work you've been doing, all this nurturing you've been doing, is Laura a keystone to whole project that you're working on?

131 A: We suggest you avoid anticipatory exercises, as realization comes after the fact.

132 Q: [Frank complains because Laura keeps taking her hand off the planchette and resting it in her lap because of recent pain issues.] *(L)* Well, I'm in pain, Frank, it's hard for me to sit here at all! Appreciate the fact that I'm in pain.

133 A: Appreciate the fact that you have been given the keys to end all this pain.[8]

134 Q: *(L)* When you say, "end all this pain", it sounds a little more inclusive than just my shoulder hurting! I mean, that sounds rather suggestive.

135 A: Yes.

136 Q: *(L)* To end all this pain ...

137 A: It all goes hand in hand.

138 Q: *(T)* Yuppers! *(L)* Well, that's ... that's scary! *(T)* Why? What's scary? It shouldn't be scary, it should be ... it should be ... *(L)* Well, you know what I mean! My poor little pitiful conscious mind thinks it's scary! Maybe some other part of me likes it. *(T)* It should be, um, satisfying to know that! It all goes together. *(V)* I wonder if hand-in-hand is literal ... *(L)* Uh-huh. And that was the big key word, all day long ... "hand-in-hand, give me your hand." *(V)* Today? *(L)* Yes, we're going here, we're going there, we're going

---

[7]Curiously, this is an instance where 'Frank is *The* Channel' was not being touted; in fact, Frank was being relegated in this remark to someone who plays a minor role in the larger drama: "just the one who awakened your sense of recognition".

[8]Here, refer to session 27 July 1996 where the Cs made the odd remark about keys. "What is Anna doing with those keys?"

to do this, we're going to do that. *(J)* Ark? *(L)* Yes. *(J)* So, do you have the keys to end all this pain? *(T)* Now, all we have to do, is find the keyring! *(L)* No, no, no! We have to find the lock! Terry, the lock! We've got to find that sucker! I mean, so what, we've got the keys? What are we going to put them in? *(T)* Yes, indeed! We've got the keys! What do we use them on? *(J)* Where's the door? And where does it go ... well, maybe not ... *(T)* Gotta find that door. We'll ask where it goes after we get the door open! *(J)* Noooo! Let's ask before!! *(T)* Watch out for the chasm beyond the door!

139 **A**: Maybe you should swim yourself silly.[9]

140 **Q**: *(T)* Start doing laps! One hundred every day. *(L)* Who is going to do them with me? *(V)* I will! *(L)* All right! You're on! How about tonight? *(V)* All right, except for every other Tuesday. *(T)* Every other Tuesday you have to swim by yourself. *(V)* What if I have a date? *(L)* No dates!

141 **A**: Your discipline may be a problem ...

142 **Q**: *(L)* I do have discipline problems ... *(V)* "You vill svim." *(L)* Who is going to come and crack the whip over me, make me get in the pool? *(T)* Be careful, they were already over the house once! *(J)* Be careful what you ask for! *(V)* I was thinking of walking in the pool, to help my hip ... *(L)* It does. Walking in the pool is very good. *(V)* Will walking in the pool help my hip get back into where it's supposed to be? Or swimming, for that matter?

143 **A**: OK.

144 **Q**: *(L)* So I'm supposed to swim myself silly ... *(T)* And then laugh a lot ... when you get silly. And have fun with it. *(L)* All right guys ... *(T)* Swim the hundred laps because you want to, not because you have to.

145 **A**: You cannot imagine the relief less poundage will bring to you.

146 **Q**: *(L)* Well, same to you, fella! Well, let me ask this. Is this swimming in circles going to make it go faster?

147 **A**: Yes.

148 **Q**: *(L)* Well, okay, we'll go for it, because I'll tell you what, I'm starving myself to death, and we're not having any movement here the last week or two. *(V)* Starving yourself to death is only going to lead to ill health. *(L)* Does anybody have any more questions? Because I'm absolutely miserable here [arm pain]. All right, let's say goodnight. Is there anything you want to impart to us in your past for us to move towards the future before we shut down for the night?

149 **A**: You need to be vigilant in your queries. Goodnight.[10]

End of Session

---

[9] In retrospect, it seems interesting that as we were trying to figure out where the 'locked door' was, the Cs interject that I should swim myself silly, keeping in mind what they had said in the previous session about swimming along with the remark about the superhypnotherapist from the 24 April 1996 session: "Laura, you need to consult a powerful, practiced, effective hypnotherapist to unlock these questions for you." And: "The locks have been installed in such a way that it is literally impossible for you to unlock them, as they were installed with full knowledge of present circumstances."

[10] I have no idea what the Cs meant by this.

September 14, 1996

The day before this session I received the following email from Jan:

> We just got back in (It's 11:45) from Tampa; we went to the UFO conference tonight with Jan & Andrew to see Linda M. Howe speak - a last minute arrangement, and didn't have time to contact you before we blew out of the house. Tomorrow night is fine for us - we will not go back to the conference as Howe was the only speaker we really wanted to hear - will give you the gories when we see you tomorrow. We had said we wanted to see how composed she & Michael Lindemann were this time around, and Michael appeared from nowhere and managed to get in between Terry & I and Jan & Andrew for Linda's lecture!!????!
>
> We saw two ladies we had met at a MUFON meeting last spring. Annette L and Anna F, of the "Gulf Breeze 6" saga. Terry has told them some about our experiences with the C's. (They told him they were initially freaked by the similarities with what they've been getting - and THEY LIVE IN GAINESVILLE — [4+2+1=7] HMMM!!) He said we were probably going to do a session Saturday. Terry asked if they would be interested in coming and Annette said that they might be. Gave them our phone number. If it's ok with you we'll make arrangements for them to come.

The prospective guests did not attend the session.

Participants: 'Frank', Laura, Terry, Jan

1 **Q:** *(L)* Hello, and who do we have with us this evening?

2 **A:** Eommna.

3 **Q:** *(L)* And where are you transmitting from tonight?

4 **A:** Cassiopaea.

5 **Q:** *(L)* We have several questions we'd like to get into tonight, and the first one has to do with Terry's health, which is a little bit ... *(T)* Flaky, to say the least! *(L)* I was going to select the word fluctuating!

6 **A:** Wheat germ.

7 **Q:** *(L)* What else? Is there anything else? Is this something he needs to add to his diet?

8 **A:** Broccoli.

9 **Q:** *(L)* What else?

10 **A:** Boil, no baking or frying. Too low on the potassium and calcium and manganese, causes mental and emotional reactions, which spur on physical declines ... Be sure to up the zinc intake.

11 **Q:** *(L)* Any more, any further on this?

12 **A**: Advice about sugar is faulty!

13 **Q**: *(L)* Okay, what is the best avenue for the sugar? *(J)* Oh, so he's not low sugar?

14 **A**: Do not eliminate, regulate with natural intake ... suggest cubes if weakness or lightheadedness appears.

15 **Q**: *(L)* So, Terry is not hypoglycemic?

16 **A**: Stop. "Hypoglycemia" is a "buzz word," nothing more.

17 **Q**: *(L)* So, they just named you hypoglycemic because they couldn't think of anything else! *(L)* Is there anything further for Terry that will help get him balanced and feeling better pretty quick?

18 **A**: Be less sedentary!!!! Exercise builds energy reserve and speeds toxin elimination.[1]

19 **Q**: *(T)* I'm going to start my walking again, because when I worked at Home Shopping, I had an hour for lunch, and I didn't want it, because I had no place to go, and nothing to do. I walked all around that complex for an hour; I was doing two miles a night. *(J)* Ask about the sleeping ... *(L)* That's all part of it ... *(T)* It's all thrown off because I'm trying to treat something I don't have ...

20 **A**: Sleep cycle will resolve itself.

21 **Q**: *(L)* And are these things going to help the hemorrhoid problem?

22 **A**: Of course! When one balances, one balances.

23 **Q**: *(T)* Good, I can get back in balance. I'm trying to treat something I don't have. Which is just messing everything up even worse.

24 **A**: Yes.

25 **Q**: *(T)* Thank you very much. I appreciate all that information. *(J)* I have a question. What is all that Nutrasweet doing to him?

26 **A**: Get rid of that! It is poison!!![2]

27 **Q**: *(T)* No more Crystal Lite? It didn't taste bad ... *(L)* Back to the RC! *(T)* No, no more RC. That's too heavy. I'll go back to 7up or something. *(J)* 7up and water. *(L)* Okay, while we're on health questions, is my swimming adequate thus far?

28 **A**: So far so good. But ... no slacking! We know when you slack, Laura, and you are only defeating your own purposes!

29 **Q**: *(L)* Well I have not missed a single night, I want you to know. And I have swam ... until ... yes, I have swam myself silly. It's just as you said, I swim myself silly, so cut me some slack here! I'm not slacking! *(T)* Where'd those missing laps go?

30 **A**: The past is also the present and the future, my dear!

31 **Q**: *(L)* Is there anything I can do to accelerate the weight loss?

32 **A**: Yes. Increase the exercise.[3]

33 **Q**: *(L)* God, I'm already swimming two hours! *(J)* What else can Laura do? *(T)* Start walking ... *(L)* I can't walk, it hurts my hip too much ...

34 **A**: Decrease the food intake.

35 **Q**: *(L)* I'm already living on two hard-boiled eggs and five stalks of celery a day! How much lower can I go?

---

[1] Obviously the Cs' dietary advice at this point was largely based on Frank's mainstream opinions and should be taken with a large dose of salt, no irony intended!

[2] At least the Cs were right about that!

[3] Which is also faulty advice based on faulty mainstream science.

36 **A**: You asked, did you not?? You did not ask if it was wise.

37 **Q**: *(L)* Well, would it be wise to decrease it any more?

38 **A**: No.

39 **Q**: *(L)* Well, at the rate I'm going ... *(J)* How about quality as opposed to quantity? *(L)* Yes. If I continue going at the rate I'm going, will I accomplish my intention?

40 **A**: It depends.

41 **Q**: *(L)* It depends on what?

42 **A**: When Arkady arrives.[4]

43 **Q**: *(L)* All right. You're making me sweat, here!

44 **A**: Good, that aids weight loss.

45 **Q**: *(T)* Sweating's good for you! Is there a place you can go for steam? *(L)* I can get in the shower and do it ...

46 **A**: How about big green salads with leafy green vegetables as opposed to eggs.[5]

47 **Q**: *(L)* Okay, we can handle that ...

48 **A**: Increases metabolic rate with no fat.[6]

49 **Q**: *(L)* Okay, so you said it depends on when Ark will arrive. Does that mean you have a clue as to when that will be?

50 **A**: Yes.

51 **Q**: *(L)* Well, are you going to tell me when that will be?

52 **A**: Nope.

53 **A**: *(T)* Of course they know when he's going to get here! *(L)* God, I feel like I've got this huge weight pushing on me. *(T)* No, it's not a weight. You're thinking of it as a weight ... *(F)* Think of it as a goal! *(T)* Yes, think of it as something you want ... *(F)* That also increases your metabolism. *(T)* Think of it positively, instead of negatively. *(F)* People who are dieting think of it as dreadful ... *(L)* I'm not thinking of it that way, I'm just feeling like I'm under a lot of pressure here. *(T)* No, you're only under the pressure you're putting yourself under, and this is something that you want, so it shouldn't be pressure, it should be ... *(F)* It should be incentive, turn it around ... *(L)* If I do the leafy green vegetables, continue the swimming and do the walking, whatever, will ... I mean, you guys obviously have sent this person into my life, so you must have a clue as to how things are going to turn out, right? You do have a clue, don't you? Are you going to tell me?

54 **A**: Open.

55 **Q**: *(L)* Do I have time...?

56 **A**: If you are dedicated, all will be well.

57 **Q**: *(L)* Is that a promise?

58 **A**: It is not necessary for us to promise anything ... you are at the controls.

59 **Q**: *(L)* And if I manage to ... what I'm trying to ... Does anybody know what I'm trying ask? *(F)* You're trying to ask if your project will be completed before

---

[4] Ark had been invited to the University of Florida at Gainesville and was in the process of applying for several grants to cover his time there. Nothing was finalized at this point.

[5] Again, mainstream advice, probably from Frank.

[6] Mainstream diet advice since proven to be wrong, probably courtesy of Frank, who considered himself a diet expert.

Ark arrives. *(T)* And they're trying to tell you it will if you want it to be. You asked if that was a promise, and they said they don't have to promise anything. They're telling you, if you want it, then that's what you'll have. And if you don't want it, it won't work. But, you've got to want it, and you've got to look at it as something you want, something you desire, not as an evil thing, not in a negative light, but in a positive light. Because this is something that you want. *(F)* Not as a burden, but as a joyous opportunity. *(T)* This is what you're all working toward. *(L)* I'm just worried I don't have enough time. *(T)* Time has nothing to do with it. *(L)* Oh, all right ... *(T)* There is no such thing as time ... You just keep doing it, and it'll ... If you keep doing it, and you keep wanting it, and you keep doing it, it will do it. *(L)* All right ... *(T)* They're not telling you, they're not promising anything, they're just telling you, "This is it, we'll do it, if you want it. But, if you don't want it badly enough, it won't happen." *(L)* Okay, switch gears. Can we switch gears now? *(T)* Yes. *(L)* Everybody ready? *(T)* Yup! *(J)* Sure. *(L)* Ark would like to put this book together with an opening chapter from you guys. Is this something we can get into, or is this something we should wait to get into, or if that's how you want it done at all? Can you give us some advice on this? We've already got a publisher who is very interested in the whole thing, and he thinks that we ought to open the whole story as a cosmic drama.

A: You must meet with Arkady before you can effectively convey any messages in a book.

Q: *(J)* In other words, he has to be here before that process ... *(L)* To do the book ... is that correct? *(J)* ... he has to be here for the process ...

A: Not to "do the book," just to do the project correctly. You see, your communications on the "Internet," "have served their purpose well," but the next chapter cannot begin until the communication levels are at the next level.

Q: *(T)* In other words, he's got to be here. You've done what you're supposed to do ... you found ... *(J)* You've met him, and you've built the foundation of a relationship on the Internet. Now it has to go to the personal level.

A: Remember, Arkady is not yet part of the conduit!!!

Q: *(L)* So, what are we supposed to do for the next few months? Just continue chit-chatting, continue building ...

A: What else can you do?

Q: *(L)* Well, that's about it, can you think of something else?[7]

A: You have communicated extensively with him, but, others have not, and neither have we, not directly, so to say.

Q: *(L)* Is there something I can do to rectify it, I mean, is there something I ought to do? Is there ... *(T)* Just keep on doing! *(L)* Give me a hint! *(T)* You're doing it! *(L)* Okay, the other night, while I was swimming, I had the thought come into my mind, as I was swimming, that number one, not only

---

[7]Ark and I were in almost constant communication, sometimes writing 25 or more emails each per day, even if only a paragraph. We discussed physics, metaphysics, philosophy, and shared our life stories. Of course, we waxed romantic a great deal and it is amazing how useful physics can be in producing romantic metaphors!

am I doing exercise, but I am generating a force field or energy vortex of some type while I'm doing the swimming. Is this correct?

70 **A**: Maybe.

71 **Q**: *(L)* Now, you said something about a hundred laps a day. Getting up to a hundred laps is a little difficult. I also had the thought that a hundred days of swimming might be a clue. Is this correct?

72 **A**: Maybe.

73 **Q**: *(J)* They didn't say no! *(T)* There you go! This is for you to discover! *(L)* Well, I know, but it just came to me while I was swimming around that it's not so much that it ... I mean, getting to the hundred laps is a good plan, but ... *(T)* Well, isn't the swimming in a circle the same as the spinning? *(L)* Yes, I mean, it's ... *(J)* It would be, wouldn't it? *(T)* Which none of us have been doing, so, the spinning is important, the circular motion is important to the whole thought process ... *(L)* Well, I've been going around in circles, man, like you wouldn't believe, I'm doing up to doing like 40 or 50 laps a day. *(J)* That's good!

74 **A**: Slacker!!! Teehee!

75 **Q**: *(J)* Fifty laps a day is great! What are you talking about? *(L)* Guys!! I started out, I could only swim around twice without dying! *(J)* Laura, Laura, they're teasing you! *(T)* Just think, the swimming, starting the walking, will help the swimming! *(L)* All right, I am motivated, guys, I'm telling you! When you guys go home, I'm going to be out in the pool! No doubt about it!

76 **A**: Mirth aids birth.

---

[8]Friend with back problems.

77 **Q**: *(T)* Well, I'm here to tell you, until Larry[8] got off his duff and stopped thinking about feeling better, and did something about it ... *(L)* You just have to go out and do it. *(T)* ... he didn't feel better. *(L)* You have to go out every day, and just start swimming around ... *(T)* It killed him, it killed him for three months, trying to walk. *(L)* I'm actually doing darned good, considering ... *(T)* You are, if you're up to 50 laps! And you only just started, what, two weeks ago? *(L)* I can do 22 without stopping! I mean, 50 is like the nightly count. *(T)* You only started two weeks ago! Getting up to a hundred is going to be hard? It only took you two weeks to get up to 50! *(L)* Well, maybe not! *(T)* Getting up to a hundred ... *(L)* Yes! *(T)* ... is going to be easy! You've made the hard part! *(L)* My other question is, is the creating of this vortex of energy somehow activating metabolism as well?

78 **A**: Yes.

79 **Q**: *(L)* I mean, is it like a cosmic liposuction?

80 **A**: It's a hell of a lot better than the endless train of "therapists" you have seen.

[The telephone rings, and the session is stopped temporarily. The phone call is from A___ (eldest daughter who had been dating Pat Z's son, Patrick) and Patrick, who want advice from the Cs.]

81 **Q**: *(L)* Okay, Patrick wants to know about him and A___. Get your paper and pencil ready now, Patrick!

82 **A**: What does he want to know?

83 **Q**: *(L)* Obviously, he wants to know if he and A___ are going to get married.

That's obviously the question.

84 **A**: Let him ask!

85 **Q**: *(L)* [Consults on the phone briefly.] Okay, he want to know, are he and A__-__ meant for each other? That's his question.

86 **A**: Vague.

87 **Q**: *(L)* Ha ha, I told you! You hate it when that happens, don't you!

88 **A**: Get to the point, Patrick.

89 **Q**: *(L)* Okay, Patrick, get to the point. What's the point, what do you want to ask? [Consults on the phone again.] Okay, Patrick wants to know if A___ is his soulmate.

90 **A**: As we have tried to explain before, there is no "one" soulmate, there are many.

91 **Q**: *(L)* Well, then, what he wants to know is ... now you say that Ark and I were each halves of a single soul. So, he wants to know, is that the same situation?

92 **A**: Open.

93 **Q**: *(L)* They're not going to tell you.

94 **A**: Ask Patrick how does she feel about him?

95 **Q**: *(L)* [Converses with him on phone.] All right, Patrick, they said to ask, how does she feel about you? Do you know? Do you have any further questions? [Converses with him on phone.] He wants to know if he's going to make a lot of money.

96 **A**: A___.

97 **Q**: *(L)* A___ is going to make a lot of money? Is that what you meant?

98 **A**: What we meant is she holds the key to this whole process.

99 **Q**: *(L)* So, in other words, you've got to listen to her, Patrick! *(T)* It's always that way, Patrick! *(L)* Anything further you want to tell Patrick?

100 **A**: Only if he asks.

101 **Q**: *(L)* All right guys, you warned me, I knew I had it coming!

102 **A**: Yes.

103 **Q**: *(L)* Is it going to work out?

104 **A**: Wait and see!

105 **Q**: *(L)* Okay, I'm giving up the floor! [Hangs up phone.] *(T)* They moved slowly on that answer! *(L)* Okay, so, basically, we're kind of on hold here, on a lot of things, waiting until Ark gets here. *(T)* Just keep working right along, and he'll just drop right in.

106 **A**: Exactly!

107 **Q**: *(J)* I have a question. Those two ladies that we met last night – how do they factor into this process? *(L)* The Gulf Breeze Six ladies? They were mentioned before, in the transcripts.

108 **A**: Vague.

109 **Q**: *(T)* Let's just let it play out, like we have been, and see what happens. *(L)* Is there any significance to the Mike Lindemann incident, where he came and sat by us at the Gulf Breeze conference, and then came and sat by Terry and Jan at the Tampa conference?

110 **A**: Yes.

111 **Q**: *(L)* Can you tell us what the significance of this was?

112 **A**: Psychic wave "undertow".

113 **Q**: *(L)* So, he's not aware of anything, he just senses it psychically? Is that correct?

114 **A**: It is pulling him in, lo may he resist.

115 **Q:** *(T)* Yes, that's right. He was standing in the aisle, looking for a seat, and Andrew and Jan went in first, and sat down. He was standing there, and he came up behind them, and when he came ... [tape turned off, portion lost] ... to the next city! *(L)* Is there anything to this *Independence Day* movie that is valid or special to any of us, other than being a good special effects movie?

A: Too vague for a pre-ending question. 116

Q: *(L)* Do you have anything to say to us before we shut down for the evening? 117

A: Ask about ID4 in the next session. Goodbye. 118

End of Session

Here I will share an exchange between Ark and me that took place a few days before this session. On 12 September 1996 (we would be married on this day in two years!) Ark wrote:

> I just talked with a reporter from local radio. He will come tomorrow 8PM and wants me to talk with him about symbols in physics. They plan to talk to astronomer, to archeologist... So there will be two minutes for the meaning and content of symbols in physics. What would Laura expect? She knows how these symbols look - a little bit, not much. She has some expectations. What should I tell? What should I stress. So that it would awake or deepen awareness of a causal listener? Any ideas? Of course I have in mind that if this is successful then perhaps later it can help in some of other way….
>
> Kisses (that cross the ocean ... faster than light)

Laura:

> My understanding of symbols, and it is just something inside me, is that they are more or less archetypal and represent larger ideas and concepts. I can't remember who wrote the story about the "plane beings" but this is what it reminds me of. If there were a world of plane beings, and somehow this world was "plastic" and a man could interact with it, how would the plane beings perceive this. If the man placed his fingers on the plane, the plane beings would perceive 5 circular phenomena. And, as he continued to move his hand through the plane, the phenomena would change with the position of the hand, like a cross-section of a CAT scan. But, the plane beings, because of their inherent limitations, could never perceive the total man attached to the hand, much less his inner life.
>
> So, symbols are like this to me. What can we really know about them? They represent larger realities that may be beyond us, or, at the very least, at the furthest edges of our awareness. Like Ouspensky's apple. If we could perceive it in its totality, it would seem like a long, red, tubular thing that begins as a point and gets larger, changing color, and then goes for a bit, finally becoming a point again before disappearing. The idea being, that an IDEA is the origin of the point that begins the

manifestation of the long, tubular apple, and the IDEA continues to exist even after the apple has come into being and gone from matter.

Another way I think about it: existence is like an oriental carpet. A thread of the carpet is a potential. A unit of consciousness is a point of illumination on a thread that moves along the thread. The threads are all there. The designs in the carpet are all there. One large design may mean a war with a lot of threads and colors involved. And, if a unit of consciousness is moving along a particular thread that progresses into this design, then there is very little that can be done to avoid it if the proximity is immediate. However, if the designs can be known, then movement, thread by thread, out of the path that leads to that design of war, can begin at a sufficient distance to avoid the pattern altogether.

So, symbols represent these realities. And symbols can help us know about them and potential pathways, and energies needed to "jump" from one thread to another, or many threads, or even to deliberately alter the design of the carpet.

Pretty simplistic, I know, but it helps me.

Kiss!

Ark:

I kiss you back. But I am not yet satisfied with your story of symbols. Because symbols in physics are MATHEMATICAL symbols. Not crop circles. Certain CONCEPTS like that of "ENERGY" I would consider also as symbols - because these can not be defined. What is MATTER? For me it is a symbol. ENERGY is another symbol. I do not know whether TIME is a symbol or not. So, as far as I see there are two kind of symbols in physics: mathematical symbols that represent precise concepts but Platonic one, and conceptual symbols like MASS, WEIGHT, ENERGY who do apply to the real world directly, but which are necessarily vague and lacking of precisions. Physics can be thought of as the science that relates these two kind of symbols... That is what comes to my mind spontaneously... Of course the math symbols relate to Ouspensky's apple and plane beings as with the help of math symbols we can DEAL effectively with concepts which very nature goes beyond the plane of our direct experience....

Now, please, be spontaneous and comment on the above.....

Laura:

It just comes to me that if crop circles and so forth, are symbols of larger IDEAS, or higher density realities, then they are like a complex thing that takes many words to express if spoken. And math symbols are these letters of these words which are equations or series of equations.

Time is going to HAVE to be a symbol because it is some sort of synthesis of energy and matter which must be just different expressions of an original singular thing. Maybe we have: The Original thing - which is greater than or equal to the first division which is into

1. energy
2. matter

and 1. is sto and free will
and 2. is sts and non-free will.

So that the tension between the two is time. But, time is NOT the original thing, it is sort of a mirror of the Original Thing. Kind of vague, I know.

> So, as far as I see there are two kind of symbols in physics: mathematical symbols that represent precise concepts but Platonic one, and conceptual symbols like MASS, WEIGHT, ENERGY who do apply to the real world directly,

Well, again we have a division: energy DOING, and what is being DONE. And the DOING and the BEING DONE results in the THING BEING DONE TO, which has no reality without the LOOKING and the REFLECTING.

> Now, please, be spontaneous and comment on the above…..

I am trying, but I feel that I am in very deep water now and you may have to rescue me!!!

Ark:

In fact you were never endangered as you know swimming by heart. The water can be of any depth and you will be doing well - provided it is not too cool. Moreover, step by step, you are also learning to swim into cooler and cooler water. But, OF COURSE, whenever you just THINK of a need of being rescued - the rescue will come!

Laura:

More: Suppose we start with gravity. We understand it as a wave, sort of, or that it expresses as a wave. But what makes this so? Wouldn't absolute gravity not be a wave at all? Wouldn't it be the no-dimensional mathematical point of non-being?

But, anyway, this gravity somehow becomes a wave... and as a wave, something in it, some characteristic, some internal mechanism, results in instability. What is this instability? What stimulates it? But, the instability results in energy expression which is light. The light is expressed, but immediately the gravity begins to act upon it and it begins to accrete, creating universes and all within them as this act of accretion and returning to stable state.

We are at some point in the middle of this process and the only way we can conjecture about it is to look in both directions by seeing what, exactly, we have present with us in our reality and then projecting it in two directions, sort of to the right and to the left. But, when we do, we will find that they ultimately meet at some point, like the mobius strip. Endlessly cycling.

And the symbols that we have in math and for concepts, are the things that describe this middle point when it is broken down to its fundamentals. But, hopefully, we will find that this breaking down enables us to both project and recapitulate what is to either side, or above, below, within, without etc. Because it is all spherical mosaic. A many layered cosmic onion which, as soon as you get to the inner layer, you find it has turned inside out and you are now at the outer layer again!

I'm sinking deeper!!!!

Ark:

Don't worry. There is still a lot of depth below... And sinking deeper and deeper is a good thing. YOU ARE ABLE to live in deep water too. Just don't be afraid. I will rescue you from whatever depth.

Laura:

But we still haven't fully addressed the symbols.

We ought to know that our world comes into being from someTHING that is "invisible." And it may not be invisible because it is so amorphous, or ethereal, exactly, it may just simply be because our psychology does not admit it. Sort of like when you have just acquired something, you NOTICE all kinds of related things. (When I was pregnant, it seemed that all I saw were other pregnant women.)

So, these symbols ought to be able to describe these realities - of necessity - so that we can have more FREE WILL in what we NOTICE. We can then expand our psychology to admit more, to have more, to DO more.

So, these symbols that describe these realms beyond are SO IMPORTANT as maps or threads that lead the human race out of the labyrinth.

And, we can see that doing this is a balancing action against that material entropy which seeks to sustain itself by opposing, or maintaining tension, by convincing us that only what we SEE with our eyes is what is REAL.

Like Homer describing the Mediterranean as the "wine dark sea." Many psychologists think that peoples of that time could not perceive BLUE and that the Mediterranean was more or less burgundy in color to them. What they think the sky looked like, I have no idea, but perhaps something similar. Anyway, expanding concepts enabled expanded perception. And just as our machines and gadgets extend our capabilities into realms that we would not ordinarily perceive, we may find that these expansions of awareness lead to internal extension so that the gadgets and machines of the present become no longer necessary, and we move to higher technologies.

So, the use of symbols to expand concepts, results in expansion of perception, which results in expansion of capabilities, including more conscious control of our environment and our ability to SEE what is best and then to DO it.

We use these symbols to build ideas. We then use the ideas to build awareness. And knowledge and awareness protect us from being cast adrift in the cosmos as seeming orphans. We reclaim our birthright by declaration through symbols.

This is why I see the symbols as important, particularly the math symbols.

I need a BIG kiss now!

Ark:

You need a BIG kiss and you get a BIG BIG one. But the subject is not yet covered. Because in physics, in math that is necessary to write down our LAWS OF NATURE, we deal with rather restricted symbols. As you know it: the most advanced mathematical expression that we know, that would perhaps take one hundred of pages to write it down in a fully expanded form (mathematicians use kind of a "zip" compression to compress hundreds of pages of symbols into ONE other symbol) - so even this more advanced equation that would describe Santilli's variable-unit-gravity-antigravity- whatsoever is only one-seventh of the full equation. So all these symbols that theoretical physics is so proud of, all these deal with our density, and only with this. There is no math known that would go beyond that. This is yet to be done. So these symbols that are used today are of restricted nature. Of course Reiki etc. uses other symbols and they perhaps go some way beyond. But is there any mystery in these equations of present day relativity or quantum mechanics? Big Psi - for Schroedinger wave function for instance. It represents the field of probabilities (read potentialities) - but there is no mystery in the symbol itself....

Water is not only deep. It is also muddied.

Laura:

I understand this, but I still think that it ALL can be known through what is available to us. At least known in abstraction. In theory. Maybe it just needs something... like adding an exponent to a number to express more power to the number. Maybe the "one seventh" of the equation is in the middle. And it just needs to be repeated with some particular expression or definition going up and an inverse process going down.

It is said that the ideas of physics influence our world in very important ways. But, the usual delay time is about 50 years for these ideas to filter down into our everyday life.

The physics of Newton resulted in the industrial revolution and the ideas that "man is a machine" and this, as we know, led to a very materialistic mode of thinking which has left man internally empty. For centuries the church had defined reality. The church was the sole arbiter of our awareness. But it was corrupt because it fell under the law of entropy.

So there was rebellion. The whole world became a question. Newton tried to answer that question. His answer reflected a distrust of religious authority. The definitions were no longer based on speculation or faith. This was because, after the corruption of the church, no one wanted to risk again having a single group in control of our reality.

But, the truth is, to a large extent, there is still a single group controlling our reality and they do so by limiting the general access of the public to the pure work of science... true science, not brainwashed science.

Symbols give us clear insight into the fact that there is something more going on than what meets the eye. The average man thinks that such ideas are unknowable. But history shows us that this is not true. History is the evolution of thought.

Symbols help to put our awareness into perspective. symbols are a way of systematically exploring our reality and building consensus about it.

The problem with quantum physics is, I think, the very uncertainty of it. This lack of a foundation has affected our culture in very significant ways. People have dealt with this uncertainty by manipulating what they think they CAN control - usually each other. Conquering and using. And this has become a preoccupation, a focus on secular and economic security to replace the spiritual security that was lost to the corruption of the church, and defined out of existence by science!!!

And, in all of this, most scientists have forgotten the original purpose: to understand our purpose and place in the cosmos.

So, the most important thing about symbols is that they can help us to reframe the question, to help us to reconsider: What is behind this life and why are we living it?

We have used symbols to create material and technological progress. Now it is time to find out why we have done this.

KISS!!!!!

At this point, we turned to discussing his application to a foundation for a grant to come to the U.S.; that required a dozen or more exchanges that day. Hopefully, this will give the reader some idea of the intensity and nature of the exchanges.

The following day, 13 September, I wrote:

Mother went to the doctor for some tests last week and then went this week for a talk with him. Her health is declining, though she is so stubborn and refuses to admit it... I am considering that she must give up her house and I will have to rearrange things for her to be here... this has advantages and disadvantages... the advantages are that I will not worry about her so much, she will have less work to do that she is becoming rapidly unable to do... expenses will be less... she will be IN the house and this will enable me to be OUT of it without making all kinds of special arrangements for someone to be with the children if I want or need to go somewhere...

The disadvantages are: she is a very controlling, obstinate, and often inconsiderate person who tends to make big issues out of things that ought to be ignored, and ignores matters of principle that ought to be addressed without delay. I love her very much and wish I could help her, but she constantly blocks me. So, it would be a situation where I would have to watch every moment... the C's have told me that she is one of the channels through which negative energies can affect me.

There is also another possibility, one I do not like and which I resist: having her move into a retirement home. She would have to give up a lot. But, either way she will have to give up a lot. If she is with me, she will have to give up to me. And she will fight this constantly with the result being that I will be drained... unless she can be made to see that she must willingly change. And if she gives up even more to go to the retirement home (which is very nice) then she will only call me and make me feel guilty every day!!!!

So, I tend to prefer to have her move in with me... having her understand that if it becomes intolerable, she will have to move to the retirement home. Perhaps this will be sufficient motivation for her to work on her controlling habits!!!!

Anyway, this is what is worrying me somewhat. Now that I have written it, it seems to have solved itself, but you may have some input for me that will help me. Help US.

The girls and I are very comfortable... but the house is big enough to accommodate all. And sometimes sacrifices are necessary. Just tell me what you think and how it seems to you so that I can DO something soon. I like to take action on things that bother me as soon as possible...

September 21, 1996

Five days before this session I had a nifty swimming experience which I described to Ark in an email as follows:

> Swimming last night was VERY interesting. After about 4 laps, the muscles began the usual burn which I knew I could push beyond. So, I did. Then, at about 15 laps I thought: "I guess I ought to stop for a few minutes and rest... maybe this is enough..." But then I thought: "No, let me see what will happen if I ignore that thought... maybe I don't HAVE to stop... what will happen if I don't... I don't really FEEL tired, so maybe that thought is just a program and I don't have to run it..." so I began to think about what dedication means and devotion... and just thought about those words for a few minutes... and I noticed that all sensations and desire to stop left me. So, I continued to swim. And, each time there was the thought to stop, I repeated the word: dedication in my mind. After a while, I noticed that the thought to stop STOPPED, and I just continued. And continued. After a while, my daughter came home and I was still going. By this time, I had been swimming non-stop for over an hour. So, I kept going... I wondered if I would reach a point where the body would stop on it's own... but it never did. After about 30 more minutes I did notice a little stiffness in my neck and shoulders, but it was not really fatigue... just stiffness. So, after WELL OVER 100 LAPS, I decided to stop. And did. And just sat for a while.

So, I felt pretty good about my physical recovery process.

Meanwhile, Ark was in the process of translating/transcribing some of his journal entries for me to read and on this occasion, there was a strange synchronicity. He sent the following to me on 16 September:

> From the Journal
> Bielefeld, Sunday **May 25, 1988**
>
> Determination is needed. Thinking with weeks and months rather than years. What is needed is setting a goal and striving to achieve it. Because as it is I am in no way different from the other people. I am drifting the same way they are drifting. The same time my only chance is a DIFFERENT way. Thus I want to change my priorities. I want to change my way of living. To change for what? I have ideal conditions. Can not be better. I am, in principle, absolutely free. So what? I see no other way than setting the goals and realizing these goals. Setting and

realizing. Setting and realizing. Otherwise there is drifting. "Life is real only when I am." If I am living consciously then I know that I am. We are setting goals, but if we are not conscious, if we are not attentive, if we are not wise - then we are drifting. Sooner or later there is a turn. I want to avoid this. But first I want to understand better what is:

DRIFTING?

Days and years are passing. I am drifting. [...] Again I am drifting. I am thinking back. What was good and what was bad? It was good when I knew where I am going. When from my depth I designed a goal and when I was striving to get it. What is my goal today? Where do I go? Where do I want to get in? Have I reconciled myself with life? Has a crystallization occurred? Am I satisfied with it? Which is my way? I have the ideal, best of the best conditions to answer this question. What do I choose? And then, how do I want to realize this choice?

I am drifting. Again I am drifting. Because first I was supposed to understand "drifting"... So first may be plan this thinking... No, better without planning, it is better if it will be based on free associations until the subject is exhausted.

Bielefeld, West Germany. Europe. Earth. Solar System. The Galaxy. Universe. That's me in this perspective. New Age is coming. Do I need a greater scale of things? No, that one is enough. So, here I am, on the planet Earth in the Solar System. Know nothing of the other living beings in the Universe. Purpose of my existence: unknown. So, a hypothesis is necessary. A working hypothesis to be falsified or confirmed. A kind of a compass. An axiom, a postulate to be verified by developing a system based on this postulate and by checking if it is useful. If it leads somewhere and not drifts in a cycle.

So, let's state the hypothesis. The only reasonable hypothesis that I can state is that one coming from the unknown system told by Gurdjieff. The system tells us that the World has a certain purpose. That not everything works well. That there are certain "bugs" in the construction. It is quite possible that using the meta-language one can prove that any program on that scale must have bugs. So the Universe is a "program", a program which has bugs, but which has a built in capacity of self-improving. There are therefore certain units that are brought into existence with this specific purpose: to self-evolve to a degree high enough to be able to find out the methods of debugging. These repairs can be only done on a local scale, therefore local units are created. Of course there are ways to act non-locally, for that one has to have some knowledge of the operating system.

This is thus the Allegory. I am such a unit. I am alive, and I am endowed with some inputs/outputs and peripherals. With some modems for communication. The computer allegory. So, potentially, I have everything necessary for a self-development. Of course, during my life certain things went wrong. Therefore certain connections are wrong, certain others are even deadly wrong. But these defects can and must be circumvented by closing certain channels and by opening of some others. Anyway I can only do what I can do - not more.

This is a general perspective. From this general perspective my aim is to save the Universe. Or rather: to help to save the Universe. And this I have to do whatever the future can be. Independently of the fact that there may be an immortal soul that can be developed by conscious effort and intellectual suffering. I have no other choice but to be helpful for saving (or debugging) the Universe.

DEBUGGING THE UNIVERSE

"In the beginning there was the word." Only today I understand this message. But also "already today". Which means we are entering now into an important era. In a sense into a final era. When to be or not to be of the Universe will be decided. This is a general perspective.

Now my role in this opus: I am a worker. I have a mission that is to be fulfilled. I have an individually designated mission. Mission to fulfill. I am sent here. Into this time, this place, in this and not in some other form. The first thing is to find and read the designated task. But there is more. There are, namely, information channels with which I can communicate with those that sent me here and that are controlling the mission. Because the higher intelligence must have some control, but it can not do the work which only I can do. So, there are certain information channels. Of course I am not able to make free use of them. I can not use them until there is a guarantee that using of these channels will not bring harm.

Summary until now:

UNIVERSE IS A COMPUTER PROGRAM
SELF-ORGANIZING SELF-EVOLVING UNITS
DEBUGGING LOCAL UNITS
MISSION HIGHER INTELLIGENCE AND COMMUNICATION CHANNELS

Of course all this process is based on the law of big numbers. That is not everything can be programmed. Statistical fluctuations must be allowed. OTHERWISE NOTHING WILL EVOLVE BY ITSELF. OTHERWISE THERE WILL BE NO SELF-EVOLUTION.

It follows thus that probabilistics, that stochastics, that element of uncertainty, element of choice is at the base of the construction of the Universe. This is interesting and I want to work on this. THIS IS VERY IMPORTANT I want to return to this point later on. But now I want to proceed further.

What is my aim, what is my goal, what is my task? What kind of work I am to perform? What kind of work I want to perform?

Universe may be a deterministic automaton, nevertheless with such a complex action that there is no other method of predicting than running the Universe to see what will happen. In this sense therefore we must be satisfied with a statistical description when we want to foresee future. Let us say this is a rough picture. But then where is there a place for free will? For choosing? For precognition? Something is therefore lacking in this picture.

WORKINGS OF THE UNIVERSE

The problem of determinism and indeterminism. The problem of free will and the problem of chance. All this relates to the problem of time and to the problem of other dimensions. Therefore I must not discuss these thing on too low a level.

So we have the following circle of problems:

TIME - CAUSALITY - DETERMINISM - CHANCE - PHASE - OTHER DIMENSIONS - QUANTUM AND CLASSICAL-COMPLEMENTARITY - INFORMATION - ORGANIZATION

What is important here is that these are general laws - these are objective. There are statistical laws that are valid "on average" and there are laws that concern each individual case. But these laws leave a certain rather big freedom. Within this freedom there is what is and within this freedom we are given free hand. Thus not everything is determined and predictions for the future have the form: IF this, THEN this, IF NOT then that.

I am living in the world based on technology, I am using this technology. We have computers, we know something about computer programs. Only now we understand what means: "In the beginning there was the word" Therefore we should not alienate ourselves from this technology. Our cognizance goes through technology - which does not exclude the fact that for "chosen" people there are other possibilities of gaining knowledge. These are possibilities that are not, however, saving all of the humanity.

Thus I am aware of the fact that I am not developing for myself. That I am not working in order to get a salvation or immortality. That I am sent here with a MISSION and my task is to add to saving of the Universe. I can do it by helping humanity. But in order to do it I need KNOWLEDGE, I need to be able to DISCERN. So the goal appears: to learn the working of the Universe, to learn about Universe, about human beings around, to learn about myself. To learn and to help the Universe. That means to help the CREATOR. To be of some help to the Creator of Everything. Everything that IS is a great thing. So, this is my ultimate goal. The goal from which all other goals stem.

Now, come back to the beginning. If this is my goal, then there should be no time for drifting, no place for pleasures. Somebody told me that I need a rest. But I do not need a rest when there is some work to be done. At each moment I can choose. Or better: there are moments when I have a choice. At these moments I have to be careful not to let things to go their way.

So, the ultimate goal is clear. Now there comes realization. It is clear, psychologically the goal is difficult. And there are all kinds of obstacles, there are phantoms that delude ... Singing of Sirens, temptation of Satan. All of the mythology is full of temptation stories. The goal is high, right, but for some reason can not be obtained by just anybody who would see it. There is a filter in action, there is a selection criterion. The goal can be reached only by some chosen, some who will pass a test, who will oppose temptations, who will prove to have enough strength, who will show that gods have them under their care. Otherwise I will perish or remain on the island of Sirens. - TEMPTATION OF SIRENS = Drifting.

I was rather stunned reading this for the reasons described in the email I sent back to Ark:

> Now: this is astonishing, to say the least. Are you sure you are human??
>
> Yesterday Tom French called and wanted me to answer questions *about my experiences of 1988 and 1989* because that is where he is in the writing.
>
> On **May 6, 1988**, I have here a copy of lab reports from the series of medical tests that were done prior to surgery that month. Don't remember the exact date of the laparoscopy and D.& C., but they were done because I had been bleeding since December the year before.
>
> For some time, at this point in my life, I had been suffering the breaking of objects in proximity to me, and it was in August of 1988 that the breaking of the car window occurred right after the vision of the cleft of the rock.[1] Somewhere in here was the breaking of the window in the bedroom, but cannot be sure exactly when. And, of course, my youngest child was conceived in 1988.
>
> In reading these pages, I was very curious to see the comparison of the universe to a computer because this is what the C's have said also. And Free will makes me think of binary code, which is one of the few math concepts I DID pick up somewhere along the way.
>
> Yesterday I was trying to explain to Tom why it seemed so important to me to understand why bad things happen... because if you don't know what everything is, how can you determine where the wrong turn was taken that led to a certain event and whether or not you could have

---

[1] See The Wave, Chapters 15 and 31.

taken a different direction, and knowing such things, could events be more statisically analyzed so that the RIGHT choices could be deliberately made... in other words, can we know how to DO by knowing precisely what we are doing now, what we have done in the past, and what it REALLY means and is?

Because, if things were just random, 50% of the time good things would happen. Yet, a careful examination of history, sociology, psychology, and so forth shows us that this is not the case. Yes, we have a host of technological improvements, but culturally we are dying... so, some of this technology, while on the surface seems to be good, is, in some way, contributory to spiritual and mental decline among the masses of people.

... To claim that our technological prowess is the standard by which our society should be measured is an outrage when 2 million children will starve to death before the year 2,000... and that number may have risen since I last checked it!!!

So, anyway, I talked for 2 hours yesterday about 1988 and what was going on in my head and about the other bizarre episodes including the night I awoke to find the room flooded with light and then later awoke to find my position reversed in the bed and my gown wet with dew from the knees down.[2]

And you are SAYING these things in 1988!!!! I am amazed.

So, the program is running...

It certainly was amazing to see what was going on in Ark's thinking in 1988, the year that so many extraordinary things were happening to me; things that led, ultimately, to the Cs, which then led to Ark.

During the entire session that follows, the sound of frogs croaking in the distance can be heard periodically. I always loved the sound of the night-singing tree frogs when I was growing up. It seems that there were a few of them living in a pipe and that amplified the sound.

Participants: 'Frank', Laura, Jan, Terry

1 **Q:** *(L)* Hello. And who do we have with us this evening?

2 **A:** Toyjiia.

3 **Q:** *(L)* And where are you transmitting from?

4 **A:** Cassiopaea.

5 **Q:** *(T)* Is there any significance to the *ID4* movie?

6 **A:** Sure.

7 **Q:** *(L)* What was the primary intention of the makers of this movie? The primary message that they attempted to

---

[2] Again, these events are described in detail in *The Wave*, Chapters 15 and 31.
[3] *The Wave* 20

convey?³

8 **A**: Infuse thinking patterns with [planchette swirled a few times here] concept of aliens.

9 **Q**: *(L)* They intended to infuse thinking patterns with concept of aliens ... was there any particular slant on aliens, per se, that was seen as desirable in the making of this movie?

10 **A**: Slant?

11 **Q**: *(L)* Slant, in other words, did they wish to present them inaccurately to confuse people, to present them as something to be feared and fought against, or to make them appear so completely erroneous, so that when actual aliens do appear, that they will not be perceived as negative?

12 **A**: Infuse.

13 **Q**: *(L)* Infuse. Just the concept, the concept of aliens in general. Okay ...

14 **A**: Part of a larger project.

15 **Q**: *(L)* And what is this project?

16 **A**: Called "Project Awaken."

17 **Q**: *(L)* And who is behind, or in charge of, this project?⁴

18 **A**: Many.

19 **Q**: *(L)* Who are the primary group, groups or individuals? I'm sure you're not going to give us individuals, but just the grouping.

20 **A**: Thor's Pantheum.

21 **Q**: *(L)* And what is Thor's Pantheum?

22 **A**: Subselect trainees for transfer of enlightenment frequency graduation.

23 **Q**: *(L)* What is enlightenment frequency graduation?

24 **A**: Think!

25 **Q**: *(L)* Enlightenment frequency graduation ... so, subselect trainees ...

26 **A**: Self-explanatory.

27 **Q**: *(L)* Well, is this group STS or STO?

28 **A**: Both.

29 **Q**: *(L)* Okay ... *(T)* Are they working at cross purposes?

30 **A**: No.

31 **Q**: *(T)* They're working together? Bipartisan?

32 **A**: No.

33 **Q**: *(J)* Are they aware of each other? Working on this?

34 **A**: Yes.

35 **Q**: *(J)* Are they screwing each other up? *(L)* No, that's going in the wrong direction ...

36 **A**: There is more to all of this than you could dream.

37 **Q**: *(T)* There's more to all of this ... were you referring to ... Who are they? Thor's Pantheum. And they're subselect trainees ... That's the group behind this movie; okay ...

38 **A**: An army of Aryan psychic projectors.

39 **Q**: *(T)* Well, that explains a lot more than Thor's Pantheum of subselect trainees! An army of psychic projectors. *(L)* And what do they project?

40 **A**: Themselves ... Right into one's head.

41 **Q**: *(T)* Into one's head ... this is better than 'Must See TV'! *(L)* Project right into one's head ... is anybody subject to this projecting?

42 **A**: Yes.

---
⁴ *The Wave* 20

Q: *(L)* And, when they project themselves right into someone's head, what does that someone perceive?

A: Inspiration.

Q: *(L)* Inspiration to what, or to do what?

A: Yes.

Q: *(L)* Yes? To do what, to do something?

A: And ...

Q: *(L)* To do something, and to understand or perceive something, is that it?

A: Yes.

Q: *(J)* To believe something? *(L)* Yes. So, how many are in this army?

A: 1.6 million.

Q: *(L)* When they're doing this projecting into someone's head, where are they projecting from?

A: Mostly subterranean.

Q: *(L)* Subterranean, so these are the people of the tunnels, the underground bases and all that sort of thing. Are they 3rd or 4th density beings?

A: Both.

Q: *(T)* Let me back up to a question here. If they can do all this projecting on their own, what was the point of the movie?

A: No, you misunderstand ... This is an intense activity, directed towards influencing the high level creative forces.

Q: *(T)* Projected against? Because this movie – if you've been following the reviews and the people talking about it – this movie has had more repeat business than any movie in years and years and years and years. People have seen it ten and twenty times! *(L)* Was there something subliminal in the movie? That opened something? *(J)* That's a good question!

A: Sure.

Q: *(L)* And was this subliminal activity with the movie designed to create an opening for this further ...

A: Not for you, but for others.

Q: *(L)* Why? Do you mean me, personally, or us as a group? *(T)* Well the movie didn't affect me.

A: Group.

Q: *(L)* What made us immune?

A: You already have the knowledge.

Q: *(T)* The movie wasn't meant for us; we already know. The movie was meant for all of those who don't understand.

A: Say hello to Gene Roddenberry.

Q: *(L)* Is Gene Roddenberry present?

A: No.

Q: *(L)* In other words, say hello to him because he was doing that sort of thing a long time ago?

A: Yes.

Q: *(L)* Is Gene Roddenberry one of these people from Thor's Pantheon?

A: No.

Q: *(L)* Why did you bring up Gene Roddenberry? *(J)* Because he was doing it in *Star Trek*?

A: Yes.

Q: *(T)* He was doing a whole different thing with *Star Trek* ... *(L)* Well, let's not get too far off track ...

A: It's not the exact "slant," it's "the concept, stupid."

79 **Q:** *(T)* Well, they don't have to get insulting here! *(L)* They weren't. Okay ...

80 **A:** "Its the economy, stupid."

81 **Q:** *(J)* We knew that! *(T)* I was just teasing. Mirth! Mirth! *(L)* Hold everything. When you say influencing high-level creative forces, do you mean as in gathering, what would you call it, gravity waves ...

82 **A:** No.

83 **Q:** *(L)* What are these high-level creative forces that are needing to be influenced, or desirable of being influenced?

84 **A:** Those in the creative arts.

85 **Q:** *(L)* So in other words, I see, this group is using their projecting ability to influence those in the creative arts to do creative things that will therefore influence the people on the planet. Is that it?

86 **A:** Yes.

87 **Q:** *(L)* And, these individuals are in the underground tunnels, and you say that they are both STS and STO.

88 **A:** We did not specify "tunnels," you did.

89 **Q:** *(T)* They said ... how did they put that? Subterranean ... *(J)* Mostly subterranean. *(T)* ... Underground. In other words, underground, as in resistance fighters–type underground, underground as in ...

90 **A:** No.

91 **Q:** *(T)* Not fighters, but the idea that they are part of the underground movement? *(L)* Subterranean as in literally under the ground?

92 **A:** Yes.

93 **Q:** *(L)* Okay, but not tunnels, then what?

94 **A:** We did not say "no tunnels" either.

95 **Q:** *(L)* Are these individuals living ... I know we said the tunnels ...

96 **A:** The point is: what happens when you assume?

97 **Q:** *(L)* We won't assume. Are there any specific things about this movie other than the general import of opening to the idea of aliens ...

98 **A:** No.

99 **Q:** *(L)* So there's no specific thing that we can pin down in this movie, and say that this might be an accurate representation of anything? It was just entertainment for that purpose?

100 **A:** Enough about the movie, already!

101 **Q:** *(T)* But they were the ones who brought it up! *(L)* Well, yes, but maybe they want us to get on to the subject of this 'Thor's Pantheon' thing? *(T)* Well, I want to make sure that we're not missing something ... *(T)* So, we're looking at some Aryan psychic projectors who are trying to stimulate people in a positive way, à la Gene Roddenberry ... *(L)* Now, that's an assumption. Can we say that they are stimulating people in a positive way?

102 **A:** Maybe.

103 **Q:** *(J)* Can we say that they are stimulating people in a negative way?

104 **A:** Maybe.

105 **Q:** *(L)* So, there's probably a little of both. And you say that we are immune to it because we already have knowledge. Now, when you say we have knowledge, do you mean just knowledge in particular about aliens and alien realities and alien potentials and so forth?

106 **A:** Yes.

107 **Q:** *(L)* Is there something more on this subject of these Aryan psychic projectors that we need to know or investigate?

108 **A:** Arkadiusz being tracked now.

109 **Q:** *(L)* By whom?

110 **A:** Grays.

111 **Q:** *(L)* And what do they plan on doing?

112 **A:** Open.

113 **Q:** *(L)* Is there anything ... Why did you tell me that? *(T)* To tell him?

114 **A:** Because it is time you talked with him more about aliens. He is not well enough informed!!

115 **Q:** *(L)* Well, I sent him the book *Grand Illusions*, I sent him the Bramley book, and I sent him a Jacques Vallee book. He's presently in the process of reading through these three books. What else do I need to say to him? He's read the transcripts; he read them in a week the whole way through.

116 **A:** And how much did he comment specifically about aliens.

117 **Q:** *(L)* Not a whole lot. Obviously there's something else you wish for me to convey to him. Since I am going to be talking to him on the phone tomorrow ...

118 **A:** The seriousness of the situation ... the reality of it ... this is not fun and games.

119 **Q:** *(L)* What specific thing can I tell him that he could do or ... How can he protect himself? Is there any specific knowledge ... But he knows these things!

120 **A:** He has been told, but the awareness is not as sharp as it should be. Ask him where his skepticism lies. All these over the road journeys now have added risk!

121 **Q:** *(L)* Well, isn't that true for all of us sitting here?

122 **A:** More so for him!

123 **Q:** *(L)* Why more so for him?

124 **A:** Because of his position and his knowledge of advanced physics!

125 **Q:** *(L)* Will awareness and knowledge ...

126 **A:** The reality must "hit home."

127 **Q:** *(L)* Anything further?

128 **A:** Much more, but you must ask.

129 **Q:** *(L)* Has he been abducted before?

130 **A:** No.

131 **Q:** *(L)* He's never been abducted?

132 **A:** No.

133 **Q:** *(L)* Is there some plan to abduct him at the present time?

134 **A:** It does not work that way.

135 **Q:** *(L)* How does it work?

136 **A:** Too complex.

137 **Q:** *(L)* Is there some attempt at the present time to modify his thinking?

138 **A:** Attempt is not right idea.

139 **Q:** *(L)* What is the right idea? Now, wait a minute, stop everything!

End of Session. *Jan's note: The session was abruptly stopped by Laura, who was upset by the line being taken. This was partly because she did not recognize the Cs' reference to the George Bush quote, "It's the economy, stupid." She thought that the C's were attacking Terry and then being negative about Ark.*[5]

---

[5] Yes, I just had a very strong reaction to this session; I did not like it one bit.

To give some idea of the external realities, a few days after this session, I wrote to Ark:

> I went over to pick the girls up from mother's and had a look around to get it in my mind just how much furniture and other things I am going to have to move. And I frankly have not the slightest clue how I am going to do it... because, whether or not my brother has arrangements made by the end of the month, I am going to have move her somewhere, even if it is temporarily here... the only things I think I will have trouble with are the bed and the sofa... can't see them fitting in the van.
>
> Then, I was talking to [my daughter] on the phone (she is over at the Z's still) and was telling her about the session and she made the remark that some people like attention but are not willing to do the work that would deserve it and attach to others who have and take credit for themselves. I think this may be a little bit true. But I am still curious as to why the rudeness was directed at Terry... probably it is as you said, conflicts between the two of them [Frank and Terry].
>
> So, while I was talking to [my daughter], Patrick Z was in the background making all sorts of weird noises - growling like a lion, horse noises... just being silly. So, I told Aletheia to ask him when he was going to go to college and make something of himself... apparently this pushed a major button.... he cursed me violently, ran out of the house, took his mother's sports car and tore down the street squealing tires etc. [My daughter] didn't know what to think. She is not used to such crazy behavior...
>
> I admit that there are people with temperamental dispositions... but I don't think this is any excuse for rudeness and irresponsible behavior. I just don't think there is a lot of hope for the kid. Yes, he got himself off of the medication, but now he has to get a grip on himself somehow. I just think his mother has played too many head games with him and with his father...
>
> Anyway, he just called and apologized. He said he just couldn't understand how someone as "kind and gentle" as I am could say something so off the wall. I explained that he should have thought about that when interpreting it... that it had to be a little joke!!!

Then later, Ark commented that it was good that Patrick began to show his true nature. I wrote back:

> I received an e-mail from Johan [a fan] and he was complaining about the fact that the C's identify learning and knowledge as the key to "salvation." He says this is just not possible for the average person who has no desire to learn or even capacity. He says that he wants "divine intervention" to save mankind, otherwise, mankind will not be saved. I think he misses the point. Why does mankind have to be "saved" at

once and immediately? Eternity is a long "time," and there seems to be no reason for it all to end just because a few humans think they have had enough. If they really have had enough, they will discover and do what is necessary to save themselves. Anyway, I will have to figure out a way to explain things to him somewhat. If I can.

Yes, I am glad Patrick blew up so that Aletheia could see. She does not need to be with someone who is so unstable.

Ark wrote back about the above-mentioned Johan:

> I think that all religions agree on the fact that there is a wide gate and a narrow gate. Different ways. Which depend on the kind of work that is being done. Notice: and from those who have little even this little will be taken away to give those that have much (I do not remember the exact words but you know them). Automatic justice is a myth, an illusion. This is the case, it seems to me, with all the deep teachings that existed through the history. One can complain about it. Or one can take it seriously and draw a lesson for himself.

And then I responded to some of the specifics of Johan's complaints about the Cs:

> > Overall, I sense it is all stick and no carrot. I just don't seem to be getting what I need to know with these guys. I appreciate the info. is not aimed at satisfiying my needs, but most of the feedback I have had so far on the original texts, is in the same vein (i.e. depressive).

> Johan, Johan, Johan!!!! If truth were pleasant, do you not think it would have been available and apparent through the centuries? Why do you think that it is all a SECRET? Because, it truly is. The satisfying and gratifying "teachings" and "carrots" have always been with us and yet have changed nothing - ever!!!!

> > There are three areas which seem to dominate. (i) Biblical or Ancient history, (ii) Intensely technical discussion on UFO technology and dimensional aspects, and (iii) our backsides are in a sling and the where's and why -fores are beyong our comprehension.

> Well, simple observation will tell you this. And remember, the questions are mostly mine, or at the very least, the subject matter is what is directed by me... so this is a reflection of my own inadequacies or strengths...

> > My problem is the continual harping on learn, learn, learn... I will make the effort, but then the subject matter must interest me. The history, technology and tails of great misery I have waded through are VERY interesting, but in an off hand way. I dont think I could bring myself to take up an intense study of these topics. My real interest would be nearer the Humanities topics.

I'm gonna go Biblical on ya here, so hang onto your hat! "For that which is known about God is evident to them and made plain in their inner consciousness, because God has shown it to them. For ever since the creation of the world His invisible nature and attributes, that is, His eternal power and divinity have been made intelligible and clearly discernible IN AND THROUGH THE THINGS HE HAS MADE. So men are without excuse -altogether without and defense or justification; because when they knew and recognized Him as God, they did not honor and glorify Him... but instead they became futile and godless in their thinking - with vain imaginings, foolish reasoning and stupid speculations - and their senseless minds were darkened.... and by them the glory and majesty and excellence of the immortal God were exchanged for and represented by images resembling mortal man and birds and beasts and reptiles... BECAUSE THEY EXCHANGED THE TRUTH OF GOD FOR A LIE.... SINCE THEY DID NOT SEE FIT TO ACKNOWLEDGE GOD OR CONSIDER HIM WORTH THE KNOWING." (Romans 1, excerpts)

"The coming of the Antichrist is through the activity and working of Satan, and will be attended by great power and with all sorts of miracles and signs and delusive marvels - lying wonders - and by unlimited seduction to evil and with all wicked deception for those who are going to perdition, PERISHING BECAUSE THEY DID NOT WELCOME THE TRUTH BUT REFUSED TO LOVE IT THAT THEY MIGHT BE SAVED. Therefore GOD SENDS upon them a misleading influence, a working of error and strong delusion to MAKE THEM BELIEVE WHAT IS FALSE in order that ALL MAY BE JUDGED WHO DO NOT LOVE THE TRUTH." (II Thessalonians, 2, excerpts)

Knowledge is the most all-encompassing of the divine attributes. God is the knower of all things, and it is our duty to become as similar to God as is possible. And, to do this, we must know as much as possible. The more we know, the more we manifest God in our lives. And it is the object of seeking to know God. Knowing God means knowing "things." There is nothing in existence that is not God. True and useful knowledge is knowledge of God, or knowledge of the cosmos because all that exists displays God and points to him. Knowledge takes a person back to God, for all knowledge is ultimately from God and leads back to him.

Entering the Garden of the next realm, or density, is the act of becoming a locus of manifestation of Godly attributes. This brings us nearer to God. This proximity is achieved on the foundation of knowledge. All happiness lies in knowledge of God, and, since all that exists IS God, can any of us say that ANY knowledge is not "worth the knowing?"

And, the question becomes: what is knowledge and what is assumption??? So many people follow only assumption and "desire to be saved from the work of gaining knowledge."

And knowledge that is useful is knowledge that can be practiced in some sense. And here there is knowledge of outward practice and inward practice. Outward practice is anything that is manifested as "work." Learning to be a mechanic is knowledge of "God the mechanic." Learning to sew is knowledge of "God the seamstress." So all sciences and history and technology is knowledge of God. And obviously, some people have more capacity and ability than others. Does this mean that those with greater capacity are more favored. Yes and no. Yes, because of him whom much is given, much is required. But no, because he who does the most with what he has is like the servant in the parable of the talents. The important thing is to do the most with what you have.

Inward practice is faith. Faith is an actual frequency that transforms the person. The never-ending trajectory of man's life in this world and the next can only be explained in terms of his constant growth in knowledge.

For the wretched, knowledge of things as they actually ARE is a searing torture, since it contradicts their beliefs and practices in this world. To people of assumption, every new knowledge, every new disclosure is a new misery. And this is because they have set their minds against God and there is conflict between the mind of the flesh which desires ease, and the will of God, which is the light of the soul.

Observing anyone, we can see that a person does not know what is within himself until it is unveiled by action and experience. Man only knows one thing after another, endlessly. This principle shows us the way to God. The most knowledgeable of knowers is he who knows that he knows what he knows and also knows that he does not know what he does not know.

That we cannot know the levels of deception and obfuscation of our realm fully is only because we are in a school. It is not necessary to know the lessons of the grade above us in order to complete the grade we are in. We only need to know that we know so little even when we know all we can obtain in the way of knowledge by diligent effort. In this way, we can look forward with joy and happiness to a graduation to the next level where we will be given opportunity to LEARN more, thereby bringing us even closer to God. "Now we see as through a glass darkly..."

And the fact that this is an eternal process, a constant cycle, an endless expansion, where all have the opportunity in their own way and time, to ultimately DO and LEARN ALL, should give peace. But, for some reason, it does not. It seems that man not only wants to not have to DO anything, he also wants God to put a period to the existence of all those who annoy him.

> Bottom line to all this: If there is going to be no Divine Intervention in all this, then too few of us will make the next density when the big crunch comes to make any difference. In which case, what the hell is all the noise about?? The millineum

> [sic] will close like a damp squib? As for the lizzies zooming in for lunch, so what? There's going to be a bit of a fight, which we will loose [sic], and then the world goes round and round some more. What's the point??

I hope I have answered some of this. It is probably true that only a few will make it to the next density. But so what? The world is NOT ENDING, there is not going to be a BIG CRUNCH, it is just a point on the cycle where some graduate and some go on with the present lessons. It is all just lessons. Learning to ride the bicycle by doing it.

And, there is one problem here. I have only sent you a portion. There is more that IS concerned with exactly these questions. When the time comes, the playing field will be level. This is the purpose of "passing through the realm curtain." Mankind is NOT helpless, he is only ignorant. Think of Dorothy in "The Wizard of Oz."

The dark forces are working very hard to make man lazy and ignorant. There is a great work to be done. People must wake up to the true condition, stop wishing for a "great rapture to the sky" where they don't have to do anything but whine for help to get out of the mess they are in. Once people wake up, then they can learn what their true powers are - how to use the Ruby slippers....

> Some of the questions I have for these C's is, what about the rest of humanity? Billions don't have access to this sort of "learning" that they are palming of on us - so what hope do THEY have??

What do you think will happen to such people? Do you think that they are going to "go to hell" for eternity? Sorry! No such place. Those who are not ready, simply have more time to do it and get ready for the next cycle.

> Despite our best efforts, this wisdom will NOT reach everybody in time and most of humanity is going to miss the bus... is that part of the grand scheme of things that we are continually over-run by these cosmic events cycle after cycle??

Pretty much. And I ask you: What else does God/Universe have to do for eternity???

> The select few that might have some hope of crashing into the next density, is hardly going to make a difference. They have said (somewhere in the texts) that the lizzie plans wont succeed in their take over (of us in 4thD I presume), but again, most will still be 3rdD squarely under their control - What is going to change??

Those who move closer to God go to the next grade and begin those lessons. But what was is and always will be just IS: world without end.

> ENOUGH! I'm making myself suicidal here...

Well, as I have said, that is a good sign. Go and get the Castaneda piece from the web page and also the entire Noah MS. Should help somewhat.

> By the way: I loved the "past life" info these C's have given you!! What a treat that must be to have access to that sort of back ground detail on yourself... and to know why things are the way they are in your very specific circumstance! I could definitely wear these guys out just asking questions in that area!

We do.

September 27 1996

In the week prior to this session there were a number of family upsets in our house including my eldest daughter breaking off her relationship with Patrick Z.[1] My next oldest daughter was worrying that my relationship with Ark would take precedence over the children. She was also worried about me dying. My brother and I had been looking for an apartment for my mother near to where he lived but there wasn't anything available. Mother, of course, was not happy with the idea, but it was clear she had to give up the rented house after Sue V had moved her mother back into a nursing home (thankfully). The decision was finally made that she would move in with me and the kids and we would keep looking for a place for her closer to me. There just weren't any other options. And so, I was busy getting the house organized for this move followed by the actual moving.

Our plans for Ark coming to the U.S. were proceeding and we were looking at late January as being most likely, though it turned out to be mid-February in the end. Ark was working hard on his research (he was back in Florence) and I was busy with the kids, the house, and swimming incredible distances in a round pool. We kept each other updated on all doings right down to the most mundane, such as what we had for lunch.

For background, on the 26th I wrote to Ark:

> I have been bothered for a few days by a nagging feeling to call a certain person whom I have not spoken to in several months: Chuck D. Chuck is a really interesting person. He was a policeman in Chicago among many occupations, and I met him because he worked with Mike H, a local Private Investigator. When I was "looking at" the murder of the little girl back in 1993, I ended up calling Mike for advice. It turned out that both of these pretty hard-nosed men were very impressed with what I had done

---

[1] Patrick's mother, Pat, has appeared in several sessions after I reconnected with her after her hypnosis session during which UFOs appeared all over the county, including over my house. See the *St. Pete Times* article by Tom French, "The Exorcist in Love" for details.

and it was the beginning of a professional and friendly relationship. I can call on either of them if I need to and they trust me completely. Chuck became closer to me than Mike because Chuck is a deep thinker and very open minded while Mike is a little more "practical."

Anyway, Chuck has even acted as a bodyguard for me on a particular memorable occasion when I was giving a lecture and received threats from the "Pleiadian/Billy Meier" aficionados. Tom French attended this particular event and was scrutinized carefully by Chuck, who had never met him, and Tom came over and asked me "Who IS that guy giving me the evil eye?" When he found out, we all had a good laugh.

So, I have been bugged by thoughts of Chuck. I knew his father had been ill, and I wondered how that was doing. So I called. It turns out that his father had died on the day I started thinking about him, which was last Friday. So we talked quite a bit and I was able to share some insights about death that made him feel better. When he gets the affairs of the father straightened out, we will get together.

Then, I received a call from Don Zanghi over in DeLand. He is a hypnotherapist who I have known for several years. He was the one who attempted to do hypnosis with me, but I'm just not hypnotizable. We have stayed in touch because we are pretty much in synch with our techniques and ideas.[2]

Several months ago he was trying to get to the bottom of the "Alien Autopsy" video and someone on the internet directed him to call me as being a person "in the know," and he was a little surprised to get this information from someone in California about me, in Florida, who he already knew! Small world.

Anyway, the aside from the "channeled" information we have about this video, there are some very bizarre experiences Frank and I had regarding it and I am positive I know the person who "leaked" it and how it was done and several other things about it. Some is evidential, some is intuition, some is synchronous happenings that point in a certain direction. Very interesting subject.

So, I talked to Don for awhile and he wants to come over for a session and I may call Leonard Sturm, the local MUFON guy in Holiday, and arrange for Don to give a little talk about what he has found out about the video. Then, he will reciprocate and I will go over to his area and give a little talk about aliens in general...

But all was not smooth. Ark and I were both aware that it might not be possible to organize our lives to be together and this ugly fact came

---

[2]Don has since gone totally New Agey. See: http://www.cassadaga.org/mapinfo/MediumPages/ZanghiD_Info.htm

up for discussion on the 26th. Ark did not see how he could divorce his wife or how he could solve the logistical problems which seemed overwhelming. There was a long, emotion-charged exchange about the realities of both our lives.

The relationship almost ended right then and I was in a horrible state. So was Ark. We both learned pretty quickly that the very thought of *not* being together was beyond bearing. Neither of us could sleep, work, function at all. A friend called shortly after and wanted to know why I looked so horrible from so much crying and I gave a very brief account. She suggested I should just call and talk instead of trying to work out an issue via email. So, I did and we made it through the crisis. Then, I wrote about the phone conversation to Ark:

> I was talking to Alex just before I called you. I was crying. I explained why. She told me I was hurting you terribly and she could feel so much pain coming either from me or you or both that she almost could not breathe. Then she said something very strange: "What happened to you in the month of September in the past that you are reliving right now???" And I couldn't think of anything. So we talked about other things a minute... and then it hit me: 22 years ago, September, I died and was brought back to life. I am not sure of the day, exactly...
>
> Last night, I swam through the entire eclipse - listening to Pink Floyd's "Dark Side of The Moon". The breeze picked up as the last edge of the moon disappeared and it was all a sort of gold shadowy effect. And I will tell you that I repeated my mantra at least several thousands of times throughout the whole event.

And then a bit later there was this:

> More bizarre stuff: I received legal papers from [my soon-to-be-ex] and he has apparently either refused to sign the ones I sent him, or is not going to sign until I sign this ridiculous document giving him full access to the children whenever he chooses and under whatever conditions he sets. On a cold day in hell!
>
> But, the interesting thing is, I called to rake him over the coals, and his mother told me he fell off the roof yesterday and broke his arm, shoulder, clavicle, and had a severe concussion!!!!
>
> That is totally bizarre.
>
> Next, this evening, one of [my eldest daughter's] co-workers who had called me a few weeks ago about some psychic energy losses, called again in a more desperate condition. I figured he could come and I would talk to him and try to get to the root of his problem. I was never really clear about his name because he spoke so softly on the phone.

He arrived, and I asked his name: Noah.[3] Okay, no cigar. But then, after listening to his whole situation, I could immediately see that what was needed was a major exorcism... and based on what he was describing, I think his head would spin at least three times and he would hurl pea soup!!!!

The last one I did, in July of 95, affected me so adversely that it was several months before I was back to some semblance of normal.

There is NO WAY I am going to do an exorcism on this kid. NONE. NADA. ZILCH!!!!

So, I made arrangements for him to call me on Monday, I will call Don Z and see if he wants to do it. So, I have to arrange for him to lecture at the Holiday MUFON, attend a session here, and talk to this kid.

As Noah was leaving, I asked him how old he was: 22.

Okay, okay. No cigar.

But, don't you think it is a little strange for someone named Noah, who is 22 and possessed, to call me and come to my house on a day where I am dealing with issues that are 22 years old that happened when I was 22????? I mean, NOAH! For God's sake!!!

I wish I could help the boy, but I am having a little trouble with being blown open myself lately and I need ALL THE PROTECTION I CAN GET!!! And I definitely don't need to go and play in the dirt with so many open wounds that are being cleaned and dressed.

Anyway. I thought you would find this a little bit interesting and you may have something come to mind as you read it that will help.

And [my ex] breaking his arm after refusing to sign my papers and writing me that nasty note...?

But yesterday was a funny day anyway... with the eclipse... and it would be even more strange if I could find out WHEN, exactly, I went to the hospital 22 years ago. I am pretty sure it was toward the end of the month, because I was in school...

Well, strange world. Very strange.

And then, we had this session. The reader will notice that, again, I'm not very revealing in my questions and I think Frank was pretty clearly antagonistic, though some small useful things were said.

---

[3] I thought it was odd that the kid's name was Noah, considering that Noah built the 'Ark' and I had written a book called *The Noah Syndrome*.

Participants: 'Frank', Laura

Q: *(L)* Hello.

A: Hello.

Q: *(L)* Have you been listening to our conversation about when Ark may arrive?

A: You have not asked for ID.

Q: *(L)* Okay, sorry. Who do we have with us this evening?

A: Lanirre.

Q: *(L)* And where are you from?

A: Cassiopaea.

Q: *(L)* Do you have any comment on when and if Ark will arrive?

A: No.

Q: *(L)* He is concerned about being able to find a permanent job here. Is this going to be a problem?

A: Not if you use your talents, as we told you to!

Q: *(L)* Is there something I am missing that I ought to be doing?

A: You "ought" to be exerting more energy toward trawling and communicating and less toward other things.

Q: *(L)* Trawling and communicating with whom?

A: Uncovering, researching, job prospects/openings.

Q: *(L)* Via the internet I should go and ...

A: And written material and "media scanning," and library, etc... We have told you that this communication has reached its maximum extent.

Q: *(L)* So, you are telling us that we have to do some stuff on our own?

A: You, Laura, you!!!

Q: *(L)* Can you give me a couple of hints as to what I am looking for?

A: You are not thinking.

Q: *(L)* Alright. I will think about it. I am not happy with the fact that I look 44 years old!

A: Vague as can be! How about a new do?

Q: *(L)* You mean my hair?

A: One.

Q: *(L)* I want to ask about this terrible ordeal we were going through the past day or two. It seemed that there were clues pointing to it being connected to what happened to me when I was 22 as well as to another lifetime. Is it related?

A: In a complex cyclical way.

Q: *(L)* What was the story about this kid named Noah who showed up here, and was 22 years old and suicidal ...

A: Coincidence.

Q: *(L)* What was accomplished, if anything, by going through this?

A: Learning.

Q: *(L)* Was it also a process of releasing stored negative energy?

A: No.

Q: *(L)* Nothing else except learning?

A: No.

Q: *(L)* I am wondering if it is possible that his traveling and our communications from and to various places reflects connections to karmic events?

A: Do not get carried away.

Q: *(L)* I am just wondering because of all the strange things that are happening.

A: Everything is a synchronous event.

41 **Q:** *(L)* Did Ark and I have a past life together in Florence?

42 **A:** Density.

43 **Q:** *(L)* What do you mean?

44 **A:** Density.

45 **Q:** *(L)* Density what? The question was: did we have a past life as I saw it in Florence?

46 **A:** Density. Lead you by the hand we do not do.

47 **Q:** *(L)* Is there a connection at another density?

48 **A:** Look.

49 **Q:** *(L)* Look what?

50 **A:** Look, discover.

51 **Q:** *(L)* When you say this communication has reached its maximum extent, do you mean it was designed and put together just to bring information, then bring Ark into the picture to benefit by it and do a particular work?

52 **A:** The communication we mean is the one between you and him.

53 **Q:** *(L)* Does that mean we should stop it now? Just break it off?

54 **A:** You need to spend more time with "Enterprise Florida." Information is readily available at your fingertips. Look 'em up! I.e. Less lovey dovey with Arky warky and more with jobby wobby, get it?!?

55 **Q:** *(L)* Very cute, guys! Another thing I have thought about is selling the house to buy another ...

56 **A:** Wrong move!

57 **Q:** *(L)* Okay. I dropped it just now! Won't even think about it!

58 **A:** Think all you want, just don't do! You arrived at this locator for a reason!!!!

59 **Q:** *(L)* I am curious about something ... Is Ark in a relationship that seems so similar to the one I was in, and is his dragging on all these years for the same reasons mine did?

60 **A:** Money.

61 **Q:** *(L)* What do you mean?

62 **A:** Everything divides.

63 **Q:** *(L)* I don't understand.

64 **A:** He has tried to get free, so far no luck.

65 **Q:** *(L)* Well, will he have luck on this? Without causing a lot of suffering?

66 **A:** If creativity prevails, he will succeed.

67 **Q:** *(L)* I am sure that she knows something. Is she aware of how unhappy he is?

68 **A:** Has been for many years.

69 **Q:** *(L)* How can she reconcile making him suffer?

70 **A:** She craves the association with "authority." One could call it the Jaqueline Kennedy Onassis syndrome.

71 **Q:** *(L)* You mean she is just there for what she can wring out of him? That's terrible!

72 **A:** Do you think a factory worker would do when she has a physicist?

73 **Q:** *(L)* Well, that means she has just been using him all these years?

74 **A:** You said it, we didn't.

75 **Q:** *(L)* Oh! That's terrible! Last week you said that something needs to 'hit home' with Ark. Was it what has already happened between us?

76 **A:** Other. He needs to understand the reality of trans-density, interdimensional, interstellar and planetary attack and contact for both STS and STO! One half of him does not yet believe!

77 **Q:** *(L)* Is something going to happen?

78 **A:** Yes.

79 **Q:** *(L)* Is it going to be upsetting to him?

80 **A:** Yes and no.

81 **Q:** *(L)* So, he will be able to handle it.

82 **A:** Yes.

83 **Q:** *(L)* Will it happen in Wroclaw, or at his residence?

84 **A:** Wait and see.

85 **Q:** *(L)* Is he married to someone who is there to keep him unaware, to monitor, or to drain his energy?

86 **A:** Yes. All.

87 **Q:** *(L)* Is she controlled by aliens?

88 **A:** Partly, but that is nothing unusual.

89 **Q:** *(L)* Well, that is not good, especially if one does not believe. I certainly did not like the experiences that convinced me.

90 **A:** Worry not. Listen and be open. Goodnight.

91 **Q:** *(L)* Goodnight.

End of Session

For the Patrick Z saga fans, I wrote to Ark the day after this session:

> [My daughter] has announced that she has told Patrick that trying is not good enough - doing is essential and that she does not usually give second chances, but that he has a second chance and must straighten up or it is curtains for him. You were right. The incident on Sunday had a lot of impact on her. So that is good.

October 1, 1996

In the days preceding this session, a number of things occurred of a very upsetting nature. Ark had sent me a link to a website he wanted me to read and give him my opinion. I wrote to him about it:

> If you had told me that the document on the Secret Government was the "Cooper Papers" I would have known immediately what it was since I already have this information to a rather extensive degree.
>
> In my MS, Noah, there are several chapters on this very subject. BUT, they were written as a result of my OWN research, and discoveries, PRIOR to any knowledge whatsoever of aliens and related matters. So, it was rather pure and uncorrupted in a certain sense, by any previous associations. I was merely seeking answers to some very strange things and came to the conclusions outlined completely isolated from outside influence. It is rather revealing.
>
> Now, as to Cooper, and related researchers - I have read most, if not all, of those things he refers to, and then some. The "Brotherhood of The Snake" is described in considerable detail in the book I sent you: "The Gods of Eden." In fact, much of what Cooper writes in this document is taken directly from the Bramley book.
>
> The main thing that is being missed by Cooper et al is the 4th density nature of the controlling aliens. If they could just come in and take over, they would have done so long ago. Obviously, there is some reason they cannot. This point is missed by many.
>
> Also, it occurred to me early on that the very nature of the subject is altogether confusing BY DESIGN. Confusion is a byproduct of lies, and we are dealing with, literally, people of the lie under control of "The Father of Lies," or STS, illusion, the downward moving part of the cycle of lessons, a principle of the Prodigal Son going to the "Far Country" and Dorothy in Oz. All the same idea.
>
> And, Free Will is important here. As I have said before, it seems that Free Will is some sort of LAW of other densities just as gravity is a law here... and may, in fact, be ontologically related.
>
> Cooper has done excellent work in putting a lot of this together, but he still is missing a major thing: even what he has uncovered, to some extent, perhaps a great extent, is part of the confusion factor, the disinformation plan.

I think that the government really knows as little about aliens as most UFO researchers who think that the govt. knows a lot. This is why the govt. is doing so many things to find out from people who do have experiences, what is going on. They MAY be developing, or trying to develop, some sort of defense technology, but this is a red herring. There is no defense of a material sort against beings from another density.

This is why your idea about the "Lizzie in the head," is so important - it is true. The battle is IN us, not just you and me, but IN all people – or, more correctly, some have chosen the STS path simply because that is where they are on the cycle, and others have chosen, at the soul level, STO. Gravity. Utilization. Unstable gravity waves. All related.

The "Stan" letter I sent you was from Stanton Friedman, the physicist who Cooper describes as a witting govt. agent. I don't think this is true. Stan may be USED, just as anyone, ANYONE, is subject to being used by 4th density technology and beings, but he has good intentions. Stan has suffered a lot of abuse by several "experts" in the UFO research field, or swamp is a better term, and he has reacted naturally, with some pretty stinging retorts. Perhaps you could write to him and open a little dialogue, just to see what would come out of it. I think it would be possibly a fruitful correspondence.

My little "source", the little old man I went to see in Orlando, the day after you first wrote to me, the old man who was a friend of the man who built the coral castle, the same old man who, I believe, had something very strange to do with the release of the alien autopsy video, the same man who may know something about gravity waves, even if he is not aware that he knows it, told me a very strange thing one day. We were discussing the fact that so many people are looking for what Frank and I call the "UFO Cadillac." You know, a solid object like a car, that you can kick the tires and hit it with a tool and it will be solid. I remarked that, if it were, in fact, extra-density technology, such rules of material manifestation may not apply… and therefore, MUFON and the government were trying futilely to find SOLID EVIDENCE. The old guy, Hilliard, replied: "Yup! They have had artifacts; but they just DISAPPEAR."

Well, my comprehension, at the moment, was that he meant that they "disappeared" into some black hole secret government project… concealed, hidden. But then he said. "Yup! They put 24 hour cameras on the stuff! Just DISAPPEARED!"

Then I realized what he was saying: It literally DISAPPEARS. Goes back to the density from which it originates… probably BY DESIGN. A different atomic state that has been artificially manipulated to enter our density… but without some continuous power, this state is lost, and it seems to us to DISAPPEAR.

So I understood immediately: there will be NO alien invasion until the planet and space sector passes into the 4th density state... BECAUSE THE ALIENS CAN ONLY SUSTAIN THEMSELVES IN OUR DENSITY WITH GREAT EFFORT. In the same way a naked, unarmed man would have great difficulty surviving in a jungle surrounded by wild beasts. Armed with his technology, he is a God among the beasts, but without it, he is helpless.

And then, of course, this started me thinking about Ouspensky's description of how animals perceive compared to how a man perceives... and I then projected this beyond myself and began to understand better our true condition in relation to these beings. So, when you said to me: "The Lizzie in your head," it had great meaning, perhaps beyond what you expected.

And some people are WILLING HOSTS to these Lizzies because the STS path, direction, position on the cycle, etc, etc, is their natural soul configuration. They have CHOSEN of their own FREE WILL, to ENTER THE ILLUSION, to go to the far country of the prodigal son. It is NATURE. It is WHAT IS. It is the balance... the black half of the yin-yang circle... the condition of the human race, the fallen Lucifer, for the past 300,000 years.

And, at the present, there are many who have learned the lessons of the Far Country, the Blind Orion seeking the cure for his blindness... and these are the ones who are "chosen, saved, the elect." These are the ones who seek knowledge, because knowledge is God. These are the ones who "have much and to whom will more be added." The ones who have chosen the STS path, OF THEIR OWN FREE WILL, will continue in this density, and will lose the little they have. Because free will is concomitant with true knowledge. The STS aliens who are "above us" are NOT beings who have "RISEN" by DARK KNOWLEDGE.... they are beings who are on their way down into the illusion as well!!! They are in ILLUSION too!!! Their illusion is that they can use their higher density position to control all the earth, and they are working hard in this direction... but the illusion blinds them, and will cause them to stumble and fall into the pit they have dug.

Yes, they have had their day, their aeon, and the human race was a willing participant... this is the true meaning of the Fall in Eden, the Blinding of Orion, the trip to Oz by Dorothy via the tornado.

So, bottom line: yes, a lot of what Cooper says is probably true. I think he is sincere. But he does not yet fully understand the nature of the BEAST.

This was followed by another email describing what was going on in general:

The moving [of my mother] has nearly finished. I tried to keep control of it and make sure things were being put in specific places as they were brought in, but after a while, there were no more places and I don't know what to do with everything!

My house looks like a furniture store!!!

And I am tired. Unimaginably tired.

I hit my head on a shelf and now have a bleeding gash on my forehead into the hair. Nearly knocked myself out!!! And I didn't even know I had broken the skin until the blood started running in my eye.

I talked to Leonard Sturm today about Don Z coming over for a talk about the alien autopsy. Also to Eugene Brown of MUFON down in Clearwater. Later I talked to Carla Santilli. She and Ruggero are now back from their trip and getting back into "the swing of things," as she put it. Will talk to R. tomorrow. She said he wanted to talk to me.

Answered the e-mail from Stan Friedman. Tried to give him a little encouragement. He does get a lot of attack. I think he is too much into 3rd level thinking, but his intentions are good and he is honest, I think.

I thought I would lie down to rest a bit. Started thinking about what the C's said about the programming done to my mind to make me destroy myself... remembered they had said the same about Karla Turner. She died of a particularly virulent and sudden cancer last January. I eulogized her in the last issue of the Aurora Journal. Her husband, Elton, sent me a beautiful photo of her and a poem she wrote just before she died.

Anyway, the C's had warned her... but she didn't listen and now she is dead.

So, I thought about that... and, for some reason, the desperation seemed to ease a little.

Then I heard the ONE THING that will pull any mother out of any state instantly - "Mommy, I'm hungry." And a soft little hand on my cheek and I opened my eyes to a pair of big blue ones in a freckled little face...

I got up and found about 7 or 8 kids in the pool... mother was resting. Peeled five pounds of carrots and put them in the steamer along with a spaghetti squash. Cut up a cabbage and put it in some beef broth, and put on a big pot of water for pasta... (sauce already made, and only needs to be heated.)

I can see I am going to feed a crowd tonight...

I put the radio outside for the kids, and they are having a grand time.

Ark then wrote to me that he had informed his wife that he wanted a divorce. I wrote and asked him why he did it now, of all times, since we had agreed to take things step-by-step. Obviously, meeting first would have been a proper first step. Apparently, his wife "knew" something was different and provoked a conflict during which he decided that he just wasn't going to lie, though he wasn't going to say who the "other person" was. His wife was convinced that it was someone in Florence and he allowed that to stand. It was true in some sense, at some level. She told him he needed to see a psychiatrist. At that point, he said, "No, I don't need a psychiatrist, I need a divorce." (My ex said the same thing to me.)

Things were made even more difficult because it was the first day of the university semester where Ark was head of a department. There was a necessity of work and that took precedence.

As mentioned in the 27 September 1996 session, my ex had fallen off a roof and injured his shoulder along with sustaining a concussion. The last I had heard, he didn't need surgery on the shoulder and was going home. With all the extra furniture in the house because of the move of my mother, I decided to call him and see if he wanted or needed any of it and find out how he was doing at the same time. I wrote the following email to Ark about it:

> I called [my ex] this evening to offer to give him some furniture to ease the crowding in the house. No answer. Several tries. No answer. I was concerned, since I know his parents go to bed very early and would not have been out. Finally an answer. His father told me they had just put him back in the hospital because he had not been able to hold anything on his stomach for two days. With a fractured skull, that is not a good sign.
>
> I called the hospital. Nurse said CT scan was negative but they were going to keep him and, if necessary, airlift him to Tampa for surgery. She let me talk to him, and he was a little vague, and very pathetic, and I felt so bad that he is like this under the circumstances.
>
> [Second oldest daughter] thinks he is going to die. I don't know. I just know that I AM NOT, NO MATTER WHAT, going to take him back in this house because he has injured himself, unconsciously, or consciously. I can see that this is where it is heading... no one else to care for him but me? guess again! ...
>
> And yes, it makes me sad and I feel very bad for him. But it really seems odd that having been disconnected from his energy source, i.e. ME, he has steadily declined. And, on the day I was working through so many issues, he falls and receives a serious injury? Just too coincidental, if you ask me.

So, those Lizzies are hard at work. But I see through their maneuvers. They have worked on me through the children, my mother, [my ex], numerous other persons... some more dangerous and blatant than others.

Still, I know it must be terrible to be in such condition and be alone.[1]

I thought about all the efforts I made over the years to get him to open and respond. And I thought about him dying. I felt pity. A lot.

And then I thought about how much it hurt to work and work, beg and plead for a single, simple, honest response from inside him... And nothing, ever...

And I wondered if the present conditions have made any change. I don't think so. His manipulations and control games are so deeply a part of him, his very nature, that I KNOW that this is just more of the same. Only, in response to the seriousness of my actions and intent, the gravity of his manipulation has reached a new level. It is amazing what the mind can do.

That is the only thing of significance from this afternoon. I cooked dinner, the children ate, I talked to Frank on the phone for a while; we'll have a session later. ... These past few days have been very stressful for both of us and it almost seems that we have unleashed some energy that is just doing its work almost without our direction or control. Quantum jumping at its finest, I guess. I expect you will have a rough time coming up, but the hardest part is over, I think.[2]

Ark wrote back:

Yes, you have a hard time now with [your ex]. Ask always your conscience, your body feelings what to do. The same I am doing. It is true what you have said that a it was a great relief for us. And, what is strange, my external situation is not in any way worse than it was before. This comes from the fact that my bonds were becoming weaker and weaker through the years. To give an example: I was not wearing the wedding ring already more than a year. I was doing much of the washing of my clothes myself - because I had the feeling that I do not want to "depend" in any way. So, you see, something was growing although could not be spelled what it was.

I slept quite well last night and today looks quite "normal". Of course I see that there will be repeated attempts to reveal the identity of the "unknown person" and to conspire to kill the relation. Here let me say that I think you should NOT reveal to [your ex] that there is another person. You have your list of reasons that we were talking about. Read it, recall it, ask your conscience, ask your body and do the best you can

---

[1] He wasn't exactly alone. He had his parents, brothers, sisters-in-law, etc.
[2] I was wrong!

but only to the extent that YOU are better with it rather than that you are worse. It is difficult (as all we do) but possible.

Whatever the circumstances: do so that you ARE more and that you DO more and that the KIDS have more of you. They will need you more and more when they see that there is more that they can get from you. They were seeing that there is very little of you that can be given to them (because you were in state of disintegration). So they did not ask. Now they will ask. And you must give to them all they ask. Their fate depends on it. And this is more important than anything. All the rest: ask your conscience, talk to the kids.

I responded:

When you write: "I see that there will be repeated attempts to reveal the identity of the 'unknown person' and to conspire to kill the relation" I am a little concerned that when such attempts fail and it becomes accepted that YOU are not using such a situation to manipulate and control, (which will be thought, as it is always natural to see everything from one's own perspective), that you DO MEAN what you say, then certain reactions will begin that will be retaliatory. This may cause you some problems in some areas. I hope not, but I am thinking of a situation of another person I knew some years ago where the relation was similar and the initial reaction of suicide and other pleadings was also similar. It seemed, in that case, that the issue was more "ownership" than anything else.

So, it may be that what you have done is precisely correct. This way there is easily available another person who can become the "blamed one" i.e. me. The wicked other woman: a siren, a temptress, who has taken away your power of discernment, and any blame for failures through the years in terms of response and nurturing on her part. She can now be free of guilt, as you will see very soon, if not already, because it is all MY fault. This is why there is the attempts to discover the identity... search and destroy the OTHER, and not look for the lack in self or the relationship.

And, of course, if it was known that it was someone who you had never even touched, then a whole team of psychiatrists would be called in!!!

But, we are in a little bit of strange territory, and are learning not to anticipate in a very graphic way. Learning this together.

And this makes me think that *anticipation, per se, is generally based on past tapes and experiences*. So, non-anticipation is casting off such limitations and admitting the possibility of miracles and events that just move in front of us and we have only to respond from inside, as in this case.

Of course, the event came into being as a result of all the little decisions and changes you were making... so, it is a good lesson in doing and being.

When you say that I should be MORE for the kids, I can say with certainty that there was certainly very little of the REAL ME, with him [my ex] in the picture.

The kids do NOT, categorically, want me to exert any effort in [my ex's] direction. Now, this is a very sad state of affairs when you think about it. I have tried hard to help them see him in a sympathetic light, but the bottom line *for them* is: if he loved them, he would not have hurt them so much, therefore since he made so much pain, he does not love them.

From my point of view, I have tried to think that he does love "in his own way." But their point is: what good is love that does not give sustenance and nurture to the object loved? Can it really be love? Is it not rather love in the sense of REALLY LIKING some physical thing because it gives status, pleasure, use, good opinion of others, and all sorts of reasons totally unrelated to the loved thing itself?

And this is part of what has hurt [second daughter] most. Her father made it clear to her that she was only lovable to him as long as she reflected well on him by her behavior, her acceptance of his control, and her appearance. If she was a "good girl" by his standards, dressed and acted to make him look good, and believed everything he told her, then he "loved" her. Any deviation brought manipulations to bring her back into the "mold." Terrible pressure to put on a sensitive and loving child. And I am horrified that I did not see that he was doing this to her. (And all of us as well, but it was more severe on her because she is so sensitive.)

And then, finally, toward the end of that day I wrote the following to Ark:

I have just suffered a terrible blow.

Jeanne R has just called to tell me that Tommy, Chloe's husband, died this morning.

A man so full of life and freedom from limitations, and joy, that everyone who knew him loved him.

I cannot believe he is dead.

And Chloe will suffer terribly. Several other friends are up there at the cabin and with her now until The Boys get there. Jeanie will fly up on the 10th and drive Chloe down here.

She is at the funeral home just now and I will call her after noon when she will be back.

I am numb.

A bit later, after I had talked to Chloe, I wrote:

I just talked to her. We cried together for a few minutes. She described everything for me. Then she remarked that it was certainly the way that anyone would like to go... a great party with friends the night before, a morning of busy-ness and doing what he liked to do, and then he went home, put on the headphones to watch television and take a short nap, and just LEFT. No trauma.

She said she had been keening (an Irish term) but now was coping. She had been down at the funeral home making the arrangements and being with him for a while.

Then she said: "The only thing he didn't do, that I think he would have liked, is go out in a blaze of glory. He always wanted to combust just to baffle people."

So we began to laugh hysterically. This is so true. Tommy would have done this if he could!

Anyway, she is hurting badly. I feel it. But she is coping. We talked about Sandra's death a little and how Frank and I talked to her after she died... so, for us, there is no doubt about where the person is and what they are doing. And that helps a lot.

And, we laughed about this being another of the DREADED OFG'S. (Opportunities For Growth)

So, there is a little peace now. I know she is okay and will call me if she needs me and I will call to make sure she is still holding up. Her friend who was at the cabin is with her, and her children and his children are all going up right away. And then she will be down here soon.

She did say that the newspaper announcement will say: "In lieu of flowers, please perform an act of kindness and generosity in Tom's memory."

And this is perfect. Exactly right.

Finally, on that same day, I received an email from Tom French as follows:

Dear Laura,

Was sitting at my desk this morning, fighting off the writing terror, preparing to stare down the blank screen, when I came across a New York Times review about a Nova show airing soon (possibly tonight) on Einstein's life. The review talks about how, at age 5, Einstein was deeply fascinated by a compass and how he later said of that fascination: "At that moment I realized that something deeply hidden had to lie behind things."

Which naturally made me think of you and your attempt to uncover the secret design of the universe, which then made me think of me and my attempt to uncover the secret epic of all our lives, which then reminded me of potato pancakes. You want to go eat some this coming Saturday?

Hope you're doing well — you're probably up to about 2,000 laps by now — hope the kids are good, hope Ark is having fun.

Still in pursuit of the grand unified narrative.

Tom

So, it was something of a chaotic period! Which brings us back to the session to hand. My second daughter wanted to sit in because she had much on her mind. She was not happy that my mother had moved in with us for a number of reasons, not the least of which was the manipulative games that went on in that dynamic. She was also suffering terribly because of what I described above about her father.

Participants: 'Frank', Laura, A___

1 Q: *(L)* Hello.

2 A: Hello.

3 Q: *(L)* Who do we have with us tonight?

4 A: Vurra.

5 Q: *(L)* A___ has wanted to sit in with us and is here tonight. Is that alright?

6 A: Yes.

7 Q: *(L)* And I suppose she has a few questions. *(A)* No.

8 A: Yes.

9 Q: *(A)* There isn't anything in particular that I want to ask.

10 A: Incorrect.

11 Q: *(L)* One thing that I know has been bothering her is that she is having trouble concentrating to the point that she cannot read. What is the problem?

12 A: Her mind is on other things.

13 Q: *(L)* And, what is that?

14 A: Ask her.

15 Q: *(L)* Well, as we go along, she will think of them. Now, something has happened: Ark has asked for divorce and apparently it was not a pleasant outcome, to say the least. From what he has said, I am thinking that she [his ex] is going to become very vindictive within the next few days. And, what concerns me is that she is going to try to discover who I am by going into his computer.

16 A: Already has tried.

17 Q: *(L)* And what was the result?

18 A: Nothing, she did not know how to get into proper file. There are passwords. She will try again until no longer able. Also snoops through printed material. But, not proficient in English.[3]

19 Q: *(L)* Thank God for small favors. I have the feeling that there is something about this situation ... that something very negative is going to happen. The reality of other-density controls will 'hit home' in a very unpleasant way.

20 A: Yes.

21 Q: *(L)* Is there anything I can do to warn him?

22 A: No.

23 Q: *(L)* And I have no idea what this feeling relates to. Looking at the [as-

---

[3] This turned out to be shockingly accurate.

trology] charts, it seems that whatever she does will be this month, probably in the next few days, because she is building steam. Anger and rage ... I don't think he really has any idea who she is, the same way I didn't know the person I was married to ... it was all my own illusion. Is this correct?

24 **A**: It is not "who she is," it is what works through her by her own choice.

25 **Q**: *(L)* So, she is a channel of attack?

26 **A**: Two more to appear at university in Wroclaw.[4]

27 **Q**: *(L)* Any clues that I can give him?

28 **A**: One is subordinate, one is authoritative.[5] Also, possibility of [his ex] trying to undermine his position at university with implications of infidelity and adultery ... both are seen as more serious breaches in Poland than here and elsewhere when it comes to one of high standing in a university level capacity.[6]

29 **Q**: *(L)* Well, I just have the feeling that she is really wanting to rip him to pieces. I can actually feel it emanating across the ocean.

30 **A**: We have detailed for you. May actually hasten things, rather than forestall as intended![7]

31 **Q**: *(L)* Is there any more you have to say on this subject?

32 **A**: Up to you. Warn, as all is not as anticipated in such detail.

33 **Q**: *(L)* I need to warn him?

34 **A**: UFOs monitoring.

35 **Q**: *(L)* Monitoring him?

36 **A**: And the situation. Also, at a human level, "the walls now have ears."

37 **Q**: *(L)* Okay, A___ is very worried about the present situation with [the current living situation]. What can we do in this situation?

38 **A**: Vague. Have A___ ask, please!!

39 **Q**: *(A)* I don't know what to ask.

40 **A**: A___ is holding back, we cannot answer.

41 **Q**: *(L)* You have to ask. *(A)* When [is grandmother and related dynamics] going to move out and will it help things?

42 **A**: Not definite. You cannot solve your problems by trying to avoid them.

43 **Q**: *(A)* I am not trying to avoid any problems. What do you mean?

44 **A**: Removing subjects does not resolve them.

45 **Q**: *(L)* What are the main subjects that need to be resolved in her mind?

46 **A**: Interplay and communication and understanding.

47 **Q**: *(L)* Anything else that can help?

48 **A**: Only if she asks.

49 **Q**: *(A)* Why do I get depressed?

50 **A**: Stress causes chemical changes.

51 **Q**: *(A)* What are my main sources of stress?

---

[4]This also turned out to be accurate.
[5]Yes indeed: a former colleague and a former Ph.D. student of Ark's.
[6]This also turned out to be accurate.
[7]This also turned out to be true. All of the actions of Ark's ex in respect of the divorce only revealed her true character more clearly and made Ark more determined than ever to get as far away from her as he could.

52 **A**: Inability to see other points of view.

53 **Q**: *(A)* Whose points of view?

54 **A**: All.

55 **Q**: *(A)* I try to see everybody's point of view. *(L)* From your own point of view. *(A)* No, I try to see what everybody is thinking and feeling, to the best of my ability.

56 **A**: No.

57 **Q**: *(A)* I don't understand. Yes, I do. *(L)* Can you help?

58 **A**: No help is desired.

59 **Q**: *(L)* Would you think that there is a possibility that you are *not* seeing the other points of view? *(A)* Sure. It's possible, but I try. Is there any way to improve this?

60 **A**: Communication.

61 **Q**: *(A)* About what? *(L)* I guess just start talking.

62 **A**: Specifically, communicate with those that bother you! Resistance is powerful.

63 **Q**: *(A)* Resisting what? You are so confusing!

64 **A**: No.

65 **Q**: *(L)* Anything else?

66 **A**: Only if desired.

67 **Q**: *(L)* Is [my ex's] injury serious and will it leave permanent damage?

68 **A**: All injuries do.

69 **Q**: *(L)* Of a major nature?

70 **A**: Semi.

71 **Q**: *(L)* Is he going to die from this as he thinks?

72 **A**: No.

73 **Q**: *(L)* What caused this accident?

74 **A**: Too complex as to root cause, but direct cause was "passing out."

75 **Q**: *(L)* Okay. Tom G passed away, and I would like to know what his state is and could we communicate with him?

76 **A**: Sleeping to adjust to the reality of afterlife in 5th density.

77 **Q**: *(L)* What was the physiological reason for his passing?

78 **A**: Electrical short circuit.

79 **Q**: *(L)* Did he suffer at all?

80 **A**: No. Did not believe in "hereafter." Are you aware of this?

81 **Q**: *(L)* No, I wasn't.

82 **A**: Will awaken, but of course, there is no "time" there.

83 **Q**: *(L)* Is there anything I can say or do for Chloe to help her through this?

84 **A**: Will recover surprisingly quickly.

85 **Q**: *(L)* Is it likely that she will move back to Florida?

86 **A**: Next year.[8]

87 **Q**: *(L)* I would really like to do something to make my baby feel better.

88 **A**: Up to A___.

89 **Q**: *(L)* Anything further for any of us?

90 **A**: No, and goodnight.

End of Session

Here I would like to add just a little memorial to Tom G. He was an extraordinary person. Tommy was an Aquarian too. Generous, loving,

---

[8] She didn't. She is still in NC.

and with a bizarre sense of humor. I once drove to their house in Ocala, and had a flat on the way. When I arrived, I asked him to recommend a garage where I could have the tire repaired. He said he would find out for me before I left the following day. Later he told me the tire was already fixed. But, he did not do *exactly* that – he had a whole new set of tires put on.

One night we sat up together and watched horror movies and drank scotch and laughed hysterically at the vampires and werewolves. Then he dragged Chloe out of bed to eat pancakes with us in the middle of the night; she just laughed and shook her head.

Tommy was raising race horses as a hobby. He had a prize horse that had accidentally impaled itself on a fence post, right in the chest. It took months to heal. Tommy nursed that horse day and night. He tried to shock me by cleaning the wound with his hands and wiping them on his jeans ... (it was *truly* disgusting) but I didn't blink an eye, and only told him that he was going to need extra detergent in the wash to get them clean again. He appreciated that, I think. I was there near Christmas one year and it was raining, and one of the mares was foaling ... so he named it 'Noah', because it was raining and he knew that I was rather obsessed with Noah and the Ark. Chloe later sent me a photo of Noah as a two-year-old.

Tommy used to say, "Everything is as it should be, and I can *prove* it – because that's the way it is!" And he would laugh. He was completely irreverent and enjoyed nothing more than shooting sacred cows.

Most of all, Tommy was special because he made Chloe happy and that made me happy.

Wherever you are, Tommy, baffle 'em!

October 5, 1996

After all the craziness of the previous week, I thought about all the chaos as a manifestation of transition, like a dissipative structure.[1] On October 2nd, my modem was fried by lightning so we were out of contact except by phone. Then the phone line got fried! That happened at the same time that Ark received an invitation to an unusual conference. He wrote:

> I have just received files from Freiburg about the conference of The Society for Scientific Exploration[2] to be held October 11-13. That is Brenda Dunne (from Princeton PEAR Lab) asked Freiburg when the conference is to be held and to send me the info. (although I knew about it before from Ezio and Joop). The moment I got the letter I immediately went to the "Director" with whom I fought not long ago asking for financial support for my going to Freiburg. There was some hesitation, he reminded me that twenty years ago when I was at Stony Brook I went crazy with this subject. I admitted it to be the fact but still insisted that I must know what other people are talking about. So, he has agreed. Which means that unless I decide otherwise, I will go to Freiburg for these three days.

Ark was also preparing and giving lectures almost every day. He wrote:

> Today I had a lecture to freshmen students. I told them that next week somebody will replace me because I am going to a conference. I can tell them what kind of a conference it is, but they are supposed to keep it secret. And then I told them. In a break I have had ten of them asking me to RECORD ALL, so that they can listen to later.

---

[1] "Ilya Prigogine developed the concept of 'dissipative structures' to describe the coherent space-time structures that form in open systems in which an exchange of matter and energy occurs between a system and its environment. Ilya Prigogine received the Nobel Prize in Chemistry in 1977 for 'his contributions to nonequilibrium thermodynamics, particularly the theories of dissipative structures.' Prigogine's primary interest was in nonequilibrium irreversible phenomena because in these systems the arrow of time becomes manifest." (http://www.osti.gov/accomplishments/prigogine.html)

[2] https://www.scientificexploration.org/

> Well, the title of my lectures is "Introduction to the word of mathematics". I am introducing them. Told them today that we will travel faster than light and that we will overcome gravity and that we will have free and clean energy. Told them never forget main questions: about God and Universe and Man. Then told them that I would never pass an entrance exam because I am not able to solve scientific problems under stress. Told them that each of them can any time come to my office for help with ANY problem or question. That does not mean that I will be able to help, but I will direct them to somebody that CAN.

My dentist called and I told Ark about the exchange:

> Sharky (Sharukh) called earlier. Seems his parents back in Bombay, have found a new marriage prospect for him and he wants me to look at the chart. This is almost a joke between us, because he never listens to what I say, but keeps asking anyway!!! The only good thing is that he does all my dental work in exchange, and the kids, too!

I read the online schedule of the Freiburg conference and wrote to Ark:

> I am thinking about the conference... Oh my, would I love to go to this one!
>
> But, anyway, the lecture entitled: "Borderlines of Creativity: Magical Ideation and the 'Dark Side' of the Brain" is the one that caught my eye. Should be interesting. I wonder if it is going to be a "logical" explanation of random firing of neurons or chemical excretions causing metaphorical states... like Sagan's explanation for the similarity of near death experiences: the reliving of the birth trauma, (you know, passing through a tunnel/birth canal, etc. Never mind that people who have been born by Caesarean have identical experiences.)
>
> Or, is it going to be a modern explication of the Sufi Imaginal World???
>
> And the following is, of course, the ONE lecture you MUST NOT MISS!
>
> "Study of Telepathy Between Rabbits."
>
> Seriously: The lectures about physiology relating to weather and/or earthquakes might be interesting. I gave a lot of attention to this for several years some time ago. I began to wonder if some physical effects I was having were related to barometric pressure, EM, or something else. So, for about 2 years I kept records of every sensation I had and then combed the news for relationships to event.
>
> This was near the time that I was regularly having prophetic dreams - almost daily - including one about the Challenger blowing up, which, of course, it did that very morning as I was watching.

The idea that prophetic dreams COULD occur nearly drove me crazy. And some of them were so MUNDANE that I wondered why such a waste of good prophetic energy on such ordinary things...

I also noticed that the symbology of the dreams was the thing I needed to understand.

Targ and Puthoff... I wonder about them. The whole remote viewing thing is highly suspect in my opinion. I had some correspondence with one of the SRI people about it. And, I discussed Courtney Brown's remote viewing experiences and explanation with Mike Lindemann. I would say that anything that can be obtained this way would be limited to 3rd density also, and therefore not pure enough for my tastes. The reason I spent so many years trying and discarding one thing after another, was the push to find that which was as uncorrupted as was possible. And most people don't understand how this has to be pushed, worked at, try this, try that... something like theories... in fact, yes, a theory.

A fellow at a MUFON meeting brought some sort of EM detecting device at a time that we were giving a demonstration of the process. It was interesting to observe the needle fly across the dial and bury itself in the opposite side each time the C's started to answer a question and then settle back to normal when anyone else was speaking. And, of course, I would like to have an explanation for the photo of the light figure over the board with the hands turned into pure light.

Well, all these are things we need to look into and find some answers for, and we will do it, but it is a lot of work.

Later I wrote:

I talked to Leonard Sturm last night (the MUFON fellow) about Don Z. He is going to talk to Eugene Brown down in Clearwater. He also told me an interesting thing: he has an older fellow who is attending his discussion group who says he SAW the [alien] autopsy video many years ago while in military service and declares it to be authentic. (I am SURE it is, but there is so much ridiculous controversy over it that I have simply kept my opinion to myself.)

On October 4th, I wrote to Ark:

Santilli called and we talked for over an hour about numerous things. He knows you are coming and is anxious to meet with you and talk etc.

I had wanted to get from him some idea of the research conditions in various places he might be familiar with. He told me about his work at Harvard and a resulting book which exposed the political controls which caused him no end of grief.

I have begun to have some ideas take shape in my mind about a direction and work that ought to be done. I will formulate some questions about this and ask the C's on Saturday night.

I tried to steer away from technical subjects because you know that I feel that I am in very deep, cold water there. But, I did bring up your work in a general way and read to him the title of the paper from Annalen der Physik about EEQT and PDD. He was very interested and wanted to read it, and I said I would give it to him to make a copy.

The political situation and suppression was what we talked about more than anything, so this gives me a little bit of a clue about some things that must be looked at with an eye to making some positive changes in the outer world.

I told him that I had been drifting a little in the past year or two, but that this entire subject interested me intensely, and maybe there was something that could be done about it. I don't really know, but I will talk to Tom French tomorrow at lunch (he is taking me to lunch) and see if there is some avenue within the press that can be utilized to help open the doors to freer and further research possibilities - it is necessary for the future of humanity, so must be looked at in terms of whether anything can be done and what. RS suggested that we can have a strategy meeting and pool our resources to make some major waves.

This session discusses mind-programming, including Greenbaum-type programming as mentioned in the 10 March 1996 session. However, as the reader might guess, considering all that was going on in the background, we started off with some personal questions. After that, it gets quite interesting.

Participants: 'Frank', Laura, Terry, Tom M, MM, V

1 **Q**: *(L)* Hello

2 **A**: Hello

3 **Q**: *(L)* Who do we have with us this evening?

4 **A**: Kournia.

5 **Q**: *(L)* And where are you from?

6 **A**: Cassiopaea.

7 **Q**: *(L)* Does anybody want to start with some questions? Do we have an open forum tonight, seeing as there are no questions?

8 **A**: You always have an open forum.

9 **Q**: *(L)* Well, seeing as how we have no specific questions, I will ask this question. I was talking with Ruggero Santilli, and he has expressed his opinion that the potential opportunities for doing research in the United States are extremely limited. I would like to know if that's necessarily ...

10 **A**: Wrong!

11 **Q**: *(L)* Good! I'm glad it's wrong! If it is wrong, can you tell us precisely in what way it is wrong, and how we can look at it to gain a better perspective?

12 **A**: There are no limits, just controls ... The knowledge gives one all the necessary tools to overcome the controls. Do not attempt to formulate words as you

write, my dear. Just "go with the flow"

13 **Q:** *(L)* Well, I'm feeling pretty darn warm; the energy is higher than I've seen it in a long time ... *(T)* Energetic little being, isn't he?! *(V)* I'm having a hard time keeping up ... *(L)* I know, it's fast. Just hang in there, sweetie. *(T)* That's what we're trying to do! *(L)* Why are we having ...

14 **A:** No meta. The.

15 **Q:** *(L)* No 'meta', 'the controls.' *(V)* Oh, I see, I had it wrong ... Thanks. *(L)* We've got some real good energy here. I'd like to ask ...

16 **A:** I see you, you see me.

17 **Q:** *(V)* What does that mean?

18 **A:** What it says.

19 **Q:** *(L)* The energy is really good. I like it. Okay, guys, we like the energy tonight. Tell us why we have such good energy tonight.

20 **A:** Tom.

21 **Q:** *(L)* And what is there about Tom?

22 **A:** Not often here.

23 **Q:** *(L)* Anything else about it? No. All right, MM took a particular type of Reiki initiation or attunement today, and I'd like to know, what was the ... she had an event occur during the attunements. I would like to know what this event was, what this condition was that she experienced.

24 **A:** She should be careful not to "spread her self too thin."

25 **Q:** *(L)* And what does that mean?

26 **A:** One does not need to cram learning, "steady as she goes."

27 **Q:** *(V)* They're punctually[3] [sic] correct, aren't they? *(L)* Yes, they are! So, is that in a sense a caution?

28 **A:** Yes.

29 **Q:** *(L)* Can you describe what it was that was taking place with her? Or define it?[4]

30 **A:** Soul bilocation.

31 **Q:** *(L)* So, it was not exactly a state, as the Sufis describe?

32 **A:** No.

33 **Q:** *(L)* And where did she bilocate to?

34 **A:** Not easily explainable.

35 **Q:** *(L)* Was it to another density or dimension? Or parallel universe or spiritual domain? *(T)* Norfolk Naval Station? [Laughter] Destination of bilocation! *(L)* Was this a beneficial event for her?

36 **A:** No. She has been ripping open the fabric too much.

37 **Q:** *(V)* Do you know what that means? *(TM)* The fabric of this dimension? *(L)* Is Terry correct? The fabric of this dimension?

38 **A:** Close. Each soul has its own patterning, which is held in place by the three bodies of existence [planchette swirls a few times] ... "thought center, spirit center and physical center," there are specific methodologies for adjusting these, and travelling into or out of other planes of existence. When one does not properly utilize these, one tears the fabric of their trilateral continuum when they seek to travel. This can be very problematic, and may lead to the soul being unable to reconnect with the

---

[3] V___ was referring to punctuation, not punctuality.
[4] *The Wave* 19

body, thus causing the physical center to perish!!!

39 **Q:** *(L)* The man who was giving the attunements, was he aware of what was happening, or what he was doing?

40 **A:** Aware only of unusual sensates.

41 **Q:** *(L)* He did this? You let him touch you? *(M)* Yes. *(L)* Oh, Jesus! *(M)* Sensations, that's what he said. He was aware of it, he just didn't know what it was. *(T)* He felt it, but he had no idea what was going on. *(M)* He just felt that it was something to do with the attunement. I guess, I mean, I don't know! *(L)* Did it have anything to do with the attunement?

42 **A:** No. It had to do with previous experiments.

43 **Q:** *(L)* Why did she see like a past-life review?

44 **A:** You described it well.

45 **Q:** *(L)* In other words, when I said that when she separated from her body, she was able to access the past-life review, just as if you were in the process of dying. *(M)* Well, experiments by who? *(L)* You!

46 **A:** You.

47 **Q:** *(L)* So, what was, what happened with this interaction that caused this to trigger right there and then? At that moment? What was the trigger?

48 **A:** Spirit center stimulus.

49 **Q:** *(L)* And what was the stimulus? Was this stimulus ...

50 **A:** The "initiation."

51 **Q:** *(L)* The initiation stimulated the spirit center. *(M)* So, what would they have me do? *(L)* Well, they aren't going to tell you that! *(M)* No? *(L)* You have to make your own mind ... *(M)* What's the proper way to go through these ... If I'm tearing my fabric, how do I not tear my fabric? *(L)* Slow down?

52 **A:** By ceasing until it is properly healed.

53 **Q:** *(L)* You've got to be healed. *(M)* Healed of what? *(T)* Healed at the rips and tears? *(L)* Well, maybe more than that ...

54 **A:** Yes.

55 **Q:** *(L)* All right, healed at the rips and tears. Approximately how long would that take? *(T)* Until it's done! *(L)* Oh, stop it!

56 **A:** Open.

57 **Q:** *(M)* Can that beam, can that portal take care of it ...[5] *(V)* Can you suggest how the rips might be healed? Is there ... *(L)* Wait a minute, wait a minute ... *(V)* Sorry!

58 **A:** It is a natural process.

59 **Q:** *(L)* MM wants to know, can the portal that she has in her house take care of helping to heal this ...

60 **A:** No.

61 **Q:** *(T)* The portal you have in your house? *(M)* I've got it in my aura, we've seen it on film. *(L)* Maybe that's part of the tear? *(M)* I don't know ... *(TM)* Look at the location of it ... *(M)* It sure is huge, and it sure is ...

62 **A:** No.

63 **Q:** *(L)* No, it's not part of the tear. *(T)* Does everybody's house have a portal in it?

64 **A:** No.

---
[5]See session 14 July 1996 for discussion of the 'portal' in MM's house.

65 **Q:** *(L)* She's got it in the photographs. Amazing. You haven't seen these photographs. These photographs will knock you out of the water. *(T)* I'm still waiting to see the photograph of the board. *(L)* I sent it to Ark. *(T)* Awwww, I'm never going to see the photograph of the board! *(L)* No, no, no! Cherie has a copy of it. She's going to make us an enlargement. *(M)* So, what am I supposed to do with this? Can the portal assist in any way? This thing in the aura, will it do me any good? I mean, what's it for, anyway...?

66 **A:** It can assist you in becoming possessed.

67 **Q:** *(M)* Well, that's just wonderful! How did it get there? *(TM)* Somebody did something bad there? *(M)* The top of my head? *(TM)* Now, wait a minute, it's in your aura? *(M)* Yes, it's on the top of my head, it comes right down. *(TM)* Ohhh!

68 **A:** No it is not a part of you.

69 **Q:** *(M)* Okay, so it just kind of likes to hang out in my aura! Loves photographing my aura. It loves to be there, we don't know what it is. *(T)* Maybe it jumps in your aura because it's photogenic! *(V)* Can it be resolved with spirit release? *(L)* No. Any personal advice for her at this point?[6]

70 **A:** Consolidate classes into three way study groupings.

71 **Q:** *(L)* What is a three way study group?

72 **A:** Combined study of three subjects.

73 **Q:** *(L)* All right, combine the study of three subjects, instead of studying them separately. So, what subjects are you teaching? *(M)* I teach healing, I teach the rays of initiation, and I teach auras.[7] *(L)* Well I guess they are saying to teach all three of them together! Have them all assemble at the same time, instead of separately. *(M)* The only one I don't do, that's really combined, I teach about healing and auras, but the other one, the one about rays of initiations, that is a separate class. It doesn't fit in! *(L)* Well, see if you can work a way to do it, like, an hour on this subject, and then we'll go on to this subject. Like a two-class school. And now we go to this, and do it all in one fell swoop, and that way, you've got about two hours. All right, anything else for her? *(T)* How about asking where this portal came from? *(L)* Yes, what was the generative source? The one in her house.

74 **A:** More than one.

75 **Q:** *(L)* Okay, there's more than one generative source. So, it's a combination of factors. Is it part of the historical site? The space-time location?

76 **A:** Yes.

77 **Q:** *(L)* Is it part of the metaphysical activities taking part in the house itself?

78 **A:** Yes.

79 **Q:** *(L)* Is it part M___ herself? And her own mental states?

---

[6] I was really leery of doing any hypnotherapy with MM due to the events described in the 17 March session.

[7] It was astonishing to me that this woman was teaching these things, considering what had come out in her hypnosis session about her 'reptilian rape' as discussed in the March 17 session. Notice also my follow-up comments to that session where I reported that she apparently had entirely forgotten everything about it!

80 **A:** Other occupants. More than her.

81 **Q:** *(M)* Do they mean live ones or dead ones?

82 **A:** Both.

83 **Q:** *(M)* That's what I thought. *(V)* How can it be removed? *(L)* What would be the best technique for her stopping activity and allowing herself to heal, and getting herself on track so that she doesn't get any real ... Jesus, can you imagine, if this kind of happened again, and you just checked out? And couldn't get back?

84 **A:** Changes in lifestyle.

85 **Q:** *(L)* Changes in lifestyle ... and what specifically? Can you list the several ...

86 **A:** No.

87 **Q:** *(M)* Oh, man! *(L)* You've got to know this yourself! You know them yourself! *(M)* Can you ask them ... *(L)* Just think about this, dear. *(TM)* The more you deny it, the worse it gets.

88 **A:** We would like to have the opportunity to discuss other issues at this session besides personal issues, as this drains the channel energy. But, we will accept limited questions from those in particular need.

89 **Q:** *(L)* I want to finish for her. Can I ask just one short, maybe a couple added to it – quick ones for MM?

90 **A:** One, please.

91 **Q:** *(L)* The question I have is, she is in a situation where she is somewhat obfuscated in her directions. It seems that many sorts of sources seek to ...

92 **A:** Obfuscation is illusion.

93 **Q:** *(L)* I know, but what I'm trying to get at for my question is yes, she's got

---

[8]See 27 November 1994 session.

all these illusions that she gets thrown at her. But, it seems to me that a person who gets this much attack ...

94 **A:** Finances would take care of themselves, miracle.

95 **Q:** *(TM)* I have a question. What is happening in my car ...*(L)* No! *(TM)* It is just a yes or no question! *(L)* Well, okay. *(TM)* Have I been abducted in my car, like Laura suggested?

96 **A:** Maybe.

97 **Q:** *(TM)* Thank you, that's all I wanted to know. *(L)* Well you should have asked it in a different way! I thought you were going to ask a mechanical question! [Laughter] It's been done! I did it! Remember, we asked about LM's truck, and he wanted to argue about it, and the next day, found out it was absolutely correct? He argued with them! They diagnosed the problem with his truck, and he argued with them: "Well they don't know anything about mechanics!" He stomped around and everything. The next day, the guy from across the street comes over and looks at it and says exactly the same thing they did! That's all it needed, just a little rubber thing stuck over a hole. [Laughter] Did he believe? No! It didn't matter to him![8] Okay, I do have one question here. I talked to Chloe the other day, and I told her what we got the other night, about Tommy sleeping, and she wanted to say that she just couldn't accept that, because so many other people have had visitations and visions and dreams and so forth of him wandering around and doing all these good deeds in the other world. Comments, please.

98 **A:** Not true.

99 **Q**: *(L)* It's not true. Then why are all these other people saying that they are seeing Tommy or having experiences with him, either in dreams or visual, or whatever, and what are these people seeing and experiencing?

100 **A**: In short, inflated opinions of ability manifest false reality.

101 **Q**: *(L)* So, these various people who think they're psychic have such inflated opinions of their own abilities that they are all calling her up and saying, "I saw him, he spoke to me ... he came to me in a dream ..." *(M)* Who is Tommy? *(L)* My girlfriend's husband just died. *(V)* Is he still sleeping?

102 **A**: Emotions directing events.

103 **Q**: *(T)* They are also just telling her what she wants to hear?

104 **A**: Yes.

105 **Q**: *(L)* So, I think I should just not say anything further about it. I was trying to say it in a more comforting way, but she, I guess, what is it ...

106 **A**: She is under emotional "cloud".

107 **Q**: *(L)* Okay, we have all given MM emotional support. We all love her, and we all see her as an important person who is being attacked from all sides. We are all here, at all times, to help you when you need it. So, therefore, you have advice, you have been promised a miracle, it may have something to do with a phone conversation I had the other day ... *(M)* Yes, that was weird! *(L)* Now, carry on! *(T)* Was there something you wanted to speak on this evening? You said there were other issues that you wanted to talk about.

108 **A**: Wait a minute ... V___, my dear, your retreat will be tremendously uplifting and positive!!! Lots of fun, too.

109 **Q**: *(V)* Yahoo! Without getting personal, and going into explanations, was the experience that I had after I fell asleep last night past-life remembrance?

110 **A**: No.

111 **Q**: *(V)* Can you tell me what it was without going into detail?[9]

112 **A**: Subconscious mind wandering.

113 **Q**: *(V)* Jesus! *(L)* Well, in her subconscious mind wanderings, was she picking up something in the atmosphere – some thought, or some fear? *(V)* I can't believe that that would come from me!

114 **A**: No. Cycling.

115 **Q**: *(L)* Can you give her anything more on this? She was very distressed about it ... You can pick it up out of my mind if you want. Her mind, whoever's mind.

116 **A**: No.

117 **Q**: *(L)* Is it anything to be concerned about as a prophetic thing?

118 **A**: No. Why would you say prophecy?

119 **Q**: *(L)* Well, she was concerned that it was something that could happen ... *(V)* No, I wasn't concerned in that way ... I'm concerned, I'm disgusted by it, and it would be much easier for me to handle if it was some kind of past-life memory than if it were something that comes from my psyche. Because it disgusts me.

120 **A**: Disgust manifested in dream state wanderings always result from repressed situations.

121 **Q**: *(L)* Ohhh, I see! Was that something that was in the air and was ... *(V)*

---

[9] As I recall, it had something to do with her son.

Repressed as in my relationship with the person?

122 **A**: Maybe.

123 **Q**: *(L)* Do you want to drop that? [Energy burst from the board: sudden, fast movement.] A couple of weeks ago you gave us a warning about Ark travelling on his over-the-road trips and possible alien monitoring. Is his intention to be fully aware and conscious and not travel at night going to help with this particular situation? This warning?

124 **A**: Maybe.

125 **Q**: *(L)* He is now of the opinion that his awareness of the state of the other person [his ex] as being possibly desirous of undermining his position at the university, that his awareness will forestall or circumvent this. How high a percentage is there of this happening, even with his awareness?

126 **A**: ? Awareness is not balanced yet.

127 **Q**: *(L)* So, his awareness is not complete yet. He is not fully aware of how deep and dark and dooey these aliens can be when they start working through people? Is that it?

128 **A**: Goin' thru the motions, babe.

129 **Q**: *(L)* What? "Goin thru the motions, babe?" What does that mean? Does that mean anything to anybody?

130 **A**: What Ark is doing, but, it is the first step to learning.

131 **Q**: *(L)* What does this mean? I don't quite get it. I'm being dense here. *(T)* We told him that this is happening, so yes, he's going through the motions for you, that he's understanding this ... *(M)* He's got to go through it completely before he understands ... *(T)* ... but it's got to really happen for it to ... *(L)* Is that it? Is Terry on to it here, that it's got to really happen ...

132 **A**: Close.

133 **Q**: *(V)* Has he been hauled out, like MM and I've been hauled out?[10] *(L)* Who the hell knows?

134 **A**: No. Not completely.

135 **Q**: *(V)* MM and I are just the lucky ones! *(T)* Such luck! *(V)* Yeah, right! That was laced with sarcasm! I do hope you heard that! *(T)* No, I didn't catch that at all, haha! *(L)* In terms of this interaction with Roger Santilli, is there anything that would be fruitful to follow in terms of trying to assist him in his work, and in his ...

136 **A**: Let events unfold.

137 **Q**: *(L)* It sounds like something is going to unfold. *(T)* Just let him do what he's going to do. *(L)* I was talking about our involvement ... *(T)* There's nothing we have to do ... *(L)* Well, okay, right ...

138 **A**: So were we.

139 **Q**: *(V)* What? What does that mean? *(L)* Okay, they also were talking about our involvement with him... *(V)* This is like taking notes in classes, you know! This is like practice! This will get me ready for the university! *(T)* Do we have to spell it out for you? [Extended laughter!] *(V)* My little finger flies sometimes, Terry, I want to tell you!

140 **A**: Mind programming.[11]

---

[10] Alleged alien abductions.

[11] Considering the topics being discussed earlier, MM's 'initiation' and 'portal' and the fact that she was still teaching after the revelations during her hypnosis session, I think that the topic of 'mind programming' was deliberate on the part of the Cs.

141 **Q:** *(L)* What about mind programming? *(T)* Is that like Fox and NBC? You know, 'Must See TV'! *(V)* This is mirth, guys! *(L)* Mind programming ... *(T)* Okay, what about mind programming? *(V)* In reference to what?

142 **A:** We thought we would just throw that onto the table.

143 **Q:** *(L)* Well, you certainly did! I guess that's what they want us to talk about! *(T)* Mind programming! As in programming of one's mind.

144 **A:** TomM received some most recently.

145 **Q:** *(L)* And who did he receive the mind programming from?

146 **A:** Cultists.

147 **Q:** *(T)* What form did it take?

148 **A:** Negative.

149 **Q:** *(V to TM)* Are you aware of this? *(T)* Not negative or positive, but what form was it presented to him as?

150 **A:** Hypnotic.

151 **Q:** *(T)* Was he awake or asleep at the time?

152 **A:** Both.

153 **Q:** *(T)* No, no. Before the hypnotics, was he awake?

154 **A:** Yes.

155 **Q:** *(L)* Was this a pre-hypnotic trigger?

156 **A:** No.

157 **Q:** *(L)* Was it hypnosis at a distance?

158 **A:** No.

159 **Q:** *(T)* How was it conveyed to him?

160 **A:** Lights, fires, chants.

161 **Q:** *(V)* Were you aware of this? *(L)* How long has it been since you've hung out with that metaphysical church, coven bunch? *(TM)* I haven't seen any of them since way back when. *(L)* Way back when, what is that, a couple of years? *(TM)* Yes. *(L)* Well, then that's still recently ... *(T)* Lights, what and chants? *(V)* [Reading:] "lights, fires and chants." *(T)* Okay, thanks.

162 **A:** Yes.

163 **Q:** *(T)* Was he with them...? *(L)* Oh, yes, he was ...

164 **A:** Yes.

165 **Q:** *(L)* This is what we were ... *(T)* I just wanted to make sure that this was not a long-distance thing... that they did it from a distance and ... *(TM)* Yes, that they still didn't have their hooks into me. *(L)* Good question, is this programming still active?

166 **A:** Close, though.

167 **Q:** *(L)* Close, though, to what?

168 **A:** Almost.

169 **Q:** *(T)* ... that this wasn't done from a distance, that he wasn't with them physically, like this, that he was somewhere nearby when they did this ... *(L)* Oh, he was close ... *(T)* He was close to them? *(L)* Right. *(T)* But he wasn't ...

170 **A:** No.

171 **Q:** *(T)* Okay, then, they weren't responding to what I was saying. *(L)* So they were doing lights, fires and chants, and he was not there?

172 **A:** Response was to "hooks".

173 **Q:** *(L)* Are some of the choices he's been making in his life in the last two years the results of this programming?

174 **A:** Maybe.

175 **Q:** *(L)* I suppose we better let him read the Greenbaum paper; everybody here has read them, right? *(M)* That's where all the accidents are coming from...? *(T*

to TM) You haven't read the Greenbaum papers yet? *(TM)* I don't think so! *(T)* Well ... *(V)* It's very enlightening, I'll have you know! *(T)* There's a person who's thrilled about this one! (T to L) Print them out and give them to him. *(TM)* I want to know: did I get married as a result of this programming?

176 **A**: Yes.

177 **Q**: *(L)* Did I get married as a result of some similar programming?

178 **A**: No.

179 **Q**: *(L)* Did M___?

180 **A**: Yes.

181 **Q**: *(V)* Did I?

182 **A**: No.

183 **Q**: *(T)* Did Terry?

184 **A**: No.

185 **Q**: *(T)* Did Frank?

186 **A**: No.

187 **Q**: *(L)* Frank never got married! *(T)* Well, I was just making sure that everybody felt like they were in on all this! *(M)* This Greenbaum program, was it due to my father?

188 **A**: Yes.

189 **Q**: *(M)* Thought so! *(L)* Remember, TomM's father was military, too! *(M)* Twenty years! [Referring to her father, a Navy SEAL.] *(T)* While I'm tossing it ... *(TM)* Was it done to my father?

190 **A**: You were "Greenbaumed."[12]

191 **Q**: *(T)* Was Jan's friend Margaret Greenbaumed?

192 **A**: Yes.

193 **Q**: *(T)* She's got all the signs ... *(L)* Was TM Greenbaumed?

194 **A**: No.

195 **Q**: *(V)* What about Violette?

196 **A**: No.

197 **Q**: *(L)* What about Frank?

198 **A**: No.

199 **Q**: *(L)* Laura?

200 **A**: No.

201 **Q**: *(L)* Terry?

202 **A**: No.

203 **Q**: *(T)* Jan?

204 **A**: No.

205 **Q**: *(M)* So, I'm the only one here that's been Greenbaumed? *(TM)* So, you got mental programming, but it wasn't Greenbaum? *(L)* I didn't know that I had mental programming ... *(TM)* They said maybe...

206 **A**: Laura had more advanced work done on her.[13]

207 **Q**: *(V)* That opens up a whole new can of worms. *(L)* And what do you mean by that?

208 **A**: Not now.

209 **Q**: *(T)* Maybe they want to go on with ... *(L)* No, they've told me before; they're not going to tell me. *(M)* Were you Greenbaumed? *(L)* No. Who did this work, can I have that? Can I know that?

210 **A**: Consortium.

---

[12]Directed at MM. This was all too frighteningly true. See the 17 March 1996 session and the chapter of *The Wave* entitled "Alligator Alley." That's the story.
[13]*The Wave* 19

211 **Q**: *(L)* Is there any possibility, to some extent, that I have overcome this influence at the present time?

212 **A**: No. Was partial, then aborted, leaving fragments of trigger response programs that have been in remission.[14]

213 **Q**: *(L)* Why was it aborted?

214 **A**: Because STO forces intervened.

215 **Q**: *(L)* And when was this?

216 **A**: Mid "fifties."

217 **Q**: *(L)* So it was when I was three or four years old. *(T)* I think we should go back to what we were talking about with TM, because they brought it up. *(TM)* Am I still receiving instructions from the programming? Am I still receiving programming from them?

218 **A**: Buried for future triggers.

219 **Q**: *(L)* Is there anything he can do to deactivate this programming?

220 **A**: Would take powerful hypnotic work. Beware of stresses of a most personal nature.

221 **Q**: *(L)* Do you mean sexual actions, activities might be triggers or connected to this?

222 **A**: Partly.

223 **Q**: *(T)* Work related. All different kinds. Anything could trigger it ... *(L)* They said personal, most personal, though ... *(T)* Well, yes ... *(V)* Wouldn't it seem like family ... *(T)* Work and jobs are very personal ... *(L)* No. Most personal is physical, you know, emotional ... *(TM)* Family ... *(T)* Your job is financial, financial security. *(L)* Well, that's right. *(V)* Is your family going to cause you stress? *(TM)* Stress, and I have not been able to hold down a job since then. *(V)* Do you live with your family? *(TM)* Not anymore! *(L)* Any further clues for him? *(T)* What was it that they ... what was given to TM? What was he told to do, or what was the mind control about? *(L)* What were the instructions?

A: Discover. 224

225 **Q**: *(T)* Is this something TM will be able to discover? Does he have enough information to work on?

226 **A**: Not by himself.

227 **Q**: *(L)* Is his wife and the baby part of the hook?

228 **A**: Yes.

229 **Q**: *(TM)* Is the hook attached to the physical, emotional, spiritual, or all?

230 **A**: All.

231 **Q**: *(TM)* Is there a physical location where it's attached in all three, in the same place?

232 **A**: You were particularly vulnerable at the time remember, this particular group[15] has an uncanny ability to get to those who have parental influences with a troubled past.[16]

233 **Q**: *(L)* Is she Greenbaumed?

234 **A**: Yes.

235 **Q**: *(TM)* Where did she receive Greenbaum programming? *(L)* Don't even ask that until you've read the Greenbaum papers. *(TM)* Never mind, disregard. *(L)* You can get all of that just

---

[14] *The Wave* "Appendix C"

[15] The coven that was behind the local metaphysical church.

[16] After this response, a phone call interrupted; the call was from TM's wife, Andrea. After brief exchange, telling her he would be home soon, we resumed.

by reading them. *(V)* Was she just coerced to make this phone call? *(L)* She was triggered to. *(TM)* Oh, I know, her father was in the Navy ... *(L)* Why are we not surprised!!!

236 **A**: Yes. And V___'s too, but fortunately in too low level a capacity.

237 **Q**: *(L)* Does the Greenbaum influence or interaction last indefinitely throughout a person's life, if something isn't done to terminate or halt it?[17]

238 **A**: Yes.

239 **Q**: *(L)* Mind programming ... Where are we going to go with this, guys? *(L)* Oh, okay, go. What were the programs? The main programs?

240 **A**: Must not say.

241 **Q**: *(L)* MM wants to know how extensive the Greenbauming was in her case. Was it extensive?

242 **A**: Yes and your husband, too!

243 **Q**: *(M)* That's just wonderful! More pleasant things this evening! *(V)* I've been sitting in your position, where I've gotten a bunch of bad news one night, and I know how you feel! *(F)* It's not really bad news, though, because it's good to know ... *(V)* It protects you to have the knowledge. But, it's tough to hear. *(TM)* Well, the next time you're doing something, and you don't know why you're doing it, it seems completely stupid, there's a thought ... *(L)* Ask yourself every time, why am I doing what I'm doing? Is it really me doing it, or am I being ... *(M)* Is there anything to cure it? Can anything be done? Now we know with him, it's hypnosis. *(T)* It is for everybody, I'm afraid. *(L)* I'm afraid, yes. Reread the Greenbaum speech.

---

[17] *The Wave* 19

244 **A**: Awareness is step number one.

245 **Q**: *(TM)* Will this Greenbauming be passed on to my son?

246 **A**: No.

247 **Q**: *(T)* It's a process; it's not hereditary. *(L)* I'm going to ask this. Don't get crazy when I ask it. Is this his son?

248 **A**: No.

249 **Q**: *(TM)* I'm not sure I understand, now. *(L)* And, since you, I mean, I had a sense of that ummm ... is this an alien-manipulated pregnancy?

250 **A**: No.

251 **Q**: *(L)* What is the scoop here in terms of that answer?

252 **A**: No scoop.

253 **Q**: *(TM)* Did she sleep with another man?

254 **A**: When?

255 **Q**: *(TM)* Around the time she became pregnant?

256 **A**: No.

257 **Q**: *(TM)* How about before we got married?

258 **A**: Yes.

259 **Q**: *(V)* I'm not understanding for a second here ... *(L)* If it's not his son, then whose son is it? *(V)* And, if she wasn't sleeping with someone else around the time she got pregnant, then ...

260 **A**: Not what we meant.

261 **Q**: *(L)* What did you mean?

262 **A**: Son not a programming trigger.

263 **Q**: *(L)* But when you said it was not his son ...

264 **A**: Son not trigger.

265 **Q:** *(L)* That's what you meant, so you didn't ... his son was not a programming trigger. *(V)* So that's his flesh and blood son ... *(M)* Oh that, it is a son. *(TM)* Okay, so it's my flesh and blood son, but not a programming trigger.

266 **A:** Right.

267 **Q:** *(T)* Andrea [TM's wife] is the trigger; one of them. *(L)* Well, TM finds himself ... we all ... I mean ... jeez! What do we do about these difficult situations that we plant ourselves in the middle of, due to programming? Then we have to extricate ourselves, at great cost and pain? Having done it already myself, I know how much pain ...

268 **A:** No need to extricate, if necessary work is done, in some cases.

269 **Q:** *(L)* If two people who are married to each other are Greenbaumed, is it possible that they could be programmed to kill each other?

270 **A:** Maybe, but not always.

271 **Q:** *(TM)* Or any two people who have had the programming?[18]

272 **A:** The programming is mainly intended to produce erratic behavior, for the purpose of "spooking" the population so that they will welcome, and even demand, a totalitarian government.[19]

273 **Q:** *(L)* So, the programming is designed to, in other words, when the people are just being erratic ...

274 **A:** Think of the persons who have inexplicably entered various public and private domains, and shot large numbers of people ... Now, you have "met" some of these Greenbaum subjects ...

275 **Q:** *(L)* Let me say this. If this is what we're saying, well, what I'm saying is, that ... Is this Greenbaum programming something that goes along the line of what I've just described a part ... a part, I don't think that's all of it ...

276 **A:** In part.

277 **Q:** *(L)* Is there also the implanted triggers to activate at a certain point in future time, to create a mass chaos, in the public domain?

278 **A:** Better to discover that one on your own.[20]

279 **Q:** *(L)* Okay, that's another one that's dangerous to know right now ... *(V)* Was the person I met last week, [name redacted], was he Greenbaumed? Has he been Greenbaumed? *(L)* He was bizarre, wasn't he?

280 **A:** Now, some history ... as you know, the CIA and NSA and other agencies are the children of Nazi Gestapo ... the SS, which was experiment influenced by Antareans who were practicing for the eventual reintroduction of the Nephalim on to 3rd and/or 4th density earth. And the contact with the "Antareans" was initiated by the Thule Society, which groomed its dupe subject, Adolph Hitler to be the all time mind programmed figurehead. Now, in modern times, you have seen, but so far, on a lesser scale: Oswald, Ruby, Demorenschildt, Sirhan Sirhan, James Earl Ray, Arthur Bremer, Farakahan,

---

[18] *The Wave* "Appendix C"

[19] Considering all that has gone on in our world since 9/11, this remark is more important than ever!

[20] *The Wave* 19

Menendez, Bundy, Ramirez, Dahmer, etc...[21]

281 **Q:** *(L)* Is there any particular individual who is currently being programmed to take a more prominent position in terms of this ...

282 **A:** Later ... you must know that Oswald was programmed to be the "patsy." So that he would say many contradictory things. Demorenschildt[22] was both a programmer and programmed. Ruby was hypnotically programmed to shoot Oswald with an audio prompt, that being the sound of a car horn.

283 **Q:** *(L)* The question has been brought up: is there some way or means that one can distinguish or discern a victim of Greenbaum or other mind programming by some clues?

284 **A:** Not until it is too late.

285 **Q:** *(L)* Was Sue V Greenbaumed?

286 **A:** Yes.

287 **Q:** *(T)* Yes, well, we kind of figured that already ... *(L)* Yes, but I was just checking here ... *(T)* Is JW Greenbaumed?

288 **A:** Yes.

289 **Q:** *(T)* And he carries guns around! Although, I'm not sure he knows how to get the cartridges in! *(L)* What about MF?

290 **A:** No.

291 **Q:** *(L)* SH?

292 **A:** No.

293 **Q:** *(L)* Anybody else got any likely suspects? *(T)* EB?[23]

294 **A:** Now you have touched on a whole other subject, my friend. At least his wife is blissfully ignorant.

295 **Q:** *(L)* What have we stumbled upon with EB? Is he a programmer?

296 **A:** Discover.

297 **Q:** *(T)* I think I'd prefer not to! *(L)* Is there anything further you'd like to add to this subject for our edification before we shut down for the night? *(V)* I'd like to know if any presidents have

---

[21] Interestingly, the Cs completely ignored the questions that were tumbling out and delivered what they considered to be most important.

[22] "George Sergius de Mohrenschildt was a petroleum geologist and professor who befriended Lee Harvey Oswald in the summer of 1962 and maintained that friendship until Oswald's death, two days after the assassination of US President John F. Kennedy. His testimony before the Warren Commission investigating the assassination was one of the longest of any witness. According to Colonel L. Fletcher Prouty, then chief Pentagon-to-CIA liaison officer, Mohrenschildt had several private lunches with former CIA Director and Warren Commission member Allen Dulles while testifying before the Warren Commission. During 1967, New Orleans District Attorney Jim Garrison interviewed Jeanne and George de Mohrenschildt as part of Garrison's prosecution of Clay Shaw. Garrison said that both of the Mohrenschildts insisted that Oswald had been the scapegoat in the assassination of President Kennedy. Garrison concluded from his conversation with them that George de Mohrenschildt had been one of Oswald's unwitting 'baby-sitters... assigned to protect or otherwise see to the general welfare of [Oswald].'" (Wikipedia, "George de Mohrenschildt")

[23] A MUFON personage.

298 been Greenbaumed? *(L)* Well, we know some probably have!

A: Yes.

299 Q: *(T)* How many have we had now? Clinton is number-what president? *(TM)* 42.

300 A: Remember, the "Greenbaum method" is one of many in existence.

301 Q: *(L)* Okay, further ... *(T)* What did it say? *(V)* You've got people getting hauled out and abducted, I mean ... *(L)* All kinds of stuff going on. *(M)* Is [name redacted] set to go off soon? *(L)* No, they told you, awareness is the first step in undoing it! Focus on that! You're aware! How many people are?

302 A: It is a veritable potpourri.

303 Q: *(L)* Any further for tonight?

304 A: There's much much much more to discuss about all of this, but if you wish to stop now, that is your choice, and we will continue later. But, it would be helpful if you begin that session on subjects not of a personal nature!

305 Q: *(L)* Can we plan to pick up on this subject next week?

306 A: Yes.

307 Q: *(L)* Would it be better if all of those present now, be present for the continuation?

308 A: Sure!

309 Q: *(L)* Well then, unless there is something else of significant importance to say before we shut down for the night ...

310 A: Tom's wife will object strenuously.

311 Q: *(L)* Anything else?

312 A: Resist.

313 Q: *(L)* Anything else? For anyone else? No? I'm ready to say goodbye.

314 A: Goodbye.

End of Session

After the session was over, I wrote a description to Ark:

> Jan wasn't there at the beginning because she took [my oldest daughter] to a Salvador Dali Surrealistic Costume Ball, and only returned late. V___ was here and young Tom M.
>
> The energy was VERY GOOD, and delivery extremely fast - was hard to keep up.
>
> Earlier in the day, the lunch with Tom French was nice, but the esteemed restaurant was a little disappointing. The potato pancakes were good, but the chocolate mousse had a VERY stale sugar wafer stuck in it for decoration and the whipped cream was not fresh either. The German potato salad was AWFUL. (I always tend to evaluate meals in restaurants by whether or not I could have produced them better myself. This one, I definitely could have improved.) The now famous owner of the restaurant, the one who asaulted a policeman who dared to put catsup on the potato pancakes, was a complete lunatic. Obviously a victim of mind programming... (laughing)
>
> We then visited the Holiday MUFON forum which was a pretty bizarre experience. Leonard Sturm was the moderator; kept asking my opinion

on a whole variety of subjects from secret government to the "end of the world." There were a couple of old ladies there, aficionados of Don Ware and Courtney Brown, the SRI guy with the remote viewing book on the market. I almost got into a serious confrontation with them because they were saying that "so many psychics are all saying the same things and there are SO MANY books on the market that support Al Bielek and the Montauk experiment and Courtney Brown..." etc. etc. I just pointed out the fact that these ideas are so OUT THERE and being POPULARIZED, that one has to consider a possible ulterior motive. The old lady was positively devastated that I would point out that the government consists of people just like her and me and everyone else... they think that the government is some sinister monolith and that EVERYONE who works for the government is some evil, mindless, drone or is involved in some conspiracy knowingly, and they all somehow manage to hide it from their family and friends.

She insisted it was true. I asked my famous question: "Says who?" She said, "The people who had the experiences." I asked what proof they had. "Well, they were there." So, I had to point out that they only SAY they were there... there is not one single shred of objective proof...

So, I was not very popular with this lady and I was almost on the verge of telling her she was a programmed drone herself when Leonard decided that I should switch to the subject of millennial issues...

Then, Ruggero's work was brought up and Leonard, who is a friend of R___, said that he was told that an Arab Cartel is possibly going to finance certain experiments. I thought this was a rather fascinating remark.

Then, Tom brought me home, I took a nap, and only awakened with the arrival of the guests for the session.

So, that is the action for yesterday and tonight.

The next morning I wrote a bit more:

Another cloudy, drippy day. Now 5 in a row, I believe. Pool will be cold today.

And I have awakened with an ear problem which is causing my jaw to be swollen so that my teeth don't meet in the back. No serious pain, but must do something immediately or it will get out of control.

Did I send you the Greenbaum Papers? If not, I will do so because it was a centerpiece for last night's session and is very important. I have had two subjects who gave evidence that this project is described accurately in these papers. And, my thought is that you ought to put them on disk and give to any and all you deem to be interested in such things. Even better if you could disseminate more or less anonymously.

I asked if something along this line had been done to me during those episodes when I was physically missing as a child. The answer was: "Laura had move advanced work done on her by the consortium, but this was only partially completed and then aborted because STO forces intervened. This left fragments of trigger response programs that have been in remission."

And the time frame was given as the middle 50's.

But, the reasons for both the attempts at programming as well as the intervention were denied to be given as "not now." Well, at least it is only fragments and in remission, but still needful of being investigated and corrected if possible.

After you read (if you have not already) the Greenbaum Papers, you will see that this programming is done along the lines of a computer program. Several cases I have read about were somewhat tragic because there was a "hidden file" that caused self-destruction of the victim before all the programs could be deactivated. When I was reading about this, I wondered if it would be possible to design a sort of psychological program that could be imprinted via hypnosis and some NLP, that would act as a sort of virus to destroy all negative programming.

It seems that more about the matter would have to be known in a certain sense, and some considerable thought given as to exactly how to go about this, but I think it could be done.

I am supposed to call Ruggero today and tell him the results of my talk with Tom French. I wish I had better news, but all Tom could offer was to talk to one of the other journalists who deals with such matters and see if he could stimulate some interest. I am going to send him an e-mail and try to spark this a bit more so that he will know that I am not going to let the matter rest without some action.

October 12, 1996

The tape of this session disappeared and has never been found, which is very frustrating. I include here the email I sent to Ark after this session giving a general description of it.

> The session was a continuation of last week on mind programming. Some of it was rather interesting because I included some questions about the 2nd cousin who is an alleged spook, who I never met in my life until I attended a MUFON meeting in Holiday, and found, to my surprise, that this man who was introduced to me turned out to be a cousin. He attached himself to me for a long time. And, I have to admit I was a little entertained by it because there was such a strong, physical similarity it was like looking at a very masculinized version of myself. And, he was VERY bright though he used his intellect speciously. It entertained me to then twist his arguments around and direct them back at him and watch him flail around for another leg to stand on!
>
> This JW, the cousin, developed an intense hatred for Frank almost immediately. He spent a lot of time haranguing me about Frank and how he was just "using" me. The way JW put it was: "Frank is a master violinist and you, my dear, are a Stradivarius. He can't resist playing you for all you are worth!"
>
> I was pretty astonished by that statement. And, when it reached the point that JW told me that, if I continued to associate with Frank, that he would have to "avoid my company," I just told him that it was too bad that he could not be a little more tolerant of others... and that was over a year ago and I haven't heard a word from him since.
>
> Anyway, I asked about this JW situation, thinking he might have been programmed. C's: "Not exactly, it was more like this: he was sent to interest you in a diversionary path that would ultimately lead down a path to 4th density STS. It was also an effort to separate you from any influences which might dissuade you from your intended interest in JW."

Also present was my physical therapist, Terry A (different from Terry R), and young Tom M who was more or less raked over the coals last session about his association with the metaphysical church coven. Apparently, Andrea let him off his leash.

Participants: 'Frank', Laura, Tom M, V, Terry A

Q: *(L)* Hello.

A: Hello.

Q: *(L)* And who do we have with us this evening?

A: Moretir.

Q: *(L)* And where do you transmit from?

A: Cassiopaea.

Q: *(L)* In an earlier session you mentioned that we ought to discuss the matter of mind control ...[1]

A: Programming is the word you need, not "control."

Q: *(L)* Tom has had some very strange events happening to him and he would like to know if he has been Greenbaumed?

A: Tom has not been "Greenbaumed," but mind programmed by those who have ties to a Wiccan organization.[2]

Q: *(L)* How does one tell if they have been programmed?

A: Pay attention to the signs.

Q: *(T)* What are the effects or intentions of this programming?

A: Difficulty keeping up with the demands and pressures of life as well as before his involvement.

Q: *(T)* Any specific signs?

A: We gave you one, now for 2: wife "acting up." Also, parental problems that have already begun.

Q: *(L)* How does one overcome or cancel this programming?

A: The same as always: Knowledge protects.

Q: *(L)* In what ways will knowledge help to cancel programming?

A: In ways directly affecting Tom.

Q: *(L)* I don't understand. How can knowledge help to cancel programming?

A: So that the awareness can be the foundation for being able to deal with situations, and possibly rectify some of them.[3]

Q: *(L)* Okay, change of subject: On a couple of occasions you mentioned a group called the Antareans.[4] Who were these people or aliens?

A: Antareans were the name given by 4th density groups in contact with the Thule Society on third density Earth, before and during World War One.

Q: *(L)* What are they called now?

A: There is no one currently labeling themselves as "Antareans," in contact with anyone now.

Q: *(L)* So, they are no longer here?

A: No, not this particular group.

Q: *(L)* Okay, I would like to know why the individual who says he is my cousin

---

[1] *The Wave* 19

[2] Mind programmers hooked up with some Wiccan groups? Yikes!

[3] This principle is much clearer nowadays with the findings of cognitive psychology as explicated in books like *Strangers to Ourselves* by Timothy Wilson; *Thinking: Fast and Slow* by Daniel Kahnemann; *When the Body Says 'No'* by Gabor Mate; *The Myth of Sanity* by Martha Stout, and so forth.

[4] See sessions 7 October 1995, 31 August 1996, and 5 October 1996.

suddenly appeared in my life when I first attended a MUFON meeting after the UFO sighting over my pool? I mean, this was a *lot* synchronous. Was he sent to spy on me?

30 **A**: Not exactly, more like this: was sent to interest you in a diversionary path that would ultimately lead you down a path to 4th density STS.

31 **Q**: *(L)* Well, you have said that MF[5] and JW were *both* involved, yet they seem to hate each other, or say they do. Was this just an attack from another direction, in case the JW attack did not work?

32 **A**: It was also an effort to separate you from any influences which might dissuade you from your intended interest in JW.[6]

33 **Q**: *(L)* Well, was I mind programmed? You said once that I was not Greenbaumed, but that something else was done. What was this?

34 **A**: The work that was attempted was more intense, but it was aborted because it turned out that your frequency resonance vibration was not proper for that particular type of "experimental" programming.[7]

35 **Q**: *(L)* Does this mean that there was something about my vibrations that caused what they were trying to do to result in positive things?

36 **A**: Possibly, in an off-hand way.

37 **Q**: *(L)* You also said that STO intervened and stopped this ... does this mean that there is some reason to protect me?[8]

38 **A**: Okay ... learning is an exploration followed by the affirmation of knowing discovery.

39 **Q**: [Question lost, but apparently a smart remark from Tom M.]

40 **A**: No comment from "the peanut gallery," please.

41 **Q**: [Question lost]

42 **A**: Not "left," Tom, "leaves."

43 **Q**: [Question lost]

44 **A**: One day, you will know this.

45 **Q**: [Question lost]

46 **A**: Neither.

47 **Q**: [Question lost]

48 **A**: Closer but not close.

49 **Q**: [Question lost]

50 **A**: There is more than one issue here.

51 **Q**: [Question lost]

52 **A**: Part of the equation.

53 **Q**: [Question lost, though I think it was something about the metaphysical church coven with which Tom M had also become involved for a short period.]

54 **A**: Through Susan.

55 **Q**: [Question lost]

---

[5]MF being the self-proclaimed UFO/Bigfoot/alien abduction expert who appears in a number of sessions.

[6]I guess I was intended by someone/something to be 'interested' in JW, and his antagonism to MF, whom I detested, was supposed to be an 'attraction'.

[7]Thank goodness!

[8]See sessions 28 October 1994, and 4 March 1995. This will come up again in future sessions.

56 **A**: This is complex, and does not "work" in the way you envision.

57 **Q**: [Question lost]

58 **A**: You are making positive moves.

59 **Q**: [Question lost]

60 **A**: Partially.

61 **Q**: [Question lost but, based on a close reading of emails to Ark, it seems that the couple of previous questions and this one were from Terry A about the bodywork he was doing on my neck and shoulders.]

62 **A**: Both. Careful there!

63 **Q**: [Question lost]

64 **A**: With what is available.

65 **Q**: [Question lost, though must have been something about the signs of attack.]

66 **A**: Your pool.

67 **Q**: [Question lost]

68 **A**: Impatience.

69 **Q**: [Question lost]

70 **A**: You are doing just fine.

71 **Q**: [Question lost]

72 **A**: Is this what you expect?

73 **Q**: [Question lost]

74 **A**: Not necessary.

75 **Q**: [Question lost]

76 **A**: Yes, but you are not showing faith or patience.

77 **Q**: [Question lost]

78 **A**: Ask A___.

79 **Q**: [Question lost]

80 **A**: Then what do you think?

81 **Q**: [Question lost]

82 **A**: Okay.

83 **Q**: [Question lost]

84 **A**: Not all.

85 **Q**: [Question lost, though it must have been something about Ark.]

86 **A**: And he is correct!

87 **Q**: [Question lost]

88 **A**: Never you mind.

89 **Q**: [Question lost]

90 **A**: Must say this.

91 **Q**: [Question lost, though it was something about Ark's situation at that moment.]

92 **A**: Because his situation is complex and precarious.

93 **Q**: [Question lost]

94 **A**: Sometimes.

95 **Q**: [Question lost, though, as far as I can recall, I was asking something about Ark.]

96 **A**: He needs you for "fine tuning."

97 **Q**: [Question lost]

98 **A**: Discover.

99 **Q**: [Question lost]

100 **A**: More through your given, and learned, talents.

101 **Q**: [Question lost]

102 **A**: Not for this session. Goodnight.

End of Session

November 23, 1996

It's over a month since the last session in October here. A number of us did meet on the 19th of October, but there was no session, just discussion as I learn from my email record. I don't find any particular reason for not having sessions during this time except that I was concentrating on the kids, the house, my health, and so forth. Patrick Z had 'run away from home', more or less, and was sleeping on the sofa in the kids' playroom. He was trying to get off the psychoactive drugs he had been taking for years that his mother insisted he needed. Maybe he did.

For the background realities, on the 23rd of October, I wrote to Ark:

> Phones were turned off when I got up 4 hours ago. I was literally wringing my hands in despair. Hard choices. Went down and paid another big portion of it with the money I had reserved for food and gas. So, we won't eat much. No extra driving. They had said that they would not turn it off if I would make another large payment on the 1st, but apparently some dark forces confused the interoffice communication, and the shut-off order was issued anyway. Now, let's hope the electric company does not become equally antagonistic.
>
> This morning was very funny, in spite of despair. I cooked the traditional Southern breakfast - and Patrick is a Yankee! So, the girls exaggerated their Southern accents and teased him mercilessly. They made him eat grits, which almost no Yankees will eat, and told him it would turn his blood Southern and he wouldn't be able to eat that horrible Northern food any more. After the food issue was exhausted, the lack of true breeding and culture of greedy, carpet-bagger Yankees was brought in, and then various battles of the war were recapitulated. So, the Civil War was fought for an hour or so, in a funny way and poor Patrick did not have a chance! Anyway, it was a lively and funny battle of wits and words!!! Patrick surrendered.

There was a great deal of turmoil in my house due to the presence of Patrick; he was an extremely negative influence. I was having a lot of trouble coping with my daughter's efforts to help him get off his meds.

Ark's arrangements to travel to the U.S. were more or less finalized, though we didn't have an exact date: we had an approximate date for his arrival in early February. Up to this point, we had been hopeful that his divorce would proceed as a more or less normal case. However, just a few days before this session we began to get an foretaste of his ex-wife's bizarre strategy: she simply claimed to be ill, got a doctor friend of hers to write a letter saying she could not appear in court, and without her appearing, the case could not proceed. At first we thought this tactic could only be employed for a little while, but I analyzed the horoscope of his ex and realized that she was going to dig her heels in and not be moved by anything or anybody. I turned out to be right.

In the meantime, of course, Ark was teaching, traveling Germany to work with colleagues there, and generally busy with running his department.

During this session, Ark participated via email. He would send his question, I would quickly type Cs' answer and send it to him for any follow-up question.

Also, this turned out to be a *most* interesting session due to the exchange about Flight 800 and EMP weapons, Courtney Brown and his remote viewing, Einstein and the Unified Field Theory *(UFT)*, and the introduction of the concept of bi-density humans. You could say that we more than made up for the wait between sessions!

Participants: 'Frank', Terry, Jan, Alice, Laura, Ark (via computer)

1 **Q**: *(L)* Hello.

2 **A**: Hello.

3 **Q**: *(L)* And who do we have ...

4 **A**: Tonno.

5 **Q**: *(L)* And where do you transmit from?

6 **A**: Cassiopaea.

7 **Q**: *(L)* We have quite a variety of questions this evening. The first is regarding the difficulties with UFL and the financial arrangements.[1] Will this work out so that he can be here the 1st of February, as planned?

8 **A**: Maybe a slight delay.[2]

9 **Q**: *(L)* And the personal finances?

10 **A**: You will see.

11 **Q**: *(L)* You said before that her[3] actions would accelerate the legal process.

12 **A**: In progress.

13 **Q**: *(L)* It looks now as though the legal

---

[1] Referring to Ark's planned travel to the U.S.
[2] This turned out to be correct: Ark arrived on 11 February.
[3] Ark's ex.
[4] Oh boy, was that ever true!

affair will not be over before he comes here ... this distresses me.

14 **A:** These are things you must wait to see.[4]

15 **Q:** *(L)* Okay, is there anything you would suggest in regard to any of his situation?

A: Slow down for strength of mind. 16

Q: *(L)* Okay, switch gears. Can you 17
comment on the strange nature of the events of the past two weeks ...

A: Learning is fun. 18

---

[5]I had described the situation to Ark in an email on the 22nd as follows:

> [I was driving my daughter to her job.] On the way there, stopped at a light, the engine sort of surged and I looked at all the gauges to see if there was a problem and saw that I had no gas. Happened to be stopped right in front of a gas place, and no one was coming, so I just turned in and got the gas. But, it startled me because I know I had just under half a tank yesterday, and the only places I drove were to the supermarket yesterday morning, and to pick [my daughter] up at 3:30. And my brother has warned me strongly not to ever let the van run out of gas because of the electronic fuel injection system.
>
> Well, it was strange. But no stranger than the story Patrick told me of waking up to find creepy little alien guys trying to pry his jaw open and that they wanted him to help them "do something" to [my daughter]. I was convinced that whatever it was, it was real to him. Then [my daughter] asked me about it while driving. I told her that I was really puzzled by everything and I wish I could figure it all out. You have to remember that Patrick's mother, Pat Z, was the subject under hypnosis on the night the UFOs were seen all over the county and directly over my house. And that we later learned that not only her husband, Vic, had been employed as a govt. scientist, but she herself had also had a high-level security clearance and worked for some department I can't remember just now. And at the present time, both of his parents seem to be deteriorating into psychotic behavior which really started when [my daughter] persuaded Patrick to quit taking the drugs his mother insisted he needed. (He quit, has had very little problem.) I actually think that, in the beginning, he thought that all parents were control freaks and manipulators like his, and I suppose that is why he had a little problem at first adjusting here.
>
> But, anyway, [my daughter] was concerned and so was I. I told her that I had a similar experience to what he described, but that the chief problem for me was that I just simply could not believe these things for a very long time. And all the books I read did not mean as much as the one or two very tiny physical traces that happened in my experience which did convince me that something was happening that had some level of objective, physical reality.
>
> I don't really know what to think. The kid is trying, but the games being played by his parents are the most vicious I have ever heard of. His father actually told his grandfather that Patrick was not his, so the grandfather ought not to send him gifts or leave him anything when he died. And this was because he was angry at Patrick, who was just a young kid at the time. And yesterday, Pat called [my daughter] at work. The receptionist took the call, and said the [daughter] was on another line. So Pat delivered a long rambling message about Vic being in critical condition in the hospital and if Patrick did not call her immediately, she was going to call the police. And, the only reason she wanted this message given to [my daughter] was because her son was living at our house and the phone had blocked her calls.
>
> Yes, I DID block her number after she called here over and over again threatening Patrick; and his sister would call and leave messages using filthy language on my answering machine.
>
> I just think that calling my daughter's job and saying all those sorts of things to a complete stranger is completely beyond the boundaries of civilized, rational behavior. That is the sort of thing that an ignorant, drunken, social misfit would do. Not an intelligent, articulate woman that Pat can be, or that I thought she was.

Q: *(L)* Was Patrick abducted in my house as he claims?[5]

A: Probe further and you will know.

Q: *(L)* Okay, talk to Patrick. Why is his mother going off into psychotic behavior?[6]

A: Not psychosis, neurosis.

Q: *(L)* Well, then I guess we are sup-

Well, I am just baffled, and that is all I can say. And I feel bad for Patrick, who seems to be handling it pretty well, but I am sure it is difficult.

[6] See previous footnote.

[7] UFO researcher of our acquaintance who went out to investigate Area 51 about six months previous to this session. I wrote to Ark about Fearon in an email on the 22nd:

> Now JW, the spook, just called again. I suppose it was to try another tactic. Yesterday's was to ask if I would do an exorcism which I refused. Today, it is a "regular spirit attachment" situation - only the guy is suicidal, and NOW, I am being offered 200 to do it (my usual fee, which I sometimes get or not, depending on the person's ability to pay, but I have never turned anyone down who could not pay, is 125 for the initial consultation and session, and a series of 3 subsequent sessions that are required at 75 per) The problem has always been that people who are in this condition are so debilitated that they have long ago lost the ability to work and then simply cannot pay anything. So, I was spending 3 or 4 days a week, exhausting myself doing this work, and getting nothing at all but further incapacitated. Which is why I decided that I cannot do it until I am completely healthy, if I decide to do it at all.
>
> Anyway, I turned down the one yesterday, and today he has another with some bucks attached, and also was massaging my ego by telling me that he lent my copy of "Life Between Life" to a fellow who used to be the Tai Chi master for the Gurdjieff school in upstate New York, and how happy he was that I made him aware of Dr. Whitton's work and so on and so on. So, this new case had an interesting thing that I thought it was odd that he mentioned: seems the guy fell on his left knee on Tuesday and broke it. So my ears perked up a little at that considering my fall on the left knee the other day...
>
> But, I don't trust all of this sudden activity all around me. I feel like there is an octopus with all sorts of tentacles trying to find an opening to me.
>
> He also informed me that Fearon Hicks was found hanged, believed to be by his own hand, in his motel room out in Nevada where he was purportedly investigating Area 51 - I had met Fearon at a conference, he was greasy and repulsive, and tried to keep touching me - but I am sorry he is dead. He was involved in the "Eddie Page Scandal" that I told you about before and I am a little hard about these things, but when people start wanting to believe in something, anything, so badly that they must grab the first dog and pony show that comes along and completely stop thinking at all, I get a little irritated. If Eddie Page had been even a little bit convincing, I could understand, but he was so blatantly a fraud!
>
> Frank and I watched a tape of him supposedly talking in his "Pleiadian" language to another person who was also supposed to be talking in the same language. Frank is very good with sounds (I am not, I don't remember a lot of what people tell me, but almost ALL of what I see or read) and he automatically was counting the sounds this guy was using and was able to repeat them back and show that the same series of 4 or 5 sounds was used over and over and over with almost no variation, yet the translation was a very complicated explanation of a Pleiadian ship construction. And the other person was making nonsense noises that sounded like a cartoon imitation of Chinese.
>
> So, is it any wonder that I avoid these people and their absurd little games and fantasies? The unfortunate thing is that people who are having some very legitimate and disturbing experiences get taken in by all this, probably as much out of fear as anything else.

posed to be figuring it out as we go ...

24 **A**: Yup!

25 **Q**: *(T)* Is Fearon H___[7] dead?

26 **A**: Yes.

27 **Q**: *(L)* Did he commit suicide as we were told?

28 **A**: No.

29 **Q**: *(L)* Was he murdered?

30 **A**: No.

31 **Q**: *(T)* Was it an accident?

32 **A**: No.

33 **Q**: *(L)* Well, how does one get hung by the neck if it is not an accident or suicide or murder?

34 **A**: He was not hung.

35 **Q**: *(T)* That's what I figured. But he *is* dead?

36 **A**: Yes.

37 **Q**: *(J)* How did he die?

38 **A**: Stroke.

39 **Q**: *(T)* Well, I can believe that. He popped every pill he could find. He was in terrible health.[8]

(T) What is wrong with my computer?

40 **A**: Offset files. Tangled web, being fed by incorrect steps to correct. Need to back up all data, then clean drive. Shortcuts won't do it, and it is not as tedious as you think. But not doing it will be![9]

41 **Q**: *(T)* Thank you ...

42 **A**: You are welcome ... Minor Cassiopaean "glitch," sorry!

43 **Q**: *(T)* About Flight 800. Pierre Salinger claims that the info floating around on the internet is accurate. He says that the Navy downed the flight.

44 **A**: Close. Pierre Salinger is an impeccable journalist and not one to "fly off the handle."

45 **Q**: *(T)* Very true. And that is why I am amazed that the rest of the journalism community is attacking him.

46 **A**: Why should you be amazed? They are "bought and paid for."

47 **Q**: *(T)* What did happen to Flight 800?

48 **A**: This was the result of an experiment gone awry. So was KAL "007" in 1983.

49 **Q**: *(L)* What was the nature of the experiment?

50 **A**: Testing of secret impulse guidance system using civilian airliner as an arbitrary "bounce" guidance target. Instead, it became the "homing" target, and a different aircraft became the bouncer. This was because the programmers did not anticipate the lower than expected altitude of the 747. Warning: this must stay in this room for the present!!!!!!!!!!! The facts will eventually be discussed by others. At that time, the danger is lifted.[10]

I told JW I would think about this second case, intending to ask you what you think. I would get paid for it and we do need the money. So maybe I should not worry about the octopus.

[8]See this forum thread for additional info:
http://cassiopaea.org/forum/index.php?topic=12503.0

[9]This suggestion was followed, and worked.

[10]See Wikipedia's article "TWA Flight 800 conspiracy theories".

Now, about KAL 007 ... that one is not dangerous to know. The plane was deliberately instructed to fly off course in order to trigger the Soviet's Pacific air defense system, to "see what they were made of" in that area. The plane was lost, but the experiment worked. They did not expect them to shoot down a civilian airliner. Now, all moving targets create electronic impulses. These can be "read" by the proper extremely high tech equipment. Older radar guided systems are subject to malfunctions in weather conditions that are severe, as one example. Also, the impulse system is an offshoot of the electromagnetic pulse experiments being carried out at Montauk, Brookings and elsewhere as part of the HAARP project! In connection with Pentagon missile tests, HAARP has many interesting tie-ins, not the least of which is your cell phone towers.

Now, the homing target can be any moving object. It can be whatever is entered on the computer. It can be a squirrel in a tree, a jogger on the beach, a building, whatever you want. The system looks for any moving target in order to establish recognition to the computer, in order to establish recognition of match pattern of pulse. TWA 800 was flying at the exact same altitude that was supposed to be designated for the "drone" craft. The drone plane was farther out at sea. The "bounce" target was to be any moving object in the air within 400 square miles.

Q: *(L)* So, TWA 800, through a series of problems, happened to find itself at the right altitude, a restricted altitude, within the parameters of the experiment. Anything further on this?

A: Not for now.

Q: *(L)* Okay, let's move on to Courtney Brown. *(T)* We all know who he is, and what he is writing about in regard to remote viewing ... what is it all about?

A: Vague.

Q: *(T)* Is the book Courtney Brown wrote, *Cosmic Voyage*, concerning the Martian population ...

A: It is true that there are underground bases on Mars, but they are Orion STS.

Q: *(T)* Are there Martians as portrayed by Courtney Brown?

A: Not exactly. He is portraying the Orion STS as the Martians.

Q: *(T)* Is Courtney Brown a government disinformation agent?

A: More as an "agent provocateur."

Q: *(T)* Is he working for the government?

A: Not directly, and remember, the government is not one entity.

Q: *(L)* Who is primarily backing Courtney Brown?

A: Rockefeller group.

Q: *(L)* Is Mike Lindemann and company part of this Rockefeller group at this time?

A: Yes.

Q: *(L)* Linda Howe?

A: No.

Q: *(T)* Did Courtney actually do remote viewing to obtain the information in the book?

A: Not really. Not needed.

Q: *(T)* Does this mean that the whole story is concocted on his part?

A: Semi. Elements of it are factual.

73 **Q:** *(T)* Yes. I could see that there were factual elements. I could also see that there was a *lot* that was questionable, that conflicts with *everything* else that has come out from other researchers. This is all totally twisted and different.

74 **A:** Close.

75 **Q:** *(T)* Is Courtney able to do remote viewing?

76 **A:** Yes.

77 **Q:** *(T)* But he did not use it with this book?

78 **A:** No.

79 **Q:** *(T)* So, the book was made up the way it is. It is a story. Some factual information, some invented information, some pure BS thrown in to fluff it out. So, the book is *not* an account of work that has come from remote viewing sessions?

80 **A:** No, but not needed.

81 **Q:** *(L)* You have said twice that remote viewing was not 'needed'. Where did he get his information?

82 **A:** Secret sources. Agents of the "nation of the third eye."

83 **Q:** *(J)* What or who is the "Nation of the Third Eye"?[11]

84 **A:** Terran civilization under the surface.

85 **Q:** *(L)* Now, wait a minute. I remember that when they said the Aryans were brought from Kantek, and that they were 'sturdier', or something like that, and I remarked that it seemed that they would be less sturdy – and the Cs answered: "on the surface". Now, that has always bothered me. I don't think they meant 'surface appearances'. Have the Aryans been glorified as the 'master race' because they are more suited to living underground?

86 **A:** Close. All types there are "Aryan."

87 **Q:** *(L)* Okay, is this a Terran underground civilization that has been 'managed' by Orions, or did it develop on its own?

88 **A:** One at a time.

89 **Q:** *(L)* Did the underground civilization develop on its own?

90 **A:** Yes.

91 **Q:** *(L)* Is it managed or manipulated by Orions as well?

92 **A:** Yes.

93 **Q:** *(L)* Are these 'managers' Orions from other densities?

94 **A:** Yes and no.

95 **Q:** *(L)* I don't understand. Are there some that are 4th and some that are 3rd?

96 **A:** The human types there are "bi-density."

97 **Q:** *(L)* Holy Shiite Moslems!

98 **A:** Grays and Lizards are 4th density. They can "visit" 3rd density, but they must keep returning to 4th in order to "regenerate."

99 **Q:** *(T)* Are you saying that the human/Aryan types can exist as long as they want in any density?

100 **A:** In 4th and 3rd.

---

[11] "The third eye (also known as the inner eye) is a mystical and esoteric concept referring to a speculative invisible eye which provides perception beyond ordinary sight." See Richard Cavendish, ed. (1994). *Man, Myth and Magic* – Volume 19. New York, NY: p. 2606.

101 **Q:** *(L)* They can move back and forth, existing with equal ease on either density?

102 **A:** Well, not with "equal ease," because 4th density is easier, naturally.

103 **Q:** *(T)* So, the information Courtney Brown was given to write this quasi-fiction book, is about the Aryans and not about the Martians?

104 **A:** "Martians" is easier to understand for the less well-informed, not to mention any discussion of the densities!

105 **Q:** *(T)* Absolutely. Martians are easier to accept. A lot easier to understand than densities! *(L)* Okay, 'Third Eye' – what is this?

106 **A:** That is what they call themselves when pressed for an explanation by surface types, such as yourselves. They were the inspiration for Masonic lore and Illuminati, too.

107 **Q:** *(L)* Does this 'Third Eye' designation have a connotation of third-eye abilities as we understand them?

108 **A:** Psychic.

109 **Q:** *(T)* Does Courtney know he has been had?

110 **A:** He has not been "had." He is under the employ of those who pull the levers, so to speak.

111 **Q:** *(L)* You said "pull the levers." Is Courtney Brown a robot, Greenbaumed, mind-controlled, implanted, or any or all of the above? *(T)* Or is he just foolish?

112 **A:** No. Not so foolish, he does not worry about paying the power bill. As Forest Gump said: "Stupid is as stupid does."

113 **Q:** *(L)* Are you implying that I am foolish or stupid because I *do* worry about paying the power bill?

114 **A:** No, we are not implying that you are stupid, or foolish, for that matter ... But, Courtney Brown is not either. Who is he hurting? And, he has hit the jackpot with this one. Knowledge can be procured by reading literature, then analyzing it.

115 **Q:** *(T)* Is the time-table that he has given correct?

116 **A:** Close.

117 **Q:** *(T)* So, the powers that be are going to follow this time table and present the Aryans as Martians?

118 **A:** No.

119 **Q:** *(L)* Are the Aryans going to present themselves as Martians?

120 **A:** Initially. In order for the Terrans to get used to the idea of EBEs.

121 **Q:** *(T)* But, they are not the good guys. Beware of Greeks bearing gifts.

122 **A:** Some of the "good guys" are identical in appearance.

123 **Q:** *(T)* Is this a subterfuge on the part of the Aryans so that they can slide in quietly and take over?

124 **A:** No, they do not need that at all. It is a way for the "government" to introduce everyone to the new reality of the existence of intelligent life all over the place, not just here.

125 **Q:** *(T)* So, they have their own agenda, but it is not what Courtney presented in the book.

126 **A:** It does not matter. The book is a somewhat altered "New Reality 101."

127 **Q:** *(A)* [Via email] Where should I turn now concerning research subjects?

128 **A:** Not very specific, but due to the constraints, we will do our best. Suggest focus on larger horizon of current search.

You are limiting yourself because of recent trend for more calculation. This is restricting you. Have you delved fully into field generators?

129 **Q:** *(A)* Which field to look at? Electromagnetic? Gravitational? Other?

130 **A:** Of course it is up to you, but why not combine the two, since they are in reality perfectly balanced and "interwoven" in nature!

131 **Q:** *(A)* Should I abandon my work on quantum theory?

132 **A:** Again, as with all, it is up to you. But, if we were you, we would not.

133 **Q:** *(A)* Should I look into the electromagnetic rail-guns problem?

134 **A:** Maybe, but first you must establish a link that you have pondered before but set aside. You set many questions aside. Patience serves the "questor of hidden knowledge" well!

135 **Q:** *(A)* Can you be more specific about the link you have in mind?

136 **A:** Yes, but we will not, because you must do the discovery here, in order for the progress to be reestablished.

137 **Q:** *(A)* Is the subject of my research at all important? If so, why?

138 **A:** Of course it is! You are on a predestined mission as you have always instinctively known. Recently though, you have developed a greater awareness of this. Self-doubts are merely the result of crises in your personal life. Please do not confuse this with your work.

139 **Q:** *(A)* Which branch of physics is closest to understanding of inter-density communications?

140 **A:** Theoretical.

141 **Q:** *(A)* Which branch of mathematics?

142 **A:** Two of them: calculus and algebra.

143 **Q:** *(A)* Should I look into zero-point energy problem?

144 **A:** That one should be "set aside." Because it will lead to a "dead end."[12]

145 **Q:** *(A)* Are the extra-dimensions beyond those of space and time relevant?

146 **A:** What "extra dimensions?"

147 **Q:** *(A)* Is time multi-dimensional? If so, is it three-dimensional?

148 **A:** Not correct concept. Time is not a dimension. This is very complex from your standpoint, but let us just say that time is "selective," or "variable."

149 **Q:** *(A)* I thank you for tonight. Any other comment to ponder about before the next session?

150 **A:** Ask, if needed, for a comment on the last responses.

151 **Q:** *(A)* Yes, a comment is needed. I am confused about space, time, Einstein's general relativity, gravitation and electromagnetism.

152 **A:** Einstein's Theory of Relativity is only partially correct. That is why we say that there is no "dimension" of time. As far as gravity and electromagnetics are concerned, we suggest a review of the as yet publicly unfinished Unified Field Theory of the same gentleman. Was it completed and put into application in secret? Hmmmmm ... And, if so,

---

[12]It's hard to tell what the Cs meant by this. Either they were suggesting that people who engage in this type of research end up dead (if they succeed), or that the subject itself is nonsense, a 'dead end'.

what are the ramifications? Maybe you could make the same discoveries.

Q: *(L)* Any last comment?

A: Slow down for strength of mind.

End of Session

November 30, 1996

Patrick Z's father died this day. Patrick was very upset and, since he was staying in our house, camping on the playroom sofa, we were upset too. I felt so sorry for him because his mother and sister were behaving like lunatics.[1]

---

[1]For those who are curious about the Patrick Z saga, which was running in the background, I wrote to Ark about it before the session as follows:

> It has been a rather "different" evening, in some ways, same in others. The usual nap before a session, and then, I woke up and came in the office and [my daughter] was crying. Seems that the story is that Patrick's mother has convinced him to jump right back into the mind-game soup using his dead father as bait. So, he is ready to quit this job he wanted so much, and which is so excellent in terms of experience and possibility for advancement, and the pay is not terrible either, (graphics and layout department of a small newspaper) and go back to running the shop that has been a bone of contention and grief, and has not made enough to pay its overhead ever since his mother bought it to tie him to her. And, on top of that, [my daughter] is EXTREMELY upset that he would even consider such a thing after the way she has behaved and threatening [daughter] and illegally harassing her at her job. And, I am sorry that I have to agree. I just think the only reason he has done what he has is because he has been feeding on [my duaghter's] energy. I SEE it, but am forced to keep my mouth shut because it is her lesson and I don't want to drive a wedge between us.
>
> What his mother is saying and doing, I have no idea. I can imagine, though. The father is conveniently dead now (JUST today!!! These people are Neanderthal!) and all is blamed on him - all behavior, all upsets, all control games, everything is going with him to the vault! And all Patrick has to do is come back to kowtow to Mama!
>
> So, what did [my daughter] do? She told him that if this was his choice, she didn't want to see him again. And then she was crying.
>
> I tried to help by telling her that she did the right thing because I just did not think he had the inner fortitude to EVER stand on his own, and that she would be feeding him energy like I did [my ex] until she hated him... and she just asked me to stop because I was making it worse. Well, I don't know what else to say. That is what I needed to hear when I was holding to a decision like that.
>
> So, she wanted me to go get her some ice cream. I didn't think that ice cream was the appropriate response, but I didn't say anything and went and got it. When I came back, Patrick was here and they are outside on the porch talking and I have no idea what is going on.
>
> He will probably try to persuade her that all is going to work, that she must make allowances for his mother and sister and all their sick behavior, and his own sick behavior going back to a proven business flop and tossing over a good job and good experience...
>
> God!!!! I hope she does not fall for it!!!!! And she is so vulnerable just now! I like Patrick. I feel VERY sorry for him. But he will NEVER do anything if he does not get free of his mother's sick obsession with him.

Again, Ark participated via email and that added a unique energy to the session.

Participants: 'Frank', Laura, Ark (via email), Terry, Jan

A: Hello

Q: *(L)* Hello, and who do we have with us this evening?

A: Jxoin.

Q: *(L)* And where are you transmitting from tonight?

A: Cassiopaea.

Q: *(L)* You said previously that time was 'selective and variable'. What, exactly, does this mean?

A: By "selective", we mean simply to think of time as if it were like your jukebox. There are many selections there, you may play them as you choose. But you need not play them sequentially, unless that is all you know. The selections are always there, are they not?

Q: *(L)* Well, that is crazy! You can't just go around having things happening in random order?!

A: Random is in the eyes of the perceiver.

Q: *(L)* What is it that causes us to only be able to perceive time in a sequential way?

A: DNA restructuring, as in the handiwork of our friends, STS 4th density.

Q: *(L)* Is there any possibility of regaining or restructuring this DNA?

A: Was there, will be again. You wanna know all there is to know about time, quantum reality, et cetera? Then it is time for you, and especially Arkadiusz, to study all that you can about the "crop circles," and closely network with those studying them directly.

Q: *(L)* Why crop circles?

A: The answers to all the questions are, or will be there.

Q: *(L)* You said that crop circles represented thoughts from 6th density. What does this mean?

A: We are compiling an almanac as well as a manual for the entire Terran population there. The reason we are doing this, is that there are millions who want to know the answers on the eve of the Grand Cycle Transformation. However, there are precious few that have chosen to try this form of communication, thus opening up a conduit.

Q: *(L)* Well, how many people are going to be able to understand?

A: But it would not be in form with Prime Level 7 Directive to limit entirely the availability of supreme knowledge!!!

Q: *(L)* So you are trying to put the entire story out there for all the world to see?

A: Not "trying," we are, my dear.

Q: *(L)* Okay, crop circles are a language, so to speak. Are they in some way related to mathematics?

A: Mathematics is the one and only true universal language.

Q: *(L)* Well, I just don't see how they can be decoded.

A: In this room is all the mental power needed, with addition of another "room" in Wroclaw, of course, that is needed to "crack" the code of our circles.

26 **Q:** *(L)* How do we start?

27 **A:** All one needs is a foundational point to build a computer program. And we have given you this already.

28 **Q:** *(L)* But nobody wants to hear what we have been saying!

29 **A:** Well, the circles are undeniable in their existence, our communication with you is deniable.

30 **Q:** *(L)* Well, if they don't want to hear it as it is channeled, what makes the crop circles different?

31 **A:** Not point. If you can crack the code, this becomes an undeniable language that is ongoing, consistent, and demonstrable.

32 **Q:** *(L)* So, you mean that if we can show what they mean, have it make sense, and then interpret others as they come into being, or show others how ...

33 **A:** Self-explanatory and yes.

34 **Q:** *(L)* At one point you mentioned that I needed to learn mathematics, which can be a years-long effort. And now, Ark is a mathematician. Was this a clue that Ark was to be part of this?[2]

35 **A:** Ark was coming into the picture all along. All is eternal, time is selective. We can see the entire jukebox menu selection at all "times."

[Break, Ark joins group via email.]

36 **Q:** *(L)* Okay, Ark has a question: "How does one distinguish an authentic crop circle from a fake one?"

37 **A:** Authentic ones are intricate in design and meticulous in the detail of their construction. The reality is that there have only been a few "fake" crop circles

---
[2] *Secret History* 12
[3] See session 2 November 1994.

in the entire history of the phenomenon worldwide, anyway.

38 **Q:** *(L)* Ark asks: "To crack the code, is it sufficient to have a collection of pictures?" I'm sure he means crop circle pictures.

39 **A:** Yes, to start with.

40 **Q:** *(L)* Ark says, to crack the code, we need an example. Can you point some out? *(T)* Example, as in crop circle pictures? *(L)* Well, no, how to crack it, or whatever.

41 **A:** Please review transcripts.

42 **Q:** *(L)* Can you tell us? I'm curious, too. What is it, is it about the using mathematics, or is it about something else?

43 **A:** You asked for interpretation of specific crop circles pictures before. Remember?!?[3]

44 **Q:** *(J)* We already did that, I already did the graphics for the ones we asked about last time. I have a whole file with nothing but crop circles. Didn't you send that to him? That's what we're talking about. We need other pictograms to ask about. *(T)* Oh, I know what we need. It's not just pictures of crop circles, we need the dimensions of the crop circles as well. You can't do anything math-wise if you don't know how big or whatever. *(A)* If Einstein's relativity is only partly correct, as pointed out last time, and this is because of the variable 'time', does this imply that the theory of relativity based on Galilei group is better than that based on Lorentz group?

45 **A:** Yes.

46 **Q:** *(L)* Why?

47 **A**: Because of the symmetric calculations they used as a basis for their efforts.

48 **Q**: *(T)* Where has the Lorentz group gone wrong?

49 **A**: Too complex to answer.

50 **Q**: *(A)* Is entropy the key concept that must be included into the unified field theory in order to include other densities into the equations?

51 **A**: Need to back up and reflect before proceeding. There is still a "missing link" that is earlier in the process. Any mathematics problem will collapse if there is a missing link.

52 **Q**: *(L)* Well if he goes back and finds that missing link, will he then need to include entropy into the equation – Into the theory – in order to include other densities?

53 **A**: Must find link before answer is given, otherwise it is useless information.

54 **Q**: *(A)* Can decoding of information from crop circles be automatized completely? Can this be done by a computer program, without human intervention, without work of mind?

55 **A**: Not likely, and what would be the benefit? Learning is necessary for progress of soul. Remember, we are not here to lead by the hand. We will help, but some answers are for you to decipher, and you have been extraordinarily good at this, my Arkadiusz, since very early childhood. This is how you are building your power center. All there is is lessons and learning is fun. More fun even than teaching.

56 **Q**: *(A)* Should I look into sonoluminescence? Are there causal time loops?

57 **A**: Q1: Yes. Q2: On the right track, now blend or unify. No polarities, please.

58 **Q**: *(T)* No polarities? *(L)* I have no ... none of us knows anything. *(T)* That's absolute. *(J)* What? *(T)* Well, if you don't have polarities, then it's absolute. It doesn't matter if the numbers are minus or plus. We're dealing in absolutes. *(A)* So, cracking the code is to be computer-assisted mind work, that is, human interpretation, assisted by computer program. Which branch of algebra will have to be used for that?

59 **A**: Not necessary to use algebra here.

60 **Q**: *(L)* Anything further on that? We should let him ask, actually ...

61 **A**: Such as?

62 **Q**: *(A)* I need guidance here. Can you give me some more specific than just work?

63 **A**: Please be more specific as to where, or with what, or how you wish to have guidance. All will be well and soon. [Ark signs off for the evening.]

End of session

December 8, 1996

At this point, Ark's arrival was finally set for February 11. There was some discussion between us as to whether or not he should allow his attorney to initiate public prosecution of his ex for stealing all his money (this episode is described in chapter 43 of *The Wave*). For the moment, we decided not to because that would simply help her achieve martyr status.

The Patrick Z saga was not yet over. He had moved back home after his father's death (keep in mind, his father was a guy who had worked on top secret research in an underground facility, and his mother had a top-secret security clearance!). On December 4th, I wrote to Ark:

> I was sitting and drinking a cup of tea when Patrick brought [my daughter] home. He was upset when he came in and said to me: "I want you to know that my mom is not vindictive! She really isn't. She has just been controlled by my dad..." and then went on to tell me that he wanted to make sure that I did not think he had "used" me. Well, I didn't know where this was coming from or what turned his switch on, so I assured him that I never thought he had used me. I asked him how he was feeling, he had a terrible, sad, bereft expression and said he was doing "terrible" because of the conflict between "the families." I asked him what he meant, because I was not aware of any conflict. He said that [my daughter] and I now had a terrible opinion of his mother and sister and they "aren't really like that," (could have fooled me!). So I just told him: "Patrick, maybe I'm cynical and disillusioned, but I have observed a lot in my 44 years. And, one of the things I have noticed is that people ARE what they are, and it is only rare and extraordinary people who can rise above what they are, see it, and make deliberate choices to be different. And being able to SEE oneself and others is essential. There cannot be any lies. And when you start seeing a pattern of lies, I can assure you, it rarely changes. I have SEEN the dynamics that operate in your family before, particularly what was between your parents, though it was carried to an extreme with them, and it is, even NOW, following a predictable course." He interrupted and said: "Tell me what is going to happen?" I said: "No, I will not. I have said before all that needed to be said. You must make your own choices now." He said: "I just wish somebody would tell me what to do!"

And that rather stunned me. It actually made me feel a little nauseous. And I knew right then that there is very little hope for the kid. And just a little bit ago when [my daughter] came to kiss me good night, she said that she has told him that if he quits his job and goes back to being run around by his mother, that all is over. And I KNOW his mother is going to bring out every ploy in the book to get him completely back and sub digito! And, being as weak as he is, I expect him to go with his mother because [my daughter] expects him to actually DO something rather than whine and have tantrums.

I told [my daughter] the other morning that yes, I feel sorry for Patrick, but I think that he is so damaged from infancy that there is almost NO way he can overcome it. And, further, that these kinds of things are a matter of CHOICE at some level.

But then I thought about it. Pat is very much like [my ex's] mother. I rather think that they were not bad mothers with their infants. Very controlling women, both of them, so maybe that is the issue. I am not sure. What I AM sure of is that the treatment a child receives in the first 3 years is CRUCIAL to their later ability to deal with life. Maybe it's toilet training? I know that [my ex's] mother criticized me severely because I was never really anxious to get my babies out of diapers - I figured they are only babies once, let them have it as long as possible. She said that [my ex] was "potty trained" at 9 months! Well, I find that hard to believe since a child does not have conscious control of the related muscles until about the age of 3. And I have heard of several tragic cases where children have actually been beaten to death by a parent because they could not control their bowels at the age of 2!!! Now that I think of it, I am almost willing to bet that Patrick was potty trained VERY early.

Ark was traveling and was unable to participate in this session. It was a good one about crop circles and Stonehenge.

Participants: 'Frank', Laura, Terry, Jan, Alice

1 **Q**: *(L)* Hello.

2 **A**: Hello.

3 **Q**: *(L)* Who do we have with us this evening?

4 **A**: Honnorra.

5 **Q**: *(L)* And where are you from?

6 **A**: Cassiopaea.

7 **Q**: *(L)* We've been discussing the crop circles, and would like to know if you have any input on that subject? Input on what we've discussed, what we think to this point, and just basically any info?

8 **A**: Must begin with specific questions.

9 **Q**: *(L)* Okay. Do the multiple perimeters represent multiple densities?[1]

10 **A**: Partly.

---

[1] What I meant was like circles within circles, each having its own perimeter.

11 **Q:** *(L)* Are the crop circles themselves like antennae, or like homing devices for energy or thought patterns?[2]

12 **A:** No.

13 **Q:** *(L)* Is the chronology of their appearance important?[3]

14 **A:** Semi.

15 **Q:** *(L)* Is their location on the planet, in terms of longitude and latitude, significant?

16 **A:** Yes and no.

17 **Q:** *(L)* In what way yes?

18 **A:** Location, not latitude and longitude ... Those are merely measure markers.

19 **Q:** *(L)* If the location is significant, what is it about the location that is significant?

20 **A:** Magnetic generators of bonding frequency.[4]

21 **Q:** *(L)* Are you saying that magnetic generators of bonding frequency are located at those places, are in those places?

22 **A:** Port through them.

23 **Q:** *(L)* Okay, location and chronology ...

24 **A:** Why have you not brought up Stonehenge?[5]

25 **Q:** *(L)* Well, we talked about Stonehenge before, that it was an energy transducer, so to speak. So, was Stonehenge put there because of the location, or did Stonehenge create ... *(T)* Why don't you just ask what it is about Stonehenge? *(L)* Okay, what is it about Stonehenge?[6]

26 **A:** Location attracted those spirit types on the proper frequency, who in turn, placed stones in proper location to receive the coded communications in code telepathically, in order not to have to chase around the countryside reading encoded pictographs.[7]

27 **Q:** *(L)* What was the technique used within the circle to receive the information telepathically?

28 **A:** [Planchette spiralled in, and spiralled out demonstrating a motion.] Transcendent focused thought wave separation.

---

[2] *The Wave* 24

[3] I would like to see a chronological catalog of images of the circles.

[4] I should have asked "bonding what to what?"

[5] It's fascinating that the Cs brought up Stonehenge in the midst of this discussion about crop circles, which, as is well known, occur most frequently in England (as far as we know).

[6] *The Wave* 58

[7] Which suggests that "those spirit types on the proper frequency" could read crop circles. Well, it seems that a number of people claim to do so, but their readings vary and therefore, one ought to be careful in placing reliance on such things. Additionally, it seems that the Cs are suggesting that crop circles were happening in this area a very long time ago. I am reminded of the dowsing work of Lethbridge as discussed in my book *The Secret History of the World*, as well as the factor that the UK seems to have a lot of 'hauntings' and the Cs have said that much of this is just 'recordings' due to the electromagnetic nature of the landscape: specific types of rocks and underground water flow.

29 **Q:** *(L)* Okay, so that you're saying that moving in a spiral ...[8]

30 **A:** The spiral serves to translate message by slowing down the wave and focusing thought wave transference energy. Utilizes/transduces electromagnetic waves, the conduit, by breaking down signal from universal language of intent into language of phonetic profile.[9] This is for multiple user necessity.

31 **Q:** *(L)* Multiple user necessity implies that a number of people must do the spiral. Is that correct?

32 **A:** No. Must hear and feel and understand precisely the same thing.[10] The molecular structure of the rock, when properly sculpted sing to you.

33 **Q:** *(L)* Is there any possibility that Stonehenge still has any capacity along this line?

34 **A:** Has fragmented energy only.

35 **Q:** *(L)* Well, that's what I would imagine. *(T)* Question: Last week you mentioned that the majority of the crop circles are real, that very few are hoaxes. Am I to believe then, that the method that is used to create the circles that everybody's looking for, that there are multiple methods being used, depending on who or what is available at the time the circle is created? In other words, Doug and Dave may have actually made legitimate crop circles, only they don't know it, because they think they went out and made it their way?

36 **A:** No.

37 **Q:** *(T)* I just wondered if there's multiple things going on here. *(L)* No, I think it's all ... *(J)* So, is there only one method for a true crop circle?

38 **A:** Reading instead of listening ... decipher rather individually than comprehend universally ... crop circles rather than Stonehenge!!![11]

39 **Q:** *(L)* Are you saying that this is the method to pursue now, since of course Stonehenge is not available?

---

[8] I was assuming that the motion demonstrated with the planchette, the spiral, was what was meant. See sessions 23 October 1994, 7 November 1994, 9 November 1994, and 29 March 1996.

[9] Curiously, this suggests that phonemes – the basis of words – have some relation to a universal language of intent, or something like an information field.

[10] This is an almost exact description of Gurdjieff's "Esoteric Circle":

> "The inner circle is called the 'esoteric'; this circle consists of people who have attained the highest development possible for man, each one of whom possesses individuality in the fullest degree, that is to say, an indivisible 'I,' all forms of consciousness possible for man, full control over these states of consciousness, the whole of knowledge possible for man, and a free and independent will. They cannot perform actions opposed to their understanding or have an understanding which is not expressed by actions. At the same time there can be no discords among them, no differences of understanding. Therefore their activity is entirely coordinated and leads to one common aim without any kind of compulsion because it is based upon a common and identical understanding." (Gurdjieff, quoted in Ouspensky, *In Search of the Miraculous*]

[11] In other words, a reversal of the Stonehenge method of listening and group comprehension.

40 **A**: How are you gonna pursue. Who is gonna believe you?

41 **Q**: *(L)* Is that it? In other words, how are we gonna ...

42 **A**: Ok, folks, let's try to picture Laura and Ark trying to drag 500 ton rocks around New Port Richey?!?

43 **Q**: *(T)* Maybe they'll drag themselves!

44 **A**: No, for that, you must "hit" the right key![12]

45 **Q**: *(L)* Sound. Actually, what I had in mind was just going to England and checking out Stonehenge itself. *(T)* You can't get near it now unless you've gotten an okay from the government; they've got it all fenced off. *(F)* Why did they do that? *(T)* Because too many people were going there, like most of the other 'ancient wonders'. They can't let people near them anymore, because it's destroying them. *(L)* They carve their names, and ... *(T)* Well, not just that, the fact that people touch them, the moisture from their skin and like that, it's deteriorating them really bad. All the traffic around it was shaking the ground. They're falling apart faster than the pyramids are falling apart. *(L)* I want to switch gears here for a few minutes ...

46 **A**: Up to you.

47 **Q**: *(L)* I have to digest it at a certain level – you get to a certain point, and you get an overload. And then I'll be able to come back and ask more about it. One thing that is pressing on my mind, and I really want to get it out of the way, and we'll see what we come to after we have a little break.

[Remainder of session redacted: a few questions relating to legal issues of insurance settlement.]

End of Session

During this period of time, Ark and I had many breaks in the communication system that was adding a lot of stress. Computers went up and down, internet connections failed, etc. We felt like we were being stalked by dark forces determined to keep us apart. That turned out to be true and the 'signs' of the breakdowns were reflecting things going on in other spheres.

A couple of days after this session, Ark commented to me that, in reading the sessions, he noticed that I was sometimes able to provoke the Cs to give more information than they previously were willing to give. In response to this, I wrote to Ark:

> "Provoke" is certainly the right word! And you WOULD NOT BELIEVE some of the tactics I think of to get them to tell me things!!! For example, they will not answer any question that implies a judgment of any kind, so I cannot ask whether this person or that person is STS or STO or whatever. But, since they do not perceive any separation between minds, and all thought is held in common, they do not object to

---

[12] A reference to moving things via sound waves.

telling me what another person thinks or is thinking about any particular subject. So, I CAN SOMETIMES ask what so-and-so thinks in regards to me and therefore discover their intentions which may be veiled. There are some exceptions to this. They would NEVER tell me anything about [my ex] and they wouldn't tell me anything about you. It is, as they say, a destined mission and NO INTERFERENCE is allowed in terms of influencing choices. The only little, tiny things they gave me in the beginning were the clues: "You are being baffled, not buffeted." And: "New." And they only gave me these because I literally PLEADED with them to help me understand what was going on.

I think one of the most interesting things they said about it was in response to a question relating to what we are supposed to DO, ultimately. They gave a rather lengthy reply:

> "Too much too soon, my dear. There is so, so, so much in store!!!!!! What have we helped you to discover so far? would you rather discontinue this operation? We have helped you build your staircase one step at a time, because you asked for it. And you asked for it because it was your destiny. We have put you in contact with those or rare ability in order for you to be able to communicate with us. Again, because you desired it, in order to realize your path. By now, you should recognize the signs... Those who display thinking patterns which in many ways deviate from that which is considered ordinary. The more unusual, the more telling. Such persons are not oriented to the earth's frequency vibrations. [Frank] is one, but not the only one, just the one who awakened your sense of recognition. We have given the signs, but they are not necessarily the same with each individual. We suggest you avoid anticipatory exercises, as realization comes after the fact. [...] Appreciate the fact that you have been given the keys to end all this pain!!!! (And this remark still startles me. It relates to something else they said a couple of years ago: 'When you are in pain, all suffer...') [...] You need to be vigilant in your quest to help Ark in his efforts to get situated here. [How best to help?] Do not rely on your own ideas of how to handle each and every situation. This will take sharing and constant monitoring of every detail, in order not to overlook anything or make mistakes due to hastily chosen directives."

And then there was the answer to what happened to me when I had the vision:

> "Balancing of half-self. [What is a half-self?] Your starter version, relating to birth karmic imprint. [What is a birth karmic imprint half-self?] What you were assigned with at onset of this incarnation. [What was the purpose of the experience?'] What you started with must be periodically balanced at apex of significant junctures."

(This little dialogue still puzzles me. If a "half-self" was the "starter version," does this mean we get to be whole together when we leave? And "assigned?" Oy! Such a puzzle!)

And, I will confess that I DID ask what you were thinking of me once. This was in August. They only said: "What do YOU think he thinks? Please answer us!" So, I said that you thought that I might be your other half. Then they said: "So where does ego enter into it? Do you think he will reject you if you are honest? We suggest you spell out to him your exact circumstances and hide nothing!"

In any event, we were some 60 days away from meeting in the flesh at this point.

Ark's correspondent Jim, who had introduced him to the Cs material, was still writing what amounted to New Age nonsense. Ark sent these emails to me asking if it was possible to connect his claims about other dimensions to anything the Cs had said. I wrote back:

I don't think you will have much success with this. I get the impression, from what remarks of his I have read, that he does not fully grasp the concept of depth in terms of density. He talks as though "dimensions" were merely technologically accessible, and those beings who traverse these dimensions he talks about are 3rd density in essence, though very advanced in technology. He talks about the human race joining other races in space travel and exploration yet does not address the issue that human beings, with few exceptions, still want to lie and are full of greed and still are killing each other in astonishing ways and numbers. It is similar to Ruggero thinking that the only reason for govt. conspiracy was the "cold war" and now everyone can just "come clean" and tell all. Doesn't it occur to them that the "cold war" and every other kind of war has been deliberately created to confuse and obfuscate? That the secrets have been there for thousands of years and ARE subject to the penetration of very few? It is, indeed, the "story of the Evil Magician." And we ARE lunch. And the only ones who get to stop being thus are the ones who figure out that this density is the "far country" of the Prodigal Son and will NEVER be anything else, and then learn how to get out of it, or are at a certain frequency when some sort of "change" occurs so that they are naturally shifted into the next density. Just the way it is. There is no point in crying for milk and a diaper change, and wanting some great, mythical being to come down and clean up our mess and do away with the bad guys and make everything shiny and new again. Isn't gonna happen. All there is is lessons. And the first one to learn is that it IS a pigsty and the only way to get out of it is to first REALIZE that it is a pigsty, and then decide to get out of it and go home. Once this is realized, the "Father" sees "from a long way" off and will begin to assist in the journey by sending out the robe and the ring via servants, while preparing the fatted calf for the ultimate feast.

> Fixing 3rd density is not the objective. Getting out of it is. And this is only done by increasing light frequency, knowledge and awareness. It is not done by watching Star Trek and having some grandiose dreams of humankind being as honorable and morally correct as Captain Picard et al and joining some 3rd density space federation, wearing nifty uniforms, and "going where no man has gone before."
>
> This may not be the whole picture, but I think it is a good part of it.

After an exchange concerning our respective marriages, Ark sent me a quote from Gurdjieff:

> "Such is the nature of man, that for your first gift - he prostrates himself; for your second - kisses your hand; for the third - fawns; for the fourth - just nods his head once; for the fifth - becomes too familiar; for the sixth - insults you; and for the seventh - sues you because he was not given enough"

On that topic, I responded:

> You know, the C's say that about 70% of the Bible, (mostly Old Testament) has been corrupted by the negative forces that dominate this world. Yet, respecting the NT, I never could find any resonance in me to "turning the other cheek." I can definitely see walking away from something unpleasant, but not staying to get hit again if you know it is coming.
>
> And on the topic of the Bible, there are many, many, absolute contradictions in there that no amount of theological interpretation can reconcile. Even St. Augustine wrote that fear must be used to inspire people to convert. And, the most unsettling thing I ever read was the Egyptian Book of the Dead which is much older than the story of Jesus etc, yet in there is almost word for word an identical myth. The main exception is that the blood that is shed for remission of sins is the birth blood of the Divine Virgin, Isis, who is impregnated by Osiris from the "heavens." And the Divine Son, Horus is also known as Iesus, and becomes the Divine Mummy, to rise from the dead to set the example for resurrection etc. St. Ireneus, says that Jesus lived to be a much older man than 33. He also decried the attempts of the church to convert pagans by making Jesus into Horus according to the "Egyptian Rites." And funny that Jesus started his ministry at the age of 30, traveled about for, as the gospels say, ONE year, and then was crucified at 33. Time must have been VERY variable then! Lots of funny stuff going on there.
>
> Yes, when I read what Gurdjieff said about humanity, I was appalled. That is one of the occasions when I threw the book against the wall. But, after I laid there and thought about it for a while, went over in my mind all that I knew and had experienced through people, I began to think that he might be right. But, of course, I did not have enough perspective

December 8, 1996

to see how it applied to me. I used to think that some people were just like cardboard cut-outs - no deeper than a quarter of an inch. And I would experiment with this by talking to people and asking questions and trying to find what was inside them and what they thought, how they thought, and so on. And I was shocked to discover that some people simply do not ever, ever, ever think about anything at all!

I will never forget a neighbor who came over to our house one day and began to talk about how inspired he was by a fictional television movie about the crucifixion of Christ. He said, "Did you know this was a TRUE story!! There was a soldier who felt sorry for Jesus and helped his family escape!!!" and he was SO amazed. So, I said him: "That is probably just a little creative license. No one knows for sure if it happened or how." He was shocked that I didn't trust this TV story. "Oh, yes, it was true! It was on TV!" I asked: "How could they know? The only thing we know about the life of Jesus is what is in the Bible and that story certainly is not in the Bible. Haven't you ever read the Bible?" His answer was: "Read? Read? No! You know you can't trust what you read!!!"

So, I gave up on that one!

December 14, 1996

The notes to the 23 November 1996 session include excerpts from an email to Ark regarding a request to do some hypnotherapy that I felt was something of a trap. Just a few days before this session, that topic came up again in an email as follows:

> I just told him that my health does not permit me to do any hypnotherapy at this time and then gave him the names and numbers of a couple of other therapists in the area.
>
> I also told him that if the guy was as bad as he says he is, it probably wouldn't do any good anyway over the long term. People don't get that way without choosing it at some level. And if the choice at that level doesn't change, all the therapy in the world isn't going to help them. And, if the choice at that level changes, they don't need the therapy. And that is what I have observed over and over again. Which is why I am so disinclined to get involved in it again. If a person really is suffering, they will do whatever is necessary to end the pain. And it usually involves gaining knowledge. If they are not at that point, no one can give it to them without effort on their part. There is no free lunch. And until we learn that, we ARE lunch.

I was working daily on the project of getting all the sessions transcribed and sending them to Ark as they were completed. In addition to the mundane accounts of our daily doings, there was some discussion of what it was going to be like to actually meet, face to face. On that topic, I wrote to Ark:

> I am not really sure HOW it will be, and am really getting curious about it. How, exactly, is half a soul supposed to feel when face to face with the other half? I have never heard of or read a precedent... so I am unable to form any real image. None of the ones I have played with seem to last very long, so I don't think they are accurate. I think that we are both so private that a lifetime of restraint will switch on no matter what, and internally there will be some sort of transducer that will operate to prevent blowing all the circuits.

Ark's attorney was trying to move the case forward but the obstructionist behavior of the ex was thwarting every move. Ark bought a book that was supposed to counsel women through divorce so that he could have some guidelines of what to expect and how best to manage things. Everything in the book turned out to be wrong. It probably would have applied to a relatively normal person, but we aren't talking about a normal person here. And nothing 'ordinary' applied here at all. Also, during this time, we experienced a lot of our emails going into some cyber black hole and never showing up at all.

Meanwhile, the home-front situation was stressful due mainly to the presence of my mother in the house. I described an episode to Ark in an email:

> And NOW, I have just finished blowing a gasket at Mother. REALLY BLEW UP! MAJOR EXPLOSION! Even slammed a door in her face. Don't know why, but didn't know what else to do either.
>
> You see, she is a controlling, negative, manipulating person. It has been like walking a tightrope keeping all under control. Since I SEE what she is doing, it cannot affect me in an ordinary way, so, it has devolved onto the kids. Just as with [my ex].
>
> I appreciate very much the fact that she has more or less taken over the kitchen and cooking except for certain things. I DO appreciate it. But she uses it as a platform of control. And, through this platform she continuously sets an example of how NOT to raise children who have faith and hope.
>
> One thing she does that has always driven me crazy is that she calls for this person or that person to "Come!" And, almost without exception, it is for an entirely useless or absurd reason. And she does not seem to care that the person, whoever it is, may be deeply involved in something that IS important, if only to them. For example: I could be sitting in the middle of a pile of papers, sorting and filing and holding things in my mind so that I can finish - and she will call "Come!" So I ask: "What do you need?" She will say: "I said Come!" So, I will dump everything and lose all my work to go and she will say: "Do you think I need to put _____ on the shopping list?" And the steam starts coming out of my ears!!!! Over and over and over she does this. And has done it all my life. It is a power trip for her.
>
> So, NOW, when she says to me: "Come!" I say: "I will only come if you tell me what you need me for and if I decide that it is more important than what I am doing now." Which REALLY makes her furious, but she can't do anything about it.
>
> So, since she can't jerk ME around, she has been doing it to the kids and I have been constantly acting as a buffer. Several times a day I have to step in and mediate.

December 14, 1996

So, today, she is cooking. [My son] doesn't eat eggs because he is allergic to them. And his stomach is sensitive sometimes. So, instead of eating what she had cooked, he declined politely and took a carrot from the refrigerator to eat instead. Well, you would have thought that he took a gold bar from Fort Knox! She went off into a VERY NASTY monologue about what a selfish and inconsiderate and all sorts of other things kid he was, and we were all going to starve because there was no more food to eat and so on and so on.

And, yes, it is understandable that she is concerned about this BUT, just yesterday afternoon we discussed exactly how we are going to manage and I made it clear that I do NOT want her to express such things in front of the children because how are they going to learn to have faith if the adults around them don't have it? And getting hysterical over where the next meal is coming from is simply a lack of faith. If there is no more food, we simply will not eat, but we will do it with faith that the condition will change.

So, I explained all of this to her, and also have repeatedly ask her not to call my children to "come!" as if they were dogs and not human beings. And I have pointed out to her that I have very definite motives behind everything I do where the children are concerned, and I would appreciate it if she would honor those objectives and support them whether she agrees or not. They are, after all, MY children.

So, when she started on this attack on [my son], I said to her repeatedly: "Mother, please drop it. We can discuss it later." (Same thing I would say to [my ex] in a similar situation.) So, after a number of repetitions from me, she finally stopped. THEN, [my son] was in the next room and she demanded "Come!" and he came and said, very nicely considering how she had abused him: "Yes, Grandma, what do you need?" And she launched off on a nasty diatribe: "What do I NEED? It's not me that needs anything! How dare you ask me what I need! You need to learn some respect and consideration and that when I cook something to eat that you better eat it or you won't have anything to eat..." and it deteriorated from there.

And I snapped. I even told her that the only reason I stayed with [my ex] so long, (who she hated BECAUSE she was used to controlling me) was because I had been well trained by her to be a doormat and that I was not going to allow her to do the same thing to my children. And then I told her that I simply could not believe that she could not remember from one day to the next the issues related to this that had been discussed, and that either she was evil or stupid. This didn't faze her a bit! She came to the door and started telling me that it was ME who didn't understand that we are on the verge of starving... so I slammed the door in her face.

Yes. I know the situation. But I also know that without faith I am lost.

And I cannot let her destroy the children's peace with her constant negativity and nasty remarks about how we are going to starve every time they put a bite of food in their mouths. I am SURE we will manage. I don't know how, but maybe I don't HAVE to know how.

And it is not like I am not AWARE of the situation, or that I do not think of anything I can DO, and do it if I can. But the point is to just see what can be done, do it, and have faith and not talk constantly about what you don't have, but look forward to unlimited possibilities and demonstrate this in thought, word, and deed. And be kind and loving to each other, especially to the children. And she just doesn't get it! And I tell her over and over and over and over again, in detail, with examples and citations...

Well, the C's told me a long time ago that she was one of the main avenues of attack against me. And, what Gurdjieff said is certainly true. When you subside to the takers, no one learns anything or gains anything. And, for me, it is of the utmost importance that the children learn in a natural way, as much as possible, both the principles of faith and of consequences.

And, even though I was almost shouting at her, I didn't say one thing that wasn't true and didn't need to be said.

She has gone to her room and shut the door. The kids have come in one by one and hugged me and kissed me and said they were sorry I was upset and they loved me. And I just wish she could understand and SEE. I want everything to work and everybody to be happy, including her, but she just can't seem to give up the controlling manipulations, or to LEARN a different way. I guess it comes down to the "no change" principle. Just isn't gonna happen. But, then, what am I going to do? I can't tolerate the constant little meannesses that come from her, especially when directed at the children. What am I gonna do?

Well, we will wait for the dust to settle and see what happens.

Jan just called and we discussed the mother situation and she made the remark that my mother is exactly like her mother was, and that she always called her mother "teflon" because not only did nothing ever "sink in" that she told her, but it also just "slid right off."

This is exactly it, and [my ex] was the same! A rather clever analogy.

She told me I was a saint to try to deal with it and I told her that my halo was on the floor in pieces right now!

Indeed, our situation was close to desperate and being physically disabled and unable to work was deeply frustrating to me. What was interesting was that quite a number of people used my situation as a criticism of the Cs. "If the Cs are real, why don't they give you winning lottery numbers?" We talked about this sometimes before sessions, though we had long been disabused of the notion that the Cs were a source that would do that and possibly interfere with our learning processes.

Just a few hours before this session, I wrote to Ark:

> Now, since I am worrying, I will just tell you. Nothing we can do about it, but I will feel better.
>
> I have to pay the phone bill tomorrow and the water bill by next Friday and I have to pay for a prescription today that the insurance won't cover. I am out of drinking water and personal products.
>
> And, I have probably 50 cents.
>
> So, there. The C's say everything will be "fine and soon." Let's see how THIS one works!!!!

Despite the fact that there were many worries on both sides, Ark and I had been discussing the 11 November 1995 session, hypnotizability, and crop circles and that is the reason I brought up those topics in this session.

Participants: 'Frank', Laura, Terry, Jan

1 **Q**: *(L)* Hello.

2 **A**: Hello.

3 **Q**: *(L)* And who do we have with us?

4 **A**: Usarro.

5 **Q**: *(L)* And where are you from?

6 **A**: Cassiopaea.

7 **Q**: [Advice to Terry and Jan about upcoming Christmas trip which had been topic of discussion before session.] *(L)* Okay, and I have been doing a tape a day, I have been an extremely good girl. I just wanted to point that out to you guys. *(T)* Send Santa! *(L)* Yes! Send Santa! *(J)* Well, Santa already came! *(L)* Oh, I know, but we want millions of dollars here!

8 **A**: Yes.

9 **Q**: *(L)* We want 'Lotto Santa'! *(T)* Yes, the regular Santa doesn't bring those kinds of things!

10 **A**: Gotta hava lotto patience!

11 **Q**: [Groans at bad pun.]

12 **A**: But, patience pays, yes?

13 **Q**: *(L)* Oh, yes it does. *(T)* Now, you've just got to find out what numbers to be patient with! *(L)* Got any numbers to be patient with? *(J)* Oh, you know they're not going to tell you that...! *(T)* ... six digits between one and 49. Take your pick, there's 13 million of them!

14 **Q**: *(L)* Along the lines of some of the things that I have been working on recently, I'd like to ask if there's any more information you can give to us about the hypnotic-opener-strobe effect,[1] and what it is preventing us from seeing. Is this one of the things that keeps us from expanding into the next density,

---

[1] See session 18 November 1995.

in terms of awareness?

15 **A:** Not related to that. You see, the souls that are affected by all these "cloaking" techniques are vibrating on a low level anyway. The point is to block those who are blockable.

16 **Q:** *(T)* We're not blockable? *(L)* Is there anything we can do to avoid this blocking? *(T)* We're not being blocked ...

17 **A:** You are not blockable.

18 **Q:** *(T)* We are not being blocked. We're beyond the blocking.

19 **A:** If you were, would you be doing this?

20 **Q:** *(T)* That type of blocking technique doesn't work on us. There may be other blocking techniques, but that particular stuff doesn't work. We either see or don't see stuff, because we are either meant or not meant to see it. We don't see UFOs anymore, because we don't need to.

21 **A:** Not necessarily true.

22 **Q:** *(L)* Okay, what is not necessarily true? Why don't we see them anymore?

23 **A:** Don't does not equal won't. If a Buick does not go by, you don't see that, either! And if you are inside, doing the laundry when Mr. Jones decides to take the old "Electra" for a spin, you do not see him, or his precious car, do you?

24 **Q:** *(L)* I don't care, I've seen enough!

25 **A:** Oh, yes, you do care!!!

26 **Q:** *(L)* Okay, yes, I care, but I've seen enough; I believe, I believe!

27 **A:** It is not up to you whether you want to see them or not. If they want you to see them, you will!

28 **Q:** *(T)* So, if they want us to see them, we'll see them!

29 **A:** Yes, and they will, and you will!

30 **Q:** *(T)* They will and we will ... yes, but, there's a blocking technique being used on people to lower the vibrational frequency to prevent them from seeing them, right?

31 **A:** The blocking technique is for many things.

32 **Q:** *(T)* So that people do not understand what's going on around them.

33 **A:** Yes.

34 **Q:** *(L)* What else?

35 **A:** That is it, in a nutshell. See and know and think or ... See, know and think that which is desired.

36 **Q:** *(L)* Yes, and you know it's there. Okay, let me jump over to this other subject of the number 33 and the number 11. Is there anything beyond what was given on 11/11/95, that you could add at this time, about any of the mathematics or the use of these numbers?

37 **A:** Prime numbers are the dwellings of the mystics.

38 **Q:** *(L)* What do you mean, "prime numbers are the dwellings of the mystics"?

39 **A:** Self-explanatory, if you use the tools given you.

40 **Q:** *(L)* How can a number be a dwelling?

41 **A:** Figure of speech. [Planchette spirals several times, vigorously.] And how interesting that we have a new "cell" phone company called: "Primeco."

---

[2] Word association by group: encryption, cells of monks, prisons, prime number divisible by one or self.

Q: *(L)* And how does a cell phone company called Primeco relate to prime numbers being dwellings of mystics?

A: Not for us to answer.[2]

Q: *(L)* Is encryption the key?

A: Oh, there is so much here. One example is: "Snake eyes" is not so good as 7,11, eh?

Q: *(T)* They are all prime numbers, too; seven and eleven. *(L)* What kinds of documents or writings ... or what would be applicable ...

A: No, Laura you are trying to focus, or limit the concept, my dear. Think of it, what is the Judaic Christian legend for the creation of a woman?

Q: *(L)* That woman was taken from the rib of Adam. That Eve was created from the rib of Adam.

A: Ever heard of a "prime rib?"

Q: [Groans.] *(T)* I hate being in kindergarten and not knowing what the subject is. Okay, prime rib. We have a prime rib, so ...

A: What happens in a "primary."

Q: *(L)* An election. You narrow down the candidates. What happens in a primary?

A: Who gets "picked" to run?

(L) Okay, keep on ...

A: "Prime Directive?"

Q: *(L)* Okay.

A: "Prime time?"

Q: *(L)* The first, the best ... and ...

A: Not point

Q: *(L)* I know that's not the point! Is what we're saying here, is that we can use these prime numbers to derive something out of something else?

A: We told you about the mystics.

Q: *(T)* They're using prime numbers to ... *(L)* Oh, okay, I get it. So, mystics ... the mystics, the mystical secrets ... dwell in the prime numbers if used as a code.

A: Name the primary mystical organizations for key to clue system.

Q: *(L)* ... key to clue system?

A: Yes.

Q: [We named: Catholicism, Christianity, Judaism, Cabalism, Sufism, The Koran, Mysteries. Laura realized that she had just set aside the book *Understanding Mysticism*, it was next to a book on Kabbalah on the bookcase in the room. Jesuits, Masons, Knights Templar, Rosicrucians.] *(L)* All right. With our little list that we're making, are we on to something, or are we completely off track?

A: Yes, now check out those crop circles photos ... any prime number combos there?

Q: *(L)* Do you mean in terms of dimension, or do you mean in composition?

A: Composition and dimensions ... anything you can find.

Q: [Discussion follows: Sacred geometries, all sects listed use prime numbers. John 3:16-19, Corinthians 13. Genesis 2:22: "rib taken from the man and made woman" – 2 is the only even prime number. 3:5: "your eyes shall be opened and ye shall be as the gods." (Eating from the Tree of Knowledge)] *(T)* ... to find a way of decoding it to get an answer, to get something, to get a message, to get something from it ... *(L)* Are we thinking in any of the lines of something we ought to follow, or are we drifting?

71 **A**: All are lines you ought to follow. Now, look at the photos on the wall! [Referring to large photocopy of a number of crop circles we had pinned to the wall.]

72 **Q**: *(L)* Okay, we're looking at them: point out something ...

73 **A**: Count the large spheres in photo three.

74 **Q**: *(L)* There are seven.

75 **A**: Yes.

76 **Q**: *(L)* And what does that photo represent?

77 **A**: Not yet.

78 **Q**: *(T)* Okay, there are seven large circles: a large central one, and then six outer ones that are smaller. Each of the six smaller circles is connected to the larger circle by a shaft, or a line, or a conduit of some kind.

79 **A**: Add large and small spheres.

80 **Q**: *(L)* Okay, there's seven. Add the large to the small and there's seven; add the little teeny ones, there's thirteen; and then even the little teeny-teeny, the little knobs on the ends, there would be six more, so that would be nineteen.

81 **A**: Yes ...

82 **Q**: *(T)* So, that's another prime: nineteen is a prime number. *(L)* Okay, they're prime numbers. And ... *(T)* Are they – just as an offshoot here – do the six circles, the first set surrounding the large circle, are those the sixth density attached to the seventh density?

83 **A**: No comment.

84 **Q**: *(T)* Okay now, and then, outside of that are smaller spheres, each one connected one to the next, in a line. We're looking at prime numbers here. What are we looking at? We've got a central one, six outer: large, six outside of that: smaller, six outside of that: tiny ... Could – and I'm just thinking off the top of my head here, nothing cast in concrete – is this a representation of ... a sphere, getting smaller and smaller ... going that way. Or, coming in, this way. Or that way and this way. Like the infinity mirrors ...

85 **A**: If you three-dimensionalize.

86 **Q**: *(L)* It would be circles, like balls, like spheres. *(T)* Ohhh, it's an axis, an x-y-z axis! A three-dimensional axis. Three-dimensionally, it would be like this [holds up hand, forefinger pointed up, thumb pointed to himself, third finger at the horizontal]. Larger, smaller, smaller ... A three-dimensional axis. Are we going somewhere with this, or am I out in left field again?

87 **A**: Yes.

88 **Q**: *(T)* I'm going somewhere with this?

89 **A**: Yes.

90 **Q**: *(T)* Ahh, I now see this as a three-dimensional object as opposed to a flat circle.

91 **A**: Do that to the others too.

92 **Q**: *(L)* Okay, we're trying to three-dimensionalize them. Now, tell us where we're supposed to be going here ... *(J)* Well, this first one is a spiral going out ... Or a DNA molecule ... *(T)* There's got to be more to it ...

93 **A**: You do not have to figure this all out tonight, just some food for thought.

94 **Q**: *(L)* Is there anything else for ...

95 **A**: Ark may be able to three-dimensionalize by computer program already.

96 **Q**: *(L)* Yes, well, let us get back to this. The crop circles, as I understand, are related to the code or the mystical prime numbers, the mystical dwellings, and that somehow, putting all of these things together, these different pieces of this puzzle, from so many different directions, will enable us to perceive, or learn, or conceive something that will enable us to do something. Is that correct?

97 **A**: Close.

98 **Q**: *(L)* Is there anything more that we could look at on this subject tonight? Because right now, I just need to think about it. You get so much, and you have to digest it. *(J)* Food for thought!

99 **A**: Well, you have enough to play with for now, so goodbye.

End of session.

After reading over and pondering the session, considering how the Cs connected various things together without actually making the connections clear, I'm still rather in the dark. One can connect the blocking of awareness via strobes and its effect on 'low vibration'-type people with the cell phone microwave towers acting as frequency blockers. But then, how do the 'prime numbers' and mystics fit together? One might assume that, because the Cs said that we were not blockable, and the evidence was our engagement in the Cs' transmissions, that we could be considered mystics, but how does one 'dwell' in a prime number? Does it mean that this prime number has something to do with frequency? And what about 'primary' and 'who gets picked to run'? Does this have something to do with graduating to another density? What does it have to do with Eve being created from Adam's rib? What does it have to do with 'cells'? Is it possible that microwaves can turn on positive DNA in 'mystics' while blocking the blockable?

It's all rather mysterious and definitely esoteric. Hopefully, someday, it will all become clear!

December 21, 1996

In the week before this session, a couple of interesting things happened. First of all, a letter was sent around on the 'Skywatch' mailing list that was alleged to be a letter from a priest to radio talkshow host Art Bell.

Date: 1996-12-11 00:33:29 EST

Dear Mr. Bell,

I have listened to your program off and on for around two years now, whenever I get "down-time". I have some disturbing information and I feel that your program would be the perfect vehicle with which to distribute what I have.

I have been under the employ of the Vatican for over five years. I have done what could best be described as counter-intelligence work, for the church. I am a man of God and please believe me when I tell you that the information I have is genuine, and very serious.

Without going into too much detail about my former employers, I will briefly tell you that I have had a Top Level security clearance in the Vatican for quite some time. Most of the work I have done regrettably falls into the realm of "black-ops", and I will not go into detail about that now.

Around six months ago, I was working at a data terminal in a highly restricted area following a case that I had just completed, when I stumbled onto something that nearly made my heart stop. Please pay attention here, this is where it gets strange.

I uncovered a heavily encrypted sub-system that was surprisingly well hidden. I found that it was only accessible through the terminal I was at, and one other terminal. (I must point out that the area I was in was not an area that I routinely used.) After two minutes of trying to get into the system, the whole lab shut itself down and I was booted off the terminal. Not wanting to raise any eyebrows, I decided to leave and come back later that night. The strange thing was, when I came back, there were ARMED guards standing sentry outside of the lab. I must say that it is not unusual to see guards roaming the Vatican, but it is very unusual for them to stand sentry at a lab, much less while armed.

Over the next month, I managed to slip in unnoticed only once. And after I had found what I came for, I understood the security.

It took me a good deal of time to break into the system, and when I did, I wished I hadn't. When I entered the system, I came across a file titled "WORMWOOD?". (Yes, with a question mark.) Thinking it to be a text file, I brought up the file with the intent of copying so I could read it later. What happened next was truly remarkable. The file sort of "deteriorated" into a series of command lines that lasted approximately two minutes. Once it was done running, there it was.

I had found a direct link-up to the Hubble space telescope. Not only that, but it was pointed directly at the comet Hale-Bopp. The program was running some kind of analysis. Taking directional notes, projecting path of travel, etc. After realizing what I had discovered, I started searching and came across an e-mail data trail that led directly to the office of the Pope himself. What was discussed, I cannot know.

Over the next two weeks, I began to uncover evidence that the Vatican is very aware of the existence of the companion, and is VERY worried about it. I began to copy files and pictures that were present at the terminal, when I found a report from the United Nations to the Vatican, as well as a report from NASA regarding their concerns.

It is very obvious to me that a great many people and entities know of the companion and are doing their best to keep quiet. VERY quiet. As the next part of my story illustrates. I had found another file that I wanted to look at, but it was independently encrypted. At the time that I discovered it, I had already been online at the terminal for some time, so I decided to copy the file encrypted, and decode it at my leisure. As I was leaving the lab, I was approached by two of the Pope's top aides and was asked to meet them later in the evening. I didn't feel comfortable about the situation, so I agreed and told them that I needed to shower, and would join them later. I haven't been back to the Vatican since.

I found out about a week later through some old friends and contacts that a contract had been placed on my life. Two days later my mother and father were killed in a car crash in France. Three days after that, my brother and sister were killed when their single engine plane went down on the East coast of the U.S. I've been on the run for a very long time now, and am still trying to decode the file that I have in my possession. Approximately ten copies have been distributed to friends in the field in the event that I should disappear. I do not fear for my life, as I am very adept at not being found, however I believe that the world needs to know of the information that I have. I would be willing to share all that I have wuth you Mr. Bell. But you need to understand that your life could be in danger if you were to go public with what I give you. I apologize for being so vague, but I feel it neccessary at this point in time.

If you would like the information, say so over the air when you get this letter. If I am not listening, someone will get the information to me, as there is no safe way for you to contact me at this point in time. I await your response.

–PRIEST–

I include this as a sample of the ways and means of disinformation. This was part of the rumor-mongering that ultimately led to the mass suicide of the Heaven's Gate cult, which was just a few months in the future at this point (March 1997). I told Ark that it "must have been written by a Jesuit who was kicked out for failing Specious Arguments 101; no pre-requisite!"

There was more, of course. Something from the *NewAge On-Line Australia Library* entitled: 'Atlantis Grid, DNA, Energy, Wormwood' from 'The House of David Teaching Centre' that I'm not going to include because it is so nonsensical it will make you dizzy to try to read it.

Ark and I were still discussing the 11 November 1995 session. I had found some interesting items in several books that I sent to Ark on the 17th:

> The annual "Troia" or maze ritual was performed yearly in Rome. Classical scholar Jackson Knight says "The Troia must have been intended to create a magical field of exclusive force, and abstract defensive entanglement."
>
> The word "Troy" seems to be derived from the Latin "troare" which comes from a Celtic root: tro, which means "to turn." The spiral maze is far more widespread than is generally recognized in academic texts. The same maze design occurs not only on the classical Cretan coins, but also occurs as a sacred symbol in ancient Rajasthan, India, and with the Hopi of America and the Nazca desert drawings.
>
> A unifying theme of mazes seems to be their use as a symbol of death and resurrection. The original Tower of Babel was supposed to have been a seven-tier mass of brickwork with a spiral stairway.
>
> The occurrence of the number seven is strikingly consistent.
>
> "Writer Geoffrey Ashe made an attempt to explain the persistent elements behind all these traditions - spiral and circle, maze, underworld and the number seven - by proposing a novel theory in which the 'ancient wisdom' behind the old myths is derived from an original centre of mysticism in the Altai mountains of central Asia. But something more potent and vital must have lain behind the 'maze urge.'"
>
> "Could the circular design of many of the mazes, suggestive of the spiral, have been symbolic of an actual force?

"The idea that maze building involved ancient sensitivity to an unknown form of energy was put forward in the 1960's by Guy Underwood, a dowser. Underwood claimed he could detect a lingering energy field rippling through the Earth's surface. This geodetic force channelled itself through underground streams, and early Man placed his sacred sites at their confluences. Underwood claims that the mysterious geodetic force often formed spiral shapes under standing stones that, through some natural law, twisted into multiples of seven coils..." (W. F. Jackson Knight, Vergil's Troy, Essays on the Second Book of the Aeneid, 1932)

In 1979 an extraordinary, and successful, experiment was carried out on a standing stone by writer Francis Hitching, mathematics professor John Taylor and Bill Lewis, one of Britain's most capable dowsers. Lewis' claim that he could detect a band of force spiralling up the stone in seven coils was confirmed by the readings of a gaussmeter, which registered anomalously high magnetic strengths at the points where Lewis had marked the stone."

"Engineer Chrles Booker used a magnetometer and found distinct fluctuations in the geomagnetic field within a stone circle at Rollright Stones. A more detailed survey showed that the magnetic pattern inside the stone circle forms a seven ring spiral, broadening as it moves outward until it leaves the circle:

"A seven ring magnetic field..."

Why did seven ring geomagnetic fields evoke important symbols of life and death to the ancients? What did they know. How did they use these forces?

And, of course, there is the maze at Chartres, connected to the Templars, and another curious fact:

"The zodiacal image for Gemini at Chartres Cathedral is swathed in mystery. The zodiacal imagery around the north door of the west front is not complete. There are only 10 signs on this arch: Gemini and Pisces are missing. They were placed on the South door of the west front.

"These two figures are both male, in the classic tradition. But, different from all other representations, they are both standing behind a huge shield. Each has one arm across the chest, in a fashion reminiscent of the arms folded in the form of a cross. This posture is probably intended to link the cathedral to the Templars - the military emblem of the shield, and the setting apart of the figures... and the fact that the Templar emblem was two men on a single horse... [The Mystery of the Great Labyrinth, Chartres Cathedral by John James; Studies in Comparative Religion, Vol. 11, No. 2. (Spring, 1977)].

One or two historians have suggested that Chartres was built with Templar funding and that much of the construction is secret symbolism.

> Another curious item that might relate to what the Cs said in that session about zodiac signs is that Aquarius was known by the Babylonians as "the Great Man." In early Christian zodiacs it was depicted as an angel with wings. The constellation is usually represented as a winged man or woman. The zig-zag lines that represent Aquarius have generally been thought to be water, but some believe it is cosmic force or electromagnetism. However, the important element is the space between the two lines - the cosmic air that permeates all things...
>
> Getting back to the subject: when Jim sent his bit about the "tube" of God with all the things about time, etc... well, maybe he was onto a little something there... in a certain sense. The Sufi idea of the worlds is that it is like a spiralling horn... that spirals back in on itself like a mobius strip... and, at a certain "turn" of the spiral, the density shifts...
>
> So, the seven turns of the spiral, as experimentally shown in what I have collected tonight, could be sort of a holographic representation of cosmic energy at an absolute level. The seven densities. But, since it is a line, each point on the line could be the point of another "spiralling horn." And, since points intrinsically have no dimension... well, they can be infinite.
>
> And, this spiralling horn of the Sufis' reminds me of the Golden Ratio and even some of the cloud figures on Jupiter...
>
> So, if something "shifts densities" into our world from another density, at what point does it do so? Is this related to quantum jumps??? Is quantum jumping related to the spiral or the numbers of 11 squared divided by phi?
>
> And, what exactly IS this number 11? Is it representative of the original division from primal gravity to gravity and Electromagnetism? And then, is light the interaction between the two? And do the numbers spiral representing levels of interaction between gravity and EM... energy exchanges???

Ark's divorce hearing was on the 17th and, as expected, his ex did not show up: doctor's note that she was ill. The issue of prosecuting her for the theft of all Ark's money was put back on the table.

Finally, an update on the Patrick Z saga from an email to Ark:

> While driving [my daughter] to work, she said that she has told Patrick that he must go home and stop sleeping on our sofa. I was a little startled at this turn of attitude, and asked why. She said that she told him that he really needs to work things out with his mother since he is always upset about it and moping. But, I think that she has finally felt that he is always draining her energy to constantly feed this emotional black hole. What she said to me was: "he is starting to get on my nerves

and I want to stay friends with him, and I know I won't if he keeps hanging all over me."

Later:

Patrick has all of his things in his truck and is ready to go, but he is having a hard time leaving. I feel more sorry for him now than before. I can't imagine having to go back home after his mother has treated him the way she has. But [my daughter] is determined. She says that he is a grown man and he shouldn't expect her to hide him from his mother, that he should be able to be strong and make his own decisions, and she is tired of taking the flak and his whining and complaining. (That's pretty much how she put it, too.)

Then, there was more on Hale-Bopp:

Now, I have a little newsletter here that comes from an astrology association in Jacksonville. There is an article on Hale-Bopp and says that there are pictures at www.ArtBell.com. So, I think I will go and look at them later.

Apparently, Dr. Courtney Brown, the remote viewer, and several others "visited" Hale-Bopp and report that there is an object trailing it that is 4 times larger than earth and is surrounded by an "unidentified gas larger than our Sun. The object appears somewhat like Saturn with rings. The object is trailing Hale-Bopp and is headed towards earth. It appears to have tunnels and it is emitting light. The surface is totally uniform and there appears to be a grid surrounding it." And then they go into the "message" coming from this object.

And, of course, all is blamed on the government... they just don't want us to know the truth, so all of humanity must beg the aliens to forgive those poor, misguided govt. people and land anyway.

Dr. Brown can be reached at www.Farsight.Org

Next this newsletter talks about the "planet Delmar" and is too hokey for me to even copy. But, the best part is that it is "invisible" to those of lesser spiritual development, because, apparently, it arrived "as foretold, in June 1982."

I sure wish somebody had told ME! I must have missed it the same way I missed the photon belt!!!

Well, I am trying to keep my mind open, but I don't want somebody to come along and dump garbage in there!!!!

Later:

I had to go and check out Art Bell. That is apparently where the "priest letter" came from because it is posted there. I read through everything, but was not terribly impressed. The pictures could have any number of explanations.

> Do you know any astronomers personally or do you know anyone who does? I would like to have a verified, expert opinion on this before I go off the deep end!
>
> And, have you heard about the amazing apparition of the Virgin Mary that has appeared on the side of a building 15 miles from me, in Clearwater??? Several stories tall, irridescence on smoked glass exterior walls. Fairly clearly defined, no doubt. I was watching it on television today and there is a large color picture in the Times.
>
> And, it is on the side of the Seminole Finance Building - a firm of Dewey, Cheatum, and Howe!
>
> Of course, there are hordes of people flocking there with their candles and rosaries and their lame and blind and whatever. So they are all down there moaning that the END is coming, imagining dire destruction and turmoil, feeling guilty as sin, crying for mercy and providing a veritable feast for the Lizzies!
>
> So, I am a skeptic. Yes, indeed. Been burned too many times.
>
> And the C's have said: "As we have explained again and again, 3rd density 'proof' does not apply. Now, listen very carefully: if proof of the type were possible, what do you suppose would happen to free will, and thusly to learning, karmic directive level 1?"

On the 19th of December, I wrote:

> I was listening to the radio in the van this morning and a woman called in and said that she had gone to see the "apparition" in Clearwater last night and that she thought it looked like someone riding a motorcycle and she couldn't understand how everybody thought it looked like the Virgin Mary.
>
> [My daughter] told me this morning that when Patrick took her to the store last night (they were gone a long time and I wondered where) that he had insisted on going down to see this "miracle" too. She said that when they got there she refused to go among the crowd of "whining people" with him and said that he had better stop running around looking for something to fix his life for him and fix it himself. She was quite a bit harder on him last night, I think.

Ark was in Germany working and he was able to put money in his MC account for me to use. However, things did not work out as we intended, as I wrote to Ark:

> I went to the supermarket. I am out of nearly everything, and I made a list and was being very careful and sticking to what was essential.
> A___ went with me and we spent over an hour getting together all that was on the list, comparing prices and so forth. Then, at the check-out, the cashier did not know how to manually enter the number. All she

knew how to do was slide the card through the slot in the machine. So, she called the manager. He had to get the written instructions on how to do it. He tried, but it did not work. So, I was getting a little desperate, so I told him to call the MC people and get a verbal approval. He said he couldn't and he was starting to be rude and I think he thought that there was something illegal going on. So, finally, he said: Well, you can either pay by check or cash. I can't help you. So, I just walked out. When I got home, I called the office of the store and explained what had happened to the head manager. He was very apologetic and said he would see what he could do. He was going to get the verbal approval and have the store deliver my groceries to me. Then he called back and said that the MC people said that I should not be using a MC if I was not an authorized user on the account. And that was that. So, I was very, very, very upset. I NEEDED to buy food. So, the Lizzies were at it again. I have NEVER not been able to feed my children.

Ark had a talk with the bank and that was sorted out.

Then, I received an email from Jason Dunlap, who was busy on the internet in those days; it was about Sheldon Nidle and the alleged Photon Belt. It's so hokey I simply can't reproduce it here, but I did ask about it in the session. And despite all the background stresses, this was a really, really interesting session! (Notice also that my mother was apparently feeling contrite about being so nasty!)

Participants: 'Frank', Laura, Alice, VG, Ark (via email)

1 **Q:** *(L)* Hello.

2 **A:** Hello.

3 **Q:** *(L)* Who do we have with us tonight?

4 **A:** Fonorrea.

5 **Q:** *(L)* And where are you from?

6 **A:** Cassiopaea.

7 **Q:** *(L)* The first question on my mind before we get to any of these other questions is: who is giving information to Sheldon Nidle about the photon belt and the mass landings that are supposed to take place on the 31st of December and the 1st of January?

8 **A:** Sheldon Nidle.

9 **Q:** *(L)* It is just coming out of his own head? He is not seeing any beings or channeling anything?

10 **A:** Okay, close enough.

11 **Q:** *(L)* I would like to ask about this fellow Jim, in a somewhat indirect way. This is a person who corresponds with Ark on a variety of subjects [and claims to have inside connections to deep government ops]. This last question that he was asked was: [reading] "Do you know about any possible relation between deep space travel and DNA structure? Or between crop circles coding and DNA coding? Have you ever been told or shown something about DNA? Like relation between time rate and the structure of our genes?" And, here is what Jim replied: "Yes, but I have been

warned not to discuss this matter where it is open to unknown ears." Could you comment on that?

12 **A**: The best thing for Ark to do is request "closed" correspondence.

13 **Q**: *(L)* Does this guy have some knowledge about DNA or crop circles?

14 **A**: Discover.

15 **Q**: *(L)* Okay, Mother, ask your question. *(Alice)* There are a lot of things that I want to know, and some, I am sure, are important, but I don't know the sequence that I want to follow.

16 **A**: Ask away.

17 **Q**: *(Alice)* So many things have happened to me, that I am wondering if something happened to my brain in this life or another that would explain my thinking.

18 **A**: More specific, please.

19 **Q**: *(Alice)* Did anything happen in another life that has caused me problems in this life?

20 **A**: The answer is yes, as with all others.

21 **Q**: *(L)* What happened to cause these mental problems?

22 **A**: Not mental, emotional.

23 **Q**: *(L)* Can you tell us a little bit about it?

24 **A**: Death of a twin in the last lifetime. Farming accident in 1880's.

25 **Q**: *(L)* How did this twin die?

26 **A**: Fell off of the ox-driven combine, driven by father. Was decapitated.

27 **Q**: *(L)* Were they male or female twins?

28 **A**: Male.

29 **Q**: *(L)* And what were their names?

30 **A**: Lucas and Lawrence. Lucas was the one that died.

31 **Q**: *(L)* Where was Mother, as Lawrence, at the time?

32 **A**: In the house.

33 **Q**: *(L)* And what kind of emotion has carried over into this lifetime?

34 **A**: Her longing is insatiable as she is always "looking for love" due to her loss.

35 **Q**: *(L)* How old was Lucas when this happened?

36 **A**: 8 years old.

37 **Q**: *(L)* How many years after this accident did Lawrence live?

38 **A**: 22 years.

39 **Q**: *(L)* Have any of the persons of that lifetime returned to interact with her in this life?

40 **A**: No.

41 **Q**: *(L)* Not even the twin?

42 **A**: Correct.

43 **Q**: *(Alice)* Emotions are not mental – there is a difference? So, my problems now are emotional and not mental?

44 **A**: Your problems are due to maladjustment.

45 **Q**: *(L)* From life to life or just this life?

46 **A**: They are the same.[1]

47 **Q**: *(V)* Did she witness the accident?

48 **A**: No.

49 **Q**: *(L)* Did she see the body after?

50 **A**: No.

---

[1] This is a very interesting idea, that maladjustments to life are always related to past-life experiences.

51 **Q:** *(L)* Was there any sense of blame or resentment directed toward her by the parents of that time?

52 **A:** No.

53 **Q:** *(L)* Was there any mental or emotional abuse that took place in that lifetime?

54 **A:** Maybe some, but it is not significant.

55 **Q:** *(L)* What steps can she take to resolve this maladjustment?

56 **A:** Awareness of the root of the problem.

57 **Q:** *(L)* Is there any other part to this event that would help her?

58 **A:** No.

59 **Q:** *(Alice)* So, all the problems that I had as a child were the result of this?

60 **A:** Some seek an environment of "punishment" in an attempt to resolve leftover issues.[2]

61 **Q:** *(L)* Did she have feelings of guilt that her twin had died and she was still alive?

62 **A:** Yes, but this was not imposed by others.

63 **Q:** *(L)* Okay, she felt guilt, and sought an environment that would punish her?

64 **A:** Close enough for hand grenades.

65 **Q:** *(L)* Where was the farm located that this incident occurred?

66 **A:** Near Cannopolis, North Carolina.[3]

67 **Q:** *(L)* Can you give us the family name?

68 **A:** O'Brien.

69 **Q:** *(Alice)* Let me ask this: all of the experiences that I had as a child were caused by this emotion where I was trying to punish myself. I have spent my lifetime trying to punish myself. Is that right?

70 **A:** Close. But remember, the point is, you sought out a environment that you perceived to be restrictive and unforgiving. Especially with your father.

71 **Q:** *(L)* Was there other karma with her father in this lifetime?

---

[2] This also is a remarkable comment. How many people live in 'punishing' situations because they choose to? It puts a rather different spin on the idea of karma.

[3] I had never heard of such a place. But, according to Wikipedia: "Kannapolis is a city in Cabarrus and Rowan counties, in the U.S. state of North Carolina, northwest of Concord and northeast of Charlotte and is a suburb in the Charlotte metropolitan area." Curiously, the Cs used the old form of the name. Again, from Wikipedia: "Early meaning and usage of the city's name was a direct reference to Cannon Mills Corporation, or James William Cannon himself. Early published name variations include 'Cannon-opolis' and 'Cannapolis'. A widely accepted origin of the word 'Kannapolis' comes from the combination of the Greek words *kanna* (reeds, not looms) and *polis* (city), which some believed meant 'City of Looms'. Dr. Gary Freeze, Catawba College history and politics department chairman, said a Concord newspaper used the name 'Cannon City' in 1906. After mill workers or newspapers called the town 'Cannapolis', J.W. Cannon asked Cabarrus County commissioners to give the town the name, but starting with a 'K'. Kannapolis historian Norris Dearmon said the K might have been to distinguish the town from his Concord mill village. Since, Freeze said, 'Jim Cannon didn't study Greek,' Cannon did not name the town 'city of looms'."

72 **A**: Maybe, but you are the one, Laura, who can best examine these issues.

73 **Q**: *(L)* What about between my mother and myself?

74 **A**: Ditto.

75 **Q**: *(L)* Well, if you guys would just tell me, it would leave me more time to transcribe tapes!

76 **A**: Learning ...

77 **Q**: *(L)* Ohhh ... *(V)* Whoops, she's growling [laughter]. *(L)* Okay. Any particular reason behind the financial difficulties I had today?

78 **A**: Not really. That will soon be forgotten.

79 **Q**: *(L)* Now, time to stop messing around. You said that "prime numbers are the 'dwelling places' of the mystics." I have been poring over this material and it occurs to me that this was put in quotes for a reason, yes?

80 **A**: We put in quotes what we want further examined.[4]

81 **Q**: *(L)* I was thinking that this could be a clue on several levels. Could it be a clue to identify people and interactions?

82 **A**: Maybe.

83 **Q**: *(L)* And, also as a means of decoding coded written material?

84 **A**: Sometimes.

85 **Q**: *(L)* Would this written material be some that is channeled? Or, more formal and general writings of mystics? Could it be, in other words, that they might write in a casual way and not be aware that they are channeling or writing in code?

[4] *Secret History* 3
[5] *The Wave* 67
[6] *The Wave* 22

86 **A**: Maybe.

87 **Q**: *(L)* I dug around about the Templars and have, more or less, come to the conclusion that they were just a smoke screen, and that something else was going on at the time that *was* important. I also think that they have been resurrected from time to time and dusted off and blamed for all this secret knowledge that is supposedly lost ... Am I on to something here?

88 **A**: Close.

89 **Q**: *(L)* Who or what brought about the end of the Knights of the Temple?[5]

90 **A**: Rosicrucians move as a "thief in the night."[6]

91 **Q**: *(L)* But, as I understand it, the Rosicrucians did not come into being until after the end of the Templars ...

92 **A**: No.

93 **Q**: *(L)* Do you mean that the information that came out, that pamphlet about 'Christian Rosenkreutz', that is a purported fable, might be correct?

94 **A**: Yes.

95 **Q**: *(L)* Well, goodness sake! The Rosicrucians advertise in magazines! Is this worldwide organization that promotes itself so blatantly ...

96 **A**: Well, the "worldwide" order is not all inclusive.

97 **Q**: *(L)* Is there an inner circle of this order that is unknown?

98 **A**: Yes.

99 **Q**: *(L)* Are the Rosicrucians connected to the Masons?

100 **A**: In a roundabout away.

101 **Q:** *(L)* Are the Illuminati connected to the Rosicrucians in any way?

102 **A:** Same.

103 **Q:** *(L)* Of the three I have named, which would be considered the one that is closest to the inner circle?

104 **A:** Not the correct concept.

105 **Q:** *(L)* Do the Rosicrucians have writings in their keeping that they, themselves, do not understand?

106 **A:** Yes. So do the Masons.

107 **Q:** *(L)* Would you say that the writings of Albert Pike might be interesting to decode?

108 **A:** Yes.

109 **Q:** *(L)* Is there any particular number sequence that could be used?

110 **A:** 353 535 ...

111 **Q:** *(L)* Is this also a genetic code?

112 **A:** Much is missing between "point A and point B."

113 **Q:** *(L)* You mean by jumping from documents to DNA?

114 **A:** Yes.

115 **Q:** *(L)* The Priory of Zion, that has been purported to be the progenitor or inheritor of the Templar tradition – is that a mystical organization of great secrecy and import?[7]

116 **A:** It is a cover for.

117 **Q:** *(L)* Another smoke-screen.

118 **A:** Yes.

119 **Q:** *(L)* Getting back to the 353 535 code: can you tell me more that will help me get to ...

120 **A:** Better turn it over to Ark.

---
[7] *The Wave* 22

121 **Q:** *(L)* So, I should leave it alone for now?

122 **A:** Good idea.

123 **Q:** *(L)* I will. I wanted to get to this other subject anyway. We know that you have said that time is an illusion in 3rd density reality – that it is the 3rd density illusion – and it is involved with our DNA, which determines how we perceive it. So, it is an illusion. Yet, somehow, this illusion converts at some point into a solid reality via some mode or operation. I would like to know at what point it converts and how.

124 **A:** You are off base. Who said it converts?

125 **Q:** *(L)* Well, we perceive a damn solid reality! There is *stuff* that if you kick it, it hurts!

126 **A:** That perception is part of the illusion.

127 **Q:** *(L)* But, that is obviously not the *total* illusion. What else is a part of this illusion? If our perception is part, then there must also be something there to be perceived, correct?

128 **A:** Yes.

129 **Q:** *(L)* Okay, what is it that we are perceiving?

130 **A:** That which you are programmed to perceive.

131 **Q:** *(L)* Is not this perception, these things we perceive as outside ourselves, are they not substance of some sort? Are they not there in some form, even if we perceive them the way we do?

132 **A:** Of course, but what does this have to do with "time?"

133 **Q:** *(L)* I am getting to that! We perceive a world 'out there'. Trees, cars,

December 21, 1996

trucks, houses, bricks, boards, blocks, people, dogs, etc., etc., etc.

134 **A**: You left out backyard barbecues!

135 **Q**: [Laughter] *(L)* Very funny! We perceive things out there. Of what are they composed?

136 **A**: Matter.

137 **Q**: *(L)* Of what is matter composed?

138 **A**: Atomic structure.

139 **Q**: *(L)* Of what are atoms composed?

140 **A**: Thoughts.

141 **Q**: *(L)* Whose thoughts?

142 **A**: Yours.

143 **Q**: *(L)* Everything?

144 **A**: Everything.

145 **Q**: *(L)* If I perceive something, and everything I perceive is composed of my thoughts, and V___ is perceiving, is everything her thoughts?

146 **A**: Yes.

147 **Q**: *(L)* What is the difference between her thoughts and my thoughts?

148 **A**: That is what binds you. You see, it is merely a program.

149 **Q**: *(L)* Is it merely a program that we think we are separate individuals?

150 **A**: Not the point.

151 **Q**: *(L)* What is the point? What binds us together? Where does the program come from?

152 **A**: Where do your programs come from?

153 **Q**: *(L)* 7th density? Ourselves? The Lizzies?

154 **A**: We are asking about the programs in your computer.

155 **Q**: *(L)* In my computer? Different places. I get them and load them in. Are programs made – do they exist like 'thought centers' – and do we just load them in ourselves?

156 **A**: Why have you forgotten? 309,000 ...

157 **Q**: *(L)* Oh. You are talking about the 'takeover' by 4th density STS. But, still, the point I am trying to get to is – yes we have DNA – but you can't reprogram DNA if there is not DNA there to begin with. If there is not something to load the program into. What is the substance of this reality that we exist in?

158 **A**: You just answered.

159 **Q**: *(L)* I don't understand.

160 **A**: You can't load it into something if there isn't something there to begin with.

161 **Q**: *(L)* Fine! What is this something that is there to begin with?

162 **A**: Your previous DNA structure.

163 **Q**: *(L)* Where did the previous DNA structure come from?

164 **A**: The previous program.

165 **Q**: *(L)* Where did that program come from?

166 **A**: Review.

167 **Q**: *(L)* Well, you once said that it was necessary to be on a planet that had a star that was getting ready to go supernova in order to molecularize physical bodies. What I want to know is: what is this process whereby thought becomes manifest as matter?

168 **A**: This is too complicated for this medium. You need another method. Something that allows for greater word usage.

169 **Q:** *(L)* But, just a clue: how does thought become matter?[8]

170 **A:** Bilaterally.[9]

171 **Q:** *(L)* What do you mean by "bilaterally"?

172 **A:** Dual emergence.

173 **Q:** *(L)* Emergence into what and what?

174 **A:** Not "into what and what," but rather, "from what and to what."

175 **Q:** *(L)* What emerges from what?

176 **A:** The beginning emerges from the end, and vice versa.

177 **Q:** *(L)* And what is the beginning and what is the end?

178 **A:** Union with the One.

179 **Q:** *(L)* What is the One?

180 **A:** 7th density, i.e.: all that is, and is not.

181 **Q:** *(L)* Now, we have managed to dance around the whole thing, and I still do not know how matter comes to be or how time ...

182 **A:** No.

183 **Q:** *(L)* How can I get where I want to go?

184 **A:** You have the basics.

185 **Q:** *(L)* Can you give me a couple more basics?

186 **A:** There are no more.

187 **Q:** *(L)* I once asked you if time was gravity.

188 **A:** Is a fence the ground?

189 **Q:** *(L)* Is gravity God?

190 **A:** No.

191 **Q:** *(L)* Is gravity 7th density?

192 **A:** No.

193 **Q:** *(L)* Where does gravity emanate from?[10]

194 **A:** Thought center.

195 **Q:** *(L)* You have mentioned thought centers of many occasions. Is there more than one?

196 **A:** All are one and all.

197 **Q:** *(L)* If you have a thought center, how do thought centers relate to 7th density, the One?

198 **A:** Exactly!

199 **Q:** *(L)* Are thought centers 7th density?

200 **A:** All is.

201 **Q:** *(L)* All is thought centers?

202 **A:** No. All is 7th density.

203 **Q:** *(L)* I think you know where I am trying to go with this and I wish you would help me out just a little ...

204 **A:** We are.

205 **Q:** *(L)* Okay. Time is an illusion. Wonderful! You have compared time to a fence ...

206 **A:** No. We compared your allusion to ours.

207 **Q:** *(L)* Let's work with this allusion. Let us say that the ground is 7th density. How would we picture time in relation to this ground?

208 **A:** As the soil.

209 **Q:** *(L)* Related to the soil, how do *we* relate?

210 **A:** Too vague.

---

[8] *The Wave* 28
[9] *Secret History* 12; *The Wave* 26
[10] *Secret History* 12; *The Wave* 26

211 **Q:** *(L)* How do created beings get painted into this picture?

212 **A:** Time is your illusion.

213 **Q:** *(L)* Yet, on one other occasion, you said that time does exist at other densities, only that it is 'selective', you can pick the time. Is that correct?

214 **A:** If you want to call it time, but it would not be the same, would it?

215 **Q:** *(L)* Okay. I am stumped. I can't go any further now. On another subject, Ark read that phosphorus is in DNA structure. Could you comment?

216 **A:** How about if you comment on the relationship of phosphorous to you?

217 **Q:** *(L)* I don't know. Is there some relationship between phosphorous and carbon?

218 **A:** Well, that is not where we were leading.

219 **Q:** *(L)* Well, phosphorous is an essential element for the brain.

220 **A:** Okay.

221 **Q:** *(L)* That is about all I know about it. I don't know enough about phosphorous.

222 **A:** So, then why not save this until later?

223 **Q:** *(L)* Next question: if there were a sufficient number of people who were working on learning how to create an alternate reality or universe, would it seem to them that there was no real 'shift' between the former one and the new one, except an internal shift of thought?

224 **A:** That is one possibility.

225 **Q:** *(L)* If we decided that we wanted a different world, could we, as even a small group, create that kind of world and have it seem that we hadn't ...

226 **A:** We have told you thus.

227 **Q:** *(L)* Is it possible that there are persons on the planet, here for some purpose, and that purpose is – say, the negativity on the planet increases to such an extent that many people will become so sick of it that they are ready to exercise their free will and make a change and they will then be open to learn from those who have come with this intent to help and teach?

228 **A:** Okay.

229 **Q:** *(L)* Well, when this Wave hits, is that going to increase the potential for the creation of a new reality, or realm?

230 **A:** Better review.

231 **Q:** *(L)* I am trying to get somewhere in particular and am trying to build the questions step by step ...

232 **A:** Ask Ark.

233 **Q:** *(L)* What do you want me to ask Ark?

234 **A:** Some of these questions, to see what he thinks.

235 **Q:** *(L)* Tell me, why he is going to know these answers?

236 **A:** It is more fun to ponder the answers, rather than the whys and wherefores.

237 **Q:** *(L)* You guys are making me a little crazy tonight.

238 **A:** Do you want to invite Ark to the discussion?

239 **Q:** *(L)* Of course. *(A)* [via email] What is the function of DNA, other than coding protein production?

240 **A:** Conductor of electricity.

241 **Q:** *(L)* Is that the only other function?

242 **A:** Well, as you know, electrical energy can have nearly endless applications. Examples ... radio waves, neuro-transceiver for thought pattern programs facilitated through electromagnetic wave transmission, etc. Method used for creation and maintenance of program illusions, such as the perception of linear time as reality.

243 **Q:** *(L)* Is that it?

244 **A:** Send that.

245 **Q:** *(A)* Should I follow the Newtonian electrodynamics thread?

246 **A:** It is up to you to follow that which you are guided to follow. This is elementary. If we were in your "shoes," we would shelve it.

247 **Q:** *(A)* Should I study the cold fusion problem?

248 **A:** Not in area of search.

249 **Q:** *(L)* Any further comment about cold fusion?

250 **A:** No.

251 **Q:** *(L)* What is cold fusion?

252 **A:** Theoretical, some recently claimed breakthroughs of dubious validity, though.

253 **Q:** *(A)* Which part of a human extends into 4th density?[11]

254 **A:** That which is effected by pituitary gland.[12]

255 **Q:** *(L)* And what is that?

256 **A:** Psychic.

257 **Q:** *(A)* Are there some particular DNA sequences that facilitate transmission between densities?[13]

258 **A:** Addition of strands.

259 **Q:** *(L)* How do you get added strands?

260 **A:** You don't get, you receive.

261 **Q:** *(L)* Where are they received from?

262 **A:** Interaction with upcoming Wave, if vibration is aligned.[14]

263 **Q:** *(L)* How do you know if this is happening?

264 **A:** Psychophysiological changes manifest.

265 **Q:** *(L)* Such as what?

266 **A:** Isn't Ark a part of this discussion?

267 **Q:** *(L)* Alright! I get the point! I was just trying to help. *(A)* I would like to know if there is a separate field beyond electromagnetism and gravitation, something similar to the Sheldrake concept of a morphological field or morphogenetic field?

268 **A:** Yes, and it is very close to that. It is apparent that Sheldrake was "in tune," as are you, Arkadiusz. But you must have faith in your thoughts, as sometimes they are assisted.

269 **Q:** *(A)* When you speak of an upcoming wave, it is a wave of what?

270 **A:** Think of it as a wave of reflection from the beginning and end point.

---

[11] *Secret History* 5, 12; *The Wave* "Appendix B"

[12] *The Wave* 26 Notice that they say "that which is EFFECTED by the pituitary gland." The pituitary gland is a small pea-sized gland that is referred to as the body's 'master gland' because it controls the activity of most other hormone-secreting glands.

[13] *The Wave* 62

[14] Which more or less takes us back to the "prime numbers are the dwellings of the mystics" session. See my comments there 14 December 1996.

271 **Q:** *(L)* Can you clarify that in more 3rd density terms?

272 **A:** No, see what the response is. It is his question, after all!

273 **Q:** *(A)* Is DNA acting as a superconductor?

274 **A:** Yes!!!

275 **Q:** *(L)* Any other comments?

276 **A:** No.

277 **Q:** *(A)* [regarding wave] But what vibrates? Energy? Aether?

278 **A:** Energy and aether are directly symbiotic.

279 **Q:** *(A)* And when it vibrates, then in which dimension?

280 **A:** The density 3 and 4 at transition junction.

281 **Q:** *(A)* If not in linear time, then in what?

282 **A:** Cyclical "time."

283 **Q:** *(A)* What measures the distance between one crest and another?

284 **A:** Ending/beginning of cycle.

285 **Q:** *(A)* Trying to understand the universe in terms of a triality, matter – geometry – information. Is it the right idea?

286 **A:** If one thinks of matter as "living" rather than "dead."

287 **Q:** *(L)* Is that it?

288 **A:** Ark questioned.

289 **Q:** *(L)* Well, excuse me for trying to help here! *(A)* Is DNA superconducting?

290 **A:** Variably.

291 **Q:** *(A)* What is electricity?

292 **A:** In what sense?

293 **Q:** *(A)* What is elementary charge?

294 **A:** Elementary means basic construct, whether directly from the natural "state," or indirectly.

295 **Q:** *(A)* What type of entity?

296 **A:** Purely substantive, as in a binder.

297 **Q:** *(A)* A warp?

298 **A:** "Warp" is incomplete concept. Remember what we said about theory of relativity.

299 **Q:** *(A)* Must I understand the nature of superconductivity? It seems to me that I must.

300 **A:** Yes and yes, definitely.

301 **Q:** *(A)* Is it correct? Is it in my reach?

302 **A:** Yes. We already answered.

303 **Q:** *(A)* That means Nobel Prize, definitely, yes?

304 **A:** We hate to say this, but ... Wait and see!!! Goodnight!

End of Session

December 28, 1996

If the reader has been following the background information I've given in previous sessions, the reasons for the questions in this one will be somewhat self-evident. It was a very trying time all the way around. For some of the specific questions in this session, the following email I wrote to Ark will provide background:

> The woman at the phone company called and said that she was going to "secure the account" until the MC people received a response from the bank in Bielefeld. So, just to find out if this was peculiar to the phone company, or the general state of affairs with the American MC network, I decided to check it out at the gas station down the street. The girl put in the number and it came back as an "invalid card." Well, this had not been a problem until the guy at the supermarket took it upon himself to call and chat with the MC people and tell me that what I was doing was "improper use" of the card. So, it seems that the American MC people must think there is some criminal here in the States running around with your card. So, they are going to protect you until they can find out for sure...
>
> Then Frank called. He had a strange experience today. He needed to find his insurance card so he could get his tags for his truck. So, he decided to go through all the mail he piles on his kitchen table. (You and I think we make messes? Nope! Nothing like Frank's mess! I have seen it!) He found two lengthy papers on mind control experiments, one of which had been mailed to me anonymously some time ago, and another that I had pulled off the net. So, he was compelled to sit down and read these. Meanwhile, all kinds of thoughts and connections were coming into his mind. The bottom line was, he wanted to call and warn me that extra care and precautions need to be taken especially NOW. In other words, we need 10,000 eyes. And he was particularly concerned about me because he doesn't think the house is secure enough, which is probably true. It is the best I can make it, though. And then he said something that is very odd for Frank because he is usually VERY tolerant of everything and everybody. He said: "We must look at everyone and everything right now as suspect. If they are okay, it won't hurt but if they are not, it could save our lives."
>
> Well, I have never heard him say something like that. But he has apparently put some pieces of the puzzle together and certain people

REALLY cause him concern. So we agreed to just keep everything very private for the time, no guests at the sessions - physically present, I mean... he also said something else. He said that he is certain that once you are here that the mental shielding will be exponentially more powerful and that forces will try to use this last window of opportunity before you come to hurt me in some way to prevent this.

Well, our charts are almost identical for the upcoming month, and we both have Mars and the Moon in the 12th house with Mars opposing Saturn in the sixth. The book says about Mars in the 12th taken alone: "Danger of injury, slander, scandal, loss of reputation or treachery from enemies. Secret enemies. Danger of injury through large animals or burglars. Saturn adverse: injuries or imprisonment, illness requiring hospitalization."

Fortunately, there are multiple positive aspects to these Mars positions which will modify the influence or make it possible to avoid it altogether if the positive energies are utilized. In both cases they are in the second and fourth houses which rule income and possessions and environmental conditions, primarily the home, and has to do with food, clothing, and household goods - that which one wishes to keep, to protect, etc.

So, for the first half of January, it may be trying for both of us. I don't want to anticipate, but forewarned is forearmed.

Participants: 'Frank', Laura, Alice, VG, AM (eldest daughter), Ark (via email)

1 **Q:** *(L)* Hello.

2 **A:** Hello.

3 **Q:** *(L)* And who do we have with us this evening?

4 **A:** Torren from Cassiopaea.

5 **Q:** *(L)* Have you not been the representative in previous sessions?

6 **A:** Remember, individual monikers are for your familiarity only.

7 **Q:** *(L)* Okay, thank you. I have a list of questions that I would like to get through fairly quickly, if possible. The first one is for VG. She is concerned about her health and would like to have a clue.

8 **A:** Study nutrition, then see doctor.

9 **Q:** *(L)* Is there anything specifically wrong that is urgent?

10 **A:** See last response.

11 **Q:** *(V)* It's too bad my doctor is an idiot.

12 **A:** Then choose another.

13 **Q:** *(L)* Is there any one thing she could do at this point that would help? *(V)* I have been bruising a lot.

14 **A:** Iron supplements help, but do not limit to that.

15 **Q:** *(V)* Is 'ruten' in conjunction with iron important?

16 **A:** What did we say 3 questions back?

17 **Q:** *(V)* I had a very disturbing dream last night. Was it processing, or a facade? I was looking at things and fixing myself. And the night before, I dreamed that Laura came swooping in to save

me from something that was scaring me to death. I woke up with my heart pounding ...

A: Best to work to purge negative influences in your life.

Q: *(L)* The dream was doing that?

A: No. That is our suggestion for VG.

Q: *(L)* What negative influences does VG need to purge?

A: Those which have tentacles leading to her representation of the past.[1]

Q: *(L)* What is her representation of the past?

A: That which in 3rd density is viewed as past.

Q: *(V)* Was the dream last night ... I was observing and looking at what I perceived as sentences and paragraphs, very logically and meticulously I was breaking things down into logical segments – once I was done doing that, I was fixing myself – my hair, my nails. Was this a positive dream? What did this dream represent?

A: When one must decipher the clues in one's life, it takes patience and reflection. As in one looking before leaping.

Q: *(V)* Back in October, I was supposed to go to a retreat that you said would be positive and uplifting. But it was cancelled at the last minute. What happened?

A: The vibrations were not in sync.

Q: *(V)* Was everybody cancelled, or was it just me?

A: From the point of view of the experience, the result is the same.

Q: *(L)* Will she go on this retreat ultimately?

A: An opportunity will present itself.

Q: *(L)* VG also had an experience the other day where she was feeling very powerful pulling sensations toward a certain person in her past. What was stimulating those sensations?

A: Physical cycle stimuli.

Q: *(V)* As in menstrual cycle?

A: Menstrual is superimposed by hormonal, is it not?

Q: *(L)* Was something outside of her stimulating the hormones?

A: Not needed.

Q: *(L)* How can she deal with this kind of stress?

A: Spiritual awareness heightening.

Q: *(V)* How do you achieve heightening of spiritual awareness?

A: This is a good vehicle, for example.

Q: *(L)* Does general acquisition of knowledge on any and all subjects also heighten spiritual awareness?

A: Yes.

Q: *(L)* So, if you are not doing it here, it does not necessarily matter, because every minute you spend learning and thinking and examining, you are heightening spiritual awareness.

A: Yes.

Q: *(L)* Okay, I had a dream about Chloe and Tommy, and Tommy had come back to life. We were on a trip in separate vehicles, and had stopped at a restaurant. Tommy had gone to

---

[1]VG continued to smoke pot and drink a lot of beer. I'm not sure if that is exactly what the Cs meant, but I think it was part of it.

the men's room and had been gone for a long time. Chloe asked me to help her find him, and I knew where he was, but she tried the door and said it was stuck and wanted me to help. I told her that it was not stuck, it was locked and, to prove it, I got the key, which somehow I had, though I had to take it off my van key ring; it was a 'master key'. And, when I unlocked the door for her, she discovered that Tommy was dead, on the toilet. This was very disturbing to me. Can you tell me anything about this dream? I was thinking, that since it was so clear, that it might have been prophetic.

48 **A**: You will learn the meaning profile of this and other dreams so well that it will be akin to reading from a road map ... Patience, my dear!²

49 **Q**: *(L)* Okay, can I ask about my other dream – about Frank and Ark and I? We were driving down the road and the school was involved – something about 'locker number 43' – there were piles of notebooks, and I had the key to get all this information ...

50 **A**: See last response.³

51 **Q**: *(L)* Okay, is the phone company going to accept the credit card?⁴

52 **A**: All will work itself out.

53 **Q**: *(L)* Well, if they don't, we are in a mess, because it was my stupid idea to do it this way ... and if they don't, my phone will be turned off and I won't even be able to contact him at all to let him know what is going on ...

54 **A**: And if that happened, what do you think Ark would do?

55 **Q**: *(L)* Well, there isn't much he could do!

56 **A**: Nonsense!! You know he would "move heaven and earth" to solve the crisis, pronto!!!

57 **Q**: *(L)* Well, that is comforting ... but I don't see how it could be done. Now, there *is* something that worries me a *lot* ... that Ark will come and not like me ...

58 **A**: Why do you think this?

59 **Q**: *(L)* Well, because I am so fat.

60 **A**: Have you led him to believe that you were skinny?

61 **Q**: *(L)* No. I told him a lot of times that I am too fat.

62 **A**: If you are worried about what Ark will think about your physical appearance, you have nothing to fear, if you have nothing to "hide," no pun intended!

63 **Q**: *(L)* Well, I want to buy some clothes ... and I want to get my final divorce paper work done ... Will I be able to settle with the insurance company before Ark comes so I can do these things?

64 **A**: Wait and see. Worry not.

---

²Well, I'm still waiting for that ability!

³Oddly, both dreams were about keys, which relates back to previous sessions where keys were discussed.

⁴With all the background detail from the previous few sessions, the reason for this question will be self-evident. I didn't have the money to pay bills, Ark had sent me a CC number and code to pay for things and had sorted things out with his bank, so they were willing, but I was having trouble getting anyone to accept this as a payment method. Obviously, without my phone line, I was cut off from the internet and the Cs' mandate to "network via internet".

65 Q: *(L)* Well, you keep saying this, and I just don't see how anything can happen the way you say it is going to happen. I am nearly going out of my mind with worry. But ...

66 A: And when have we been wrong?

67 Q: *(L)* Not *yet*!

68 A: How many demonstrations do you need?!? We told you to tell Ark everything way back, as you measure time, if you recall. You were suspicious then, but you did follow the suggestion, and see what happened? We will not be joyous if you are not able to develop greater faith.

69 Q: *(L)* Well, that makes me feel like I *have* to have faith or I will let everyone down.

70 A: No, you do not "have" to do anything ... It is just that it will be disappointing if you become blocked.

71 Q: *(L)* Okay, but there was something else that happened then. When I told Ark all those things, he went to the bank and discovered that he had been wiped out ... she took every damn dime. So, where did faith get us then?

72 A: No. When we suggested it, it was well before that event. And, she did not take "every damn dime."

73 Q: *(L)* Well, close enough. Never mind. I don't want to know any more on that subject. Okay, change of subject: what is the source of the apparition – allegedly of the Virgin Mary – on the building down in Clearwater?

74 A: "Apparitions" are not important as to their "source" but rather their result.

75 Q: *(L)* Well, is it STS or STO or just a chemical anomaly? But you say that is not important – the result is. What is the result?

76 A: Have you not witnessed it?

77 Q: *(L)* Well, I can't tell what is in the hearts and minds of people, all I see is a lot of people making money off of it. How can I know whether ...

78 A: Then you must think that the result of the UFO/alien phenomenon is that a "bunch of people are running around and buying silly rocks."

79 Q: *(F)* Obviously there are a lot of different results. Most could be buying the silly rocks, but others could be learning from it either for STS or STO. *(L)* So, the results of anything is strictly the result of the configuration of the individual?

80 A: Yes.

81 Q: *(L)* But it still begs the question: Is it truly an apparition of the Virgin Mary?

82 A: Well, is it possible for you to differentiate between that which is an apparition, and that which is not. And does it really matter? Or, is "apparition," merely a classification? Or a "label?"

83 Q: *(V)* Is it really there?

84 A: Are you? Are we? Is George Bush? Or is he an apparition?

85 Q: *(V)* AM wanted to ask about her upset stomach and the pain she has had for the past few days.

86 A: Ask her to ask.

87 Q: *(AM)* Why is my stomach in such a bad state the last couple of days?

88 A: Not your terminology.

89 Q: *(AM)* Why has my stomach been so upset the past week or two, whenever I eat, and why do I have these headaches with it?

90 A: What else has happened in the past "week or so?"

91 **Q:** *(AM)* You are asking me? I don't know.

92 **A:** We are asking you to ask aloud, and more importantly, ask yourself, for therein lies your answer!

93 **Q:** *(AM)* What is the remedy to correct it?

94 **A:** What is the underlying cause?!?!

95 **Q:** *(AM)* I'm confused. I'm asking questions and they are asking me questions. *(V)* Are you stressed over something major? *(AM)* I'm always stressed.

96 **A:** No.

97 **Q:** *(AM)* It's not stress?

98 **A:** Your response was incorrect. When you said "I'm always stressed." Really??? This much??? We don't think so!!!

99 **Q:** *(L)* Does it have to do with Patrick? *(AM)* Does it have to do with my dislike of Patricia and Shayna?

100 **A:** Partly.

101 **Q:** *(AM)* I dislike them intensely. What is the other part?

102 **A:** Work related. Career direction related.

103 **Q:** *(AM)* I also dislike my job. Is the other part of my physical problem, the fact that I see my job as a dead end?

104 **A:** Yes.

105 **Q:** *(AM)* What can I do to correct this?

106 **A:** See the bigger picture.

107 **Q:** *(AM)* I don't understand that. It is not clear enough for me.

108 **A:** Current events will mean little, eventually. "This too, shall pass."

109 **Q:** *(AM)* Is one of the solutions to steer clear of Patrick's family?

110 **A:** Then, all your life, you will need to "steer clear" of a lot of things. Better to learn to let "bad" things fall off your back, as in the proverbial duck's water!

111 **Q:** *(L)* I don't understand. You told *me* to avoid these people!

112 **A:** You react differently.

113 **Q:** *(L)* Well ... I can be around them ... it doesn't bother me. I just don't choose to because I don't want their vibrations all over me. *(AM)* I don't have to talk to them, do I?

114 **A:** That is not the point. One does not need to let others bother them, if one can learn to regulate absorption. Not unsolvable.

115 **Q:** *(AM)* How can I take steps to get to the point where I can deal with them, but not so that they make me sick? It is very difficult for me to do this. It literally makes me sick.

116 **A:** Learn to laugh at that which currently disturbs you. After all, it is comical, when you think of it. Stop taking everything so seriously!!!

117 **Q:** *(AM)* I always thought that I was able to deal with everything, but these people absolutely nauseate me. And, then I get mad at myself because I react to them. Usually I wouldn't react to them. I would not even acknowledge their existence! *(L)* What makes it so personal? *(AM)* They are so low on the evolutionary scale that they don't even see their own evil. They think that if anyone else sees the disgusting way they behave as wrong, that there is something wrong with that person, and not them!

118 **A:** Then, picture them as squawking dodo birds.

119 **Q:** *(AM)* It is very difficult.

120 **A**: Not if you try.

121 **Q**: *(AM)* What steps should I take to relieve my work stress? Do I need to start looking for another job? Is there something I can do there to make it less stressful?

122 **A**: All are good possibilities, but, look at these things as joyous challenges, rather than drudgeries.

123 **Q**: *(AM)* Am I in danger of being replaced in my job? Are they looking to replace me?

124 **A**: What danger? Is this the chairmanship of Ford Motor Company??

125 **Q**: *(AM)* Is Patrick at the point where he can see his mother and sister as people with shortcomings, or will he always be blindly devoted and unable to see their faults?

126 **A**: Too many thought patterns at once.

127 **Q**: *(AM)* Is Patrick at the point now where he can clearly see what his mother is doing? See her faults?

128 **A**: Best way for one to "see" faults is for one not to be reminded by others.

129 **Q**: *(AM)* Will he ever be able to be healthy and break away from her control, and go out on his own?

130 **A**: Well, that is quite a "wish list," but see last response.

131 **Q**: *(AM)* Then, the best way for me to deal with this is to cut off all connection with Patrick and his family, correct?

132 **A**: We would never limit your options thusly!

133 **Q**: *(L)* Why is Patrick being dragged through the mud this way, if that is what is happening?

134 **A**: Why is attack, and the particular victim, ever important?

135 **Q**: *(L)* Is it because Patrick is supposed to learn to overcome these things?

136 **A**: Close enough.

137 **Q**: *(L)* Okay, so Patrick has to learn on this, and the best way you can help him is by backing off. *(AM)* From Patrick, too?

138 **A**: When one protests, one facilitates the building of barriers that are an integral part of the attack. For one to have revelation, one must "step back," and view the picture without prejudice!

139 **Q**: *(AM)* Well, I think that my lesson in all of this is that I need to learn that there are going to be people in this world that I will need to deal with, and I need to learn how to do it now. The world is full of these kinds of people.

140 **A**: Or that you can deal with them without letting it affect you.

141 **Q**: *(AM)* It is very difficult. *(V)* Is Patrick this important? *(AM)* The thing is after I got him off the drugs, after all of this happened, it really wasn't him anymore, it was me. I felt that something was happening ... usually people don't affect me like this ... *(L)* Did you hear what you just said? *(AM)* What? *(L)* "When I got him off the drugs." *(AM)* Is that bad? *(L)* He didn't do it himself. *(AM)* I know he didn't. And he knows he didn't. He tried before ... *(L)* Is it any good this way? That he didn't do it himself? *(AM)* I think so. While he was on them, his mom and his sister had complete control of him. He is 300 per cent better ... the only difference between Patrick and his family is that he knows there is a problem and he wants to get help. *(L)* I think he thrives on the continuous drama of it. Crisis after crisis. Drama Queen City! Is there

a karmic relationship between Patrick and AM?

142 **A**: Yes.

143 **Q**: *(L)* Can you tell us what it is?

144 **A**: Let it unfold. Remember, all there is is lessons.

145 **Q**: *(L)* Will you tell us the number of lifetimes they have had together?

146 **A**: Oh, how about 4?

147 **Q**: *(L)* Well, that is not much. *(V)* Would exploring this help now?

148 **A**: Maybe, "Mom" has that talent. Go "under" to rise above.

149 **Q**: *(AM)* Okay, thank you. I have to go to bed.

150 **A**: Good Night AM.

151 **Q**: *(L)* Now, we have a question from Ark ... for his sister. Can you find her?

152 **A**: We can "find" anybody.

153 **Q**: *(L)* Okay, she would like to ...

154 **A**: But she wants us to advise her regarding business decisions ... hmmm, seems she is quite capable, a good organizer and very pragmatic. Better advice could be reserved for other arenas.

155 **Q**: *(L)* Such as?

156 **A**: Quest for knowledge.

157 **Q**: *(L)* So she should be asking about spiritual matters and not material things?

158 **A**: Yes. She is a dynamic business woman ... for us to advise at this juncture could harm, as we would not wish to be a crutch for those currently most capable.

159 **Q**: *(L)* Anything that you wish us to convey to her?

160 **A**: Does channeling when in garden.

161 **Q**: *(L)* She does?

162 **A**: Advanced.

163 **Q**: *(L)* What do you mean?

164 **A**: This particular subject. Remember, souls of alike frequency vibration often travel together. Tell her to go ahead as already intentioned, it will work just fine.

165 **Q**: *(L)* Anything else for her?

166 **A**: Nope.

167 **Q**: *(A)* [via email] Years ago in Hamburg, while working on Unified Field Theory I had the impression I am being watched. Was it indeed the case?

168 **A**: Yes.

169 **Q**: *(L)* By whom?

170 **A**: Not yet.

171 **Q**: *(A)* Was my idea of that time sound and worthwhile to pursue further now?

172 **A**: Yes.

173 **Q**: *(L)* Is there any general comment you can make to Ark about any of these things?

174 **A**: Isn't it fun, Ark, to have heightened awareness ... To be able to piece together more and more?

175 **Q**: *(L)* Ark wants to know about Hoagland ...

176 **A**: Let Ark ask in form he chooses.

177 **Q**: *(A)* Should I seek contact with Hoagland concerning the paper by Modanese?

178 **A**: Best approach is to groove the contact with Hoagland enough so as to have open forum with him and have free exchange of ideas on all possible subjects. Suggest you make him aware of how your particular field, background and angle of experience can further quest.

179 **Q:** *(A)* Is following this link a) safe, b) right?

180 **A:** Well, safety is not determined by what is followed, but rather how followed.

181 **Q:** *(L)* Okay, while we are waiting for Ark's response, I have a question. I am *burning* up! What is the reason for this unbearable heat I am suffering?[5]

182 **A:** Heat means 4th density bleedthrough.

183 **Q:** *(L)* I am about to die of heat, and I know it is cold in here. When you say 4th density bleedthrough, what do you mean?

184 **A:** Oozing of faint reflections of new reality.

185 **Q:** *(L)* Do you mean new or altered or changed bodies?

186 **A:** Review.

187 **Q:** *(V)* Are the night sweats connected?

188 **A:** Maybe.

189 **Q:** *(V)* Are the night sweats I have hormonal?

190 **A:** Maybe.

191 **Q:** *(V)* How come I can't get a straight answer?

192 **A:** Seek and find, tis fun!

193 **Q:** *(L)* Back some time ago, I went unconscious in the chair, nearly passed out, anyway, and Ark sent me a message and said that he *saw me there!* What happened?[6]

194 **A:** Haven't you learned?

195 **Q:** *(L)* Well ... is there any activity a person could do to stimulate their DNA to become superconductive?[7]

196 **A:** No need. You would like to find an activity to stimulate [your youngest child] to grow up faster?

197 **Q:** *(L)* Of course not! She's just a *baby!* She needs to have fun! Oh, I get it. Okay. Now, Frank had a funny feeling about MM [Greenbaum-programmed individual previously mentioned] the other day. Was he getting a message about her?

198 **A:** Yes.

199 **Q:** *(L)* Did she know I was cancelling her for some reason other than the excuse I gave?

200 **A:** She had some suspicion.

201 **Q:** *(L)* Is there some danger to us at this time from her, as Frank perceives?

202 **A:** Yes. Always be vigilant and proceed with caution!

203 **Q:** *(V)* Has she come by to spy on us? *(L)* Does it matter? *(V)* Well, it does

---

[5] *The Wave* 3

[6] This was a very strange experience. I went into a state that can only be described as semi-consciousness. I tried to stay in observer mode and forced my eyes to open and saw that everything around me was like living light. It was such an interesting state that I didn't resist it and was only snapped out of it by the computer sound that I had mail. Ark wanted to know what the heck I was doing, because he had just been walking down a corridor in the university and saw me walking toward him and then I disappeared. It happened a second time when he was in Wroclaw. I was very intrigued by this bilocation. I wasn't consciously doing it, but it was apparently happening.

[7] *The Wave* 12

if she is crazy and has a gun! Can you define this danger?

204 **A**: There are many possibilities.

205 **Q**: *(L)* Well, can you list the top three?

206 **A**: Physical, psychic, spiritual.

207 **Q**: *(V)* You mean she would ...

208 **A**: Be open to all possibilities as pathways of attack.

209 **Q**: *(L)* Is it true that when Ark is here, that our protection level will increase exponentially?

210 **A**: Yes.

211 **Q**: *(V)* All of us?

212 **A**: Any and all.

213 **Q**: *(A)* [via email] I am confused about time. You said relativistic physics must be redone because it assumes unnecessary symmetry. What symmetry do you have in mind?

214 **A**: Unnecessary symmetry? You asked about a particular project or theorem being examined, and those involved. We said that it was on the right track, so long as the symmetrical aspects were dropped as an absolute. Meaning the framework of the project was too narrowly focused.

215 **Q**: *(A)* You suggest that what I was trying to do in Hamburg was a worthwhile pursuit, but I was assuming even more symmetry than Einstein's relativity.

216 **A**: Then don't assume. Remember, symmetry, by its very nature, combines both realms of possibility. It is all inclusive, rather than inharmoniously exclusive.

217 **Q**: *(A)* Is there some anti-gravitational effect in the levitron toy?

218 **A**: Not "in" the levitron toy. Rather "through" the toy. The toy is just the vehicle.

219 **Q**: *(L)* Well, should we spend 40 bucks on this thing? *(V)* How does it work? *(L)* I don't know!

220 **A**: Antigravity is deceivingly simple.

221 **Q**: *(L)* So, the guy who is advertising it is not cheating?

222 **A**: Not correct concept.

223 **Q**: *(L)* What is the correct concept?

224 **A**: See last response for clue.

225 **Q**: *(L)* So, you aren't going to tell me any more about it?

226 **A**: Ark is the questioner, yes?

227 **Q**: *(L)* Okay. Well, he thanks everyone ... and says good night. *(Alice)* I fell recently and would like to know what caused me to fall in the driveway?

228 **A**: Vertigo.

229 **Q**: *(Alice)* Is it a continuing ailment?

230 **A**: Intermittent.

231 **Q**: *(Alice)* When I had that terrible pain in my foot, in church, what caused that?

232 **A**: Thrombosis.

233 **Q**: *(Alice)* I seem to be having trouble with my memory ... is this related to the emotional issues you told me about?

234 **A**: Check dietary considerations. These can either enhance or forestall the ageing process.

235 **Q**: *(Alice)* What is wrong with my leg?

236 **A**: Circulatory disruptions; see previous response.

237 **Q**: *(Alice)* Will my eyes get any better?

238 **A**: Ditto.

239 **Q**: *(V)* My grandmother recently died. How is she?

240 **A**: Okay.

241 **Q**: *(V)* I know that was a lame question, but is there any opportunity of speaking to her? *(L)* No! I'm not gonna channel your grandmother! I don't even know her! You can ask about her ... *(V)* Is there a message for me from my grandmother?

242 **A**: Maybe, at another juncture.

243 **Q**: *(L)* Why another time?

244 **A**: She is not ready now.

245 **Q**: *(V)* Is she sleeping as you described Tom?

246 **A**: There, time exists not.

247 **Q**: *(L)* But you said she is not ready *now*, but then you say time exists not? What is the deal here?

248 **A**: What was the first word of the previous response?

249 **Q**: *(V)* Okay, there as opposed to here. Where is she?

250 **A**: Fifth density.

251 **Q**: *(L)* Why do I not want to channel other entities ... that was a strong response that just sort of jumped out ... is it correct?

252 **A**: Yes.

253 **Q**: *(L)* Why?

254 **A**: It would be like trudging through the saw palmetto bush thickets, at night, barefoot!

255 **Q**: *(L)* Well, that is a good way to step on a rattlesnake!

256 **A**: Maybe.

257 **Q**: *(V)* Has 4th density Earth been in existence as long as 3rd density Earth?

258 **A**: Not correct concept.

259 **Q**: *(V)* Does 4th density Earth exist?

260 **A**: Yes.

261 **Q**: *(V)* And there are human beings ...

262 **A**: All exists always.

263 **Q**: *(L)* Where is the 4th density Earth, aside from being in 4th density?

264 **A**: Another realm.

265 **Q**: *(L)* Are there 4th density 'us' existing *now* on this 4th density Earth?

266 **A**: Yes. Us.

267 **Q**: *(V)* When you are on 4th density and look at the sun, do you see the same thing we see here? When you look at the moon, do you have the same visual experience?

268 **A**: No. Awareness is broader.

269 **Q**: *(L)* Well, what would you see when looking at the sun?

270 **A**: Entire visual spectrum.

271 **Q**: *(L)* You mean we would be able to see all the things that we can now only see with instruments? Like the corona, the solar wind, et cetera?

272 **A**: The entire sphere from all possible angles of realization?

273 **Q**: *(L)* Would we be able to *hear* the sun?

274 **A**: If chosen.

275 **Q**: *(L)* What does the sun sound like?

276 **A**: Not answerable.

277 **Q**: *(L)* Do planets and suns talk to each other? Are they angels and archangels?

278 **A**: Laura, let us not go over the "deep end." [Laughter] Boys are all snails and puppy dog tails ... Girls are really sugar and spice, and everything nice ...

279 **Q**: *(L)* So, you are making fun of me!

280 **A:** Sure, why not?

281 **Q:** *(L)* Well, are there such things as archangels?

282 **A:** Maybe.

283 **Q:** *(L)* Well, if there are such things as archangels, how would we perceive them?

284 **A:** Too complex.

285 **Q:** *(L)* Okay, do different individuals have connections to different archangels? *(V)* Yes, are our souls born from different archangel realms?

286 **A:** No. The soul was never created. Was/is/always will be.

287 **Q:** *(V)* Well, I can't grasp that ... I mean, creation ... *(L)* There is no creation; All just *is*. *(F)* Well, there are cycles. *(V)* Well, where does the substance come from. *(L)* Doesn't come from anywhere. Just thoughts in the mind of God. I mean, what else does God have to do for eternity but dream? We are the dream. *(V)* Can you comment on my struggle to understand this?

288 **A:** What is the struggle? It will come. Okay, folks, for now, goodnight.

End of Session

This was the last session of 1996. It was 44 days before Ark would arrive, but we won't be covering that in this volume. But, just so the reader won't be left hanging entirely, I'll include here some of the final emails between Ark and myself in 1996.

Ark and I both decided to read some of the Richard Hoagland materials. After finishing a lengthy piece, I wrote:

> Have finished Hoagland. Had a number of thoughts as I went through. There was a lot of technical jargon that I simply did not know so could not understand some references, but I had enough of a grasp to know what was going on. I think Richard is good in many respects, but he also seems to be rather obsessive in some ways and that can be dangerous.
>
> One of my questions is: if a reputable scientist has supposedly been forced to recant or withdraw AFTER a paper has been published giving the fundamentals of a certain direction of research, and Hoagland might possibly be cranking the public to play with these toys, why is Hoagland still out there???
>
> I mean, we have to consider the apparent fact that even one of the richest men in America, Ross Perot, with all his capacity for protection in a material sense, was essentially silenced regarding his bid for the presidency. He withdrew from the race one day, suddenly, and the next gave some lame excuse, and it was obvious that the man was severely shaken.
>
> I have more questions about certain things, but will save them until I print the thing and can jot notes in the margins.

Ark responded:

Yes, this Hoagland is a puzzle. But it is a puzzle that, I believe, can not be neglected. I thought whether I should try to contact him or not. And I think I should. All in the open. Well, "almost" all.

I was thinking about C's answer to my question about Hamburg. There was no rational basis at all for thinking I was watched. But I was really afraid and was checking if my papers were moved during the night etc. But I was sure it was paranoidal. Because WHY? It is true that I was was working on a unification of gravitation with electromagnetism. But NOBODY knew that - except if somebody could read my thoughts. So this answer is strange. I did not expect a "yes" here. Although I noticed C's answers are never of that kind that they tell something really new - so that one would be SURE they really KNOW something. Probably it must be so, otherwise it would contradict Directive number I do not remember. By the way: what are these directives? Did they ever list them?

I responded:

But, if you consider psychic spying, strictly from the 3rd density level... add to that 4th density manipulations and interactions with 4d and 3d... I will tell you some VERY bizarre events that happened to us that CONVINCED us that either my house was bugged or somebody was reading our minds or listening to our conversations.

And, wasn't it in Hamburg that your hands were going numb? Might there be some connection between the emotional states in you, which would be related to manipulated external conditions and experiences, and an attempt to deflect you from that course?

And, actually, they have told a number of things that NONE of us could possibly have known. These things involve rather complicated series of events that proved the correctness of what they had said in startling ways.

I think they want to help by making us think in new ways. Goodness knows, if they had not repeatedly said things to me about the internet, you would NEVER have found me. It will be a lot easier when you are here and we can really take things apart minutely. ... In a sense, they did go a little beyond to prod me repeatedly to use the internet... Also, it will REALLY help for me to finish the tapes. Will try to get a couple done this afternoon and evening. Get myself back on schedule.

Another day. Tomorrow is day 43 on the countdown - a prime number, isn't it? It was the number on the locker full of notebooks in my dream.

On the 30th of December, I received an email from Jason Dunlap, who was constantly harassing me because the C's did not agree with his daily channel-o-choice – especially when Hale-Bopp was the topic. Below is his email with my interline responses:

Dear Laura,

> According to the info you sent, the C's consider Hale-bopp a non-event, and I'm wondering if things have changed in light of the new information about the comet.

Well, as in the case of the photon belt, we will have to wait and see, won't we? Not too long, either!

> There is so much astronomical data relating to it's "companion", it being artificial, and tons of info about a transmission coming from it, etc.

Could it be DIS-information? Once again, we will see.

> I don't see how it's re-appearance in Jan./feb is going to be simply "the passing of a nice comet". There was no mention of the companion object which wasn't discovered by us until Oct., but it seems that they would have mentioned it if it was significant.

If you go to www.hale-bopp.com, you will find that the original claim of the companion object was in November. Additionally, you will read more than one side of the story.

And, since at this point, the C's are running at about 90% when they DO say something, (leaving 10% for trans-density distortion) I am quite comfortable with what they have said about it. But, that is me. You have not had the personal validating experiences that I have had. And, after these many years pursuing the "truth," I have to say that very little impresses me about the continuous wild claims that pile up year after year. A little simple truth now and then is refreshing. But truth is often intimidating because it takes away the buffers of rationalization in which most people like to hide to find comfort.

> Are they saying that there is no such object, that it is all imagination and nonsense based on errors in observation?

Yep.

> I find this really hard to believe.

Belief is a choice. It has nothing to do with truth.

> I've talked to scientists that claim a big coverup, because it is real and it is coming this way in a few months.

Are scientists immune to disinformation? Carl Sagan, rest his soul, was a primary source of disinformation and was considered to be one of the most eminent scientists of this country. Do you care to name your sources? Do THEY wish to be named?

As before, time will tell. And I put my money on the Hale-Bopp Flopp.

But, it is FUN to try to figure out who is who, and who is doing what, isn't it?

Laura

And, of course, the Cs turned out to be right.

Apparently, the credit card was made to work, though there is no email discussing it. There are references to several phone calls between us, so it must have been discussed there. In any event, there are no further references to such issues.

The final emails show that the year ended on a note of great hope; Ark's arrival was getting closer and closer and we both settled down to doing our respective work. You could say that the end of 1996 was the end of our old realities and in 1997, Forever began, thanks to the Cs!

Chapters of "The Wave"

"The Wave" originally was a series of articles written by Laura Knight-Jadczyk for the Internet only. These articles have been expanded and published as a series of volumes (1–8), in paper and in electronic formats. Over the years, a number of editions have been produced for each of these volumes. Some of these editions do not have chapter numbering, and for some, the chapter numbering has been re-started from one. However, the chapter titles are identical in all editions. For this reason, the following table summarizes all chapters of *The Wave* Series and gives chapter number, chapter title, and shows into which volume a particular chapter number has been included (VP = volume number in print, VE = volume number in electronic format), and where a chapter can be found on the Cassiopaea website. Please refer to the bibliography, section "Esotericism", for additional details about the volumes of *The Wave*.

Nr.	Chapter Title	VP	VE	http://cassiopaea.org/
1	"Riding The Wave"	1	1	/the-wave-chapter-1
2	"Multi-Dimensional Soul Essences"	1	1	/the-wave-chapter-2
3	"Dorothy and The Frog Prince"	1	1	/the-wave-chapter-3
4	"The C's go for a 'Test Drive'"	1	1	/the-wave-chapter-4
5	"Perpendicular Realities"	1	1	/the-wave-chapter-5
6	"Animal Psychology"	1	1	/the-wave-chapter-6
7	"Laura Falls Into the Pit"	1	1	/the-wave-chapter-7
8	"Everywhere You Look..."	1	2	/the-wave-chapter-8
9	"The Beast of Gévaudan"	1	2	/the-wave-chapter-9
10	"The Truth Is Out There"	2	2	/the-wave-chapter-10
11	"Roses Grow Best In Manure"	2	2	/the-wave-chapter-11
12	"All There Is Is Lessons"	2	2	/the-wave-chapter-12
13	"Some Further Remarks"	2	2	/the-wave-chapter-13
14	"Candy Will Ruin Your Teeth"	2	2	/the-wave-chapter-14
15	"He Hideth My Soul..."	2	2	/the-wave-chapter-15
16	"Laura Finds Reiki"	2	2	/the-wave-chapter-16
17	"Wandering In 3rd Density"	2	2	/the-wave-chapter-17
18	"A Trip to 'Alligator Alley'"	2	2	/the-wave-chapter-18
19	"Dr. Greenbaum"	2	2	/the-wave-chapter-19

20	"Black Lightning Strikes"	3	3	/the-wave-chapter-20
21	"Roswell Revisited"	3	3	/the-wave-chapter-21
22	"The Nexus Seven"	3	3	/the-wave-chapter-22
23	"Lucifer and the Pot of Gold"	3	3	/the-wave-chapter-23
24	"The Bacchantes Meet Apollo"	3	3	/the-wave-chapter-24
25	"A Walk in Nature"	3	3	/the-wave-chapter-25
26	"The Tree of Life"	3	3	/the-wave-chapter-26
27	"Stripped to the Bone"	3	3	/the-wave-chapter-27
28	"Technicians of Ecstasy"	4	4	/the-wave-chapter-28
29	"The 3-5 Code"	4	4	/the-wave-chapter-29
30	"Grape Wine In a Mason Jar"	4	4	/the-wave-chapter-30
31	"The Priory of Sion"	4	4	/the-wave-chapter-31
32	"Torah, Kaballah..."	4	4	/the-wave-chapter-32
33	"Introduction"	5	5	/the-wave-chapter-33
34	"The Channel"	5	5	/the-wave-chapter-34
35	"A Strange Interlude"	5	5	/the-wave-chapter-35
36	"A Vile Superstition"	5	5	/the-wave-chapter-36
37	"Critical Channeling"	5	5	/the-wave-chapter-37
38	"The Feminine Vampire"	5	5	/the-wave-chapter-38
39	"The Court of Seven"	5	5	/the-wave-chapter-39
40	"Secret Agents from Alpha 1"	5	5	/the-wave-chapter-40
41	"The Realm of Archetypes"	5	5	/the-wave-chapter-41
42	"The Tradition"	5	5	/the-wave-chapter-42
43	"The Head of Bran"	5	5	/the-wave-chapter-43
44	"The Crane Dance"	5	5	/the-wave-chapter-44
45	"The Gulf Breeze"	5	5	/the-wave-chapter-45
46	"The Theological Reality"	5	5	/the-wave-chapter-46
47	"Semiotics and the Content Plane"	5	5	/the-wave-chapter-47
48	"The Juvenile Dictionary"	6	6	/the-wave-chapter-48
49	"Frequency Resonance Vibration"	6	6	/the-wave-chapter-49
50	"Shifts in the Matrix"	6	6	/the-wave-chapter-50
51	"The Psychomantium"	6	6	/the-wave-chapter-51
52	"The Cryptogeographic Being"	6	6	/the-wave-chapter-52
53	"Strange Birds"	6	6	/the-wave-chapter-53
54	"Glimpses of Other Realities"	6	6	/the-wave-chapter-54
55	"Albert Einstein, Free Energy..."	6	6	/the-wave-chapter-55
56	"Intolerance, Cruelty..."	6	6	/the-wave-chapter-56
57	"It's Just Economics"	7	7	/the-wave-chapter-57
58	"Alien Reaction Machines"	7	7	/the-wave-chapter-58
59	"An Encounter with the Unicorn"	7	7	/the-wave-chapter-59
60	"The Unicorn's Closet"	7	7	/the-wave-chapter-60
61	"Ira's Inner Cesspool"	7	7	/the-wave-chapter-61
62	"Secret Games at Princeton"	7	7	/the-wave-chapter-62
63	"Murdering the Feminine"	7	7	/the-wave-chapter-63
64	"Crossing the Threshold"	8	8	/the-wave-chapter-64

65	"The Way of the Fool"	8	8	/the-wave-chapter-65
66	"The Zelator"	8	8	/the-wave-chapter-66
67	"Food for the Moon"	8	8	/the-wave-chapter-67
68	"As Above, So Below"	8	8	/the-wave-chapter-68
69	"The Whirlpool of Charybdis..."	8	8	/the-wave-chapter-69
70	"You Take the High Road..."	8	8	/the-wave-chapter-70
71	"If I Speak in the Tongues..."	8	8	/the-wave-chapter-71
72	"Nonlinear Dynamics of Love..."	8	8	/the-wave-chapter-72

Recommended Reading

This is a subset of the "Recommended Reading" list at
http://cassiopaea.org/forum/index.php/topic,33 092.0.html

9/11

- Griffin, David Ray – *The 9/11 Commission Report: Omissions And Distortions*, Olive Branch Pr 2004
- Griffin and Falk – *The New Pearl Harbor: Disturbing Questions About the Bush Administration and 9/11*, Interlink Pub Group 2004
- Quinn and Knight-Jadczyk – *9/11 The Ultimate Truth*, Red Pill Pr 2006
- Wood, Judy – *Where Did the Towers Go? Evidence of Directed Free-energy Technology on 9/11*, The New Investigation 2010

Ancient Civilizations

- David-Neel, Alexandra – *Magic and Mystery in Tibet*, Dover 1971
- Dunn, Christopher – *The Giza Power Plant: Technologies of Ancient Egypt*, Bear & Company 1998
- Firestone, West, Warwick-Smith – *The Cycle of Cosmic Catastrophes: How a Stone-Age Comet Changed the Course of World Culture*, Bear & Company 2006
- Fox, Hugh – *Gods of the Cataclysm: A revolutionary investigation of man and his gods before and after the Great Cataclysm*, Aardwolfe Books 2011
- von Hassler, Gerd – *Lost Survivors of the Deluge*, Signet 1978
- Muck, Otto – *The Secret of Atlantis*, HarperCollins 1979

Astronomy

- Clube and Napier – *The Cosmic Serpent*, Universe Pub 1982
- Clube and Napier – *The Cosmic Winter*, Blackwell Pub 1990
- Knight-Jadczyk, Laura – *The Apocalypse: Comets, Asteroids and Cyclical Catastrophes*, Red Pill Pr 2012
- Velikovsky, Immanuel – *Worlds in Collision*, Paradigma Ltd 2009

Bible History

- Davies, Philip R. – *The Origins of Biblical Israel (Library Hebrew Bible/Old Testament Studies)*, T&T Clark 2009
- Finkelstein and Silberman – *David and Solomon: In Search of the Bible's Sacred Kings and the Roots of the Western Tradition*, Free Pr 2007
- Garbini, Giovanni – *History and Ideology in Ancient Israel*, Crossroad Pub Co 1988
- Mack, Burton – *The Lost Gospel: The Book of Q and Christian Origins*, HarperOne 1994
- Mack, Burton – *A Myth of Innocence: Mark and Christian Origins*, Augsburg Fortress Pub 1998
- Silberman, Neil Asher – *The Bible Unearthed: Archaeology's New Vision of Ancient Israel and the Origin of Its Sacred Texts*, Touchstone 2002
- Thompson, Thomas L. – *The Mythic Past: Biblical Archaeology And The Myth Of Israel*, Basic Books 2000
- Thompson, Thomas L. – *The Messiah Myth: The Near Eastern Roots of Jesus and David*, Basic Books 2005

Cassiopaea Experiment

- Koehli, Harrison – "The Cs Hit List 01: Prophecy, Prediction, and Portents of Things to Come", *Signs Of The Times*, sott.net/article/236777
- Koehli, Harrison – "The Cs Hit List 02: Space and Weather Science Gone Wild", *Signs Of The Times*, sott.net/article/237356
- Koehli, Harrison – "The Cs Hit List 03: History Is Bunk", *Signs Of The Times*, sott.net/article/238372
- Koehli, Harrison – "The Cs Hit List 04: Nature, Nurture, and My Monkey Genes", *Signs Of The Times*, sott.net/article/239307
- Koehli, Harrison – "The Cs Hit List 05: Dr. Greenbaum and the Manchurian Candidates", *Signs Of The Times*, sott.net/article/240587
- Koehli, Harrison – "The Cs Hit List 06: Let's Do the Planetary Twist to the Tune of the Brothers Heliopolis", *Signs Of The Times*, sott.net/article/242280
- Koehli, Harrison – "The Cs Hit List 07: Sun Star Companion, Singing Stones and Smoking Visions", *Signs Of The Times*, sott.net/article/244819
- Koehli, Harrison – "The Cs Hit List 08: Of Oracles and Conspiracies: TWA 800, 9/11, H1N1, and VISA", *Signs Of The Times*, sott.net/article/247080
- Koehli, Harrison – "The Cs Hit List 09: DNA, Rational Design and the Origins of Life", *Signs Of The Times*, sott.net/article/250256

Esotericism

- Campbell, Joseph – *The Hero with a Thousand Faces*, Princeton University Pr 1972
- Chittick, William – *The Sufi Path of Knowledge: Ibn al-'Arabi's Metaphysics of Imagination*, State University of New York Pr 1989
- Hall, Manly – *The Secret Teachings of all Ages*, Wilder Publications 2009
- Knight-Jadczyk, Laura – *Amazing Grace*, Red Pill Pr 2012
- Knight-Jadczyk, Laura – *Riding the Wave: The Truth and Lies about 2012 and Global Transformation* (The Wave Series Vol. 1), Red Pill Pr 2010
- Knight-Jadczyk, Laura – *Soul Hackers: The Hidden Hands Behind the New Age Movement* (The Wave Series Vol. 2), Red Pill Pr 2010
- Knight-Jadczyk, Laura – *Stripped to the Bone: The Path to Freedom in the Prison of Life* (The Wave Series Vol. 3), Red Pill Pr 2010
- Knight-Jadczyk, Laura – *Through a Glass Darkly: Hidden Masters, Secret Agendas and a Tradition Unveiled* (The Wave Series Vol. 4), Red Pill Pr 2011
- Knight-Jadczyk, Laura – *Petty Tyrants & Facing the Unknown: Navigating the Traps and Diversions of Life in the Matrix* (The Wave Series Vol. 5/6), Red Pill Pr 2011
- Knight-Jadczyk, Laura – *Almost Human: A Stunning Look at the Metaphysics of Evil* (The Wave Series Vol. 7), Red Pill Pr 2009
- Knight-Jadczyk, Laura – *Debugging the Universe: The Hero's Journey* (The Wave Series Vol. 8), Red Pill Pr 2012
- Ouspensky, P. D. – *In Search of the Miraculous: Fragments of an Unknown Teaching*, Harvest/HBJ 1977

Information Theory, Metaphysics and Evolution

- Davies and Gregersen – *Information and the Nature of Reality: From Physics to Metaphysics*, Cambridge University Pr 2010
- Hardy, Alister – *The Living Stream: Evolution and Man*, Harper & Row 1965
- Milton, Richard – *Shattering the Myths of Darwinism*, Inner Traditions 1997
- Morgan, Elaine – *The Scars of Evolution: What Our Bodies Tell Us About Human Origins*, Oxford 1990
- Nagel, Thomas – *Mind and Cosmos: Why the Materialist Neo-Darwinian Conception of Nature Is Almost Certainly False*, Oxford University Pr 2012
- Pierce, John R. – *An Introduction to Information Theory: Symbols, Signals and Noise*
- Shiller, Bryant M. – *Origin of Life: The 5th Option*, Trafford Pub 2006

Health

- Keith, Lierre – *The Vegetarian Myth: Food, Justice and Sustainability*, PM Press 2009
- Mate, Gabor – *When the Body Says No: Exploring the Stress-Disease Connection*, Wiley 2011

History

- Baigent and Leigh and Lincoln – *Holy Blood, Holy Grail: The Secret History of Christ & The Shocking Legacy of the Grail*, Dell Trade Paperbacks 2004
- Baillie, Mike – *Exodus to Arthur: Catastrophic Encounters With Comets*, B T Batsford Ltd 1999
- Baillie, Mike – *New Light on the Black Death*, Tempus 2006
- Carotta, Francesco – *Jesus Was Caesar: On the Julian Origin of Christianity: An Investigative Report*, Aspekt 2005
- Garnier, John – *The Worship of the Dead, or the Origin and Nature of Pagan Idolatry and Its Bearing Upon the Early History of Egypt and Babylonia*, Chapman & Hall 1904
- Knight-Jadczyk, Laura – *The Secret History of the World: And how to get out alive* (Secret History Series Vol. 1), Red Pill Pr 2005
- Knight-Jadczyk, Laura – *Comets and the Horns of Moses* ("Secret History" Series Vol. 2), Red Pill Pr 2013
- Langer, Walter C. – *The Mind of Adolf Hitler: The Secret Wartime Report*, Basic Books 1972
- Lescaudron and Knight-Jadczyk – *Earth Changes and the Human Cosmic Connection* (Secret History Series Vol. 3), Red Pill Pr 2014
- Malkowski, Edward F. – *Ancient Egypt 39,000 BCE: The History, Technology, and Philosophy of Civilization X*, Bear & Company 2010
- Momigliano, Arnaldo – *On Pagans, Jews, and Christians*, Wesleyan 1987
- Shreeve, James – *The Neandertal Enigma: Solving the Mystery of Modern Human Origins*, Avon 1996
- Sitchin, Zecharia – *The 12th Planet*, Harper 2007
- Thompson and Cremo – *The Hidden History of the Human Race (The Condensed Edition of Forbidden Archeology)*, Bhaktivedanta Book Pub 1999
- Wilkens, Iman – *Where Troy Once Stood: The Mystery of Homer's Iliad & Odyssey Revealed*, St Martins Pr 1991

Hyperdimensions

- Abbott, Edwin A. – *Flatland: A Romance of Many Dimensions*, Signet 1984
- Kaku, Michio – *Hyperspace: A Scientific Odyssey Through Parallel Universes, Time Warps, and the 10th Dimension*, Anchor 1995
- Ouspensky, P.D. – *Tertium Organum: A Key to the Enigmas of the World*, Vintage 1981
- Rucker, Rudy – *The Fourth Dimension: A Guided Tour of the Higher Universes*, Houghton Mifflin 1984

Politics and Pathocracy

- Allen, Gary – *None Dare Call It Conspiracy*, Gsg & Assoc 1971
- Douglass, James W. – *JFK and the Unspeakable: Why He Died and Why It Matters*, Touchstone 2010
- Klein, Naomi – *The Shock Doctrine: The Rise of Disaster Capitalism*, Picador 2008
- Knight-Jadczyk, Laura – *JFK: The Assassination of America*, Red Pill Pr 2013
- Prouty, L. Fletcher – *JFK: The CIA, Vietnam, and the Plot to Assassinate John F. Kennedy*, Skyhorse Pub 2011
- Prouty, L. Fletcher – *The Secret Team: The CIA and Its Allies in Control of the United States and the World*, Skyhorse Pub 2011

Psychology

- DiSalvo, David – *What Makes Your Brain Happy and Why You Should Do the Opposite*, Prometheus 2011
- Donaldson-Pressman, Stephanie – *The Narcissistic Family: Diagnosis and Treatment*, Jossey-Bass 1997
- Golomb, Elan – *Trapped in the Mirror: Adult Children of Narcissists in their Struggle for Self*, William Morrow & Co 1995
- Hort, Barbara E – *Unholy Hungers: Encountering the Psychic Vampire in Ourselves & Others*, Shambhala 1996
- Kahneman, Daniel – *Thinking, Fast and Slow*, Farrar, Straus and Giroux 2013
- McRaney, David – *You Are Not So Smart: Why You Have Too Many Friends on Facebook, Why Your Memory Is Mostly Fiction, and 46 Other Ways You're Deluding Yourself*, Gotham 2012
- Simon, George K. – *Character Disturbance: the phenomenon of our age*, Parkhurst Brothers 2011
- Stout, Martha – *The Myth of Sanity: Divided Consciousness and the Promise of Awareness*, Penguin 2002

- Wilson, Timothy D. – *Redirect: The Surprising New Science of Psychological Change*, Little, Brown and Company 2011
- Wilson, Timothy D. – *Strangers to Ourselves: Discovering the Adaptive Unconscious*, Belknap Pr 2004

Psychopathy

- Babiak and Hare – *Snakes in Suits: When Psychopaths Go to Work*, HarperBusiness 2007
- Brown, Sandra – *Women Who Love Psychopaths: Inside the Relationships of inevitable Harm With Psychopaths, Sociopaths & Narcissists*, Mask Pub 2010
- Cleckley, Hervey – *The Mask of Sanity: An Attempt to Clarify Some Issues about the So-Called Psychopathic Personality*, Literary Licensing 2011
- Hare, Robert D. – *Without Conscience: The Disturbing World of the Psychopaths Among Us*, Guilford Pr 1999
- Lobaczewski, Andrzej – *Political Ponerology: A Science on the Nature of Evil Adjusted for Political Purposes*, Red Pill Pr 2007
- Stout, Martha – *The Sociopath Next Door*, Harmony 2006

Religion

- Hoyle, Fred – *Origin of the Universe and the Origin of Religion (Anshen Transdisciplinary Lectureships in Art, Science, and the Philosophy of Culture, Monograph)*, Moyer Bell 1997

Spiritualism

- Ashe, Geoffrey – *The Ancient Wisdom: A Quest for the Source of Mystic Knowledge*, Macmillan 1997
- Baldwin, William – *Spirit Releasement Therapy: A Technique Manual*, Headline Books 1995
- Barrett and Hyslop – *Evidence Of Survival After Death*, Kessinger Publishing 2010
- Blum, Deborah – *Ghost Hunters: William James and the Search for Scientific Proof of Life After Death*, Penguin Books 2007
- Davis, Vance A. – *Unbroken Promises: A True Story of Courage and Belief*, White Mesa Pub 1995
- Doyle, Arthur Conan – *The History of Spiritualism*, Fredonia Books 2003
- Carrington and Fodor – *Haunted People: The Story Of The Poltergeist Down The Centuries*, Kessinger Publishing 2006
- Ebon, Martin – *Prophecy in our Time*, New American Library 1968

- Elkins, Rueckert, McCarty – *The Ra Material*, L/L Research 1984
- Fiore, Edith – *The Unquiet Dead: A Psychologist Treats Spirit Possession*, Ballantine 1995
- Fodor, Nandor – *The haunted mind: A psychoanalyst looks at the supernatural*, Garrett Pub 1959
- Garret, Eileen – *Many Voices: The Autobiography of a Medium*, Putnam Pub
- Kardec, Allan – *The Spirits Book*, White Crow Books 2010
- Lethbridge, T. C. – *The Power of the Pendulum*, Penguin Books 1991
- Marciniak, Barbara – *Bringers of the Dawn*, Bear & Company 1992
- Martin, Malachi – *Hostage to the Devil: The Possession and Exorcism of Five Contemporary Americans*, HarperOne 1999
- Roll and Storey – *Unleashed: Of Poltergeists and Murder: The Curious Story of Tina Resch*, Pocket Books 2007
- Stevenson, Ian – *Twenty Cases Suggestive of Reincarnation*, University of Virginia Pr 1980
- Vickers, Brian – *Occult Scientific Mentalities*, Cambridge University Pr 1986
- Whitten and Fisher – *Life between Life*, Grand Central Pub 1988
- Wickland, Carl – *Thirty Years Among the Dead*, White Crow Books 2011
- Wilson, Colin – *The Siren Call of Hungry Ghosts: A Riveting Investigation Into Channeling and Spirit Guides*, Paraview Press 2001

UFOs/Aliens

- Bramley, William – *The Gods of Eden*, Avon 1993
- Corso, Philip – *The Day After Roswell*, Pocket Books 1998
- Dolan, Richard – *UFOs and the National Security State: Chronology of a Cover-Up, 1941–1973*, Keyhole Pub 2009
- Dolan, Richard – *UFOs and the National Security State: The Cover-Up Exposed, 1973–1991*, Keyhole Pub 2010
- Fort, Charles – *The Complete Books of Charles Fort*, Dover 1974
- Fowler, Raymond E. – *The Andreasson Affair: The Documented Investigation of a Woman's Abduction Aboard a UFO*, Wild Flower Pr 1994
- Fuller, John G. – *The Interrupted Journey*, Dial Pr 1967
- Jessup, Morris – *The Case for the UFO*, New Saucerian Books 2014
- Knight-Jadczyk, Laura – *High Strangeness: Hyperdimensions and the Process of Alien Abduction*, Red Pill Pr 2008
- Moulton Howe, Linda – *Glimpses of Other Realities Vol. 1: Facts and Eyewitnesses*, LMH Prod 1993

- Moulton Howe, Linda – *Glimpses of Other Realities Vol. 2: High Strangeness*, LMH Prod 1998
- Keel, John – *Operation Trojan Horse*, Anomalist Books 2013
- Keel, John – *The Mothman Prophecies*, Tor 2002
- Keel, John – *The Eighth Tower*, Anomalist Books 2013
- Picknett and Prince – *The Stargate Conspiracy: The Truth about Extraterrestrial life and the Mysteries of Ancient Egypt*, Berkley 2001
- Redfern, Nick – *Close Encounters of the Fatal Kind: Suspicious Deaths, Mysterious Murders, and Bizarre Disappearances in UFO History*, New Page Books 2014
- Sanderson, Ivan T. – *Invisible Residents: The Reality of Underwater UFOs*, Adventures Unlimited Pr 2005
- Strieber, Whitley – *Majestic*, Tor 2011
- Turner, Karl – *Into the Fringe: A True Story of Alien Abduction*, WordMean 2014
- Turner, Karl – *Taken: Inside the Alien-Human Agenda*, WordMean 2013
- Vallee, Jacques – *Passport to Magonia: On UFOs, Folklore, and Parallel Worlds*, Contemporary Books 1993
- Vallee, Jacques – *Dimensions: A Casebook of Alien Contact*, Anomalist Books 2008

Books and DVDs from Red Pill Press

Visit redpillpress.com for more information!

The Secret History of the World, Vol. 1

... and how to get out alive

Laura Knight-Jadczyk

If you heard the Truth, would you believe it? Ancient civilisations. Hyperdimensional realities. DNA changes. Bible conspiracies. What are the realities? What is disinformation?

The Secret History of The World and How To Get Out Alive is the definitive book of the real answers where Truth is more fantastic than fiction. Laura Knight-Jadczyk, wife of internationally known theoretical physicist, Arkadiusz Jadczyk, an expert in hyperdimensional physics, draws on science and mysticism to pierce the veil of reality. Due to the many threats on her life from agents and agencies known and unknown, Laura left the United States to live in France, where she is working closely with Patrick Rivière, student of Eugene Canseliet, the only disciple of the legendary alchemist Fulcanelli.

With sparkling humour and wisdom, she picks up where Fulcanelli left off, sharing over thirty years of research to reveal, for the first time, The Great Work and the esoteric Science of the Ancients in terms accessible to scholar and layperson alike.

Conspiracies have existed since the time of Cain and Abel. Facts of history have been altered to support the illusion. The question today is whether a sufficient number of people will see through the deceptions, thus creating a counter-force for positive change - the gold of humanity - during the upcoming times of Macro-Cosmic Quantum Shift. Laura argues convincingly, based on the revelations of the deepest of esoteric secrets, that the present is a time of potential transition, an extraordinary opportunity for individual and collective renewal: a quantum shift of awareness and perception which could see the birth of true creativity in the fields of science, art and spirituality. *The Secret History of the World* allows us to redefine our interpretation of the universe, history, and culture and to thereby navigate a path through this darkness. In this way, Laura Knight-Jadczyk shows us how we may extend the possibilities for all our different futures in literal terms.

With over 850 pages of fascinating reading, *The Secret History of The World and How to Get Out Alive* is rapidly being acknowledged as a classic with profound implications for the destiny of the human race. With painstakingly researched facts and figures, the author overturns long-held conventional ideas on religion, philosophy, Grail legends, science, and alchemy, presenting a cohesive narrative pointing to the existence of an ancient techno-spirituality of the Golden Age which included a mastery of space and time: the Holy Grail, the Philosopher's Stone, the True Process of Ascension. Laura provides the evidence for the advanced level of scientific and metaphysical wisdom possessed by the greatest of lost ancient civilizations - a culture so advanced that none of the trappings of civilization as we know it were needed, explaining why there is no 'evidence' of civilization as we know it left to testify to its existence. The author's consummate synthesis reveals the Message in a Bottle reserved for humanity, including the Cosmology and Mysticism of mankind Before the Fall when, as the ancient texts tell us, man walked and talked with the gods. Laura shows us that the upcoming shift is that point in the vast cosmological cycle when mankind - or at least a portion of mankind - has the opportunity to regain his standing as The Child of the King in the Golden Age.

If ever there was a book that can answer the questions of those who are seeking Truth in the spiritual wilderness of this world, then surely *The Secret History of the World and How to Get Out Alive* is it.

Comets and the Horns of Moses

The Secret History of the World, Vol. 2
Laura Knight-Jadczyk

The Laura Knight-Jadczyk's series, The Secret History of the World, is one of the most ambitious projects ever undertaken to provide a cogent, comprehensive account of humanity's true history and place in the cosmos. Following the great unifying vision of the Stoic Posidonius, Laura weaves together the study of history, mythology, religion, psychology and physics, revealing a view of the world that is both rational and breathtaking in its all-encompassing scope. This second volume, Comets and the Horns of Moses, (written in concert with several following volumes soon to be released) picks up the dangling threads of volume one with an analysis of the Biblical character of Moses – his possible true history and nature – and the cyclical nature of cosmic catastrophes in Earth's history.

Laura skillfully tracks the science of comets, revealing evidence for the fundamentally electrical and electromagnetic nature of these celestial bodies and how they have repeatedly wreaked havoc and destruction on our planet over the course of human history. Even more startling however, is the evidence that comets and cometary fragments have played a central role in the formation of human myth and legend and the very concept of a 'god'. As she expertly navigates her way through the labyrinth of history, Laura uncovers the secret knowledge of comets that has been hidden in the great myths, ancient astronomy (and astrology) and the works of the Greek philosophers. Concluding with a look at the political and psychological implications of cyclical cometary catastrophes and what they portend for humanity today, Comets and the Horns of Moses is a marvel of original thought and keen detective work that will rock the foundations of your understanding of the world you live in, and no doubt ruffle the feathers of the many academics who still cling to an outdated and blinkered view of history.

Earth Changes and the Human-Cosmic Connection

The Secret History of the World, Vol. 3
Pierre Lescaudron and Laura Knight-Jadczyk

Jet Stream meanderings, Gulf Stream slow-downs, hurricanes, earthquakes, volcanic eruptions, meteor fireballs, tornadoes, deluges, sinkholes, and noctilucent clouds have been on the rise since the turn of the century. Have proponents of man-made global warming been proven correct, or is something else, something much bigger, happening on our planet?

While mainstream science depicts these Earth changes as unrelated, Pierre Lescaudron applies findings from the Electric Universe paradigm and plasma physics to suggest that they might in fact be intimately related, and stem from a single common cause: the close approach of our Sun's 'twin' and an accompanying cometary swarm.

Citing historical records, the author reveals a strong correlation between periods of authoritarian oppression with catastrophic and cosmically-induced natural disasters. Referencing metaphysical research and information theory, *Earth Changes and the Human-Cosmic Connection* is a ground-breaking attempt to re-connect modern science with the ancient understanding that the human mind and states of collective human experience can influence cosmic and earthly phenomena.

Covering a broad range of scientific fields, and including over 250 figures and 1,000 sources, *Earth Changes and the Human-Cosmic Connection* is presented in an accessible format for anyone seeking to understand the signs of our times.

The Wave 1 – "Riding the Wave"

... The Truth and Lies about 2012 and Global Transformation
Laura Knight-Jadczyk

As 2012 fast approaches, opinions about what to expect on this much-anticipated date are sharply polarized. Will humanity experience a global, spiritual transformation? Cataclysmic Earth Changes? Or both? Or nothing? If Earth and its inhabitants are scheduled for some life-changing or life-ending event, we should ask ourselves what we know and how we know it, and how to prepare for our future.

Drawing on decades of research into history, religion, and the esoteric, Laura Knight-Jadczyk introduces the concept of "the Wave" to describe the possible phenomena behind all the hype surrounding global transformation. *Riding the Wave* not only collects the most probable scenarios we may face in the near future – it provides the context to make it all intelligible.

With roots in the science of hyperdimensions made popular by physicist Michio Kaku and the Fortean theories of the late John Keel, *Riding the Wave* suggests that many of the noticeable changes to our world in the last century are symptoms of the approaching Wave. From climate change, extreme population growth and technological development, as well as novel social and political movements, to the advent of UFO sightings, crop circles, and a variety of otherworldly experiences, something is up on the Big Blue Marble, and it all seems to be leading to a sea change in the way we see and interact with the world. The only question is, will it be for the better or the worse?

An intimate blend of science and mysticism, this volume of Laura Knight-Jadczyk's Wave Series initiates the process of unveiling the truth about life on Earth, and the man behind the curtain...

The Wave 2 – "Soul Hackers"

... The Hidden Hands Behind the New Age Movement
Laura Knight-Jadczyk

Why are we here? Why do we suffer? If this is an infinite school, what are we here to learn? And why do our efforts at "fixing" our lives often do exactly the opposite? As mystic and researcher Laura Knight-Jadczyk writes in this volume of her expansive Wave Series: "when you ask a question – if the question is a burning one – your life becomes the answer. All of your experiences and interactions and so forth shape themselves around the core of the answer that you are seeking in your soul. In [my] case, the question was: 'How to be One with God,' and the answer was, 'Love is the answer, but you have to have knowledge to know what Love really is.'"

Soul Hackers is a deeply personal and insightful account of this very process – of burning questions and transformative answers. Through the story of her own struggle with mainstream and alternative religion and the solutions they claim to offer, Knight-Jadczyk lays bare the problems inherent in the New Age movement as a whole – from Reiki, Wicca, and the phenomenon of channeling, to the very real problems of spirit attachments, mind control, and otherworldly predators posing as benevolent beings. She asks what it really means to "create your own reality." Is it merely self-hypnosis, or is something more hidden in this New Age truism?

The answers lie in the very nature of the Wave – the cosmic force and fabric of personal and collective evolution. For anyone wishing to understand the deeper meaning and reality of the human experience, and what our very near future may very well have in store for us, *Soul Hackers* provides a map to our symbolic reality and the knowledge necessary to weather the approaching storm.

The Wave 3 – "Stripped to the Bone"

... The Path to Freedom in the Prison of Life
Laura Knight-Jadczyk

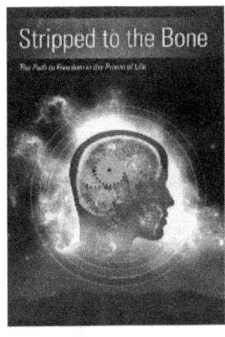

Media propaganda. Official cover-ups. Dishonest science. "Non-lethal" weaponry. Mind control technology. Racial stereotypes. Social engineering. Religious programming. The cold pursuit of profit. And the unrelenting pull of materialism... In a world where "freedom" is exported at the barrel of a gun, true freedom seems more like a distant fairytale, blocked for us in more ways than we can imagine.

In *Stripped to the Bone,* author Laura Knight-Jadczyk lays bare the forces seeking to keep humanity in a prison of its own creation. She lucidly describes evil's place in the cosmos, from the dark world of political conspiracy and government mind control to the reality behind the UFO phenomenon. But in response to the grim state of affairs on the Big Blue Marble, she also asks: Is there a solution? What can we learn from those who came before us? *Stripped to the Bone* suggests that this knowledge was not only known and widely practiced in humanity's prehistory, but that it can be rediscovered.

Through her extensive reading on all things esoteric, Knight-Jadczyk maintains that by knowing our limitations, we may overcome them. In this volume of her acclaimed Wave Series, she tears down our illusions about freedom and the idea that it can be won in any war. Rather, the path to freedom is an inner battle against the many limitations placed on our ability to choose by official culture, our own beliefs, and the forces behind the reality of our everyday experience.

By showing us our own limitations she also succeeds in presenting anew the real possibilities and true potential of a free humanity.

The Wave 4 – "Through A Glass Darkly"
... Hidden Masters, Secret Agendas and a Tradition Unveiled
Laura Knight-Jadczyk

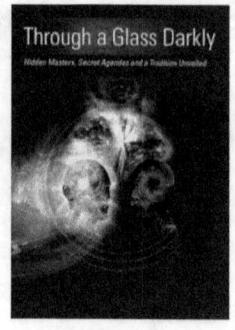

Behind the surface of everyday life lie secrets that have been kept from the eyes of the humanity. In every field of knowledge, we seem to take a wrong turn, coming to conclusions that are diametrically opposed to the truth of the matter. It seems that true science, history, the purpose and aim of human life, our past and potential futures are all off limits to public consumption. How can this be the case, and can these truths come to be known?

In *Through a Glass Darkly*, Laura Knight-Jadczyk continues to make it clear that nothing is what it appears to be. From the stories stitched together to make up our own personal identities to the myths of history on which nations are founded, we live in a sea of lies and half-truths. Just as we lie to ourselves and each other about who we really are, often putting ourselves in the best light possible, there are those who manufacture, manipulate, and shape current and past events to suit their own vested interests. And the current events of today will become the history of tomorrow, erroneously shaping our notions of who we are as a people, just as those of the past have done before.

But behind this sorry state of affairs, the truth awaits discovery. In this fourth volume of her series *The Wave or Adventures with Cassiopaea*, Knight-Jadczyk follows the trail of the hidden masters of our planet, exposing the agenda behind the alleged secret society, the "Priory of Sion", and that mystery's connections with alchemy, Oak Island, and the Kabbalists of old. In the process she reveals aspects of the tradition kept under wraps by these very groups. By exposing the agendas and conspiracies of the elite, we can come to know the truth about ourselves, and why it is has been kept hidden.

The Wave 5 & 6 – "Petty Tyrants & Facing the Unknown"

... Navigating the Traps and Diversions of Life in the Matrix

Laura Knight-Jadczyk

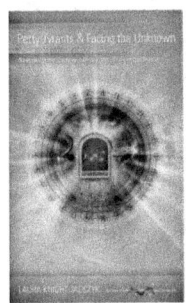

From the myths of romance to the tales of the hero's journey, the quest for knowledge and being has always been portrayed in terms of struggle. Far from home, the hero faces obstacles and tests of his or her courage, will, and cunning. But how do the labyrinths and monsters of these 'messages in a bottle' from our remote ancestors relate to our lives in the 21st century? In an age of mass media, the worldwide web, and multinational corporations, how do these archetypal dramas play themselves out?

In these two volumes of her revolutionary series, *The Wave or Adventures with Cassiopaea,* Laura Knight-Jadczyk continues her project of laying bare the nature of our reality. Through her own experiences and interactions over the course of the Cassiopaean Experiment, many of which just go to show that truth is stranger than fiction, Laura describes the real-life dynamics only hinted at in myth. Most importantly, she gives the tools and clues necessary to actually read the symbols of reality: the theological substrate in which our ordinary psychological motivations are embedded.

With these stunning revelations, Shakespeare's famous words take on a whole new meaning: "All the world's a stage, and all men and women merely players."

First published on her groundbreaking website cassiopaea.org, *Petty Tyrants & Facing the Unknown* have now been fully revised and packaged together in one attractive volume. For anyone interested in the world of esoteric knowledge, studies in the paranormal and everything 'alternative', or even just curious about life in general and its possible significance and meaning, these volumes are a must-read.

The Wave 7 – "Almost Human"

... A Stunning Look at the Metaphysics of Evil

Laura Knight-Jadczyk

In this volume of her prescient Wave series, Laura Knight-Jadczyk brings order to the chaotic and labyrinthine world of murder, conspiracy, and the paranormal. In a unique and probing synthesis of science and mysticism she presents a detailed series of case studies and application of her hypothesis of hyperdimensional influence.

From interpersonal relationships and their expression of archetypal dramas to the vectoring of human behaviour to achieve hyperdimensional purposes, *Almost Human* reveals the mechanics of evil, how it creeps into our lives, and what we need to be aware of in order to avoid it.

The case studies of John Nash, the schizoidal creator of Game Theory, and Ira Einhorn, the New Age psychopath who murdered his girlfriend, are the window through which Knight-Jadczyk unravels the intricate web of deception, aims, and counter-aims of the Powers That Be.

Almost Human is essential reading for anyone wondering why our world is becoming increasingly controlled and our freedoms more restricted.

The Wave 8 – "Debugging the Universe"

... The Hero's Journey

Laura Knight-Jadczyk

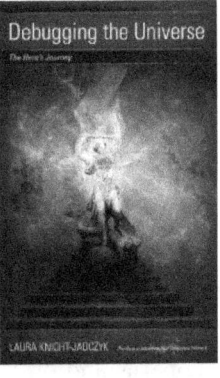

The Path of the Fool, the Hero's Journey, the Great Work – by whatever name it takes, the path of self-development and growth of knowledge is one fraught with difficult lessons and intense struggle. But what exactly is the nature of those lessons, and what insights can the latest advances in modern science provide for us along the way?

Debugging the Universe takes us into the heart of what it means to be human, from the molecules of our DNA to our life purpose and true place in the universe, and everything that separates us from embodying that higher potential. Explored within are real-life applications of the Hero's archetype, the relevance of neuroscience and the 'molecules of emotion', the hidden meaning behind the enigmatic symbols of esoterica, and what it means to live inside a complex system: the universal breath of chaos and order.

This volume concludes the publication in print of Laura Knight-Jadczyk's unparalleled and controversial magnum opus: *The Wave or Adventures with Cassiopaea*. Originally published online at www.cassiopaea.org, The Wave is a fully modern exposition of the knowledge of the ancients, with subjects ranging from metaphysics, science, cosmology, and psychology to the paranormal, UFOs, hyperdimensions and macrocosmic transformation.

"High Strangeness"

... Hyperdimensions and the Process of Alien Abduction
Laura Knight-Jadczyk

High Strangeness: Hyperdimensions and the Process of Alien Abduction is an enlightening attempt to weave together the contradictory threads of religion, science, history, alien abduction, and the true nature of political conspiracies. With thorough research and a drive for the truth, Laura Knight-Jadczyk strips away the facades of official culture and opens doors to understanding our reality.

The Second Edition includes additional material that explains the hyperdimensional mechanisms by which our reality is controlled and shaped by 'alien' powers. The self-serving actions of unwitting puppets – psychopaths and other pathological types – who may have no knowledge that they are being used, become the portals through which an agenda that is hostile to humanity as a whole, is pushed forward.

High Strangeness takes the study of ponerology into a whole new dimension!

"9/11 – The Ultimate Truth"

Joe Quinn and Laura Knight-Jadczyk

In the years since the 9/11 attacks, dozens of books have sought to explore the truth behind the official version of events that day - yet to date, none of these publications has provided a satisfactory answer as to **why** the attacks occurred and who was ultimately responsible for carrying them out.

Taking a broad, millennia-long perspective, Laura Knight-Jadczyk's *9/11: The Ultimate Truth* uncovers the true nature of the ruling elite on our planet and presents new and ground-breaking insights into just how the 9/11 attacks played out.

9/11: The Ultimate Truth makes a strong case for the idea that September 11, 2001 marked the moment when our planet entered the final phase of a diabolical plan that has been many, many years in the making. It is a plan developed and nurtured by successive generations of ruthless individuals who relentlessly exploit the negative aspects of basic human nature to entrap humanity as a whole in endless wars and suffering in order to keep us confused and distracted to the reality of the man behind the curtain.

Drawing on historical and genealogical sources, Knight-Jadczyk eloquently links the 9/11 event to the modern-day Israeli-Palestinian conflict. She also cites the clear evidence that our planet undergoes periodic natural cataclysms, a cycle that has arguably brought humanity to the brink of destruction in the present day.

For its no nonsense style in cutting to the core of the issue and its sheer audacity in refusing to be swayed or distracted by the morass of disinformation that has been employed by the powers that be to cover their tracks, *9/11: The Ultimate Truth* can rightly claim to be **the** definitive book on 9/11 - and what that fateful day's true implications are for the future of mankind.

The new Second Edition of *9/11: The Ultimate Truth* has been updated with new material detailing the real reasons for the collapse of the World Trade Center towers, the central role played by agents of the state of Israel in the attacks, and how the arrogant Bush government is now forced to dance to the Zionists' tune.

JFK: The Assassination of America

Laura Knight-Jadczyk

Anyone who has taken the time to study the facts about that fateful day in Dallas, TX, November 22, 1963, will already know that John F. Kennedy was deliberately murdered by a cabal of psychopathic warmongers who were opposed to his plans for a more peaceful world. This ebook written by Laura Knight-Jadczyk brings into focus how the convergence of greed and the power-mad forces of big oil, organized crime, and the military-industrial complex brought about the destruction of JFK. Drawing on an early analysis of Kennedy's assassination, *Farewell America*, which was produced by a French intelligence group, Mrs. Knight-Jadczyk brings a deeper understanding of this tragic event by placing it in the light of the psychopathic motivations of these criminal elements. *JFK: The Assassination of America* shows a world that could have been, and a great man silenced by forces who will stop at nothing to keep that world from becoming a reality.

Amazing Grace

Laura Knight-Jadczyk

Laura Knight-Jadczyk has lived intimately – and mysteriously – with the world of spirit. In *Amazing Grace*, Laura takes us back to her beginnings in a Gulf Coast Florida childhood, mapping the first decades of her extraordinary search for an objective reality of spirit, of the play of forces that exist as a subtext to the lives of all human beings – a journey toward knowledge and understanding.

From her first experiences with a terrifying Face at the Window in childhood, to her work as an exorcist, chronicled by Pulitzer Prize–winning journalist Thomas French in the *St. Petersburg Times*, Laura relates the many experiences in her search for the existence of truth about our reality, which forced her to recognize the validity of perceptions beyond those of materialism.

This is also the story of how the Cassiopaeans came to be a part of her life. Their channeled messages, which include important concepts of physics and the underlying nature of reality, have drawn the attention of intellectually advanced yet spiritually hungry people from all over the world. This is not just the story of one woman's experience with personal quantum jumps from one reality to another, but is also the greater story of the potential that exists in every seeker. We have the potential to discover the genuine existence of spirit and the play of the archetypal forces of the world, and to connect with them in a dynamic way. Amazing Grace, or Quantum Future, can be a reality in our lives.

The Apocalypse: Comets, Asteroids and Cyclical Catastrophes

Laura Knight-Jadczyk

For untold millennia, comets and asteroids have struck fear into the hearts of humankind. Their stark radiance was observed everywhere with a sense of impending doom, interpreted as signs of the gods' judgment, omens of plague, mass destruction and the end of time. Astronomers recorded their appearance the world over, building large scale observatories to track their movements and predict their ominous arrival. What was it about these majestic wonders of the heavens that inspired such dread? Was it simply a product of mere superstition and social hysteria?

The latest scientific analysis and historical analysis strongly suggest otherwise. Our ancestors knew something we have since forgotten, their secrets deeply embedded in the archaeological record and the myths passed on throughout generations. And we have only begun to unravel their mysteries ...

Spurred on by the discovery of a little known letter of warning to the European Office of Aerospace Research and Development by astrophysicist Victor Clube, author Laura Knight-Jadczyk began an in-depth research project to get to the bottom of the very real threat to humanity posed by these celestial visitors. In *The Apocalypse: Comets, Asteroids, and Cyclical Catastrophes*, Knight-Jadczyk shares what she found: historical evidence for mass destructions, comet-borne plagues, and repeated cover ups littering our past, as well as clues that a similar fate may be fast approaching.and repeated cover ups littering our past, as well as clues that a similar fate may be fast approaching.

The Noah Syndrome

Laura Knight-Jadczyk

"As it was in the days of Noah ..."

Technological progress married with moral decay. A people enraptured by the trivial and superficial, entrenched in a culture of materialism and endless warfare. A civilization whose time has come. If a phrase defines the condition of our era, it is this: The Noah Syndrome.

After twenty-six years, Laura Knight-Jadczyk's unpublished book is now in print for the first time. And it's more relevant than ever. Drawing on prophecies ancient and new - from biblical narratives to modern-day visionaries - yet grounded in cutting-edge scientific discoveries about earth's cataclysmic history, this book presents a remarkable vision of humanity's dramatic past and extremely hazardous future.

The Noah Syndrome also introduces the concept of quantum cosmic metamorphosis - the spiritual ark that may carry us through the coming catastrophe. If our past is the key to our future, as Laura suggests, heeding the counsel in these pages could mean the difference between transformation and destruction.

Evidence of Revision

Quantum Future Group

Evidence of Revision is a six part documentary containing historical, original news footage revealing that the most seminal events in recent American history have been deeply and purposefully misrepresented to the public. Footage and interviews provide an in-depth exploration of events ranging from the Kennedy assassinations to the Jonestown massacre, and all that lies between.

The footprints left in this archival footage reveal the coordinated, clandestine sculpting of the America we know today. Evidence of Revision proves once and for all that history has been revised even as it was written!

Part 1: The Assassinations of Kennedy and Oswald
Part 2: The why of it all referenced to Vietnam and LBG
Part 3: LBJ, Hoover and others: what so few know even today
Part 4: The RFK assassination as never seen before
Part 5: RFK assassination, MKULTRA and the Jonestown massacre
Part 6: The assassination of Martin Luther King

6 parts – 3 DVD set – Region-Free DVDs – Watch on any DVD player or computer anywhere in the world.

Newly subtitled in English, Spanish, French and Polish – the documentary is filmed in English, the subtitles are for clarity due to archival footage on which the audio is, at times, unclear. Duration: 10 hours 25 minutes.

Éiriú Eolas, An Amazing Stress Control, Healing and Rejuvenation Program

Laura Knight-Jadczyk

Are you stressed? Do you suffer from chronic fatigue, conditions that your doctor cannot diagnose or that he thinks are "all in your head"? Are you in physical pain more often than not? Is your system toxified from living in today's polluted environment? Do you wish you could face life's challenges with greater calm and peace of mind? Would you like to actually feel healthy, happy and pain-free every day?

Introducing Éiriú Eolas (pronounced "AIR-oo OH-lahss"), the amazing scientific stress-control, healing, detoxing and rejuvenation program which is THE KEY that will help you to change your life in a REAL and immediately noticeable way:

Proven benefits of the Éiriú Eolas Program include: instantly control stress in high energy situations, detox your body resulting in pain relief, relax and gently work through past emotional and psychological trauma and regenerate and rejuvenate your body/mind.

Éiriú Eolas will enable you to rapidly and gently access and release layers of mental, emotional and physical toxicity that stand between you and a healthy, younger feeling and younger looking body!

Subtitles available in: English, Danish, German, Spanish, Greek, French, Croatian, Italian, Dutch, Polish, Russian, Serbian, Turkish and Vietnamese!

Red Pill Press
info@redpillpress.com
www.redpillpress.com

Index

309,000 years ago, 163

abduction, 2, 6, 7, 19, 22, 33, 34, 59, 75, 80, 168, 169, 191, 328, 341, 434
acupuncture, 27, 188
alien
    craft, 5, 7, 9–11, 18, 22, 44, 79, 241, 242, 347, 348
aliens, 1–3, 14, 15, 33, 34, 39, 45, 46, 58, 74, 75, 101, 117, 127, 152–154, 171, 174, 177, 191, 205, 206, 208, 238, 239, 242–244, 284, 287, 289, 290, 298, 303, 305–308, 321, 328, 332, 340, 341, 345, 382, 399, 434
    grays, 6, 99, 208, 290, 349
    reptilian, 73, 74, 79
angels, 41, 405, 406
    guardian, 41
anger, 1, 2, 4, 13, 37, 43, 44, 48, 89, 92, 100, 107, 108, 113, 116, 124, 127, 152, 175, 194, 222, 223, 225, 275, 310, 315, 333, 340, 345, 347, 348, 378, 396, 401, 403, 404, 406, 418, 420, 431
Antareans, 261, 333, 340
anticipation, 235–237, 311
antimatter, 180, 181, 190, 191, 195, 197
Aryan, 287, 289, 290, 349, 350
astral projection, 38
astrology, 15
Atlantis, 145, 176, 238, 243, 248, 253, 379, 415
attack, 17, 37, 52, 64, 65, 80, 84, 85, 87, 96, 122, 133, 134, 152, 162–164, 194, 222, 244, 290, 303, 308, 315, 327, 341, 342, 347, 369, 370, 401, 404, 435
    expect, 37
aura
    energy, 22
    imprint, 22, 26
    record, 22
aura camera, 23, 25, 27, 204, 212, 238

Bible, 97, 143, 144, 171, 180, 231, 242, 244, 364, 365, 416, 423
bilocation, 253, 323, 403
bloodline, 94, 95
Bluebeard [story], 114, 115, 137
Bundy, Ted, 13, 14, 16, 93
Byrd, Admiral, 262

Caesar, Julius, 171, 320, 418
Camp David, 7–10
cataclysm, 97, 141, 435, 439
cattle mutilations, 14, 154
Celts, 260
channeling, ii, 1, 13, 18, 20, 21, 25, 26, 38, 68, 84, 135, 158, 161, 163, 201, 215, 384, 387, 402, 428
choices, 17, 56, 63, 100, 104, 108, 124, 142–144, 163, 172, 173, 199, 206, 210, 216, 238, 282, 283, 285, 286, 315, 329, 335, 343, 353, 357, 362, 367, 407, 408
chupacabras, 45–47, 154
Coincidences, 250
comet, 69, 71, 72, 98, 226, 229–231, 233, 241, 378, 408, 425, 426, 438
    cluster, 71, 72, 98, 226, 229–231

conduit, 26, 66, 67, 85, 117, 172, 190, 238, 270, 354, 360, 374
consciousness
    mosaic, 205
    sub, 2, 5, 22, 39, 116, 135, 188, 222, 327
consortium, 7, 97, 123, 124, 175, 208, 330, 337
Coral Castle, 91, 182, 183, 188, 224
crop circles, 189, 274, 354–356, 358–360, 371, 373–375, 384, 385, 427
Crowley, Aleister, 178

dark matter, 228, 233
dead dude [5th density discarnate spirit], 21, 67
Deception, 99
deception, 41, 97, 139, 172, 207, 215, 293, 294, 423, 432
denial, 2, 134, 139, 236
density, 6, 7, 15–19, 21, 22, 26, 38, 40–42, 46–49, 56, 58, 64, 66–71, 81, 94, 95, 97, 98, 104, 124, 134, 135, 138, 141–145, 151, 153, 154, 156, 158, 163, 164, 171, 173, 174, 180, 181, 183, 185–191, 195, 197–199, 204, 206, 207, 211–213, 226, 232, 236, 238, 240, 244, 246, 248, 249, 254, 255, 263, 274, 277, 288, 293–295, 302, 303, 305–307, 314, 316, 321, 323, 333, 339–341, 344, 349–351, 354, 356, 358, 363, 364, 371, 374, 375, 381, 383, 388–393, 397, 403, 405, 407, 408
    1st, 21, 185, 343, 344, 384
    2nd, 41, 141–143, 212, 319, 339
    3rd, 6, 7, 15, 17, 18, 21, 22, 26, 40, 41, 47, 56, 68, 69, 71, 97, 98, 141, 156, 163, 164, 171, 174, 180, 183, 185, 187, 189, 191, 195, 197–199, 207, 212, 236, 238, 240, 255, 263, 288, 308, 321, 333, 340, 349, 363, 364, 383, 388, 393, 397, 405, 407, 411
    4th, 6, 15–17, 19, 21, 22, 40, 58, 66, 71, 94, 95, 97, 138, 141–144, 149, 151, 153, 154, 163, 180, 185–191, 195, 197, 198, 204, 206, 211, 213, 226, 244, 249, 288, 295, 305–307, 321, 333, 339–341, 349, 350, 354, 357, 389, 392, 403, 405, 407
        bleedthrough, 96, 186, 249, 403
    5th, 15, 21, 38, 47–49, 67, 70, 135, 174, 185, 187, 213, 244, 316, 405, 417
    6th, 21, 26, 41, 42, 56, 94, 151, 156, 185, 195, 240, 244, 354, 374
    7th, 21, 181, 197, 254, 374, 389, 390
    candidates, 26, 373
Denver Airport, 117
destiny, 42, 163, 164, 185, 202, 263, 264, 362, 424
diet, 27, 255, 268, 404
dimensions, 2, 46, 47, 58, 74, 81, 134, 153, 156, 165, 181, 188, 191, 275, 284, 292, 303, 323, 351, 355, 363, 373–375, 381, 393, 411, 419, 421–423, 427, 432–434
dimensions vs. densities, 47
disinformation, 135, 176, 305, 348, 379, 408, 423, 435
DNA, 154, 163, 164, 173, 186–188, 190, 200, 219, 354, 374, 375, 379, 384, 385, 388, 389, 391–393, 403, 416, 423, 433
    alteration, 163, 164
dreams, 15, 36–38, 41, 47, 48, 59, 73, 79, 91, 92, 97, 113, 116, 121, 131, 135, 149, 173, 200, 206, 221, 223, 253, 287, 320, 321,

326, 327, 364, 396–398, 406, 407

emotions, 62, 66, 75, 87, 90, 91, 93–95, 113, 115, 121, 132, 133, 135, 155, 175, 188, 194, 206, 219, 221, 240, 247, 256, 258, 267, 299, 327, 331, 381, 385, 386, 404, 407, 433, 441

faith, 4, 56, 84, 85, 90, 143, 207, 209, 223, 236, 258, 260, 263, 278, 294, 342, 368–370, 392, 399
Flight 800 [TWA 800], 243, 344, 347, 348, 416
Fort Detrick, 9, 10
frequency resonance vibration [FRV], 133, 138, 212, 263, 264, 362, 372, 402
future, 20, 36, 236, 243, 265, 268, 283, 284, 322, 379, 435
  shaping, 236

gene pool, 138
Ghost, 22, 420, 421
God, 21, 47, 70, 77, 107, 119, 143, 169, 171–173, 175, 182, 197, 198, 211, 230, 238, 254, 255, 260, 268, 269, 293–295, 300, 305, 307, 314, 320, 353, 377, 381, 390, 406, 415, 421, 428
government, 3, 6, 7, 9, 11, 19, 21, 33, 45, 58, 73, 81, 97–99, 139, 154, 174, 243, 249, 306, 333, 336, 348, 350, 361, 382, 384, 429, 435
  secret, 19, 21, 33, 58, 73, 81, 97, 154, 262, 305, 306, 336
grammar, 27
gravity, 100, 101, 140, 149, 179–184, 186, 188–191, 193–197, 199, 201, 204, 210, 222, 229, 231, 232, 275, 277, 289, 305, 306, 310, 320, 351, 381, 390, 404
  waves, 101, 179–181, 183, 184, 190, 191, 193, 194, 196, 197, 199, 201, 204, 210, 222, 231, 289, 306
  unstable, 101, 180, 181, 190, 191, 196, 197, 199, 210, 306
Greenbaum programming, 33, 34, 73, 75–77, 79, 80, 123, 204, 249, 250, 322, 329–337, 340, 341, 350, 403, 411, 416
Grey beings, 70, 208

HAARP, 58, 98, 145, 175, 176, 190, 249, 348
Hale Bopp, 71
Headless Valley, 64
higher self, 5, 77
Hitler, 205, 261, 333, 418
Holocaust, 205
hypnosis, ii, 1–3, 5, 7, 27, 74, 75, 77, 79–81, 168, 297, 298, 325, 328, 329, 332, 337, 345, 428
  regression, 27

Ibn al-Arabi, 167, 172, 179, 180, 209, 256
Illuminati, 350, 388
illusions, 24, 69, 70, 107, 123, 163, 173, 180, 189, 292, 305, 307, 315, 326, 357, 388, 390–392, 423, 429
indigenous people, 260

Jesus, 42, 170, 171, 175, 324, 326, 327, 364, 365, 416, 418
judgment, 211

Kantek, 70, 349
karma, 68, 87, 199, 200, 256, 301, 362, 383, 386, 402
Kennedy, John F., 174, 175, 177, 243, 302, 334, 419, 436, 440
knowledge, ii, 1, 6, 16, 21, 26, 27, 38, 45, 64, 98, 101, 104, 110, 117, 118, 123, 124, 126, 143, 144, 164, 168, 172, 174, 179, 180, 187, 195, 205–209, 211, 239, 250, 265, 277, 282, 284,

288–291, 293, 294, 305, 307,
322, 332, 340, 351, 354, 360,
364, 367, 385, 387, 397, 400,
402, 424, 425, 428–431, 433,
434, 437
Koran, 180, 209, 373

learning
    cycle, 206–209
    directive, 57, 67, 104, 124
lessons, 15, 42, 47, 185, 186, 198,
205–207, 210, 212, 216, 219,
225, 292, 294, 295, 305, 307,
311, 353, 356, 363, 401, 402,
433
Level One, 68, 221
Lizard beings, 61, 62, 64, 67, 73, 75,
118, 208, 243, 307, 310, 349,
383, 384, 389
love and light, 76, 78, 189, 207, 210

mantid beings, 239
Mars, 3, 18, 240–244, 246, 247, 348,
396
    Cydonia region, 246, 247
Masons, 373, 387, 388
Master Race, 263
melatonin, 174
Melchizedek, 171
memory
    screen, 22
Mercury retrograde, 11
Monroe, Marilyn, 177
Montauk [project], 175, 208, 336, 348

names of God, 172
Nazi Germany, 206, 221
Nephilim beings, 45, 70, 71, 87, 118,
206
Nidle, Sheldon, 18, 39, 242, 384
nordic beings, 23, 94, 95, 97, 100, 118,
208

Oak Island, 140, 430
Oort cloud, 229–231

Orion, 118, 153, 239, 250, 261, 307,
348, 349

pain killers, 27
Paramahansa Yogananda, 47, 48, 70,
72, 211
past life, 4, 206, 221, 241, 296, 302
Paul [apostle], 171, 242
perception
    linear, 189
personal questions [discouragement to
ask], 68, 135, 224, 225, 322,
335
Philadelphia Experiment, 176, 191
photon belt, 18, 39, 382, 384, 408
physicality, variable, 21, 154, 240
playing field, 189, 206, 295
pollution, 140
portals, 37, 62, 66, 87, 133, 134, 155,
190, 191, 211–213, 324, 325,
328, 434
power center, 94, 356
prayer, 42
prediction, 39, 40, 68, 69, 284, 416
prejudice, 15, 40, 51, 56, 57, 66, 85,
210, 401
pressure
    psychological, 28
prime numbers, 372–375, 387, 392, 407
Project Awaken, 287
proof, 1, 5, 39, 68, 336, 383
prophecy, 40, 97, 204, 230, 327, 416,
420
    calendar dates, 211
psychic projectors, 287, 289, 290

quantum jump, 233, 236, 381, 437
quantum physics, 180, 199, 278

Ra material, 238, 239
realm border, 98, 186, 190, 206, 211,
230, 231
Reiki, 23, 27, 34, 255, 256, 277, 323,
411, 428
robot person, 93, 95, 122, 135, 136,
242, 350

Roddenberry, Gene, 288
Rosicrucians, 373, 387, 388

sacred geometry, 238, 246, 248
sleep, 173
sleep disorder, 27
soul, 15, 36, 69, 87, 95, 108, 134, 135, 140, 142, 154, 162, 173, 174, 194, 206, 207, 209, 210, 219, 225, 240, 254, 256, 272, 283, 294, 306, 307, 323, 356, 367, 372, 402, 406, 408, 428
   alignment, 95
   progress, 87
spirit release, 21, 27, 48, 51, 119, 259, 325, 420
staircase, 263, 264, 362
Star Trek, 288, 364
STO, 48, 66, 67, 98, 124, 151, 189, 195, 210, 236, 281, 287, 289, 303, 306, 331, 337, 341, 361, 399
Stonehenge, 118, 358–361
STS, 41, 48, 64, 66, 67, 86, 95, 98, 104, 115, 117, 123, 124, 138, 142, 144, 153, 163, 180, 189, 195, 204, 207, 210–212, 239, 261, 287, 289, 303, 305–307, 339, 341, 348, 354, 361, 389, 399
subliminal, 22, 288
Sufis, 167, 179, 180, 182, 183, 185, 188, 209, 211, 320, 323, 373, 381, 417
   The Sufi Path of Knowledge [Chittick], 167, 179, 185, 209, 211, 417
symbolism, 186, 187, 380
synchronicity, 14, 36, 44, 80, 150, 189, 190, 205, 215, 237, 253, 281, 298, 301, 341

telekinesis, 16, 19
theological reality, 5, 104, 105, 107, 110, 114, 123
Theory of Relativity, 351
Thor's Pantheum, 287

Thule society, 94, 95, 100, 118, 261, 333, 340
time
   missing, 22
   passage, 70
   timelessness, 189
twin sun [theory], 226–229, 231, 233

UFO, 1, 2, 5, 7, 13, 14, 16, 18, 23, 40, 59, 61, 79, 83, 91, 92, 96, 117, 127, 169, 170, 177, 203, 238, 240, 242, 267, 292, 297, 298, 300, 306, 308, 315, 321, 334, 335, 339, 341, 345, 346, 372, 399, 421, 422, 427, 429, 433
underground, 3, 6, 10, 21, 137–141, 144, 145, 204, 241, 257, 260–262, 288, 289, 348, 349, 357, 359, 380
   bases, 6, 137, 139, 145, 257, 261, 262, 288, 348
   cities, 139, 140, 260, 261
   tunnels, 7, 9–11, 288, 289, 320, 382
Unified Field Theory, 344, 351, 402

Virgin Mary, 11, 39, 42, 383, 399

Wanderers, 239, 240
warfare, 9, 10, 138, 439
wave, 15, 16, 19, 21, 46, 48, 58, 101, 146, 175, 179–181, 183, 184, 190, 191, 193–197, 199, 201, 204, 208, 210, 222, 231, 232, 237, 244, 246, 272, 275, 277, 289, 306, 322, 359–361, 375, 392, 393, 411–413
   traveling, 190
will
   free, 42, 44, 45, 68, 91, 104, 116, 124, 133, 141, 163, 207, 210, 225, 228, 250, 275, 284, 285, 305, 307, 383, 391
   strong, 22
window fallers, 46